Politics, U.S.A.

Politics, U. S. A.

Cases on the American Democratic Process

Andrew M. Scott and Earle Wallace
The University of North Carolina, Chapel Hill

4th Edition

Macmillan Publishing Co., Inc.,
NEW YORK

Macmillan Publishing Co., Inc.
866 Third Avenue, New York, New York 10022

Library of Congress Cataloging in Publication Data

Scott, Andrew MacKay, ed.
    Politics, U.S.A.

    Includes bibliographical references.
    1. United States—Politics and government—
Addresses, essays, lectures. I. Wallace, Earle,
joint ed. II. Title.
JK21.S3   1974   320.9'73   73-5285
ISBN 0-02-408220-1

Printing: 2 3 4 5 6 7 8   Year: 4 5 6 7 8 9 80

Preface

This volume of "cases" on politics and the American political system has been designed specifically for use in the introductory course on the American political system. The case approach has much to recommend it. A good case will engage the student's interest—a prerequisite for effective learning. A good case makes it clear that "government is people"—men and women thinking, calculating, torn by conflicting desires, occupying offices of greater or lesser importance, making decisions, playing out the roles they have defined for themselves. Because of the basic purpose of a textbook, it is difficult for it to convey to the student a full understanding of the human element in politics and government.

A case often provides an excellent way of bringing out basic issues. If it concerns a conflict situation, words and arguments come from the mouths of the protagonists. The student may identify with one or both sides in the dispute and in so doing improve his understanding of what is involved. Students sometimes identify so thoroughly with one side or the other that they engage in "role playing" during the discussions. The ability of students to project themselves imaginatively into situations and to learn from this experience often increases markedly over a period of time. The knowledge that an actual situation is involved, and not merely a hypothetical one, causes even the skeptical student to be willing to project himself to at least some extent.

The case approach also encourages thought and discrimination. The analysis of one situation after another helps a student learn how to think about government and politics. (With luck, the habit of analysis might carry over into other areas of activity as well.) Because the student is thinking and perceiving for himself, and not simply accepting authority, knowledge and understanding gained are more likely to be retained beyond the next examination.

The case approach, moreover, has the advantage of allowing the student greater freedom in developing his own perceptions about politics and government. A case provides data against which he can check his ideas or ideas expressed by his textbook or instructor. Although the instructor may not find his task eased by the use of a case book, he will certainly find it made more exciting. The student will be thoroughly engaged and the instructor will not need to fight to maintain interest. He will also find it more effective to draw issues and "principles" directly from the case under discussion rather than from a body of anonymous data with which the student is not familiar and the accuracy of which he must take on faith.

Although the case approach is an extremely useful teaching tool, there are certain problems connected with it. If it provides an unsurpassed means of giving students a feeling for the processes and problems of government and politics, it leaves much to be desired in presenting a discussion of governmental structure. Textbook and case book, therefore, bear a complementary relationship, each providing what the other cannot.

A second limitation of this approach is that, as historians have been accustomed to note, there is no such thing as getting "all the facts." Even if this were a possibility, the ensuing account would be too boring and trivial to read or think about. In the preparation of any case, some of the facts will be included and a great many more left out. Which are to be included and which excluded will depend upon the skill, perceptions, purposes, and viewpoint of the individual preparing the case. Sometimes the author will try to give a balanced presentation, and other times this will be no part of his purpose. If a case is written by a participant in the events described, one must expect him to try to justify the role that he played in those events. This by no means destroys the value of the case, and may increase it, for the case will then provide insight into the actor's motivation and his interpretation of the events in which he played a part. If a case is thoroughly one-sided, students can usually be relied on to see this. Not infrequently they may argue that the hero in a case is really the villain of the piece, or vice versa.

In preparing this book, the editors discovered that the total volume of case material available was enormous. They also discovered that it was uneven in its coverage, some areas having been dealt with quite often in cases, others having been virtually ignored. This has influenced our selections.

A good deal of frankly partisan material has been included and we have not worried very much about immediately offsetting one such piece by a selection representing the opposite view. Instead, we have tried to achieve a balance when the volume is taken as a whole. It is in the nature of things that not everyone will agree that we have succeeded. It is our experience, however, that the critical faculties of students develop very quickly to the point where they no longer need to be solemnly warned before they read a selection that it may be slanted.

We have tried to find cases that are vivid, that give the volume variety, and that make their point without being unduly long. While we have not regarded it as an ironbound rule, most of the cases used in this volume deal with matters that are fairly recent. Our material on Watergate is an example of this attempt to be as topical as is possible in a college text. Exceptions have been made only for cases where the personalities are particularly interesting or well known and where the events involved are of historical significance.

Because of the interest of the editors in using timely material, the fourth edition of *Politics, U.S.A.* contains sixty-four new selections and retains only four selections from the previous edition. It goes without saying that our search for case materials has taken us into some unlikely places. There are a good many items included that were not regarded as "cases" by their authors but that serve our purposes very well.

Also, we have concentrated on materials available from sources easily accessible to the student, now and in the future. We know that most students in the introductory course in American government will not become professional political scientists and will have neither the interest to read professional journals nor easy access to them; therefore, the experience of analyzing cases drawn from popular sources that today's students will continue to read after graduation should be of lasting value.

Most of our selections carry their original titles. In some instances, however, we have devised our own titles, either because the selection was an untitled excerpt from a larger work or because the original title was less suitable for the purposes of this volume.

We wish to express our gratitude to the many persons who have made this book possible: to the authors and publishers who have given us permission to use their materials; to the editorial and production departments of Macmillan; to Scott Keeter for his research assistance; and especially to Elaine Wallace for her devotion to the countless details of manuscript preparation for all four editions.

Chapel Hill   A. M. S.   E. W.

Contents

Chapter 1

We the People: The Context of American Politics 1

    The Politics of Change *Samuel Lubell* 2

    The Unfinished Business of America *Look Magazine* (Interviews with John W. Gardner, George C. Wallace, Rev. Jesse Jackson, Gen. James M. Gavin, George Wald, and Bella Abzug) 16

    Conservatism May Have a Future After All *A. James Reichley* 25

    What YOU Can Do—NOW *Ebony Magazine Editorial* 35

    The Legacy of Paternalism *Nathan Hare* 38

    A Federal Judge Digs the Young *Judge Charles E. Wyzanski, Jr.* 45

Chapter 2

The Constitutional Background: The Politics of the "More Perfect Union" 52

    The Declaration of Independence *Thomas Jefferson* 54

Politics 1787: A Case Study in Democratic Politics   *John P. Roche*   57

Chapter 3
The Cities and the Environment   81

Revenue Sharing: Game Plan or Trick Play?   *Allen S. Mandel*   82
Municipal Monopoly   *E. S. Savas*   88
Racially Tense Cairo, Illinois: Quiet but Loathing   *Andrew Wilson*   98
It's Blacks Who Must Stop Crime   *Orde Coombs*   102
The Lesson of Forest Hills   *Roger Starr*   107
Saving the Crusade   *Peter F. Drucker*   115
Gasps for Help from Smog City   *Business Week Magazine*   126

Chapter 4
Politics, Pressure, and Payoffs   129

Can a Nonpartisan Lobby Find a Role in Politics?   *Natalie Davis Spingarn*   130
Why Ma Bell Still Believes in Santa   *Nicholas Johnson*   138
Beyond the ITT Case   *Harlan M. Blake*   144
The Grassing of America   *Barnard Collier*   153
$100,000 Gift to Nixon Campaign Is Traced to Texas Corporation   *Bob Woodward and Carl Bernstein*   158

Chapter 5
Politics and the Media   162

A White House Aide on Control of the Press   *Herbert G. Klein*   163
The Sam Ervin Show   *Laurence Leamer*   167
Electronic Journalism   *John Chancellor*   178
Electronic Schizophrenia: Does Television Alienate Voters?   *Robert MacNeil*   183
Television and the First Amendment   *Fred W. Friendly*   193

Chapter 6
Political Parties, Campaigns, and Elections   199

Primaries: Trial by Ordeal   *Eugene McCarthy*   200
The Democratic Party: Part Way to Reform   *Mary Meehan*   205

What Did We Learn from the Polls This Time?   *Martin Mayer*   213
Democrats Defected in Droves   *William Chapman*   221
The Meaning of the President's Landslide
    Vermont Royster   223

WATERGATE   227
    Statement on *The Washington Post*   *Clark MacGregor*   229
    A Refusal to Believe It All   *Haynes Johnson*   231
    The Minds of the "Managers"   *Richard J. Whalen*   240
    Can a President Govern Effectively Who Systematically
        Alienates Himself from the Rest of Official Washington?
        Nelson W. Polsby   245
    The Swelling of the Presidency   *Thomas E. Cronin*   250

Chapter 7

Congressional Politics   261

On Becoming a United States Senator   *James L. Buckley*   262
One Day in the Life of Guy Vander Jagt (R.-Mich.)   *John Corry*   275
Amphetamine Politics on Capitol Hill   *James M. Graham*   294
The American Constitution and the Air War   *Anthony D'Amato*   311

Chapter 8

The President and the Executive Branch   321

Nixon II: Power Seesaw   *Elizabeth Drew*   322
The Balance of Mutual Weakness   *Henry Brandon*   329
Nixon's Haldeman: Power Is Proximity   *Christopher S. Wren*   343
The Convenience of Secrecy   *Francis E. Rourke*   351
Spiro   *Frank Trippett*   356

Chapter 9

Courts, Judges, and Justice   363

Birth of Judicial Review   *Marbury v. Madison*   365
The Role of the Courts: Conscience of a Sovereign People
    Judge J. Skelly Wright   370
The Case of the Pentagon Papers: Knee Deep in the "Political
    Thicket"   *New York Times v. United States*   378
The Trial Judge   *Harry W. Jones*   383
The Bail System: Money Justice   *Lynn Walker*   403
Does the Law Oppress Women?   *Diane B. Schulder*   408

Chapter 10

Civil Rights: Liberty and Authority   424

Hello Dolly: A Case for Selective Incorporation   *Mapp v. Ohio*   426

Your Phone Is a Party Line   *Ira Glasser and Herman Schwartz*   436

No Right to Liberty   *In Re Gault*   446

The Case of Demetrio Rodriguez   *William Allen*   456

Freedom of Speech for Bigots?   *Brandenburg v. Ohio*   461

Should Government Prescribe Morality?   *Stanley v. Georgia*   462

Is There a "Private" Right to Discriminate?   *Jones v. Alfred Mayer Co.*   464

Chapter 11

The Politics of Discrimination and Liberation   467

The Women's Liberation Movement: Its Origins, Structures, and Ideas   *Jo Freeman*   468

NOW Bill of Rights   480

Redstockings Manifesto   481

The White Niggers of Newark   *David K. Shipler*   483

Black Politics at the Crossroads   *Alex Poinsett*   493

No Hope in Woodlawn   *Seth S. King*   500

Chapter 12

Foreign and Military Policy   507

The Convenience of "Precedent"   *Francis D. Wormuth*   508

Congress and Foreign Policy   *Arthur S. Miller*   516

In Search of Kissinger   *Joseph Kraft*   524

Diplomatic Notes   *Leslie H. Gelb and Morton H. Halperin*   538

Silent Vietnam   *Orville Schell, Jr.*   548

Chapter 1

We the People: The Context of American Politics

This book is concerned with the American political system. It asks: What is that system? How does it work? In what ways is it changing? What makes it democratic?

But a political system does not exist in isolation. It is always embedded in a culture, which provides the context the system operates in. An important component of the culture is the political part, the element this chapter is concerned with. The political culture of a nation consists of the ideas, traditions, assumptions, and accepted rules of the game that make up the framework within which the political system functions. Unless one understands the political culture, one cannot comprehend the system itself.

The political culture appears to be relatively stable if viewed from the perspective of passing political events. But if observed longer, it, too, will be seen to evolve. For example, the context of American politics in the mid-1970's is very different from that of the early 1960's. In fact, recently, the context itself has been evolving somewhat rapidly. Rules-of-the-

game that seemed unchallengeable a few years ago have now been contested. Assumptions that seemed firm have lost their hold. New groups have emerged or are emerging into political consciousness. New issues have become the focus of attention, and old and established coalitions have broken up. The cases in this chapter discuss some of the more prominent features of the context of current American politics, note the changes that have taken place, and suggest some of the practical implications of the new developments.

The Politics of Change

Samuel Lubell

1. Lo, the Coalition-Makers

This book is an effort to bring into focus the strange new politics of impatience which seized hold of this nation and has transformed the tempo and character of American politics.

The nature of this transformation is not easily labeled. One might begin by captioning it as a near-revolutionary quickening of the whole of American political life, as if time itself had been abruptly shortened.

But then one would have to hasten to note that this speedup in our political reflexes has plunged us into disruptive conflict over the reshaping of our society; it has also brought the beginnings, at least, of both a voter revolution and a realignment of our parties unlike any experienced in our history.

To the politicians creating a new majority coalition seems mainly an exercise in reshuffling the party loyalties of key voting blocks. But the compulsive force twisting our political insides and restructuring both parties is the fact that rapid change has become the prime political disturber of our time.

In its first turbulent stage, the reeling impacts of uncontrolled change pushed us off balance as a nation, wrenching much of society out of control and leaving us more divided than we dared admit. During the last years of the Johnson Administration, we were making decisions like a giant Gulliver hopping on one foot.

Source: *The Hidden Crisis in American Politics* (New York: W. W. Norton & Company, Inc., 1971), pp. 17–38. Reprinted from *The Hidden Crisis in American Politics* by Samuel Lubell. By permission of W. W. Norton & Company, Inc. Copyright © 1970 by W. W. Norton & Company, Inc.

In struggling to regain our national balance, we naturally tend to pull back toward more "normal" times. But we are carried into the 1970's on a whole train of unresolved crises which we have been unable—or unwilling—to reconcile. Much of our society is being reshaped to continue battling these conflicts indefinitely.

It is these unresolved conflicts which President Richard Nixon is trying to ride and guide so they will bring into existence a new Republican majority.

Virtually the whole of our society is caught up in the "crisis" around which this book is structured—the deepening hostilities between whites and blacks; air-polluted, crime-stalked cities; the "generation gap" which has been transformed into a crisis of our universities; the resistances to the Vietnam war and how they have projected into a new isolation which pressures for far-reaching changes in foreign policy; the battle to reorder our priorities and to reallocate our economic resources, a struggle made all the more bitter by the slowness in checking inflation.

Each of these conflicts has been headlined repeatedly. Still, what remains elusive is a sense of their lasting impacts, how they have locked together to form what might be termed the politics of a polarized nation that has chopped away so much of the past, now irrevocably gone, has shaken psychological attitudes through the country and still runs on uncontrolled. It is our inability to reconcile these conflicts that divide us that I see as the hidden crisis in American politics today.

Eight points of departure from the old politics of stability stand out:

1. How quickly an unresolved crisis becomes a conflict on the run which can hardly be caught up with.

All the conflicts examined in this study share a common proliferating quality, generating their own momentum and taking on new forms as they rush along. In the process, old choices of action that are being debated get foreclosed, usually leaving only harsher options.

With our racial crisis most of us can still remember when gradual desegregation would have been acceptable to Negroes generally. Currently, though, a new form of territorial racial conflict is taking over our cities, with whites and blacks separated into expanses of "turf" so large that effective school and residential integration is pushed out of reach. Gary, Cleveland, and Newark have already been split into polarized halves, with more such polarizations on the way.

We often argue as if prejudice and bigotry were the only enemies. Yet the main force structuring this new racial crisis is residential mobility, which continues unchecked.

When the white exodus to the suburbs began after World War II, it had little to do with race. But the suburban migration soon found itself linked up with two other happenings of the 1950's—the northward drift of Negroes displaced by the mechanization of cotton, and the surging racial militancy stirred by the Supreme Court's desegregation decision. All three time-locked together to transform our cities, break down urban government, and now threaten to nullify the Supreme Court's school-desegregation decision.

Who would have thought when William Levitt put up the first of his Cape Cod houses on Long Island that he would become part of a process which would enable Mississippi Senator John C. Stennis to demand equal enforcement of desegregation in the North, hoping that this would provide an out for the South?

Other conflicts of more recent origin display the same proliferating quality. The youth crisis, which might have been eased by sensible draft reform, radicalized much of a whole student generation, pushing our universities into deeper turmoil that became further aggravated by black-studies agitation. At stake now is nothing less than what kind of intellectual legacy will our colleges and universities be able to transmit to further generations.

The Vietnam battling between "doves" and "hawks" is also being perpetuated, as colleges and universities are turned into anti-war shelters and opposition to military spending is pressed as a crusade to "regain civilian control of our society" and release funds for social spending.

2. These conflicts on the run have plunged us into zealous combat to remake American thinking, pressed with an intensity not known in this nation since the pre-Civil War period.

Reasoned argument and orderly debate have been shoved aside by efforts to impose beliefs through force, by violence, control of government, and other uses of power.

Black power, student power, George Wallace power—all the varied demands for power—seek to rearrange other people. In fighting back, many of the people who were being rearranged have dug in to resist all change.

That may be the real meaning of "polarization"—to take shelter in hardened silos, to create a situation that others will be forced to accept because they cannot change it.

3. This battling has been targeted largely at our institutions, with the public schools, universities, the draft, the police, churches, the welfare system, perhaps in the future whole cities serving as successive staging area.

Partly this reflects the fact that these agitations have sought lasting changes in basic social relationships; in our zeal to get at each other, we have been ready to break down institutions that stood in the way.

But rapid change also turns society's points of entry into special fronts of vulnerability, and at least two of the raging conflicts have been basically entry assaults.

Negroes, banging at every door they can reach, are demanding entry en masse in place of the old pattern of each individual making it on his own.

Less clearly recognized, the so-called "generation gap" has been primarily concerned with how to find a meaningful place in society for greatly enlarged numbers of young people.

In a single year—1965—the count of young people reaching eighteen leaped from 2,769,000 to 3,739,000. By 1970 the number between eighteen and twenty-four was half again as high as in the 1950's.

Certainly, from at least 1965 on, every policy of government should have sought to speed the absorption into society of these youthful millions. Instead, the escalation of the Vietnam war and a failure to change the draft caged those millions back onto the campuses. Much of a whole generation has been left at odds with a society that has stared in bewilderment at the on-goings in the university zoos.[1]

Revealingly, some students in our highest institutions of learning and blacks on the streets reacted with similar, near-revolutionary violences. Both tried to seize and transform whatever part of society they could reach, the blacks by asserting "black nationalism" in the ghettos, the college students by occupying buildings and demanding that universities be "restructured."

It may be one of the "laws" of unreconciled conflict that it lunges at whatever can be reached, without plan or rationality.

4. No longer can we be sure which of the self-correcting strengths of American democracy still prevail.

We have been accustomed to believe that economic progress overcomes or eases social ills. The unprecedented boom of recent years has yielded remarkable benefits, quadrupling in a single decade the number of families with incomes over $10,000 and reducing by nearly half the proportion of families at the statistical "poverty" level. However, this prosperity has also quickened racial frictions in our cities and is eroding the effective power of all government, aggravating political conflict generally.

In the process, loyalty to all political parties has been loosened, which in turn is changing voter psychology.

Virtually all elements in society appear to have been strengthened so they are better able to fight one another politically, to be more assertive of their rights and self-interests, readier to press their claims upon each other and against the government. It is as much our strengths as our weaknesses that divide the nation.

5. The crisis has been one of management, that is, of a managed society —call it mismanaged if the results seem displeasing.

Through its 1954 desegregation decision, the Supreme Court, without

[1] My manuscript included this term before Vice-President Agnew's reference to "a whole zoo of dissidents." Mr. Agnew does not sense the caged-off feeling of so many collegians.

quite realizing it, put the government into the business of managing racial relations in much of the country. The enterprise brought the most dramatic racial advances in our history, but it also backlogged desires for political revenge that are now being cashed in.

With the tax reduction of 1964, the nation moved officially into a managed economy. For one spectacular year, the performance of the "Keynesian revolution" seemed miraculous, as economic growth soared and tax revenues increased even though federal tax rates had been lowered. Economists became the newest of our high priests.

But the "model" by which the economy was being managed proved inadequate. It never was programed for the pressures of even a limited war. Booming the economy also unloosed great economic and social demands too costly for local governments to support. Burdening local government further were inflationary rises in costs and the high interest rates used to curb inflation.

"Economic stability" was the ideal talked of by both the new economists and the old money managers, but structural changes in our economy seem to be transforming us into a claimant society in which we fight one another for tax cuts and favored government programs, over what share of the tax dollars are to go to missiles, schools, space, or the wider distribution of food stamps. Once the most bitter economic warring was waged by business and labor; today it seems to be the military-industrial complex against the health-education-research complex.

Nor have we been content to leave the driving to Washington. A managed society, as will be seen, generates new compulsions upon the citizenry to take an active hand in the managing.

Southerners battle to end the government's efforts to enforce desegregation, while civil rights advocates would intensify them. Some would extend economic controls; others would throw them off; still others would take them over and charge a commission for the greasing job. In the universities, economists still teach of the wondrous promises of Keynesian economics, while the marketplaces pull back toward McKinleyism.

6. A new structure of political bargaining has come into being in the struggle for political visibility, to make oneself seen and heard.

The great peace and civil rights marches on Washington have been the TV spectaculars which illustrate the huge scale on which attention-getting is being organized.

But the proddings for voter recognition also come from how our society is being reorganized. The greater the powers exercised by government the harsher become the costs of being neglected or overlooked.

Visibility is also a means of protesting against the selection and rejection processes by which our society is run, against the draft, against racial discrimination, against inflationary price rises. As its structure of political bargaining is extended through the country, the unorganized are spurred to organize; political activity has become less orderly, spilling into the streets.

For their part the managers of society try to control who and what is to become visible. Where Presidents Kennedy and Johnson pushed the "war on poverty" before the cameras, President Nixon tends to ease it out of the picture, and to up-front his "war on crime."

As one by-product effect, the relationship between the government and the people is becoming something of a psychological contest, which is changing the arts of government in many subtle ways. It is a feedback contest; while the politicians try to manipulate the voters, the people try to manipulate their politicians.

7. We seem to be losing the ability to moderate and compromise the conflicts that divide us.

The question must be asked whether we really want to come to terms among ourselves? Certainly during the Johnson and Nixon years dissension has been pushed to the surface and made more visible than areas of agreement.

What has happened to the fabled "middle ground" in American politics? Is it still there?

President Nixon has pictured himself as a "centrist" politically; yet the near-fatal weakness that almost lost him the 1968 election lay in his effort to hold the middle ground without any policies or programs that could bring compromise. The same riddle dominates his presidency. Can he really "bring us together again" or is he improvising his own partisan patch-work of disunity?

8. For the first time since the Civil War the effectiveness of our foreign policy has come to hinge on domestic conciliation.

In his Guam doctrine, Nixon began the hazardous process of reducing our military commitments abroad to use more of our resources at home. Done well, this process could prove highly beneficial, but how long will it take? And while we turn inward, what will happen in the rest of the world? How long can we stay divided without inviting troubles abroad and without impairing our ability to act on behalf of peace?

At some point in this process the adjustments made abroad will have to be balanced by domestic reconciliation. But there is no party coalition in command of a sufficiently stable majority to be able to advance a unifying set of policies. The coalition-makers in both parties are organizing to intensify political competition.

Taken together, these eight departures add up to a drastically different kind of politics than we have ever known. My emphasis on conflict should not be interpreted as meaning that it is bad in itself. Quite the opposite. Conflict is indispensable for needed change and for continued progress.

What is deeply troubling is that we seem simultaneously to be intensifying conflict and to be weakening our powers of reconciliation. Unless this spiral is broken we risk being torn apart as a nation, with catastrophic consequences for the whole world.

The choice is not quiet against change. No matter who sits in the White House—and who pickets it—drastic and far-reaching changes will continue to rock our society. The choice, as I see it, is whether hasty "solutions" will be imposed by whoever happens to be in power, or whether we can bring these conflicts under manageable control and, in doing so, learn how to manage the fresh changes that are certain to come tumbling in upon us.

Accelerated change quickens political passions and tends to make people impatient of facts that do not support the cause they favor. Probably I haven't escaped this contagion completely. Still, in examining what rapid change is doing to American life, I have followed the processes of change wherever they have led, reporting my findings whether they were pleasing or not, and trying to label my biases as the narrative runs along.

In analyzing these conflicts I combined intensive research into the nature of the problems with systematic interviewing of people caught up in these conflicts. Through these interviews I sought particularly to trace what effects these conflicts are having on the competition between our major parties to build a new majority coalition. How are old voter loyalties being altered? Are these changes moving us closer or farther apart as a nation?

One could look on this book as a sequel to *The Future of American Politics,* which told the story of how the famed Roosevelt coalition was brought together into a new Democratic majority that dominated American politics for so long. Has that coalition been broken for good? Can it still be revitalized? What sort of new majority coalition is Richard Nixon trying to put together and how would it transform American politics if he succeeds?

2. Time As a Political Force

Although staggering problems confronted both presidents, Nixon can be said to have come into office in circumstances almost exactly opposite to those which prevailed when Franklin Roosevelt became president.

In 1933 the whole American economy had come to a halt; when Nixon was inaugurated nothing seemed to be standing still. Yet in both eras the American people gave evidence that they had not lost that personal ingenuity which enabled many of them to go about their affairs regardless of the government's doings.

When Roosevelt, as his first official act, closed all the banks in the country, a million Americans were not inconvenienced. They had learned during the Depression years to live without money by bartering their services for food and shelter.

For Nixon, of course, the great economic battle has been billboarded as inflation. Still, after more than a year of his efforts, an unrevealed number of Americans were using credit cards to pay taxes, which had been levied supposedly to curtail credit and spending.

From barter to credit cards represents quite a social leap. Writing about such prodigious changes and conflicts on the run requires new ways of organizing our thinking, with new concepts especially adapted to change.

One such concept that proved particularly helpful to me was the realization that rapid change makes time itself a political force.

Political time leaves virtually nothing untouched. As a result, sensitivity to time lights up obscure corners, yielding a keener sense of the deeper dimensions of all our problems.

Why, for example, has the battle to shape public opinion been pressed with such fierce, even fanatical tenacity? From my interviewing it was not surprising to discover that the views held by many voters reflected their upbringing, how they had been brought up to think about war, race, and money.

Digging more deeply, though, revealed that we are also divided by clashing visions of what the future should be like.

We might find it easier to compromise if we were not so conscious that the future is being molded by our daily actions and what is done *now* will have lasting effects.

At times, our capacity to overload the future is staggering. Take the much-advertised "fiscal dividend" that is supposed to become available as the economy grows and federal tax collections jump. One might suppose that the prospect of such a bonanza—as much as $15 billion year after year—would encourage greater flexibility in handling economic problems. Actually, it appears to have made our economy more rigid. Programs for spending the "dividend" are organized by competing claimants, and often the money is committed long before it becomes available.

When President Nixon came into office he had the politician's natural desire to launch a new program or two that could be headlined "Nixon did it." But Johnson had put a down payment on every political promise in sight. In a budget of more than $190 billion, Nixon's aides had trouble scraping together a few loose billions.

Another blinder on our political vision has been the practice of organizing our thinking of most public problems in terms of money. This remains the frame within which the debate over "reordering our priorities" rages, of how to shift tax dollars from one use to another.

But an effective sense of priorities requires time tags, which spell out what is to be done into units of time, as well as price tags.

Actually, much of the turmoil that divides us so furiously is over the use of time rather than money. Since all of our more critical conflicts are carriers of past neglects, each comes up at us as a double crisis, at two differing time-dimensions.

At one time-level—always on stage and highly visible—are all the clamorous pressures for "action now," with the varied tactics of impatience wheeled into belligerent display—marches and strikes, sit-in demonstrations and staged confrontations, northern and southern style.

But at another time-level, with each major conflict we find submerged, even hidden, neglects which have gone unrepaired for too long. Altering these long-range underlying forces is unavoidably a slow process, but if they are not dealt with, much that is attempted at the visible time-level could be nullified.

Basic to our whole crisis is that we have lost the proper balance between these two time-levels, between what is made visible and acted on and the deeper neglects we cannot seem to reach. Confrontations try to quicken the use of time, but often the actions taken are poorly thought through; simultaneously, evasions hold back long-overdue changes. As a result, orderly evolutionary change has been forced to yield to disruptive, spasmodic change.

Thinking in terms of time also provides a more sensitive basis for appraising Nixon's political strategy.

His first, current time-stage might be captioned: "To finish dividing the Democrats." One tactical problem Nixon faces is that the forces of realignment have been running most rapidly in the South, and yet to form a nationally spread majority Nixon needs to gain additional strength in the North and West.

This problem reflects the fact that the New Deal coalition has not collapsed in one heap, in the manner of the one-horse shay, but broke down at one enormously important point, that of racial conflict.

In fashioning his coalition, Franklin Roosevelt transformed the Democrats into a party whose main appeal was economic. By suppressing racial and religious prejudices beneath a stronger, Depression-born sense of economic interest, he was able to bring into a new majority both white and black workers, southerners and northerners, the children of immigrants and of the native-born.

In the South, this coalition of white workers and Negroes collapsed completely in 1968, Hubert Humphrey doing worse than any Democratic presidential candidate since Reconstruction. But in the North, the New Deal alliance, although suffering heavier losses than generally realized, held together with sufficient strength so Humphrey was almost able to win the presidency.

Since 1952 the Republicans have gained two U.S. senators and twenty-four congressional seats in the South, which remains the one region where large numbers of new Republican supporters can be recruited quite quickly. Nixon's problem has not been whether to pursue a southern strategy—he did that all through 1968—but how to do so, and more crucial, with what timing?

My own reading of Nixon's disposition is that he is seeking the broadest possible coalition, with political living space for both Strom Thurmond and Jacob Javits, Barry Goldwater and Nelson Rockefeller, John Tower and Charles Percy, plus, if possible, some Negroes.

But realignments are often shaped by the voters they attract. When Roosevelt was elected in 1932 there was a wide array of voting groups which had been looking for a party that could serve their economic interests. To the one-time supporters of Al Smith, former socialists, frustrated trade unionists, hard-pressed farmers, the varied minority elements in the cities—to all of them—the New Deal Democratic Party was exactly what they had dreamed of to realize long-held aims.

With the realignment that Nixon has been pressing, voters generally have been waiting to see how his economic policies and Vietnam turn out. But one voting element—the white southerners—has been itching to lay its hands on a new party. The Supreme Court's ultimatum to desegregate "at once" quickened its desires to use the Republican Party to fight the Court and hold back desegregation.

As political forces are running in the South, the decisive issue in 1972 is likely to be headlined:

NIXON CAN CHANGE THE COURT

This lure of a sympathetic "Nixon Court," I see as the key to his southern strategy. Handled effectively, it could lock up the South's 128 electoral votes, perhaps for good. That would be the political equivalent of Sherman's march to the sea, cutting the Confederacy in two. The Democrats would be divided so that the New Deal coalition could not be restored in its old form.

But it is possible that these gains could come too rapidly in relation to Nixon's strength outside of the South. Pro-civil-rights senators have had the votes to block his court nominations.

At stake in the 1970 Senate elections is whether enough liberal Democrats are beaten to give Nixon clear confirming power. A White House strategist examining the list of Democratic senators coming up for re-election would mark for defeat with double checks at least five names: Albert Gore in Tennessee, Ralph Yarborough in Texas, Harrison A. Williams, Jr. in New Jersey, Vance Hartke in Indiana, and Quentin N. Burdick in North Dakota.

A premature Nixon confrontation with the present Court would risk splitting the liberal Republicans in the North. Without being planned that way, New York City's 1969 mayoralty election turned into a test run of such a conservative strategy, when John Lindsay, rejected by the Republicans as their candidate, went on to be re-elected with liberal Republican and overwhelming Negro and Puerto Rican support. In that election, much of the voter following of both parties was reshuffled in a manner reminiscent of the Civil War period.

In its first time-stage, in short, the Nixon presidency has sought not political reconciliation, but a sharpening of divisions in the nation. The demolition of the old New Deal structure had to come first, to clear the ground for the erection of the new shining Republican edifice. The Democrats, for their part, have been equally intent upon sharpening prevailing dissensions. No pattern of possible victory for either party in 1972 can resolve our unreconciled conflicts. Even if Nixon were to win by a landslide, many of the voters supporting him would be doing so primarily to give him more time to deal with what are generally recognized as enormously difficult problems. Nor would he have brought into existence a stable and lasting Republican majority. After 1972 there would still lie ahead the testing of whether Nixon would be able to shift into the second time-stage of really bringing the nation together into a new unity.

3. The Quest for Unity

In plotting their strategies both the Republicans and Democrats have come to rely heavily on public opinion polls and computer analysis. But at least one crucial influence will remain unpredictable for several years, no matter what questions are asked by the pollsters or what data is fed into the computers.

This influence is the weakening of party loyalty generally, stimulated, as will be seen later, by prosperity, the changed role of government, and the emergence of a new generation of voters. As a result, dramatic voter swings from one election to the next have become almost a regular occurrence; but that is very different from gaining the sustained voter support which is essential to build and hold a stable and lasting party majority.

These ready-to-shift voters may refrain from giving either party a lasting majority until one of the parties manages to demonstrate that it can unite this sorely divided country.

This emphasis on unifying ability as a test of our political parties, readers should be warned, reflects a bias I have held to in all my political writings. The real drama of American politics, as I have seen it, has always lain in the ceaseless struggle for national unification, in our constant striving for that "more perfect union." This has always been a distinctively American problem because of our immense geographical expanse and the astonishing variety of people drawn to our shores.

Unifying a great nation like ours once it has become divided has never been an exercise in image-making or public relations. Always the unifying process has been one of conflict and reconciliation, touching virtually everything that was happening, as broad as the sweep of American history.

The label pinned onto the majority party has been relatively unimportant, whether it was considered "liberal" or "conservative," whether the party's leaders were politically clever or virtuous. The decisive factor has been the party's capacity to serve as the means through which the nation's needs for unification could be met.

During the era of Republican dominance after the Civil War, unification had to be achieved through physical expansion across the continent; the "impatient ones" were the robber barons, the railroad builders, and assorted monopolists.

The formation of the New Deal coalition was essentially an "adventure in social unification" which brought together into a new majority all of the once-despised "minority" elements—the unemployed, both white and black, along with the children and grandchildren of the former immigrant elements, debt-burdened farmers, and other victims of the Depression.

Today the American need remains one of social unification, but on the basis of a far more intimate involvement and under more perilous conditions than any which have ever prevailed in our history.

We are not a sick society. We have become an undergoverned and overmanipulated one. Part of our troubles reflects, I suspect, the fact that we have become perhaps the most demanding people in all history, asking more of each other than human imperfections enable us to deliver. Our productive wealth and technological skills sharpen this dilemma, since we cannot plead scarcity or ignorance as an alibi. It is largely to be able to demand more of each other that we exaggerate some of our dissensions and difficulties.

Another aspect of our troubles is a deeply rooted habit of letting conflicts "work themselves out" or to "let time cure all ills." But the sweep of uncontrolled change during recent years has generated new disunities and vulnerabilities in the country.

Two distortions that have developed and which clash fiercely for the allocation of tax resources, are also giving a strange sectional twist to party realignment. Looking to the Democrats are the northern cities, overburdened with lopsided concentrations of Negro populations. In the South and Southwest, where Republicans are gaining strength, is concentrated much of our defense technology, whose costs in missile and nuclear development unbalance the rest of the economy.

Both of these distortions are national problems, requiring national solutions, but since each is centered in a different area, they tend to give our parties conflicting geographic orientations.

Age has become another new force for disunity. Each year between now and 1984, the eligible voting population will be enlarged by nearly four million new twenty-one-year-olds. For many of these youths entry into society must still be reconciled with the protective walls that have been erected by older people.

Wherever one looks at American society today, high potential is confronted by high tension; full employment by inflation; vast expectations of what government can do by vast fears of what government may do.

It is at this screamingly high pitch of conflict that the American nation must be unified, not in tune with the slow time of accepted tradition, but in terms of acute self-awareness and impatience.

Where all of it will come out remains uncertain. Still, I am reasonably optimistic and feel that some years from now we will be able to look back upon these impatient years as part of a larger drama of a great nation adjusting its political habits and institutions in a time-shortened world.

Profound adjustments will have to be made. Our parties, if they are to succeed in performing their customary unifying role, are likely to be transformed.

Three new sensitivities which both parties will have to acquire can be discerned:

1. Both parties will be adjusting to the many novel political relationships that arise from our having become so highly managed a society. As our first president-manager, Lyndon Johnson undertook to manage the economy, racial relations, and a war, all at once. He left behind a legacy, impressive in its accomplishments but equally impressive in the demands that were stirred for safeguards against the excesses of too much White House management.

Nixon has been brewing a different managerial mix—what he hopes will be a "strict constructionist" Supreme Court, more power for the states, more concern for balanced budgets—all of which are designed to be visibly different from the Johnsonian memories.

But the test of unity comes through performance, not rhetoric. Will the Nixon mix sustain economic prosperity, bring racial peace and freedom from war?

2. The parties will also be struggling to adapt to the quickened pace of time. Here again the example of Lyndon Johnson has been serving as a point of departure. Under Johnson, the Democratic majority was given a push toward becoming an impatient coalition, which whipped itself on to undertake too much, too quickly. This spurring urge may have reflected Johnson's own restless energies and prodigious ability to manipulate everything his hands could reach. There was also the competing and goading presence of Robert Kennedy, who had pitched his political appeal to the most impatient voting elements.

It would be a nice literary touch to depict Nixon as building a "patient coalition" in contrast with the Johnson-Kennedy effort. But that would not be accurate despite Nixon's emphasis on lowered voices.

His major actions, all deliberately timed, vary strangely in their pacing. Efforts to slacken the enforcement of school desegregation in the South suggest a slower tempo but they also risk ending the whole integration effort, which would represent a new kind of impatience. Similarly, the spacing of troop withdrawals from Vietnam suggests slower action but they seem also to reflect a determination to stay in Asia whose implications are uncertain.

Nixon's new family assistance plan is a fine example of careful progress; he seems to have moved quite quickly to commit us to a long-range expansion of the ABM missile program.

My overall impression is of a president testing public opinion and congressional roll calls to determine how fast he can move toward goals he has not fully revealed to the people. Also it may be that the only coalitions possible these days are impatient ones.

3. Both parties will also have to come up with a workable answer to the question of what the voters can expect from the processes of politics and what should be considered beyond the reach of politics.

These decisions—what is left in, what is dropped out—could prove the most revealing political actions to watch, since they reflect so closely how a managed society operates. The computer can be taken as a symbol. Computer experts have a favorite wisecrack—"garbage in garbage out," which is their way of saying that what is programed into the machine determines what comes out on the printout.

If something is left out, it is as if it does not exist. The struggle to be included in the programing could become among the most crucial of all our conflicts.

This suggests another concept that might be helpful in judging change: to pay special attention to the acts of selection that are going on around us —by our leaders, by ourselves, by other people. These decisions will point to how the future is being shaped.

Every president, of course, feels that he must do many things he does not relish to gain and consolidate his power, but that once the rough battling is over, he will be able to "rise above politics," be more statesmanlike, and put his ideals to work.

This is certainly true for Richard Nixon as it was for Franklin Roosevelt and other presidents; and should be kept in mind as one weighs the Nixon actions and policies. But a managed society brings one difference which our political leaders have not yet learned. Thus far the programing of a managed society has proven far more rigid than one less subject to management. Once something is left out of the computers it is not easily gotten in.

The stubbornness of inflation and the extent of dissension in the nation suggest that we have been overloading our government.

But whose expectations are to be dropped out of the government computers and whose are to be left in? Pressures for government action will vary enormously if the Supreme Court's desegregation decisions are obeyed, defied or sidetracked; if employment and prices run high or low, if we really reduce our commitments abroad or plunge in somewhere because of some "communist" happening.

More than one election, perhaps more than one presidency will probably be required to develop the unifying balance of what controls are to be applied and where permissive policies should run free, what time tempo is best for the nation, what government should not try to do.

If our entanglements were simply domestic there might be little need to worry over how long this process would take. But at stake in our struggle for social unification is also our own and world survival.

The domestic troubles of Soviet Russia and Red China yield us an uncertain span of time to complete this process of reducing our foreign commitments and coming to terms among ourselves. Will we make it? Or will the spectacle of a divided, distracted America encourage the kind of adventurism abroad that could bring on the war we dread to think about? Or will the urgencies of foreign affairs be used to justify over-quick "solutions" at home?

That, in essence, is the ordeal of national unification that I have tried to describe in this book. Where do we stand in this race between unity and disruption? What is it we are witnessing today—the breakdown of this country, or the self-conflict of a nation determined to preserve its freedoms as it takes the measure of what unity requires?

Let us begin with the voters themselves and why the failure of image-making in the election of 1968 was a portent of so much to come.

THE UNFINISHED BUSINESS OF AMERICA

Look Magazine

Just what shape the bicentennial celebration will take, five Fourth of Julys hence, remains unclear. But it seems to us that the occasion of our 200th anniversary could more profitably encourage thought on the shape of the nation itself: What kind of society are we? What kind should we be?

Source: *Look* (July 13, 1971), Vol. 35, pp. 57–61. *Look* Magazine, copyright © Cowles Communications, Inc., 1971. Reprinted by permission.

Accordingly, LOOK asked a number of Americans for their ideas about the things we might do for ourselves while we wait for the big birthday party.

John W. Gardner
CHAIRMAN, COMMON CAUSE

We will not accomplish our shared purposes as a nation without drastically renewing our political and governmental institutions—making them responsive and accountable to the citizenry. We have the kind of system that will permit us to do that, if we have the courage, if we have the honesty, and if we're willing to do the hard, pointed things that have to be done.

One example: If we could have lobbying-control statutes, campaign-financing controls, and statutes requiring full disclosure of conflicts of interest in the Federal Government and every state legislature, we would transform the political landscape of this country.

Whenever you talk about access, responsiveness, accountability, you have to bring it down to the things that prevent and obstruct these things. And the access of people to power is blocked by the access of *money* to power. What you can see most vividly in every state legislature today is what some critics call the third house of the legislature: the lobbies. They're in effect the same groups that indulge in campaign spending, and the extent that they stand as sort of a Chinese Wall around the legislatures diminishes access on the part of the people.

Second example: The seniority system in the Congress of the United States is a direct denial of the principle of accountability. The power structure of Congress is the committee chairmen. Not the majority leader, not the Speaker, but the chairmen of the powerful committees. They never have to stand for election before their fellow party members, their peers. There's no way their peers can hold them to account.

I could multiply examples, but the point I want to make is this: at the time of our founding as a nation, a group of men who were essentially citizens—not professional civil servants, not professors of public administration but essentially a banker, several lawyers, farmers and so on—sat down and worked out a system that was really extraordinarily impressive from a point of view I take very, very seriously: it was almost uniquely designed to accommodate change. But the institutions within that system are just as vulnerable to decay as *any* human institution; they couldn't be otherwise.

But we have proceeded to neglect this marvelously flexible system, shamefully. Who spends time worrying about his city council or state legislature? And yet, the public interest is being done in every day in these bodies, and in the Congress and the regulatory agencies. It's ironic that a people who will fight and die for the principles of self-government will ignore the instruments of self-government.

You look at a state legislature and you see the obscene conflicts of interest that exist in that body. You see that 24 state legislatures meet only every two years. It's almost incredible: the sessions are too short, the bills get jammed through, there's no way the citizen can know when a hearing is scheduled. . . . So I'm not speaking of generalities. There are specific things that can be changed.

But in the case of political and governmental institutions, the shake-up, the process of renewal, has to start with the citizens. It can't come from anywhere else. If we'd waited for a civil rights movement, or a peace movement, or a conservation movement to emerge from the innards of the bureaucracy, we'd still be waiting.

So I think the most important thing we can do by 1976 is to go back to the idea that citizen-statesmen created this country—and citizens have to renew it.

George C. Wallace
GOVERNOR OF ALABAMA

I have great faith in the collective wisdom and judgment of the mass of the American people. I feel that by our 200th birthday, our country will have stabilized and settled down, and the small minority group that wants to destroy this society—a society that most people in other parts of the world would like to emulate—that their moment will have passed, because of the insistence of the American people that we get on and stop all of this attempt at violent change. People believe in change, but it ought to be done through the constitutional context that's open to anyone if he has a majority viewpoint.

I think we'll have a lot to celebrate, even with all the things happening that I don't like in our country. I've been critical of many actions of the Government, but no country has ever given as much blood or treasure in defense of freedom in the world as has the United States, with no territorial aggrandizement plans at all.

We can reach new heights in industrial production in five years; and by that time, we should change the tax structure. You're beginning to get a great hue and cry about these private foundations: people putting their wealth into foundations has resulted in higher taxes for the average workingman and businessman; and by 1976, I think we could have a more equitable tax structure to celebrate.

The people in this country, through their elected representatives, can put the Supreme Court in its place. They can have its authority to determine every phase and aspect of people's lives—they can have that authority limited.

And I think the problems of race will be accentuated in the large cities above the Mason-Dixon line, and more progress and good race relations will exist in the southern parts of the country, and that we Southerners will be praying that people in other parts of the country can solve their problems.

I think there could be an effort on the part of the Government to disperse industry, so that all of our population will not become one great urban mass on the Eastern Seaboard, or in the Los Angeles area, or around the Great Lakes. We must do this or we'll compound our economic and social problems; the abnormal growth of large urban areas without proper planning is not good.

I think industry and government at all levels can join together in an effort to clean up the environment, both air and water, with a reasonable approach. (Not the approach of some ecologists today who, if they closed down all industry, would put everybody out of work.)

I hope the country will realize in the immediate future that the optimism of some of the doves, in predicting that the Communists' strategic-weapons buildup will slow down, has been false optimism, and that the Soviets are not only reaching parity but they're going to be superior.

The only way you can guarantee generations of peace is to be so strong militarily, offensively and defensively, that no nation would ever do anything but *talk* with you. Now, we're fast approaching the point where they will do all the talking and we'll have to do the listening. . . .

So I hope that by 1976, this country would have overrun these extremist peace folks who themselves are causing a situation to exist where there will *be* no peace. And I hope that this big drive against the military-industrial complex will be seen for what it is. Now, as far as cost overruns and waste in defense go, I'm just as much against war profiteering as anybody else is: I've advocated a war-profits tax even now, in an undeclared war. But we cannot, because of profiteers, let our defenses get to the point where there'll be no profit for *anybody* in our country. I think everything else we've been talking about will be for naught if that happens.

Also, by 1976, the Government will have realized that it has failed in an attempt to run the public school systems of our states. The people will have demanded a return of local control and called for reason and logic to prevail instead of busing and social experimentation—this will be demanded on a non-discriminatory basis without mistreating any group of people.

By 1976, this nation's technology and industrial know-how can provide the consumer goods for the masses of our people and a high standard of living, and at the same time have us in such a superior position—defensively and offensively—that there can be no World War III.

Rev. Jesse Jackson
DIRECTOR, OPERATION BREADBASKET

In my opinion, there are three things we can do to make the Two Hundredth Anniversary Celebration worth celebrating. They are: First, implement the total and complete withdrawal of United States troops from Southeast Asia *this year*. Second, cut the military budget at least by 25 percent and redirect these funds into the cities, which are near bankruptcy. And third, end the current "welfare" payments to General Motors, Lockheed, Boeing and the Wall Street investment houses. There are about 50 major corporations in this class, each of whom has been getting more than $100 million a year over the past several years from the Federal treasury. These welfare payments to the rich take the form of "defense contracts." It seems to me that this is a gross misuse of the taxpayers' money. These large corporations should be allowed to sink or swim in the good old "free enterprise" tradition rather than looking to welfare handouts from the Government in order to guarantee their profits and dividends to stockholders.

(And none of the defense contractors who has been appealing for welfare has demonstrated any willingness to shift from a war economy to a peace economy. There was no suggestion that they could now make hospital beds or build schools. There's no commitment there. So the nation needs to develop, by 1976, a national *will* toward peace.)

These three steps are an absolutely essential condition to prevent this nation from becoming a military state. To achieve them will probably take the better part of the next five years, since we would be naïve to think that the opponents of such changes will not put up stiff resistance. Nevertheless, they are possible of achievement if we mobilize young voters, who number 25 million and will be voting for the first time in the 1972 elections, together with the black community, Chicanos, women power and the unemployed into a kind of progressive third force. The empowerment of these constituents, who have been locked out and denied really representative government, has been the central purpose and outlook guiding our Operation Breadbasket program in Chicago and other urban centers. The old-line Democratic and Republican clubhouse politicians represent a force for preserving the status quo, while the George Wallace movement represents a second political force for carrying the nation backward to the "good old days." So, the nation needs this new political *third force,* which in numbers represents a majority of the population, capable of moving the nation forward, resuming the effort to fulfill the ideals of the Declaration of Independence. Such a progressive political force ought, in the national interest, seriously to consider running a black presidential candidate in the 1972 elections, selected from among the number of highly qualified persons now in public life. Or the appointment of a black or Indian U.S. Attorney General, who would be assigned to enforce the laws that have been passed over the last 20 years to insure that justice would be indivisible.

By 1976, we should be considering a woman for the highest office in the land as well. If Indira Gandhi can run India, if Golda Meir can run Israel, there are women in America who could do it. We must fight male chauvinism as much as racism or militarism.

By 1976, the cradle of democracy should not only have full voter registration for all of its citizens, but should have *automatic* voter registration—just as you're automatically registered when you're born and you're automatically taxed. If you have automatic taxation, but you don't have automatic representation, you have tyranny.

As an act of national conscience, it seems to me we also have a moral obligation to begin undertaking responsibility for rehabilitating Vietnam, Laos and Cambodia; rebuilding homes, hospitals, farms and cities that have been destroyed by U.S. bombings. Such a program should be channeled through some appropriate United Nations agency.

Our nation needs the restoration of moral leadership in the White House, which has been missing since the assassination of President Kennedy eight years ago. Only a political movement with both vision and commitment toward ending militarism, racism, male chauvinism and poverty can create the milieu that will make the Two Hundredth Anniversary of the founding of the United States worth celebrating.

Gen. James M. Gavin
CHAIRMAN, ARTHUR D. LITTLE, INC.

The first thing we have to do is restore our society to a state of peace, by extricating ourselves from our involvement in Southeast Asia and reducing our commitment in Europe. And I'm not talking about isolationism: the world's too small—it's a global village, of course—for isolationism. No one's isolated from his neighbor now.

Next, the improvement of the domestic condition. I have very strong feelings about two things concerning the national condition—and when I speak of the national condition, I refer to our problems of housing, health care, education, transportation, the deterioration of our major population centers. . . .

I see revenue sharing as only a stopgap measure, because when you get to this point, obviously a proper system doesn't exist for providing adequate revenue for the states and the cities. To come up with the necessary revenue, I think we need what some people call a TVA system: a tax-value-added system. We now have a mountainous number of taxes of which most people are unaware—whether it's a tax on cigarettes, or gasoline, or theater admissions or whatever. These are discriminatory . . . cigarette smokers are catching it at the moment because the public accepts it, but these are essentially discriminatory.

Well, human society has arrived at a point where it can be so productive, with present automation and machine installations, that we ought to do away with all this mess and simply put a tax on each step in the manufacturing process—each increment of labor—all the way up. It'll mean a tremendous source of funds, and in a way, this would no longer be a tax, just a dividend from the productivity of our society.

Next, we have a remarkable system for getting money from the citizenry through the Internal Revenue Service—through its computers, through its regional organization, it's damn near flawless. We have a marvelous way of administering justice through the Federal court system. We have wonderful ways of keeping track of the economy through Federal economic regions. We have the country beautifully organized to do all of these things—even the armed forces have regional organizations: Army areas, naval districts, and so on. But when it comes to administering to the most critical problem of all—welfare—and responding to the social needs, how do we do it? Through an antiquated political structure, the administration of which is transient in character, staffed by political hacks.

Now, this is absolute nonsense—it's so wrong you can hardly believe that we do it this way. We must have a *regional* welfare organization, manned by competent, politically sensitive and capable appointees. The Federal Government should divide the country up into perhaps three major areas: east, middle, west. Each of these should be broken up into maybe three or four subregions, headed by a retired governor, or the equivalent —a man of honesty, integrity, of proven ability and leadership, but who's sensitive to political needs. He should have at his disposal a computer system at least equal to the IRS', which gets the money *out* of the system, to distribute it and respond to needs.

With these two major changes—a more effective national taxing program and a more efficient system for administering to the nation's social needs, I'd have high hopes that the country could administer its own resources well. These changes aren't going to come about right away, but in five years, we could get them done. We could do tremendous things for this country before 1976.

Its holdings are vast. It has $250 billion in assets, probably as much acreage as New York state. It's larger than any financial institution in the world.

The only way you can get rid of its stranglehold over this country is to make the political power structure more responsive to the people that have been excluded. You have to organize a new political coalition to do it. You've got to see that young people, who now have 25 million new votes, register that vote and insist on a stake in that power structure. They've been feeling that either they don't care or that they're going to have a revolution. They've got to opt for power *in* the structure to create social change. And women are going to have to be organized. They're examining their political, social and economic stations in life. They want change, and for that, they must have political power.

And working people are beginning to realize that their bosses, their leaders, their elected representatives are not acting for them. They've carried the burden of this war more than others. First their sons were killed in greater proportions. Then their pay got taken away in higher taxes. And now they haven't got jobs.

This is where the hope of democracy and our Constitution and the American dream really lies. If we don't organize political power, and begin to put *people* into the power structure, instead of politicians, then I think there'll be nothing to celebrate.

George Wald
PROFESSOR OF BIOLOGY, HARVARD

Our task now, in a sense, is to repossess America, to try to regain the American tradition, which has been badly eroded in recent years. We have a generation of young people who, because they've never known anything else, think that certain practices that have come into our country only since World War II have always been there—that they're part of the American tradition, whereas in fact they do it enormous violence.

The very thought that we could have become a country with, by now, 23 years of compulsory military service, a kind of permanent draft—nothing could be more un-American. There were generations of immigrants who came from Central Europe and Russia to escape compulsory military service. Now we have it, in peacetime and wartime alike.

There's been a very serious erosion of our judical procedures. Justice in our courts has become, for one thing, frightfully expensive. And just very recently, many new practices have come in that harass and imprison people without due process—such matters as detention while awaiting trial in overcrowded calendars, excessive bail, the Government's bringing people to trial on preposterous and ill-prepared charges—charges that are eventually dismissed, but, in the course of the trial, a contempt citation will succeed in jailing them anyway.

We once represented a kind of beacon light to the world, and all the world looked to us for things that Americans were proud of and I hope will be proud of again—our sense of human liberty, justice, generosity. I think we no longer quite represent these things as we did, but rather great wealth, great power, great greed. And so, if we're to be proud of our country again, I think a great many fundamental changes need to be made—so fundamental as to constitute a continuance of the American Revolution. No revolution is permanent and we need to renew ours.

I think we shall have little to celebrate in 1976 if we still have compulsory military service; if we're still supporting, as part of what's called the "free world," the largest collection of military dictatorships ever assembled; if we're still, habitually, voting not for candidates we genuinely desire and believe in, but for the lesser evil; if it still costs huge sums to get justice in American courts; if it still costs ever so much more—astronomical sums—to be elected to public office; if poverty is still hereditary, as it is now—not through the operation of genes, but through malnutrition, bad living conditions, inadequate schooling; if racial injustice is still rampant.

I think we need to get out of the Vietnam war rapidly and completely, but I think that, shameful as it is, the Indochina war is only symptomatic of a situation that needs fundamental correction. I think we need to get rid of the draft, but in doing that I think we need to cut back drastically the size of the armed forces, which are at an unprecedented level. The American tradition is an all-volunteer army, but a *small* one.

We need—this is crucial—to cut back sharply the so-called defense budget; we need to demilitarize our present position. We've turned into a kind of armed camp.

But these are all negative things. The postive program everyone knows: better health care—our health care costs us more and brings us less than that of any other advanced nation in the world; better schools; more and better and cheaper housing; better nutrition—we know now officially that 10 to 20 million Americans regularly go hungry; better mass transportation —too many cars on the road; and dealing with pollution is another problem.

So there are all these problems, all do-able things, and indeed we know how to cope with them. The necessary thing is to follow through, to do the things that thoughtful and well-meaning and patriotic Americans *want* to do.

Bella Abzug
CONGRESSWOMAN (D., N.Y.)

You have to change the political power structure, which I think can be done within two elections. As we approach our 200th anniversary, it seems to me shocking that the power structure is so limited.

The thing that struck me most when I came to Congress—although I knew that we were only 13 women in the Congress, representing 51 percent of the population, and only 13 blacks (a symbolic baker's dozen of each) and very few other minorities—was that essentially we had very few young people in Congress, and no people who represented the working person. It's a middle-aged, middle-class, white male power structure; no wonder it's been so totally unresponsive to the needs of this country for so long.

If we're talking about the 200th anniversary of our country, about chartering real freedoms, you can't do that if the legislative body of the country isn't a free body. And it's not, if it doesn't reflect the diversity and dynamics of this country—if all classes are not represented, and all sexes and all ethnic groups.

There will be nothing to celebrate unless we restore real democracy to this country. What we're suffering from is a *crisis* in democracy: politically, socially and economically. Let's not kid ourselves. You can't have economic democracy in a country that is one of the richest in the world but in which 15 million people still hunger, in which people are still without adequate housing.

And you don't have a social democracy either. The elderly, for example, are totally shortchanged in this country. People who put in their whole lives working are afraid to walk the streets because of the drug problem that we've no funds to fight. They're afraid to go into a store to buy a piece of fruit, because the prices are so high. They don't know if they'll be able to pay their rent; it's rising out of sight.

We don't have a political democracy. You have the right to vote, but that's not serious if there's no opportunity for you to determine the course of government. We've permitted the military machine to take over governing us, silencing democracy. It's become the arm of Government that dominates the political structure.

CONSERVATISM MAY HAVE A FUTURE AFTER ALL

A. James Reichley
Research associate: Patricia Langan

On the basis of highly visible political developments, U.S. conservatism appears to be in retreat and disarray. President Nixon, elected with conservative support, has violated one conservative dogma after another: aversion to deep deficits in the federal budget, resolute opposition to the major Communist powers abroad, and nonintervention in the economy at home. What's more, the attempt by some ideological conservatives to rally

Source: *Fortune* (July 1972), pp. 44–47; 105–106. Reprinted from the July 1972 issue of *Fortune* Magazine by special permission; © 1972 Time Inc.

opposition to Nixon behind Ohio Congressman John Ashbrook in this year's Republican primaries has proved a humiliating flop.

And yet there are underlying political and social forces at work that seem capable of moving the U.S. in a conservative direction. Traditional liberalism is losing ground, even in its old big-city strongholds, because of its seeming inability to deal adequately with contemporary social problems. The new radicalism, rising on liberalism's left, is frightening or offensive to many middle-of-the-road voters. On the race question, the social costs of efforts to achieve complete integration have risen beyond what even many liberals are willing to pay. Unsafe streets, unruly youth, dirty movies, spreading use of drugs, are all doing their bit to win converts to conservatism. So is the emergence of a "counterculture" that challenges the moral outlooks of practically all traditional religious or ethnic groups. The startling vote for George Wallace in many of this year's Democratic presidential primaries grew in part out of the race issue, but also expressed a widespread anger among working-class whites at having their values scorned.

These forces working for conservatism have emphatically *not* increased public backing for economic or foreign-policy doctrines of the kind preached by, say, William Buckley's *National Review*. The Nixon Administration's economic and international initiatives, which some avowed conservatives deplore, have actually strengthened the President's appeal for most of those who are moving in a conservative direction on social issues. Nor is social conservatism, as some liberals fear, creating a climate favorable to police-state repression. Most potentially conservative voters favor tough law enforcement, but hold on to traditional democratic ideals. Even Governor Wallace, before he was shot, had begun to add the code phrase "with justice" to his cries for "law and order."

Conservatism, in other words, now has a golden chance to achieve political success—*if* it gives up rigid adherence to laissez-faire economics and belligerent anti-Communism, *and* offers continuation of a generally free and open society. But then, in the view of some fundamentalist conservatives, it would no longer be conservatism.

The Heart Reinforcing the Head

Like liberalism, conservatism has taken on so many varied and even contradictory meanings that nobody any longer is quite sure what it stands for. Some political analysts have suggested that the meanings of both "conservative" and "liberal" are now so muddled that the terms tend to confuse rather than clarify, and should be abandoned. No discussion of modern politics, however, can go far without them. There certainly exists a body of opinions, attitudes, and principles that is now summed up in our minds, however vaguely, by the word "conservative."

To a large extent, the varied manifestations of conservatism can be traced to two basic strains: a conservatism of the head, growing out of common sense and the will to survive; and a conservatism of the heart, growing out of affection for the familiar, the traditional, the persons and places among which one finds one's roots. In general, conservatism of the head and heart are found in the same people and tend to reinforce each other. A politician who for practical reasons is wary about making basic changes in a social system is likely also to exhibit strong emotional attachment to its institutions and traditions.

Conservatism of the head, of course, is related to the natural tendency among those who are well off to look out for their own vested interests. This cource of conservatism is little mentioned by conservatives themselves. But the current spread of conservative attitudes is due in part simply to general affluence. As so astute an authority as George Meany has pointed out, working people who rise on the economic scale begin to worry about defending their own stakes in the system.

Even those who are not particularly well off, however, have an interest in the maintenance of social order. Street crime bears more heavily on the poor than on the well-to-do. Liberal remedies for dealing with the "causes" of disorder have not worked (partly, liberals would maintain, because they have not really been tried). As a result, many working-class families are now turning to politicians who promise tougher law enforcement. The Gallup Poll shows that even among persons with incomes of less than $5,000 a year, more than one-third regard themselves as conservatives.

Conservatism of the head, at least in its more sophisticated form, does not oppose social change, but argues that change should come gradually and rise organically out of natural social processes. There are so many unknown variables at work in the operation of society, conservatives say, that no one can tell in advance what effects a given change imposed from above will lead to. Radical efforts to remake society, such as those recommended by Plato or Marx, are sure to turn out differently from what their advocates intended—often with catastrophic results for persons and institutions caught up in these experiments.

This kind of argument underlies the philosophy of "strict constructionism" that President Nixon says he looks for in prospective Supreme Court appointees. "Strict construction" is not, as its critics charge (and as even some of its apologists appear to believe), based on the view that the Supreme Court must stay within the limits of what is specifically written in the Constitution. Nor need the Court confine itself to the exact ideas that appear to have been in the minds of those who drafted the Constitution or various amendments. The Constitution obviously contains broad moral concepts such as "cruel and unusual punishments" and "due process of law," whose content is bound to change with the evolution of social thought.

But the strict constructionist argues that the courts should be restrained in applying these general moral directives, leaving their interpretation wherever possible to the workings of the legislative and executive branches, which are politically responsible to the people. The meaning of "due process of law" at any given time should reflect broad social consensus, rather than the opinion of an individual jurist, or even the views of an intellectual elite.

A weakness of conservatism of the head—when it comes to gathering popular support—is its negative aspect. Don't try too hard to make things better, it seems to say, or you are likely to make them much worse. This may under some circumstances be good advice, but it tends to sound crabbed, particularly to the young. And it cannot have much appeal for those who believe that things are not likely to get much worse for them under any circumstances.

These difficulties are to some extent overcome by the other form of conservatism—conservatism of the heart. Even in the most cosmopolitan or sophisticated societies, a great many people still seem to yearn, perhaps instinctively, for an orderly environment in which to conduct daily life, roots in a particular piece of the earth's geography, inclusion in a family, and the sense of belonging to a community—and even for some kind of religious explanation for the basis of existence. (Emotion can work against conservatism, too. Most people, particularly during adolescence and early adulthood, are also moved by a seemingly contrary set of yearnings—desires for adventure, independence, revolutionary change. From this latter set, of course, springs the other half of the human story.)

Conservatism of the heart supplies the emotional mortar without which any society would quickly fall apart. When natural feelings of loyalty and affection are undermined, social chaos looms. This kind of conservatism, however, also has its share of liabilities. A comparatively minor fault is its weakness for clinging to forms and structures that are no longer suited to deal with current needs. More seriously, roots of both racism and belligerent nationalism can grow in the affinities that men feel for others who share the same inherited past.

The Expanding White "We"

In present-day U.S. politics, conservatism of both the head and the heart have been strengthened by the emergence of the so-called "social issue." In part, this is a reflection of white concern over problems rising out of racial difference. The Wallace vote in this year's primaries reads like a seismograph of racial tensions. But for many people, the race problem is a less important cause of social conservatism that distress and anger over current challenges to social and cultural traditions. Many middle-class people, in fact, are *restrained* from moving toward conservatism by reluctance to take a position identified as antiblack. Manifestations of the new radicalism—communes, women's lib, drugs, pornographic films, demonstrations, flag burning, the whole gamut—have helped drive together traditional culture groups that previously emphasized their differences. White Protestants, Catholics, and Jews, working class as well as middle class, have begun to conclude that they may after all share a sort of culture in common. The white "we" is expanding.

This rapprochement among traditional culture groups is being aided by the easing of old disputes. For instance, the decline of confidence among almost all groups in the effectiveness of the public schools has reduced resistance among non-Catholics to the Catholic demand for some kind of government financial assistance for parochial schools. This shift has made it politically practical for the Nixon Administration to court Catholic opinion on the issue. Weakening Catholic opposition to birth control (though not to abortion) has removed another cause of friction between Catholic and non-Catholic conservatives. On moral and cultural issues that provoke national controversies, conservatives of all groups are now often able to stick together. For example, the drive by some Protestant denominations to restore prayer to the public schools is supported by many conservative Catholics.

Each of the traditional religious cultures had some inherently conservative traits—as the very fact of their being traditional would imply. Protestantism, though radical in origin, has been the nation's dominant culture group from the start, and many Protestants have a large stake in the maintenance of established institutions. Moreover, some of the new radicalism's particular targets, such as the "work ethic" and puritan moral codes, are offshoots of Protestant tradition. Catholicism, because of its own authoritarian structure and its organic view of society, tends naturally to conservatism. Traditional Catholic identification with the Democratic party has reflected the fact that the economic and social establishment has been largely Protestant. Even Judaism, which in the U.S. has been predominantly liberal and has produced many radicals, grows out of a tradition that emphasizes such conservative values as family ties and social decorum.

The New Soft-Shells

Among intellectuals, too, a form of conservatism is attracting new adherents. As social commentator Irving Kristol observes, a good many former liberal intellectuals are reacting against the excesses they see around them. Most of these (some of whom still call themselves liberals) are drawn to a new camp of what may be called "soft-shell" conservative intellectuals, in contrast to the "hard-shells" such as Milton Friedman, Edward Banfield, and many of the writers for *National Review*. Prominent soft-shells include Daniel Moynihan, Nathan Glazer, and Oscar Handlin at Harvard; Alexander Bickel at Yale; Morton Kaplan at the University of Chicago; and William Gerberding at U.C.L.A. The soft-shells tend to be more pragmatic and more humanitarian than the hard-shells. They emphasize social responsibilities as well as personal rights, and are less doctrinaire in opposing government intervention to help solve economic or social problems.

Blacks have so far shown little inclination to join the conservative coalition. The evolving black culture recognizes some bonds with the white counterculture—some aspects of which in fact derive from attitudes and forms of behavior first explored among blacks. But many blacks draw back from the nihilistic direction in which the new radicalism seems to be moving. And with the growth of the black middle class, a drift to conservatism might be expected to follow. What stands in the way is the continuation of discrimination based on race. Blacks can hardly miss the point that to some extent they are what traditional white groups are uniting *against*. So long as conservatism has racial undertones, there will be few black conservatives.

Only a minority of white conservatives now discernibly favor racial discrimination. But the potential for racism inherent in conservatism is one of the most serious problems that conservatives have to contend with. This is not because they need a great many black votes to win elections—in the short run, there may be more to be gained, as some conservative theoreticians have suggested, by appealing to the racial fears and aversions of white voters. But a movement that achieved power through such appeals would probably lead to an intensification of violence, certainly to a thickening of guilt and anger. Society would sink further into turmoil and dissension— the very stresses that conservatives claim they can moderate.

Transgressing the Faith

For conservative ideologues, it is understandably frustrating to discover that growth in strength for one kind of political and social conservatism has in no way advanced their own most cherished doctrines. They did not, after all, labor in the vineyards for so many years to put a President responsive to the views of Henry Kissinger and Pat Moynihan in the White House. Not surprisingly, many of the ideologues agree with the verdict of William Rusher, publisher of *National Review*. "Mr. Nixon," he says, "is not only not a conservative; he is, on rigorous analysis, the central obstacle to a healthy conservative movement in this country, and for the country's sake he must go."

These fundamentalists accuse Nixon of transgressing two of the most important elements in the conservative faith: laissez-faire economics and militant anti-Communism abroad. There is no doubt that he has moved away from these doctrines as conservatives generally expressed them in the 1950's and the 1960's. What is in doubt is whether these particular formulations are *essential* to conservatism, or whether they merely represented conservative responses to a particular set of facts at a particular time, subject to revision as new facts appeared.

The laissez-faire theory of economics, based on the belief that social progress grows out of free competition in the marketplace, has a tangled political history. During the nineteenth century it was generally regarded as a *liberal* doctrine, opposed to the conservatism represented by such leaders as Metternich and Disraeli. Only after the rise of socialism and other collectivist philosophies did laissez faire begin to wear conservative colors.

In the U.S., starting with the New Deal, a good many conservatives gradually accepted modifications of laissez faire. Responding to this drift, a "new conservatism," rigidly committed to laissez faire, began to take shape during the 1950's. This movement found its intellectual voices in *National Review* and the so-called Chicago school of economists. For a short time in 1964 it became the official philosophy of the Republican party. It now serves as dogma for the small group of stalwarts gathered behind Congressman Ashbrook.

A Goal Business Can Never Accept

The Ashbrook conservatives never tire of expressing astonishment and indignation over the failure of business to rally to their cause. Tom Winter, editor of *Human Events,* a conservative weekly newspaper published in Washington, raises a typical lament: "If the conservative movement had to depend on the business community, it wouldn't exist. Don't businessmen see the dangers in government controls? Too many are shortsighted, and willing to go along with anything for immediate gain."

Businessmen do indeed tend to trim their ideological sails to the prevailing social and political winds. But this is merely to say that they are more attached to practical realities than to abstract ideas—a common conservative characteristic. By its very nature, business is drawn to a moderate and flexible version of conservatism. All over the free world, businessmen give most of their political support to nonideological conservative parties. Business has every reason to fear too rapid or unpredictable alteration in the structure of society. While it can accommodate many liberal and even radical values, business can never accept the goal of enforced equality for everybody, toward which modern radicalism appears to be moving.

This natural inclination to conservatism, however, does not imply that business will oppose government intervention in economic matters at all times or in all places. Quite the contrary. Under some conditions, business will welcome the intervention of government as a stabilizer of economic and social change. In hopes that inflation could be slowed without severe restraint on economic growth, business has given general support to Nixon's imposition of wage and price controls.

Similarly, there is little basis for arguing that consistent conservatism requires eternal hostility to the Soviet Union or Communist China. The policy of containment of Communist aggression was a response to the perceived international facts of life following World War II. Containment was not uniquely conservative. Most liberals gave it their support. Some prominent conservatives, including Herbert Hoover and Robert Taft, opposed it, favoring instead a return to prewar isolationism. The containment policy as such was derived from sober calculation of national interest. But militant opposition to Communism was also motivated by a much more idealistic—much more romantic—set of goals: extending freedom all over the globe, preserving "democratic" regimes outside the iron and bamboo curtains, "making the world safe for diversity."

The changes in foreign policy instituted by Nixon may be said to represent the triumph of Metternichian realism over Wilsonian idealism in the U.S. world outlook. This shift may not be wholly desirable—carried too far, it could be a very bad thing for both the U.S. and the rest of the world—but it can hardly be called a retreat from conservatism.

Perfect Freedom for the Perfect

Law enforcement is one subject on which Nixon and the conservative ideologues still find much to agree. The ideologues praise his Supreme Court nominations (usually with the exception of Carswell, in whose "mediocrity" they found little to rejoice). And they support the Administration position on such police-power issues as wiretapping and no-knock entry. Some conservatives are bothered by the apparent contradiction between their advocacy of economic freedom and their willingness to accept some contraction of civil liberties to strengthen the police. Most, however, defend the latter on grounds of "practicality." Congressman Philip Crane of Illinois, a brainy young conservative who represents Chicago's North Shore suburbs, expresses an old conservative doctrine when he says: "Perfect freedom would require perfect people. In the light of history, we know that without the maintenance of order and virtue in society, no freedom is possible."

Reaction against crime and disorder is one of the principal factors now drawing middle-of-the-road voters toward conservatism. The 1970 elections, contrary to general impression, showed the strength rather than the weakness of law enforcement as a political issue. Despite the sluggishness of the economy, the over-all result of the congressional elections was moderately conservative. In New York, Ohio, Maryland, Tennessee, and Texas, candidates markedly more conservative than the incumbents they replaced won seats in the U.S. Senate—more than offsetting conservative losses in Illinois and California. In 1971, according to calculations made by *Congressional Quarterly,* the coalition of conservative Republicans and southern Democrats was significantly more successful in both houses of Congress than at any time during the past ten years.

But the law-enforcement issue, as the 1970 elections also showed, can be overdone. Middle-of-the-road voters do not respond favorably to being addressed as though they were potential vigilantes. Particularly in the crucial state of California, the Republican concentration on "law and order" in the days just before the election actually lost votes. And attempts to portray such moderate liberals as Adlai Stevenson in Illinois, Quentin Burdick in North Dakota, and Howard Cannon in Nevada as accomplices of crime and disorder were bound to backfire.

Pondering the election returns in December, 1970, the President himself decided that the Republican stance in the campaign had been too negative. While feeling that the Republicans had done about as well as could be hoped given the condition of the economy, he recognized that excessive emphasis on law and order had lost more than it had gained in major industrial states vital to his re-election. Partly as a result, he made broad reform of government the theme of his State of the Union message the following month. Adopting Disraeli's example (suggested to him by Moynihan), he set out to make the conservative party the party of reform.

Since that time, several elections have been won on all-out law and order appeals—notably, the election last fall of Frank Rizzo as mayor of Philadelphia and Edward Hanrahan's renomination as state's attorney of Cook County in this spring's Illinois Democratic primary. These were special situations. But Nixon may be tempted by them to return to strident emphasis on law and order. If he does, he will kick away much of his potential attraction for moderates.

Opportunity in a Radical Turn

The reformist strategy is probably conservatism's most promising route to political success. Conservatives need have no fear that by accepting change they are in danger (as both *National Review* and Ashbrook have charged) of becoming indistinguishable from liberal Democrats. The whole political wasteland through which Nixon is now venturing is a product of the virtual collapse of New Deal liberalism. The basic New Deal approach —essentially, as Senator Kenneth Keating used to say, "to find a problem and then throw money at it"—has been found wanting when applied to national problems, including unemployment, race relations, the condition of the cities, education, population distribution, health care, and crime.

If conservatism is to have a future, conservatives will have to seek means of dealing with these problems within the framework of basic American principles. In this pursuit there should be no hesitancy over making use wherever possible of institutions and devices that remain from the New Deal, Fair Deal, New Frontier, or Great Society. If most of these institutions failed finally to accomplish their intended missions, some of them have nevertheless performed socially valuable tasks, and should be continued as parts of a sounder over-all structure.

Politically, conservatives can benefit from the radical turn now being taken by some liberal politicians. One of the great difficulties faced by moderate conservatives in the U.S. in recent years has been differntiating their approach from that of moderate liberalism. Under Adlai Stevenson, John Kennedy, and Lyndon Johnson, the Democrats strove to be the party not of a single class but of the general national interest. Now, under the inspiration of the "new populism," many national Democratic politicians are again taking up the rhetoric of class war and the role of dividers of society. Conservatives, as a result, have the opportunity to claim the high ground of broad national unity.

Pragmatic conservatism—of the kind represented by Nixon and such close associates as John Connally and Melvin Laird—runs the danger of becoming so flexible as to lose touch with principle altogether. Yet the pragmatic approach has a much better chance than doctrinaire rigidity of advancing conservatism's two most important objectives: maintaining social order and keeping social change to a rate that does not exceed the capacity of human institutions and the human spirit to adapt. Neither of these aims —growing out of the basic principles of conservatism of the head and conservatism of the heart—is indissolubly linked to the political dogmas of the 1950's or the economic interest of any particular group. On the contrary, continuity of the conservative tradition now depends on the willingness of conservatives to become instruments of change.

What YOU Can Do—NOW

Ebony Magazine Editorial

A stormy debate is raging over the state of the black movement. This debate, insofar as it is political rather than personal, serves a useful purpose. In fact, it speaks well for the soul of black America that so many men and women are concerned and are actively participating on the level of dialogue. But for this dialogue to bear fruit millions of individuals are going to have to assume personal responsibility for the movement in their private and public lives. In other words, the dialogue is positive if it reminds us of our personal responsibilities. But it is a waste of time and energy if it is not based on an understanding that the black movement is not a spectacle to be applauded or booed from afar but the very movement and breath of our lives.

We stress this point because the black movement is in danger of becoming a spectator sport. An ominous manifestation of this fact is the large number of people who like to stand on the sidelines, awarding Brownie points to the gladiators, not knowing—perhaps not even caring—that the struggle involves their survival. Another manifestation of the same fact is the tendency to blame all problems on the presence or absence of certain leaders with certain personal traits. To be sure, there is a crisis of black leadership, but that crisis is a function of the crisis of black followership. In the long run, people get the kind of leaders they deserve. And it is appropriate, under certain circumstances, to reason from the qualities of the leaders to the qualities of the followers.

Liberation Voyeurism

Viewed from this standpoint, the question of the state of the black movement assumes a new and challenging aspect. And within the context of this new perspective, we can say that one of the major problems today is the problem of the large number of people who do nothing else except debate the problem of black leadership. Stated in a somewhat different way, the major problem is not what X leader or Y leader has done but what have you done and what are you prepared to do for yourself and for your children and your children's children.

Because of the danger of the hour, because of the enormity of the obstacles and the paucity of our resources, we can no longer afford spec-

Source: *Ebony* (May 1972), p. 96. Reprinted by permission of *Ebony* Magazine, copyright 1972 by Johnson Publishing Company, Inc.

tatorship and liberation voyeurism. Nor can we afford the pleasant illusion that somebody else is going to shoulder our burdens and save us from ourselves.

The time has come for every black person to assume responsibility for himself and for all his brothers and sisters.

The time has come, as one author said recently, for us "to stop acting like spectators at our own funeral."

Contrary to the common impression, the Black Revolution is not an event unrelated to your life. On the contrary, the Revolution is doing what you are doing, and the Revolution is not doing what you are not doing. The Revolution is in your heart and your mind; it depends on your legs and arms; it rises and falls with your action or lack of action.

Control Your Space

Faced with this fact, many men and women throw up their hands and ask: "But what can I do?" The answer to that question is simple. You can become an example, a model, a witness. You can stand wherever you are and demand the rights and responsibilities of manhood and womanhood. That's not Vernon Jordan's task. It's not Ralph Abernathy's task or Jesse Jackson's task. It is inescapably your task, and nobody else can do it for you.

What can you do?

You can control and transform the space you occupy. You can make your voice heard in the chorus of liberation.

To be specific, it is your duty to study social processes and appraise issues so you can speak from a background of informed opinion. It is your responsibility to know yourself and your situation. To this end, you can and should buy black books, black art and black periodicals.

The important point here is that it is your first responsibility to know yourself and to understand yourself. And your second responsibility is to commit yourself by choosing a terrain and an organization. If organization A does not please you, don't waste your time denouncing that organization at cocktail parties and in bars. It would be more productive to use that time and energy supporting organization B or C. And if you don't like organizations A, B, C, D and Z, if you don't think anybody is doing anything, then it is your duty to hire a hall and proclaim your own doctrines. The response or lack of response will tell you which way the wind of history is blowing.

It is important in this regard for us to understand the politics of supporting organizations. Support is not a single contribution or attendance at an annual meeting. Support is participation in the life of the organization and the formulation of its policy.

There are other things you can do now. You can:

- Register and vote.
- Patronize black-owned businesses and black professionals and artisans.
- Monitor the program of local schools by participating in the PTA and other organizations.
- Volunteer for work with black youth and black indigents.
- Contribute regularly to black-owned organizations and institutions. If you can buy a fifth of whiskey, you can give $10 for black protest. black welfare and black education. If you can support a dance or a dinner, you can give regularly to black institutions.

A Personal Agenda

This is only an outline of the possibilities. And it should be said immediately that a man or a woman living at the height of responsibility will not seek guarantees and prepackaged one-two-three plans. Freedom is not given to people who need a one-two-three outline in order to act. Your agenda is in your situation. Your agenda is in your city, your neighborhood, your home. Liberation, like everything else, begins at home.

One-two-three outlines apart, it is evident from what we have said that the power of a group is a function of the power of its individual components.

A black man or a black woman coping with an impossible situation by rearing children and creating a strong black family life is black power.

A teacher stretching the minds of children and expanding their horizons is black power.

A student getting his head and soul together is black power.

An institution, guided and controlled by blacks within the perspective of the strengthening of the total black community, is black power.

A child saved is black power.

Something put away for an emergency, something given in love to support a black institution, something ventured, something wagered in defense of black manhood and black womanhood: these things, all of them, are the foundations of power, and they are all within your realm of responsibility.

What can you do?

You can empower black people by empowering yourself.

You, and only you, can say: Let there be black unity, black power, and black liberation—and let it begin with me.

THE LEGACY OF PATERNALISM

Nathan Hare

Last year, Harvard University social scientists David Riesman and Christopher Jencks published a devastating article in the *Harvard Educational Review* on the failure of the American Negro college. It created a furor in Negro college circles. The anxious reaction of Negro college administrators and professors led to a number of lively, high-level faculty meetings and private threats—to my knowledge never carried out—to debate Riesman and Jencks in print.

I do not think that the professors' hesitancy was simply a product of the fact that most of them had never published anything before. Rather, it is that they know, as I do, that Riesman and Jencks were as accurate as outsiders could manage to be. I know because I graduated from a Negro college—Langston University, housed in an all-Negro town in Oklahoma —taught for seven years at two Negro colleges (Virginia State College in Petersburg and Howard University in Washington, D.C.), and lectured at many others across the country where I had occasion to observe classroom behavior and engage students in casual conversation. I had stayed on at Howard University for six full years—against the advice of friends, relatives, and former professors—because of a keen interest in helping to educate black students. It was my belief that they would become the leading black individuals of the future, and that the entire race and the world would benefit from whatever they became.

Because I cannot bear to watch what Negro colleges as a whole are doing to their students, it is not my ambition—after a decade of teaching in them—ever to teach in a Negro college again. This view is shared by several other black professors I know. What is wrong with Negro colleges today? What are the sources of emerging Negro college student unrest and frustration?

Part of the answer may be traced to the history of Negro colleges and the nature of their founding and motivation. A few grew out of abolitionist sentiment in the North but quickly became favorite places for guilt-ridden white slave-masters to send away their illegitimate offspring. Most early Negro colleges, however, were founded in the South by the missionary movement and religious groups interested in recruiting and training teachers and preachers for missionary work in this country ("home mission") and Africa. They had the objective, writes Earl Conrad in *The Invention of the Negro,* "not only of teaching the freedmen how to read and write, but, by bringing the learning in the form of the Bible, to temper this teaching, perhaps to moderate the freedman as well as free him."

Missionary-run colleges, for the most part, eventually folded, or were taken over or duplicated by state governments, but Negro colleges, to this day, have never escaped the missionary influence. Most are teachers colleges with an occasional school of theology attached, though many, predictably, are called universities. Students insist that they are more properly "puniversities," and complain that A&M (Agriculture and Mechanical) are Athletics and Music colleges; A&I (Agriculture and Industrial), Athletics and Ignorance; and A&T (Agriculture and Technical), Athletics and Tomism.

As idealistic white teachers and administrators retreated, they were replaced by "colored" personnel who quickly instituted the mores of the plantation and sought to ape the academic trivia and adolescent fanfare of white colleges. These newcomers were mainly descendants of free blacks or "house nigger" slaves (those who worked in the house instead of the field and became domesticated emulators of upper-class Southern white manners). They longed to be accepted at all costs by white society and modeled their lives to approximate white thinking and behavior—even toward their own race—shunning association and identity with the lower class.

Thus, according to Riesman and Jencks:

> instead of trying to promote a distinctive set of habits and values in their students, they were, by almost any standard, purveyors of super-American, ultra-bourgeois prejudices and aspirations. Far from fighting to preserve a separate subculture, as other ethnic colleges did, the Negro colleges were militantly opposed to almost everything which made Negroes different from whites, on the grounds that it was "lower-class."

These colleges accepted the unalterable superiority of all aspects of white middle-class culture and came to favor Greek and Roman classics, for example, over the study of African civilization or the history of black Americans. Many still maintain that "there is no such thing as Negro history or a distinct history of black people." After a Negro professor returned from a full year in Greece and Italy with slides "to prove that there were colored people in ancient Greece and ancient Rome," a student was heard to remark: "So what? Now they're going to blame us colored for the fall of Rome."

Only recently have Negro colleges begun to permit jazz musicians and blues singers, long accustomed to performing at white colleges, to appear on campus. Similarly, light skin color as a badge for admission to exclusive clubs and campus queen courts has been slow to die. Students are cajoled to lose their "flat talk" and "brogue" and learn to "talk proper" (that is, like whites).

One student claimed to have had a roommate from Mississippi who, after going through this transformation, went home for a visit and fell into association with his old cronies there:

> One day they went to the corner store, where pickled pigs' feet were sold from a jar. Whereas once he would say to the storeman, "Gimme some o' them feet," now he said in ultra-polite tones: "Puh-lease, may i [ah-ee] hawve some of those fibulatibias?" The fellows thought he had turned funny on them.

A single white professor is enough to raise the heated correction from some irate Negro professor that his college "is not a Negro college." Yet, as early as 1949, a white faculty wife wrote, in *Social Forces,* of the difficulty white and Negro professors experience in relating to one another. The Negro professors are generally conservative, by comparison, except for lip-service adherence to "civil rights" causes, and they resent their white liberal colleagues' relative success with the students. At a national "black" student conference held at Tuskegee Institute about two years ago, the faculty chaperons for every visiting black student group were white!

Negro professors as a group prevail as mute robots who value their professions only for pecuniary and prestigious rewards; they possess little true interest in knowledge and books beyond the assimilation of matter necessary for the interpretation, padding, and prefunctory transmission of their graduate school professors' lecture notes. They supplement these, where necessary, with personal anecdotes and conjectures on the race question and, when these run out, typically require their students to take up the remainder of the semester teaching for them via "oral reports" and "panel discussions."

The time saved in this way is wasted on house parties, dawn dances, harvest balls, carnival balls, and "coming out" (introducing their offspring to "society") affairs. Inasmuch as they depend on television and the movies for their major contemporary exposure to white middle-class norms and values, these professors place considerably more stock in expensive cars and fancy furnishings than on books and academic materials. They acquire most of their knowledge and lecture fuel from the daily press and mass-circulation magazines, although many belong to popular book clubs and even have "studies" filled with complimentary textbooks and readers acquired along with those borrowed from the college library or accumulated during graduate school days. The major activities in these "studies" are drinking, cat-napping, and "relaxing"—in that order. Frequently, they seek respite through house parties, where they play "bid whist," penny pinochle (or more recently, bridge), and pathetically strive to master the latest teen-age dance crazes.

In a quantitative study published in the *Journal of Negro Education,* I found that Negro professors, while looking down on their students as incapable of learning because of their "poor backgrounds," are generally regarded by their students as inadequate individuals who know neither how to teach nor much of anything to teach if they did know how. Almost none ever publish, except for an occasional condensation of their doctoral dissertations into an article or two (often their thesis abstracts word for word) and letters-to-the-editor. Those who publish significantly are regarded as "geniuses" or contemptuously are said to be showing off in search of publicity.

Although there have been recent efforts to "raise standards" by increasing the proportion of students flunked, grades given by these professors usually mean very little and may even be changed to permit some student to make the grade-point average required to join the fraternity or sorority to which the professor belongs. Fraternity devotion approximates —and for some, replaces—religious fanaticism and frenzy. On "frat days," the student children of the black bourgeoisie, still under the influence of these professors, hold gaudy pow-wows and "war dances" comprising a caricature of tribal festivities in Tarzan movies, with the only difference being the mode of dress and the language of the lyrics (converted blues tunes). Yet they are the students most ashamed of their blackness and most inclined to reject their African ancestry.

As integration at the college level increased (about half of all black college students now attend predominantly white colleges) the black bourgeoisie increasingly began to send their children to white colleges. The late sociologist E. Franklin Frazier complained to me, as we were walking across Howard University's campus one spring morning shortly before his death some years ago, that for forty years he for one had been unable to teach the black bourgeoisie or their children anything. Today, however, about half of all Negro college students come from families with incomes below $4,000. Frazier once wrote prophetically in his book, *Black Bourgeoisie:* "As the children of the Negro masses have flooded the colleges, it was inevitable that the traditional standards of morals and manners would have to give way."

Thus, although the protest at Negro colleges sometimes takes the form of black power cries (often exaggerated or concocted by administrators and public relations officials playing to public sentiment), the fight on Negro college campuses—in contrast to more nationalistic tendencies on white campuses—more accurately reflects a desire to escape the doldrums of black bourgeoisie dalliance and administrative tyranny and mismanagement. Although I am a black power advocate, born to the breed long before it grew fashionable, white allies at Howard—about the only ones within the faculty—knew and accepted the fact that black power was not the true issue there, though necessary as a tactic in the quest for general freedom.

Even where Negro college student protesters may be seen chanting "black power," it is mainly a rallying cry. Closer inspection of their demands reveals divergent provocations. Howard students, who launched the fad this year of briefly taking over administration buildings, finally wrangled some concessions out of their administrators. These concessions revolved around the following: the freedom to bring liquor into the dormitories (they always did so freely even if they didn't have the freedom), and the opportunity, in the case of girls, to take as many as three "unexplained" weekends. However, a cutback in the stiff prerequisites for the existing course in Negro history also is being "considered." When students at Pennsylvania's Cheyney State College chased the administration out of its building, they demanded a state investigation of school policies. The students thrown out of Louisiana's Grambling College merely wanted less emphasis on athletics and more on academics.

Black students on Negro campuses are merely rejecting the paternalism (some say "maternalism") of their administrations and, like the black race generally, seeking a new direction. They resentfully contend that their particular college is "the Negroest of Negro colleges," by which they mean that they are as white as any college now extant. Although the sad truth is that Negro colleges are fundamentally grotesque caricatures of white colleges, there is more to their problem than that.

The unfortunate fact is, as Riesman and Jencks observed, "oppression corrupts the oppressed as well as the oppressors," and so it is with Negro college administrators, who generally operate with an Amos 'n' Andy approach, laboring under a system of second-hand power manipulated by white remote control. Although their boards of trustees frequently include a token number of Negro members, they invariably reflect the wishes of white politicians who dole out the bulk of their operating funds. To compensate for the resulting sense of powerlessness as administrators of white decrees, Negro college presidents develop a "chieftain complex," sustained by a cliquish, rubber-stamp oligarchy of lesser administrators. The dirty work of the administrative process may be handed down to a dean, though students nonetheless may have to go to the president to, say, get a course changed.

Seldom are regulations, let alone acceptable codes of behavior, fully and clearly spelled out. Consequently, it is not always possible to tell just who has the power in a particular instance. When six professors were bounced last summer from a leading Negro university in Washington,

D.C., the dean (who opposed the firings in writing, but had to sign the letters of dismissal whose contents had been dictated to him) blamed the vice president. The vice president blamed the president during the legal testimony, and the president in turn blamed the vice president, who pointed out that the dean sent the letters.

The volatile nature of administrative control intensifies faculty and student dependence on whimsical administrative directives, producing an insouciant state of powerless docility in which administrators heavy-handedly rule the minutest aspects of campus life. Once while I was teaching at Virginia State College, the chairman of my department interrupted my class to warn me that the deans would decimate me if they should ever catch me leaning against the desk instead of sitting behind it while lecturing. At Howard University, for example, the deans take turns making the rounds of classrooms scolding professors before classes containing some student caught smoking a cigarette. The dean at one college I attended habitually visited classrooms, occasionally challenging professors on material presented to the class.

Professors who attempt to oppose these bonds of political and academic weakness run counter to administrators' preference for tranquility over progress and accordingly are "de-hired" (that is, not reappointed, a technical firing) as contracts terminate. Contracts typically take the form of business letters and are seldom issued before August, when most hiring is done, of any given year. However, the failure to receive a letter of non-reappointment is traditionally regarded as an "assumptive contract."

Students similarly are denied any place in helping to determine their destinies. On small Southern campuses, female students employed as part-time maids by faculty wives may be snatched from the classroom for unfinished chores. A student may be expelled for publicly calling the president of a neighbor college an Uncle Tom. Troops will be rushed in to compel students to accept the de-emphasis on scholarship while students are flunked out in droves to "raise standards." Students may be required to attend Sunday chapel while faculty members are compelled to sign in to meetings. Some administrators may haunt lovers' lanes with flashlights looking for copulating students but, like an objectionable number of their subordinates, demand sexual favors from students for academic returns. Many students complain that it is "necessary to have a good body as well as a good mind" in order to graduate.

Since administrators extend only puppet power to official student governments, most students disdain to take an active part in routine campus politics or even to vote in campus elections. Thus the student selected to office seldom represent genuine choices of the student bodies they serve, and, except for occasional sham attempts to be relevant to student interests, serve largely antithetical goals. Students seeking self-determination accordingly feel impelled to take matters into their own hands and force the administration to serve them.

In all the Negro colleges I have visited, I found students who wanted to know, as one of them put it recently, how to "break this administrative grip." At a college in South Carolina I was kept up all night long convincing students who had had enough, to stay on in school so that someday, somehow, they might move into a better position to bring about some change.

A college registrar, before fleeing midyear to a white university, once showed me figures indicating that his college, despite a high flunkout rate, lost more students each year who earn a "C" average and above than students with less than a "C" average. We could only speculate on the fact that most major leaders of black revolutionary groups such as SNCC (Student Nonviolent Coordinating Committee), RAM (Revolutionary Action Movement), and the Black Panthers, were above-average, frequently honor students, in predominantly Negro or junior colleges, before dropping out in disgust. I have many times watched helplessly while my best students began to disdain most of their other classes and proceeded to flunk out.

A student at a leading Negro college finally managed to graduate, after some hesitancy by his professors; then, after making *Who's Who in America* that self-same year, he returned to his campus, where he was moved to remark that it should be burned down and cotton planted in its place, so that at least some economic benefit could accrue. Instead of teaching white colleges the methods of a new and genuine freedom, Negro colleges merely compounded the most deplorable errors of white college ways.

It is ironic but not inexplicable that my own efforts to help make education relevant to black college students have brought me finally to a white college campus. It comforts me sadly to know that, as this goal is achieved on white campuses, Negro colleges will feel obliged to ape them.

A FEDERAL JUDGE DIGS THE YOUNG

Judge Charles E. Wyzanski, Jr.

It is rather strange that the generation gap is thought of as something to be regretted. In my book, conformity is generally more to be regretted, and a search for unity is already a denial of the divesity of human life. The creativity of God as he created Adam involved a gap. And indeed, it is the kind of challenge that comes from the electricity which crosses the gap that makes life meaningful.

Long ago, in a not very different spirit, the ancient Greek philosopher Heraclitus said, "That which opposes, also fits"; and while what he said may proleptically have had Freudian implications, it is ordinarily thought he was talking of a bow and arrow. I don't know whether the young are the arrow, but I am quite certain that there is no reason for anybody to regret the kind of challenge which comes from difference. Indeed, could there be a clearer indication of a static and decadent civilization than one in which each generation followed the pattern of the previous one?

We are, of course, well aware that this is no ordinary change from one generation to another. Indeed, what we are going through can be compared only with what happened at the end of the eighteenth century, with the American and French Revolutions; what happened in 1848, or nearly happened; what happened in 1917. We are in a great cataclysmic change, one of the most profound in world history, and lucky we are to live in this period.

Harold Howe 2d, U.S. Commissioner of Education, talked recently about the possibility that the colleges were to blame, not the students, for what has been going on at Ohio State, Columbia, Boston University, in Paris and Italy. Wherever you are, you cannot pick up the morning paper without finding that the student revolt is spreading in every corner of the globe. In Paris, in Germany, with the attack on Axel Springer and his newspapers; in Italy, with its closed universities; at Barnard, where *The New York Times* exposed a single child and her parents to an invasion of privacy that it would have condemned editorially if anybody else had done it; at Boston University, where a courageous president told the students they were right about their demand for a larger representation of Negroes in the student body; at Radcliffe College, where students are seeking to be admitted to the board of trustees; at Columbia University, where one can see how justified students were in resenting a proposed gymnasium that would have a separate entrance for Harlem residents and which would be built on land leased

Source: *Saturday Review* (July 20, 1968), pp. 14–16; 62. Copyright © 1968 by Saturday Review, Inc. First appeared in *Saturday Review,* July 20, 1968. Used with permission.

at a ridiculously low price. Mr. Howe is right—perhaps the colleges should look at themselves as well as their students.

Certain aspects of the student revolt are much overrated by the commercial press and money-seeking exploiters: sex, drugs, and dress. Most people know what hypocrites the previous generation were. They did not have to wait for the biography of Strachey to know that Keynes and the Bloomsbury set, who determined the intellectual tone of the first quarter of the twentieth century, were hardly in the Sunday school copybook tradition. What Proust and Robert de Montesquiou represented, as we have recently been told in clear language, is that France was no different from Britain. And what person who lived as a young man between World War I and World War II wants to file a certificate as to the errors of Professor Kinsey?

We did not have to wait for the young generation in order to be aware that from the beginning of mankind premarital and post-marital sex have not been lived according to the graven tablets handed down to Moses. What is it that made sex such a dangerous activity in earlier years? Was it not conception and venereal disease? And are they not both, by technological advance, much altered in our society? What reason have we to be so certain, so terribly certain, that sexual chastity is the most desirable state at all stages of a man's and a woman's life? I don't believe it. Neither did the Greeks. Neither did the Asians. A particular Western sect, inspired by a religious leader without sexual experience, foisted that notion on the Western world. Is it not time to reconsider that idea?

And what of drugs? I make no case in behalf of marijuana, but who could tell how many more people have died on the roads in the last year as a result of marijuana than as a result of alcohol. Who could tell me more people have died as a result of marijuana than as a result of cancer caused by cigarette smoking? Is there anybody who doubts that the commercial motives of our society promote the sale of tobacco and the sale of alcohol, and that anybody who came from Mars or Venus or some remote place would find it absolutely impossible to decide on what basis we as a society had outlawed marijuana and not tobacco or alcohol? Have you any doubt in your own mind that it is merely habit and profit that make us of the older generation so content to live in a society where alcohol and tobacco freely circulate, and marijuana is outlawed?

Oh, we go to church, do we? Why? For social and commercial reasons and for consolation in time of trouble. But do we go with faith and conviction and discipline and self-denial? Which of us? From the day that Darwin and Huxley opened the doors and science walked into the church and we walked out, which of us has had that kind of faith which represents a deep commitment to that denial and sacrifice and discipline which are the essence of religion?

It is quite right that the young should talk about us as hypocrites. We are. And it is quite right that they should note that our hypocrisy is embedded in our materialism.

So we are critical of the young. Have they not far more reason to be critical of us? And what have we done to get them on the right path from the beginning? Most of us were quite content to have them undergo a permissive kind of education in which not merely the *quadrivium* and the *trivium,* but the whole core of humanistic learning was not part of their deep education. We allowed them pretty much, in their early primary and secondary stages, to have the kind of education from their schools and their peers which they wanted because we were not sufficiently convinced of our own beliefs. And they knew it.

We brought them up in a society in which we no longer believed in either the carrot or the stick. Nor did they. Our society afforded them as children, in their occupations as babysitters and otherwise, a salary rate sufficient to assure them a minor kind of affluence and independence. They walked as they pleased because they had the money, the very root of independence. Then, vastly and suddenly, and quite rightly, we expanded the total educational system so that we flooded the colleges and the universities of the nation at a rate at which nobody could possibly absorb.

Mark Hopkins at one end of the log and the student at the other? Doesn't it sound like a prehistoric fable? Which university student today is in a one-to-one relationship with anybody on the faculty? Which one has any kind of personal relationship in a large university? Was it not certain that men and women of any character would resent these institutions and seek some sort of outlet other than the formal ones in which they were treated like commuters in a subway train?

What is to be said about these young people, plus and minus? And those of us who sit where we hear both sides or many sides of the question know that truth is never or almost never all on one side. Let us give the young, first of all, credit for being right about their concern. They, at least, know that there can never be, in a growing society, a philosophy of consensus. They realize, to return to Heraclitus, that "strife is the source of all things." Growth implies discord as well as advance.

What the young care about is a deeper kind of democracy than some of us have been willing to accept. The French in their immortal division talked of liberty, equality, and fraternity. May one not say that in my generation the accent was heavy on the first? And we do not need to turn to Lord Acton to know that he who emphasizes liberty is he who is already priviledged. Liberty means one thing if you are already in the top place and something very different if you are low on the scale.

Many know the classic remark of Mr. Justice Maule, phrased somewhat differently by Anatole France, when Justice Maule was faced by a divorce case in the nineteenth century. At that time in England you were free to get a divorce if you took a very lengthy and expensive proceeding in the Probate, Divorce, and Admiralty Court. And there was before Justice Maule a poor man, poor of purse and poor of spirit, who had not gotten a divorce but had married again. Justice Maule said, "It is the glory of England that the law courts are open alike to the rich and the poor." The glory of the law which treats alike the rich and the poor is no glory. It is a sham. And the society which pretends that it gives liberty to all without being concerned with equality and fraternity is a sham.

The young are quite right that equality and fraternity are necessary for democracy and a kind of understanding of what people are like. We in this country stand too close to know how right the young men are. If you look from a distance at what goes on in the United States, there is much sense in the concern that the young have about our total order. It is no accident that the young and the Negro are allied, and this is not pure sentimentalism. It is an awareness that in our civilization the litmus paper is black.

The young marched with the black, and now the young are not wanted. The black do not want us, nor are they wrong. One of the things that we must face up to, just as a parent must face up to it with respect to a child, is that when one is struggling for freedom and identity, sometimes one must do it alone. The rejected, sympathetic, kindly person—the parent or white man—does not understand; but it is his fault. It is part of the process of growing up to grow on your own.

There are those who don't like the phrase "black power." It's a very correct phrase. Anyone who really studies democracy will find out that democracy is pluralistic in character. It is those already in power who scorn the pressure groups. But it is pressure groups—whether they be voter leagues formed by women, labor unions formed by workers, black organizations fomed by colored people—that in the end count and enter into the total social fabric. Democracy is a struggle based not only on high ideals; it is power against power. There is an overarch of principle, but the overarch is to hold the ring firm while the contestants battle it out within the limits authorized by the organized society.

The young are not wrong, either, in their wonder about the scope of violence. I tread on very dangerous ground here, and I beg indulgence as a quasihistorian and not as a judge. I ask you to reflect carefully on the Boston Tea Party, on John Brown and the raid on Harpers Ferry, on the sit-down strikes in 1937 in the plants of General Motors. Every one of these was a violent, unlawful act, plainly unlawful. In the light of history, was it plainly futile? There are occasions on which an honest man, when he looks at history, must say that through violence, regrettable as it is, justice of a social kind has worked itself out. Does that mean that I think that violence is right? Most certainly I answer ambiguously. I cannot know; none of us can know until long after this time has gone. But I warn those who think that violence is right because history, in the three instances that I have cited, and many others that one might mention, has shown that violence worked—I warn them that violence will lead to McCarthy I or McCarthy II. To which Senator's philosophy, if either, will this nation respond?

What I invite is caution. The young are right not to take too seriously our statement that they must always behave lawfully, but we who are older are also right to say, "We have lived through reaction, and we know what a price you will pay if you are wrong. And we remind you of the words of Charles Morgan that liberty is a room which can be defined only by the walls which enclose it." The young have a great responsibility. They cannot define liberty except in terms of limitation. Believe me, I do it every day!

The ultimate problem which the young face is whether they have the courage to be radical enough to face the implications of what they are doing. I fear not one bit what they have done so far, provided they go further.

In that wonderful play, even if it was a failure on Broadway, by Peter Ustinov, called *Halfway Up the Tree,* there was a British colonial officer who went abroad and left behind his wife and his two children. One was his son who went to Oxford and dressed like a hippie and was having a homosexual relationship with another fellow while they were carrying around a guitar which neither of them could play. The daughter was pregnant, by which of several men she wasn't sure. The colonial fellow returned —he was of my venerable age—and he wasn't disturbed by what his young had done, but he was a little concerned that the boy didn't know how to play the guitar and the girl didn't know how to keep house. If they had taken the first step, they must be prepared for the second. To show them how he felt about it, he went and lived up in a tree and took care of his own food needs and learned how to play the guitar. Well, it is all quite in point.

The young can be as radical as they like, but they must carry the consequence. It isn't enough to overthrow us. They have to establish themselves. It is one of the elements of life that there will be an establishment. They may not like ours—and I don't think they much care for the Communist one because they have seen how that works—but have they thought through what kind of establishment they want?

I am quite sure that one of the things they will have to do is to rearrange the property structure of this nation. As any good lawyer will tell you, property is only an idea—*meum* and *teum. Meum* and *teum* are just a lawyer's idea. The things themselves are things. They don't belong to anybody except as we create the relationship.

There is no doubt that our social structure now works in a most undesirable way. Among the 80 per cent—and it is pretty nearly that—who have the benefits of our system, it works surprisingly well. Effort, at least if followed in paths of conformity, will in the long run yield affluence and security. Or at any rate, one will have an automobile! But if one is in the lowest 20 per cent, he is caught. He may proceed to gain a little, but the gap between him and the 80 per cent is not like the generation gap; it is like the gap between the underdeveloped and the developed nations—constantly growing and creating tensions and creating an envy which will surely lead to disaster.

I speak not in favor of a negative income tax, about which I understand far too little. Nor do I endorse a particular measure of any sort of redistribution or any particular kind of program of health, education, and welfare. I merely say to those who are young that it isn't enough to love your neighbor. You had better be concerned about how your neighbor will be in a position to love you.

What I have talked about doesn't get very close to specifics. But I do know something about what life presents. It presents a riddle that has no answer and never will. In Erwin Schrödinger's phrase, it is a circle that always will have a gap.

Each generation is faced with a challenge of making some kind of sense out of its existence. In advance it knows from the Book of Job and the Book of Ecclesiastes and the Greek drama that there will be no right answer. But there will be forms of answer.There will be a style. As ancient Greece had the vision of *acrete* (the noble warrior), as Dante and the Medievalists had the vision of the great and universal Catholic Church, even as the founding fathers of the American Republic had the vision of the new order which they began, so for the young the question is to devise a style—not one that will be good *semper et ubique,* but one for our place and our time, one that will be a challenge to the very best that is within our power of reach, and one that will make us realize, in Whitehead's immortal terms, that for us the only reality is the process.

Chapter 1
SUGGESTED TOPICS FOR CLASS DISCUSSION

1. What are some of the prominent issues in American politics at present? Which of these issues were viewed as important ten years ago? Are there common characteristics of the issues that have grown in importance?
2. What political beliefs are undergoing change? Are Americans now as content with the working of the political system as they were ten years ago? Is their confidence as great as it was in such political institutions as Congress, the Presidency, and the courts?

3. What would be the area of agreement among today's conservatives? What about liberals? Do people who regard themselves as "liberals" find it easy to agree on the meaning of liberalism? If not, what is the source of the definitional difficulty?
4. What are some of the major political changes that have taken place in the last ten years? To what extent are these changes associated with shifts in the attitudes or perceptions of major groups of Americans?

Chapter 2

The Constitutional Background:
The Politics of the "More Perfect Union"

On June 7, 1776, Richard Henry Lee of Virginia offered in the Second Continental Congress the following resolution:

> *Resolved, that these United Colonies are, and of a right ought to be, free and independent States, that they are absolved from all allegiance to the British Crown, and that all political connection between them and the State of Great Britain is, and ought to be, totally dissolved.**

Thomas Jefferson was appointed chairman of a committee that included John Adams, Benjamin Franklin, Robert Livingston, and Roger Sherman to draft an appropriate document. On June 28, 1776, the Declaration of Independence was offered to the Congress.

* *The Federal Convention and the Formation of the Union of the American States,* Winton U. Solberg (ed.) (New York: Liberal Arts Press, 1958), p. 32.

Not all the delegates representing the colonies were ready to take this irrevocable step. New England leaders were impatient, and Virginia was ready to support the break; but New York and Pennsylvania were lukewarm and there were controversies in other colonies. In general, the conservatives, the well-to-do, who had the most to lose from a revolution—whether successful or not—were fearful of the "mob" and opposed the more radical leadership. After considerable debate the Declaration was adopted on July 4.

It would be difficult to overstate the importance of the Declaration to American constitutionalism It expressed the beliefs of the American people in the natural and inalienable rights of man, a philosophy that justified rebellion against tyranny and announced that governments derived authority only from the consent of the governed.

The Constitutional Background

It is no service to the members of the Constitutional Convention who gathered in Philadelphia in May, 1787, to make their work little more than a triumphal procession. Their achievement was magnificent because they faced staggering problems. When they gathered for the first session, it was not even clear that representative government was a viable concept when applied to a nation of so great an extent. The decisions and arrangements that are now so well known to every schoolboy lay hidden in the shadowed future.

> *All was doubtful and uncertain. It was clear that Americans would now go their way independent of England, but it was not clear which way the path would lead. Would they successfully assume the "separate and equal station to which the Laws of Nature and of Nature's God" entitled them, or would they be absorbed by a foreign power, be torn apart by internal strife, or sink into impotence and thence into despotism—the ideal of self-government proving unattainable? Did Shay's Rebellion represent the handwriting on the wall? Could several million people, with varying interests, spread over a vast territory, actually govern themselves on republican principles? Could the proud and independent state governments be combined with a central government and, if so, how? ***

In a time of troubles, such as the present, it is helpful to see how the events of an earlier era appeared to the men of the time. As late as July 10, 1787, George Washington, president of the Convention,

* Andrew M. Scott, *Political Thought in America* (New York: Holt, Rinehart and Winston, Inc., 1959), p. 93.

was moved to write, "I almost despair of seeing a favourable issue to the proceedings of the Convention and do therefore repent having had any agency in the business. . . ." † Yet patience, reason, tolerance, and a willingness to compromise eventually resulted in the document known as the Constitution.

† Max Farrand, *Record of the Constitutional Convention* (New Haven, Conn.: Yale University Press, 1911), Vol. 3, p. 56.

THE DECLARATION OF INDEPENDENCE

Thomas Jefferson

In Congress, July 4, 1776

The unanimous Declaration of the thirteen united States of America,

When in the Course of human events, it becomes necessary for one people to dissolve the political bands which have connected them with another, and to assume among the Powers of the earth, the separate and equal station to which the Laws of Nature and of Nature's God entitle them, a decent respect to the opinions of mankind requires that they should declare the causes which impel them to the separation.

We hold these truths to be self-evident, that all men are created equal, that they are endowed by their Creator with certain inalienable Rights, that among these are Life, Liberty, and the pursuit of Happiness. That to secure these rights, Governments are instituted among Men, deriving their just powers from the consent of the governed, That whenever any Form of Government becomes destructive of these ends, it is the Right of the People to alter or to abolish it, and to institute new Government, laying its foundation on such principles and organizing its powers in such form, as to them shall seem most likely to effect their Safety and Happiness. Prudence, indeed, will dictate that Governments long established should not be changed for light and transient causes; and accordingly all experience hath shown, that mankind are more disposed to suffer, while evils are sufferable, than to right themselves by abolishing the forms to which they are accustomed. But when a long train of abuses and usurpations, pursuing invariably the same Object evinces a design to reduce them under absolute Despotism, it is their right, it is their duty, to throw off such Government, and to provide new

Source: *The Federal and State Constitutions*, Benjamin P. Poore (ed.), Part I, pp. 1–6. *The Federal Convention and the Formation of the Union of the American States*, Winton U. Solberg (ed.) (New York: Liberal Arts Press, 1958), pp. 34–38.

Guards for their future security.—Such has been the patient sufferance of these Colonies; and such is now the necessity which constrains them to alter their former Systems of Government. The history of the present King of Great Britain is a history of repeated injuries and usurpations, all having in direct object the establishment of an absolute Tyranny over these States. To prove this, let Facts be submitted to a candid world.

He has refused his Assent to Laws, the most wholesome and necessary for the public good.

He has forbidden his Governors to pass Laws of immediate and pressing importance, unless suspended in their operation till his Assent should be obtained; and when so suspended, he has utterly neglected to attend to them.

He has refused to pass other Laws for the accommodation of large districts of people, unless those people would relinquish the right of Representation in the Legislature, a right inestimable to them and formidable to tyrants only.

He has called together legislative bodies at places unusual, uncomfortable, and distant from the depository of their Public Records, for the sole purpose of fatiguing them into compliance with his measures.

He has dissolved Representative Houses repeatedly, for opposing with manly firmness his invasions on the rights of the people.

He has refused for a long time, after such dissolutions, to cause others to be elected; whereby the Legislative Powers, incapable of Annihilation, have returned to the People at large for their exercise; the State remaining in the mean time exposed to all the dangers of invasion from without, and convulsions within.

He has endeavoured to prevent the population of these States: for that purpose obstructing the Laws for Naturalization of Foreigners; refusing to pass others to encourage their migration hither, and raising the conditions of new Appropriations of Lands.

He has obstructed the Administration of Justice, by refusing his Assent to Law for establishing Judiciary Powers.

He has made Judges dependent on his Will alone, for the tenure of their offices, and the amount and payment of their salaries.

He has erected a multitude of New Offices, and sent hither swarms of Officers to harass our People, and eat out their substance.

He has kept among us, in times of peace, Standing Armies without the Consent of our legislature.

He has affected to render the Military independent of and superior to the Civil Power.

He has combined with others to subject us to a jurisdiction foreign to our constitution, and unacknowledged by our laws; giving his Assent to their Acts of pretended Legislation:

For quartering large bodies of armed troops among us:

For protecting them, by a mock Trial, from Punishment for any Murders which they should commit on the Inhabitants of these States:

For cutting off our Trade with all parts of the world:

For imposing taxes on us without our Consent:

For depriving us in many cases, of the benefits of Trial by Jury:

For transporting us beyond Seas to be tried for pretended offences:

For abolishing the free System of English Laws in a neighbouring Province, establishing therein an Arbitrary government, and enlarging its Boundaries so as to render it at once an example and fit instrument for introducing the same absolute rule into these Colonies:

For taking away our Charters, abolishing our most valuable Laws, and altering fundamentally the Forms of our Governments:

For suspending our own Legislatures, and declaring themselves invested with Power to legislate for us in all cases whatsoever.

He has abdicated Government here, by declaring us out of his Protection and waging War against us.

He has plundered our seas, ravaged our Coasts, burnt our towns, and destroyed the lives of our people.

He is at this time transporting large armies of foreign mercenaries to compleat the works of death, desolation and tyranny, already begun with circumstances of Cruelty & perfidy scarcely paralleled in the most barbarous ages, and totally unworthy the Head of a civilized nation.

He has constrained our fellow Citizens taken Captive on the high Seas to bear Arms against their Country, to become the executioners of their friends and Brethren, or to fall themselves by their Hands.

He has excited domestic insurrections amongst us, and has endeavoured to bring on the inhabitants of our frontiers, the merciless Indian Savages, whose known rule of warfare, is an undistinguished destruction of all ages, sexes and conditions.

In every stage of these Oppressions We have Petitioned for Redress in the most humble terms: Our repeated Petitions have been answered only by repeated injury. A Prince, whose character is thus marked by every act which may define a Tyrant, is unfit to be the ruler of a free People.

Nor have We been wanting in attention to our British brethren. We have warned them from time to time of attempts by their legislature to extend an unwarrantable jurisdiction over us. We have reminded them of the circumstances of our emigration and settlement here. We have appealed to their native justice and magnanimity, and we have conjured them by the ties of our common kindred to disavow these usurpations, which would inevitably interrupt our connections and correspondence. They too have been deaf to the voice of justice and of consanguinity. We must, therefore, acquiesce in the necessity, which denounces our Separation, and hold them, as we hold the rest of mankind, Enemies in War, in Peace Friends.

We, therefore, the Representatives of the united States of America, in General Congress, Assembled, appealing to the Supreme Judge of the world for the rectitude of our intentions, do, in the Name, and by Authority of the good People of these Colonies, solemnly publish and declare, That these United Colonies are, and of Right ought to be Free and Independent States; that they are Absolved from all Allegiance to the British Crown, and that all political connection between them and the State of Great Britain, is and ought to be totally dissolved; and that as Free and Independent States, they have full Power to levy War, conclude Peace, contract Alliances, establish Commerce, and to do all other Acts and Things which Independent States may of right do. And for the support of this Declaration, with a firm reliance on the Protection of Divine Providence, we mutually pledge to each other our Lives, our Fortunes and our sacred Honor.

JOHN HANCOCK.

(and Delegates of New Hampshire, Massachusetts Bay, Rhode Island, Connecticut, New York, New Jersey, Pennsylvania, Delaware, Maryland, Virginia, North Carolina, South Carolina, Georgia)

POLITICS 1787: A CASE STUDY IN DEMOCRATIC POLITICS

John P. Roche

Over the last century and a half, the work of the Constitutional Convention and the motives of the Founding Fathers have been analyzed under a number of different ideological auspices. To one generation of historians, the hand of God was moving in the assembly; under a later dispensation, the dialectic (at various levels of philosophical sophistication) replaced the Deity: "relationships of production" moved into the niche previously reserved for Love of Country. Thus, in counterpoint to the Zeitgeist, the Framers have undergone miraculous metamorphoses: at one time acclaimed as liberals and bold social engineers, today they appear in the guise of sound Burkean conservatives, men who in our time would subscribe to *Fortune,* look to Walter Lippmann for political theory, and chuckle patronizingly at the antics of Barry Goldwater. The implicit assumption is that if James Madison were among us, he would be President of the Ford Foundation, while Alexander Hamilton would chair the Committee for Economic Development.

Source: "The Founding Fathers: A Reform Caucus in Action," *The American Political Science Review* (December 1961), Vol. 55, No. 4, pp. 799–816. Footnotes omitted. Reprinted by permission.

The "Fathers" have thus been admitted to our best circles; the revolutionary ferocity which confiscated all Tory property in reach and populated New Brunswick with outlaws has been converted by the "Miltown School" of American historians into a benign dedication to "consensus" and "prescriptive rights." The Daughters of the American Revolution have, through the ministrations of Professors Boorstin, Hartz, and Rossiter, at last found ancestors worthy of their descendants. It is not my purpose here to argue that the "Fathers" were, in fact, radical revolutionaries; that proposition has been brilliantly demonstrated by Robert R. Palmer in his *Age of the Democratic Revolution*. My concern is with the further position that not only were they revolutionaries; they were also democrats. Indeed, in my view, there is one fundamental truth about the Founding Fathers that *every* generation of Zeitgeisters has done its best to obscure: they were first and foremost superb democratic politicians. I suspect that in a contemporary setting, James Madison would be Speaker of the House of Representatives and Hamilton would be the *éminence grise* dominating (*pace* Theodore Sorenson or Sherman Adams) the Executive Office of the President. They were, with their colleagues, *political men*—not metaphysicians, disembodied conservatives or Agents of History—and as recent research into the nature of American politics in the 1780's confirms, they were committed (perhaps willy-nilly) to working within the democratic framework, within a universe of public approval. Charles Beard *and* the filiopietists to the contrary notwithstanding, the Philadelphia Convention was not a College of Cardinals or a council of Platonic guardians working within a manipulative, predemocratic framework; it was a *nationalist* reform caucus which had to operate with great delicacy and skill in a political cosmos full of enemies to achieve the one definitive goal—popular approbation.

Perhaps the time has come, to borrow Walton Hamilton's fine phrase, to raise the Framers from immortality to mortality, to give them credit for their magnificent demonstration of the art of democratic politics. The point must be reemphasized; they *made* history, and did it within the limits of consensus. There was nothing inevitable about the future in 1787; the *Zeitgeist,* that fine Hegelian technique of begging causal questions, could be discerned only in retrospect. What they did was to hammer out a pragmatic compromise which would both bolster the "national interest" and be acceptable to the people. What inspiration they got came from their collective experience as professional politicians in a democratic society. As John Dickinson put it to his fellow delegates on August 13th: "Experience must be our guide. Reason may mislead us."

In this context, let us examine the problems they confronted and the solutions they evolved. The Convention has been described picturesquely as a counterrevolutionary junta and the Constitution as a *coup d'état,* but this has been accomplished by withdrawing the whole history of the movement for constitutional reform from its true context. No doubt the goals of the constitutional elite were "subversive" to the existing political order, but it is overlooked that their subversion could have succeeded only if the people of the United States endorsed it by regularized procedures. Indubitably they were "plotting" to establish a much stronger central government than existed under the Articles, but only in the sense in which one could argue equally well that John F. Kennedy was, from 1956 to 1960, "plotting" to become President. In short, on the fundamental *procedural* level, the Constitutionalists had to work according to the prevailing rules of the game. Whether they liked it or not is a topic for spiritualists —and is irrelevant: one may be quite certain that had Washington agreed to play the De Gaulle (as the Cincinnati once urged), Hamilton would willingly have held his horse, but such fertile speculation in no way alters the actual context in which events took place.

When the Constitutionalists went forth to subvert the Confederation, they utilized the mechanisms of political legitimacy. And the roadblocks which confronted them were formidable. At the same time, they were endowed with certain potent political assets. The history of the United States from 1786 to 1790 was largely one of a masterful employment of political expertise by the Constitutionalists as against bumbling, erratic behavior by the opponents of reform. Effectively, the Constitutionalists had to induce the states, by democratic techniques of coercion, to emasculate themselves. To be specific, if New York had refused to join the new Union, the project was doomed; yet before New York was safely in, the reluctant state legislature had *sua sponte* to take the following steps: (1) agree to send delegates to the Philadelphia Convention; (2) provide maintenance for these delegates (these were distinct stages: New Hampshire was early in naming delegates, but did not provide for their maintenance until July); (3) set up the special *ad hoc* convention to decide on ratification; and (4) concede to the decision of the *ad hoc* convention that New York should participate. New York admittedly was a tricky state, with a strong interest in a *status quo* which permitted her to exploit New Jersey and Connecticut, but the same legal hurdles existed in every state. And at the risk of becoming boring, it must be reiterated that the *only* weapon in the Constitutionalist arsenal was an effective mobilization of public opinion.

The group which undertook this struggle was an interesting amalgam of a few dedicated nationalists with the self-interested spokesmen of various parochial bailiwicks. The Georgians, for example, wanted a strong central authority to provide military protection for their huge, underpopulated state against the Creek Confederacy; Jerseymen and Connecticuters wanted to escape from economic bondage to New York; the Virginians hoped to establish a system which would give that great state its rightful place in the councils of the republic. The dominant figures in the politics of these states therefore co-operated in the call for the Convention. In other states, the thrust toward national reform was taken up by opposition groups who added the "national interest" to their weapons system; in Pennsylvania, for instance, the group fighting to revise the Constitution of 1776 came out four-square behind the Constitutionalists, and in New York, Hamilton and the Schuyler ambience took the same tack against George Clinton. There was, of course, a large element of personality in the affair: there is reason to suspect that Patrick Henry's opposition to the Convention and the Constitution was founded on his conviction that Jefferson was behind both, and a close study of local politics elsewhere would surely reveal that others supported the Constitution for the simple (and politically quite sufficient) reason that the "wrong" people were against it.

To say this is not to suggest that the Constitution rested on a foundation of impure or base motives. It is rather to argue that in politics there are no immaculate conceptions and that in the drive for a stronger general government, motives of all sorts played a part. Few men in the history of mankind have espoused a view of the "common good" or "public interest" that militated against their private status; even Plato with all his reverence for disembodied reason managed to put philosophers on top of the pile. Thus it is not surprising that a number of diversified private interests joined to push the nationalist public interest; what would have been surprising was the absence of such a pragmatic united front. And the fact remains that, however motivated, these men did demonstrate a willingness to compromise their parochial interests in behalf of an ideal which took shape before their eyes and under thier ministrations.

As Stanley Elkins and Eric McKitrick have suggested in a perceptive essay, what distinguished the leaders of the Constitutionalist caucus from their enemies was a "Continental" approach to political, economic, and military issues. To the extent that they shared an institutional base of operations, it was the Continental Congress (thirty-nine of the delegates to the Federal Convention had served in Congress), and this was hardly a locale which inspired respect for the state governments. Robert de Jouvenal observed French politics half a century ago and noted that a revolutionary deputy had more in common with a nonrevolutionary deputy than he had with a revolutionary nondeputy; similarly one can surmise that membership in the Congress under the Articles of Confederation worked to establish a Continental frame of reference, that a congressman from Pennsylvania and one from South Carolina would share a universe of discourse which provided them with a conceptual common denominator vis à vis their respective state legislatures. This was particularly true with respect to external affairs: the average state legislator was probably about as concerned with foreign policy then as he is today, but congressmen were constantly forced to take the broad view of American prestige, were compelled to listen to the reports of Secretary John Jay and to the dispatches and pleas from their frustrated envoys in Britain, France, and Spain. From considerations such as these, a "Continental" ideology developed which seems to have demanded a revision of our domestic institutions primarily on the ground that only by invigorating our general government could we assume our rightful place in the international arena. Indeed, an argument with great force—particularly since Washington was its incarnation—urged that our very survival in the Hobbesian jungle of world politics depended upon a reordering and strengthening of our national sovereignty.

Note that I am not endorsing the "Critical Period" thesis; on the contrary, Merrill Jensen seems to me quite sound in his view that for most Americans, engaged as they were in self-sustaining agriculture, the "Critical Period" was not particularly critical. In fact, the great achievement of the Constitutionalists was their ultimate success in convincing the elected representatives of a majority of the white male population that change was imperative. A small group of political leaders with a Continental vision and essentially a consciousness of the United States' *international* impotence, provided the matrix of the movement. To their standard other leaders rallied with their own parallel ambitions. Their great assets were (1) the presense in their caucus of the one authentic American "father figure," George Washington, whose prestige was enormous, (2) the energy and talent of their leadership (in which one must include the towering intellectuals of this time, John Adams and Thomas Jefferson, despite their absence abroad); and their communications "network," which was far superior to anything on the opposition side, (3) the preemptive skill which made "their" issue The Issue and kept the locally oriented opposition permanently on the defensive; and (4) the subjective consideration that these men were spokesmen of a new and compelling credo: *American* nationalism, that ill-defined but nonetheless potent sense of collective purpose that emerged from the American Revolution.

Despite great institutional handicaps, the Constitutionalists managed in the mid-1780's to mount an offensive which gained momentum as years went by. Their greatest problem was lethargy, and paradoxically, the number of barriers in their path may have proved an advantage in the long run. Beginning with the initial battle to get the Constitutional Convention called and delegates appointed, they could never relax, never let up the pressure. In practical terms, this meant that the local "organizations" created by the Constitutionalists were perpetually in movement building up their cadres for the next fight. (The word "organization" has to be used with great caution: a political organization in the United States—as in contemporary England—generally consisted of a magnate and his following, or a coalition of magnates. This did not necessarily mean that it was "undemocratic" or "aristocratic," in the Aristotelian sense of the word: while a few magnates such as the Livingstons could draft their followings, most exercised their leadership without coercion on the basis of popular endorsement. The absence of organized opposition did not imply the impossibility of competition any more than low public participation in elections necessarily indicated an undemocratic suffrage.)

The Constitutionalists got the jump on the "opposition" (a collective noun: oppositions would be more correct) at the outset with the demand for a Convention. Their opponents were caught in an old political trap: they were not being asked to approve any specific program of reform, but only to endorse a meeting to discuss and recommend needed reforms. If they took a hard line at the first stage, they were put in the position of glorifying the *status quo* and of denying the need for *any* changes. Moreover, the Constitutionalists could go to the people with a persuasive argument for "fair play"—"How can you condemn reform before you know precisely what is involved?" Since the state legislatures obviously would have the final say on any proposals that might emerge from the Convention, the Constitutionalists were merely reasonable men asking for a chance. Besides, since they did not make any concrete proposals at that stage, they were in a position to capitalize on every sort of generalized discontent with the Confederation.

Perhaps because of their poor intelligence system, perhaps because of overconfidence generated by the failure of all previous efforts to alter the Articles, the opposition awoke too late to the dangers that confronted them in 1787. Not only did the Constitutionalists manage to get every state but Rhode Island (where politics was enlivened by a party system reminiscent of the "Blues" and the "Greens" in the Byzantine Empire) to appoint delegates to Philadelphia, but when the results were in, it appeared that they dominated the delegations. Given the apathy of the opposition, this was a natural phenomenon: in an ideologically nonpolarized political atmosphere, those who get appointed to a special committee are likely to be the men who supported the movement for its creation. Even George Clinton, who seems to have been the first opposition leader to awake to the possibility of trouble, could not prevent the New York Legislature from appointing Alexander Hamilton—though he did have the foresight to send two of his henchmen to dominate the delegation. Incidentally, much has been made of the fact that the delegates to Philadelphia were not elected by the people; some have adduced this fact as evidence of the "undemocratic" character of the gathering. But put in the context of the time, this argument is wholly specious: the central government under the Articles was considered a creature of the component states; and in all the states but Rhode Island, Connecticut, and New Hampshire, members of the national Congress were chosen by state legislatures. This was not a consequence of elitism or fear of the mob; it was a logical extension of states'-rights doctrine to guarantee that the national institution did not end-run the state legislatures and make direct contact wtih the people.

With delegations safely named, the focus shifted to Philadelphia. While waiting for a quorum to assemble, James Madison got busy and drafted the so-called Randolph or Virginia Plan with the aid of the Virginia delegation. This was a political masterstroke. Its consequence was that once business got under way, the framework of discussion was established on Madison's terms. There was no interminable argument over agenda; instead the delegates took the Virginia Resolutions—"just for purposes of discussion"— as their point of departure. And along with Madison's proposals, many of which were buried in the course of the summer, went his major premise: a new start on a Constitution rather than piecemeal amendment. This was not necessarily revolutionary—a little exegesis could demonstrate that a new Constitution might be formulated as "amendments" to the Articles of Confederation—but Madison's proposal that this "lump sum" amendment go into effect after approval by nine states (the Articles required unanimous state approval for any amendment) was thoroughly subversive.

Standard treatments of the Convention divide the delegates into "nationalists" and "states'-righters," with various improvised shadings ("moderate nationalists," and so on), but these are *a posteriori* categories which obfuscate more than they clarify. What is striking to one who analyzes the Convention as a case study in democratic politics is the lack of clear-cut ideological divisions in the Convention. Indeed, I submit that the evidence —Madison's *Notes,* the correspondence of the delegates, and debates on ratification—indicates that this was a remarkably homogeneous body on the ideological level. Yates and Lansing, Clinton's two chaperons for Hamilton, left in disgust on July 10th. (Is there anything more tedious than sitting through endless disputes on matters one deems fundamentally misconceived? It takes an iron will to spend a hot summer as an ideological *agent provocateur.*) Luther Martin, Maryland's bibulous narcissist, left on September 4th in a huff when he discovered the others did not share his self-esteem; others went home for personal reasons. But the hard core of delegates accepted a grinding regimen throughout the attrition of a Philadelphia summer precisely because they shared the Constitutionalist goal.

Basic differences of opinion emerged, of course, but these were not ideological; they were *structural.* If the so-called "states'-rights" group had not accepted the fundamental purposes of the Convention, they could simply have pulled out and by doing so have aborted the whole enterprise. Instead of bolting, they returned day after day to argue and to compromise. An interesting symbol of this basic homogeneity was the initial agreement on secrecy: these professional politicians did not want to become prisoners of publicity; they wanted to retain that freedom of maneuver which is possible only when men are not forced to take public stands in the preliminary stages of negotiation. There was no legal means of binding the tongues of the delegates: at any stage in the game a delegate with basic principled objections to the emerging project could have taken the stump (as Luther Martin did after his exit) and denounced the Convention to the skies. Yet Madison did not even inform Thomas Jefferson in Paris of the course of the deliberations, and available correspondence indicates that the delegates generally observed the injunction. Secrecy is certainly uncharacteristic of any assembly marked by strong ideological polarization. This was noted at the time: the *New York Daily Advertiser,* August 14, 1787, commented that the ". . . profound secrecy hitherto observed by the convention [we consider] a happy omen, as it demonstrates that the spirit of party on any great and essential point cannot have arisen to any height."

Commentators on the Constitution who have read *The Federalist* in lieu of reading the actual debates have credited the Fathers with the invention of a sublime concept called "Federalism." Unfortunately, *The Federalist* is probative evidence for only one proposition: that Hamilton and Madison were inspired propagandists with a genius for retrospective symmetry. Federalism, as the theory is generally defined, was an improvisation which was later promoted into a political theory. Experts on "Federalism" should take to heart the advice of David Hume, who warned in his *Of the Rise and Progress of the Arts and Sciences* that ". . . there is no subject in which we must proceed with more caution than in [history], lest we assign causes which never existed and reduce what is merely contingent to stable and universal principles." In any event, the final balance in the Constitution between the states and the nation must have come as a great disappointment to Madison, while Hamilton's unitary views are too well known to need elucidation.

It is indeed astonishing how those who have glibly designated James Madison the "father" of Federalism have overlooked the solid body of fact which indicates that he shared Hamilton's quest for a unitary central government. To be specific, they have avoided examining the clear import of the Madison-Virginia Plan, and have disregarded Madison's dogged inch-by-inch retreat from the bastions of centralization. The Virginia Plan envisioned a unitary national government effectively freed from and dominant over the states. The lower house of the national legislature was to be elected directly by the people of the states with membership proportional to population. The upper house was to be selected by the lower, and the two chambers would elect the executive and choose the judges. The national government would be thus cut completely loose from the states.

The structure of the general government was freed from state control in a truly radical fashion, but the scope of the authority of the national sovereign as Madison intitially formulated it was breathtaking—it was a formulation worthy of the Sage of Malmesbury himself. The national legislature was to be empowered to disallow the acts of state legislatures, and the central government was vested, in addition to the powers of the nation under the Articles of Confederation, with plenary authority wherever ". . . the separate States are incompetent or in which the harmony of the United States may be interrupted by the exercise of individual legislation." Finally, just to lock the door against state intrusion, the national Congress was to be given the power to use military force on recalcitrant states. This was Madison's "model" of an ideal national government, though it later received little publicity in *The Federalist*.

The interesting thing was the reaction of the Convention to this militant program for a strong autonomous central government. Some delegates were startled, some obviously leery of so comprehensive a project of reform, but nobody set off any fireworks and nobody walked out. Moreover, in the two weeks that followed, the Virginia Plan received substantial endorsement *en principe;* the initial temper of the gathering can be deduced from the approval "without debate or dissent," on May 31st, of the Sixth Resolution, which granted Congress the authority to disallow state legislation ". . . contravening *in its opinion* the Articles of Union." Indeed, an amendment was included to bar states from contravening national treaties.

The Virginia Plan may therefore be considered, in ideological terms, as the delegates' Utopia, but as the discussions continued and became more specific, many of those present began to have second thoughts. After all, they were not residents of Utopia or guardians in Plato's Republic who could simply impose a philosophical ideal on subordinate strata of the population. They were practical politicians in a democratic society, and no matter what their private dreams might be, they had to take home an acceptable package and defend it—and their own political futures—against predictable attack. On June 14th the breaking point between dream and reality took place. Apparently realizing that under the Virginia Plan, Massachusetts, Virginia, and Pennsylvania could virtually dominate the national government—and probably appreciating that to sell this program to the "folks back home" would be impossible—the delegates from the small states dug in their heels and demanded time for a consideration of alternatives. One gets a graphic sense of the inner politics from John Dickinson's reproach to Madison: "You see the consequences of pushing things too far. Some of the members from the small States wish for two branches in the General Legislature and are friends to a good National Government; but we would sooner submit to a foreign power than . . . be deprived of an equality of suffrage in both branches of the Legislature, and thereby be thrown under the domination of the large States."

The bare outline of the *Journal* entry for Tuesday, June 14th, is suggestive to anyone with extensive experience in deliberative bodies. "It was moved by Mr. Patterson [*sic*, Paterson's name was one of those consistently misspelled by Madison and everybody else] seconded by Mr. Randolph that the further consideration of the report from the Committee of the whole House [endorsing the Virginia Plan] be postponed til tomorrow, and before the question for postponement was taken. It was moved by Mr. Randolph seconded by Mr. Patterson that the House adjourn." The House adjourned by obvious prearrangement of the two principals: since the preceding Saturday when David Brearley and Paterson of New Jersey had announced their fundamental discontent with the representational features of the Virginia Plan, the informal pressure had certainly been building up to slow down the steamroller. Doubltess there were extended arguments at the Indian Queen between Madison and Paterson, the latter insisting that events were moving rapidly toward a probably disastrous conclusion, toward a political suicide pact. Now the process of accommodation was put into action smoothly—and wisely, given the character and strength of the doubters. Madison had the votes, but this was one of those situations where the enforcement of mechanical majoritarianism could easily have destroyed the objectives of the majority: the Constitutionalists were in quest of a qualitative as well as quantitative consensus. This was hardly from deference to local Quaker custom; it was a political imperative if they were to attain ratification.

According to the standard script, at this point the "states'-rights" group intervened in force behind the New Jersey Plan, which has been characteristically portrayed as a reversion to the *status quo* under the Articles of Confederation with but minor modifications. A careful examination of the evidence indicates that only in a marginal sense is this an accurate description. It is true that the New Jersey Plan put the states back into the insitutional picture, but one could argue that to do so was a recognition of political reality rather than an affirmation of states' rights. A serious case can be made that the advocates of the New Jersey Plan, far from being ideological addicts of states' rights, intended to substitute for the Virginia Plan a system which would both retain strong national power and have a chance of adoption in the states. The leading spokesman for the project asserted quite clearly that his views were based more on counsels of expediency than on principle; said Paterson on June 16th: "I came here not to speak my own sentiments, but the sentiments of those who sent me. Our object is not such a Government as may be best in itself, but such a one as our Constituents have authorized us to prepare, and as they will approve." This is Madison's version; in Yates's transcription, there is a crucial sentence following the remarks above: "I believe that a little practical virtue is to be preferred to the finest theoretical principles, which cannot be carried into effect." In his preliminary speech on June 9th, Paterson had stated ". . . to the public mind we must accommodate ourselves," and in his notes for this and his later effort as well, the emphasis is the same. The *structure* of government under the Articles should be retained:

Because it accords with the Sentiments of the People [Proof:] 1. Coms. [Commissions from state legislatures defining the jurisdiction of the delegates]
2. News-papers—Political Barometer. Jersey never would have sent Delegates under the first [Virginia] Plan—
Not here to sport Opinions of my own. Wt. [What] can be done. A little practical Virtue preferrable to Theory.

This was a defense of political acumen, not of states' rights. In fact, Paterson's notes of his speech can easily be construed as an argument for attaining the substantive objectives of the Virginia Plan by a sound political route, that is, pouring the new wine into the old bottles. With a shrewd eye, Paterson queried:

Will the Operation and Force of the [central] Govt. depend upon the mode of Representn.—No—it will depend upon the Quantum of Power lodged in the leg. ex. and judy. Departments—Give [the existing] Congress the same Powers that you intend to give the two Branches, [under the Virginia Plan] and I apprehend they will act with as much Propriety and more Energy. . . .

In other words, the advocates of the New Jersey Plan concentrated their fire on what they held to be the *political liabilities* of the Virginia Plan—which were matters of institutional structure—rather than on the proposed scope of national authority. Indeed, the Supremacy Clause of the Constitution first saw the light of day in Paterson's Sixth Resolution; the New Jersey Plan contemplated the use of military force to secure compliance with national law; and finally Paterson made clear his view that under either the Virginia or the New Jersey systems, the general governmnt would ". . . act on individuals and not on states." From the states'-rights viewpoint, this was heresy: the fundament of that doctrine was the proposition that any central government had as its constituents the states, not the people, and could reach the people only through the agency of the state government.

Paterson then reopened the agenda of the Convention, but he did so within a distinctly nationalist framework. Paterson's position was one of favoring a strong central government in principle, but opposing one which in fact *put the big states in the saddle.* (The Virginia Plan, for all its abstract merits, did very well by Virginia.) As evidence for this speculation, there is a curious and intriguing proposal among Paterson's preliminary drafts of the New Jersey Plan:

Whereas it is necessary in Order to form the People of the U.S. of America in to a Nation, that the States should be consolidated, by which means all the Citizens thereof will become equally intitled to and will

> equally participate in the same Privileges and Rights. . . it is therefore
> resolved, that all the Lands contained within the Limits of each state
> individually, and of the U.S. generally be considered as constituting one
> Body or Mass, and be divided into thirteen or more integral parts.
> Resolved, That such Divisions or integral Parts shall be styled Districts.

This makes it sound as though Paterson was prepared to accept a strong
unified central government along the lines of the Virginia Plan if the existing
states were eliminated. He may have got the idea from his New Jersey
colleague Judge David Brearley, who on June 9th had commented that the
only remedy to the dilemma over representation was ". . . that a map of
the U.S. be spread out, that all the existing boundaries be erased, and that
a new partition of the whole be made into 13 equal parts." According to
Yates, Brearley added at this point, ". . . then a government on the
present [Virginia Plan] system will be just."

This proposition was never pushed—it was patently unrealistic—but
one can appreciate its purpose: it would have separated the men from the
boys in the large-state delegations. How attached would the Virginians have
been to their reform principles if Virginia were to disappear as a component
geographical unit (the largest) for representational purposes? Up to this
point, the Virginians had been in the happy position of supporting high
ideals with that inner confidence born of knowledge that the "public interest" they endorsed would nourish their private interest. Worse, they had
shown little willingness to compromise. Now the delegates from the small
states announced that they were unprepared to be offered up as sacrificial
victims to a "national interest" which reflected Virginia's parochial ambition. Caustic Charles Pinckney was not far off when he remarked sardon-
ically that ". . . the whole [conflict] comes to this: Give N. Jersey an
equal vote, and she will dismiss her scruples, and concur in the Natil.
system." What he rather unfairly did not add was that the Jersey delegates
were not free agents who could adhere to their private convictions; they
had to take back, sponsor, and risk their reputations on the reforms approved by the Convention—and in New Jersey, not in Virginia.

Paterson spoke on Saturday, and one can surmise that over the weekend
there was a good deal of consultation, argument, and caucusing among the
delegates. One member at least prepared a full-length address: on Monday,
Alexander Hamilton, previously mute, rose and delivered a six-hour oration. It was a remarkably apolitical speech; the gist of his position was that
both the Virginia and New Jersey plans were inadequately centralist, and he
detailed a reform program which was reminiscent of the Protectorate under
the Cromwellian *Instrument of Government* of 1653. It has been suggested
that Hamilton did this in the best political tradition to emphasize the moderate character of the Virginia Plan, to give the cautious delegates some-

thing *really* to worry about; but this interpretation seems somehow too clever, particularly since the sentiments Hamilton expressed happened to be completely consistent with those he privately—and sometimes publicly —expressed throughout his life. He wanted, to take a striking phrase from a letter to George Washington, a "strong well mounted government"; in essence, the Hamilton Plan contemplated an elected life monarch, virtually free of public control, on the Hobbesian ground that only in this fashion could strength and stability be achieved. The other alternatives, he argued, would put policy-making at the mercy of the passions of the mob; only if the sovereign was beyond the reach of selfish influence would it be possible to have government in the interests of the whole community.

From all accounts, this was a masterful and compelling speech, but (aside from furnishing John Lansing and Luther Martin with ammunition for later use against the Constitution) it made little impact. Hamilton was simply transmitting on a different wavelength from the rest of the delegates; the latter adjourned after his great effort, admired his rhetoric, and then returned to business. It was rather as if they had taken a day off to attend the opera. Hamilton, never a particularly patient man or much of a negotiator, stayed for another ten days, and then left, in considerable disgust, for New York. Although he came back to Philadelphia sporadically and attended the last two weeks of the Convention, Hamilton played no part in the laborious task of hammering out the Constitution. His day came later when he led the New York Constitutionalists into the savage imbroglio over ratification—an arena in which his unmatched talent for dirty political infighting may well have won the day. For instance, in the New York Ratifying Convention, Lansing threw back into Hamilton's teeth the sentiments the latter had expressed in his June 18th oration in the Convention. However, having since retreated to the fine defensive positions immortalized in *The Federalist,* the Colonel flatly denied that he had ever been an enemy of the states, or had believed that conflict between states and nation was inexorable! As Madison's authoritative *Notes* did not appear until 1840, and there had been no press coverage, there was no way to verify his assertions, so in the words of the reporter, ". . . a warm personal altercation between [Lansing and Hamilton] engrossed the remainder of the day [June 28, 1788]."

On Tuesday morning, June 19th, the vacation was over. James Madison led off with a long, carefully reasoned speech analyzing the New Jersey Plan which, while intellectually vigorous in its criticisms, was quite conciliatory in mood. "The great difficulty," he observed, "lies in the affair of Representation; and if this could be adjusted, all others would be surmountable." (As events were to demonstrate, this diagnosis was correct.) When he finished, a vote was taken on whether to continue with the Virginia Plan as the nucleus for a new constitution: seven states voted "Yes"; New

York, New Jersey, and Delaware voted "No"; and Maryland, whose position often depended on which delegates happened to be on the floor, divided. Paterson it seems, lost decisively; yet in a fundamental sense he and his allies had achieved their purpose: from that day onward, it could never be forgotten that the state governments loomed ominously in the background and that no verbal incantations could exorcise their power. Moreover, nobody bolted the convention: Paterson and his colleagues took their defeat in stride and set to work to modify the Virginia Plan, particularly with respect to its provisions on representation in the National Legislature. Indeed, they won an immediate rhetorical bonus; when Oliver Ellsworth of Connecticut rose to move that the word "national" be expunged from the Third Virginia Resolution ("Resolved that a *national* Government ought to be established consisting of a *supreme* Legislative, Executive and Judiciary"), Randolph agreed, and the motion passed unanimously. The process of compromise had begun.

For the next two weeks, the delegates circled around the problem of legislative representation. The Connecticut delegation appears to have evolved a possible compromise quite early in the debates, but the Virginians and particularly Madison (unaware that he would later be acclaimed as the prophet of "Federalism") fought obdurately against providing for equal representation of states in the second chamber. There was a good deal of acrimony, and at one point Benjamin Franklin—of all people—proposed the institution of a daily prayer; practical politicians in the gathering, however, were meditating more on the merits of a good committee than on the utility of divine intervention. On July 2nd, the ice began to break when through a number of fortuitous events—and one that seems deliberate— the majority against equality of representation was converted into a dead tie. The Convention had reached the stage where it was "ripe" for a solution (presumably all the therapeutic speeches had been made), and the South Carolinians proposed a committee. Madison and James Wilson wanted none of it, but with only Pennsylvania dissenting, the body voted to establish a working party on the problem of representation.

The members of this committee, one from each state, were elected by the delegates—and a very interesting committee it was. Despite the fact that the Virginia Plan had held majority support up to that date, neither Madison nor Randolph was selected (Mason was the Virginian), and Baldwin of Georgia, whose shift in position had resulted in the tie, was chosen. From the composition, it was clear that this was not to be a "fighting" committee: the emphasis in membership was on what might be described as "second-level political entrepreneurs." On the basis of the discussions up to that time, only Luther Martin of Maryland could be described as a "bitter-ender." Admittedly, some divination enters into this sort of analysis, but one does get a sense of the mood of the delegates from these choices

—including the interesting selection of Benjamin Franklin, despite his age and intellectual wobbliness, over the brilliant and incisive Wilson or the sharp, polemical Gouverneur Morris, to represent Pennsylvania. His passion for conciliation was more valuable at this juncture than Wilson's logical genius, or Morris's acerbic wit.

There is a common rumor that the Framers divided their time between philosophical discussions of government and reading the classics in political theory. Perhaps this is as good a time as any to note that their concerns were highly practical, that they spent little time canvassing abstractions. A number of them had some acquaintance with the history of political theory (probably gained from reading John Adams's monumental compilation *A Defence of the Constitutions of Government,* the first volume of which appeared in 1786), and it was a poor rhetorician indeed who could not cite Locke, Montesquieu, or Harrington, *in support* of a desired goal. Yet up to this point in the deliberations, no one had expounded a defense of states' rights or the "separation of powers" on anything resembling a theoretical basis. It should be reiterated that the Madison model had no room either for the states or for the "separation of powers": effectively *all* governmental power was vested in the national legislature. The merits of Montesquieu did not turn up until *The Federalist;* and although a perverse argument could be made that Madison's ideal was truly in the tradition of John Locke's *Second Treatise of Government,* the Locke whom the American rebels treated as an honorary president was a pluralistic defender of vested rights, not of parliamentary supremacy.

It would be tedious to continue a blow-by-blow analysis of the work of the delegates; the critical fight was over representation of the states, and once the Connecticut Compromise was adopted, on July 17, the Convention was over the hump. Madison, James Wilson, and Gouverneur Morris of New York (who was there representing Pennsylvania!) fought the compromise all the way in a last-ditch effort to get a unitary state with parliamentary supremacy. But their allies deserted them, and they demonstrated after their defeat the essentially opportunist character of their objections—using "opportunist" here in a nonpejorative sense, to indicate a willingness to swallow their objections and get on with the business. Moreover, once the compromise had carried (by five states to four, with one state divided), its advocates threw themselves vigorously into the job of strengthening the general government's substantive powers—as might have been predicted, indeed, from Paterson's early statements. It nourishes an increased respect for Madison's devotion to the art of politics, to realize that this dogged fighter could sit down six months later and prepare essays for *The Federalist* in contradiction to his basic convictions about the true course the Convention should have taken.

Two tricky issues will serve to illustrate the later process of accommodation. The first was the institutional position of the executive. Madison argued for an executive chosen by the National Legislature, and on May 29th this had been adopted with a provision that after his seven-year term was concluded, the chief magistrate should not be eligible for re-election. In late July this was reopened, and for a week the matter was argued from several different points of view. A good deal of desultory speechmaking ensued, but the gist of the problem was the opposition from two sources to election by the legislature. One group felt that the states should have a hand in the process; another small but influential circle urged direct election by the people, election by state governors, by electors chosen by state legislatures, by the National Legislature (James Wilson, perhaps ironically, proposed at one point that an electoral college be chosen by lot from the National Legislature!), and there was some resemblance to three-dimensional chess in the dispute because of the presence of two other variables, length of tenure and re-eligibility. Finally, after opening, reopening, and re-reopening the debate, the thorny problem was consigned to a committee for resolution.

The Brearley Committee on Postponed Matters was a superb aggregation of talent, and its compromise on the executive was a masterpiece of political improvisation. (The Electoral College, its creation, however, had little in its favor as an *institution*—as the delegates well appreciated.) The point of departure for all discussion about the Presidency in the Convention was that in immediate terms, the problem was nonexistent; in other words, everybody present knew that under any system devised, George Washington would be President. Thus they were dealing in the future tense, and to a body of working politicians the merits of the Brearley proposal were obvious: everybody got a piece of cake. (Or, to put it more academically, each viewpoint could leave the Convention and argue to its constituents that it had *really* won the day.) First, the state legislatures had the right to determine the mode of selection of the electors; second, the small states received a bonus in the Electoral College in the form of a guaranteed minimum of three votes, while the big states got acceptance of the principle of proportional power; third, if the state legislatures agreed (as six did in the first presidential election), the people could be involved directly in the choice of electors; and finally, if no candidate received a majority in the College, the right of decision passed on to the National Legislature, with each state exercising equal strength. (In the Brearley recommendation, the election went to the Senate, but a motion from the floor substituted the House; his was accepted on the ground that the Senate already had enough authority over the executive in its treaty and appointment powers.)

This compromise was almost too good to be true, and the Framers snapped it up with little debate or controversy. No one seemed to think well of the College as an *institution;* indeed, what evidence there is suggests that there was an assumption that once Washington had finished his tenure as President, the electors would cease to produce majorities and that the Chief Executive would usually be chosen in the House. George Mason observed casually that the selection would be made in the House nineteen times in twenty, and no one seriously disputed this point. The vital aspect of the Electoral College was that it got the Convention over the hurdle and protected everybody's interests. The future was left to cope with the problem of what to do with this Rube Goldberg mechanism.

In short, the Framers did not in their wisdom endow the United States with a College of Cardinals—the Electoral College was neither an exercise in applied Platonism nor an experiment in indirect government based on elitist distrust of the masses. It was merely a jerry-rigged improvisation which has subsequently been endowed with a high theoretical content. When an elector from Oklahoma in 1960 refused to cast his vote for Nixon (naming Byrd and Goldwater instead) on the ground that the Founding Fathers intended him to exercise his great independent wisdom, he was indulging in historical fantasy. If one were to indulge in counterfantasy, he would be tempted to suggest that the Fathers would be startled to find the College still in operation—and perhaps even dismayed at their descendants' lack of judgment or inventiveness.

The second issue on which some substantial practical bargaining took place was slavery. The morality of slavery was, by design, not at issue; but in its other concrete aspects, slavery colored the arguments over taxation, commerce, and representation. The "Three-Fifths Compromise," that three-fifths of the slaves would be counted both for representation and for purposes of direct taxation (which was drawn from the past—it was a formula of Madison's utilized by Congress in 1783 to establish the basis of state contributions to the Confederation treasury), had allayed some northern fears about southern over-representation (no one then foresaw the trivial role that direct taxation would play in later federal financial policy), but doubts still remained. The Southerners, on the other hand, were afraid that congressional control over commerce would lead to the exclusion of slaves or to their excessive taxation as imports. Moreover, the Southerners were disturbed over "navigation acts," that is, tariffs, or special legislation providing, for example, that exports be carried only in American ships; as a section depending upon exports, they wanted protection from the potential voracity of their commercial brethren of the eastern states. To achieve this end, Mason and others urged that the Constitution include a proviso that navigation and commercial laws should require a two-thirds vote in Congress.

These problems came to a head in late August and, as usual, were handed to a committee in the hope that, in Gouverneur Morris's words, ". . . these things may form a bargain among the Northern and Southern states." The committee reported its measures of reconciliation on August 25th, and on August 29th the package was wrapped up and delivered. What occurred can best be described in George Mason's dour version (he anticipated Calhoun in his conviction that permitting navigation acts to pass by majority vote would put the South in economic bondage to the North—it was mainly on this ground that he refused to sign the Constitution):

> The Constitution as agreed to till a fortnight before the Convention rose was such a one as he would have set his hand and heart to. . . . [Until that time] The 3 New England States were constantly with us in all questions . . . so that it was these three States with the 5 Southern ones against Pennsylvania, Jersey and Delaware. With respect to the importation of slaves, [decision-making] was left to Congress. This disturbed the two Southernmost States who knew that Congress would immediately suppress the importation of slaves. Those two states therefore struck up a bargain with the three New England States. If they would join to admit slaves for some years, the two Southern-most States would join in changing the clause which required the 2/3 of the Legislature in any vote [on navigation acts]. It was done.

On the floor of the Convention there was a virtual love feast on this happy occasion. Charles Pinckney, of South Carolina, attempted to overturn the committee's decision, when the compromise was reported to the Convention, by insisting that the South needed protection from the imperialism of the northern states. But his southern colleagues were not prepared to rock the boat, and General C. C. Pinckney arose to spread oil on the suddenly ruffled waters; he admitted that:

> It was in the true interest of the S[outhern] States to have no regulation of commerce; but considering the loss brought on the commerce of the Eastern States by the Revolution, their liberal conduct towards the views of South Carolina [on the regulation of the slave trade] and the interests the weak Southn. States had in being united with the strong Eastern states, he thought it proper that no fetters should be imposed on the power of making commercial regulations; *and that his constituents, though prejudiced against the Eastern States, would be reconciled to this liberality*. He had himself prejudices agst the Eastern States before he came here, but would acknowledge that he had found them as liberal and candid as any men whatever. [Italics added]

Pierce Butler took the same tack, essentially arguing that he was not too happy about the possible consequences but that a deal was a deal. Many southern leaders were later—in the wake of the "Tariff of Abominations" —to rue this day of reconciliation; Calhoun's *A Disquisition on Government* was little more than an extension of the argument in the Convention against permitting a congressional majority to enact navigation acts.

Drawing on their vast collective political experience, utilizing every weapon in the politician's arsenal, looking constantly over their shoulders at their constituents, the delegates put together a Constitution. It was a makeshift affair; some sticky issues (for example, the qualification of voters) they ducked entirely; others they mastered with that ancient instrument of political sagacity, studied ambiguity (for example, citizenship), and some they just overlooked. In this last category, I suspect, fell the matter of the power of the federal courts to determine the constitutionality of acts of Congress. When the judicial article was formulated (Article III of the Constitution), deliberations were still in the stage where the legislature was endowed with broad power under the Randolph formulation, authority which by its own terms was scarcely amenable to judicial review. In essence, courts could hardly determine when ". . . the separate States are incompetent or . . . the harmony of the United States may be interrupted"; the National Legislature, as critics pointed out, was free to define its own jurisdiction. Later the definition of legislative authority was changed into the form we know, a series of stipulated powers, *but the delegates never seriously reexamined the jurisdiction of the judiciary under this new limited formulation.* All arguments on the intention of the Framers in this matter are thus deductive and *a posteriori,* though some obviously make more sense than others.

The Framers were busy and distinguished men, anxious to get back to their families, their positions, and their constituents, not members of the French Academy devoting a lifetime to a dictionary. They were trying to do an important job, and do it in such fashion that their handiwork would be acceptable to very diverse constituencies. No one was rhapsodic about the final document, but it was a beginning, a move in the right direction, and one they had reason to believe the people would endorse. In addition, since they had modified the impossible amendment provisions of the Articles, (the requirement of unanimity which could always be frustrated by "Rogues Island") to one demanding approval by only three-quarters of the states, they seemed confident that gaps in the fabric which experience would reveal could be rewoven without undue difficulty.

So with a neat phrase introduced by Benjamin Franklin (but devised by Gouverneur Morris) which made their decision sound unanimous, and an inspired benediction by the Old Doctor urging doubters to doubt their own infallibility, the Constitution was accepted and signed. Curiously, Edmund Randolph, who had played so vital a role throughout, refused to sign, as did his fellow Virginian George Mason and Elbridge Gerry of Massachusetts. Randolph's behavior was eccentric, to say the least—his excuses for refusing his signature have a factitious ring even at this late date; the best explanation seems to be that he was afraid that the Constitution would prove to be a liability in Virginia politics, where Patrick Henry was burning up the countryside with impassioned denunciations. Presumably, Randolph wanted to check the temper of the populace before he risked his reputation, and perhaps his job, in a fight with both Henry and Richard Henry Lee. Events lend some justification to this speculation: after much temporizing and use of the conditional subjunctive tense, Randolph endorsed ratification in Virginia and ended by getting the best of both worlds.

Madison, despite his reservations about the Constitution, was the campaign manager in ratification. His first task was to get the Congress in New York to light its own funeral pyre by approving the "amendments" to the Articles and sending them on to the state legislatures. Above all, momentum had to be maintained. The anti-Constitutionalists, now thoroughly alarmed and no novices in politics, realized that their best tactic was attrition rather than direct opposition. Thus they settled on a position expressing qualified approval but calling for a second Convention to remedy various defects (the one with the most demagogic appeal was the lack of a Bill of Rights). Madison knew that to accede to this demand would be equivalent to losing the battle, nor would he agree to conditional approval (despite wavering even by Hamilton). This was an all-or-nothing proposition: national salvation or national impotence with no intermediate positions possible. Unable to get congressional approval, he settled for a second best: a unanimous resolution of Congress transmitting the Constitution to the states for whatever action they saw fit to take. The opponents then moved from New York and the Congress, where they had attempted to attach amendments and conditions, to the states for the final battle.

At first the campaign for ratification went beautifully: within eight months after the delegates set their names to the document, eight states had ratified. Only in Massachusetts had the result been close (187–168). Theoretically, a ratification by one more state convention would set the new government in motion, but in fact until Virginia and New York acceded to the new Union, the latter was a fiction. New Hampshire was the next to ratify; Rhode Island was involved in its characteristic political convulsions (the legislature there sent the Constitution out to the towns for decision by popular vote and it got lost among a series of local issues); North Carolina's convention did not meet until July, and then postponed a final decision. This is hardly the place for an extensive analysis of the conventions of New York and Virginia. Suffice it to say that the Constitutionalists clearly outmaneuvered their opponents, forced them into impossible political positions, and won both states narrowly. The Virginia Convention could serve as a classic study in effective floor management: Patrick Henry had to be contained, and a reading of the debates discloses a standard two-stage technique. Henry would give a four- or five-hour speech denouncing some section of the Constitution on every conceivable ground (the federal district, he averred at one point, would become a haven for convicts escaping from state authority!). When Henry subsided, "Mr. Lee of Westmoreland" would rise and poleax him with sardonic invective. (When Henry complained about the militia power, "Lighthorse Harry" really punched below the belt: observing that while the former governor had been sitting in Richmond during the Revolution, *he* had been out in the trenches with the troops and thus felt better qualified to discuss military affairs.) Then the gentlemanly Constitutionalists (Madison, Pendleton, and Marshall) would pick up the matters at issue and examine them in the light of reason.

Indeed, modern Americans who tend to think of James Madison as a rather desiccated character should spend some time with this transcript. Probably Madison put on his most spectacular demonstration of nimble rhetoric in what might be called the "Battle of the Absent Authorities." Patrick Henry in the course of one of his harangues alleged that Jefferson was known to be opposed to Virginia's approving the Constitution. This was clever: Henry hated Jefferson, but was prepared to use any weapon that came to hand. Madison's riposte was superb: First, he said that with all due respect to the great reputation of Jefferson, he was not in the country and therefore could not formulate an adequate judgment; second, no one should utilize the reputation of an outsider—the Virginia Convention was there to think for itself; third, if there were to be recourse to outsiders, the opinions of George Washington should certainly be taken into consideration; and, finally, he knew from privileged personal communications from Jefferson that in fact the latter *strongly favored* the Constitution. To devise an assault route into this rhetorical fortress was literally impossible.

The fight was over; all that remained now was to establish the new frame of government in the spirit of its Framers. And who were better qualified for this task than the Framers themselves? Thus victory for the Constitution meant simultaneous victory for the Constitutionalist; the anti-Constitutionalists either capitulated or vanished into limbo—soon Patrick Henry would be offered a seat on the Supreme Court and Luther Martin would be known as the Federalist "bull-dog." And, irony of ironies, Alexander Hamilton and James Madison would shortly accumulate a reputation as the formulators of what is often alleged to be our political theory, the concept of "Federalism." Also, on the other side of the ledger, the arguments would soon appear over what the Framers "really meant"; while these disputes have assumed the proportions of a big scholarly business in the last century, they began almost before the ink on the Constitution was dry. One of the best early ones featured Hamilton versus Madison on the scope of presidential power, and other Framers characteristically assumed positions in this and other disputes on the basis of their political convictions.

Probably our greatest difficulty is that we know so much more about what the Framers *should have meant* than they themselves did. We are intimately acquainted with the problems that their Constitution should have been designed to master; in short, we have read the mystery story backward. If we are to get the right "feel" for their time and their circumstances, we must, in Maitland's phrase, ". . . think ourselves back into a twilight." Obviously, no one can pretend completely to escape from the solipsistic web of his own environment, but if the effort is made, it is possible to appreciate the past roughly on its own terms. The first step in this process is to abandon the academic premise that because we can ask a question, there must be an answer.

Thus we can ask what the Framers meant when they gave Congress the power to regulate interstate and foreign commerce, and we emerge, reluctantly perhaps, with the reply that (Professor Crosskey to the contrary notwithstanding) they may not have known what they meant, that there may not have been any semantic consensus. The Convention was not a seminar in analytic philosophy or linguistic analysis. Commerce was *commerce*—and if different interpretations of the word arose, later generations could worry about the problem of definition. The delegates were in a hurry to get a new government established; when definitional arguments arose, they characteristically took refuge in ambiguity. If different men voted for the same proposition for varying reasons, that was politics (and still is); if later generations were unsettled by this lack of precision, that would be their problem.

There was a good deal of definitional pluralism with respect to the problems the delegates did discuss, but when we move to the question of extrapolated intentions we enter the realm of spiritualism. When men in our time, for instance, launch into elaborate talmudic exegesis to demonstrate that federal aid to parochial schools is (or is not) in accord with the intentions of the men who established the Republic and endorsed the Bill of Rights, they are engaging in historical extrasensory perception. (If one were to join this E.S.P. contingent for a minute, he might suggest that the hard-boiled politicians who wrote the Constitution and Bill of Rights would chuckle scornfully at such an invocation of authority: obviously a politician would chart his course on the intentions of the living, not of the dead, and count the number of Catholics in his constituency.)

The Constitution, then, was not an apotheosis of "constitutionalism," a triumph of architectonic genius; it was a patchwork sewn together under the pressure of both time and events by a group of extremely talented democratic politicians. They refused to attempt the establishment of a strong, centralized sovereignty on the principle of legislative supremacy, for the excellent reason that the people would not accept it. They risked their political fortunes by opposing the established doctrines of state sovereignty because they were convinced that the existing system was leading to national impotence and probably foreign domination. For two years they worked to get a convention established. For over three months, in what must have seemed to the faithful participants an endless process of give-and-take, they reasoned, cajoled, threatened, and bargained amongst themselves. The result was a Constitution which the people, in fact, by democratic processes, did accept, and a new and far better national government was established.

Beginning with the inspired propaganda of Hamilton, Madison, and Jay, the ideological buildup got under way. *The Federalist* had little impact on the ratification of the Constitution, except perhaps in New York, but this volume had enormous influence on the image of the Constitution in the minds of future generations, particularly on historians and political scientists who have an innate fondness for theoretical symmetry. Yet, while the shades of Locke and Montesquieu *may* have been hovering in the background and the delegates *may* have been unconscious instruments of a transcendent *telos,* the careful observer of the day-to-day work of the Convention finds no overarching principles. The "separation of powers" to him seems to be a by-product of suspicion, and "Federalism" he views as a *pis aller,* as the farthest point the delegates felt they could go in the destruction of state power without themselves inviting repudiation.

To conclude, the Constitution was neither a victory for abstract theory nor a great practical success. Well over half a million men had to die on the battlefields of the Civil War before certain constitutional principles could be defined—a baleful consideration which is somehow overlooked in our customary tributes to the farsighted genius of the Framers and to the supposed American talent for "constitutionalism." The Constitution was, however, a vivid demonstration of effective democratic political action, and of the forging of a national elite which literally persuaded its countrymen to hoist themselves by their own boot straps. American pro-consuls would be wise not to translate the Constitution into Japanese, or Swahili, or treat it as a work of semi-Divine origin; but when students of comparative politics examine the process of nation-building in countries newly freed from colonial rule, they may find the American experience instructive as a classic example of the potentialities of a democratic elite.

Chapter 2
SUGGESTED TOPICS FOR CLASS DISCUSSION

1. What basic ideas concerning the nature of both government and society are expressed in the Declaration of Independence?
2. Why were such great lengths taken in the Declaration of Independence to make revolution appear to be a *legal* action?
3. Could the Declaration of Independence be classed a radical and dangerous

document? It insists that when men differ with their government, they have
not only the *right* but the *duty* to revolt. Could any society exist if these ideas
were widely held? Does this mean that Americans have never really subscribed to the doctrines that are so frequently quoted as the foundations for
American liberty?

4. What are the fundamental points John P. Roche makes about the process
by which the Constitution was created? If his analysis is correct, does this
change your view of the worth of the Constitution?

Chapter 3

The Cities and the Environment

The problems of the environment and those of the city have much in common. The city, like the environment, is a complex and delicate organism. The way in which each functions is little understood. However, we do understand that the complex processes of each are easily disrupted. Goods and services flow through the intricate interlocking networks of a city, and blockage at any of a large number of points will affect the working of the system as a whole. A city is at the mercy of a variety of groups of men who perform special functions. These men, with no ill-will toward their neighbors, can bring a city to its knees if they choose. The environment, too, is vulnerable to the actions of special groups of men. Generally, these men are not deliberately trying to pollute or despoil the environment; they are pursuing what they conceive to be their own interests, and, in so doing, damage to the environment is a side effect. The governing of a metropolis involves a succession of crises or threatened crises: too much snow, too little rain, too much garbage, too few jobs, too much smog, too little sense of community, too many strikes, too little money for community needs, and so on. It appears that the management of the broader environment will also provide mankind with chronic crises.

Both city and environmental problems have historical roots, and there is no chance of dealing adequately with either unless significant changes in contemporary attitudes and practices occur. How are men to live in the cities they have built? Are we in the process of making cities unliveable? What is the best way to tackle the problems of the city? What costs will be involved and how should burdens be shared? What should be done to prevent further environmental deterioration? What are the choices open to mankind and what are the costs associated with each choice? Are we in a race with time? Are environmental problems increasing faster than man's capacity to find solutions? What political actions need to be taken if men are to have a chance of dealing with the problems of the cities and the environment?

REVENUE SHARING: GAME PLAN OR TRICK PLAY?

Allan S. Mandel

One of the top items on President Nixon's legislative agenda this year is his general revenue sharing proposal. Too bad. The good intentions of its designers and backers are matched only by their failure to come to grips with the fundamentals of the problem they are trying to correct.

This is not totally unexpected. State and local tax and expenditure policy is a rather dull topic. That's part of the reason for the state and local mess we're in. Few people, especially politicians, can stay awake long enough to inform themselves on the subject. Yet understanding this area is of great importance, since federal-state-local tax and expenditure relationships vitally affect the quality of life in an urban, industrial society.

Basically the analysis of the matter is a simple one. There is an old economic dictum that for each policy goal the government needs a separate policy tool. The government's first job is to decide on a set of goals and then find the best policy tool for each goal.

This may sound somewhat academic. But it is not irrelevant. If government policy does not flow from a sensible and complete underlying

Source: *Society* (May 1972), Vol. 9, No. 7, pp. 4, 6, 8. Published by permission of Transaction Inc. from *Society,* Vol. 9 (May 1972). © 1972 by Transaction Inc. Allan S. Mandel is on the faculty of the Lyndon B. Johnson School of Public Affairs of the University of Texas at Austin.

theory it is likely to misfire unless we are very lucky. And it is best not to have to rely on luck.

In recent years economists have made impressive advances toward specifying possible goals of intergovernmental fiscal relations and the tools to reach them. The best overall analysis to date has been done by MIT's Lester Thurow who has laid bare the basic economic "workings" of a federal system. From his analysis and that of his predecessors, modern economics now teaches that economic involvement by the national government in the affairs of state governments, and state intervention in local government activities, properly comes about for three reasons.

• *The need to adjust for spillovers.* A spillover occurs when an activity carried on in one political jurisdiction confers unpaid-for benefits upon people in other jurisdictions. For instance, if a person with 16 years of education paid for by the taxpayers of California moves to Illinois, the citizens of Illinois receive the benefits of all that education—the immigrant's increased productivity, his enhanced potential for contribution to community life—at no cost.

A publicly financed smallpox vaccination program in New York benefits the citizens of New Jersey because it lessens the chances of an epidemic developing in New York and spreading across the Hudson. But New Jersey taxpayers receive this benefit for nothing.

The problem is that in deciding how much to spend on education, public health or other spillover-connected activities such as sewage disposal and air pollution control, a state considers (and rightly so) only the benefits that fall inside the state. Illinois taxpayers presumably would be willing to pay for the benefits they receive from California education if they had to. But there is no way that California, or any single state, can compel payment. What results is the widespread feeling that less is spent on education, public health, sewage disposal and air pollution control than consumers of these goods and services desire.

The best solution to this problem is a matching grant from the federal to the state government to finance spillover-producing activities. The state pays for the percentage of benefits going to its citizens, from elementary-secondary education, for example. The federal government, acting for those who live outside the state, pays the state government for the percentage of benefits reaching outside its borders.

• *The need to provide merit wants.* A "merit want" is Harvard economist Richard Musgrave's term for publicly financed goods and services "considered so meritorious that their satisfaction is provided for through the public budget, over and above what is provided for through the market and paid for by private buyers." Examples might be publicly subsidized health care, housing, education and food. This is a controversial rationale for government intervention because it can be held to go against the doctrine of consumer sovereignty. But to the extent that society, as a matter of national policy, wants to ensure at least minimum levels of the various possible categories of merit wants, the best policy tool is a lump-sum grant. This is a federal grant to the state government with no matching provisions. It is better than a matching grant because the response of states to matching grants would be likely to vary. Washington would have to offer a different matching ratio to each state in order to bring about the desired outcome.

• *The need to provide equal treatment for equals.* The suggestion that taxpayers with equal incomes should be taxed equally sounds reasonable enough. But this is difficult to carry through in a federal system. Taxpayers in poor states must pay higher tax rates than their neighbors with the same incomes in rich states in order to obtain the same level of public services. The frequent result is that taxpayers in poor areas have the worst of both worlds. They pay high rates and receive inferior public services.

One reason for altering this situation is a humanitarian concern for equity. But there are other, more practical reasons. Price distortions, large-scale migration and the spread of crime and social unrest are produced or encouraged by the existence of rich and poor areas side by side.

Economists are not in agreement on the best way to handle this problem. There is agreement, though, that the least expensive way to do it is with an instrument specifically designed for the task. One possible solution is to give each state a lump-sum grant equal to the difference between need and fiscal capacity, where need is defined as an adequate level of public services and fiscal capacity as the revenue yielded in the state by a model state tax system. The problems in making these concepts operational are formidable but not insurmountable. To increase political acceptability, only a percentage of the gap between need and capacity might be filled in, with the percentage increasing over time.

Closely related to equal treatment of equals is the subject of "vertical equity," which is economists' shorthand for the problem of the overall distribution of income in society. This is something which has concerned political philosophers for some time. To Marx it meant "to each according to his needs." To Locke it entitled a person only to as much property as he could use to "advantages of life." To some it means that a man is entitled to as much as he can get, regardless of how much it is or how he came by it.

America today is somewhere between the polar cases. We have welfare payments and a federal income tax with progressive rates. But in 1960 the poorest 40 percent of American families still shared only 18 percent of the national income. The richest 40 percent enjoyed 65 percent of it. There has been no improvement since World War II. The base of the federal income tax is riddled with loopholes. And the shortcomings of the welfare system have been well documented.

So there is room for improvement. There is also demand for improvement. What are today's domestic social tensions about if not the distribution of income?

The best policy tool for affecting the distribution of income is a federal personal income tax revitalized by the elimination of loopholes and the addition of negative tax rates. The question of vertical equity, if it is handled properly, does not require federal intervention in state affairs. It is best handled by the federal government alone.

The three aforementioned goals and policies require federal grants to state governments for the purposes of adjusting for spillovers, providing for merit wants and establishing equal treatment of equals. State grants to local government should be based on these same three principles. What emerges is a two-tiered relationship in which grants are made from federal to state governments and then from state to local governments. Each grant is tailored specifically for one of the goals.

One notable feature of this set of policies is that President Nixon's general revenue sharing proposal did not make the list. That, indeed, is the moral of this story. There is no place in a proper designed federal system for Heller-Pechman-Nixon general revenue sharing. The reason is that it violates the first principle of policy making—that expenditures must be related to specific goals.

What revenue sharing does is to say we will take 1.3 percent of the federal income tax base each year and give it to the states. Each state's share will be based on its relative population, with a slight bonus or penalty if a state taxes more or less heavily than the national average.

Now what do 1.3 percent of the tax base, relative population and relative tax effort have to do with spillovers, merit wants and equal treatment of equals, which modern economics has shown to be the real reasons for economic intervention by the national government in the affairs of state and local governments? The answer is nothing. And the reason is that a three-pronged problem requires a three-pronged solution. Revenue sharing, a single policy instrument, is being called upon to solve problems that should be handled by three separate sets of policy tools, each with a one-to-one relationship with the problem it is supposed to handle. All that revenue sharing has going for it is simplicity. But the problems it is supposed to solve are complex. It is ironic that the very people who accuse others of advocating simplistic solutions to complex problems are in this instance guilty of the crime themselves.

The most important virtue claimed for revenue sharing is the redirection of money from high-income to low-income areas, that is, equal treatment of equals. Some light is shed on how well revenue sharing will accomplish this goal in a recent paper by Richard Musgrave and Mitchell Polinsky. They found that under the Nixon plan only 55 percent of the funds would go to the states with needs greater than fiscal capacity. And only 42 percent of the excess needs at the state level would be filled.

Things will be even worse once the funds are passed on to local governments. Under one of the two options local governments would receive the money in proportion to the amount of taxes they raise locally. Consider two communities with the same population and tax rates. One community is rich and the other poor. The rich community would receive more in shared funds than the poor one. The result is perverse.

There is no way of predicting what would happen under the second option, which gives states and their localities a small bonus if they work out their own agreements.

Musgrave and Polinsky found the areas most in need of outside assistance to be the low-income states and urban areas within high-income states. The latter combine relatively high incomes with even higher needs. Revenue sharing, while it would give some help to these areas, falls far short of alleviating their distress. And, by giving considerable money to cities and states with fiscal capacities greater than needs, it diverts funds from New York City and Detroit and sends them to Scarsdale and Grosse Pointe.

The second most important claim for revenue sharing is that it will increase the level of state-local spending. It seems plausible to argue that grants from the national to state and local governments would raise their expenditure levels. But this argument ignores the fact that taxes must be paid to finance those grants. Economic theory suggests that in the long run the spending rate could be higher, unchanged or even lower, depending upon how states' expenditures from their own sources react to the higher level of federal taxation necessary to finance the revenue sharing grants.

In any event, any stimulus is not likely to be large. How many governors will be able to resist following the lead of Governor William Milliken of Michigan, who recommended, should revenue sharing be adopted, that his state's "share of new money be used to reduce the tax increase" outlined in his 1971–72 budget message?

What is the way out? The malaise of state and local government in the United States is too severe to be cured by a placebo. Unless strong medicine is prescribed the physician may someday be judged to have been guilty of malpractice.

At the federal level we now have from 140 to 1,315 grant programs, depending on who is doing the counting. Most are inadequately funded. The system was well intentioned, but it is not rational. It just grew.

It should be replaced by a carefully designed and adequately funded system of matching and lump-sum grants, each of which should be tailor-made for the accomplishment of one of the aforementioned goals. To do away with excessive numbers of programs, grant categories should be broadly defined.

This will result in the proper redistribution of funds from the federal to the state level. But what happens once the funds reach the states? The national goals cannot be achieved unless funds are rationally redistributed within each state. One way of ensuring this is to make part or all of the federal grant conditional upon the state's enacting its own program of matching and lump-sum grants keyed to the three goals.

Since the revenue side is at least as great a problem as the expenditure side in states and cities, consideration should also be given to making the grants conditional upon state and local tax reform. Greater reliance upon income taxes and less on property taxes, a requirement that state and local tax incidence be proportional or progressive rather than regressive, and substitution of land-value taxes for current property taxes are all strong candidates for state-local tax reform.

The emphasis in this discussion upon intergovernmental relations may leave the impression that there will be nothing left for states and localities to decide. If so, the impression is false. After the reorganization suggested here has taken place, states and localities will still be free to decide all matters of state and local interest. What is more, they will have enhanced resources with which to put those decisions into effect.

Finally, just as important as the three federal-state-local goals is the attainment of vertical equity. The best instrument is a federal income tax purged of loopholes and augmented by a set of negative rates to replace our current welfare system.

Federal-state-local fiscal relations are in crisis. The causes of the crisis are fairly well understood and the policies that could end it are known also. But for some reason President Nixon has seen fit to recommend a "solution" which is so inadequate as to make one question either his understanding of the problem or his desire to solve it.

Our whole intergovernmental structure has become so irrational that a basic rebuilding is necessary if cities and states are to perform their functions adequately. To beat the political bushes selling revenue sharing as the best we can come up with would be laughable if it weren't being done by the president of the United States. As he himself might say under different circumstances, "You can't win by a trick play if you have the wrong game plan."

Municipal Monopoly

E. S. Savas

Our cities are not working well. Sanitation, safety, transportation, housing, education—even electricity and telephones—all seem to be failing. The taxpayer complains about waste, inefficiency, and mismanagement, and blames his public servants.

In part, the problems derive from the fragile nature of modern society, which is so variously complex and interconnected. Just think of all the different people—from farmer to supermarket clerk—whose efforts must mesh in order for a slice of bread to reach your table. Any one participant could break the chain, including the man whose guild card authorizes him (and only him) to pump gas into the baker's delivery van. Nevertheless, we manage to get our daily bread after all. That's because there are many sources of flour and numerous individual bakeries: no one has an effective monopoly. Furthermore, products can be stockpiled, and so there's always fertilizer, wheat, flour, and even bread and frozen rolls, stored at various points in the system.

The city, however, is uniquely vulnerable to service shutdowns—and it doesn't have the options of moving to the South, starting a branch in Hong Kong, or going out of business. After all, a principal function of government is to provide, or at least regulate, those services that by their very nature are monopolies; and so the city furnishes public sanitation, police, and fire services, while the state government regulates the private power and telephone companies. These are all monopolies of a crucial sort, for their services—unlike flour—cannot be stockpiled or imported.

Therein lies a key problem of American cities: monopolies, whether public or private, are inefficient. Since most city agencies are monopolies, their staffs are automatically tempted to exercise that monopoly power for their own parochial advantage—and efficiency is rarely seen as an advantage. When a municipal monopoly no longer serves any interest but its own, the citizenry is left quivering with frustration and rage. The inefficiency of municipal services is not due to bad commissioners, mayors, managers, workers, unions, or labor leaders; it is a natural consequence of a monopoly system. *The public has created the monopoly, the monopoly behaves in predictable fashion, and there are no culprits, only scapegoats.*

Monopoly systems are also inherently unreliable because of their vulnerability to strikes and slowdowns. Legislators who do not seem to understand the fundamental workings of the system continue to demand that

Source: *Harper's Magazine* (December 1971), pp. 55–60. Copyright © 1971 by Minneapolis Star and Tribune Co., Inc. Reprinted from the December 1971 issue of *Harper's Magazine* by permission of the author.

public employees behave as though they did *not* possess monopoly power. The New York State legislature, for example, persists in drafting futile no-strike edicts, and is now hailing compulsory arbitration as the latest cure. That's like King Canute asking the sea to pretend it's a pond and telling the tides they must cease and desist. The U.S. Congress did much the same thing—and achieved equally spectacular failures—in its naïve dealings with monopolies such as the Postal Service and the railroads.

Employee groups favored with a monopoly can always arrange work slowdowns and carefully contrived absenteeism to achieve the effect of a strike, while getting around no-strike laws and avoiding prosecution. The government is then left with trying to prove there was a conspiracy when a tenth or a third of the work force suddenly took ill or started diligently following some obscure, trivial, but time-consuming work-safety rule.

In this situation, the urban public often lacks even the most basic defenses of a community: when much of the municipal work force lives outside the city proper, they and their families do not feel the effects of strikes and slowdowns at first hand, and are not subjected to social pressure from their friends and neighbors to resume their duty of providing vital services.

Roll Call, Lunch Breaks, and Washing Up

Evidence of malfunctioning municipal monopolies is all around us, and although the specific examples here are drawn from New York, the picture is, or soon will be, similar in other cities across the country.

Over the past ninety years, for instance, New York has constructed an elaborate organization called the Department of Sanitation and given it a monopoly over the collection of household refuse. Unlike most municipal monopolies, however, there is here a standard for comparison—the regulated (and unionized) private cartmen who collect refuse from stores, restaurants, and other commercial establishments. The comparison is instructive: it costs Sanitation almost three times as much to collect a ton of garbage as it costs the private entrepreneur. Furthermore, the average Sanitation truck is out of commission more than 30 per cent of the time; the private truck is out only about 5 per cent of the time. The explanation is obvious: if you own a mere one or two trucks, as most cartmen do, and your livelihood depends on them, you make sure they stay in working order.

An explanation of the threefold difference in collection costs is also simple, and derives from such embarrassingly old-fashioned concepts as close supervision and good management, motivated by the lure of profits. The more refuse a private cartman picks up in a day, the more money he makes. In the municipal monopoly, there is absolutely no connection between the two.

Household refuse collection is not the only monopoly granted to the

Department of Sanitation; it also has exclusive responsibility for snow removal. Here, too, the dead hand of monopoly is evident. In an eleven-hour work shift, only about six hours of actual plowing is done. The rest of the time is consumed in roll call, starting up, lunch breaks, coffee breaks, warm-up breaks, fueling breaks, driving to and from the plow routes, and washing up.

Nowhere does the inexorable inefficiency of municipal monopolies come through more clearly than in the following incredible statistic: between 1940 and 1965, the number of policemen in New York City increased by 50 per cent (from 16,000 to 24,000), but the *total* number of hours worked by the entire force in 1965 was actually *less* than in 1940. The increase in manpower was completely eaten up by a shorter work week, a longer lunch break, more vacation days, more holidays, and more sick leave. By comparison, during the same period, the length of the average work week throughout the U.S. declined by only 8 per cent.

The monopoly nature of police, fire, and sanitation services has produced work schedules totally unrelated to public needs. Until Mayor Lindsay successfully persuaded the state legislature to pass the "fourth platoon" bill—and it required a major effort on his part—state law called for an equal number of policemen working on each tour of duty. Small wonder that there was "cooping," or sleeping on the job; there simply wasn't much work to be done at 4:00 A.M. But neither the Mayor nor the Police Commissioner could reduce the graveyard shift and switch men to other tours of duty. "If you want more police available at 8:00 P.M., hire more police," was the legally sanctioned reply.

The most absurdly run New York City monopoly is mass transit. Seventy per cent of all mass transit rides occur during rush hours, and therefore few bus drivers and conductors are needed between rush hours. But just try to push through any efficient "split-shift" scheduling of manpower. Instead, some bus drivers for the state-operated Metropolitan Transportation Authority work *eight* hours a day but are paid for *fourteen*. They are compensated handsomely for the "hardship" of taking a paid four-hour Mediterranean-style break in the middle of their eight-hour work-day. Imagine where baseball would be if the hot-dog vendors insisted on being paid for a forty-hour week, fifty-two weeks a year.

Of course, no rundown of the municipal monopolies would be complete without mentioning education. It is enough to point out that a 50 per cent increase in the number of teachers, and the addition of one para-professional for every two teachers, has produced only a slight reduction in class size. The teachers have simply reduced their work hours and passed on some of their duties. Parents can judge for themselves whether the result has been better teacher preparation and better education for their children.

A different example of a malfunctioning municipal system is one invisible to the average citizen. Over the past century, the city has constructed an elaborate, time-consuming, costly bureaucratic system of checks and balances designed to assure that the government gets fair value in its purchases and to protect against corruption in contracting for supplies and equipment. However, the consequence is a long delay in securing bids, ordering goods, and paying bills. Requests are prepared and submitted to bidders on an approved list. Sealed bids are received and opened ceremoniously, contracts are awarded, purchase orders are prepared and issued, goods are received, several different agencies check to see that the right goods were delivered in good condition to the right place at the right time, payment is authorized after a proper invoice is received and cross-checked, and finally a check for payment is grudgingly issued by the city treasury months later.

The result of all this red tape is that many potential vendors refuse to do business with the city, while those who do charge higher prices to make up for their additional costs and trouble. Thus, a strategy intended to *increase* competition and *reduce* the cost of goods has precisely the opposite effect of *reducing* competition and *increasing* cost.

Much of the malfunctioning of municipal monopolies can be attributed to the fact that the civil service system itself is defective. The system was originally designed to promote quality in public service by providing security for the individual employee and freedom from external influences. Unfortunately, this has come to mean freedom to be unresponsive to the changing needs of society. The problem shows up all over the country in the form of uncivil servants going through preprogrammed motions while awaiting their pensions. Too often the result is mindless bureaucracies that, to the embittered taxpayer, appear to function solely for the convenience of their staffs rather than the public whom they are supposed to serve.

In civil service there is virtually no connection between an employee's performance and his reward; raises are automatic, and an employee cannot be dismissed without an extraordinary and time-consuming effort. Instead of a merit system there is a seniority system. Promotions occur incestuously from within, based on examinations that attempt—but fail—to measure performance. The Civil Service Commission in New York recently severed one of the last vestigial links between performance and reward when it abolished a rule requiring a favorable appraisal of an employee in his current job before he could be promoted. In the meantime, the able and devoted civil servant—and there are many—is often no better rewarded than the incompetent slacker and finds himself vilified by the public for the negligence and lethargy of his colleagues.

It is not only rank-and-file employees who are tempted to abuse their monopoly power; monopoly agencies tend to develop their own separate goals and values. Thus, in a paradoxical and unintended way, it turns out that a severe housing crisis can actually be *good* for a housing agency, in the same odd sense that dirty streets are *good* for a street-cleaning department, high crime is *good* for police, a drought is *good* for a water department, traffic congestion is *good* for a traffic department, and an epidemic is *good* for doctors and hospitals. No one wills it that way, but the system rewards the crisis area with money, growth, visibility, and prestige —the chance to be a hero. This can lead to brinkmanship, an appealing tactic that is readily available to a monopoly.

Of course, all the remarks about the publicly operated municipal monopolies apply equally well to the privately operated municipal monopolies. Brinkmanship is being exercised when a local electric utility warns that its equipment will (be allowed to?) deteriorate unless its demands for higher rates are met. Or when it predicts (threatens?) a blackout unless it is permitted to build a dam, power station, or transmission line at a particularly scenic spot.

Refuse-Collection Vouchers

So much for this brief but depressing catalogue of runaway municipal monopolies, both public and private. What can be done about this state of affairs? How can the inefficiencies of our public services be corrected?

There are three major strategies for relaxing the stranglehold of the municipal monopolies:

- Increase the supply of organizations and people authorized to provide the services.
- Reduce the demand for these services.
- Break up the monopolies into smaller pieces.

The first approach—increasing the supply of organizations and people who are authorized to provide municipal services—is an obvious remedy in the area of refuse collection. Under competitive bidding a city could contract with private carting firms to collect refuse from certain routes or in certain areas. This is the way it's done in Boston and it was the practice until 1929 in parts of New York, where the idea is now being examined anew.

A more drastic approach would be to issue a refuse-collection voucher to a property owner when he pays his property tax. He would then have the choice of using his voucher to purchase service from either his sanitation department or a private firm. Competition for his voucher would be based on the quality and quantity of service—convenience, cleanliness, quietness and frequency of service, and the amount picked up. Of course, the competition ought to work both ways. A store owner should also have the option of buying his service from a sanitation department; in most cities at present he can be serviced only by private industry.

The voucher system is also being used experimentally in some cities to provide competition to the education monopoly. Under this system, a family receives a voucher good for one year's worth of grade-school education, for example, and can use the voucher to enroll the child in any certified private or public school. The school subsequently converts the voucher to cash by turning it in to the public agency that issued it.

One might argue that a completely competitive system of education could lead to such diversity in curriculum and achievement that students transferring or being promoted to other schools would be badly served. There is no reason for anguish; higher education in the United States is a good example of a competitive system, with both private and public colleges in many different state systems, yet these problems do not arise in any serious form. Regulation of all schools would continue to be exercised by government boards, which would prescribe general standards for curriculum and reading achievement, for example, while leaving the pedagogical details to the individual schools. The function of the state would be to inspect, measure, and report on the performance of the different schools.

Certainly, competition is not practical for all municipal services. In particular, it is difficult to see how the dangerous duties of police and fire departments could be performed competitively. However, some activities other than catching criminals and putting out fires do lend themselves to competition, even though the competition would come from other public servants. Civilians could perform more of the work currently assigned to uniformed patrolmen and firemen that doesn't require their special skills. An obvious area is traffic control. Meter maids in New York's Traffic Department could direct traffic, but there is predictable pressure from the police to prevent this from happening. Even in parking enforcement, the Traffic Department's agents do not have authority to issue tickets for "no parking" violations; that remains the private preserve of the police—and incidentally guarantees the latter the extralegal fringe benefit of parking with impunity in no-parking zones.

The second major strategy for relaxing the stranglehold of the municipal monopolies is to reduce the demand for their services. There are three possible ways to accomplish this:

- Shrink the monopolies.
- Change our consumption habits for these services.
- "Do it yourself."

Shrinking the refuse-collection monopoly means reducing the number of eligible customers. For example, a city could drop its traditional "free" service to tax-exempt properties and to institutions such as schools, hospitals, and large apartment buildings. These customers would then arrange for their own pickups, using commercial services.

The scope of the traditional education monopoly is shrinking—albeit on a minute scale—as students drop out of high school and subsequently enroll in privately financed street academies and high-school-equivalency programs in the armed forces and in the business world; surely such programs ought to be encouraged. In the same vein, junior colleges throughout the country are stressing remedial programs whose net effect is to provide the high-school education that was not provided by the high schools. Perhaps this responsibility should be formally transferred, by permitting students to enter junior college after two or three years of high school. As for vocational high schools, it is likely that they could be replaced by modern industrial unions or corporations that have a vested interest in training skilled workers to fill expected job openings. Shrinkage may also occur at the lower end of the educational spectrum, if day-care centers expand to assume the functions of kindergartens.

In the field of electric power, one way to shrink the scope of the monopoly is to separate power generation from power distribution. Legislation should make it possible for a city to buy power from any appropriate generating plant, and to rely on the local utility only for the use of the distribution network.

Another way to limit the demand for certain monopoly services is to change the public's consumption habits for such services. For example, in order to reduce a city's vulnerability to power blackouts and brownouts, it would be helpful to reduce the peak demand for power. One way to achieve this is by a pricing policy that would make people pay more for the power they draw during peak periods and give them a bargain on the electricity they use during low-demand periods. This would require some technical changes in electric meters, but it can be done; in fact, such a system is in effect in France.

Finally, the "do it yourself" philosophy makes sense for some municipal services. For example, the Association for a Better New York, out of exasperation and at its own expense, has started cleaning the streets (in addition to the sidewalks) in front of its member buildings. One way to reduce the need for more preventive police patrol is to encourage more citizen patrols, tenant patrols, auxiliary police and the like to work in cooperation with the police. Already in many urban neighborhoods residents are, in effect, levying a special tax on themselves and purchasing guard services or volunteering for guard duty for their block or building—and thereby buying protection at a much lower cost than the municipal monopoly could provide.

So far we have discussed various ways to increase the supply and reduce the demand for monopoly services. Together these two strategies would reduce the number of failure-prone parts in our vulnerable city systems.

In addition, there is a third strategy. These public systems could be made more reliable by breaking them up into smaller geographical pieces. That way, if a little system breaks down in a Bronx neighborhood, maybe it won't affect Harlem; a street-cleaning slowdown in Brooklyn Heights could still mean clean streets in the financial district. Neighborhood government, a concept much in vogue, offers precisely this opportunity. One doesn't even have to invoke the ideals of "participatory democracy" or "power to the people." Neighborhood government makes sense even on such prosaic grounds as potential reliability, efficiency, and effectiveness.

Suppose that a neighborhood were to receive a modest supplemental budget that could be expended at the direction of some sort of neighborhood government council. One could then imagine the following dialogue between the neighborhood body and the city's street-cleaning department:

CITIZENS: *We would like to spend $100,000 more this year for cleaner streets. What will that buy us?*

DEPARTMENT: (*thumbing through the city's official rate book*) *Umm, let's see now . . . oh, yeah. For $100,000 you get one truck, three men, and a broom.*

CITIZENS: *What? For $100,000 all we get is one lousy truck, three men, and a broom? Forget it. We can get a better deal by setting up our own local Municipal Services Corporation!*

But there is a more drastic and far-reaching way to break up the monopoly and to restructure the public service in a manner that simultaneously builds up the neighborhood concept and takes advantage of the dawning "do it yourself" awareness in urban communities.

Before describing it, however, it is useful to step back and view urban problems in the following way: the urban dweller is dissatisfied because he feels that he cannot influence the quality of his immediate environment—he cannot effectively influence the safety of his family, the education of his children, the behavior of his neighbors, the appearance of his physical surroundings, the cleanliness of his block, the purity of his air, or the adequacy of local transportation.

The problem arose when the Industrial Revolution brought about a separation between the place of residence and the place of work. As more and more people started working at sites distant from where they lived, they could no longer pay attention to the immediate environment around around their homes and had less reason to interact and cooperate with their neighbors. They started paying people to educate their children, police their streets, protect their property, pick up their litter, and so forth. In other words, we've been "contracting out" for our local needs, but we've done it without writing very good specifications for the work to be done and without establishing very good systems for measuring the performance of the contractors who are doing the work on our behalf.

With that view in mind, consider these two facts and translate them for any city in the nation:

- New York City has about 400,000 employees.
- New York City has about 60,000 residential blocks.

Then start speculating about converting one-seventh of this work force into block workers. Imagine the effects of one full-time worker on each block whose job would be to monitor services, organize a block association for self-help, and generally work to improve life on that block. I'm not suggesting a Red Guard commune, where everybody on the block falls out for calisthenics at 6:00 A.M. and afterwards marches into the community mess hall for breakfast, but think of the possibilities.

Crime could be reduced by a voluntary escort service and by informal street and building patrols whose members would not be too embarrassed or too uninvolved to help a woman screaming for her life. Block parties and other functions organized by the block worker would increase the street movement, create a sense of community, and otherwise make the block a safer place. Drug pushers would look for more hospitable hangouts. Social pressure on litterers, superintendents, tenants, homeowners, merchants, illegal parkers, and cleaning personnel would produce cleaner streets and sidewalks. Fire-prevention programs and even fire drills could be carried out on blocks subject to the daily threat of fires, and this might also reduce the number of false alarms. Parents' associations and local school boards would have a good mechanism at their disposal to build an informed constituency and increase their influence over the remaining education monopoly. In tenement areas, the block worker could organize tenant groups to improve housing conditions and to work with landlords and the police to improve building security. Ad hoc recreation activities, after-school learning centers, and volunteer day-care facilities would inevitably be started. Merchants using predatory practices would be more likely to be exposed than they are today. Repairs to streets, sidewalks, hydrants, lights, signs, and even public telephones could be ordered promptly by the block worker and followed up to make sure they were done.

All this could be accomplished with nothing more sophisticated than lists of tenants and phone numbers, access to a mimeographing machine, and Scotch tape for posters. Right now we've got police, sanitation, fire, education, housing, recreation, social services, consumer affairs, highways, traffic, and other departments whose job it is to produce these results. Proportional reductions in these agencies, and switching to block workers, might accomplish a lot more, in the final analysis, where it really counts: in the taxpayer's daily life.

The cost of such a program could be further offset by assigning the block worker to perform minor departmental inspections and to read water meters. The local utility company might pay to have him read its utility meters on that block. And here is a far-out approach to federal revenue sharing that Wilbur Mills hasn't mentioned: the worker could be paid by the Postal Service to pick up mail at the post office and deliver it to the residents on that block.

The block worker would emerge as a sort of concierge, a benign busy-body with formal active responsibility for improving the "livability" of the block. The block has lacked such a person ever since modern technology eliminated the lamplighter and the watchman on foot; now no one (except the postman—a very specialized service employee from a distant government) has a daily duty to perform on the block.

A skeptic might point out that this is nothing but a return to the ward-heeler style of government, and would be disastrous. Nonsense. In the first place, to reduce the potential for conventional political activity, the job could be restricted to qualified people who live outside the immediate political district where they work, and they could be made subject to a local version of the Hatch Act. In the second place, the danger of a local thug somehow taking command in an area is no different from the similar danger today, or the danger of corrupt local public servants and officials. In the third place, the excesses of the inefficient ward heelers of a century ago required reform in the way of centralization, professionalization, and a merit-based civil service. Now that we have carried out those reforms— and are left victimized by monopolistic, unresponsive, meritless systems— it's time for a change.

If these changes are made, no doubt the time will come again, in another half-century or century, when the disadvantages of the block-level system advocated here will outweigh its advantages. At such time in the distant future, a change toward a new system—a system that meets the needs of those new conditions—will again be in order, for there is no such thing as a manmade system that works well for all eternity.

Racially Tense Cairo, Illinois: Quiet but Loathing

Andrew Wilson

CAIRO, Ill.—Following the course of some unhappy marriages, the conservative whites and militant blacks in this town have progressed from raucous brawling to quiet loathing.

The time for dramatic confrontations seems to have yielded to a time of tight-lipped, emotional disengagement.

After an absence of more than two years, blacks began, six months or so ago, to shop again at the central business district, where the white merchants who dominate the town's political structure are to be found.

Shopowners in the business district report that they now have as many black customers as they ever had, and this claim is supported by the fact that revenues from the city's sales tax are back at the level they were prior to the black boycott of the business district.

None of the major demands that the militant United Front announced in launching the boycott has been met. The merchants haven't hired any more blacks. Whites continue to monopolize all classes of city jobs except for street maintenance and garbage collection. To serve a population that is nearly 40 per cent black, Cairo has one—semi-retired—black policeman, and no black firemen.

Even so, the United Front allowed the boycott to peter out. It gave up the practice of holding weekend rallies and parades to reinforce the boycott. It stopped trying to embarrass or intimidate black shoppers through car patrols of the business district.

Shortly after the quadrennial city council elections in the spring of last year, Pete Thomas, the then mayor of Cairo, confided his fear to this reporters that a major racial blood-letting on the streets of Cairo had become inevitable.

The moderate white candidates who had supported Thomas in his efforts to give blacks a greater voice in city government were soundly defeated by members of an arch-conservative white group called the United Citizens for Community Action, which bears its initials and the defiant emblem—crossed U.S. and Confederate Flags, encircled by the mottos: "Citizens Councils—States' Rights—Racial Integrity"—on a large sign over the door of its headquarters in the heart of the business district.

Not only has no blood been spilled since then, but there has been no repeat of the noisy nighttime gun battles that made headline-news around the country in 1969, 1970 and early 1971.

Source: *The Washington Post* (September 25, 1972), Section A3. © The Washington Post. Reprinted by permission.

Somehow no one was ever injured seriously or arrested in the course of any of those affairs anyway. But their cessation has given both sides something to cheer about.

The United Front is glad to be rid of the state police, which kept as many as 100 men here—or one policeman for every 60 inhabitants—for long periods of time.

According to the Front, the state police confiscated weapons from blacks but not whites, arrested marchers illegally and in other ways abused the Front and the black community generally.

Many whites are equally glad to be rid of the hordes of reporters who used to sweep into Cairo, along with reinforcements for the state police, the morning after every big shootout.

When the U.S. Civil Rights Commission held a three-day hearing here this March to examine the root causes of the town's problems, only one or two out-of-town papers sent reporters.

The feeling is strong among officials and whites generally that their town has been unjustly portrayed in the national news media as a brutal, lawless, racist community.

Gone with the boycott, marches, nighttime gun battles, reporters and state policemen, is the ad hoc committee-special meeting fever that once gripped the town.

According to Cairo Police Chief Bill Bowers and several other white officials, Cairo is peaceful because the United Front is broke.

Counter-Arguments

"The United Front has tried to shroud its deeds under the guise of doing something for the poor, but they've always been interested strictly in their own financial gain," says Bowers.

"Just like anybody else, when they could no longer get the financial gain they were looking for, they began looking for something else to do.

"They stopped disrupting this town and let it go back to being the peaceful place it always was before they got here."

It is almost an infallible law in this town that for every argument put forward by the one side, there is an equal and opposite counter-argument advanced by the other side.

Thus, it is no surprise to hear a United Front spokesman maintain that Cairo is peaceful because the city administration is broke, or close to it.

According to Preston Ewing of the Front, the top city and county officials have begun to behave properly and to instruct the police to do likewise because they have found that illegal arrests, improper searches and seizures and other attempts to harass blacks have resulted in a costly barrage of lawsuits being brought against them by the United Front, aided by a local public interest law firm and the Cairo Public Defenders office.

It is true that the United Front has been forced to curtail some activities —such as publishing its own newspaper—because contributions from state-wide church organizations, the main source of financial support, have tapered off.

But the organization is hardly on its last legs. With most of the people who put it together in 1969 still active, the United Front has redirected its energy.

"We feel the social aspect of the struggle has been won," says Charles Koen, the Front's executive director.

"This has been the longest, most successful boycott in the history of the country. The merchants are three—going on four—years behind. We've shown what can be accomplished through a united effort.

"Now we're interested in economics—in housing and building up the black community, in self-help and self-development."

A staff report to the U.S. Civil Rights Commission stated the basic facts about economic conditions in Cairo and surrounding Alexander County:

• "Although poverty is a serious problem throughout the area, blacks are in much worse shape than whites. The median county income for white families is about $6,400; for black families, only $2,800. . . .

• "Cairo ranks second in the state among comparable cities in its proportion of substandard housing. . . .

• "The average value of a house in Alexander County is less than $7,000. . . . Housing owned and occupied by blacks has a median value of only $5,000."

It is in this context that Koen's designation of the boycott as part of the "social" rather than the "economic" aspect of the United Front's endeavors should be understood.

Cairo's business district is little more than a clutch of old-fashioned mom-and-pop stores. It is not, even potentially, a prime economic mover. It supports the merchants and their families and that's about all.

Most or all of the city council seats are usually occupied by these same merchants—this, presumably, because of their natural solidarity and daily contact with the rest of the community.

But measured against the hard economic problems of joblessness and poverty, the internal resources of the city government are pitifully scant.

If the council, for instance, were to decide to redistribute city jobs (64) to reflect the town's racial composition (37.5 per cent black), blacks would gain 10 jobs (going from 14 to 24).

Turning from confrontation to "self-development," the United Front set up a non-profit corporation which is presently building the first new houses seen in Cairo in many years.

Backed by $224,000 in bank loans guaranteed by the Farmer's Home Administration (FHA), the Cairo Non-Profit Housing Corporation has already built seven houses and plans to complete 10 more this month and another 10 the next.

Under FHA Section 502, persons buying the homes pay little or no down payment on 33-year mortgages with monthly interest, insurance and other charges limited to 20 per cent of family income and running as low as 1 per cent.

The Cairo Chamber of Commerce liked the idea enough to copy it. Under its sponsorship, a private construction company is scheduled to complete 30 homes under Section 502 before the end of the year.

According to both builders, prospective buyers are lined up waiting to grab the new houses. The Cairo Non-Profit Housing Corp., which has a biracial board, sold its first house to a white woman.

Without a big boost in employment, the new houses may simply add—by displacement—to the city's already plentiful supply of old, abandoned houses.

Efforts are being made to line up new businesses and industries in the area by the Mississippi-Ohio Valley Regional Planning and Development Commission.

Three federal departments—Housing and Urban Development, Commerce, and Health, Education and Welfare—are supplying most of the pump-priming money.

The commission is a five-county outgrowth of an organization called PADCO, which has been operating for the last two years in Alexander and adjacent Pulaski County and still exists as the most active division within the commission.

The commission's three professional officers divide their time between courting outside business leaders, offering technical assistance on land acquisition and other matters to firms wanting to move into the area, and advising and typing up loan packages for new and existing businesses.

Noland Jones, PADCO's executive director, reports encouraging, though hardly decisive, two-year results for Alexander and Pulaski counties:

300 new jobs; 30 new business operations including 21 in Cairo; a new printing company in Cairo employing 50 people and a new lumber mill nearby also employing 50.

The record is not quite so impressive as it might seem. For instance, many of the new businesses were retail shops in Cairo's business district which simply replaced others that closed during the boycott.

Only four of the new businesses opened with PADCO-arranged Small Business Administration loans are owned by blacks.

But progress has been made. Illinois State Employment Service statistics show that unemployment in the two counties was 9.6 per cent the first half of this year, compared with 12 per cent for the first half of last year.

And, there are other faint signs that things are getting better in Cairo and its environs.

For the first time in three years, for instance, Cairo high school's traditional football rivals from nearby cities have decided it is safe enough for them to come to Cairo to play.

It's Blacks Who Must Stop Crime

Orde Coombs

According to the police records I can assume that the moment Dr. Wolfgang Friedmann was stabbed to death in September near Columbia University, I was talking on the telephone to an old friend who had been mugged the afternoon before on the streets of Washington. This woman, black and 72 years old, is the essence of Christian fortitude. She has no close relatives, lives on her Social Security checks, bakes me a pecan pie whenever I go to visit her and constantly sings praises to her God. She was, in fact, on her way home from cleaning the pews of her storefront church when two young blacks asked her for money.

As she speaks through puffed lips, she tells how she gazed at the teenagers, spat on the ground and moved on. One tugged at her pocketbook while the other hit her on the mouth and on the back of the head. She remembers crying out for help and receiving, before she passed out, a kick in the ribs. She had looked at the clock before she left her church, and so she knows that she must have been lying on the sidewalk for 10 minutes before another old, black woman passed by, pulled her to her feet and then walked tremblingly with her two blocks to her house.

My old friend lives on a street that has known better days but is certainly not a slum. It was early afternoon when her attackers struck, and since there is always a line of unemployed black men in front of a barber shop one block away, it is unlikely that no one saw her assailants, or saw her lying face down on that hot pavement, bruised and dazed. She has always been a woman with a sense of humor and so, in retrospect, she says that she is sure some people saw her on the ground, but they "must have thought I was a wino or a junkie. Perhaps my clothes wasn't too clean," she adds. "Maybe I need a new bleach." She went home, washed her face, painted

Source: *The Washington Post* (December 3, 1972), p. B-1. © The Washington Post. Reprinted by permission.

iodine on her lips, bolted her doors and prayed. She did not call the police. She had survived for the time being and will redouble, if that is possible, her faith in God. She has no one else. She does not believe that the police can protect her from wanton attack, and she does not think her fellow blacks care if she bleeds to death in front of them.

This woman's experience has become so commonplace in the black ghettos that, even if she had reported it, only the most cursory questions would have been asked by the police and no great attempt would have been made to find her assailants. One can safely assume that, unlike the mugging of Dr. Friedmann, hers would have brought forth no editorials and no mayor would have angrily commented on her misfortune. The reasons are obvious. Dr. Friedmann died. He was white and prominent. My friend lives. She is black and poor.

But it is precisely her blackness and her poverty that must compel those of us who are black to put an end to the epidemic of crime which is raging through our urban communities and threatens to stunt our growth unless we quickly do something about the menace.

Simple Self-interest

In the past year the following incidents have occurred to black people close to me: A cousin, 70 years old and suffering from a lymphatic disorder, is knocked down and robbed of $10 by two young blacks at 4 in the afternoon on Decatur Street in Brooklyn. A girl friend, 26 years old, is dragged by her hair behind a hedge near the Clinton Avenue Apartments in Brooklyn. Her assailant is a black man in his early twenties and her muffled screams attract the attention of two old men who chase the ambusher away. A friend, male, 36 years old, is returning to his apartment on Central Park West when two black junkies pull a knife on him in his vestibule and relieve him of his money and his watch.

Is it any wonder that a black woman who has been in Harlem politics for a quarter of a century and who has more than her share of spunk and bravery tells me that "After Nixon, the person I fear most in the world is the ghetto black teenager"? And her friend, a lawyer's wife who was determined to raise her children in Harlem, finally, after a series of incidents, gives up when her 10-year-old son is robbed of $3 on a sunny day in front of Harlem Hospital by two middle-aged black women! She shakes her head and, as she pours me coffee and packs her belongings, says: "There is no hope. I can stay here because I know how to fight, but I can't stand to look at the fright in my children's eyes."

It seems clear to me that we have now hit some kind of nadir in our communal lives, and that the only solutions to crime in our parts of this city rest in our hands. We must end crime, not because the statistics reveal that we proportionately get arrested for more crimes than whites—everyone says that policemen, black and white, advance their careers on the broken heads of powerless young blacks—but because our growth as a black nation and our survival in this country depend on our extirpation of this cancer.

It is, then, out of simple self-interest that we must take a hard look at our condition. If we are honest, we will realize that no society matron retches in horror at the thought of personal ambush as often and with as much feeling as our overworn grandmothers who have grown frightened of their grandchildren. We cannot talk of advancement in this country unless we lessen crime in our communities, for the specter of disorder inhibits our trust in each other, reduces our stirrings of commonality, breaks down our fledgling thrusts toward unity and robs us of the gains—and there were some—of the Sixties.

A Walk Through Harlem

Consider these events that I witnessed on a recent Saturday on 118th Street and Lenox Avenue: I was on my way to Muhammad's Mosque No. 7 when suddenly out of a bar and on to the sidewalk two black women fell fighting. The smaller one whipped out a razor and cut through the nose of the larger one. Then she calmly wiped off the razor on her trousers, put it in her bosom and walked off. The victim whimpered quietly, then pulled her-self up while trying to prevent the blood from washing away her severed nose. As she staggered about, a bartender came out of the bar, cursed her, hailed a taxi and took her to Harlem Hospital. The beat went on. No one even gathered around to look at the pool of blood soaking into the broken sidewalk. Everyone had seen it all before.

One block farther south, that same gray afternoon, I saw two young hoodlums accost an old black man who seemed to be something of an anachronism in his stained red tie and black fedora. The old man waved his trembling fists at them while some younger men gathered around and laughed at him. I could not hear what the two hoodlums said, but whatever it was elicited a loud cackle from the sidewalk loiterers, much slapping of the palms and cries of "right on!" The old man hobbled off, sure in the knowledge that if anyone decided to kill him right there because the color of his tie was offensive to that person's eye, he would die, a helpless nigger, alone on the Harlem sidewalk and in full view of his fellow blacks. When I ran up to him and asked what was going on, he looked at me with his eyes pinched in terror and said: "Don't kill me, please. Don't kill me."

It is this fatalism, this absolute belief that one stands alone in the face of one's attackers, that is most eroding to the spirit of all our Harlems. And it is quite easy to see where this slow disintegration of commonality leads. How can we get together to spell out our political aims, to worship and to organize if every time a black man ventures out of his home he must look behind every garbage can for a potential ambusher? How can we measure our progress if each man runs away from his brother, fearing, through experience, that on every black ghetto street there is the possibility of death?

How did we get to this place where we spend our lives shaking from fear of rapacious attacks by our brothers and sisters? The journey is not difficult to trace. Heroin rides through our communities, an unconquered monarch popping off our children at will, and we seem powerless to stop his march. And with the rise in the incidence of drug addiction has come a loss of respect for all authority and an end to discipline.

It is easy enough to understand why many young black people have grasped the chance to abuse and disrespect whites, for the whites have, quite simply, been erecting barriers to our physical and psychological emancipation ever since we entered these Western boundaries. And once their authority to damage us was lessened, we were only too pleased to trumpet our distaste for them since they had done very little to compel our respect.

I don't know why educated liberal whites cannot understand that our freedom from the altar of white supremacy would mean the end of our attraction for them—for the legacy of coercion and pain can never be ameliorated by smiles of welcome. And just as one does not ask the progeny of German Jews to embrace German Protestants, so should one resist the urge to ask contemporary American blacks to smile—except for profit— in front of American whites.

This state of affairs will not end soon, and whites are really powerless to do anything about it. Police sweeps are only alien forays through a conquered land, and the conquered know that they must obey only until the hated presence turns its back.

Since the symbols of white authority cannot end the disorder in our ghettos, it is up to us, blacks who care about the black future, to impose an order where none exists today. And *we* have to do it, for our lives have always been worth less than white ones in the eyes of our country, and our country does not really care about the chaos in our neighborhoods as long as that anarchy does not spill over the lines of demarcation. *We* have to do it because we cannot ask our old people to spend the rest of their lives passing through a gauntlet of muggers.

We can begin to turn this dreadful tide only if we immediately confront the fact that, no matter how discriminatory life is, one's problems cannot be resolved by a stiletto in somebody's chest. And we can stop finding excuses for criminality and not allow it to mask itself by any other name. We must find the truths in such old, commonsensical propositions as that nothing lasting is won without sacrifice and that even if discrimination ended tomorrow, there would be no shortcuts to achievement.

Just as we took to the Southern streets to protest in the Sixties against segregation, so should we now stand in our Northern streets to insist that our tax dollars flood our neighborhoods with lights and policemen. The latter will perhaps never learn the difference between brutality and firmness, but we need their presence to give us a breathing spell while we devise plans to rid our communities of the ambushers who are emboldened by our silence.

The Heroin Epidemic

No question of crime can be raised without exploring dope addiction. It must, quite simply, be recognized that in the black ghettos of our country, heroin addiction is no longer something that happens to people across the street. It is an epidemic that has consumed the best and now threatens the rest. If we were menaced by bubonic plague or smallpox, our response would be immediate. We would quarantine the victims and end the epidemic. This is what we must now do to the addicts in our midst. They must be swept off the streets and placed in addiction villages in the deserts of the West. And the pushers of heroin must know that once they are caught they will spend the remainder of their lives in the dungeons that we call prisons.

If the liberals cry about constitutional rights, chase them back to Scarsdale, for they do not quake every time they saunter out of doors. Of course I know that if this is done to addicts, it can be done to alcoholics, to homosexuals and to all blacks. But we can only fight one battle at a time, and we are fighting, now, for our lives. The addicts of Harlem now control more turf than they did 10 years ago in spite of the millions of dollars spent for rehabilitative programs.

So what alternatives have we? Methodone maintenance? In the first eight months of this year, there were 946 narcotic deaths in New York City, an increase of 63 from the same period last year. With the expansion of the methadone treatment centers there has been an increase in methadone-related deaths: 45 in 1970, 330 in 1971, and projections from the Medical Examiner's office indicate that every day this year someone will die from too much methadone.

Well, what about heroin maintenance? The experimentalists are standing in the wings ready to use black bodies in the interest of white tranquility and science. We should legalize heroin, the arguments go, because there is no other way to stop muggings and roll back crime in the cities. And the propagandists tell us that if heroin is legally available to those who need it, we will immediately wipe out the profits of the pushers and organized crime. It sounds so simple, but this is a panacea that we, as black people, should fight until we drop. For what we need is not the prolonged and easy orgasm of a high, not the illusory retreat from the brutal realities of our lives, but more and increasing doses of black-enforced discipline.

Let us take a look at where we are headed. If the government will not protect us and if the police cannot, then it follows that black citizens will have to protect themselves. And where does this lead? To black vigilante groups that would try to make Harlem calm. Already there have been meetings to discuss the necessity of forming secret societies to end crime. The participants feel that drugs have created monsters out of their brothers. These brothers—hiding behind their weaknesses and using the sorry history of white brutality and sentimentality as a shield—have made crime a vocation.

Nothing in urban life is simple, but I know that we cannot wait until discrimination ends before we rid our communities of crime, for discrimination against blacks will, perhaps, never end. We can no longer excuse crime because of society's inequities, for we will not live to see the end of those injustices. We stand menaced by our kith and kin. All our nobility and all our endurance, which have brought us to this place, will be corroded by the unremitting fear of the muggers who hide behind every lamppost. It is inconceivable to me that we who have prevailed in spite of the barbarism of white people should, in the last quarter of the century, stand as mute spectators to our doom.

THE LESSON OF FOREST HILLS

Roger Starr

The conflict triggered by the attempt to build a low-income public-housing project in the Forest Hills section of New York has raised a great many difficult and unpleasant issues. Underlying all of them, however, is the general question of "scatter-site housing"—the policy, that is, of deliberately placing low-income housing in middle-income neighborhoods. Considering how much resistance this policy can stimulate, and how much bitterness follows each demonstration of resistance, there has been astonishingly little effort to examine the ideas behind it. On the contrary, the value of scatter-site housing has simply been taken as self-evident by many liberals, by many officials of the federal government, and by many members of Congress. So much has this been the case that one is hard-put to find a clearly stated rationale for the policy that can be examined and considered on its merits. Nevertheless, the absence of such a rationale has not prevented the Department of Housing and Urban Development from placing

Source: *Commentary* (June 1972), Vol. 53, No. 6, pp. 45–49. Reprinted by permission.

the power of the federal government behind scatter-site housing by effectively forbidding the disbursement of any further federal subsidies for housing in areas in which black or poor people already live.

In general, the advocates of scatter-site housing seem to believe that sprinkling low-income families in relatively expensive neighborhoods will make a significant contribution to the advancement of the poor (and particularly the non-white poor) in American cities. If, by definition, scatter-site housing cannot be numerically significant, its significance must be symbolic: it must demonstrate that higher-income families stand ready spontaneously to embrace these newcomers, or that city officials will force their acceptance. The wrath of Forest Hills soured the symbol, and in the turbulent aftermath it should have become clear that the city's elected officials cannot paste smiles of welcome on the faces of their belligerent constituents. Nor are they likely to try, easily preferring to abort any similar proposal that might provoke a similarly surly response.

But by no means do all proponents of scatter-site housing regard the difficulties over Forest Hills as conclusive. Some seek to explain these difficulties by attributing them to the size of this particular project. Forest Hills, involving three high-rise buildings and 840 families, may indeed be too big, but there is little evidence that a smaller project would have engendered less vigorous opposition. Thus a project approved for the Lindenwood area of Queens has now been killed by local opposition even though it was to hold little more than half the people of the Forest Hills project, in buildings only about one-third as high.

Others have attributed the trouble in Forest Hills to bigotry which, they argue, deserves little or no consideration. It would be hard to maintain convincingly that there are no bigots in Forest Hills, but racial bigotry cannot be the reason why a black middle-class group living in the Baisley Park neighborhood of Queens objected strongly to a 200-unit scatter-site project planned for that area in the same year as the Forest Hills project. In fact, the Baisley Park opposition, with the support of the same New York State NAACP chapter which has been very outspoken in castigating the present opponents of Forest Hills, succeeded in having the project withdrawn from consideration even before it came to a public hearing. At a private meeting in the office of the then Borough President of Queens, I heard people who claimed to be representatives of the Baisley Park neighborhood saying almost exactly the same things which the alleged representatives of the Forest Hills residents now say. They told the Borough President that the project was to be put in their neighborhood because the Mayor didn't care about their views, felt they were powerless, and was quite prepared to sacrifice them and their homes and their property values to his political ambitions.

Still another argument is that scatter-site housing would have been entirely successful in Forest Hills if there had been more "involvement" of the "community" from the beginning. Yet one of the specific irritants arose from too much, not too little, local consultation. As a portent of architectural wonders to come, the original design of the project was widely shown in the area after the plan had been approved. When this design turned out to be too expensive for federal subsidization, the consultation itself was taken as proof of an intent to deceive the local people.

IF IT has always been hard to find a clearly stated rationale in writing for scatter-site housing, one could get at some of the reasons behind the policy in conversation with the New York City officials who were responsible for the original development of the program in 1966. These officials held the view that a neighborhood which contains people with a wide variation of incomes is *better* than an economically homogeneous neighborhood; and they further believed—as apparently federal housing officials have also come to do—that government has the right and the duty to foster the development of such heterogenous neighborhoods.

The enthusiasm of New York's officials for scatter-site housing did not rest simply on the effects they expected it to have on the mostly non-white poor people who would be moved into more prosperous neighborhoods inhabited mostly by whites. They believed that scattering low-rent units in middle-class areas would also have a healthy effect on the middle-class residents of those areas who would perforce become more tolerant and more worldly—more, in short, like residents of the West Side of Manhattan, from which the key figures in the Lindsay administration's early housing program themselves largely came.

The West Side of Manhattan, lying roughly between 59th and 125th Streets, and between Central Park and the Hudson River, becomes crucial to any discussion of housing integration not only because the impulse to scatter-site housing started there, but because it actually reflects, perhaps uniquely among American neighborhoods, a consistent pattern of juxtaposition of high-rent and low-rent housing. Only one city block separates the luxurious apartment houses of Central Park West from the tenements of Columbus Avenue; only a few steps separate those same tenements from the stone row houses that were built on the side streets for exclusive occupancy by the single families who could afford them. The elevated railway that once ran up Columbus Avenue blighted the avenue for any but low-income families. But for the more prosperous, there was Central Park West and Riverside Drive and West End Avenue, as well as the side streets—all made practical by excellent up- and down-town public transportation. This basic pattern of land use persisted, even after the side-street houses were converted into rooming houses or tiny apartments and filled with Puerto Ricans and blacks in the years following the end of the Second World War.

As a result of these demographic changes, the central shopping thoroughfare of the West Side, upper Broadway, offers the observer a uniquely human mixture that might be characterized as a realization of the dream of American pluralism. The shoppers include blacks, Puerto Ricans, and whites of differing ethnic origin; the stores, restaurants, and cafés run the gamut of all the many groups whose members now inhabit the West Side. Economically, too, the West Side is heterogeneous. Its major urban-renewal project, which sought to replace the Columbus Avenue tenements with modern apartment houses and to enable the side-street row houses to revert to single-family occupancy, included more than 2,500 low-rent public-housing units in its final plans. At least that many poor families had been living in the area before the renewal started.

To enjoy the apparently happy juxtaposition of so many different ethnic and socioeconomic groups, however, it is well to remain on the cluttered sidewalks of Broadway. For the exciting but on the whole harmonious vista of Broadway is not sustained in the rest of the area. The West Side, historically, produced a bumper crop of private schools so that the row-house and elevator-apartment families could mitigate with social distance their physical propinquity to their poorer neighbors. The split between private-school families and public-school families still continues; the public schools, with rare exceptions, attract few of the higher-income children. The febrile political life of the West Side confirms the suspicion that the human mix of varied income groups disturbs as many as it pleases; there is undiminished tension between the leaders of the low-income groups, or at least those who claim leadership, and the higher-income groups, generally over the question of how much low-income housing will, in the final analysis, be permitted in the urban-renewal area.

No matter how entertaining, then, one may find the spectacle of Broadway, it remains difficult to point to one concrete social result of the intermingling of diverse income groups, one sign of effective social action, which would not otherwise have taken place. Whether the upper-income residents are more tolerant than their counterparts in economically homogeneous neighborhoods is doubtful. And at the other end, it is almost impossible to find one measurable difference between the pride, energy, political awareness, or social mobility of the low-income residents of the West Side and the low-income residents of the Lower East Side, or Harlem, or Brownsville in Brooklyn.

Despite all this, the Department of Housing and Urban Development has promulgated guidelines based on the assumption that the case for locating low-income housing in middle-income neighborhoods has been made and proved.

Since the establishment of the public-housing program in 1937, the federal government has opted to put public housing on inexpensive land, thus generally reinforcing the way in which members of different social classes "naturally" distribute themselves in the cities. The government did this without ever considering the existence of social class. It simply limited the amount of money that could be spent on each apartment in a public-housing development. Although no words explicitly mandating this policy appeared in the public-housing law after 1948, the intent of the law was obvious. Dwellings had to be economical in "construction and administration" if they were to be subsidized; and the administrators extended this statutory language by establishing a dollar limit (which could, however, occasionally be waived) on the total cost of development, including land.

If not for the intensifying national concern with racial equality, the federal housing agencies would probably have continued to avert their gaze from the realities of social class in the United States. But race could not be ignored. In the immediate postwar years, the FHA discouraged mortgage bankers from making loans in interracial neighborhoods because, as an insurer, FHA worried that mortgages in interracial communities were intrinsically unsafe. After great pressure had been applied by Presidents Kennedy and Johnson, FHA appraisers and officials decided they could safely ignore race. Nondiscrimination in housing became for the first time official federal policy. When non-discrimination failed to bring many racially-integrated neighborhoods into existence, some commentators blamed the income difference between the median white and the median black family. The 1970 census indicates drastic reduction in this difference, but recent federal housing policy has increasingly been based on an implied contrary theory to the effect that racial differences in income will be ever-lasting.

On the assumption that the goal of housing policy should be racial integration, and given the theory of permanent income difference between the races, the conclusion drawn by the federal government was irresistible —government policy must seek to obliterate the significance of income to housing location. On this syllogistic base, mandating an attack on the class structure of American cities, the federal government founded the scatter-site housing policy embodied in the new HUD guidelines.

The HUD list contains eight separate categories on which a housing proposal may be rated as *superior, adequate, or poor;* a rating of *superior* gets priority over a rating of *adequate* in the award of federal subsidies, while a rating of *poor* in any category disqualifies the proposal from any subsidy at all.

Only two of these categories—the second and third—concern us here. Category Two, entitled "Minority Housing Opportunities," permits officials to rate as *superior* only those proposals which would open up areas for "minority-group" residence in which there are few or no members of such groups now living. The wording of the criterion specifically excludes from a *superior* rating any project which would stand in an existing racially-mixed area except if the area were part of an officially planned redevelopment, and it could be proved that "sufficient, comparable opportunities exist for housing for minority families, in the income range to be served by the proposed project, outside the area of minority concentration." Obviously, if there were such housing opportunities already available elsewhere, it would be unnecessary to rebuild the slum in the first place.

Otherwise the best a project in a racially-mixed area can hope for is a rating of *adequate,* and then only if it can be shown that "the project will not cause a significant increase in the proportion of minority to non-minority residents in the area." As a footnote, the guidelines require that these stipulations must be "accompanied by documented findings based upon relevant racial, socioeconomic, and other data and information." This means that if any sponsor—a government agency, a nonprofit group, a profit-motivated builder, whatever—wishes to erect a government subsidized apartment house in a racially-mixed area, the sponsor can get approval only after demonstrating that the racial distribution of the new tenants will be in the same proportion as the racial distribution already obtaining in the area. If the government believes anyone can promise this without installing a quota system for tenant selection, it has failed to explain how.

AS FOR a project in an area of minority-group concentration, it can be considered *adequate* only if it is necessary "to meet overriding housing needs." An explanatory note points out that a need resulting from exclusionary practices elsewhere does satisfy the criterion. This last seems fair enough, given the premises. It does not seem fair, however, that a proposal for subsidized new housing to be built in an area, say, of black concentration must be disapproved even if, demonstrably, the people living in that area want to remain there and also want an opportunity to improve the quality of their housing. Is improving housing quality to be considered an "overriding housing need"? The federal government tells every minority group in the nation that its members are free to live wherever they want, yet under this rule, if they want to live in the neighborhoods in which they are already living, they had better be able to show that they are camping on the sidewalk.

Thus, by an irony which is becoming familiar in other fields of government activity as well, measures aimed at expanding the freedom of non-whites are actually having the effect of limiting that freedom. In this case, government policy allows non-whites the choice of living in predominantly non-white areas—a choice which many might wish to make and should certainly have the right to make—only at the sacrifice of any chance to get better housing. A judgment has been rendered to the effect that a neighborhood composed predominantly of non-whites is not good enough to deserve federal support, whatever may be the wishes of its members.

Furthermore—and here we have another irony emerging from Washington's integrationist activism—the implied promise, that the federal government will supply adequate housing for non-whites in predominantly white sections, is itself illusory. Although the federal government has the power to prevent housing from being built, it has no power to force the construction of housing in a local area over the expressed will of the government of that area. Thus, the suspicion arises that one reason for the development of the new guidelines of site selection may be the desire of the present Housing administration—following, no doubt, policy established in the White House or the Budget Bureau—to avoid paying out subsidies for new housing. The federal pocketbook will be protected on both flanks. Local governments will not wish to build in areas that are not already occupied by non-whites, and the federal guidelines will forbid them to build anywhere else, on sites which are mixed or occupied predominantly by minorities. There being nowhere else to build, nothing will be built.

As Category two of the HUD guidelines seeks to promote racial integration, Category Three seeks to promote socioeconomic integration. This category, "Improved Location for low(er) Income Families," starts bravely with a few general assertions amounting to a pledge by the government to provide "low(er) income" households with a wide choice of locations. Incidentally, that e.e. cummings-like word "low(er)" serves to remind the reader that government guidelines apply not merely to public housing for low-income families, but also to other forms of subsidized housing which is offered to families with somewhat higher incomes. In the peculiar language that takes shape on the electric typewriters of government, "lower" means "less low than low." Low-income housing is for people whose income is as low as possible, and who therefore are eligible for public housing. Lower-income housing, however, is for families whose income is generally below the median level, which includes many whose income is still too high for low-income public housing.

Once we have scrambled over this curious linguistic barrier, we come to the two final objectives: that subsidized housing should be served with all the facilities and utilities that unsubsidized housing is served with; and that subsidized housing should be "reasonably accessible" to job opportunities. These, in a simpler day, would have been the two primary requirements for selecting housing location. Now, however, they have become subsidiary to the objective of separating some subsidized housing from other subsidized housing, of dividing some low-income people from other low-income people. Here again, as with racial integration, a realistic appraisal of the government's actual powers in this field leaves one wondering what choice it is really in a position to offer. Since it cannot *require* housing to be built in a particular location, its refusal to permit federally-subsidized housing to be located "in a section characterized as one of subsidized housing," may well mean that federally-subsidized housing will not be built anywhere at all. Surely this provision will prevent the systematic upgrading of low-income neighborhoods, even if they are favorably located with respect to jobs and transportation.

Obviously, no one would want to locate a single subsidized project by itself in the midst of a decayed low-income neighborhood. Once the neighborhood is decayed and no longer economically self-sustaining, only federal subsidies can possibly resuscitate its housing. But the federal guidelines, placing their primary emphasis on integrating low-income families into unsubsidized middle-class neighborhoods, would rule out placing subsidized buildings—not only public housing, but any kind of subsidized buildings— in sufficient proximity to protect each other from the decayed surroundings.

IT SHOULD BE easy to bring forth a more constructive set of housing policies than these, leaving aside that gloomiest of all dismal subjects, the *who* and *how* of economic subsidization of housing. As to the end and purpose of housing subsidization, surely this government investment should be measured by the level of housing choice truly made available rather than by the degree of racial and economic integration achieved in the policy directive.

The cornerstone of housing choice must be a program which will make impossible the exclusion of families from access to housing because of their race or nationality. This must be as true in Forest Hills (where exclusionary practices must in part be responsible for the scarcity of black families) as everywhere else. But there is a great difference between effectively banning discrimination and exclusion on the one hand, and numerically mandating racial or economic integration on the other. The former lies within the practical scope of governmental activity. The latter—if it accomplishes anything at all—merely impedes the exercise of personal choice by black or white.

Second, government subsidy programs should be made available for those who need better housing, and cannot obtain it without subsidy, *wherever* these people may want to live, provided that the housing offers suitable access to transportation, education, and job opportunities. These utilitarian criteria come first, because given a flourishing economy, they provide the means by which social classes are, in fact, rearranged and their memberships pooled. The effort to accomplish the same objective by spatial rearrangement mistakes the nature of the problem; and, worse, it fools no one.

Third, government subsidy programs must come to terms with the fact that there are households in the city which, for whatever reasons, are unable to live in a housing development without presenting a serious danger to their neighbors and to the building itself. At present cost levels, and with the present inadequate level of supply, it seems absurd to give these families good housing, which they then grievously damage, while other families who could use the housing fruitfully wait on endless lines. The assurance by Chairman Simeon Golar of the New York City Housing Authority that all prospective tenants of the Forest Hills project would be carefully screened to keep out the destructive was a step in the right direction—and a most unusual one in the present climate. So too is the complex subsidy formula developed in the housing bill recently passed by the United States Senate which, properly administered and adequately funded, should be of great help in providing new houses for families of limited income. (If a similar program could be developed for existing buildings, the help might even be greater, but that is another story.)

Simply because Forest Hills produced so much bad feeling, the priorities suggested here might be taken as a formula for social peace. It would be nice if, indeed, they worked out that way, but they should not be taken to be non-controversial. If subsidized housing is to be located where job opportunities exist, that housing may well be placed in areas in the city, or outside it, where low-income families will be living for the first time. Possibly —perhaps probably—perhaps inevitably, the opposition to their prospective arrival will be just as hard as that of Forest Hills, and just as clamorous. But the objective is different. While the scatter-site program expresses primarily a symbolic objective, the siting of housing to make economic opportunity available follows traditional American attitudes toward work and human dignity and social mobility. It may, in the end, be harder to mobilize opposition to it simply because, using the value system of the potential opponents themselves, it makes such very good sense.

SAVING THE CRUSADE

Peter F. Drucker

Everybody today is "for the environment." Laws and agencies designed to protect it multiply at all levels of government. Big corporations take full-color ads to explain how they're cleaning up, or at least trying to. Even you as a private citizen probably make some conscientious effort to curb pollu-

Source: *Harper's Magazine* (January 1972), pp. 66–71. Copyright © 1972, by Minneapolis Star and Tribune Co., Inc. Reprinted from the January 1972 issue of *Harper's Magazine* by permission of the author.

tion. At the same time, we have learned enough about the problem to make some progress toward restoring a balance between man and nature. The environmental crusade may well become the great cause of the Seventies— and not one moment too soon.

Yet the crusade is in real danger of running off the tracks, much like its immediate predecessor, the so-called war on poverty. Paradoxically, the most fervent environmentalists may be among the chief wreckers. Many are confused about the cause of our crisis and the ways in which we might resolve it. They ignore the difficult decisions that must be made; they splinter the resources available for attacking environmental problems. Indeed, some of our leading crusaders seem almost perversely determined to sabotage their cause—and our future.

Consider, for example, the widespread illusion that a clean environment can be obtained by reducing or even abolishing our dependence on "technology." The growing pollution crisis does indeed raise fundamental questions about technology—its direction, uses, and future. But the relationship between technology and the environment is hardly as simple as much anti-technological rhetoric would have us believe. The invention that has probably had the greatest environmental impact in the past twenty-five years, for instance, is that seemingly insignificant gadget, the wire-screen window. The wire screen, rather than DDT or antibiotics, detonated that "population explosion" in underdeveloped countries, where only a few decades ago as many as four out of five children died of such insect-borne diseases as "summer diarrhea" or malaria before their fifth birthday. Would even the most ardent environmentalist outlaw the screen window and expose those babies again to the flies?

The truth is that most environmental problems require technological solutions—and dozens of them. To control our biggest water pollutant, human wastes, we will have to draw on all sciences and technologies from biochemistry to thermodynamics. Similarly, we need the most advanced technology for adequate treatment of the effluents that mining and manufacturing spew into the world's waters. It will take even more new technology to repair the damage caused by the third major source of water pollution in this country—the activities of farmers and loggers.

Even the hope of genuine disarmament—and the arms race may be our worst and most dangerous pollutant—rests largely on complex technologies of remote inspection and surveillance. Environmental control, in other words, requires technology at a level at least as high as the technology whose misuse it is designed to correct. The sewage-treatment plants that are urgently needed all over the world will be designed, built, and kept running not by purity of heart, ballads, or Earth Days but by crew-cut engineers working in very large organizations, whether businesses, research labs, or government agencies.

Who Will Pay?

The second and equally dangerous delusion abroad today is the common belief that the cost of cleaning the environment can be paid for out of "business profits." After taxes, the profits of all American businesses in a good year come to sixty or seventy billion dollars. And mining and manufacturing —the most polluting industries—account for less than half of this. But at the lowest estimate, the cleanup bill, even for just the most urgent jobs, will be three or four times as large as all business profits.

Consider the most efficient and most profitable electric-power company in the country (and probably in the world): the American Power Company, which operates a number of large power systems in the Midwest and upper South. It has always been far more ecology-minded than most other power companies, including the government's own TVA. Yet cleaning up American Power's plants to the point where they no longer befoul air and water will require, for many years to come, an annual outlay close to, if not exceeding, the company's present annual profit of $100 million. The added expense caused by giving up strip mining of coal or by reclaiming strip-mined land might double the company's fuel bill, its single largest operating cost. No one can even guess what it would cost—if and when it can be done technologically—to put power transmission lines underground. It might well be a good deal more than power companies have ever earned.

We face an environmental crisis because for too long we have disregarded genuine costs. Now we must raise the costs, in a hurry, to where they should have been all along. The expense must be borne, eventually, by the great mass of the people as consumers and producers. The only choice we have is which of the costs will be borne by the consumer in the form of higher prices, and which by the taxpayer in the form of higher taxes.

It may be possible to convert part of this economic burden into economic opportunity, though not without hard work and, again, new technology. Many industrial or human wastes might be transformed into valuable products. The heat produced in generating electricity might be used in greenhouses and fish farming, or to punch "heat holes" into the layer of cold air over such places as Los Angeles, creating an updraft to draw off the smog. But these are long-range projects. .The increased costs are here and now.

Closely related to the fallacy that "profit" can pay the environmental bill is the belief that we can solve the environmental crisis by reducing industrial output. In the highly developed affluent countries of the world, it is true that we may be about to de-emphasize the "production-orientation" of the past few hundred years. Indeed, the "growth sectors" of the developed economies are increasingly education, leisure activities, or health care rather than goods. But paradoxical as it may sound, the environmental crisis will force us to return to an emphasis on both growth and industrial output—at least for the next decade.

Overlooked Facts of Life

There are three reasons for this, each adequate in itself.

1) Practically every environmental task demands huge amounts of electrical energy, way beyond anything now available. Sewage treatment is just one example; the difference between the traditional and wholly inadequate methods and a modern treatment plant that gets rid of human and industrial wastes and produces reasonably clear water is primarily electric power, and vast supplies of it. This poses a difficult dilemma. Power plants are themselves polluters. And one of their major pollution hazards, thermal pollution, is something we do not yet know how to handle.

Had we better postpone any serious attack on other environmental tasks until we have solved the pollution problems of electric-power generation? It would be a quixotic decision, but at least it would be a deliberate one. What is simply dishonest is the present hypocrisy that maintains we are serious about these other problems—industrial wastes, for instance, or sewage or pesticides—while we refuse to build the power plants we need to resolve them. I happen to be a member in good standing of the Sierra Club, and I share its concern for the environment. But the Sierra Club's opposition to any new power plant today—and the opposition of other groups to new power plants in other parts of the country (e.g., New York City)—has, in the first place, ensured that other ecological tasks cannot be done effectively for the next five or ten years. Secondly, it has made certain that the internal-combustion engine is going to remain our mainstay in transportation for a long time to come. An electrical automobile or electrified mass transportation—the only feasible alternatives—would require an even more rapid increase in electrical power than any now projected. And thirdly it may well, a few years hence, cause power shortages along the Atlantic Coast, which would mean unheated homes in winter, as well as widespread industrial shutdowns and unemployment. This would almost certainly start a "backlash" against the whole environmental crusade.

2) No matter how desirable a de-emphasis on production might be, the next decade is the wrong time for it in all the developed countries and especially in the U.S. The next decade will bring a surge in employment-seekers and in the formation of young families—both the inevitable result of the baby boom of the late Forties and early Fifties. Young adults need jobs; and unless there is a rapid expansion of jobs in production there will be massive unemployment, especially of low-skilled blacks and other minority group members. In addition to jobs, young families need goods—from housing and furniture to shoes for the baby. Even if the individual family's

standard of consumption goes down quite a bit, total demand—barring only a severe depression—will go up sharply. If this is resisted in the name of ecology, environment will become a dirty word in the political vocabulary.

3) If there is no expansion of output equal to the additional cost of cleaning up the environment, the cost burden will—indeed, must—be met by cutting the funds available for education, health care, or the inner city, thus depriving the poor. It would be nice if the resources we need could come out of defense spending. But of the 6 or 7 per cent of our national income that now goes for defense, a large part is cost of past wars, that is, veterans' pensions and disability benefits (which, incidentally, most other countries do not include in their defense budgets—a fact critics of "American militarism" often ignore). Even if we could—or should—cut defense spending, the "peace dividend" is going to be 1 or 2 per cent of national income, at best.

But the total national outlay for education (7 to 8 per cent), health care (another 7 to 8 per cent), and the inner city and other poverty areas (almost 5 per cent) comes to a fifth of total national income today. Unless we raise output and productivity fast enough to offset the added environmental cost, the voters will look to this sector for money. Indeed, in their rejection of school budgets across the nation and in their desperate attempts to cut welfare costs, voters have already begun to do so. That the shift of resources is likely to be accomplished in large part through inflation—essentially at the expense of the lower-income groups—will hardly make the environmental cause more popular with the poor.

The only way to avoid these evils is to expand the economy, probably at a rate of growth on the order of 4 per cent a year for the next decade, a higher rate than we have been able to sustain in this country in the postwar years. This undoubtedly entails very great environmental risks. But the alternative is likely to mean no environmental action at all, and a rapid public turn—by no means confined to the "hard hats"—against all environmental concern whatever.

Making Virtue Pay

The final delusion is that the proper way to bring about a clean environment is through punitive legislation. We do need prohibitions and laws forbidding actions that endanger and degrade the environment. But more than that, we need incentives to preserve and improve it.

Punitive laws succeed only if the malefactors are few and the unlawful act is comparatively rare. Whenever the law attempts to prevent or control something everybody is doing, it degenerates into a huge but futile machine of informers, spies, bribe givers, and bribe takers. Today every one of us in the underdeveloped countries almost as much as in the developed ones

—is a polluter. Punitive laws and regulations can force automobile manu-facturers to put emission controls into new cars, but they will never be able to force 100 million motorists to maintain this equipment. Yet this is going to be the central task if we are to stop automotive pollution.

What we should do is make it to everyone's advantage to reach en-vironmental goals. And since the roots of the environmental crisis are so largely in economic activity, the incentives will have to be largely economic ones as well. Automobile owners who voluntarily maintain in working order the emission controls of their cars might, for instance, pay a much lower automobile registration fee, while those whose cars fall below accepted standards might pay a much higher fee. And if they were offered a sizable tax incentive, the automobile companies would put all their best energies to work to produce safer and emission-free cars, rather than fight delaying actions against punitive legislation.

Despite all the rhetoric on the campuses, we know by now that "capital-ism" has nothing to do with the ecological crisis, which is fully as severe in the Communist countries. The bathing beaches for fifty miles around Stockholm have become completely unusable, not because of the wicked Swedish capitalists but because of the raw, untreated sewage from Com-munist Leningrad that drifts across the narrow Baltic. Moscow, even though it still has few automobiles, has as bad an air-pollution problem as Los Angeles—and has done less about it so far.

We should also know that "greed" has little to do with the environ-mental crisis. The two main causes are population pressures, especially the pressures of large metropolitan populations, and the desire—a highly commendable one—to bring a decent living at the lowest possible cost to the largest possible number of people.

The environmental crisis is the result of success—success in cutting down the mortality of infants (which has given us the population explosion), success in raising farm output sufficiently to prevent mass famine (which has given us contamination by insecticides, pesticides, and chemical fer-tilizers), success in getting people out of the noisome tenements of the nineteenth-century city and into the greenery and privacy of the single-family home in the suburbs (which has given us urban sprawl and traffic jams). The environmental crisis, in other words, is very largely the result of doing too much of the right sort of thing.

To overcome the problems success always creates, one has to build on it. The first step entails a willingness to take the risks involved in making decisions about complicated and perilous dilemmas:

• What is the best "trade-off" between a cleaner environment and unemployment?

• How can we prevent the environmental crusade from becoming a war of the rich against the poor, a new and particularly vicious "white racist imperialism"?

• What can we do to harmonize the worldwide needs of the environment with the political and economic needs of other countries, and to keep American leadership from becoming American aggression?

• How can we strike the least agonizing balance of risks between environmental damage and mass starvation of poor children, or between environmental damage and large-scale epidemics?

An Environmental Crime?

More than twenty years ago, three young chemical engineers came to seek my advice. They were working for one of the big chemical companies, and its managers had told them to figure out what kind of new plants to put into West Virginia, where poverty was rampant. The three young men had drawn up a long-range plan for systematic job creation, but it included one project about which their top management was very dubious—a ferroalloy plant to be located in the very poorest area where almost everybody was unemployed. It would create 1,500 jobs in a dying small town of 12,000 people and another 800 jobs for unemployed coal miners—clean, healthy, safe jobs, since the new diggings would be strip mines.

But the plant would have to use an already obsolete high-cost process, the only one for which raw materials were locally available. It would therefore be marginal in both costs and product quality. Also the process was a singularly dirty one, and putting in the best available pollution controls would make it even less economical. Yet it was the only plant that could possibly be put in the neediest area. What did I think?

I said, "forget it"—which was, of course, not what the three young men wanted to hear and not the advice they followed.

This, as some readers have undoubtedly recognized, is the prehistory of what has become a notorious "environmental crime," the Union Carbide plant in Marietta, Ohio. When first opened in 1951 the plant was an "environmental pioneer." Its scrubbers captured three-quarters of the particles spewed out by the smelting furnaces; the standard at the time was half of that or less. Its smokestacks suppressed more fly ash than those of any other power plant then built, and so on.

But within ten years the plant had become an unbearable polluter to Vienna, West Virginia, the small town across the river whose unemployment it was built to relieve. And for the last five years the town and Union Carbide fought like wildcats. In the end Union Carbide lost. But while finally accepting federal and state orders to clean up an extremely dirty process, it also announced that it would have to lay off half the 1,500 men now working in the plant—and that's half the people employed in Vienna. The switch to cleaner coal (not to mention the abandonment of strip mining) would also put an end to the 800 or so coal-mining jobs in the poverty hollows of the back country.

There are scores of Viennas around the nation, where marginal plants are kept running precisely because they are the main or only employer in a depressed or decaying area. Should an uneconomical plant shut down, dumping its workers on the welfare rolls? Should the plant be subsidized (which would clearly open the way for everybody to put his hand in the public till)? Should environmental standards be disregarded or their application postponed in "hardship" cases?

If concern for the environment comes to be seen as an attack on the livelihood of workers, public sympathy and political support for it is likely to vanish. It is not too fanciful to anticipate, only a few years hence, the New (if aging) Left, the concerned kids on the campus, and the ministers in a protest march against "ecology" and in support of "the victims of bourgeois environmentalism."

Third World Ecology

In the poor, developing countries where men must struggle to make even a little progress in their fight against misery, any industry bears a heavy burden of high costs and low productivity. Burdening it further with the cost of environmental control might destroy it. Moreover, development in these countries—regardless of their political creed or social organization, in Mao's as well as in Chiang Kai-shek's China and in North as well as in South Vietnam—cannot occur without the four biggest ecological villains: a rapid increase in electric power, chemical fertilizers and pesticides, the automobile, and the large steel mill.

That poor countries regard those villains as economic saviors confronts us with hard political choices. Should we help such countries get what they want (industrialization), or what we think the world needs (less pollution)? How do we avoid the charge, in either case, that our help is "imperialistic"? To complicate matters, there is a looming conflict between environmental concern and national sovereignty. The environment knows no national boundaries. Just as the smog of England befouls the air of Norway, so the chemical wastes of the French potash mines in Alsace destroy the fish of the lower Rhine in Belgium and Holland.

No matter what the statistics bandied about today, the U.S. is not the world's foremost polluter. Japan holds this dubious honor by a good margin. No American city can truly compete in air pollution with Tokyo, Milan, Budapest, Moscow, or Düsseldorf. No American river is as much of an open sewer as the lower Rhine, the Seine, or the rivers of the industrial Ukraine such as the lower Dnieper. And we are sheer amateurs in littering highways compared to the Italians, Danes, Germans, French, Swedes, Swiss, and Austrians—although the Japanese, especially in littering mountainsides and camp grounds, are clearly even more "advanced."

If not the worst polluter, however, the U.S. is clearly the largest one. More important, as the most affluent, most advanced, and biggest of the industrial countries, it is expected to set an example. If we do not launch the environmental crusade, no one else will.

We shall have to make sure, however, that other nations join with us. In the absence of international treaties and regulations, some countries— especially those with protectionist traditions, such as Japan, France, and even the United States—may be tempted to impose ecological standards on imports more severe than those they demand of their own producers. On the other hand, countries heavily dependent on exports, especially in Africa and Latin America, may try to gain a competitive advantage by lax enforcement of environmental standards.

One solution might be action by the United Nations to fix uniform rules obliging all its members to protect the environment; and such action is, in fact, now under official study. The United States might help by changing its import regulations to keep out goods produced by flagrant polluters— allowing ample time for countries with severe poverty and unemployment problems to get the cleanup under way. We have good precedent for such an approach in our own history. Forty years ago we halted the evils of child labor by forbidding the transportation in interstate commerce of goods produced by children.

Such a course, however, will demand extraordinary judgment. Unless we persuade other nations to join with us—and set an example ourselves —we may well be accused of trying again to "police the world."

Choosing the Lesser Evils

The hardest decisions ahead are even more unprecedented than those we have been discussing. What risks can we afford to take with the environment, and what risks can we *not* afford to take? What are the feasible trade-offs between man's various needs for survival?

Today, for example, no safe pesticides exist, nor are any in sight. We may ban DDT, but all the substitutes so far developed have highly undesirable properties. Yet if we try to do without pesticides altogether, we shall invite massive hazards of disease and starvation the world over. In Ceylon, where malaria was once endemic, it was almost wiped out by large-scale use of DDT; but in only a few years since spraying was halted, the country has suffered an almost explosive resurgence of the disease. In other tropical countries, warns the UN Food and Agricultural Organization, children are threatened with famine, because of insect and blight damage to crops resulting from restrictions on spraying. Similarly, anyone who has lately traveled the New England turnpike will have noticed whole forests defoliated by the gypsy moth, now that we have stopped aerial spraying.

What is the right trade-off between the health hazard to some women taking the pill and the risk of death to others from abortions? How do we balance the thermal and radiation dangers of nuclear power plants against the need for more electricity to fight other kinds of pollution? How should we choose between growing more food for the world's fast-multiplying millions and the banning of fertilizers that pollute streams, lakes, and oceans?

Such decisions should not be demanded of human beings. None of the great religions offers guidance. Neither do the modern "isms," from Maoism to the anarchism popular with the young. The ecological crisis forces man to play God. Despite the fact that we are unequal to the task, we can't avoid it: the risks inherent in refusing to tackle these problems are the greatest of all. We have to try, somehow, to choose some combination of lesser evils; doing nothing invites even greater catastrophe.

Where to Start

Cleaning up the environment requires determined, sustained effort with clear targets and deadlines. It requires, above all, concentration of effort. Up to now we have had almost complete diffusion. We have tried to do a little bit of everything—and tried to do it in the headlines—when what we ought to do first is draw up a list of priorities in their proper order.

First on such a list belong a few small but clearly definable and highly visible tasks that can be done fairly fast without tying up important resources. Removing the hazard of lead poisoning in old slum tenements might be such an action priority. What to do is well known: burn off the old paint. A substantial number of underemployed black adolescents could be easily recruited to do it.

Once visible successes have been achieved, the real task of priority-setting begins. Then one asks: 1) what are the biggest problems that we know how to solve, and (2) what are the really big ones that we don't know how to solve yet? Clean air should probably head the first list. It's a worldwide problem, and getting worse. We don't know all the answers, but we do have the technological competence to handle most of the problems of foul air today. Within ten years we should have real results to show for our efforts.

Within ten years, too, we should get major results in cleaning up the water around big industrial cities and we should have slowed (if not stopped) the massive pollution of the oceans, especially in the waters near our coastal cities.

As for research priorities, I suggest that the first is to develop birth-control methods that are cheaper, more effective, and more acceptable to people of all cultures than anything we now have. Secondly, we need to learn how to produce electric energy without thermal pollution. A third priority is to devise ways of raising crops for a rapidly growing world population without at the same time doing irreversible ecological damage through pesticides, herbicides, and chemical fertilizers.

Until we get the answers, I think we had better keep on building power plants and growing food with the help of fertilizers and such insect-controlling chemicals as we now have. The risks are now well known, thanks to the environmentalists. If they had not created a widespread public awareness of the ecological crisis, we wouldn't stand a chance. But such awareness by itself is not enough. Flaming manifestos and prophecies of doom are no longer much help, and a search for scapegoats can only make matters worse.

What we now need is a coherent, long-range program of action, and education of the public and our lawmakers about the steps necessary to carry it out. We must recognize—and we need the help of environmentalists in this task—that we can't do everything at once; that painful choices have to be made, as soon as possible, about what we should tackle first; and that every decision is going to involve high risks and costs, in money and in human lives. Often these will have to be decisions of conscience as well as economics. Is it better, for example, to risk famine or to risk global pollution of earth and water? Any course we adopt will involve a good deal of experimentation—and that means there will be some failures. Any course also will demand sacrifices, often from those least able to bear them: the poor, the unskilled, and the underdeveloped countries. To succeed, the environmental crusade needs support from all major groups in our society, and the mobilization of all our resources, material and intellectual, for years of hard, slow, and often discouraging effort. Otherwise it will not only fail; it will, in the process, splinter domestic and international societies into warring factions.

Now that they have succeeded in awakening us to our ecological peril, I hope the environmentalists will turn their energies to the second and harder task: educating the public to accept the choices we must face, and to sustain a world-wide effort to carry through on the resulting decisions. The time for sensations and manifestos is about over; now we need rigorous analysis, united effort, and very hard work.

GASPS FOR HELP FROM SMOG CITY

Business Week Magazine

The postmistress of Riverside, Calif., Mrs. Ruth Gurley, reports that a while ago a postman returned from his rounds and proclaimed, "Boy, it's sure smoggy out there." Then, she says, he dropped his bag and collapsed. Riverside's virulent smog has become so serious an occupational hazard for postmen that last week the director of the postal district ordered a halt on mail deliveries during the city's increasingly frequent smog alerts.

Higher authorities later reversed the order. But the postmen's plight illustrates what many of Riverside's 146,000 residents have been saying for a couple of years—that their desert city, 60 mi. east of Los Angeles, has the country's worst smog problem. Some of the locals have even called their community Smog City, U.S.A.

Riverside's smog forces school children to stay inside during recess. On days of heavy smog, the radio broadcasts warnings to residents to avoid physical strain. Riverside's poisonous air is said to be withering property values, and it is severely damaging crops in the area.

PLEA TO SACRAMENTO. The smog's ravages prompted Riverside Mayor Ben Lewis, along with the mayors of neighboring communities, to appeal last month to Governor Ronald Reagan to declare their region a disaster area and to ban the sale of gasoline and the use of cars during smog alerts. Lewis has also asked Reagan to consider ordering that all cars in Southern California be converted to burn natural gas or propane, a plea that is not likely to get results.

Meanwhile, Riverside is moving in that direction on its own. This year it became the first city in which a driver can have his car converted and get its tank filled with natural gas. But these steps are unlikely to open more than a slit in Riverside's smog blanket, much of which drifts in from elsewhere.

Riverside did not always have heavy smog. In 1961, it recorded air below recommended purity levels on 91 days. Last year, the air was foul on 207 days. "Most of the smog is created by automobiles in Los Angeles," says Dr. James Pitts, director of the University of California's statewide Air Pollution Research Center in Riverside. "Sea breezes have always blown it out this way, but clean air from relatively undeveloped Orange County would also blow up here and ventilate it." But Orange County has been heavily developed in the past decade—and, says Pitts, "Now, all we are getting is dirty air from both places."

Source: *Business Week* (July 29, 1972), pp. 19–20. Reprinted by permission.

LOCKED IN. Once the smog arrives over Riverside, it is trapped there by the San Bernardino and San Jacinto mountains. Sunlight produces a photochemical reaction in the smog that creates peroxyacetyl nitrate. The chemical damages human tissue and plants.

The city calls smog alerts when the photochemical oxidant level exceeds .27 ppm of air. It called 50 alerts last year. "I believe we are facing a medical problem," says Ray Berry, Riverside's superintendent of schools. "We can already see it in these children. If it gets any worse, we may have to think about washing the air before inside use." Robert Zweig, president of the Riverside County Medical Assn., says that, increasingly, his patients complain of smog-related illnesses.

Riverside County lost $5.2-million of last year's $143-million crop harvest to smog. The loss included all of the county's watermelons, 35% of its grapefruit, 40% of its lemons, and 50% of its grapes. As a result, the horticulture of the area is being transfigured. Flower growers have left, along with growers of watermelons, lemons, grapes, and other vulnerable crops.

Thomas Crocker, an associate professor of economics at the University of California's Riverside campus, claims that the pollution is deflating property values. The *Riverside Press-Enterprise* bears out Crocker's bleak appraisal. One realtor told the paper that 15% to 20% of his business came from homeowners who were selling because of the bad air. Says Gerhard N. Rostvold, an economic researcher who has studied Riverside County: "The population of Riverside should grow to 200,000 by 1990. If it weren't for the smog, it would be 50,000 more."

SILVER LINING. Robert Tremaine, manager of business development for the Riverside Chamber of Commerce, sees a silver lining through the smog. "People would rather live here and bitch about it than live up to their tails in snow. And they appreciate things more," he says. "The other day it was clear and we went up to the mountain to see the sunset. Ten years ago, it would have been just another sunset." Besides, he adds, "Smog is not much of a detriment to business."

The state's Air Resources Board, however, says the smog in Riverside is getting worse because of the wind patterns, even though smog conditions in Southern California generally are improving. That is little consolation to Riverside residents—and to those of nearby communities. "It is starting to get into the desert now," says UCR's Pitts. The nearby resort of Palm Springs, for example, had 984 hours of substandard air last year, compared with 198 the year before.

"The public spirit is at an all-time low because of frustration," asserts Zweig. Says Mayor Lewis: "Sacramento doesn't think this is an emergency, but we are relying on winds around here to see who will have the worst smog. The dam is ready to break."

Chapter 3
SUGGESTED TOPICS FOR CLASS DISCUSSION

1. Try to make an inventory of the major problems of a typical city today. On which of these problems is significant progress being made?
2. Why is progress so slow?
3. What are the different kinds of "costs" involved in making an attack on this cluster of urban problems?
4. Where will the financial costs of this attack rest? How are relations between the various levels of government—federal, state, and local—involved in this question? Is this a problem for the cities? for the federal government? for the states?
5. The problems of the cities and of the environment are linked in what ways?
6. Who is responsible for the environmental crisis?
7. Is technology the source of the problem or is it the solution to the problem?
8. Would a sharp reduction in production and Gross National Product be one way of attacking the environmental problem? What are some of the difficulties associated with this approach?
9. Which environmental problems seem to be the most urgent? How can a start be made on these at the local level? at the national level?

Chapter 4
Politics, Pressure, and Payoffs

What we now call pressure groups *or the more polite descriptive term* interest groups *have been with us since the organization of the first government under George Washington. Indeed, the first President expressed concern that "factions," seeking their own selfish interests, might undermine the Republic.*

Whatever term is applied, there is a natural instinct among those having common attitudes and interests to organize in order to pursue their own goals by influencing those who make public policy. In addition, such organizing is protected by the first amendment to the Constitution: "Congress shall make no law . . . prohibiting . . . the right of the people peaceably to assemble, and to petition the Government for a redress of grievances." This phrase has long been held to protect groups that assemble and organize for a variety of purposes.

All organized groups who seek to influence public policy do it in the name of the public good—whatever is good for them is automatically good for the public. Obviously, this is not always true, and is perhaps even rarely the case. There is a bewildering array of organized groups in modern society, and they have been credited with wielding enormous power, so much so that they have been variously called "the invisible government," and "the fourth branch of government."

This view is probably overdrawn. Nevertheless, there is justification for concern over the amount of influence exercised by such groups. Should the concern lead to greater regulation and public disclosure of the groups' activities? How often does the result of lobbying actually lead to decisions benefitting the few? In what forms do payoffs come? Are these payoffs relatively harmless to the public interest, or do they, by enriching some, deprive many more?

The cases in this chapter reveal how some interest groups work, and raise some of the issues just mentioned.

CAN A NONPARTISAN LOBBY FIND A ROLE IN POLITICS?

Natalie Davis Springarn

In these past months of political partisanship, the last thing you might have expected was to find a nonpartisan organization, Common Cause, coming into its own.

Yet as the campaign lumbered along, this issue-oriented lobby seemed at last to have found the right horse to ride and began carving out an election year role of its own, turning abstract "electoral process" issues like campaign spending and party reform into a very lively show.

Six days before the election, its suit to force the fund-raising arms of the Committee for the Re-election of the President to disclose the sources of pre-April 7 contributions of more than $10 million resulted in success. A consent decree dramatized its intensive efforts to focus public attention on the slipshod way this country has been funding its election campaigns.

Operating on a $3.7 million budget ($2.7 million for program and $1 million overhead for serving and acquiring members), Common Cause may not have become the "third force" it set out to be. Its membership has dipped slightly, from 232,000 in October, 1971, to just over 200,000, as was expected with an election attracting activists into the partisan fray. But the Cause is still unprecedented in size for a two-year-old lobby. More

Source: *The Washington Post* (November 19, 1972), p. B-5. © The Washington Post. Reprinted by permission.

scrupulous than most, it reported spending more money on lobbying—$847,850–than any other organization last year.

Its third floor offices in one of those concrete-and-glass M Street buildings are a far cry from the humble walkups and hand-me-down desks traditional with public interest lobbies cautiously husbanding the contributed dollar. Volunteers flock in each day, telephoning around the country, typing, filing, sorting zip codes.

There is a "boiler room" where young men and women in jeans and minis last summer worked on questionnaires sent to both parties' convention delegates and alternates (Name? Address? Zip code? Congressional district? Miami hotel? Member of Common Cause? Would you be willing to assist Common Cause with its convention efforts?). There is a "situation room," three walls of which this fall were covered with charts listing candidates for office throughout the country. There is a telephone "peace center" where Cause members worked to boost end-the-war legislation.

From Talk to Action

There is, neither last nor least, John William Gardner, still speaking of a more lofty world, a world of excellence, self-renewal and revitalized institutions; he can articulate the dream. But sometimes the abstractions which have so irritated his critics give way to factual argument, as when he confronts tough House Administration Committee Chairman Wayne Hays on the nitty-gritty of campaign spending.

"John has become aware," explains a Midwestern congressman, "that though it is important to define goals, it is not enough. To be effective on substantive matters one must pay greater attention to the political process." Certainly this former HEW secretary, Urban Coalition and Carnegie Foundation head is showing more of an appetite for issues politicking than he ever did before. He makes that call. He sees that congressman. Though not exactly kissing babies, or sipping twilight bourbon and branch water in Capitol hideaways, he has come far from the days when his staff despaired that he would ever grab the ball to make an urgent call to the speaker.

Gardner receives no salary, although his income from lecture fees, book royalties, stock dividends and foundation consulting is a comfortable $50,000 a year. Though he travels around the capital in a chauffered limousine ("That peoples' lobbyist doesn't march up the Hill like Coxey did," quipped one observer), his registered Republican face is only one of many among the display of 50 staffer snapshots on the office bulletin board.

The staff he heads, most in their thirties, includes just enough Republicans to justify the "non-partisan" label ("I had never really met a Democrat before," confessed former Republican National Committee aide Pam Curtis. "I used to think they were all bums."). As the campaign began,

Reuther-trained Jack Conway, on whose office walls hang pictures of John and Robert Kennedy, advised anyone with an itch to take part to quit. Several did, including Connecticut's savvy Anne Wexler, who went first to the Muskie, then the McGovern, cause, and wound up directing the Democrats' voter registration effort.

Since Conway joined up as president, second-in-command and operation chief a year ago last March, the Cause's organizational plans have crystalized. There are and will be no chapters, no auxiliaries, no structured meetings of subordinate units out across America. Members, the consensus runs, have been chaptered to death; they are active, involved people, bored with boards. Instead, Common Cause will remain loosely organized, a citizen's network divided by congressional district and by state.

David Cohen, who at 35 resembles a taller and younger Pierre Salinger, doubles as director of field organization and lobbyist. Conway brought Cohen to Common Cause. Fred Wertheimer, 33, whose balding, mustached face illustrated a *Saturday Review* cover on lobbying last spring, serves as legislative director. He used to work for liberal Rep. Silvio Conte (R-Mass.) and for the House Small Business Committee (as minority counsel). Tom Mathews, a veteran newspaperman and public relations official, is special assistant to Gardner for public relations and completes the Common Cause high command.

Other staffers, like Georgianna Rathbun, former *Congressional Quarterly* legislative editor, who edits the handsome Cause newsletters, David Dawson, comptroller, and Ken Guido, former University of Kentucky law professor, help earn the group high marks for professionalism. Guido is playing an increasingly significant role (with general counsel Mitchell Rogovin of Arnold and Porter) as the Cause moves deeper into court actions as a way of achieving its goals.

Directors Decide

Fifteen dollars is a high price to pay for belonging to a Cause group. Some assert the organization would do better with the less affluent and young if it lowered its dues, or at least adopted an additional lower student fee. But $15 it will probably remain, at least until the Cause feels it can start to reach out toward a wider constituency. What does the member get for this sum?

Certainly not the usual uncertain joys of membership debating at meetings, reading the minutes, running for office, amending resolutions, participating in that camaraderie church programs call "fellowship." What Common Cause strives, to give its members for their $15 is a chance to work on the team, plus effective representation in the capital's competitive centers of power.

Members are polled occasionally for their views on crucial issues. These polls are advisory only; they guide a 15-member executive committee and 42-member board of directors in selecting between six and eight issues each year. The Cause has just completed its own election; the board has been enlarged and is now less VIP- and status-oriented. Partisan elected officials like New York's Mayor John Lindsay and Cleveland's former Mayor Carl Stokes (who served on the board of the Urban Coalition Action Council, Common Cause's predecessor) are gone this election year; the board now includes grassroots Cause leaders like Vermont's Susan Paris and California lawyer Michael Walsh, as well as Betty Furness, Leonard Woodcock and League of Women Voters chief Lucy Benson. This change may help placate members who have wanted more of a say on policy; there is sensitivity to complaints that a group so deeply concerned with citizen participation makes its own key decisions in a small committee room.

Thus far, regional offices have been set up in Boston, San Francisco and New York to service local groups; three more regional desks are manned from Washington. Thirty-four states have either organized or are organizing state program advisory committees. Very few state groups have paid staff. The real lobbyists are the people in the states and regions who are called on, in an issues fight, to put the heat on carefully selected "swing" congressmen. The word goes out from Washington through the newsletter or special bulletins, or by telephone (on leased lines) to Common Cause telephone coordinators in each congressional district. The coordinator contacts between 15 and 20 "activators." Each "activator" in turn contacts about 10 telephoners. The telephoners ask members to write or call their congressman.

Look at Common Cause's own estimate of how it is dividing the third of its budget going toward policy matters this year, and you can guage its sense of direction: 35 per cent into campaign finance monitoring; 25 per cent into end-the-war; 15 per cent into the Equal Rights amendment; 10 per cent into congressional reform, and the remaining 15 per cent divided among D.C. home rule, welfare reform, no-fault insurance, a consumer protection agency, clean water, and a few miscellaneous activities.

Campaign Spending

The turning point for the Cause came last year when a federal judge, over the combined opposition of the Republican and Democratic national committees, ruled that the Cause had standing to sue to force compliance with campaign spending limitations. Passage of the new federal elections law—for which it had lobbied strenuously—made this ruling moot. But as the days rolled toward and past the April 7 date on which the new law was to go into effect, the Cause perceived a serious gap, and moved to fill it.

Fred Wertheimer, who directs the campaign monitoring project, explains that the new law did not change the enforcement mechanism: "It didn't change the fact that government officials had to go to court to prosecute offenders and never did. And it didn't give us a way of getting information about sources of funds to the public; it left this job, on which enforcement actions could be based, to the media. They cannot do it alone; it's too massive."

Until the nation's system of financing elections is changed to one with public subsidies and tax credits instead of concentrated private contributions, Wertheimer argues, someone must do this job: "We live in a corrupted political system: It allows people who want preference from the government to provide financial aid to precisely those people who they are asking for a favorable political decision. The new law helps deal with this problem. It is comprehensive in its requirements of disclosure and we want to get compliance with it; we want to force candidates to make their financial resources clear."

The Cause sought in diverse ways to influence the electoral process and to surface the issue of campaign financing for national debate:

• Common Cause claims it had 1,000 volunteers, 300 of them in Washington, working in its campaign monitoring project. Their aim was to set up files on every candidate in the country, get copies of the financial disclosure reports the new law requires (the filing of periodic reports of receipts and expenditures and identification of contributors of more than $100 by name, address, occupation and principal place of business), analyze the reports and issue press releases on the results. Statewide analyses distributed in September and October gave detailed information about Democratic and Republican, conservative and liberal contributions. The Cause reported, for example, that candidates in Massachusetts' 5th Congressional District primary had raised the largest amount for any one district, a total of more than $413,000, with Democrat John Kerry, former head of Vietnam Veterans Against the War, leading the field of 15 by more than $75,000. (Kerry won his primary but lost in November.)

• Shortly after the first deadline under the new elections law, April 17, Gardner flew to Columbus, Ohio, and in a television press conference read off the names of 69 congressional candidates he said had failed to file proper disclosure statements. By Aug. 30, the Cause had filed formal complaints with the clerk of the House against 286 House candidates who it said had not properly filed reports on campaign income and expenditures in the primaries—128 Democrats, 98 Republicans and 19 minor party candidates. Other complaints were filed against the Committee to Impeach the President and *The New York Times* (the proper information, the Cause charged, was not included in an advertisement; the Justice Department has moved against the group inserting the ad).

• In early May, Wayne Hays, stung at his inclusion in the group of noncompliers, ordered the cost of reproducing disclosure reports filed under the new federal campaign financing law increased from the original 10 cents to $1 a page: The Cause promptly sued the clerk of the House for establishing prohibitively high charges for copies. The court ruled for Common Cause, and the price went back to 10 cents a page.

• In June, Hays called Gardner before his House Administration Committee, ostensibly to testify on proposals to change the new law and reduce the number of reports a congressional candidate must file (Gardner strongly opposed this step). But most of the questioning centered on the Cause's efforts to expose nonfiling candidates and on the congressmen's charges that the Cause had listed from 17 to 26 filers as nonfilers. The exchange was harsh (Hays, who blamed the mails and claimed his report was only one day, not a week, late, spoke of "bold, barefaced lies," and gave each committee member the chance to castigate Gardner). Even those friendly to Gardner still speak of the difficulties and complexities inherent in filing under the new law, both in Washington and in the states, and wonder whether the Cause jumped overhastily into accusing noncompliers.

• As part of its monitoring project, the Cause compiled and constantly updates a special interest file. On July 28, it released information on money stockpiled in political funds controlled by corporate and labor executives, lobbying and trade associations: Organized labor had $4,244,000 on hand for the campaign; business and industry some $3,699,000; agricultural interests more than $1,900,000; the medical profession $1,270,000.

• In early August, the Cause sued TRW, Inc., a large defense contractor, in a major challenge to corporate and union committees set up to collect contributions for joint, centrally controlled political funds. The suit was settled: TRW, headed by early Cause contributor Simon Ramo, agreed to dissolve its Good Government Fund. The Cause then advised a hundred other contractors what had happened. Ken Guido's phone rang busily over the next weeks as businessmen and their lawyers sought information about the suit, and tried to find out how long they would have before the Cause sued them, too.

• On Sept. 19, the House Administration Committee showed its concern; without holding public hearings, it reported out a bill, supported by the Justice Department, specifically to remove the grounds for the Common Cause suit from the elections law. Cause lobbyists fought in vain to keep the measure from being rushed through the House, but succeeded in the Senate when Majority Leader Mike Mansfield refused to schedule it and Sens. William Proxmire, George Aiken and Robert Stafford blocked floor efforts to attach it as an amendment to another measure.

• Common Cause staffers traveled to Miami Beach for both political conventions last summer. In July, they helped persuade Democratic platform writers to endorse reforms in congressional seniority, secrecy, conflict of interest, campaign financing and regulation of lobbying, and are credited by Rep. Donald Fraser (D-Minn.) with helping work out a compromise delaying for two years sweeping reforms in the new Democratic Party charter. In August, Cause proposals gained no recognition in the Republican platform, although a platform subcommittee had adopted recommendations for ending seniority and for a strong lobby disclosure bill. Ironically, neither party showed any interest in a Cause proposal, first advanced last February, to reform the selection of vice presidential candidates by having running-mate preferences aired well before the conventions.

• On Sept. 6, Gardner announced the Cause suit to force disclosure of the names of contributors to President Nixon's reelection campaign before the new elections law became effective April 7. The suit, based on reporting requirements under the old law, followed months of calling on all presidential candidates to disclose their contributions. Most did so; President Nixon, Sen. Henry Jackson (D-Wash.) and Rep. Wilbur Mills (D-Ark.) did not.

The White House apparently tried to delay or deter filing of the suit. At the last minute, Leonard Garment, special consultant to the President, called Gardner to ask for details. Two hours later, a second call advised him that a reply to a four-week-old Gardner letter to Campaign Director Clark MacGregor was on its way. The letter, delivered to Gardner's suburban home the night before the filing, suggested a meeting possibly to "clear the air." The Republican position was that the fund-raising committee was not covered by the law during the period in which the money was collected, since its function was solely to support the President's renomination. The papers were nonetheless filed.

At one point, committee attorneys wrote to the Internal Revenue Service asking for an investigation of the Cause's tax-exempt status. On Nov. 1, a federal judge approved an out-of-court agreement under which the committee agreed to make public a partial listing of contributors before election day. The Cause, in return, consented to delay of the trial until after the election.

Who Gets the Credit?

Until the Hamilton-Whelan end-the-war-on-a-date-certain provision went down to defeat in early August, Common Cause lobbying increasingly centered on its efforts to put the House on record, for the first time, against the Vietnam war. It had several things going for it: This was an issue its members supported vehemently—as Doris Cadoux of Scarsdale put it, "People who would never work under the peace symbol will work with Common Cause." And new House reforms enabling members to ask for and get recorded teller votes on amendments made that unwieldy body more responsive to constituents' pressures.

What's more, the peace groups had heretofore concentrated on the Senate, with its broader foreign policy powers. So as the Washington staff orchestrated this fight, as it tried to strike a fruitful balance between inside action on the Hill and outside pressures from the field, it aroused less resentment from other organizations than it had in other battles—the defeat of the SST, for example, or the achievement of the 18-year-old vote. Some felt that the Cause, seeking new members, had often claimed credit for accomplishments many had lobbied to achieve.

The Cause has learned to be more careful than it used to be in the credit-claiming game. It defers to others for leadership on selected issues— to the League of Women Voters on welfare reform, for instance, or to the labor movement on public service employment.

As it opens its third year, some Common Causers hope to move further into state legislative reform, building on the record of the successful Colorado project, for instance. (There, Cause members blocked a power rate increase and joined with the Colorado Labor Council to put several reform initiatives on the November ballot; most were rejected, but a legislative reform package was approved.) Others prefer to remain largely in the national arena, concentrating perhaps on congressional reform.

"We're in damned good shape, considering that the country goes ape every four years," says Jack Conway. "When Congress meets again in January it will be ripe for a change. There will be many new faces. We want to tackle the committee system and similar issues."

Gardner, who usually stays a step ahead of his critics, says that historically citizens' "cause" groups have made themselves felt in the United States. But in truth, unless they joined the political system as the Populists did when they formed a political party, they were single-issue groups—the suffragettes, the prohibitionists, the peace or civil rights movements—concentraing their passions and their power.

More, than ever now, when events are so complex, an issue has to reach out and hit you in the face. It is hard to do that with six or eight common issues. Perhaps the Cause has found its issue in political process reform, and can sustain interest in it beyond the drama of the partisan battle. Perhaps the real question for John Gardner, and for the organization he chairs, is whether, in pluralistic America, there are any causes that are truly common.

Why Ma Bell Still Believes in Santa

Nicholas Johnson

Christmas came a little early for Ma Bell last year—to be precise, two days early. On December 23, the Federal Communications Commission announced its decision to dismiss its six-year-old inquiry into AT&T's rate base and operating expenses, while continuing its generous effort to set ever higher rates of return for Bell. (Two of the seven commissioners, H. Rex Lee and I, dissented, and Commissioner Robert Bartley concurred "reluctantly.") The commission, which acknowledged that it hadn't been doing much to regulate the telephone company anyway, as usual chose a "graveyard time" to announce an important decision—the late afternoon of the last working day before Christmas—in the hope that the press would not particularly notice the announcement. Journalists, as well as consumers and public officials, are bored and confused by the subject of regulation of public utilities—or at least so the FCC thought, and no doubt AT&T officials thought so too.

After that holiday weekend, AT&T stock went nicely up, and telephone executives could gather round the hearth a few days later to toast what promised to be a vintage new year.

In the next few weeks a storm of public protest boiled up, stunning the majority of the FCC, which had never really understood the consumer movement or correctly measured its powerful influence on the press, citizens, and Congressmen. The first day Congress reconvened after the Christmas holiday, the AT&T matter came up for floor discussion. Even the Department of Defense, on behalf of all the federal executive agencies, said that without an inquiry the fairness of long-distance phone rates could not be determined. What had seemed to the FCC majority as merely a more candid way of dealing with business as usual ("As long as we're not really going to conduct a hearing anyway," one commissioner had said, "why not just cancel it?") was publicly denounced. On January 28 the FCC reinstituted the inquiry, and on February 1 Chairman Dean Burch was trying to explain to the Senate Commerce Committee why an investigation that involved billions of dollars in phone company charges had been dropped in the first place.

Before trying to unravel the implications of the December 23 decision

Source: *Saturday Review* (March 11, 1972), Vol. 55, pp. 57–60. Copyright © 1972 by Saturday Review, Inc. First appeared in *Saturday Review,* March 11, 1972. Used with permission. Nicholas Johnson is the author of two books: *How to Talk Back to Your Television Set* (Atlantic-Little, Brown; Bantam, 1970) and *Test Pattern for Living* (Bantam, 1972).

and the January 28 reversal, we must understand a little about the economics of the Bell System and the FCC's so-called "rate regulation." It's not all that complicated. The Communications Act of 1934 gives the FCC the responsibility of regulating the rates of "common carriers by wire." The act states that these rates must be "just and reasonable" and that proposed rate increases must be "in the public interest." Any charges not in the public interest are prohibited. As it works out, the FCC sets the long-distance rates and state commissions set local rates.

Telephone rates are based on three variables: Bell's capital investment, or "rate base" (the value of the poles, your telephone, and so forth), the "rate of return" (or profit) on that capital investment, and Bell's expenses.

First, consider the rate of return. Suppose the FCC, after a hearing, decides that Bell should get, say, 7 per cent as a fair return on its investment. Taking Bell's capital investment figure, compute 7 per cent of it. Then, figure out how much revenue all our telephone bills have to generate so that, after all expenses are paid, Bell will be left with that 7 per cent figure as profit. Finally, figure out what long distance telephone rates must be to provide their share of the money. Conceptually, it's a relatively simple process.

You would think that, since the public interest is the guiding criterion for this calculation, Ma Bell would use FCC hearings to tell us how the public will be better off in terms of faster dial tones, fewer busy signals, and more telephone installations if we would grant an 8 per cent return as opposed to a 7 per cent one. Right? Wrong. I asked a Bell attorney at the 1967 rate hearing how service would be affected if the company got 4 per cent—or 10 per cent. He was totally unprepared for such a question.

Instead, the hearings are concerned almost exclusively with the marketability of Bell stocks and bonds—stock prices and rates of interest. Ever higher stock prices are assumed to be necessary for the phone company to raise new money for construction. For some reason, the commission seems to buy this reasoning, in spite of the evidence that the quality of telephone service has declined during the very years Bell has enjoyed its highest earnings.

The size of Bell's capital investment, the rate base itself, may have a far more substantial effect on telephone rates than the rate of return. If we assume that Bell has a legitimate capital investment of $50-billion and is entitled to a 10 per cent rate of return, that's a $5-billion profit. An 8 per cent rate of return would give the company $4-billion—and the subscribers a $1-billion saving. But suppose the $50-billion figure is too high. Suppose that for any number of reasons—unreasonable depreciation practices, paying Western Electric, Bell's wholly owned subsidiary and supplier, too much for equipment, or counting items of operating costs as capital investments—Bell has inflated its rate base. Even at the higher 10 per cent figure, if the company's rate base ought to be valued at $20-billion, its return is only $2-billion—rather than $4- or $5-billion. I don't charge that Bell has done any of these things. I don't know any more than you do. The point is that nobody else at the FCC knows either and that the commission has not yet made any real effort to find out.

Let's look at an example. What's the rate base value of the telephone instrument in your home? Bell purchased that phone from Western Electric, whose phones are produced only for Bell and are the only ones Bell buys. And Western Electric's price—including Western's *profit*—has never been regulated by the commission. As far as the Bell System is concerned, these purchases are merely bookkeeping entries. Bell's incentive, in general, is to put as much value as possible on a rate base item because every dollar "in the ground" immediately starts earning its own rate of return. When that dollar includes Western's *profit,* it means AT&T is making two profits on the same piece of equipment—a rate of return on a rate of return. The FCC's trial staff—the agency's "prosecuting attorneys"—now urges the commission to consider Western Electric's rate of return in any decision on AT&T's over-all rate of return.

Most of your phone bill doesn't have anything to do with Bell's profits, but with the third variable, "expenses"—$13-billion of them. How much do the executives get paid—in salaries, stock options, expense accounts? Is there a cheaper way of installing a telephone than sending a man to take out the old phone one day and another man to put in an identical one in the same apartment two days later? Advertising, policies on accelerated depreciation, use of employees, and maintenance costs all go into Bell's expenses. You're paying every month for those telephone trucks you see running around your town—and the public relations firm that told Bell it was time to give up on the drab green paint and the nineteenth-century company emblem. The FCC is supposed to be ensuring that Bell—and you —are not paying too much. In the thirty-eight years since the 1934 act, the agency has yet to complete a single hearing examining expenses. We have always simply accepted the figures supplied by Bell itself. At best, that is a lot of trust in Bell's multibillion-dollar infallibility.

Finally, there is the manner in which AT&T apportions its phone rates among different classes of customers. FCC's jurisdiction over long-distance service is not limited to individual subscribers' calls. It includes rates for "free" (flat rate) long-distance calls (Wide Area Telephone Service, or "WATS" lines), TELPAK (cheaper-by-the-dozen rates for private lines), and other large corporate uses of long-distance lines for transmission of voice, picture, and computer data. In 1964, when AT&T earned a 7.5 per cent rate of return on its total long-distance investment, the rates charged reflected a rate of return ranging from 10 per cent for individual long-distance consumers like you and me to 0.3 per cent for corporate TELPAK users.

In years of off-again, on-again hearings, starting in 1965, the commission has been unable to come to grips with any of these questions essential to regulation. All that came out of the first two years' work was the determination of a reasonable rate of return and a few rate reductions, although not enough, as it turned out, to bring Bell down within the range determined by the commission to be reasonable. The commission really never did get around to Bell's capital investment, expenses, and the apportioning of rates. Then, in 1969 and without a hearing at all, the commission granted Bell a new, higher rate of return. Finally, in November 1970, Bell filed substantially higher rates still, and the FCC ordered the new hearing. None of the big issues were settled when the commission dismissed that part of the hearing that would have dealt with those larger issues last December.

Struggling to come up with explanations of this dismissal, the FCC majority said it had neither the staff nor the budget to carry out an AT&T hearing. The commission implied that priorities made it impossible to readjust on-going projects in order to find the funds necessary to conduct proper inquiry. It seemed to me the public indignation was predictable. Chairman Burch was surprised, however. In a letter to members of Congress, he said that the commission did and would regulate Bell "vigorously and effectively" through private, cozy, closed-doors chats with Bell officials—or "continuous surveillance," as the commission prefers to call them.

Bell officials were of mixed mind about the decision. AT&T Vice President for Federal Relations E. B. Crosland said that the decision to dismiss the hearing into rate base items was "encouraging, because it should lead to a prompt commission decision" on the now pending rate increase case, and he applauded the long record of success of the FCC's practice of "thorough regulation without excessive costs and extended hearings." But AT&T Board Chairman H. I. Romnes later backtracked and called the dismissal "very unfortunate." As a Bell lawyer put it, the decision was embarrassing, because it "made it appear as if Bell isn't regulated." It is always unfortunate for an unregulated monopoly when the public learns the truth.

Now that the hearing is to be reopened, will it finally deal with all the real issues of regulating Ma Bell? It likely won't be as broad a hearing as the one originally planned, nor can we expect it to be accomplished as soon as we had hoped. Chairman Burch told the Senate Commerce Committee in January that he couldn't even indicate a starting date.

The FCC still doesn't know where it is going to get the manpower to conduct the inquiry. Indeed, it has admitted that it doesn't even have the resources or expertise to determine what resources it will need. After all, the commission has never done so large a study before, and it is difficult, if not impossible, to find a suitable model. If the commission intends to proceed with the investigation using its current resources, or with just a few additional staff members, it will surely be engaged in what Chairman Burch called "window dressing."

Senator Fred Harris and Congressman William Ryan, as well as Senator Philip Hart and Congressman Jonathan Bingham, have introduced bills to give the commission the necessary funds. When given an opportunity to support the Harris-Ryan bill, and accept the funds, Chairman Burch, in a letter to Senator Harris, declined even to comment on his proposed legislation.

What, in fact, has been the FCC's budget position? In fiscal year 1972 Congress gave the FCC all the money it requested. Indeed, for fiscal 1973, after the criticism of the commission, the Office of Management and Budget insisted the commission take more than it had asked for AT&T regulation. Thus, if the FCC does not in fact have sufficient funds to conduct an investigation, the responsibility rests with the commission itself. It is hard to plead poverty when you get all you ask for, and more, and refuse to accept a $2-million gift from Senator Harris and Congressman Ryan.

What is the meaning of the AT&T caper? At least the days of bluntly "dismissing" such hearings seem to be over. But telephone users will continue to suspect, with some reason, that they are being charged more for long-distance service than the law permits. Beyond that, state public utility commissions, most of which have even fewer resources than the FCC, will be under pressure to permit excess charges for local and intrastate service as well. Many of them were legitimately concerned by the commission's admission of inability to regulate Bell.

It is difficult to predict precisely the dollar benefits that could come to you and me from the reopened inquiry. In establishing a rate base and expenses, there are, for example, hundreds of accounting decisions that affect your telephone bill—among them the proportion of debt and equity financing, using (or not using) accelerated depreciation, and the methods of evaluating property. But for the consumers dealing with a monopoly, these are more than "accounting practices." In an industry whose annual revenues are roughly twice the yearly income tax collected by all fifty states combined, a fraction of a per cent here and there may amount to millions of dollars in phone-bill savings.

There are implications to this whole affair that are bigger than our phone bills, however. The history of nonregulation of AT&T is a bad omen for the current efforts at broader economic regulation. Public utilities regulation is the closest working model we have to the current Phase II wage and price controls. In both, the guiding criterion is "fair and reasonable" profits, and the controlling question is where the balance should be struck between corporations and consumers. In both, the regulated industries are well organized and capable of hiring the finest lawyers and economists to plead their cases, while the affected public is essentially unrepresented. The inadequacies and biases of public utility regulation do not speak optimistically for the success of the much vaster Phase II regulation. If the FCC cannot effectively regulate one company, how can we expect to accomplish meaningful regulation of the entire economy by the Wage, Price, and Rent boards?

The short-lived FCC dismissal of the AT&T hearing is only part of the current pattern of governmental deference to large corporations at the expense of the small consumer. Other examples include the continuing reluctance to re-examine, in a serious way, the Internal Revenue Code with its capital gains taxes, oil depletion allowances, prepaid interest deductions, bad debts reserves, tax-free municipal bond income, investment credits, and other "special interest" loopholes. The tax code, through these provisions, gives those earning more than $25,000 each year a "welfare payment" of at least $4,000 annually; those earning below $3,000 a year get $16 in such "welfare." The oil-import quota costs the consumer an additional 5 cents a gallon in gasoline prices. The maritime subsidy gives big ship companies and shipyards benefits estimated at $750-million annually from the Treasury, with no advantage to consumers or taxpayers whatsoever. The continuing refusal to require quality labeling of canned goods (labels describing the grade of the product, measured against government standards) produces a 20 per cent increase in the cost of such items. In virtually every area where government affects business, there is a battle between consumer interests and corporate interests, and the corporate interests generally win hands down. Publicity aside, the trend in the day-to-day decisions in government during the past three years is against the consumer on every front.

Possibly the most distressing aspect of this corporate-consumer imbalance is that those who make such decisions often honestly believe they are acting in the public interest. Just as supporters of the SST argued that the project provided jobs, and opponents of the recently vetoed day-care legislation felt the family was being threatened, so those who applaud the commission's decision in the AT&T case believe we are protecting the investments of countless "little people."

Maybe so. But if that is the justification, let those who make the decisions say so. If the public interest is to be found in some secondary gain, let the choice between the alternative ways of attaining that gain be given to the public. If American automobile production is to be encouraged not because it produces the best product for the money (it clearly doesn't) but because the planned obsolescence creates jobs and stimulates economic growth, let the American people decide that's the way they want to do it. If we can't—or won't—regulate AT&T, let's consider breaking it up into manageable pieces, or perhaps nationalizing it, and then find another way to support those who are holding its shares.

Some would argue that our decision to reinstate the AT&T rate base hearing is a step in the right direction. I would like to share their optimism, but in my eight years in Washington I have seen too much that leads me to believe otherwise. Until the finance company comes to repossess the Christmas loot, Ma Bell is going to go on believing in Santa Claus.

BEYOND THE ITT CASE

Harlan M. Blake

Dita Beard, the flamboyant Washington lobbyist for the International Telephone and Telegraph Company, opened up into the headlines a situation whose broader implications deserve public attention.

Mrs. Beard's unwilling celebrity resulted from an alleged admission (in conversations with an aide of columnist Jack Anderson) to a political deal between ITT and the Republican party. Supposedly, her cocktail-party conversation with former Attorney General John Mitchell, and an ITT promise to make a hefty contribution, through its Sheraton Hotel subsidiary, to the San Diego Republican party convention, were instrumental in getting ITT's antitrust cases favorably settled. But although it is clear from sources other than Mrs. Beard that getting a favorable antitrust settlement was the subject foremost in the minds of ITT officials during the summer of '71, it is at least an equally plausible hypothesis that the San Diego gift was regarded as a more generalized investment in political goodwill with the Republican party. The fact that Mr. Republican Party happened also to be Attorney General of the U.S. (instead of Postmaster General, once the pattern) was a happy coincidence, for ITT if not for the public interest.

Thus the focus of attention must shift to Richard W. McLaren, Assistant Attorney General in charge of the Antitrust Division of the Justice Department, whose "primary responsibility" it was, to use his own words, to exercise "the broad discretionary authority" to decide whether or not to settle the cases. If McLaren's settlement was a good one from the point of view of public policy, as he claims, and if it is credible that the list of factors he says he took into account is complete, the case for or against

Source: *Harper's Magazine* (June 1972), pp. 74–78. Copyright © 1972, by Minneapolis Star and Tribune Co., Inc. Reprinted from the June 1972 issue of *Harper's Magazine* by permission of the author. Harlan M. Blake is Professor of Law, Columbia University School of Law.

improper influence will have to be decided on other evidence. For example, Deputy Attorney General Richard G. Kleindienst's apparent initial attempt to conceal his role in the settlements and ITT's speedy destruction of files may be persuasive to some. If on the other hand McLaren, too, seems to have been less than fully candid, this would point strongly toward pressures, although quite likely subtle ones. It would not, of course, prove that arrangements for the San Diego convention were decisive, although it would seem to suggest that generally ITT's influence in high places is dangerously pervasive.

Since McLaren's earlier honesty and toughness had impressed all observers, it is not pleasant to be forced to conclude that his statement of reasons to the Senate committee was not persuasive. To evaluate the credibility of his testimony it is important to know more about the cases involved and about the recent history of antitrust enforcement policy. To begin, one should note that McLaren *did* change his mind rather abruptly. Briefs on appeal of the ITT cases to the Supreme Court had already been written and filed, and every speech and public pronouncement by Antitrust Division officials in months prior to July 1971 made it clear that the division thought the cases were soundly based and were going to be won.

The legal question involved was whether ITT's acquisitions in 1969 of Automatic Canteen Corporation, the nation's largest food-vending concern; of Grinnel Corporation, the nation's largest supplier of fire prevention (sprinkler) systems; and of Hartford Fire Insurance Company, the nation's second largest fire insurance company, were violations of the antimerger law, Section 7 of the Clayton Act. That statute was amended and strengthened in 1950 by the Celler-Kefauver bill after lengthy Congressional hearings into increasing concentration in the U.S. economy. Before it could be an effective tool in the hands of the Justice Department, however, the language of the new law required definitive interpretation by the Supreme Court. In 1962 this was achieved. The famous *Brown Shoe* case defined strict standards for the legality of horizontal mergers (between competing firms) and for vertical mergers (between a firm and an important supplier or customer).

In short order, thanks to Justice Department enforcement of these rigorous new standards, horizontal and vertical mergers among large companies virtually ceased. But the trend toward increasing concentration in the economy did not subside. During the 1960s the number of mergers rapidly increased. From record levels in 1966, the number of mergers doubled in two years to over 4,000 in 1968. Furthermore, the proportion of large firms acquired by even larger ones increased even more rapidly than the acquisition rate. The total asset value of acquired firms rose from $4 billion in 1966 to $12 billion in 1968; 110 of *Fortune*'s 500 largest industrial corporations of 1962 had by 1968 disappeared by merger. The mergers were largely of the "conglomerate" variety, in which there are no important horizontal or vertical relationships between the acquiring and acquired corporations. In a speech delivered shortly after taking office, McLaren noted that "the pace and scale of the current merger trend can be ignored only at the risk of serious and perhaps irreversible damage to our competitive economy, to wit, undue economic concentration. . . ."

The most aggressive conglomerate of the past twelve years, and probably of all time, has been ITT. In 1955 ITT was a firm whose considerable size was concentrated primarily in overseas communications systems. It ranked as the eightieth U.S. industrial corporation, but its $500 million in annual sales were largely outside the domestic market. By 1971 ITT had soared to ninth in rank, with sales of $5.5 billion, largely in domestic markets. This growth within the United States was accomplished not through adding to the productive capacity or employment levels of the economy by new investment or building new plants. It was accomplished almost entirely by buying up existing businesses. Since the arrival of Harold S. Geneen as ITT's president in 1959, the company acquired 110 or more domestic companies (as well as fifty-five foreign firms), by trading its highly leveraged common and convertible preferred shares for those of the acquired firm.

Among its better known acquisitions were Continental Baking Co., Sheraton Hotels, Avis Corporation, Levitt & Sons, and Rayonier. At a meeting early in 1969, the ITT Board authorized acquisitions of an additional twenty-two domestic corporations and eleven foreign corporations. Geneen had established himself as the industrial empire builder *par excellence*—a man whose scale of operations challenged that of the legendary John D. Rockefeller, Sr., and surely surpassed any other figure of the era of the "robber barons," whose operations frightened Congress into enactment of the original antitrust law, the Sherman Act, in 1890.

Geneen's development as master *conglomerateur* was helped along by the coincidence that between 1965 and 1968 the Antitrust Division was headed by a Harvard law professor, Donald F. Turner, who took the position, based on his earlier writings, that conglomerate mergers should be dealt with, if at all, by special legislation rather than by antitrust enforcement. Turner neither sought legislation nor filed complaints in conglomerate cases, although he did help divert Geneen's attempted takeover of the American Broadcasting Company.

The day Richard McLaren emerged from Chicago antitrust law practice to take his oath as antitrust chief for the Justice Department, things changed. McLaren had no doubt that Congress had intended that the antitrust laws should be applied to all classes of mergers, including conglomerates, and he was convinced that the Supreme Court would agree if it were provided the opportunity. He promptly gave Attorney General Mitchell a speech to deliver that contained the following warning:

> The danger that super-concentration poses to our economic, political and social structure cannot be overestimated. . . . The Department of Justice may very well oppose any merger among the top 200 manufacturing firms . . . [or] by one of the top 200 manufacturing firms of any leading producer in any concentrated industry.

Since ITT ranked ninth among manufacturing firms, and had made itself the nation's star "super-conglomerate" through acquisitions, it seemed clear that if Mitchell meant what he said, ITT's days of empire-building were numbered. Within weeks of taking office, McLaren faced a situation that put this policy to the test. ITT had announced plans to acquire Automatic Canteen, the nation's largest food vendor. McLaren decided to bring suit in Chicago to secure an injunction against the merger. However, Kleindienst —acting for Mitchell, since an ITT division had been one of Mitchell's clients in his law practice—refused to approve the filing of the suit. According-ing to a report of Ralph Nader's antitrust investigators, Kleindienst re-sponded to White House intervention following a lobbying campaign di-rected at "White House staff close to Nixon" by "ITT, aided by New York investment houses which would greatly profit if the merger were com-pleted . . ." The Nader report concludes that the suit was filed later, after the merger was consummated, only because McLaren had gone to the White House to make clear the strength of his conviction that the suit should be brought.

The Nader evaluation seems plausible since, shortly before the an-nouncement of the ITT-Automatic Canteen merger, McLaren had filed suit, with no reported difficulty, against Ling-Temco-Vought's proposed acquisition of Jones & Laughlin Steel. Since LTV ranked below ITT on the *Fortune* list and J&L ranked sixth among steel producers, compared to Automatic Canteen's dominant first position in its industry, the ITT ac-quisition would seem to have been even more clearly exposed to attack. Mr. Ling, a Texas friend of Lyndon Johnson, might have done better if political history had been written differently.

Having won this important victory, McLaren filed a series of conglom-erate suits. The most important were two more filed against ITT in August 1969, when temporary injunctions were sought in the District Court for Connecticut to prevent its acquisition of Grinnell Corporation and Hart-ford Fire Insurance Company. Geneen was not to be dissuaded by only one lawsuit against the Automatic Canteen acquisition—and the reason soon became clear. Although Grinnell was expendable—indeed, Grinnell, con-veniently found in the same (Connecticut) judicial district as Hartford, may have been sought by ITT partly with the thought of later relinquishing it in plea-bargaining negotiations with the Antitrust Division—the billion-dollar annual cash flow of the insurance company would be an important factor in ITT's financing of past and future acquisitions.

As it almost always does in merger cases, the government lost the initial rounds with ITT in the trial courts. Still, its prospect of eventual victory was excellent. Even ITT attorney Lawrence G. Walsh was reported to have advised his client that it was probable that the Antitrust Division's appeals would succeed in the Supreme Court. There was good reason for his prophecy: in *each* of seven merger cases after *Brown Shoe,* the Supreme Court had found it necessary to reverse a district court's decision adverse to the government. The Antitrust Division had never lost a merger case in the Supreme Court since the Celler-Kefauver amendment in 1950. Neither had the Federal Trade Commission, which had litigated two conglomerate cases there. In the one merger appeal decided since Nixon's appointment of Justices Burger and Blackmun, they too joined a unanimous court in deciding for the government; as usual, the district court was reversed.

There are reasons for this pattern. District court judges are accustomed to dealing in the "hard" facts of mail fraud, drug distribution, damage claims, and the like. They find it difficult to "find" so nebulous a fact as that a merger causes a "probability of injury to competition," the criterion of the merger law. The Supreme Court, more attuned to questions of public policy, has no such difficulties. Furthermore, lawyers representing defendant corporations in the trial court are the best in the locality, and even in the country, often well known to and respected by local judges. Frequently, in terms of sheer manpower they outnumber the antitrust staff many times. Too, district court judges, often chosen from among successful local attorneys, are likely to share a similarity of outlook on business matters with their former colleagues.

These facts, and close study of the district court decisions in the three ITT cases, reveal no basis for Solicitor General Erwin Griswold's reckless statement before the Senate Judiciary Committee that the government would probably not have won the cases if the appeals had been taken. This was clearly not the view entertained by McLaren at the time, it was not the view of government lawyers handling the Grinnell and Hartford cases, and it is not a view likely to be shared by a careful student of the Supreme Court's handling of merger cases, which Griswold, it is fair to add, did not claim to be.

The Change of Mind

It is against this background that we must evaluate McLaren's statement regarding his change of mind about the desirability of going forward with the cases. Keep in mind that McLaren's decision to move strongly against conglomerates was far and away the most important decision and accomplishment of his entire term of office. He had fought and won permission to bring the cases. For two years or more he had consistently pressed them all the way through trial. None of the other conglomerate cases he had brought remained a suitable vehicle for appeal to the Supreme Court. On two of the three ITT cases, however, the Supreme Court was ready to hear argument. The badly needed clarification of the law that its opinions probably would have provided almost certainly would have embodied Richard McLaren's most important contribution in public service.

The reasons given by McLaren to the Judiciary Committee for changing his mind about settlement of the litigation were (1) that ITT's financial condition—its debt capacity and credit rating—would be jeopardized if it were denied access to the $1 billion annual cash flow of Hartford; (2) that the adverse effect on the stock market, and on the owners of ITT and Hartford shares, might be severe; and (3) that the effect on the international balance of payments might be adverse. None of these reasons, as McLaren presumably knew, could be taken seriously.

First, the twelve-page report in which these arguments were made, prepared in two or three days for a reported fee of $242 by Richard J. Ramsden, a financial analyst recommended to McLaren by the White House's ambassador-at-large to Wall Street, Peter Flanigan, was not—in content, in sponsorship, or in circumstances of authorship—objectively persuasive.[1] Most of it reads like the kind of research report on a company put out every day by the major brokerage houses. In addition, these are the kinds of arguments that every antitrust lawyer knows by heart and marks in desperation when his arguments "on the merits" are not strong enough to prevail. They are likely to be effective only with men who lack experience in the ways of the world, or who are looking for an excuse to be persuaded.

1) The possibility of an adverse effect on access to the capital market is not a factor that can be taken into account since it is present in every antitrust suit worth prosecuting; monopoly profits or cartel gains, at the expense of consumers, always improve the looks of financial statements and reduce credit risks. Was ITT's elaborate financial structure so shaky during the summer of '71 that it would have been "crippled financially," as McLaren said he feared, if it had been required eventually to divest itself of Hartford? If so, it was surely the best-kept secret in the history of corporate finance. During 1971, in spite of the pending appeals and McLaren's known opposition to settlement, ITT shares were much stronger than they had

---

[1] On April 17 Ramsden testified to the Committee that the Justice Department had made too much of his report.

been a year earlier. A number of Wall Street's most respected investment houses and brokerage firms were acquiring ITT shares or recommending them to clients. It is difficult to conceive of data that would be persuasive to any sophisticated observer in the face of this contrary evidence provided by the attitudes of the financial community expressed in the most sensitive and best-informed marketplace in the world. The worry about a stock-market debacle thus was a red herring, and it is not credible that McLaren was persuaded by it.

What seemed to worry McLaren most was ITT's assertion that it had paid a $500 million "premium" for the Hartford stock but took Hartford's assets onto its books at book value. To sell Hartford stock would result in a loss, and ITT would incur capital-gain tax liabilities.

As to this argument, one may note that it has been standard practice in conglomerate takeovers for the acquiring firms to pay a substantial "premium" for the acquired, in that shares selling (or convertible to shares selling) at twenty-five times earnings (like ITT's) were exchanged for shares selling at fifteen times earnings (like Hartford's). This reduces the former's price/earnings ratio on paper by adding to its earnings account more proportionately than to the number of new shares issued in the exchange. Thus everybody gets rich without adding anything to the real productivity of the economy. This was the kind of empire Geneen was building (for which services, at $812,000 per year, he was surely the best-paid executive in the nation). But if this kind of defense is accepted by the Antitrust Division and the courts, there will seldom be a conglomerate case in which relief can be obtained, except where the government is fortunate enough to secure a temporary injunction to prevent the transaction in the first place.

2) The Ramsden report was equally weak in arguing excessive injury to stockholders. First, this argument is faulty in the same respect as the prior one. No shareholder has any vested right to stock values arising from anticompetitive circumstances. Furthermore, most of the risk to ordinary investors had been absorbed by arbitrage buying and selling during the previous year by sophisticated speculators betting, in effect, on the outcome of the litigation.

Most important, in the event that Hartford were to be ordered divested two or three years hence, the courts have plenty of discretion in choosing plans that prevent injury to the innocent (for instance, by spreading small public offerings over a period of time). Such a plan was developed in 1961, when duPont and its shareholders were ordered to divest themselves of sixty-three million shares of General Motors stock, 23 per cent of the total. Counsel for duPont predicted calamity on Wall Street and enormous losses for defendant shareholders—none of which, of course, came to pass. The

Supreme Court warned in that case, however, that "adverse tax and market consequence" arguments could not be decisive:

> Those who violate the [antimerger] Act may not reap the benefit of their violations and avoid an undoing of their unlawful project on the plea of hardship or convenience.

3) Even less is it credible that the Treasury Department offered a balance of payments argument that could have been persuasive. First, the Treasury now states that its report to McLaren was only informal and casual. Second, such a report could not have been seriously made without the most detailed analysis of ITT's financial structure and its relationship with, and the condition of, several dozen important overseas subsidiaries. No one claims that this was done.

Finally, the balance of payments argument is the reddest and smelliest herring in the entire weaponry of businessmen seeking special treatment in antitrust matters. Even Ramsden's report described the possibility only as "some indirect . . . effect." (The argument is now being trotted out again by Flanigan in the cause of legislation, now being pushed by the Wall Street wing of the Administration, that would exempt export cartels generally from antitrust surveillance.)

Tired Trustbuster

As an antitrust lawyer, McLaren must have known well that even if somehow troubled by one or more of these arguments, he could not accept them without violating every tenet of antitrust policy. The U.S. economy is not a planned economy; it is based on the assumption of markets working freely and well enough without extensive government regulation and controls. That is the central policy and objective of the antitrust laws and their administration. The Supreme Court has made it clear that the antitrust rules presume that neither the courts nor the prosecutor shall sit in continuing surveillance over justifications for every price decision in every industry. Neither does Congress presume to make the Justice Department the ultimate arbiter of issues of domestic and international economic policy. The courts must ultimately define the content of the law on the books, subject to supervening legislative change. If Congress decides to move from a relatively free market economy toward a more highly planned system, and finds the antitrust laws inappropriate or inconsistent with that approach, legislative redress may of course be undertaken. Until that day, any Attorney General, or Deputy, or Assistant, who becomes convinced by the economic theories of John Kenneth Galbraith, or Herbert Spencer, or

Joseph Schumpeter, or Karl Marx, or Richard Ramsden, in deciding about the impact of antitrust proceedings on balance of payments, stock-market activity, unemployment, or patterns of sunspots, should be persuaded to resign forthwith. Exotic economic philosophies are not part of the job description.

If we assume that McLaren's real reasons for deciding the ITT questions were not those he has publicly provided, it does not follow that he was responding to specific knowledge of a "deal," nor even to overt pressures. No one has suggested the former, or is likely to. His antagonist response to decisions by Kleindienst that he regarded as improper was demonstrated at the outset of his campaign against conglomerates—in the ITT-Canteen suit.

Thus it seems quite conceivable that, when the signals of interest in high places concerning the ITT settlement began to appear—Kleindienst's repeated intercession, the indication of White House interest through Flanigan, the communication from ITT's Walsh (also, one almost hesitates to note, chairman of the American Bar Association committee on judicial selection)—McLaren may simply have felt too worn down in the apparently endless battle to keep the antitrust machinery functioning in such highly politicized surroundings. Rather than fight yet another round, possibly exhausting completely his presumably already depleted supply of goodwill, and perhaps placing in jeopardy the budgetary well-being of the Antitrust Division and its career staff, he may have persuaded himself that the Ramsden and Treasury "reports" were more credible and relevant than they would have appeared to another observer. That he was, indeed, understandably disillusioned and weary of battle at this stage is borne out by his retirement six months later to accept a hurried appointment to a federal district court judgeship.

The underlying problem is much deeper than the internal politics of the Justice Department, and it is one that should be squarely and promptly faced. During and since World War II there has been growth at an exponential rate of the variety and importance of federal government decisions that vitally affect the profitability of businesses, the power of labor unions, the effectiveness of multifarious organized special-interest groups. Their response has been to establish in Washington innumerable special lobbying and favor-seeking organizations. Hundreds, perhaps thousands, of special interest groups and large corporations, including ITT, maintain offices in Washington—in ITT's case with an extravagant annual budget. Enormous sums are spent to win lobbyists solid favor and influence with legislators and members of the Administration, perhaps from the White House down. Their presence and influence may have become so pervasive that for many public officials—including administrative and law-enforcement agencies and the courts—it has become virtually impossible to make, and then make stick, a decision in the public interest that runs counter to the lobbyists' special interests.

The worst offender and quickest to jump to the bidding of special interests in the antitrust area has unfortunately been Congress. In recent years, after adverse Supreme Court decisions, the banking lobby has twice demanded, and promptly got, special legislation seeking to exempt bank mergers from usual antitrust standards. After successful Antitrust Division proceedings against unnecessarily anticompetitive joint advertising agreements between newspapers, the publishers' association demanded virtually complete exemption from the merger laws, and got legislation providing most of what it wanted. The patent bar has fought hard, and is still hopeful that it will eventually get, special-interest legislation that would greatly weaken antitrust surveillance over restrictive patent licensing. Among special-interest bills currently moving ahead in Congress is one to reverse the results of twelve years of antitrust proceedings, and four Supreme Court decisions, against El Paso Natural Gas Company's anticompetitive acquisition of its major potential competitor in supplying natural gas to California. Another, sponsored by Flanigan and supported by export trade interests, would permit exporters to form cartels, largely exempt from public-interest antitrust surveillance.

With much of the Administration, and especially the Department of Justice, more aggressively politicized than, perhaps, ever before in history, and with richer lobbyists than ever before playing for higher stakes, the public interest may be a lost cause. At any rate, the top-priority item on the agenda of all who are concerned about the integrity of government should be how to reverse the trend of which the ITT settlement is only a small evidence.

THE GRASSING OF AMERICA

Barnard Collier

Dear Mr. and Mrs. Stroup:

It's good to be able to tell you that your son, Keith, is okay. He said you have been a little worried about the kind of life he's fallen into in Washington and about whether he might get arrested and perhaps hurt his

Source: *Saturday Review* (July 29, 1972), Vol. 55, pp. 12–14. Copyright © 1972 by Saturday Review, Inc. First appeared in *Saturday Review of the Society,* July 29, 1972. Used with permission.

law career and his future. Don't worry. He's safe; he's making $18,000 a year for running a very legal Establishment (his word) lobby. Lobbying for any thing or cause is legal in Washington as long as you register, and few people here see anything very strange about it when Keith says, "I'm the lobbyist for marijuana."

He retains a great respect for his roots. It sometimes sounds as if he hates the Midwest, but I suspect that underneath he doesn't. He'll say things like, "Oh, Lord, I didn't think anybody around here even knew where southern Illinois was," and "I went through all that middle-class, midwestern stuff in high school and college." But don't let that embarrass you; it doesn't bother anybody here, where it's fashionable to say belittling things about rural parts of the country. That kind of cosmopolitan conversation tends to diminish with age, and Keith is still just twenty-eight.

Keith looks good. His hair was a little long when I saw him, about down to his shoulders, but he cut it for the Democratic Convention in Miami Beach. He operated a booth where he passed out literature and "educated" the delegates and the press about the marijuana laws and why they ought to be abolished on the federal level. Keith didn't get a crew cut, but he must have been very presentable in a necktie, suit, and lawyerish eyeglasses.

If Miami Beach had turned into a Chicago, you can be sure Keith would have had no part in it. He's not that kind of man, as I'm sure you know. Marijuana has not addled his brains. He says, "The freaks who say that marijuana is a peace drug and that everybody should turn on to save the world embarrass me intellectually. Marijuana doesn't do anything to change my policy outlook." His policy outlook, Keith said, is much the same as that of most people back in Mount Vernon, Illinois, and you might get yourself prepared to welcome him back home in not too many years.

I'd say he'll need five or so more years of seasoning in Washington; let him get to know more contacts in the big government agencies and in the Congress; perhaps he will even take a marijuana case up to the Supreme Court, and with luck he'll win it. Then he'll be ready to come home with a solid reputation behind him: staff aide to Senator Everett Dirksen; staff counsel of the National Commission on Product Safety; lobbyist for the American Pharmaceutical Association; graduate of Georgetown Law School; married; children.

He said, "I'll tell you what I wanted back when I was taking political science at the University of Illinois. I wanted to come to Washington, get some polish, and go back home to be a politician. I like Washington. I own a nice house near Dupont Circle, which is a good neighborhood, and my wife works with me here at the office. I've had some good offers back home, and so far I've turned them down."

Keith told me, Mrs. Stroup, that you said he's going about this thing in a good way. You were right. If ever there was a clever and effective means of going about lobbying for marijuana, Keith has found it.

His offices are located on the first floor of a townhouse on Twenty-second Street, a good address. No sign on the door says what's inside. You wouldn't be hesitant about walking in. If you know you are entering the offices of the marijuana lobby, you feel as though the police are taking your picture going in and out. But Keith's headquarters look like any ordinary young lawyer's office.

There are big posters on the wall that show a police billy club and a big, green sprig of marijuana. In big, black letters on top, one poster says: PENALTY FOR POSSESSION OF MARIJUANA (FIRST OFFENSE). Underneath this, there's a list of the fines and jail terms for each state. In Texas, for example, the sentence is two years to life for simple possession. Texas is the worst. Keith says there are 691 people in jail in Texas for marijuana possession, with an average sentence of nine years. The poster is tremendously scary to anyone who might smoke marijuana, and it won't encourage anyone in his right mind to smoke it who hasn't already.

Keith makes it perfectly clear to nonsmokers of marijuana that he is not a marijuana salesman. His job is to lobby for "the people, the consumers, who are the ones that buy and use marijuana." He says he is in the Ralph Nader tradition of public interest law (students at Georgetown Law School get academic credit for working for him on marijuana-related cases), and he looks out for the interest of the approximately twenty-four million unseen Americans who, according to conservative estimates, are marijuana consumers. As Nader does for automobiles, Keith advocates quality control for marijuana so that unscrupulous growers, wholesalers, and dealers do not fleece the buying public. "Marijuana quality runs from .05 per cent of the active ingredient, tetrahydrocannabinol, in domestic grass to as high as 7 per cent in marijuana imported from Vietnam," he said. "Also, some of the marijuana is laced with adulterants such as heroin, LSD, strychnine— which is a deadly poison but gives a high—catnip, and even animal tranquilizers." He said some marijuana he once smoked must have contained an animal tranquilizer because he got so relaxed on it that he could hardly hold his head up. He is against this kind of consumer deception.

Keith says the reason he smokes marijuana is for recreation, against the law or not. He says the law is wrong, not him, and as a good lawyer he intends to prove it in court if necessary.

He has no intention of getting arrested for smoking marijuana, or for anything else, if he can help it. Keith said: "Smoking marijuana should be thought of as we think of alcohol. It's a recreational drug, a drug of choice. It's what I use weekends instead of alcohol, which kills your brain cells." When Keith smokes, he does it in private places where no policeman would have probable cause to break in and arrest him. "I've thought about it very carefully," Keith said. "I'm sure it wouldn't be considered probable cause by a judge just because I say I *have* smoked marijuana. The police would have to weigh the good it would do our cause if I am illegally arrested, against the small harm it would do to me personally. If they are reasonable men, and they are, they will decide not to arrest me."

Back to Keith's office. He has a secretary; his diplomas are on the wall. He has shelves of serious books pro and con marijuana, so people can get both sides of the story. He has some law books mixed in with the marijuana books so that potential clients don't forget he is a practicing lawyer. His desk is neat (by most standards); there is a photograph of President Kennedy and his brother Robert on the wall. Pinned to a big bulletin board is a collection of marijuana memorabilia. I say memorabilia because Keith says those posters and arm patches and stickers will be worth something someday. As you know, old political buttons and stickers are becoming increasingly valuable at antique fairs.

The way Keith goes about his lobbying job is to use "moral force" against the legislators to get anti-marijuana laws repealed. He explained that there isn't enough money around from legitimate sources to do a really first-class job of lobbying for practically anything, much less something as unpopular as marijuana. About 85 per cent of the American people have never smoked marijuana, Keith says. "Those are the people we have to educate. We assume that people who have smoked marijuana are on our side, even if they are not active."

Most of the money for Keith's work comes from the Playboy Foundation, which is associated with *Playboy* magazine's founder, Hugh Hefner, who wants the use of marijuana made a matter of personal choice, like sexual intercourse. Two other lawyers run offices in New York City and Phoenix, Arizona, under the lobby's name, NORML, for National Organization for the Reform of Marijuana Laws. Playboy can expect to get back a portion of its investment in NORML, because it sells the marijuana posters I described before and other marijuana-oriented materials. Keith says NORML is getting "more into the merchandising end of the business" itself. At present NORML sells such items as marijuana bumper stickers and stamps (they look like Easter seals) for letters. He also had some very nice-looking marijuana-leaf golden lapel pins in the office. They are rather elegant and look like they'll sell. Keith seems to have a good head for business.

One of his most serious lobbying problems, and one of the reasons Keith says he must sell marijuana souvenirs to raise money, is that the $100,000 a year from the Playboy Foundation, plus the $5 or $7 annual dues for subscribers to the NORML publications (about 6,000 of them, Keith says), is not enough to take senators, congressmen, assemblymen, and other government people out to lunch and dinner.

Government people like to be wined and dined. If they aren't, they think a lobby is poor and weak. By most Washington lobbying standards NORML is poor and weak, so Keith must rely heavily on "moral" and "intellectual" persuasion. This is going after flies with vinegar, and Keith knows it. But he states his position very clearly: "I am on the morally defensible side of the issue. Some issues have a right and wrong side. This issue has a wrong side, and I am opposed to it. I'm not into becoming a martyr. No. Our power is of a strange variety but a real one. People who are on the right side of such issues will know what I mean."

The important legal moves Keith is making center around the recent filing of an administrative action against the Bureau of Narcotics to have marijuana removed from the most dangerous drugs list and moved down to a Number Five (Roman numeral V) category along with such drugs as cough medicines. This would be just a step short of taking marijuana away from federal control altogether, which Keith wants but admits may be unrealistic to talk about in the near future. Complete decontrol of marijuana on a federal level would leave the matter to the individual states. Keith says that in many states all penalties for the private use of marijuana might be abolished by referendum "after the people are educated."

If and when the federal government stops bothering about marijuana, Keith feels that there must be state laws that would inhibit (he knows that, as with liquor, prohibition is impossible) adolescents from obtaining it too openly or freely. I asked him why he felt adolescents should not be permitted to smoke marijuana if it does not harm adults, and he said: "Marijuana may seem like a lot of fun to kids, but maybe they'll start to think that fun is all there is."

Keith takes a very balanced and controlled view of everything, and the work he puts out is worthy of the Playboy Foundation's confidence in his legal and business sense. His newsletter, called *The Leaflet,* is not a mimeographed underground handout. Not only is it printed on excellent heavy paper, it is nicer looking than most cigarette company literature, and it's a lot more interesting and better written. *The Leaflet,* which is done by professionals, lets its subscribers and those on its mailing list know every two months about the latest marijuana developments. It also contains a coupon for marijuana seals and bumper stickers that reads, "Rush me . . . zonko bumper stickers (2 for $1)."

Within the next month or so Keith is planning to hold "The People's Pot Conference" at a site somewhere near Washington. He has had a lot of trouble getting property owners to rent him space. "They take one look at our name, and they say, 'Go away, we're not interested.' But we'll get a place and hold a serious program about how we can really repeal the marijuana laws."

Meanwhile, Keith makes speaking engagements at meetings of Jaycees and similar organizations. He appears in a suit jacket and necktie and gets a good reception. A lot of people, like the Jaycees, are eager to know about marijuana, and they don't mind hearing about it from Keith, who looks like he knows what he is talking about, is no radical, and speaks maturely and well. There is no need to worry about Keith.

Yours truly,
Barnard Collier

P.S. NORML's letterhead, which you may have seen, is perfect. Keith may answer the telephone, "Normal, this is Keith speaking," but the letterhead reads: "R. Keith Stroup, Esq."

$100,000 GIFT TO NIXON CAMPAIGN IS TRACED TO TEXAS CORPORATION

Bob Woodward and Carl Bernstein

The FBI has established that $100,000 given to President Nixon's campaign—a donation that surfaced during the Watergate investigation—originally came from a corporate bank account in Houston.

Campaign contributions by corporations are illegal. FBI sources said this week that this contribution was so well disguised that it is virtually impossible to prove wrongdoing.

The $100,000 came from the First City National Bank account of the Gulf Resources and Chemical Corp. on April 3.

At the time, Gulf Resources' major subsidiary, an Idaho mining operation, was under pressure by the Federal Environmental Protection Agency to correct extensive water and air pollution problems. Since then the pressure has diminished.

The $100,000 contribution came to light when it was learned that $89,000 of it, in the form of four Mexican cashier's checks, was deposited in the bank account of Bernard L. Barker, one of the five men seized in the Watergate raid on the Democrats' headquarters June 17.

The money has been traced from Gulf Resources to the Nixon re-election committee in a series of four complicated steps. Government law enforcement sources, in describing the procedure, said it is similar to that used by organized crime leaders to conceal secret payments.

Maurice H. Stans, the finance chairman of the Nixon re-election campaign, personally approved the secret transfer of the funds through Mexico,

Source: *The Washington Post* (October 6, 1972), pp. A-1, A-36. © The Washington Post. Reprinted by permission.

according to a confidential report prepared by the House Banking and Currency Committee staff last month.

"The entire transaction involves the payment of an apparently inflated fee to a Mexican lawyer through the company's subsidiary—which has been out of business for two years. We'll never figure it out and it's the hardest kind of case to prove," one law enforcement official said.

Richard Haynes, attorney for Gulf Resources, said all the transactions involving the $100,000 were perfectly proper and include no illegal activity.

Haynes confirmed the findings of the FBI, in which the money reportedly moved in these steps:

1. Gulf Resources, whose president, Robert H. Allen, is the chief Nixon fund-raiser in Texas, transferred $100,000 on April 3 from its corporate account to its subsidary in Mexico called Compania de Azufre Veracruz, S.A. (CAVSA), a sulfur company.

(CAVSA discontinued operations in December, 1969, and Gulf Resources took a $12,688,000 tax write off that year because the business became inactive according to records at the Securities and Exchange Commission. The subsidiary, however, maintains administrative personnel in Mexico City for financial transactions.)

2. CAVSA then turned the $100,000 over to Manuel Ogarrio Daguerre, a Mexico City attorney, saying it was payment for legal services.

FBI sources said they strongly suspect the legal fee was inflated. Haynes, the Gulf Resources attorney, did not deny this, but noted that it would be "nearly impossible to penetrate" because the reason for such fees is protected by the confidentiality of the attorney-client relationship.

3. Ogarrio, or a representative, then converted $89,000 of this money to four cashier's checks and $11,000 to cash. The $100,000 was then sent back to Texas and became part of $700,000 in Nixon contributions that were rushed to Washington in an oil executive's suitcase on April 5, just two days before a stricter campaign contribution disclosure law took effect.

4. Donations by foreign nationals are illegal. Ogarrio—at least on paper—made loans amounting to $100,000 to several Texans. These persons, the names of whom have not been publicly revealed, then became the contributors to the Nixon committee.

Haynes, the Gulf Resources lawyer, said as a result of these transactions the $100,000 was "not a corporate contribution or one from a Mexican national."

He said the money was not a campaign contribution when it reached Ogarrio. "Then if it is his dough, he can do anything with it," Haynes said.

Government sources said the four Mexican cashier's checks were later deposited in the bank account of Barker, one of the Watergate suspects, to avoid the federal gift tax. On $89,000, the gift tax would be about $6,300, according to an Internal Revenue Service spokesman.

"It had nothing to do with the financing of Watergate," one knowledgeable Republican source said. He said the checks were converted to cash so the $89,000 could be divided into separate contributions of $3,000 or less, the maximum that can be given free of gift tax.

The government sources said that G. Gordon Liddy, at the time the finance counsel to the Nixon committee, had Barker cash the checks so they could never be traced as campaign contributions by the IRS.

Barker, a Miami real estate agent with extensive CIA contacts, and Liddy, a former White House aide and FBI agent, are two of the seven men who were indicted Sept. 15 in the Watergate bugging incident.

In the weeks before the $100,000 transfer of funds from Gulf Resources, environmental problems over air and water pollution were mounting for the company's chief subsidiary, the Bunker Hill Co.

On March 29, five days before the transfer began, EPA informed Bunker Hill that it would impose stiffer air pollution control standards on the company's lead and zinc mining operation in Kellogg, Idaho.

Bunker Hill had $86 million in sales last year. Ray Chapman, director of public relations for the firm, said last week that "the survival of the company could be determined by the decision on air pollution standards."

Bunker Hill's position with the EPA has improved considerably since the transfer of funds from Gulf Resources to Mexico.

First, no stiffer air pollution standards have yet been imposed.

Second, the EPA has recently reversed an earlier decision and will not sue Bunker Hill on water pollution, according to the EPA regional general counsel.

On April 18, when a suit was still threatened, Bunker Hill signed a consent agreement with Idaho, adopting the state's water pollution control standards.

At least one EPA official, Leonard A. Miller, director of enforcement in the Northwestern states region, criticized the Idaho standards, calling them insufficient.

Ted Rogowski, general counsel for EPA in the region, said EPA officials were unaware of the Bunker Hill-Idaho agreement when it was made. "Goddamn, what's going on!" Rogowski said was the general reaction when EPA representatives learned of the agreement.

Nevertheless, Rogowski said, EPA will not press for stronger water standards. "Within two weeks we'll agree . . . we're on the verge of agreement for quite the same [water standards] as the state," he told a reporter last week.

Asked why EPA seemed satisfied with the relaxed standards, Rogowski said: "They are a good company. They are spending more money, millions of dollars to correct the problems."

Miller, head of the enforcement division of EPA said that Bunker Hill "is one of the most significant water polluters in the area," discharging an average of 93 per cent of all zinc and lead found in the Coeur d'Alene River.

This makes the river "very, very, very toxic," killing all the fish in it and bringing the levels of zinc in the river to the point where the water becomes unsafe to drink, according to Miller. He said Bunker Hill discharges 12,000 pounds of zinc in the river each day.

The U.S. Attorney for Idaho, Sidney E. Smith, was contacted last week by telephone to inquire why the proposed water pollution suit against Bunker Hill was dropped. Smith said he would check his file and call back. He never did, and four separate attempts to reach him again were unsuccessful.

The stiffer air pollution control standards proposed on March 29 have not been imposed on Bunker Hill.

Chapter 4
SUGGESTED TOPICS FOR CLASS DISCUSSION

1. Articles in this chapter have discussed two kinds of corporate bigness that the government has sought to regulate: (a) the vertically and horizontally integrated monopoly exemplified by AT&T and (b) the newer type of "conglomerate" such as ITT. What kind of threat does the first pose? What problems are raised by the second? What factors have contributed to the growth of conglomerates? Should the federal government play a more aggressive role in fostering economic decentralization?
2. ITT is also a multinational corporation. What conflicts of interest might be created by the operation of such corporations? What are some of the problems faced by national governments in trying to regulate the economic activity of large multinational corporations?
3. In the article on AT&T, the author suggests that Bell Telephone might be nationalized to correct certain abuses. What kinds of change might this produce? How might the interests and behavior of a nationalized corporation differ from those of a federally regulated private firm?
4. Business, labor, and professional organizations often devote much effort to lobbying. What happens to the broader public interest as a consequence of special interest lobbying?
5. Citizens' lobbies, such as Common Cause, seek to represent the general public. How representative are such groups? How do they determine the "public interest"? How does it happen that Common Cause has chosen to focus on electoral reform while the groups taking their cues from Ralph Nader concentrate on corporate reform?
6. The federal government guides economic activity by various techniques such as fiscal policy, monetary policy, regulation of exports, imports, and payments, and corporate regulation. Should it seek to do more, or less? Should it try to expand its economic planning, or to curtail it? Why?

Chapter 5

Politics and the Media

One can rarely know the principal events of his time directly. As a rule he can know the events only as they are transmitted to him via the media. The media provide the means by which information and frequently interpretation are communicated to members of the public. Therefore, the media cannot escape having a great influence on American politics. The only question, therefore, is what kind of an impact should the media have, and the answers will vary. For example, an Administration in power is likely to charge that the reporting of the media is biased. Spokesmen of the media, on the other hand, will point out that the Administration always wants to look good and therefore tries in various ways to use the media to project a favorable image. It is part of the responsibility of the media, they would argue, to play the role of critic and not be seduced or pressured into becoming a part of the White House's public relations program.

Television, though the newest of the media, may have a greater impact on politics than any other form, and it brings with it a special set of problems and characteristics. For many candidates, television has become the preferred way of campaigning, and this places heavy emphasis on appearance and on having a "television personality." Is there more emphasis than is desirable? Television reporting tends to gravitate toward action and the dramatic. Is there more action and drama than is desirable? The cases in this chapter explore these and other issues.

A WHITE HOUSE AIDE ON CONTROL OF THE PRESS[1]

Herbert G. Klein

A recent Supreme Court decision compelling newsmen to divulge information from confidential sources to grand juries has renewed interest in the free press/fair trial controversy.

On the one side is the traditional right of the press to gather and publish news and opinion as it sees fit. On the other is the equally traditional right of the judicial system to obtain any and all evidence needed in carrying out thorough criminal or civil proceedings.

While current law clearly supports the government's position, we must not forget the maxim that "hard cases make bad law." As you know, there are some situations where the public interest is better served by negotiations and self-restraint than by judicial mandate, and where it is in the interests of all concerned to avoid a confrontation and an imposed settlement.

The Department of Justice has historically been cautious in subpoenaing the press. This caution was reflected by former Attorney General John N. Mitchell in February, 1970, when he said he regretted "any implication" that the federal government "is interfering in the traditional freedom and independence of the press." Mr. Mitchell said his policy was to negotiate with the press prior to the issuance of subpoenas, in an effort to maintain a balance with respect to free press/fair trial interests. In August, 1970, the Attorney General issued the first set of departmental guidelines for use by Justice Department attorneys in requesting courts to subpoena the media. The guidelines were met with approval from both the bar and the journalistic societies.

Source: *The Washington Post* (September 21, 1972). © The Washington Post. Reprinted by permission.

[1] Excerpts of remarks by Herbert G. Klein before the Hastings School of the Law, San Francisco. Mr. Klein is director of the Office of Communications for the Executive Branch at the White House.

Attorney General Richard G. Kleindienst has since said that these guidelines, which state that the Department of Justice "does not consider the press an investigative arm of the government" and which require specific approval by the attorney general before a subpoena is issued to a member of the press, "have been successful in resolving the problem" of media concern. He has pledged to continue to follow the guidelines.

The fundamental purpose of the First Amendment is to enlighten the public. It would seem to follow that if the public has the right to receive information, the press should have the right to disseminate information. But the Supreme Court has never actually recognized the newsman's right to gather news. In the past, decisions by the Court dealt only with the newsman's right to *publish* news. In 1935, the right to gather news was recognized by a Federal Court of Appeals, but the decision was later reversed by the Supreme Court, on grounds other than the First Amendment. Therefore, while the Supreme Court has had dozens of cases involving freedom of expression, it had never before decided a case directly on the question of press subpoenas.

You can appreciate the uproar that took place earlier this year when the Supreme Court made its 5-to-4 decision, holding that the First Amendment does not shield a reporter automatically from having to disclose information or sources to a grand jury. Newsmen feared that their confidential sources would hesitate to offer information if they knew there was danger of losing their anonymity. Editors claimed that broad subpoenas would impose heavy administrative requirements on their news departments. Cameramen and reporters said they felt they would be viewed as government agents and subjected to harassment when covering certain public events.

In an effort to counteract these repercussions and continue to protect the confidentiality of their sources and information, five major news organizations joined together to support a proposal entitled the "Free Flow of Information Act." This Joint Media Committee, as it is called, is comprised of the American Society of Newspaper Editors; the Associated Press Managing Editors Association; National Press Photographers Association; Radio-Television News Directors Association; and Sigma Delta Chi, professional journalistic society.

. . . Their proposal is intended to provide broad but not unlimited protection to all who gather information for publication or broadcast. It is similar, but not identical, to nearly two dozen newsmen's "shield" bills introduced in the 92nd Congress. It states that those who gather such information "shall not be required" to disclose their information or its source to any official federal body.

The proposal, for which the Joint Media Committee began immediately to seek congressional support, further provides that a federal district court may remove the protective "shield" if it finds "clear and convincing evidence" that:

- The writer or broadcaster probably has information relevant to a specific law violation;
- there are no other means of obtaining the necessary information, and
- there is a "compelling and overriding national interest" in making the information available to the investigative body.

Such determinations by a federal district court could be appealed through the federal court system.

Eighteen states have already adopted similar "shield" laws providing newsmen with varying degrees of immunity from state or local investigative bodies. I would like to go on record as favoring the shield laws, but I believe there is a real question as to whether the timing is correct to gain passage of an adequate law by the Congress. . . . I would only point out that Congress came within an eyelash of supporting Congressman Staggers' effort to cite for contempt the President of CBS for his refusal to release film out-takes. I oppose further regulation of the media.

I would urge journalistic societies to proceed as rapidly as possible with additional state shield laws in order to provide the media with necessary protection while Congressional action is under study.

If a random group of lawyers had been asked a couple of years ago to define the legal rights of newsmen in refusing to testify under subpoena, to protect their sources, the answer from most probably would have been "none." But the highly visual cases of Earl Caldwell of the *New York Times,* Paul M. Branzburg of the *Louisville Courier-Journal,* and Paul Pappas of WTEV-TV in New Bedford, Massachusetts, have gone a long way in changing this.

Mr. Caldwell and Mr. Pappas were called to testify about black conspirators. Mr. Caldwell was covering the Black Panther party in the San Francisco area. The grand jury called him in to investigate possible threats against the President and the violent overthrow of the government. Mr. Caldwell refused to comply with the subpoena.

Mr. Pappas was allowed to spend a night in Black Panther headquarters in New Bedford during some racial uprisings in 1970. It was agreed that if there were a raid, he would report on police methods; but if there were no raid, he would write nothing. As it turned out, no raid took place and he wrote no report. Later, he was subpoenaed to give information about the Panthers. He refused and was held in contempt.

Mr. Branzburg was subpoenaed after writing articles dealing with the marijuana trade. Mr. Branzburg would not enter the grand jury room, claiming that the First Amendment shielded him from making testimony. The Supreme Court of Kentucky ruled against him and he appealed to the U.S. Supreme Court.

These incidents illustrate two things: that the government has usually issued subpoenas to the press to obtain information about political conspirators, and that the information being subpoenaed usually went well beyond the *identity* of a confidential source. Both elements are important, but the second is having more impact because it is broadening the area of conflict between the government and press. In so doing, it is making obsolete most of the legislation that has been passed in prior years dealing with this relationship.

In all of these considerations, we must make certain we protect the right to the individual and of the media to dissent in a lawful way.

A traditional part of the American system is a press that is free to criticize. However, I should add that, too often, the press fails to recognize that officials of the government also have the right to be critical of the press. We in this Administration will continue to exercise that right—on a specific basis, not a blanket basis—and we expect that the press will do the same.

In a general way, I think we should be looking at what measures are necessary to protect the notes of reporters and the out-takes of film. We should also continue to recognize that newsmen have duties *as citizens*. In this day and age, there is constant danger of over-regulation, particularly as it refers to the broadcast industry. With the introduction of cable and other innovations, which have widened the broadcast spectrum, I believe the time has come to consider *less* regulation, not more.

In the Associated Press case, the Supreme Court said, ". . . a free press is the condition of a free society." I think we can safely say that we have more freedom of speech and freedom of press in this country than has any other country of the world. The United States has 6,000 radio stations, 650 television stations, 1,800 daily newspapers, the theater, motion pictures, books, magazines, periodicals, and an underground press. Indeed, it is the very *strength* of this media that is helping to establish the rights on subpoena power.

THE SAM ERVIN SHOW

Laurence Leamer

Senator Sam Ervin, Jr., always gets good and wound up talking about the dangers that computers pose to personal liberty, and so, last May, he'd been glad enough to come down to Atlantic City to address the farewell luncheon of the Joint Computer Conference. He inclines to think of computer technicians as men employed at dark sorceries, arranging data on coded tapes and thus threatening ordinary citizens with a web of secret information. Mindful of the insidious technology available to the members of his audience, the Senator gave them one of his best speeches. He offered Biblical quotations and some of his best down-home North Carolina stories, but none of it took too well. The Senator is not a sophisticated raconteur, and anyway, everybody was in a hurry to leave.

No one really should have expected the computer experts to take to Ervin, for the North Carolina Senator is just too confounded old-fashioned. He is a lover of good food, of bourbon and ginger, and hard work; and now, in his seventy-fifth year, the food and liquor, if not the work, show in his face. He has jowls deep as a goiter, a nose that glows red on color television, age lines running down the sides of his nose and along his chin much as they do on a ventriloquist's dummy, heavy eyebrows that angle almost rakishly down toward his nose, and a thick mane of white hair that appears not the absence of color but its quintessence. In a word, his face is a perfect caricature of the old-time Southern Senator, and when cartoonists draw his face, often they will soften his features, not exaggerate them.

Driving back to Washington in a spring drizzle with three of his subcommittee aids, Senator Ervin wasn't worrying about the reception the computer experts had accorded him. He was rambling on with Rufus Edmisten, a North Carolinian and a pretty decent yarn-teller himself, reminiscing about some old boy they had known back in the mountains. Then, out of the blue, Ervin turned to Lawrence Baskir, chief counsel and staff director of the Constitutional Rights Subcommittee: "You know, Larry, I think we better have hearings on the First Amendment and freedom of the press. Why, I think we should come right out and say that television should be as free as newspapers. If it's not a question of freedom of the press, then it's a question of freedom of speech."

Thus the provenience of the hearings held last November by Ervin's Constitutional Rights Subcommittee, hearings that were later scheduled to

Source: *Harper's Magazine* (March 1972), pp. 80–86. Copyright © 1972 by Laurence Leamer. First published in *Harper's Magazine*. Reprinted by permission of The Sterling Lord Agency, Inc.

resume in February. The Senator didn't need to explain anything to Baskir. The staff members are very much *his* people, and Ervin knew they would set up a free-press hearing that would do him proud and conform to *his* vision of what freedom of the press is all about.

Learning of Liberty

Sam Ervin's notion of liberty has evolved from his life in Morganton, North Carolina (population 10,000). Morganton sits on the western edge of the Piedmont Plateau. It's still the kind of place where a man can go up to his neighbor and speak his mind; a man can even start his own newspaper if he pleases, and if he wants to write that the moon is made of blue cheese, that's fine too, and anyone who agrees with him can buy the paper.

As a boy Sam Ervin was addicted to learning and toy soldiers, his face full of twitches, his arms full of books. His father taught him that the worst threat to liberty comes from government, and he helped to instill in the boy a sense of independence and individuality as fierce as his own, a sense that tangled with his son's shyness and reserve, and that he wore camouflaged, cloaked in the mores and language of the town.

When he returned to Morganton in 1922, Harvard law degree in hand, Ervin still had those simple country ways. He still had eyebrows that jittered up and down when he got nervous, and an occasional stutter, and in court he depended on his wits and his stories, and not on any sort of thundering oratory.

In those years when Sinclair Lewis was writing of Babbitt and Main Street, Ervin was a town booster, a patriot, a joiner, commander of the local National Guard unit, a member of the Masons, the Knights of Pythias, the Junior Order, the Sons of the American Revolution, the Society of the Cincinnati. His was a patriotism and a boosterism that so far transcended the puerile, self-serving ideals of the emerging industrial and commercial order that they scarcely should be spoken of in the same language. He could almost always be found with a book in his hand, learning of his country, his county, or his people. He traced his people back to their Scotch-Irish origins and their arrival in the colonies in 1732, and he traced back the genealogies of his uncles, aunts, even distant relatives—all taproots to his past. He was not searching out nobles, notables, the making of a family crest, but a deepening of his sense of the uniqueness and richness of the American experience.

Ervin's vision of a free press is both simple and profound; simple because his ideas do not venture far from the world of the Founding Fathers and the early printing presses, profound because no matter how the media might defame his beliefs, his region, his very being, his struggle to maintain a free press continues with unabated zeal.

His particular interest in the present hearings was also encouraged by Walter Cronkite, who, at about the same time the Senator spoke to the computer technicians, came to the Old Senate Office Building to expound the troubles of television news broadcasting. It was natural that Cronkite should come to Ervin, for the Senator and his staff already had conducted hearings on the threats to freedom implied by computers, government dossiers, and the Army's surveillance of civilians.

What Cronkite came to tell Ervin the Senator already believed: television should be as free as possible from governmental control. In his earlier hearings, as in almost every speech, the Senator had described the modern battle between freedom and slavery as one being fought in a thousand government offices—with newfangled legislation, bureaucratic initiatives, and computer printouts as the weapons of tyranny, and the Constitution as the last, best, and only defense of liberty.

In the Pentagon Papers case, for the first time in the history of the Republic, the government had sought, prior to publication, to restrain a newspaper from printing critical documents. Police were posing as newsmen, and the courts themselves had been subpoenaing the notes of professional journalists. Television had endured similar harassments.

A Jeffersonian liberal to the very marrow of his bones, Ervin *knew* that as long as government kept even one small finger on freedom of the press, the day might well come when government would reach out and crush that freedom in its fist. The Senator is given to hyperbole, and he believes the nation to be in the midst of a grave Constitutional crisis. To Ervin the Constitution is the most precious of American possessions, and he speaks of it with language and emotion that are rarely heard these days even on the Fourth of July.[1]

Cronkite's lament thus was heard by a man who believed that television had to be a free marketplace for ideas as well as products. Liberal meddlers had already ended tobacco advertising on television. Since tobacco itself wasn't illegal, Ervin believed the action to be unconstitutional, and many legal scholars agreed with him. Then there was the fairness doctrine that said if you aired one side of an issue, you had to give somebody a chance to air the other side. One U.S. Court of Appeals had gone so far as to rule that consumer groups had to be given air time to run ads countering

---

[1] In this perspective, it is no irony that Sam Ervin, adamant defender of the First Amendment, is also the Senate's most brilliantly effective opponent of civil rights legislation. He takes as his dictum Justice Brandeis's statement that "the greatest dangers to liberty lurk in the insidious encroachment by men of zeal, well-meaning, but without understanding." In his tenacious defense of State's Rights, Ervin is the best that Southern conservatism has to offer; his tragedy is the tragedy of his age and his class and the ideas they lived by. His hometown has passed him by now; his grandson attends an integrated school; and the people there, black and white alike, are proud that the racial situation has worked out as well as it has.

commercials for high-powered autos and leaded gas. Now Women's Lib groups, ladies from Boston upset about children's television, New Leftists, kooks, pressure groups of all kinds were lining up to get on the air. Conservatives, for their part, were talking about laws to make sure television acted "responsibly." They were all good-minded people out to improve society, but Ervin knew they would end up destroying the very freedom they were tinkering with.

Lost Irony

When Bill Pursley, a dedicated young lawyer on the Constitutional Rights Subcommittee staff, began putting together a list of witnesses for the hearings, he took account of the Senator's opinions. The list of witnesses practically wrote itself. He couldn't have just one network president, although he felt one would be sufficient; he had to ask all three. It wouldn't be right to invite just Walter Cronkite, so he asked all the network anchormen. Then, let's see, there were the press associations, certain prominent Constitutional scholars, and by the time he'd gotten through there just wasn't that much time for anyone who might be critical of the networks.

With this remnant of time, Pursley had to be especially careful. Ervin was seeking to educate the Senate, and nothing could be worse than having some freaky radical jump up and down in front of the television cameras making the Senator out as the guardian of the underground press, the Daniel Ellsbergs, the Jerry Rubins of the world.

The hearings would be, then, as Lawrence Baskir, the chief counsel, said, "a version of freedom of the press cleaned up for the Establishment." They would proceed as ritual drama, in which, to a large extent, reality is predetermined. (There is nothing devious about this. Senator Ervin runs as fair and open a hearing as is found in Congress, but all hearings develop a kind of legal brief intended to convince Congress and the American people of whatever it is the committee wants to announce.)

Because the mass media accept the *reality* of Congressional hearings, in much the same way shopgirls once accepted the reality of professional wrestling, Ervin and his subcommittee entered into the customary collusion between press and government. The hearings that were to have raised the most profound questions of press freedom became a convenient pseudo-event that various commentators, journalists, and politicians could exploit for their own purposes.

The irony was lost on Ervin. He distrusts the modern theories of the press advanced by people such as Walter Lippmann and Nicholas Johnson, the outspoken commissioner of the Federal Communications Commission. Lippmann once observed that the television networks are so powerful that it is as if there were only three printing presses in the entire country, a situation the Founding Fathers hardly could have envisioned. The Johnson argument holds that the networks constitute an information oligarchy (60 per cent of the American people say they get most of their news from television) and that instead of a free marketplace of ideas the networks operate a closed shop, run by people to whom controversy is anathema because it interferes with the business of selling things. "You simply have to make a distinction between government controls designed to enhance freedom and to restrain it," Johnson has said in response to the Ervin argument against government intervention. "The antitrust laws are regulations that allow free enterprise to function. That's the kind of regulation we're talking about."

The law appears to support Johnson. In the 1934 Communications Act, Congress decided that the best way to apportion the public airwaves was to have the FCC make private licensees the temporary custodians of particular frequencies. The licensees would be free to make a profit, but in exchange the public interest had to be served.

It is the FCC's mandated duty, then, to see that this greatest of communications media does not become, or indeed remain, merely a conduit for selling soap and razor blades. "It is the right of the viewers and listeners, not the right of the broadcasters, which is paramount," wrote Justice Byron White in expressing the Supreme Court's opinion in the 1969 *Red Lion* decision, the most important and eloquent expression of this modern free-press theory. "It is the purpose of the First Amendment to preserve an uninhibited marketplace of ideas in which truth will ultimately prevail, rather than to countenance monopolization of that market, whether it be by the government itself or a private licensee. It is the right of the public to receive suitable access to social, political, esthetic, moral and other ideas and experiences which is crucial here. That right may not constitutionally be abridged either by Congress or by the FCC."

Fooling with Realities

Perhaps the most revealing encounter of the hearings took place on the third day. Several hundred spectators, half a dozen television cameras, and more than a score of reporters crowded the Senate caucus room. Senator Ervin hardly noticed. Innocent of the ways of the media, Ervin never realized that his staff had scheduled the committee witnesses to obtain maximum publicity. On the third day the witness would be Walter Cronkite.

In their approach to the television cameras, no two men could offer a more perverse contrast than Ervin and Cronkite. Ervin's deep, lumbering mind would have served him well over a century ago alongside a Webster or a Calhoun on a Senate floor where debate was charged with vitality and importance. He believes that the reality of a political event is conveyed by the vigor of the ideas and the truth of the arguments, not by the presence of the media. In this he is almost an anomaly, not only in the Senate but among Americans generally. Even so conservative a man as Robert Byrd of West Virginia will play to the television cameras, having several paragraphs of sharp, graphic prose stitched into his usually florid speeches, an addition that reads like a television commercial—which, in a sense, is what it is. Ervin will have none of that. With his long, rambling stories and broad forensic gestures, he is an unmitigated disaster on television.

He hurried into the caucus room just after 10:00 A.M., taking his place at the enormous felt-covered committee table that extended through half the length of the room. He was the only member of the subcommittee who bothered to appear on time. Sitting alone at the vast table, he began in a voice that seemed hesitant, an old man's voice. He welcomed Cronkite with his customary stateliness of phrase.

Cronkite read from a prepared statement, his text as lean and crisp as that of the *CBS Evening News*. A man thoroughly familiar with the medium of television, he did not raise his voice. He pumped his every sentence full of spontaneity and earnestness. He caressed the medium, playing with it: and the lights stayed on him, the cameras gorging themselves with good film.

"There are things we are not doing that we ought to do," Cronkite began. "There are challenges we have not fully met."

Cronkite had little choice but to read his testimony. The etiquette of Congressional hearings requires that witnesses provide neatly mimeographed statements to pass out to committee members, staff, and particularly the press. The Washington press corps feeds off press releases, news briefs, PR handouts, and prepared statements, and some reporters turn surly if a witness should dare speak extemporaneously.

Americans seem unable to give to another man's ideas and feelings anything that borders on complete attention, and practically everyone in the room was zooming in on Cronkite, then Ervin or a cameraman, a face somewhere, a moment or so scanning the room, back to Cronkite, fooling with the realities of the hearing much the way one fools with a home movie camera. Probably no one in the room was listening to the testimony with quite Ervin's intensity. Many Senators will sign letters, catch up on minor paper work, even daydream at hearings, but when Ervin is truly involved with a hearing he has an intensity of concentration that is awesome. They are no ritual to him. He learns from his witnesses; and in other hearings on other days, he has learned things that have led directly to legislation.

In the past few years, almost despite himself, Ervin has become something of a minor hero to the national press. The issues he speaks to are of such importance that he just can't be ignored. For the most part Ervin is pictured as an eighteenth-century libertarian, an absolutist on questions of civil liberties, and an avowed opponent of strong government. This is as much a caricature of Ervin as was the earlier view that he was simply a racist. Ervin's libertarianism is, in fact, both constrained and subtle; his struggle to preserve the meaning of the Constitution in a century rapidly approaching 1984 is both magnificent and rather limited.

It was perhaps inevitable that the media would stereotype Ervin anew since in recent years he has made his national reputation through his sub-committees, the committee system being in large measure a client of the media. In the past two decades, primarily by exploiting the media, Con-gressional committees have achieved unprecedented and often nonlegisla-tive power. They have come to serve as a surrogate press, but they are rarely neutral or benign in their interest.

By merely reporting what committees do—not what they don't do—the national media caricature the whole governmental process. Ervin's hearings on the Army's surveillance of civilians, for instance, appeared to be a frontal attack on the forces of illiberalism and the developing tyranny by dossier. That it was Sam Ervin, a hawk, a proponent of big military spending, a Southern conservative, in a word a patriot, who was heading the attack gave the hearings an unimpeachable credibility. In articles and editorials the press heralded their newfound champion of civil liberties, but the press did not know or care to know that Senator Ervin had placed clear limits on just what his subcommittee was to delve into.

"They Help Us Find Our Way"

How could we be improved by outside monitors without destroying the independence which is essential for a free press?" Cronkite asked. "Vice-President Agnew was right in asserting that a handful of us determine what will be on the evening news broadcast, or for that matter, which he didn't specify, in the *New York Times,* or the *Christian Science Monitor,* or the *Wall Street Journal,* or anywhere else. Indeed, it is a handful of us with this immense power, power that not one of us underestimates or takes lightly."

Cronkite is the great switchman shuttling the truth on and along his track at CBS as best he can, a noble, good, and modest man, as impartial and fair as can be, or so his testimony implied. He danced through the pages, in turn concerned, worried, earnest; and he called for an end to the fairness doctrine.

Ervin's questioning, a colloquy really, seemed to meander on all around the issues but, when transcribed and placed in the written record, it would serve to deepen Cronkite's and Ervin's view of press freedom. Ervin never even hinted that the scarcity of network news and information programs, which during the last fiscal year took up 2 per cent of total broadcast time, might have helped prevent a full and frank discussion of public issues. Nor did he ask questions that would have led one to realize that Cronkite had been less than candid. The CBS newscaster's performance had been masterly, but at times he had ridden that well-traveled border between deviousness and truth where public-relations men make their living. He said there was far more diversity in radio and television than in print; however, as Fred Friendly, once Cronkite's superior as president of CBS News and now the Ford Foundation's television consultant, suggested in testimony two weeks later, such assumptions were "suspect." Cronkite talked of "the wired cities of tomorrow" when with cable television we "will have an almost unlimited number of channels available," but he did not mention that the networks are fighting to cripple cable television.

While Ervin and Cronkite were having their discussion, Senators Roman L. Hruska of Nebraska; Hugh Scott of Pennsylvania, the Senate minority leader; and Ted Kennedy of Massachusetts came into the room and sat down at the committee table. At least one or two of the Senators may have been attracted to the hearings solely by the scent of the media. Scott, it turned out, had never attended a Constitutional Rights Subcommittee session before, and he would not appear again at these free-press hearings. Kennedy, who had spent something less than an hour at the previous day's session, would not return either. Hruska was making his first appearance also.[2]

After Hruska asked several questions, Ervin called on Senator Scott. Unfortunately, several of the television cameramen were changing film reels.

"Thank you, Mr. Chairman," Scott said. "I will try not to say anything important, Walter, until the cameras come back on."

"I was wondering how you fellows stand these lights," Cronkite said over the laughter of the audience.

"We can stand the lights in view of what they connote because they help us find our way," Scott said.

"Maybe we are like our old partner, a Reconstruction lawyer in North Carolina," said Senator Ervin. "A lawyer lost a point of law arguing before him and he said that the more lights you shed upon him the louder he got. Maybe that is our condition."

"I think that when I attend some of the executive sessions of the Judiciary Committee," the minority leader said, and asked several questions.

Senator Kennedy came next. "I want to extend a warm welcome to Mr. Cronkite as well," he said, "and apologize that I was unable to be here for

[2] Senator Hruska did appear regularly from that day on and from his conservative perspective made as large a contribution to the hearings as anyone other than Ervin. Strom Thurmond (S.C.) was the only other Senator ever to attend. The other subcommittee members are: Birch Bayh (Ind.), Robert Byrd (W. Va.), Hiram Fong (Hawaii), John McClellan (Ark.), and John Tunney (Calif.).

your statements and for your comments." The Massachusetts Senator began by asking Cronkite whether the networks had been intimidated by the Vice-President's attacks and by other harassments—the same question, as he pointed out, that he had asked Dr. Frank Stanton, the president of CBS, the day before. Next Kennedy asked a question that had been handed him by a subcommittee staff member. After receiving an answer he thanked Cronkite once again.

None of the Senators asked Cronkite the questions that would have prevented his testimony from becoming solely a platform for the networks' view of freedom. They did not seem to know that this should have been a debate of historic proportion, that there was a decision known as *Red Lion,* that this was the first opportunity Congress and the American public had had truly to grapple with these monumental issues.

The Senators could have had an opportunity to learn something of the other major First Amendment theory, since the morning's second witness was Jerome Barron, professor of law at George Washington University. Professor Barron's theory of public access to the media has made him the best-known scholarly proponent of this contemporary free-press theory. The subcommittee staff had only called Barron the previous afternoon, and he had not had time to prepare a formal statement: "I was lucky that I was able to hear most of Mr. Cronkite's testimony this morning, and I think the best way for me to start is perhaps to give my reaction to it. I might borrow something from you, Senator Ervin, to frame that reaction. You said the First Amendment was drafted not only for the brave but for the timid, and I would like to put an addendum to that. The First Amendment was not drafted for the broadcast networks, and yet I think really that is a conclusion which we got from Mr. Cronkite's testimony."

Even before Barron began talking, Senators Scott, Hruska, and Kennedy left the room. While he was talking the television cameramen were gathering up their equipment, slamming film cameras into boxes. At least half the reporters had left or were leaving, and most of the audience was slowly shuffling out of the room.

"I have said before in print," Barron continued, "that I think that it is one of the great public relations triumphs of the twentieth century over the eighteenth that the broadcasters have managed to identify themselves so completely with the First Amendment. I think the problem comes because we are groping for a Constitutional theory which will somehow be adequate to the communication problem of the twentieth century. I think all of our difficulties stem from a rather myopic view of what freedom of speech means in broadcasting. I think the conventional view has been that freedom of speech in broadcasting is exhaustive when the freedom of speech of the communicator is protected. In other words, if Dr. Stanton, Mr. Cronkite, Mr. Reasoner, Mr. Brinkley had their say, then freedom of speech in

America is safe; but they are three or four people out of 200 million. I don't think it is conspiratorial or anything like that; it is a combination of the marriage of technology and the pressure of the concentration of the economic system, which has given them this enormous power. I don't accuse them of seeking it, I realize in many ways they just find themselves at the throttle, but our problem is, what are we going to do about it. . . . And it is nothing short of amazing to me for a representative of broadcasting to contend that now they should be free from all regulations and yet they don't suggest everybody should be licensed anew as an original proposition. To that extent they are not willing to abdicate or abandon government aid."

Barron is a man full of all that confounded liberal *smartness,* a man who, as the Senator might put it, believes that all the wisdom in God's creation is found on the banks of the Potomac, and Ervin had no use for his ideas. Yet he questioned him with just the same civility and purpose that he had shown to Walter Cronkite. The Senator hadn't noticed the cameras before when they were grinding away, and he didn't notice them now when they were quiet, and he spent a good half hour drawing Barron out, giving the man a chance to develop his case as fully and as pronoundly as he could. He didn't quit until one o'clock or so when he called a lunch break so he could go over to the Capitol barbershop for his daily shave.

A Commercial for the Networks

There had been something so admirable, so likable, about Senator Ervin and the manner in which he conducted the hearings. Even those mountain stories, he couldn't resist telling them but then he would hurry through, the words spilling down his chest so that much of the time it was impossible to understand, but everyone would laugh anyway. When he talked of the meaning of a free press—unaware of reporters or cameras or anything but his ideas, as if his very words might reaffirm belief in liberty—he was truly inspiring. He believed that the ideas of a Jerome Barron or a Nicholas Johnson had a brilliance to them that had not worn into wisdom, and that there was a danger to liberty in their solutions, but he did not see that they had come far closer than he to understanding why freedom of the press in America is so often such a sham.

He did not see that in this anonymous, urban society the mass media are the vocal chords of free speech. One hundred thousand demonstrators can march in Washington against the Vietnam war, but unless their protests make the evening news they have no reality. Ervin believed ultimately in the goodwill of free men, and he believed that in the long run broadcasters would be fair. He did not see that television is so powerful, and the diversity of ideas in America so wide, that no man or small group of men can be given total control. He just did not see this, and he did not see that in his free-press hearings Professor Barron and his ideas had been denied their freedom of speech.

That evening on the network news programs, the TV reporters merely introduced their films of Walter Cronkite and his reasoned appeal for freedom of the press, followed by what appeared to be probing questions from Senators who, in fact, had not even heard Cronkite's full testimony. Ervin's hearings had been turned into a commercial for the networks, and by the end of the first week he began receiving letters from people back home asking why he was supporting the liberal networks. He wrote back saying that he was only supporting freedom of the press; he did not understand how his very lineup of witnesses had made it easy for the networks to use him and his beliefs.

NBC covered the hearings for seven of the eight days and ran testimony from seven witnesses who in a broad sense could be considered pro-industry as against two who were not. Christie Basham, Washington producer of the *NBC Nightly News,* was trying to do what in the network's sense of the word was a fair and responsible job, but once she accepted the reality of the hearings she just could not. "We tried to cover different points," she says. "We had a long cut of Cronkite partially because he was animated. By watching Cronkite's testimony you wouldn't have gotten the story of the hearings but you would have learned something. You would have learned what Cronkite feels about television. That's more valuable than what an outsider feels. Of course, it's an interesting question whether we should be covering such hearings at all." In fact, if NBC, CBS, or ABC really had cared to define the free-press issue by doing their own reporting, they could have done so in less than half the total time they spent on the hearings. The same could be said for the print media since its coverage of the hearings was by no means superior to television's.

During the hearings the public learned almost nothing about this historic debate over the nature of the First Amendment; and Sam Ervin, a man for whom ideas and beliefs are almost tangible, helped to foist clichés and half-truths on the nation. For years the integrity of his beliefs and of his earnest struggle to protect the Constitution had prevented him from becoming one of the manipulators or the manipulated. But with his new fame and the urgency of his struggle, he, too, was now part of the media apparatus.

Once Ervin and his subcommittee grew dependent on "news," they were living in a world where there were few boundaries between reality and unreality, and truth has the consistency of cotton candy.

Electronic Journalism

John Chancellor

"My fellow Americans, tonight I want to talk with you about a subject that is both painful and important. We live in a time when many of our basic institutions are changing, and often in directions we don't like. We have seen this in our schools. We have seen it in the courts. We have seen it even in some churches. And, my friends, we see it perhaps most vividly of all in the press and on television.

"We have been engaged in a long and dreadful conflict in Southeast Asia, a conflict made all the more protracted and all the more difficult because many of our citizens at home have felt they could not support the war. One must ask why. Why were the American people, who were steadfast in World War Two and resolute during the Korean War, so divided on Vietnam? Perhaps it was because they were told only the negative side of that story, the destructive side, while the courage of our fighting men and the nobility of our goals were ignored.

"My friends, the facts were twisted and the whole story not told, and the blood is on the hands of the twisters—in the press and on television. . . ."

Who said that? Nobody—yet. But a growing number of those who report the news are becoming aware that someone, either a Democrat or a Republican, may say something like it in 1972.

A Johnson Administration official has said that if there had been television news cameras at the Anzio beachhead during World War Two, the public would have withdrawn its support of the war. Richard Nixon has said that he will be satisfied as long as he gets the chance to present himself *directly* to the American people. And any stump speaker of either party will tell you that knocking the papers and the commentators always gets a good hand these days.

The controversial CBS News program *The Selling of the Pentagon* didn't help. Some of the editing in that show came dangerously close to the ethical line, in my view, and the uproar that followed in the Congress made matters worse. CBS compounded the problem by issuing an almost theologically complicated directive to its news staff on how to edit film—a directive that made the network look guilty as charged. CBS was courageous in its refusal to turn over private papers on the program to a Congressional panel; but its victory in that fight left a lot of people in Congress more hostile to television news than they had been before.

Source: *Playboy* (January 1972), Vol. 19, pp. 121, 216–217. Reprinted by permission of International Famous Agency for John Chancellor. Copyright © 1972 by HMH Corp.

The publication of the Pentagon papers was held up for two weeks by the courts—a demonstration of prior restraint unprecedented in our history. American freedom involves the right of a person to publish what he pleases; though he may go to jail for it later, he can't be stopped beforehand. But the Pentagon papers *were* stopped, temporarily, at least, and the opinions written by the Supreme Court Justices who finally allowed publication are by no means reassuring to us First Amendment types. In fact, it can be argued that in both *The Selling of the Pentagon* and the Pentagon-papers disputes, we won the battle but moved in the direction of losing the war.

Walter Cronkite says he thinks there is a conspiracy in the Administration to discredit the news media, and maybe he's right, but I see the current anti-news campaign as more fundamental to the character of the President and the men close to him. Nixon is leading an adversary Administration, one that sees the world as a patchwork of battlefields, or football fields, in which the good guys are playing the bad guys in a thousand different contests. There is little room for amelioration or compromise in this viewpoint, hardly any possibility of "bringing us together," since everything is seen in terms of one side against another, winning or losing.

One of the conflicts is the Government versus the news media. Since the President himself is fond of sports analogies, let us recall that for years he stood outside the ball park asking to play in the big leagues. And after getting in, his team got into trouble in the second inning. He was watching television during the peace marches; the White House was having a very hard time. Manager Nixon sent someone out onto the field to say the umpires were fixed. That someone, of course, was Vice-President Agnew, in his first attack on the newspapers and network instant analyzers.

A word about instant analysis, since I am the senior man on that assignment for NBC News. Who are we, Agnew demanded to know, to appear on television after the President and tell the people what he has just said? Well, for one thing, quite often the people don't *understand* what he has said. An example of this was Nixon's sudden midday appearance not long ago, when he read a very carefully worded statement of agreement with the Russians to move ahead on the limitation of strategic nuclear weapons. The statement had to be identical with one being issued in Moscow, which meant that, like most diplomatic language, it had a sort of Delphic quality about it. It had to be analyzed and explained—immediately—and that's just what we did. When we engage in that kind of instant analysis, or talk about Henry Kissinger's secret mission to Peking, the White House is all smiles. But when we say that the President ducked some questions at a news conference, there is a certain amount of glaring the next day. In that sense, the President's men are very human.

But the Vice-President is something else: He is close to being European —and radical—in his attitude toward the media. In many countries of the world, the newspapers are run by and for political parties. Many state-operated television systems are controlled by the politicians who happen to be in power—the government-run, government-censored television news operation of Gaullist France being a vivid example. What characterizes the news in these party newspapers and on these politically controlled television programs is bias; the news is put out by true believers *for* the faithful—and it usually ends up not being news. In some countries, one must go through four or five papers a day, reading between the lines, to get a coherent idea of the real news.

Mr. Agnew would take us in that direction. It seems to be his assumption that all journalists are dominated by their prejudices—right-wing journalists and left-wing journalists alike. When the Vice-President says it might be valuable to see the people who broadcast the news every evening examined by a panel who would question them on their personal political beliefs, he is saying that you can't understand the news unless you know the political values of the people reporting it. That is a very European view, and it ignores the fact that American journalism is known throughout the world for its unusually high ethical and professional standards.

One of the basic elements of the New Journalist is his commitment to a political idea; he is identified with one side of the story and interprets it from that side. This isn't reporting, it's essay writing, and it has produced, from Jonathan Swift to Nat Hentoff, some first-rate essays—but not good daily journalism.

Would we be better off if we had a left-wing Associated Press and a right-wing United Press International? Or a right-wing CBS and a left-wing NBC? I don't think so. Moreover, the professional craftsmen who process the news in daily journalism would themselves reject that, since it would conflict with the centrist politics most of them embrace.

I am a member of the extreme center, and that's because my life has shaped my politics. I have been a reporter all my life, and my experiences as a reporter have given me a set of political beliefs. I began as a police reporter, the classical basic training, and I saw crime, corruption, brutality and racism. I was a war reporter, and I learned about men and courage and waste and tragedy. I was a foreign correspondent, and I learned how other countries and other people organize their lives. I lived in Moscow and learned what totalitarianism means and how journalism can be twisted and distorted by forcing it to serve what are called the needs of the state, I was a political reporter, and I learned the differences between oratory and truth, between the promise and the payoff. I was a Washington correspondent, and I learned one or two things about power, how it is gained and how it is used.

I have spent 20 years in professional association with problems, conflict and change, and there are thousands like me—men and women who are paid to go out into the field and see how the society is working. What kind of people are we? We have a basic distrust of officials, bureaucrats and politicians. We have a deep dislike of fools and phonies, and probably a greater admiration than most for the occasional good man or woman. We tend to side with the underdog, with the poor and the oppressed. And we favor activists who try to bring about social change, since journalists know more than most people that the society is in profound need of renovation.

At the same time, most journalists reject radicalism and violence, simply because we have seen too much of it to believe that it can work. And, in my experience, most reporters don't join causes nor political parties, perhaps because we are forced to listen to too many speeches. So the group of journalists I know best, who cover national and international affairs, are people of the center, perhaps more skeptical and pragmatic than the average American, but reasonably close to the norm in a moderately liberal country.

Critics of journalism never take into account the fact that journalists are moved by ordinary emotions. The American people respected Eisenhower; so did the press. The American people loved John F. Kennedy; so did the press. The American people were suspicious of Lyndon Johnson; so was the press. About half the American people don't seem to like Richard Nixon, and that's probably the breakdown in the press.

Popular Presidents get a good press, and even a popular action by an unpopular President will get a good press. The Nixon Administration may believe that it's dealing with a hostile press, but what about the general reaction to Kissinger's visit to Peking? Or to the wage-price freeze? In truth, the Nixon Administration is getting quite a *good* press in many ways. Nixon is winding down the war, and most of the newspapers and radio and television programs are treating him with respect on that score. His foreign policy, from disarmament to the Middle East, is reported and discussed with little criticism. Nixon got a very bad press when he sent the names of Haynsworth and Carswell up to the Senate; but, looking back on it, even some Nixon loyalists admit that the two nominations were a mistake. In fact, the President is not getting the special attention he deserves in the areas of race, poverty and the cities.

The attacks on the press and on television by Agnew and other politicians are made in defense of an Administration that has, in the main, been treated with fairness. To what degree is that fairness a result of the Agnew attacks? From where I sit, the answer is—not much. The network news programs seem to be operating as they were before the attacks. The major newspapers and magazines seem about as they were, although one or two conservative columnists are doing better, in terms of circulation, than before the Agnew attacks. That's good, and if Agnew is responsible, he deserves our thanks. But in news coverage generally, we have not entered an Agnew era of a muzzled and subservient press. The disastrous "incursion" into Laos is an example: That was a gamble that failed badly, and there was no lack of critical comment (partially caused by the Government's own heavy-handed attempt to restrict the coverage).

Yet, having said this, no journalist is unaware of the hostility toward our craft that exists in the minds of many Americans. It's difficult to say whether this is growing or diminishing. A recent Harris Poll on the public's confidence in the network newscasts was very encouraging, but the over-all indications are mixed. The fact is that the world is in a period of hard times, and most of the news is bad. This makes life especially hard for television journalists, since we are the ones in the living rooms every night with the bad news.

It's especially hard because the television set is a brutal way to get the news. You can read a newspaper when you want to; you have to take a television report when we give it to you. You can skip the war news in a newspaper and read only the comics, if that's your mood. The options on a television news program are to sit through the war news or to turn off the program. You can't duck it, or put it away for another time.

This situation isn't going to change until we get some good news, and there isn't much of that on the horizon. The end of the Vietnam war is likely to help, but offsetting that could be a series of nasty political campaigns this year. The cities are still falling apart, crime is a disaster, the blacks and other minorities are still shut out of the mainstream and millions of young people are trying to get some genuine satisfaction out of a dehumanizing life.

Against this background, there is no shortage of politicians willing to say that the divisions in our society are the result of the news media telling it like it isn't; powerful men in both parties will do that if they get into political trouble. There is no shortage of true believers, right-wing and left-wing, who condemn the media because the centrist American press does not share nor fully reflect their views. And there is no shortage of weak, venal and incompetent newspapers and television news programs, particularly on a local level, that make thoughtful citizens question their sources of information.

This is a distressing combination, especially in a time of intense social change. It has been said that journalism should give men a picture of the world upon which they can act. That has never been more difficult than it is today. The most important element of journalism is trust: trust between sources and journalists, trust between journalists and the public. And trust, alas, is what we seem to have too little of these days.

Electronic Schizophrenia:
Does Television Alienate Voters?

Robert MacNeil

During a snowstorm on a Saturday morning a few weeks before the New Hampshire primary, Mary McGrory of the *Washington Star* followed two young McGovern canvassers up the stairs of a walk-up apartment in one of the French Canadian wards of Manchester. They sat at the kitchen table talking to the middle-aged housewife about Senator McGovern and his policies. The television set was on in the background. They asked what she thought was the most important issue this year.

"Oh, stopping the war up there," the housewife said, gesturing vaguely toward the television set.

"Well, that's what Senator McGovern is for. He wants to stop the war," the canvassers pointed out.

"He can't do that," she protested. "Only the President can do that."

"But Senator McGovern is running for President."

"Oh," the woman said, "I didn't know that."

How could she not have known? She did not live in a remote farmhouse beyond the White Mountains. She lived in the state's biggest city served by a widely read, if somewhat idiosyncratic, newspaper and by several television and radio stations. And McGovern had been actively campaigning in New Hampshire for over a year.

The incident was chastening to the young canvassers who trudged off through the snow to knock on more doors. It should also be chastening to anyone who confidently sets out to discuss the effect of television journalism on the electoral process.

It is so easy to assume that because there is a television set in practically every household in the land the information it pumps out will stick in the minds of the viewers. It is also easy to assume that because the millions are more securely "hooked" by television than by any other leisure activity (2.50 hours per person per day average viewing in 1971) and that because a growing percentage of Americans depend on television to know what is going on in the world (60% in 1971) the journalistic activities of the medium must have a colossal political effect.

That may be so. Certainly that is what all sorts of people—learned, qualified or not—have been assuming for years, and the literature of their speculation is prodigious. But it remains speculation.

Four years ago, after a thorough study, I concluded in my book, *The*

Source: *Politéia* (Summer 1972), Vol. 1, No. 4, pp. 5–10. Reprinted by permission.

People Machine (Harper & Row, 1968), that "the real impact of the (television) medium on the American democratic process is still too sparsely documented or analyzed to justify sweeping conclusions." As far as I can determine, that is still the case.

That does not inhibit politicians who view the medium as one entity (entertainment, journalism and paid political advertising) from leaping to vivid, even exotic conclusions. Harley Staggers, Chairman of the House Interstate and Foreign Commerce Committee, said during hearings last year that the television networks "can ruin every President and every member of Congress." Such assumptions or fantasies are implicit in the campaign of intimidation directed at the networks by the Nixon Administration. If the fulminations of Vice President Agnew have slackened off recently, the torch has been passed to presidential aide, Pat Buchanan. In a recent interview on Public Television, he raised the possibility of some form of anti-trust action against the networks to counter what he called the "monopoly . . . of a single point of view and a single political ideology."

The same Administration had no hesitation in trying to use the same television networks blatantly for its own propaganda purposes by discriminating against print journalists in coverage of the President's visit to China.

Clearly, whether television journalism is a decisive influence on our electoral processes or not, many important politicians *believe* it might be and act accordingly. That is one reality.

Another reality is a paradox. Despite all the attempts of politicians, especially during the Nixon years, to discredit and vilify television journalism, public trust and confidence in television as a source of information has actually grown—and grown, moreover, at the expense of public confidence in government and politicians.

Pat Buchanan accuses the networks, among the media, of being alienated from the point of view of the American people. That assumption is not supported by the latest research.

Since 1959, Burns Roper has been conducting regular national surveys to determine public attitudes toward television and the other media. He has found a remarkably steady growth in the percentage of Americans who say they get most of their news about what is going on in the world from television, rather than from radio, newspapers or magazines. The percentage rose from 51% in 1959 to 64% in 1964, fell (as all media did) after the traumatic year, 1968, but by January, 1971, had climbed again to 60%, while newspapers, magazines and radio continued their relative decline.

More interestingly, Roper's survey has traced the relative credibility of the media over the same period. His question has been: "If you got conflicting or different reports of the same news story from radio, television, the magazines and the newspapers, which of the four versions would you be most inclined to believe?"

In 1959, newspapers were the first choice with 32% and television second with 29%. But while newspaper credibility has continued to sink from that figure, television's has consistently gained. Even in November, 1968, during the peak of the outcry about television's handling of the Chicago convention, 44% of Americans regarded television as the most credible medium. By January, 1971, after two years of attacks by Agnew, the percentage had risen to 49%.

So, despite all the political attempts to discredit television journalism, despite all the theories about the American public instinctively and primitively wishing to punish the bringer of bad news, television is increasingly the medium people rely on for news and the medium in which they increasingly put their trust.

In June, 1971, pollster Louis Harris surveyed national attitudes toward the quality of news reporting from Washington. Asked whether they thought television was fair in reporting news of the Nixon Administration, 64% said yes, while only 20% said it was unfair.

There is one final, and ironic, piece of evidence. The *New York Times* reported on May 25 the results of an Oliver Quayle poll. A total of 8,780 people in 18 states had been asked about the degree of trust they placed in certain public figures. Vice President Agnew (the scourge of television) was rated 50%. President Nixon's rating was 57%. The highest rating of all went to Walter Cronkite, with 73%.

That is where one should start in looking for the possible political effects of television journalism. By 1972, after a quarter-century of growth, television journalism is the most popular, and most highly trusted journalistic medium this country offers and it is seen to be fair. With those facts in mind, it should be an act of basic political common sense for politicians to accept television journalism as an open marketplace for their ideas and to stop trying to hold it up to public scorn. By approaching the medium constructively rather than destructively, politicians could have a considerable influence in making television journalism a lot better than it is.

For there is another side of the picture. Television is clearly the most pervasive and vivid medium of political communication today. It is also the most trivial, superficial and, in a sense, irresponsible.

A certain degree of superficiality is inevitable in a mass medium. But there is no inherent limitation requiring television to rejoice in its present superficial treatment of news and public affairs. Television is not forced by the nature of the medium to limit informational programming to 2% of prime time broadcasting, as Columbia University's "Survey of Broadcast Journalism 1970–71" reveals. But it does so because of its commercial greed. Television news "shows" (the vocabulary is significant) do not have to bewilder us with a multiplicity of brief, unbackgrounded items; they do it to produce a show-business pace and to avoid straining the attention span of the average viewer. The medium does not require newsmen to laugh inanely with each other or to throw snowballs around the studio (as I recently saw them doing on a news program in Florida); they do it to make their shows more entertaining, to enhance the ratings, to attract advertisers.

Television is irresponsible not when it does its journalistic duty but because it shirks that duty so often. Under the Communications Act of 1934, television is required to operate "in the public interest." Informational programming, programs about the real world as opposed to fictional, fantasy, escapist programs, are indisputably in the public interest. But although 60% of the American people say they depend on television to tell them about the real world, the industry permits them very limited glimpses. True, television occasionally performs expensive prodigies of journalism at moments of great public interest—space shots, summit meetings, political conventions. But the day-to-day events are treated cursorily at best, and from 7:30 to 11:00 P.M., commercial television continues to feed on a diet of mediocre fiction.

So, this is the context in which the search for political effects of television journalism should be made: a popular and trusted medium, embattled by Administration critics; the chief purveyor of political and other information to the American masses but on a relatively superficial level most of the time.

I believe that the context itself has a certain, though immeasurable, political effect. The level of public information and the motivation to seek information both have a bearing on political behavior, as we shall see in more detail below. If the medium on which the masses are dependent for information chooses to minimize its journalistic role, that presumably has an effect on the amount of information the public absorbs and on the quality of public understanding of the political issues of the day.

Moreover, although it cannot be documented, I suspect that millions of people do not perceive the informational programming television does offer as essentially different in tone or texture than the rest of what comes at them out of the box. Indeed, the journalistic side of television has been at pains for years to shape the form of its news programs so as to conform as nearly as possible to the patterns of entertainment programs: the commercial interruptions are as frequent and abrupt; there is the same premium on picture and action; newscasters, whether trained journalists or not, have the same qualities of glibness and charm as entertainment personalities; and a great effort is made to avoid straining the audience's intellectual attention span, already conditioned by the overall output of the medium over many years. Furthermore, many of the most popular fictional programs deal with subject matter that is relevant to the real world described in the news but deal with it in a romantic and often highly prejudiced manner. Two obvious examples are the plethora of fictional series dealing with medicine and police work. Both areas involve major areas of controversy in political life today—the quality of American health care and the effectiveness and legitimate extent of the police role. Yet, as frustrated writers of these serials have often complained, these programs reduce all such issues to a bland soup of reassurance in which virtually all doctors are selflessly dedicated miracle-workers and all policemen paragons of virtue and good citizenship. Since such programs vastly outweigh in quantity television's few journalistic attempts to examine these issues objectively, I assume the total impact of the medium is to give the unsophisticated viewer at least a distorted picture of reality.

It is interesting to note the sustained reverence for the medical profession in American society as revealed by Louis Harris' comparative survey of public confidence in major institutions in 1966 and 1971. During those turbulent years, confidence in every institution listed slipped dramatically. For example, in 1966, 62% of Americans said they had a great deal of confidence in the military. By 1971 it had plummeted to 27%. The Congress had fallen from 42% to 19%, education from 61% to 37%, organized religion from 41% to 27%. The institution which was highest in public esteem (72%) in 1966 was medicine, and it was the institution which slipped least in the 5 years, falling to 61%. Clearly, the events of the late '60's did not shake the public faith in medicine as drastically as in other fields. Yet there has been no lack of public and political complaint about short-comings in American medicine. Is it far-fetched to think that the sheer quantity of romantic medical fiction on television has simply wiped out news reports of the realities? If so, then clearly there is a political effect.

With this context in mind, let us break down into categories what real effect on the electoral process television journalism could possibly have. I think there are four basic areas: the first two operating chiefly *between* election campaigns, the latter two principally as a result of actual campaigns.

IDENTIFYING CANDIDATES. By bringing lesser-known personalities before the gaze of millions who do not follow politics intimately, television journalism may give such figures identity and credibility which are prerequisites for office-seeking. There is little doubt that television conveys an impression of personality and character far more vividly than all but the most inspired print journalism. Even viewers only casually interested in politics are liable after a certain amount of television exposure to feel they "know" a public figure far better than if they had merely read about him. Politicians aspiring for office, and their advisers, are anxious to get such exposure on news programs, especially those programs like *Face the Nation, Issues and Answers,* and *Meet the Press,* which show them in a setting reserved for "important" people. In this area, television behaves very much as newspapers do, the criteria for exposure being newsworthiness. At the national level that criterion can be very narrow, often confining the field to a small "club" of already famous people.

CHOOSING ISSUES. By the same criterion of newsworthiness, television journalists, like the newspapers, play a major role in setting the parameters of public debate on the issues. In the words of Dr. Ithiel de Sola Pool, Chairman of the Political Science Department at M.I.T.: ". . . the media are doing exactly what they should be doing, news story by news story. They are recognizing the issues, identifying issues, and thereby making them issues. The power of TV is the immediacy, the rapidity, the overwhelming force that it has in doing this, in taking an event and immediately turning it into an issue on which sides are chosen."

There are ways, other than its vividness and immediacy, in which television works on issues differently than the better print media. Because of the time limitations it imposes on any news treatment, television is liable to present any issue very baldly and thus oversimplify it. By its legal requirement to be fair, the industry feels the need often to present sides of an issue in something like mathematical balance. It may often seem that there are equal sides to every issue, pro and con, which is rarely the case. Television journalism may thus help to create artificial polarities in the public mind.

But where television is weakest is in devoting enough time and care in trying to explain the background complexities to issues.

INCREASING VOTER TURNOUT. The television industry, in earlier days, used to claim that its efforts had substantially increased voter turnout. This is one area that has been quite well studied and the findings have been negative or inconclusive. In one study William A. Glaser of Columbia University concluded that "newspaper reading may be more effective than television watching in affecting turnout and in affecting the fulfillment of intention to vote."

AFFECTING ELECTION RESULTS. It is probably futile to ask whether television journalism of and in itself can influence the way voters behave on any election day. There are always simply too many interacting variables: the coverage by other media; the competence and objectivity of the television station or network in question; the effectiveness and amount of paid television advertising by the candidates; the nature of the issues; the relative strengths of the candidates; their telegenic qualities; the success of their campaigns in attracting television news coverage of their activities and, finally, whether or not there are televised debates.

I do not know of any campaign, local, state or national, in which it could be said that bias by a television station or network decisively affected the outcome of an election. Edith Efron's painstaking mathematical analysis of network coverage of the 1968 Presidential election in *The News Twisters* attempts to prove that the national networks were biased against Richard Nixon. If they were, they were unsuccessful in swinging the election against him. While there may be some truth in the frequent charge that the network news departments contain a disproportionate number of so-called Eastern liberals, the news personnel are on the whole too cautious and too professional to be caught up in any conspiracy, conscious or not, to inject consistent bias into coverage of a campaign.

There are, however, some aspects of the manner in which television news works which, together with other forces might have an influence on a campaign. They are worth noting.

Television, for a variety of reasons, does less original reporting than the newspapers and this applies to politics as well as to general news. Television tends to follow the pack; it is often reactive. It will cover stories after they have appeared in an influential newspaper or magazine. Television may thus have the effect of reinforcing the points that a print journalist has made and communicating them to a wider and different audience. If the print journalist has slanted the story, or told only part of it, a lazy or rushed television crew may do the same. This is far more likely to happen in the news departments of less competent local television stations than in the networks.

Television has a hunger for action which can be filmed. If a campaign were turning on complex economic issues, for example, voters would be less likely to hear those complexities on television than to see them in the press. If one candidate had an interest in attacking or oversimplifying the issues, and the other in making a complicated defense, the former candidate might benefit from television's tendency to reduce its nightly coverage to a couple of minutes of campaign action with a few snippets from the day's speeches. The recent California primary contest between Senators McGovern and Humphrey is an example. The nightly news coverage tended to consist of brief snatches of rhetoric, of traded charges and counter charges. Humphrey's interest was clearly in raining fairly simplistic attacks on McGovern's highly complicated economic proposals—to depict them as wildly radical. McGovern was not adept at presenting his economic ideas clearly. Even in the televised debates, which went into far more detail, it was difficult for a voter to understand clearly what the two men were talking about. Fortunately perhaps for McGovern, the election actually appeared to turn on deeper questions of image and credibility.

There is another way in which television's hunger for filmable incident can affect the course of a campaign. For several years now astute campaign managers have realized that what a candidate does on the stump may be far less effective than what he does on television, especially what he can manage to do on television news programs. There he is relieved of the expense of commercials, freed of the taint of image making, and he appears in a context of credibility. His campaign incidents thus have the aura of news. These managers have also discovered that local television stations need to "fill up" their one-hour evening news shows and can be fairly easily seduced into covering almost any incident which makes good pictures. Hence the arrival of the pseudo event as standard campaign procedure, a happening devised to attract television coverage in good time to be processed and edited for the evening news programs. In effect, television is asking the campaign "please fill this space." Campaign managers adept at that will benefit.

Senator Muskie's appearance on a flatbed truck in front of the *Manchester Union Leader* to berate its publisher, William Loeb, was such an event, although notoriously it backfired. Curiously, however, the political impact of Muskie's crying did not come through the television film but through print reporting. CBS had extremely good close-up shots of Muskie, his face half-averted, large flakes of snow falling on his shoulders, his voice constricted. But by itself, the film did not convey the story that the political reporters filed. In the film he looked rather upset. In print he broke down and wept.

There is yet another way in which the nature of television news allows manipulation during a campaign. Many local stations are willing, incredibly it seems, to let a candidate give them his own film or videotape coverage of himself campaigning. And the stations run it in their news programs!

All these mechanical realities are well known to the professionals who run political campaings and, to the extent that these are exploited and television journalism manipulated, they may be having an effect on the political process.

But I would like to conclude by speculating about an aspect of television that gets too little attention: who television really talks to.

For many years political scientists have attempted to define "the floating voter" and there is a widely accepted hypothesis about him. One part of the hypothesis is stated by Philip E. Converse of the Survey Research Center at the University of Michigan: "Not only is the electorate as a whole quite uninformed, but it is the least informed members within the electorate who seem to hold the critical balance of power, in the sense that alternations in governing party depend disproportionately on shifts in their sentiment . . . it is easy to take the stable vote for granted. What commands attention as the governor of party success at the polls, and hence administration and politics, is the changing vote. And "shifting" or "floating" voters tend to be those whose information about politics is relatively impoverished." (From *Elections and the Political Order,* John Wiley, New York, 1966)

Converse goes on to argue that as the flow of political information has increased in this century, especially through the "spoken media," voting trends show swings of increasing amplitude between the parties at the national level.

These observations hold really important implications for the political impact of television. The floating voter is a person with weak motivation to seek political information. The people with the highest motivation, and with more stable partisan identity, seek the most information. Typically they fall into the section of the population with the most education and they rely predominantly on the print media.

While television network research has shown that the audience for their news programs represents something very close to a cross section of the entire population in socio-economic terms, that audience also contains a high proportion of people who read newspapers and magazines very little. So it is probable that the people who decide elections, the floating voters, are the same people who depend more or less exclusively on television for their political information.

Richard Scammon further defines them as the Lower Middle Class. Because they are relatively disinterested in politics and relatively uninformed, they make up their minds very late in a campaign. Media consultants imported increasingly into political campaigns during the 1960's brought with them from Madison Avenue the knowledge that the less people care about something, the more easily they believe what they are told about it. Putting together these facts about the weakly motivated floating voter, dependent on television, inclined to make a late decision trivially, provided the rationale for much of the so-called new media politics.

But the same facts may tell us something about the effect of television journalism. I wonder, in fact, whether television has not done a great deal to stir up in the electorate what it is fashionable this year to call "alienation." The 1966–71 Harris survey on faith in institutions quoted earlier and almost any attitude poll taken by candidates this year reveals widespread disenchantment with political institutions, deep mistrust of politicians as a breed and a conviction that government has consistently lied to the people. These attitudes are concentrated, according to Senator McGovern's pollster, Pat Caddell, in the same socio-economic group we have been discussing, the Lower Middle Class, the floating voter, the people dependent on television.

It is through television that they will have absorbed the traumas of the past decade. They will have vivid visual memories of riots, wars, assassinations and urgent Presidential appeals, glimpsed through the reassuring twilight of *Perry Mason, Bonanza* and *Marcus Welby.* Is it any wonder that they feel disconnected? Television has wooed them for a generation by concocting a womb-warm fantasy of America, a dream world of nice people, solving all problems in the wild west, or the hospitals or the Peyton

Places of their lives and solving them *simply* with guns, or aspirins, or fists or laxatives or deodorants—but solving them.

Into this fantasyland, however, television journalists kept bursting with increasing frequency during the sixties, like cold strangers breaking down the door, letting in the noise and stink of a dangerous and complicated world outside. Their bulletins were often brief with little to prepare you for the horrors they told of—our kids were fighting another war and *losing,* they were burning the flag, they were tearing up the universities, they were shouting obscenities at the cops, and the taxes were going up and crime was going up and the blacks were all over the place and President Johnson and President Nixon kept breaking in and saying "believe me, it will be all right." But it didn't get all right. It just got worse. Yet every evening there was television trying to pretend that the good old America of *High Chapparrall* and *Dr. Kildare* and *I Love Lucy* was still there.

If anything was calculated to induce schizophrenia, this conditioning would. And television journalism did little to help people understand. The better educated people, whose college years had given them some sense of history and perspective were disturbed too, but they could go outside television to books, newspapers and magazines, for deeper explanations of what was happening to the country. The others were trapped and confused.

Every critic of television journalism has complained that where the industry fails most is in explaining the news, putting events into perspective, telling the "why." Yet the people who depend on television for their information need such perspective more than the others. It may well be that we are now reaping the harvest of that neglect.

The people who depend on television trust it, as we noted earlier, but they look at the entire output of the medium, not just the pockets of news. Taken as a whole, that output has presented a disconnected and schizophrenic view of America. On the one hand the industry was trying to do its duty journalistically, on the other it was trying to be a more efficient vehicle for commercials. Given the nature of its devoted watchers, and their probable role as floating voters, it would be very surprising if television has not contributed substantially to the disorientation and volatility of the 1972 election scene.

Television and the First Amendment

Fred W. Friendly

"The spirit of liberty . . . is the spirit which is not too sure it is always right." Judge Learned Hand wrote that, and it's a fitting foreward for one willing to take "A Second Sober Look" at the relationship of broadcast journalism to all the protections of the First Amendment.

Last fall, in collaboration with a Columbia law professor, I began teaching a new course, "Journalism and the First Amendment." In preparation for this, I spent the past year re-examining a lifetime of convictions and assumptions concerning the First Amendment and my profession. I have concluded that the First Amendment, like the Bill of Rights, is a cornerstone, but not a completed building. To paraphrase a nineteenth-century professor of Constitutional law, Woodrow Wilson: "It is a root, not a perfect vine. . . . It is the sap-center of a system of government vastly larger than the stock from which it has branched. . . ."

I believe, with all my heart and conscience, in the spirit of the First Amendment. To say that I believe the absolute letter of that law should automatically be applied to twentieth-century technology would be simplistic and unfair to James Madison and his fellow framers of the Bill of Rights. It would be, to borrow from Mrs. Malaprop, "to anticipate the past."

There is every evidence that the drafters of the First Amendment were being purposefully ambiguous. We must resist the temptation to put our own libertarian words in their mouths. The canon, "Congress shall make no law . . . abridging the freedom of speech or of the press. . . ." presupposes a community of equals, which is the very core of the Constitution and the Declaration of Independence. Yet, when Congress passed the Communications Act of 1934, it implicity created an electronic community where some citizens are more equal than others.

The premise of the First Amendment is that free expression will flourish as long as: 1) government remains neutral; 2) everyone has the same tools and/or access to those tools. When the government, through the FCC, disturbs that delicate balance and enfranchises several citizens to operate the equivalent of a super public-address system that can, in effect, drown out that multitude of diverse and robust voices, then the ground rules may have been changed. The federal government, because of the limitations of the electromagnetic spectrum, had no choice in the 1920s and 1930s but to issue radio licenses. But in giving some citizens this awesome responsibility

Source: *Saturday Review* (January 6, 1972), Vol. 55, pp. 46–47, 55. Copyright © 1972 by Saturday Review, Inc. First appeared in *Saturday Review,* January 6, 1972. Used with permission.

and unique privilege, it, by definition, denied these rights to others. The open market place of ideas became more dynamic but limited.

Indeed, the gift of this license can be considered a form of "prior restraint," as the courts have stated, and if one wanted to pursue a legal point, one could argue that the Communications Act and the First Amendment have been on a collision course. The Blackstonian principle against "prior restraint," so simply restated in our First Amendment, foreclosed the divine right of kings and governments to license only selected printers and publications. The Communications Act, although clearly forbidding FCC censorship of radio and television communications, necessarily bestows, licenses on some but denies them to most others. The franchise holder, as the gatekeeper to the biggest soapbox in town, becomes an adjudicator of everyone else's First Amendment rights. Walter Lippmann once put it another way: "Suppose there were only three printing presses in the nation, to whom would you give that responsibility?"

The government, having made this major alteration in the system by which we communicate, has an obligation to make certain the system is used well and used enough. To say that is not to imply that the Senate or the House of Representatives or the FCC has any place in the "content" business. It *does* have an obligation to make sure, as Edward R. Murrow once put it, that "licensees don't welch on their promises"—promises not to please all the people all the time, but to use the system to communicate, not just to amuse and to sell goods.

At a time "when what the American people don't know could kill them," high officials who are critical of broadcasters for doing their best remain virtually silent about their worst, which is clearly visible almost every night in prime time. If the Vice President of the United States were one-tenth as concerned with the low level of nighttime entertainment as he is with the performance of Cronkite or Brinkley or Reynolds, his motives might not be so suspect. If some members of Congress were as concerned with the selling of violence and superfluous medicine as they were with *The Selling of the Pentagon,* the debate over slanting the news might be more understandable.

I am far more distressed with attacks on the news media from the Vice President and certain members of Congress than I am with the Communications Commission. Most of the time the FCC has been a tower of Jell-O, more concerned with citizens' band radio and marine frequencies than with the crucial communications that shape our lives. But there have been some notable exceptions. Some of my former colleagues may not like what I am about to say, but the truth is that the threat of government action after the quiz show scandals in 1959 and 1960 is what caused "CBS Reports," NBC's "White Paper," and other documentary programs to be placed on the nighttime schedule. And now that the threat has receded, the programs have gone back to the intellectual ghetto, receiving only occasional nighttime exposure.

When I hear some broadcasters complain about the chilling hand of FCC intervention, I share their concern. But frankly, I perceive very little FCC meddling in newsroom activities. The chilling hand that concerns me far more is the corporate concern for maximizing profit. It is this profit drive that causes the network evening news programs to remain a half hour in length, when every newsman and producer knows full well they should last an hour.

It is the dollar sign, not the government's censorship stamp, that has caused the termination of all weekly scheduled documentaries and public affairs in prime time. The news organizations of the three major networks are capable of far more professional journalism than ever gets on the air, and the frustration of many practitioners is hardly a secret. Vice President Agnew, for all his denunciation of broadcast journalism, has not really influenced the cancellation or abridgment of a single program. The real censor remains high cost of air time.

My position is that the First Amendment should apply to broadcast journalism, but I also believe that the broadcast industry must meet the Bill of Rights halfway. There ought to be an electronic Bill of Rights, but to make that work there would have to be an electronic "Bill of Responsibility." Broadcasters would have to give their professional consciences "equal time" with their corporate balance sheets. The Fairness Doctrine, Section 315, and the FCC's requirements for diverse programing are nothing more than substitutes for this Bill of Responsibility, and they are not adequate. The Fairness Doctrine is awkward to enforce and demeaning to the FCC and the broadcast profession.

I think that the equal-time provision of Section 315 of the Communications Act is counterproductive and causes less public access, less debate, not more. And the programing requirement is sampled only at license renewal time, and even then it is seldom successfully met.

Frankly, I don't believe the Fairness Doctrine works very well. If the doctrine is enforced in broad and general terms, it represents no more than the credo of an honest journalist. If—and this has sometimes been the tendency—the doctrine is applied fastidiously by the FCC, the potential for abuse is enormous. In the hands of a lazy management or a timid journalist, the doctrine is a convenient excuse for doing nothing. On balance, I suppose that the Fairness Doctrine is a necessary evil in a technology of scarcity —an ultimate restraint against the broadcaster who might abuse his public trust. But I look forward to the day when, with broad-band cable capacity, we have sufficient television channels so that the doctrine will not be necessary.

Nor do I believe that Congressional or FCC investigators have any place in the newsroom or second-guessing the editing of documentaries. Frank Stanton was on solid ground in refusing to give up film outtakes and other unused material from *The Selling of the Pentagon*. Judging from the number of policy changes made by the Defense Department as a direct result of that broadcast, Mr. Staggers and his subcommittee should be asking why there aren't more investigative documentaries.

Congress has a responsibility to make certain that the long range promises affecting the public interest are honored. It has no place in the newsroom or in monitoring individual programs. It is unfortunate that the House of Representatives decided that issue on political grounds before the courts had a chance to decide it on Constitutional grounds.

I think the subpoenaing of a reporter's notes, whether he be a print or broadcast reporter, is a futile exercise that is as unproductive as it is unconstitutional. The plain fact is that experienced reporters leave very few relevant facts in their notebooks or on the cutting room floor. Prosecutors looking there for admissible evidence will do better to spend their time in more fruitful pursuits. In truth, the subpoenaing of reporters' notes is attempted much more for harassment than in search of light. Incidentally, I think the Pearson Bill, S1311, is an excellent step in the right direction, but it is really only a beginning.

The use of false press credentials by police officials who seek cover seems to me as fraudulent and dishonest as the false use of police badges by newsmen. Both practices are inexcusable; both should be unlawful.

Repealing the Fairness Doctrine or improvising other patchwork alterations in the communications structure will not reorder the priorities of the First Amendment. Specifically, it is the piecemeal approach that has made us face a situation where Presidents of the United States can avoid debating their challengers by hiding behind the equal-time provisions. It is the absence of an electronic Bill of Rights that caused CBS News to spend far more money and energy defending *The Selling of the Pentagon* than in producing it. It is the absence of an electronic Bill of Responsibilities that necessitates broadcast editors compressing complex issues to such a point that too often they must maximize heat at the expense. of light. Television is so unfair to its own journalists in the distribution of air time that it can't possibly be fair to everyone.

It is the lack of an adequate communications policy that requires politicians to mortgage their consciences to raise anywhere from $10,000 to $50,000 for a few minutes of air time, which in most other democracies is provided free to candidates for office. It is the absence of a communications policy that subverts the newly established Public Broadcasting Service to second-class status by denying almost half of our major cities the use of a VHF (very high frequency) public television transmitter. Think of the irony. Congress and the foundations pour tens of millions of dollars of funds into public broadcasting while *Sesame Street, The Advocates, Masterpiece Theatre,* and the other refreshing public broadcasting programs cannot be seen in approximately 45 per cent of American homes. The Washington-Baltimore area, with a total of seven commercial VHF stations and not one public VHF license, is a constant reminder of the high price we all pay for bad planning.

The situation has reached such proportions that in Los Angeles recently even $15-million raised in the philanthropic and business worlds, could not ransom a commercial VHF channel for the public sector. Half the children of Los Angeles still cannot watch Big Bird or the other characters of *Sesame Street.*

The absence of a long-range communications policy causes the nation to improvise and stumble from one crisis to another. Television regulations grew out of radio law, just as the term "public interest, convenience, and necessity" was borrowed from Interstate Commerce Commission language pertaining to grain elevators.

If we continue to improvise, we shall never break out of the thicket that slows our progress. Even today when broad-band community cable could put fifty or sixty channels into every home, could end the constricting limitations of the VHF quasi-monopoly, could change television as much as television changed radio, we are bogged down in jurisdictional controversies between cities and states, between the states and the FCC, betwen the FCC and the White House. Cable television, the wired city, could virtually eliminate limited access and the other problems that now make it difficult to apply all of the principles of the First Amendment to broadcasting.

It *could happen* if we reorder our priorities and re-create the kind of long-range communications policy that can carry us into the next century.

To change this course we need a knowledgeable citizens' commission to question and report on where we have been. After thirty-seven years, how well has the Communications Act served the nation? Has the FCC been a threat to journalistic independence? Has it been a goad for progress? Should a new agency be created exclusively for telecommunications? Is the First Amendment compatible with a semi-closed franchised system? What should replace the Fairness Doctrine? Should vast conglomerates be allowed to own television stations and/or cable systems? (After all, aren't our banking institutions limited in the kinds of corporations they may acquire?) Should members of Congress be permitted to own stock in conglomerates which own powerful broadcast operations? How can public broadcasting be provided a long-term finance plan completely insulated from government and foundation control?

We need a serious study of all these problems, not by government and not by the broadcast industry, but by a panel of concerned and learned citizens. In Britain the Pilkington Commission of 1962 evaluated the long-range performance of the BBC, and similiar surveys constantly are being made.

I am not recommending an examination of day-to-day content, and certainly not an inspection of broadcast practices on any one program. I am talking about performance for a decade. It is precisely this kind of long-range evaluation that will keep opportunists from sharpshooting practices that take aim at individual journalists and documentaries.

Merely reciting the litany that broadcasting deserves all the protection of the First Amendment will not make it true. Like patriotism, integrity, and marriage, it is better upheld in the demonstration than the recitation. Much more thought and work, much more self-examination on and off the air, much more access to air time for those who believe they have been wronged by television and radio are essential. For communications to be truly free, there must be opportunities to vent the steam that builds up in what Jefferson called "the most certain and legitimate engine of government."

Senator Sam Ervin, in his eloquent statement at the beginning of his recent hearings on Constitutional rights and journalism, had a sentence that ought to be on the first page of a book that I hope he, or someone else, will write about these landmark hearings: "If the First Amendment principles are not held to apply to the broadcast media, it may well be that the Constitution's guarantee of a free press is on its deathbed." The outcome of this issue lies not only with those in high places who make communications policy, but also with those who make programs.

The First Amendment will apply when the broadast schedule is worthy of it. Did the Founding Fathers mean what they seemed to be saying? Had they ever dreamed of broadcasting, would they have included it under the protections of the First Amendment? Perhaps the best answer to that is another question: Do *broadcasters* mean what *they* seem to say about their responsibility to the public in their applications for license renewal?

Chapter 5
SUGGESTED TOPICS FOR CLASS DISCUSSION

1. Why are media and administration spokesmen so often at odds?
2. Is there a tendency for television reporting to introduce certain kinds of distortion? What kinds? Why?
3. What responsibilities should the media have in their political role? Are the responsibilities of the press, radio, and television the same? How well do the media meet these obligations?
4. There is evidence to indicate that many persons receive most of their information about the political scene from television. How might the perceptions of television viewers differ from those of newspaper readers?
5. Events do not select, report, and interpret themselves for the media. Human beings are involved in making these judgments. What are some of the factors that may influence the persons involved?
6. Issues relating to "freedom of the press" are frequently before the public eye. Why can't the issues be settled once and for all?

Chapter 6
Political Parties, Campaigns, and Elections

Political parties play an indispensable role in the American political sys-
tem. Indeed, it could be said that the system could not operate without them.
They offer candidates, hold primaries under state direction, select Presi-
dential candidates, and offer programs through national conventions. The
Legislative and the Executive Branches are organized on a party basis;
almost all judges, both elected and appointed, are chosen on the basis of
their party affiliations.

In addition to the functions just described, political parties offer the only
means to hold government accountable—the wide dispersion of powers, the
large number of elective offices, and the relative independence between
branches of government make it nearly impossible to hold individual office-
holders responsible or accountable. Parties can be held to both. Finally, the
party system provides the basis for decisive and orderly changes in govern-
ment.

These essential functions provided by parties are made more effective

199

by the two-party system. In the last half century there have been attempts by third parties to gain a political foothold, but because their primary interests have been so narrow, the two major parties have been able to absorb the third party programs and their supporters. Nevertheless, because of a relatively weak party loyalty, both of the major parties must appeal to a variety of social, economic, ethnic, religious, and sectional interests. This makes it impossible for either of the major parties to assume doctrinaire positions, which in turn leaves them open to charges such as "there is not a dime's worth of difference between them."

The electoral process is the very heart of any democratic political system. This makes feasible what is called popular sovereignty: the capacity of the governed to control those who govern. Fixed terms of office and established times for elections make it possible for the electorate to keep or reject those in office.

Because of the central role played by elections, anything that has an important influence on the electoral process is important to the functioning of the political system as a whole: the characteristics and background of candidates; the nominating system, including both primaries and conventions; the strategy of campaigning; the high cost of running for office; polls and their impact upon candidates; campaigns by public relations experts; the intangibles that sometimes surface during a campaign and that may have a decisive influence on the election itself.

The cases selected for inclusion in this chapter illustrate various aspects of political parties and the electoral process.

PRIMARIES: TRIAL BY ORDEAL

Eugene McCarthy

The Democratic primaries this year have been expensive and exhausting and to say the least—or the most—inconclusive as to both issues and candidates. They have shown that the Democratic party is greatly divided, if not confused, and that no one candidate is likely to come to the convention with a clear mandate.

They have done little to clarify the issues. In Florida, the race was principally for the school board, and in Wisconsin for county or city assessor.

This is not to fault the primary system itself. There is no reason to be-

Source: "A Hard Look at Primaries," *Politéia* (Summer 1972), Vol. 1, No. 4, pp. 15–17. Reprinted by permission.

lieve that if there were no primaries, and that if the traditional practices of caucuses followed by county, district, and state conventions were being followed in all states, this year the picture would be much clearer. It is difficult to demonstrate that presidential primaries within the Democratic party over the last twenty years have had many positive results, either in the determination of issues or in the selection of candidates. The one exception was 1960, the year in which John Kennedy established himself as a candidate through victories over Senator Humphrey in the Wisconsin and the West Virginia primaries and then went on to win the nomination and the November election. There is no solid reason, however, to believe that the primaries apart from the person determined the political events of that year, or to believe that Senator Humphrey, had he won the same two early primaries, would have been nominated.

In 1952, Senator Kefauver challenged President Truman in early primaries. Truman did not challenge and announced that he would not run again. Senator Kefauver then went on to win twelve primaries. Yet he was not nominated to be the candidate of the Democratic party. Again in 1956 he won nine primaries, challenging Adlai Stevenson. He was the vice presidential candidate that year, but not because of his primary showing. He won the nomination in the convention when Stevenson opened the choice of Vice President to the convention.

In 1964 there were no significant primary challenges. In 1968 there were. In that year President Johnson, after a mixed decision in the New Hampshire primary, after Senator Robert Kennedy had declared his candidacy and two days before the Wisconsin primary, which he subsequently lost by a vote of approximately 56% to 44%, announced that he would not be a candidate for re-election.

What might have happened if Senator Kennedy had not been assassinated or if President Johnson had not withdrawn no one can know. In the convention in August of that year in Chicago, the Democratic party chose not only to ignore but to positively reject the primary results both as to candidate and as to the issue of the war. The convention chose then Vice President Humphrey, who had competed in only two primaries and had lost both, and whose support came principally from states that had not held primaries. This support was supplemented by delegates from states like Indiana and Nebraska, who after the death of Senator Kennedy chose to ignore what the primaries had indicated.

What then is to be said for primaries? Are they an expensive political side show which does little more than fill the gap between the end of the winter sports season and the time when the baseball season becomes serious? Do they contribute anything really worthwhile to the political process, or would they if they were conducted in some other way?

I have no certain answers. Minnesota adopted a presidential primary designed to make Harold Stassen a front runner at least for a short time. The law was in effect from 1942 until 1956. It was repealed after two bad experiences (that is, in the judgment of party leaders). One was Eisenhower's near defeat of Harold Stassen in the 1952 primary; the second was Kefauver's defeat of Adlai Stevenson in the 1956 primary, despite the fact that Stevenson had been the Democratic nominee in 1952 and had in 1956 the full support of the party organization, the endorsement of Senator Humphrey and of the then Governor of the state, Orville Freeman.

What has happened in that state since neither proves nor disproves that the action taken after 1956 was good. The Republican party in convention without a primary was bitterly divided over the Goldwater choice in 1964, and there was sharp division over my candidacy and that of Senator Humphrey in 1968.

One or two things do seem clear about primaries.

The 1952 and the 1968 experiences indicate that an incumbent President who is successfully challenged in primaries is, either for political or for personal reasons, not likely to run for re-election.

Primaries also have eliminated some candidates early in the political year, or at least before the conventions of the parties: Stassen, for example, in 1948 when he was done in by Dewey in Oregon, and possibly Senator Muskie in Wisconsin in 1972, although this is not conclusive. Muskie may not be politically dead but only sorely wounded. He may lie down and bleed awhile and then rise to fight again, as did the hero in the medieval ballad. Whether it is good to have candidates eliminated early in a campaign year along the campaign trail is not certain, unless the objective is simply elimination and the nomination is to go to the one who survives, a kind of political trial by ordeal.

If primaries have not proved much about candidates what have they done in the past as to the issues? There is no evidence that they have affected issues. In 1948 there was no real test in primaries on the issue of civil rights. That test came at the convention itself. In 1960, the year primaries did have determinable bearing on the selection of the candidate, there was no significant division among Democrats on the issues. In 1968 the primary test was on the issue of the Vietnam war. Though the results were conclusive, the party in convention chose to ignore them.

Despite the fact that little positive good can be attributed to the primaries as a way of picking presidential candidates or formulating platforms, it does not follow that they should be eliminated. Neither does it follow that there should be more primaries, or that there should be a national primary.

The idea of a national primary is the worst of all proposals. Senator Mansfield and Senator Aiken, after one of their regular Senate Restaurant breakfasts, proposed such a primary. A national primary would at most quantify the failures and inadequacies of present primary practices. It would be difficult to administer, would certainly require a series of run-offs, and would probably cost more than the present primaries cost. Since there could be no selection of primaries on the part of candidates, it would give even greater advantage to candidates who have private fortunes or who have large financial backing.

A national primary would discourage state political organization and activities and would encourage the proliferation of political parties since the easier way might well be to run under a new party banner rather than to make the effort required in a national primary. It would probably result in the formation of essentially the same substructure of politics that now goes into national elections. There would certainly be caucuses to support candidates, and possibly primaries to pick primary candidates. The last state of politics might become worse than the first.

The ways of democracy are not simple, clear, and direct. William Stafford, a poet from Kansas, has warned that "if you purify the pond, the lilies die." What one proposes to do about primaries depends in large part on what one conceives to be the role of major parties in American politics and on the function and desirability of what is called a two-party system. It is in this context (the one in which most judgments and proposals about primaries are today being made) that the primary should be made into an effective means for clarifying party positions and picking candidates.

Primaries should not be an instrument for the capture of a party by a faction or by individuals for personal use or for aims not generally consistent with the party tradition. A political party, as Woodrow Wilson wrote, should not be an organization to be taken over and used, but an organism alive to issues and to people. Thus, although the liberal Republicans did not have a right to take over the Republican party in 1964, they did not deserve the Goldwater candidacy which was retrogressive and counter to new forces which were alive in the Republican party. In the same way, the Democrats should not have been forced in 1968 to support a military policy in Vietname which contradicted what that party had committed itself to in 1964, a policy against which it had stood since at least 1945.

At some point in the process of choosing presidential candidates and determining party platforms, there should be a break in the straight-line, popular, arithmetical choice. Persons or a party must be made responsible to the public. This was the principle incorporated into the method of the electoral college as provided in the Constitution. Responsible persons were to be chosen as presidential electors. They, in turn, were to make responsible selections and to be held answerable to their constituencies. This principle, I believe, is sound and should be the basis of primary laws as it is in principle the basis of proceedings in non-primary states.

Among existing primaries, the New York primary comes closest to conformity. In that primary, the names of presidential candidates are not on the ballot, nor even identified or associated with delegate candidacies. The delegate's name alone is formally taken to the voters for judgment. The delegate or his party or his candidate must inform the public who the delegate is, if that is necessary, or whom he supports, if that is necessary. The delegate once chosen is not legally committed to any candidate, although he may have personal and moral commitments. These delegates then go on to the national convention, at which candidates are picked and the platform is written.

This procedure not only conforms to the electoral college procedures of the United States Constitution and to the caucus system where the caucuses are open and democratic, but it also opens the way to greater participation on the part of voters since it does not require their physical presence at caucuses. It can offset the imbalance that often arises in caucuses because of the physical effort of some factions or persons to get people to the caucuses and consequently could result in a more democratic participation.

This kind of primary could be used to experiment with the wider use of absentee balloting and with spreading of the voting time over several days, experiments which might then be used as bases for changing voting practices in general elections.

I would make two other suggestions.

One is that the amount of money to be spent in primaries should be limited overall, but not the amount that might be spent on any one form of communication. More importantly the amount that any person can contribute should be absolutely limited. The new federal law limits only contributions from the candidate or his immediate family.

Existing legislation affecting primaries, as well as legislation relating to party processes which favor existing parties and which tend to underwrite the two-party system should be challenged on constitutional grounds.

One of the worst forms of discrimination is the requirement in several states that independent efforts and new parties must file their petitions for electors much earlier than the two major parties name their electors.

Ten of the states and the District of Columbia either have no statutory provision for independent electors or specifically forbid independent electors. (Three states forbid independent electors altogether. This seems directly contrary to the intent of the founding fathers in writing the electoral college provision.)

The way must be kept open to outside challenge from new political movements.

"Taxation without representation is tyranny" was the cry of James Otis at the time of the American Revolution. Unrepresentative politics, which leads to unrepresentative government, may not be tyranny but it is not the strength of democracy.

THE DEMOCATIC PARTY: PART WAY TO REFORM

Mary Meehan

A Presidential candidate in Florida received 42 per cent of the primary vote and 93 per cent of the delegates to the national convention. In California another candidate received 44 per cent of the vote and 100 per cent of the delegates. That candidate also won 41 per cent of the vote in Rhode Island and 100 per cent of the delegates. With 30 per cent of the vote in Wisconsin he took 80 per cent of the delegates.

Insurgents in the state of Washington won major support in precinct caucuses but were shut out at the state convention. In Illinois, a Presidential candidate did not run in the preferential primary and had delegate candidates for only thirteen of the sixty-two Chicago seats; yet he received most of the delegates from Chicago. The same candidate skipped the preferential primary in Indiana, yet was supported by many Indiana delegates on credentials and platform votes. A favorite son in the District of Columbia warned the major candidates to stay out of his primary; he then captured all of the D.C. delegates and used them for a backroom deal.

Does that sound like 1968? It does indeed, but it all happened in the great reform year of 1972. The results in Florida favored George Wallace. The outcome in Washington favored Henry Jackson. The results in California, Rhode Island, Wisconsin, Illinois, Indiana and the District of Columbia favored George McGovern.

The drive for reform of the Democratic Party began in 1968, when anti-war Democrats were treated unfairly almost everywhere. Peace folk from the North and West made common cause with blacks from the South who had also been shut out of the process. They lost most of their credentials challenges in Chicago. But a resolution providing for a reform commission slipped through under the leadership of Iowa's Harold Hughes.

When the reform commission was appointed in 1969, Senator McGovern was made its chairman and Senator Hughes its vice chairman. (Rep. Donald Fraser was appointed chairman when McGovern resigned early in 1971; but by then the commission's major decisions had been made.) The other members ranged from reformers to regulars and from doves to hawks.

The commission's mandate was vague; it was a general order to study the delegate selection process and recommend changes to assure broader citizen participation. The commission was also instructed to aid state parties in meeting the Call to the 1972 Democratic convention, which would forbid

Source: *The Nation* (January 8, 1973), p. 47–51. Reprinted by permission.

use of the unit rule in choosing delegates and would require that the selection process be open to public participation within the calendar year of 1972. But the 1968 turmoil had in a sense provided its own mandate. Simply stated, it was to move toward a "one Democrat, one vote" standard in selecting Presidential candidates.

The McGovern commission required certain reforms—such as open slate making and timely selection—to benefit all Democratic voters. These reforms, commission enthusiasts kept saying, opened the process to rank-and-file voters, but the commission made a small mistake: it failed to guarantee that all the votes of the rank and file would be counted.

The commission required convention states to select at least 75 per cent of their delegates at a level no higher than the Congressional district, thus providing some representation for political minorities. But the same requirement was not imposed on primary states. California and a few other states continued to give all the delegates to the person who won the primary, whether by majority or plurality. This meant that a majority of those who voted in the primary might be entirely unrepresented at the national convention—precisely what happened to the 56 per cent of California Democrats who voted for someone other than McGovern.

Other primary states awarded delegates to the winner of each Congressional district, but gave extra delegates to the candidate who won a statewide plurality. This system usually gave some representation to the runner-up, but did not produce a "one Democrat, one vote" result. In Florida, the outcome was almost as distorted as it would have been in a winner-take-all primary. In Ohio, Hubert Humphrey divided the district delegates almost evenly with McGovern, but because he held a small margin in the statewide vote, Humphrey won all the thirty-eight delegates elected at large.

The reform commission also allowed several states to confuse voters by holding preferential primaries but selecting delegates through a convention process. McGovern delegates from Indiana, where McGovern did not even run in the preferential primary, were bound to vote for preferential winners Humphrey and Wallace for the Presidential nomination. But they were free to vote against them on credentials and platform issues. They did so, and may have surprised Indiana voters who thought their vote in the preferential would be decisive.

The McGovern commission developed an obsession with women and minorities as delegates. It said that racial minorities, women and young people had been underrepresented at the 1968 convention. It could have remedied this injustice by insisting on an open process and a "one Democrat, one vote" rule. Instead it attempted social engineering, requiring state parties to encourage the presence on state delegations of minority group members, women and young people "in reasonable relationship" to their presence in the state's population.

The commission had difficulty explaining what it meant by "reasonable relationship," perhaps because the members themselves were not sure what they meant. Senator McGovern "at first agreed that a quota system had been adopted. But after lunch, he persuaded the gathering to declare unanimously that no such system had been intended." (*The New York Times,* November 20, 1969.) McGovern later explained, "The way we got the quota thing through was by not using the word 'quotas.' We couldn't have gotten quotas." (*National Journal,* June 19, 1971.)

The result of such double talk was great confusion in the state parties and the Presidential campaigns. No one knew exactly what percentage of delegates had to be women, under 30, black, or Chicano. Some state parties wrote quota systems into their own rules; others tried to reach a "reasonable relationship" in practice; others just ignored the guidelines on this question. Presidential campaigns also did their own interpreting, but often at the risk of credentials challenges.

Though a member of a group whom the "reasonable relationship" guideline is supposed to assist, I have never been convinced that the commission was justified in imposing it. It seems artificial and paternalistic to give us what we would be better off winning on our own. The first emphasis should have been on issue representation. If you assure everyone full and fair participation, the natural result is for minorities to organize their strength on the basis of issues important to them. Black candidates for delegate would run on such issues as assured income and a serious approach to the unemployment problem. Women might run on issues like equal employment, day care, etc. The young might talk about educational reform and the legalization of marijuana. Or women and minorities could run on other issues that seemed more urgent to them. Many of them entered politics on the peace issue and still have it as their chief concern.

Quota advocates might argue that their approach produced real gains on issues, but I am not sure they can prove it. It is true that the 1972 Democratic platform had a good plank on women's rights, a good one on bilingual education, and many strong statements on civil rights. Yet the first two issues were striking in the 1972 platform chiefly by comparison with the 1968 platform, which hardly set a high standard. And regardless of delegate selection methods, all recent platforms have had good statements on civil rights.

But the minority report calling for a $6,500 assured income for a family of four was defeated at the 1972 convention, and that was the most important issue for many black people. The defeat of the minority report left them with the usual patchwork of New Deal-New Frontier-Great Society programs that have not worked.

Feminist leaders complained about the manipulation of women delegates at the convention. They rightly questioned the value of being used as window dressing. Despite all we heard about the young delegates, there was no debate over legalizing marijuana. It is not a frivolous issue: the effect of the marijuana prohibition on the young probably has been second only to the effect of the war. The issue was ignored, apparently, in deference to McGovern's chances in November.

Liberals and radicals were supposed to rejoice at the sight of so many young people, black people, brown people and women at the 1972 convention. Yet the question was bound to arise: Once you get them there, what are they supposed to do? Just take their orders from George Mc-Govern? Is that so much better than taking orders from Richard Daley?

There is something demeaning about becoming a delegate primarily because of ethnic background, or sex, or age. This condition probably made some of the delegates less independent than they should have been. A young Chicano delegate told *The Washington Post:* "Well, how the hell I made it I don't know. Mostly I think I made it as a token Mexican and for a while this really hurt my ego. But whatever star guided me here I am indebted forever. I have already learned so much that textbooks will never seem the same."

The minority guideline protected only some minorities. Poor people, for example, were not included. The assured income proposal was defeated partly because the 1972 convention was overwhelmingly middle class and upper-middle class. The white ethnics also lacked special protection. A literal reading of the minority guideline seems to include ethnic and religious minorities; but it was interpreted in 1972 to include only racial minorities. It will have its real test when the ethnics start organizing. Democrats will then be so busy calculating quotas for Italians, Poles, Czechs, Lithuanians, Ukrainians, Croats, Slovenes, Greeks, Irish—and maybe even WASP's —that issues may be forgotten entirely. Suppose that a woman is of Greek descent but married to an Italian: for which national origin does she count? If a man is half Irish and half Polish, but has a Polish surname, does he count half and half or strictly Polish or what? The quota system may become a parody of itself and finally fall of its own weight.

When the McGovern commission met late in 1969, it was deadlocked on whether to require proportional representation on issues (as indicated by candidate preference). The commission tackled the question again in November, when a proposal to require proportional representation was soundly defeated. Harold Hughes, Patti Knox and David Mixner cast the only votes for the proposal. Commission member Fred Dutton, who had argued for more young delegates and women delegates, led the fight against proportional representation on issues. Dutton seemed to think that winner-

take-all was a fine practice. Senator McGovern, who had previously supported the concept of proportional representation, was not willing to require
it for 1972. He apparently thought the issue needed more debate within the
party. The commission finally passed a resolution urging, but not requiring,
proportional representation.

In 1972 four states and the District of Columbia had winner-take-all
primaries on a statewide basis. The four states were California, Oregon,
Rhode Island and McGovern's own South Dakota; Senator McGovern won
all four. The District of Columbia winner, Walter Fauntroy, soon led his
delegates into the McGovern camp. Had the delegates from these five primaries been allotted on a proportional basis, McGovern probably would
not have become the Democratic nominee.

The District of Columbia and South Dakota were two of only three
places where favorite sons won primaries in 1972. Proportional representation in the District would have been a healthy check on Walter Fauntroy's
ambition. In South Dakota it might have provided a little competition for
George McGovern. But California, with its 271 delegates, was the big prize.
State Democratic leaders there wanted to keep winner-take-all in order to
continue California's great power in national party affairs.

In April 1972, the Center for Political Reform and individual supporters
of Ashbrook, Chisholm, Humphrey, Jackson, Lindsay, McCarthy, Mc-
Govern, Muskie, Nixon and Yorty brought suit in California's supreme
court to end the winner-take-all in that state. They asked for proportional
allocation of delegates according to the results of the primary to be held
in June. The state supreme court declined to hear the case, and for some
reason the Center did not follow its initial plan of appealing to a federal
court. Another suit was brought in federal court by another group after the
primary, but was quickly dismissed. In the end, the only recourse for those
who opposed winner-take-all was an appeal to the Credentials Committee.
Such an appeal was made by California delegate candidates who had been
pledged to Chisholm, Humphrey, Jackson and Muskie.

McGovern fans were wrong when they said no one had challenged
winner-take-all before the California primary. And they missed the point
when they said it would be unfair to their candidate to take away some of
the delegates he had "won" because he had "played the game" on the assumption it would be winner-take-all. Party reform was supposed to favor
the voters, not the candidates. About 56 per cent of the Democrats who
voted in the California primary—that is, more than 2 million Democrats—
voted for candidates other than McGovern.

The Credentials Committee decided in favor of the 2 million voters; but
the full convention reversed the committee and decided for McGovern.
Speaking for the McGovern cause, Assemblyman Willie Brown cried that
he wanted "to stand before you in my just due, with my 271-man delega-

tion, and cast the votes of that unanimous 271-man delegation. And I don't think I deserve any less. . . . Give me back my delegation!" This reminded me of John Connally's fight for the unit rule at the 1968 convention. Brown, like Connally, seemed to regard his state's delegation as a personal possession. Others thought that a delegation, if it belonged to anyone, belonged to the voters who elected it.

The Chicago challenge was another case of reform gone haywire. Illinois has a preferential primary that is unrelated to delegate selection. A candidate may choose to enter the preferential, or run some delegate candidates, or do both. Edmund Muskie and Eugene McCarthy chose to do both. George McGovern stayed out of the preferential but fielded some delegate candidates.

Illinois law permits a delegate aspirant to run pledged to any person without that person's consent. Noncandidate Edward Kennedy may have been startled to find that twenty people in Chicago pledged themselves to him when they ran for delegate. And the Chicago Muskie campaign was plagued with overfiling and with fake Muskie candidates who were intent on confusing the Daley machine instead of aiding the Maine Senator.

Muskie won the Illinois preferential with more than 60 per cent of the vote. Most of the delegates were elected by Congressional district. Muskie won fifty-nine by district, including three in Chicago. McCarthy, partly because of greater stress on the preferential, won no delegates. McGovern won thirteen—all of them outside Chicago.

The other winner was Mayor Daley, who emerged with fifty-nine uncommitted delegates from Chicago. Daley's fifty-nine were soon challenged by Alderman William Singer, Rev. Jesse Jackson and other anti-Daley people. The hearing officer sustained their charge that the Daley organization had violated McGovern commission guidelines. Violations included secret slate making and underrepresentation of minorities and women. The Credentials Committee, and later the full convention, barred the Daley delegation and seated the Singer-Jackson group in its place.

The successful challenge delegation included blacks, Chicanos and women in proportion to their presence in Chicago's population. But Mike Royko, anti-Daley columnist of the *Chicago Daily News,* had a serious complaint about the new delegation. In an open letter to Alderman Singer, Royko said: "As I looked over the names of your delegates, I saw something peculiar. It might not be noticeable to somebody from another part of the country, but it jumps out at a native Chicagoan. There's only one Italian name there. . . . And only three of your fifty-nine have Polish names. . . . Your reforms have disenfranchised Chicago's white ethnic Democrats, which is a strange reform. . . ."

But the major shortcoming of the Singer delegation was that it did not represent Chicago's primary vote. Had the challengers followed the preferential vote, they would have split about 63 per cent Muskie to 37 per cent McCarthy—that is, thirty-seven Muskie delegates and twenty-two McCarthy delegates. Had they followed the primary vote on delegates, the majority would have been Daley people. But since they excluded all the Daley votes as impure, they could have divided according to the vote for non-Daley delegates. Leaving out the Daley votes and the votes for three Muskie delegates elected in Chicago and not challenged, the Chicago delegate vote broke down this way: Muskie, 44 per cent; Kennedy, 19 per cent; McCarthy, 15 per cent; McGovern, 11 per cent; uncommitted (non-Daley), 8 per cent; others, 3 per cent.

So how did the Singer delegation actually break down on Presidential preference? Just before the convention, this way: McGovern, 69 per cent; uncommitted, 22 per cent; Muskie, 5 per cent; McCarthy, 2 per cent; Chisholm, 2 per cent. There is really no way to justify a delegation so unrepresentative of a primary vote.

The Democratic Party may be too divided—and too tired—to pull itself together again. Institutions, like people, do run out of steam eventually. A party that has lasted more than 150 years should not be ashamed to acknowledge the symptoms of advanced age. But if the Democratic Party is dying, one could not guess this from observing the lively fight in progress for its control. The party could at least set an example for other institutions by providing fair rules for the fight.

The 1972 Democratic convention did require more reforms. It also provided for another reform commission, which is chaired by UAW leader Leonard Woodcock, and has forty-eight members. The new commission could become a peacemaker of sorts—if all factions of the party understand the stake they have in the "one Democrat, one vote" standard. The last two national conventions have provided this lesson for all who want to learn it.

The 1972 convention required that delegates to the next convention "shall be chosen in a manner which fairly reflects the division of preferences expressed by those who participate in the Presidential nominating process. . . ." A brief discussion in the Rules Committee, which proposed this change, suggested that it would forbid winner-take-all on both state and district levels. Certainly the Woodcock commission can interpret the new provision to require proportional representation on all levels.

Primary states can follow the example of Michigan, which in 1972 selected its delegates on the basis of the primary vote. Or they can let slates run in a primary and later pare themselves down to the percentage of the vote they have won in the primary. Convention states can assure proportional representation by following the example of Iowa, which has an excellent caucus system that is fair to all voters and candidates. Or they might copy other convention states that have adopted cumulative voting.

The 1972 convention passed a new provision that will encourage more participation by poor people. It required the Democratic National Committee to establish a special fund to pay expenses of delegates who otherwise could not attend the 1976 convention. And it suggested holding the next convention on a university campus in order to provide low-cost food and lodging for delegates. The 1972 convention also required that delegates to the next convention be real supporters of the candidates for whom they must vote. If properly enforced, this will unscramble systems that now allow a state convention to contradict a state primary.

The Woodcock commission is bound to face a major battle over the quota system. If it is expanded to include all economic and ethnic groups, it will become a mathematical monster. It will also encourage more divisiveness in the party without assuring real gains for minorities. And it may even reach the point of holding minorities down to certain levels, so that where blacks make up 10 per cent of a state's population only 10 per cent of the delegation may be black (because 90 per cent is allocated to other minorities).

An alternative is to abolish the quota system, for which there is much to be said. Proportional representation on issues can provide the protection needed by women and minorities. If a minority believes that no Presidential candidate answers its needs, it can field slates committed to its own issue positions but not committed to any candidate. If Presidential candidates fail to respond to the needs of minorities, they will be faced with black slates, women's slates, Italian slates, and so forth. That threat should assure sensitivity to minority interests.

It would not make sense to abolish one quota system only to impose another. There have been hints that party leaders may try to guarantee their own participation in the next convention. Many of them were defeated in 1972 delegate contests because they ran under the banner of losing Presidential candidates. They did not enjoy the experience; but even party leaders can get used to democracy.

Another good topic for the Woodcock commission is vote fraud. If it were cited as a specific basis for challenging any delegation, that would be a long step toward making the party honest. The 1972 convention did not deal with the problem of selecting challenge delegations, and it is something the Woodcock commission should face. The same standards of fairness that are used to unseat a delegation should be applied to any delegation that tries to replace it.

Unfair election procedures in 1968 hurt the left wing of the Democratic Party. The unfair procedures that remained in 1972 hurt the right wing and the Center. It is anyone's guess what might happen in 1976. But each faction can best serve its own interest by working for changes that will insure fairness to all. Then, at last, the voters will decide. Not the candidates, not the lawyers, not the young pros or the old pros. The voters.

What Did We Learn from the Polls This Time?

Martin Mayer

In prospect, one thing was perfectly clear about the forthcoming 1972 campaign: it would mark the apotheosis of social research as an election tool. The machinery had been perfected. The 1970 census and the reports on it had been designed to facilitate subsequent research; maps of census tracts lay about offices thick as autumn leaves; random number tables cluttered the bookcases. A pollster drawing a sample could be confident that it accurately represented the population almost to the degree that a doctor is confident the smear on the slide accurately represents the patient's bloodstream.

Thousands of really trained, experienced, efficient, conscientious interviewers were available for hire all around the country, and in case anybody ran short the larger established research houses (noblesse oblige) had organized an informal exchange procedure by which any one of them could draw on the field staff of the others. Questionnaire construction was still an art, but the sub-art of pre-testing a questionnaire before sending it into the field was nearing the status of a science. Polling, in fact, had become much more cut-and-dried than most human activities. "Any systematic person could replicate what we do," says The California Poll's Mervin Field, a non-swinging San Franciscan in exile from Princeton. "Systematic polling is paying attention to details. If you will pardon the reference to Vince Lombardi, you have to block and tackle every day."

Moreover, politicians had come to recognize the value of information: nobody wanted distorted polls anymore, or was likely to muddy the waters by proclaiming the inaccuracy of public-opinion research in general. In the depths of the agony of the McGovern collapse, when the wounds were still fresh, the most ardent spokesmen for that unfortunate campaign did not seek to deny that the published polls were more or less right—at least as of the day they were taken: of course, the spokesmen kept saying, that was

Source: *New York* (November 6, 1972), pp. 55–59. Reprinted by permission of Curtis Brown, Ltd. Copyright © 1972 by The NYM Corporation.

a week ago and things have changed so fast during the last week. . . .

Nevertheless, published poll results, nearly all from reputable operations that tell exactly what they are doing, became themselves an "issue" (whatever that means) in the 1972 elections. It was even seriously proposed that such polls be prohibited, as they recently have been in British Columbia. (This is by no means the first time around for the idea of de-legalizing polls in America—in the early 1930s, Congressman Walter Pierce of Oregon introduced a bill to forbid publication of the *Literary Digest* straw ballot or anything like it, on the ground that its accuracy perverted the political process.) Mostly, the proposals to investigate polling in 1972 were like the proposals made in the British Parliament in June 1971 to investigate the weather bureau: the proposer didn't like the poll results, just as the M.P.s hadn't liked the weather.

No doubt public-opinion polls, even election polls of a simple binary-choice variety, have been, can be and are abused. Political advertising specialist Joseph Napolitan tells a story of hornswoggling Sargent Shriver out of a run for the Maryland gubernatorial nomination by plastering the state with advertising for incumbent Marvin Mandel just before Shriver took a poll to measure his chances. This story, if true, reflects only marginally more discredit on Shriver than it does on Napolitan, because any politician with a few grains of sense should know that polls taken in the spring before a potential candidate has become a real candidate (let alone a campaigning candidate) must show a sizeable lead for the better-known man, usually the incumbent in any less than Presidential office. That's why the McGovern forces persisted in the face of their 5 per cent ratings. Oliver Quayle, who polls for NBC and for candidates (and supplies newspaper columnists with questionnaires and experienced interviewers to help them make their own special polls), says that "any politician who would make a decision based on a springtime poll as to who would win this election has got to be an idiot." People should not praise Napolitan, maybe he shouldn't even praise himself, for advising his client to spend $50,000 on the assumption that Shriver was an idiot.

Polls are obviously misrepresented in the reporting. Good reporters are scientists *manqué;* at heart, without thinking about it, they apply Occam's Razor, trusting the simplest story, and they follow Lord Kelvin's rule that if you can put a number on something you really know about it. The purpose of scientific numbers is that they predict what will happen under similar conditions in the future. Publication of poll results produces a crazy definition of victory in primary elections—not whether a candidate in fact wins or loses, but whether he does better or worse than the published polls said he would. This definition is good only for toy elections like primaries; when real office is at stake the rules change. The use of primaries as a way to choose candidates, always a dubious proposition practically, has become dubious in theory, too.

Of course, all opinion researchers insist that they don't *predict* elections: heaven forfend. As Mervin Field put it in a never-published letter to *The New Yorker* shortly after McGovern's lead over Humphrey had shrunk from 20 per cent in his and others' polls to about 6 per cent on primary day, "A poll is simply a description of the public mood at a given time—in other words, an observable fact at that time." But we all predict what will happen tomorrow on the basis of what happened today; even David Hume, the most cheerful of men, was driven to despondency by serious consideration of the idea that you really never can tell.

By early October, there was enough difference between different polls to create talking points against all of them. Field showed Nixon only 14 points ahead in California, while Yankelovich showed him 31 points up; Gallup and Harris showed McGovern gaining, slowly and slightly, while Sindlinger showed him falling even further behind. Different polls will usually show somewhat different results (the mathematics of sampling promise a high order of probability that a correctly drawn sample will be *near* the truth, not on it, and even careful polls following the same basic procedures, like Gallup's and Harris's, should be a few percentage points apart most of the time). But in this case the different numbers also reflected differences in procedure. Yankelovich, polling 16 states, had a much smaller sample for California alone than Field did; Sindlinger was using telephone interviews rather than personal contact, which presumably warps results somewhat in favor of the Republican candidate by leaving out all those too poor to have telephones. (But Sindlinger also has a trick question—a "dimension," he calls it—that would have saved the polls from their Truman/Dewey mistake: he asks people not only which candidate they plan to vote for but also which candidate they would like to see win. In 1948, a fair number of people who said they were going to vote for Dewey also said they hoped Truman would win; in spring 1972, in the McGovern-Humphrey primary contest, Humphrey did better on the loyalty test than on the how-will-you-vote test. In fall 1972, Nixon was doing just as well on the one as on the other.) In any event, nobody interested merely in who was going to *win* the election could find any reason to doubt the certainty of the result from any of the polls. McGovern's own poll, conducted by people who told each respondent they were working for McGovern before asking him for his preference, showed Nixon with a clearly unsurmountable lead.

Everyone around McGovern seems to feel that his bad showing in the polls has created a self-reinforcing prophecy—that he can't raise money because nobody thinks he will win (Sindlinger finds 5 per cent or less believing that McGovern will win), and that Democrats who would otherwise return to the fold are encouraged to stay off the reservation because they know they have so much company. Everyone around Nixon feels that the polls are dangerous to him because they encourage sympathy for the underdog and will give members of the President's "new majority" the feeling that they don't have to take the time and trouble to vote. Both attitudes are supported by instinct rather than information. When the Gallup Poll was fairly new and results were printed only in those newspapers that bought it, some academic researchers went looking for differences in voting behavior between people who knew the poll results and people who didn't; and they found that such knowledge made no difference at all. As Gallup likes to point out, Goldwater did about as well as expected in California even though a goodly percentage of the votes there were cast after all the networks had declared Johnson the winner.

It is by no means too early to say that McGovern's weakness as a candidate was not a result of his poor showing in the polls; his poor showing in the polls was the result of his weakness as a candidate. But the influence of the polls on this election—and their danger in subsequent elections— goes far beyond the sledgehammer question of their accuracy in forecasting how hard McGovern is going to be hit.

What was going to make the polls so important in 1972, after all, was not their measurements of who's ahead, but the chance they would give the candidates to be right before the event; to tailor their political approach to public feelings about "the issues," as formulated in slogans; to avoid offending the *Geist* of the politics of their time; to follow rather than to lead. "Polls are now an essential," Charles W. Roll Jr. and Albert H. Cantril write in their book *Polls*. "The candidate who usually prevails is the one who most effectively responds to the concerns of the people, and there is no better way to learn of these concerns than through opinion research."

Uncovering public attitudes toward "issues" is much trickier than straight election stuff, because the form of the question influences the attitudes apparently expressed. Asked if he could think of any occasion when opinion research did harm, Yankelovich said he thought that for a critical three to six months Lyndon Johnson was seriously misled about popular attitudes on Vietnam by polls showing that overwhelming majorities "had confidence" in the President's conduct of the war. Confidence, Yankelovich said, "is the last thing to erode: when you 'lose confidence' in an employee, you fire him. By asking the least sensitive question, the poll-takers concealed a great deal of unease about the war." Questions about "abortion" (an English word almost as negative as "black") draw one set of responses; questions about "a woman's right to control her reproductive facilities" draw different responses.

But neither the Nixon nor the McGovern researchers were likely to paint themselves into such corners. They were sophisticates: the academic orientation of the McGovern movement and the advertising orientation of the Nixon campaign came together here. Because both parties would be seeking to exploit the same "issues," as revealed to them by polling, the contest would rest on public perception of personalities. That would be

McGovern's strength, the academicians said. As Arthur Schlesinger Jr. wrote in *The New York Times Magazine* for publication the weekend Eagleton was pushed under for the third time, people don't like Nixon, and everybody who came to know McGovern would love him.

But McGovern had a peculiar *Geist* problem. George Gallup likes to recall that when he started polling in Iowa as a boy there was really only one issue in American politics: the Civil War. The Democrats were the Southern party, give or take some immigrants; the Republicans were the Northern party, and almost always won, the North being more populous than the South. Roosevelt changed these alliances, and made social class and status a major factor in determining party loyalty. In 1960, Simulmatics, a university-based research operation, did a study for Kennedy assuming that there were only two factors in the Kennedy-Nixon election—party loyalty and religion. Analyzing other people's polls state by state, the computer-based Simulmatics study told Kennedy in early September that he had already lost all the votes he would lose because of his Catholicism, but had not yet gained the votes he might gain. Several million dollars were then spent to buy time on local television stations in heavily Catholic areas, to show filmed excerpts of Kennedy's confrontation with Norman Vincent Peale and assorted Protestant ministers in Houston toward the beginning of the campaign. The Kennedy family felt it was money well spent. Simulmatics got a lot of business from the Government (and from friendly foreign governments) after Kennedy won.

McGovern's *Geist* problem was that he had won his nomination as the peace candidate, and all the polls proclaim that the nation perceives the Republicans as the peace party. This sounds like terrible nonsense in 1972, but there is folk wisdom behind it. The United States has fought four wars in this century, and every one of them was started in a Democratic Administration; no war has been started by a Republican Administration. Eisenhower sat by when Castro conquered Cuba and told the French they would have to hack it alone in Indochina; Johnson sent the Marines to the Dominican Republic and put half a million Americans in Vietnam. Nixon's rapprochement with China and the Soviet Union heightened the public feeling that the Republicans keep the country out of trouble.

On the other hand, the Depression and most of the bad recessions have occurred in Republican Administrations; folk wisdom says that the economy sours under the Republicans, sweetens under the Democrats. Without exception, the polls that say the Republicans will do better in foreign affairs also say the Democrats will do better domestically. Social research told McGovern to play to his party's strength, to go "pork-chopping," as this year's lingo has it; and the accumulated wisdom and rage of Tony Lewis and Tom Wicker were not enough to change the campaign pattern dictated by the polls.

But social research also tells McGovern he must be careful about how he attacks Nixon's domestic record. Having called for "fundamental change" in his primary campaign and in his early speeches as a candidate, he is now told to lay off that line. "What plays through the interviews over and over again," says Peter D. Hart, a sober young pollster who has *The Washington Post* as his chief acknowledged client, "is the statement that McGovern wants to change things too much, too fast."

"McGovern's greatest liability is what happened at the convention," says Yankelovich—a baggy man with graying hair and a thin mustache, wearing thick glasses, everybody's family doctor, who makes his living by telling industry about changing social attitudes, but this year is polling for *The New York Times* and *Time* magazine. "In our research on the primaries, almost nobody saw him as a radical. Immediately after the convention, lots of people saw him as a radical." That's death—less than 2 per cent of the American people consider themselves radicals. (Nearly 40 per cent consider themselves "conservatives," and half of that 40 per cent also consider themselves "Democrats.") So McGovern has been busily occupied denying that he's a radical. "What plays through," says Peter Hart, "is that he's a radical and he's indecisive. . . ."

On the biggest decision of all—Eagleton—the McGovern campaign went against the information in the polls, and suffered horribly by doing so. One of the highest ranking black officials in the Federal Government, himself a Democrat, spoke for many more people than he knew when he discussed the Eagleton affair: "Here's this fellow running for President who says he's all for the oppressed, the black, the Chicanos, the women, the poor. And there's somebody on his ticket who's being pushed around by the real oppressors of this society, the press and television and Jack Anderson, and what does this fellow do? He cuts the man off at the knees."

In the six days after the story of Eagleton's illness broke, Sindlinger found that 65 per cent of his cumulative telephone sample of 1,964 had talked about the matter, and only 10 per cent of those who talked lacked an opinion. Some 61 per cent thought Eagleton should stay on the ticket, while 29 per cent thought he should be dropped. Worse, from McGovern's point of view, most of those who thought Eagleton should go planned to vote for Nixon regardless. Among those who planned to vote for McGovern, three-quarters thought Eagleton should be kept; among those who were undecided, four-fifths thought he should be kept. Sindlinger starkly summarized the situation in his weekly report on what people are talking about: "To remove Eagleton from the Democratic ticket would do great damage to McGovern's chances of winning in November."

By Labor Day, Lou Harris, looking for something that might give the impression of a contest, was reduced to asking respondents whether they thought Nixon *ought* to win by a landslide. Somehow he thought it mildly encouraging for McGovern that only 35 per cent of the Democrats in his sample thought the President was entitled to a landslide. Looking into October, the researchers were intrigued by the prospect of a Senate debate on busing. More than half the small minority who said they planned to vote for McGovern were violently opposed to busing, and he simply couldn't go their way, because he couldn't. As it happened, McGovern was able to go through the week of the busing debate without mentioning the subject.

Except for its downgrading of the war as an "issue," then, social research made surprisingly little difference in the 1972 campaign. "When you have a close election," Yankelovich said, "the question of how you appeal to the Irish, what you say to the farmers, how you handle the Jews, might make an enormous difference. But that's all tactical maneuver. McGovern is so far behind that these tactical maneuvers can't help him."

Richard Nixon did not need polls to tell him that his best campaign tactic was simply to play President; and McGovern, who had never in any pre-convention poll won the support of as much as 30 per cent of his own party, obviously had to turn a sharp right and woo the unions and the bosses if he was to have any chance at all. This obviousness may not be truth, of course: Lou Harris believes McGovern might have done much better, or much less badly, if he had stuck with his initial "change-oriented" constituency. (Obviousness never impresses a pollster: "The prevailing-wisdom people in the New York-Washington axis," Harris says, "are almost always wrong about what the American people are thinking.") Some purely technical elements of timing were undoubtedly influenced by the techniques of polling: the McGovern people started their television spots early in a desperate hope of influencing the Gallup Poll to be taken the weekend of September 23; and the same poll was undoubtedly the reason the Nixon people launched their house-to-house canvass the previous Saturday.

Some polls did deliver new kinds of information. Yankelovich got into this year's election because *The New York Times* had been shocked to learn from subsequent polls that many of those who had voted for Eugene McCarthy in New Hampshire in 1968 had thought they were voting for *Joe* McCarthy. Yankelovich was doing very well measuring attitudes for industry to help management plan future marketing and personnel policies, and *The Times* hired him this year to check on what voters in primary elections thought as they were leaving the polling booth. One of the discoveries of his studies was that the Wallace vote was probably not available to any other Democratic candidate, but the columnists and editorial writers of *The Times* ignored it, and kept talking of a populist revolt. His later studies during the election campaign, though, convinced these worthies, glumly, that the country was sliding right (included in the Yankelovich questionnaire is a simple item about whether people consider themselves conservative, moderate or liberal, and a lot of complicated items about positions on particular "issues" to crossruff against the self-label and the choice of candidate). It would be interesting to know the extent to which this information was discussed at the luncheon of *Times* executives and McGovern that preceded his decision to say in New York that he would make crime the "number-one priority" of his Administration.

If the Democrats persist in permitting a heavy influence from academics in their inner council, and retain the "reform" rules that produced this summer's convention and the nomination of so poor a candidate, their abdication of all prospect of victory will make polling irrelevant and elections unexciting for a long time to come. But the interest in winning is likely to return when the party is no longer facing an incumbent President running for re-election in a prosperous year, and then both sides may well make much more profound and dangerous use of the mountains of data now accumulated almost accidentally by virtually continuous exploration of the moods of the American people. To go around the country telling special-interest groups what they want to hear is an exercise everybody expects of a political candidate, and nobody worries about it too much. To calculate a campaign to match all the half-consistent, half-conflicting attitudes that make a public mood at a given time would be a corruption of the political process that democracy might not survive. Yet both candidates this year were clearly willing to do just that, if necessary. Not the least of Nixon's advantages this year was the fact that he could sit back and allow his "new majority" to project their attitudes onto him while McGovern had to seek the expansion of his minority through older, self-contradicting accretions of promises.

In his greenhouse at home and on the huge, ornately carved dining table he uses as a desk at the office, Sindlinger keeps a loudspeaker and a gadget that allows him to feed the speaker from any of the phones his interviewers use. Because he spends hours every day listening in, he is probably closer to the feel of daily public response than any other boss of a polling operation. "You've got a very intelligent group of people in this country," he says, "and they're selfish like a pig." A political life *openly* dominated by selfishness is very nearly the last thing the country needs.

Democrats Defected in Droves

William Chapman

One out of every three Democrats voted for President Nixon in November to provide the largest defection from either party in at least two decades, according to a Gallup organization poll.

The post-election poll found that 33 per cent of Democrats abandoned their party to vote for Mr. Nixon. The rest voted for Sen. George S. McGovern.

It amounted to the largest defection from a party to the other party's presidential candidate in the 20 years since the Gallup organization began making post-election surveys to determine how particular groups had voted.

The defection of Democrats this year was even larger than in 1952 when 23 per cent of them crossed party lines and abandoned Adlai E. Stevenson to vote for Dwight D. Eisenhower.

Also, Mr. Nixon almost set another record for attracting independents —those who decline to state any party affiliation. In November, 69 per cent of the independents voted for Mr. Nixon, the Gallup poll showed, approximately equalling the 70 per cent independent vote which Mr. Eisenhower won in 1956.

Polling Dates

The post-election survey of 1,462 persons was conducted from Nov. 10 to Nov. 13.

It confirmed many of the pre-election predictions which anticipated a shattering of the traditional Democratic coalition that was composed of Catholics, blue-collar workers and minority groups.

The only segment maintaining Democratic loyalty was composed of blacks. The Gallup poll found that 87 per cent of the blacks who voted favored McGovern, approximately the same proportion that voted for Sen. Hubert H. Humphrey in 1968.

These were the other results of the Gallup post-election poll:
* Blue-collar workers, who comprise more than a third of the electorate, voted for Mr. Nixon by a margin of 57 to 43 per cent. That bloc normally is Democratic. Mr. Nixon received only 35 per cent of that vote in 1968 and Humphrey got 50 per cent. Gov. George C. Wallace received the remaining 15 per cent four years ago.

Source: *The Washington Post* (December 14, 1972), p. A–4. © The Washington Post. Reprinted by permission.

How Americans Have Voted Since '52
Vote By Groups in Presidential Elections Since 1952
(Based on Gallup poll survey data)

	1952 STEVENSON %	1952 IKE %	1956 STEVENSON %	1956 IKE %	1960 JFK %	1960 NIXON %	1964 LBJ %	1964 GOLDWATER %	1968 HHH %	1968 NIXON %	1968 WALLACE %	1972 MCG %	1972 NIXON %
NATIONAL	44.6	55.4	42.2	57.8	50.1	49.9	61.3	38.7	43.0	43.4	13.6	38	62
Men	47	53	45	55	52	48	60	40	41	43	16	37	63
Women	42	58	39	61	49	51	62	38	45	43	12	38	62
White	43	57	41	59	49	51	59	41	38	47	15	32	68
Non-White	79	21	61	39	68	32	94	6	85	12	3	87	13
College	34	66	31	69	39	61	52	48	37	54	9	37	63
High School	45	55	42	58	52	48	62	38	42	43	15	34	66
Grade School	52	48	50	50	55	45	66	34	52	33	15	49	51
Prof. & Business	36	64	32	68	42	58	54	46	34	56	10	31	69
White Collar	40	60	37	63	48	52	57	43	41	47	12	36	64
Manual	55	45	50	50	60	40	71	29	50	35	15	43	57
Under 30 years	51	49	43	57	54	46	64	36	47	38	15	48	52
30–49 years	47	53	45	55	54	46	63	37	44	41	15	33	67
50 years & older	39	61	39	61	46	54	59	41	41	47	12	36	64
Protestants	37	63	37	63	38	62	55	45	35	49	16	30	70
Catholics	56	44	51	49	78	22	76	24	59	33	8	48	52
Republicans	8	92	4	96	5	95	20	80	9	86	5	5	95
Democrats	77	23	85	15	84	16	87	13	74	12	14	67	33
Independents	35	65	30	70	43	57	56	44	31	44	25	31	69
Members of labor union families	61	39	57	43	65	35	73	27	56	29	15	46	54

• For the first time since at least the mid-thirties a majority of organized labor voted for a Republican presidential candidate. About 54 per cent of members of labor union families voted for President Nixon this year. That was at least 10 per cent more than any Republican candidate has received in the previous five elections.

• The votes of younger persons were almost evenly divided, with McGovern and Mr. Nixon drawing approximately the same amount of support for those between 18 and 30 years of age.

• Although Catholics previously had given Democratic presidential candidates a majority of their votes, they divided them evenly between McGovern and the President this year, Mr. Nixon received 52 per cent of the Catholic vote on Nov. 7. Four years ago, he won only 33 per cent.

Not since 1956, when Mr. Eisenhower won about half of the Catholic vote, had a Republican candidate fared so well in that category.

THE MEANING OF THE PRESIDENT'S LANDSLIDE

Vermont Royster

The first question is, Why? The second question is, What does it mean?

It is difficult to be sure why President Nixon won re-election by such an astounding margin, not because reasons are lacking but because there are so many of them:

The fact that he was an incumbent, and only rarely have we turned out Presidents in office. The impressiveness of his overall record, particularly in foreign affairs. The accidents of the campaign, including the last-minute developments toward peace in Vietnam. The appearance of "radicalism" in the McGovern program. The ineptness of the Senator's own campaign. The skill with which Mr. Nixon campaigned loftily from the White House. And the possibility—of which there are some signs—of a basic shift in the attitude of people towards the role of the federal government in the nation's affairs.

The second question is equally difficult for much the same reasons.

If the election turned on the particularities of the campaign, then the results reveal no more than an ad hoc decision between these two particular candidates. That is, it was a political decision good for this campaign only.

Source: *The Wall Street Journal* (November 9, 1972). Reprinted with permission of *The Wall Street Journal.*

On the other hand, if the particularities were less important than an underlying movement away from the political philosophy of the New Deal-Fair Deal-Great Society, then this election could indeed mark a great political watershed, comparable in significance to that of 1932.

And for those who would leap to great conclusions within 24 hours of the returns, there's the complication that Mr. Nixon's party was badly mauled in the state and local races. Despite the Republican presidential victory, the Democrats kept control of both Houses of Congress.

Yet for all the complications and cross-currents, there are a few clues of significance. One lies in what has happened inside the Democratic Party. Another can be glimpsed from the trend of national voting over the past third of a century, if you don't let the ripples obscure the tide.

By all the usual political expectations, the Democratic Party had great ones this year. For four years the economy has been, and still is, plagued by unemployment, high taxes and inflation, to the discontent of the people. Many of the government's programs—notably welfare—had become monstrosities to anger the people. The administration in office has been sullied by scandals, of which Watergate was only the latest and not necessarily the most important. Abroad there was the draining, frustrating war that might be ended but could not be won.

On the surface, then, things seemed made to order for the opposition party. The Republican administration appeared to be in much the same trap as the Democratic one in 1952, when the voters decided that they had "had enough" and turned it out.

Every poll right up to election eve showed President Nixon apparently vulnerable on the traditional "gut" issues. On keeping the economy healthy the latest Harris poll showed 60 per cent of the voters negative on Mr. Nixon; 54 per cent negative on his handling of pollution; 61 per cent negative on crime and law and order; 69 per cent negative on his handling of taxes and spending.

But these advantages proved seeming only. His critics notwithstanding, President Nixon by election day had won the respect of the majority, if not their affection, for his decisiveness and his willingness to grapple with hard decisions. This coupled with the fact that he was already President would have probably made it difficult for any Democrat to defeat him.

Senator McGovern, moreover, compounded these difficulties with an appearance of ineptitude. He changed his mind too many times about too many things, from Senator Eagleton to his Asian policy to his economic program. He also grew querulous as his frustrations mounted. How much of a factor this was no one can be sure but it must have been appreciable.

There was another and more important factor. Senator McGovern and his supporters completely misread the people's discontent. Somehow they were persuaded by the noise of the anti-Vietnam demonstrators, left-wing theorists, rebellious youth, angry blacks and the like that the country was ready for a revolution in politics.

Consequently, Senator McGovern mistook the dissatisfactions about Vietnam for a willingness to cut-and-run; his solution was simply to quit and beg Hanoi to be charitable. He mistook the unhappiness with the welfare program for a willingness to embark on what appeared to be an even bigger welfare program.

Similarly, he misread the people's weariness with the high cost of arms for a willingness to dismantle our defenses, mistook an interest in reform for an acceptance of revolutionary changes in everything from taxes to social legislation.

At the same time he ignored many of the people's real grievances. School busing is no doubt an overblown issue. What it symbolizes is not. People have grown resentful at having the long arm of the federal government reach out to dictate to local school boards, zoning commissions and city halls.

By seeming not to understand these resentments, Mr. McGovern left the impression he had little sympathy with them and this only increased the resentments. It was the totality of all of these things that created the image of the Senator as a "radical."

Given all that, the chances are that the Democrats lost this election at Miami by nominating a man with an illusion about the mood of this country. There remains the question of why the party—which was for so long in tune with the people's feelings—nominated such a candidate.

The explanation for this lies in what happened to the Democratic Party, or rather what has been happening to it over a long period of years.

The conventional view of American politics is that the so-called Roosevelt coalition, born in the 1930s, has held its grip on the voters through Truman, Kennedy and into the Johnson years, with the Eisenhower period a brief interruption much like the Cleveland period during the long years of Republican ascendancy.

The actual record mars this conventional picture. In fact, Democratic power hit its peak in 1936 and has been eroding ever since. Even Roosevelt himself won by successively smaller margins in 1940 and 1944. The 1948 Truman victory was spectacular only in its surprise; it was a paper-thin victory.

So too was Kennedy's margin over Mr. Nixon on Mr. Nixon's first try. Lyndon Johnson did win by a landslide, but in that election—as in this one —there was the added factor that the losing candidate was inept and seemingly too radical. It's clear in retrospect that the Johnson sweep did not mean what it then seemed to mean.

Moreover, during much of this period we had a divided government. Truman, Eisenhower and now Nixon have had one or both Houses of Congress controlled by the other party.

What this record suggests, therefore, is a steady erosion of the Democratic power based on the coalition of labor, urban bosses, farmers, ethnic groups including especially the blacks, the intellectual community and traditional Southern Democrats.

That coalition could be, and was, patched together for particular elections, but each time with more difficulty. There were always inherent contradictions in it: what do farmers and urban bosses have in common? There was also the fact that much of what had to be done to pacify one or the other of these groups tended to alienate another group, and also the large, if somewhat amorphous, middle-class voters.

Besides, much of the New Deal-Fair Deal-Great Society programs failed to live up to their promises. They neither cured unemployment nor diminished social unrest: they added new problems of inflation and ever-rising taxes. Some, such as the many welfare programs, aggravated the very problems they were intended to solve.

In 1972 the patchwork unravelled. Senator McGovern went to Miami with a minority of the primary votes and hardly any support from either the party regulars or the leaders of the old party power groups; labor, for instance, or Southern Democrats or urban bosses.

Yet he achieved a sort of *coup d'état* first, because, he skillfully used the party rules he had written and, secondly, because the rest of the party was divided and confused.

That division and confusion was symptomatic. It was clear at Miami, if not before, that the national Democratic Party had lost its sense of direction. With the old war-cries no longer effective, the Muskies and the Humphreys knew not which way to turn. Senator McGovern and his supporters did. They had the power of evangelical certainty.

As it turned out, it was the evangelism of a cult. When this election is fully analyzed it will show, I suspect, that the millions who did vote for Senator McGovern were simply expressing lingering Democratic loyalties or were moved by strong anti-Nixon feelings. McGovern politics as such called forth very little response from the people.

This election, then, buried the old Democratic politics. What is not clear—indeed what is very fuzzy—is whether, as some think, it marks the emergence of a new Republican majority.

Neither the record of past elections nor the results of this one prove such a thesis. If past elections have shown the voters progressively less willing to continue the Democratic mandate, they have shown no inclination to give one to the Republicans.

In this election President Nixon can claim a personal victory but it is certainly not a Republican one. Even the size of his own victory is clouded by the particularities of this campaign. Senator McGovern contributed as much to it as Mr. Nixon.

It's clouded in other ways, too, for even Senator McGovern did not misjudge the people in everything. They do want honesty in government, good conduct from their officials. Morality in government is a perfectly valid issue, and the hints of scandalous behavior in the administration have taken their toll in public opinion.

Senator McGovern used it with some effect. It was almost the only issue he had. That he could not use it more effectively can be accounted for only by the impression he left in other ways that he was out of step with his times.

Nevertheless, it is an issue that will remain to haunt the Republicans until, or unless, the President exorcises it. It will be one more obstacle in the way of convincing the public that Republican leadership can bring an uplift of the spirit, that they have a party to which all man can repair.

That is a measurable obstacle. Those same polls that showed Senator McGovern distrusted, showed the Democrats as a party more trusted than the Republicans. And so long as that feeling prevails the Republicans will not be a true majority party. Voters will think them handy as an alternative when Democrats are out of step; they will be inclined to return to the Democratic fold when the aberration has passed.

Thus on the morrow of the election some tentative answers. Richard Nixon has clearly won a vote of confidence, his margin enhanced by the particularities of the campaign. For the Democrats, an era has passed. The old politics is worn out; the national party no longer speaks for the American people, as it once did so surely.

But there has as yet been no transference, from either the disaffection with the Democrats or from the respect won by President Nixon, to a new and durable allegiance to the Republican Party.

The country remains, as it has for years past, on a political teeter-totter board, unwilling for the time being to give either party a clear mandate to govern. For that decision, the nation waits.

WATERGATE

As this volume goes to press, the events and activities that have come to be known as "Watergate" continue to unfold week by week, and the end is not yet in sight. It is already clear that corruption and criminal activity for political ends have infected the Nixon Administration beyond anything ever known before in the federal government. Beyond that general fact, however, there are more questions than answers. What can we learn from these revelations? What do they reveal about American politics and American society? Is it true in any sense that a society gets the kind of government that it deserves?

As Thomas Cronin points out in the article reprinted in this section, the Presidency has become progressively bureaucratized so that a whole new layer of administration now exists between the President on the one hand and cabinet secretaries and their departments on the other. This staff, attached to the White House, has shown an increasing tendency to encroach on the work of the departments. Did this centralization increase the likelihood that Watergate could take place? Did President Nixon's preferred style of operation—channeling virtually all communication and decisions through a very few trusted subordinates such as H. R. Haldeman and John Ehrlichman—make it harder for him to control the Presidential establishment and, in that way, increase the likelihood of Watergate? If it is fair to say that a President normally sets the moral tone of his Administration, where did Richard Nixon fail and why?

In order to attain the Presidency a man must have well-developed instincts for the acquisition of power. Once in office, however, what restraints are there on those instincts? Clearly, in these days of complex government, a President must have an apparatus to help him govern, but what is to restrain him from creating a personal apparat *and surrounding himself with* apparatchiki *whose primary characteristic is personal loyalty and readiness to advance the career of their patron, and hence their own careers, by virtually any means they deem effective?*

It is not yet possible to foresee the restrictions on the Presidency that may follow from Watergate, but it seems likely that the role of the President vis-à-vis Congress will be clarified. Specifically, there will probably be clarification of the war-making power, the power of impoundment, and the doctrine of executive privilege.

The need for stronger legislation concerning fund raising and campaign practices has also become clear. The aftermath of Watergate has made many Americans aware that it is almost impossible to change Presidents between elections save in the case of the President's death. Regardless of waning public confidence, if a President chooses to remain in office he will almost certainly be able to serve out his term. Impeachment, like all ultimate weapons, is almost too terrible to use unless national catastrophe seems imminent. However, how effective can a President be who has lost the confidence of a major segment of the American people, and what may be the costs to the nation if he remains in office?

Watergate is a morality tale, and regardless of the formal legislative and other changes that may grow out of it, it will have an impact on the Presidency for a long time to come. The public may learn to measure candidates in new ways, and those who succeed to the office will be sensitive to a set of sins and errors that must be avoided at all costs.

Statement on The Washington Post

Clark MacGregor

According to the Gallup, Harris, Sindlinger, and Yankelovich polls, the political leftist movement known as McGovernism is about to be repudiated overwhelmingly by the American people. As it should be. But, frustrated, twenty-six points behind in the polls, with three weeks to go, George McGovern—and his confederates—are now engaging in the "politics of desperation"; we are witnessing some of the dirtiest tactics and hearing some of the most offensive language ever to appear in an American presidential campaign.

Lashing out wildly, George McGovern has compared the President of the United States to Adolf Hitler, the Republican Party to the Ku Klux Klan, and the United States Government to the Third Reich of Nazi Germany. His personal assaults on the President have been characterized by such terms as "most corrupt," "murderous," and "barbaric," and his running-mate has served as an echo chamber.

And *The Washington Post*'s credibility has today sunk lower than that of George McGovern.

Using innuendo, third-person hearsay, unsubstantiated charges, anonymous sources, and huge scare headlines—the *Post* has maliciously sought to give the appearance of a direct connection between the White House and the Watergate—a charge which the *Post* knows—and half a dozen investigations have found—to be false.

The hallmark of the *Post*'s campaign is hypocrisy—and its celebrated "double standard" is today visible for all to see.

Unproven charges by McGovern aides, or Senator Muskie, about alleged campaign disruptions that occurred more than six months ago are invariably given treatment normally accorded declarations of war—while proven facts of opposition-incited disruptions of the President's campaign are buried deep inside the paper. When McGovern headquarters in California was used as a boiler room to rally hard-core anti-war militants to confront the President—that was apparently of no significance to a newspaper which has dispatched a platoon of reporters to investigate charges that somebody sent two hundred pizzas to a Muskie rally last spring.

> Why hasn't *The Washington Post* investigated—The Molotov cocktail discovered on October 8th at the door of the Newhall, California, Nixon Headquarters?

Source: "Clark MacGregor's Statement on *The Washington Post*," *The Washington Post* (October 24, 1972). © The Washington Post. Reprinted by permission.

The extensive fire damage suffered September 17th to the Nixon headquarters in Hollywood, California?

The arson of September 25th which caused more than $100,000 in damage to the Nixon headquarters in Phoenix, Arizona?

The extensive window breaking and other trashing this fall at Nixon storefronts in New York City, Arlington, Massachusetts, and Los Angeles County?

While the *Post* itself openly and actively collaborated in the publication of stolen top secret documents of the Government of the United States sixteen months ago—today, it is faking shock and outrage at some obvious volunteers who were allegedly spying on Larry O'Brien.

Like George McGovern, who personally encouraged Daniel Ellsberg to commit the deed for which he faces a possible 115 years in a Federal Penitentiary—*The Washington Post* is a hypocrite. While each crime is reprehensible, which is the more serious? Stealing top secret documents of the Government of the United States; or allegedly stealing Larry O'Brien's political papers?

The purpose of the *Post* campaign is clear: To divert public and national attention away from the real issues of this campaign—peace, jobs, foreign policy, welfare, taxes, defense and national priorities—and onto the phony issues manufactured on L Street and in McGovern headquarters.

It is said that this is a dirty campaign, but all the dirt is being thrown by only one side. The mud slinging, the name calling, the unsubstantiated charges, the innuendos, the guilt by association, the character assassination, the second-hand hearsay are all tactics exclusively employed by the McGovernites and their apologists. President Nixon will remain on the high road, discussing issues of real concern to the American people in a fair, forthright, and hard-hitting manner. The American people will apply a single standard in judging the performance of Richard Nixon and George McGovern, even though that essential fairness is not exhibited by *The Washington Post* and a few others.

A Refusal to Believe It All

Haynes Johnson

The Watergate, shortly after midnight, Sunday, June 18, 1972: Frank Wills, 24, slim, black, an $80-a-week security guard who lived in a one-room Washington apartment, was patrolling alone that night. The other guard who was supposed to be on duty had left early. Wills was checking the bottom level of the building when he noticed tape placed over the latches of two doors so the doors wouldn't lock when closed. He removed the tape and continued on his rounds. It hadn't struck him as suspicious: "I thought it might be maintenance men." Still, "just to make sure," he returned about 10 minutes later.

This time he found the locks on all the doors of the level taped open. He immediately went to the lobby and called the metropolitan police. After the police arrived, they discovered the locks on upper floor levels also had been taped and that the 6th floor suite occupied by the Democratic National Committee had been tampered with and opened. "When we went inside all the office lights were on and we saw men speaking in foreign accents moving around and crawling on the floor," a policeman said. All the men were well-dressed, all were wearing rubber surgical gloves.

The police confiscated lock-picks, door jimmies, a walkie-talkie, a short-wave receiver, 40 rolls of unexposed film, two 35-millimeter cameras, three pen-sized tear gas guns and an array of sophisticated eavesdropping equipment capable of picking up and transmitting all conversations, including those over telephones. They also seized $2,300 in cash, most in $100 bills, with the serial numbers in sequence. One of the suspects was carrying an application blank of the kind the Democrats had been sending to college newspapers for issuance of press credentials for their presidential nominating convention to be held three weeks later in Miami Beach. In the address books carried by two of the five men police noted the name of someone called "Hunt." Beside Hunt's name one of the suspects had written "W.H." Another noted Hunt's association as "W. House."

The White House, about 9:15 Monday night, April 30, 1973: President Richard M. Nixon was sitting behind his desk in the Oval Office, flanked by a bust of Lincoln and the American flag, reporting to the American people on what "has come to be known as the Watergate affair." The President was in the midst of his address when he said: "Looking back at the history of this case, two questions arise: How could it have happened—who is to

Source: *The Washington Post* (May 6, 1973). © The Washington Post. Reprinted by permission.

blame?" Moments later, he said: "I will not place blame on subordinates, on people whose zeal exceeded their judgment and who may have done wrong in a cause they deeply believe to be right. In any organization the man at the top must bear the responsibility. That responsibility, therefore, belongs here in this office. I accept it."

The President had taken the responsibility, but still the larger questions lodged between those two events remained unanswered: How—and why—did it happen? What was to be accomplished at such risk? How could so many of the President's men—men he himself had carefully picked for their loyalty and dedication—betray their public trust? What degree of damage has Watergate done to Richard Nixon personally, to the office of the presidency, and to the judicial process? And, perhaps the most perplexing piece of the puzzle, why did it take so long for Watergate to make any impact on the country?

It is not as though nothing has been known about Watergate for the past 10 months. Indeed, within days after the break-in last June many of the critical elements in the case had already appeared in the press.

In less than a week it had been established that E. Howard Hunt, the former CIA agent, had been hired by the White House after a recommendation from a key Nixon adviser, Charles W. Colson; that Hunt had refused to answer questions by FBI agents in connection with the Watergate break-in; that Bernard Barker, his longtime CIA associate arrested at the Watergate, had attempted a year before to obtain blueprints of the Miami Beach convention hall and its air-conditioning system; that big money was involved, that it flowed to a Miami bank, and that Barker withdrew large sums in $100 bills; that James McCord, now established as a high-ranking veteran CIA agent and previously a toiler for the FBI, had been hired not just by the Committee for the Re-election of the President, but in October, 1971, by the Republican National Committee; that forgeries and diagrams of the two large ballrooms to be used for George McGovern's Florida convention headquarters figured in the case; that there had been other break-ins—one also at the Watergate, in the offices of Sargent Shriver, Patricia Harris and Max Kampelman, all prominent in national Democratic Party affairs; and, in the most bizarre touch of all, that Martha Mitchell was saying publicly she would leave her husband John unless he left the Nixon re-election effort because of "all those dirty things that go on."

Despite all this, there was no public outcry.

Enter G. Gordon Liddy

Within two weeks after the break-in other damaging information had come to light. There was the discovery of a loaded pistol, diagrams of the

Democratic National Committee headquarters and electronic eavesdropping devices in Hunt's office within the White House complex. There was Mitchell's own resignation as director of the Nixon campaign apparatus. And it was learned—and printed—that Hunt had been gathering considerable information about Sen. Edward M. Kennedy's accident at Chappaquiddick.

Still no public outcry.

Within a month the name of G. Gordon Liddy had entered the case, and his association with the White House and the re-election committee had been established. Phone records dating back to March, 1972, showed that Barker had made at least 15 calls to the Nixon campaign organization in Washington headquartered at 1701 Pennsylvania Ave. NW, just across from the White House.

August, after the Democrats had met and chosen George McGovern as their presidential nominee and the month the Republicans gathered to again nominate Mr. Nixon, brought further major disclosures. On August 1, The Washington Post reported that a $25,000 check had been given personally to Maurice Stans, the former Secretary of Commerce who had become the President's chief fund-raiser in his re-election campaign. The check, in turn, was deposited in Barker's Miami bank account. Questions about secret funds and huge publicly unaccounted campaign donations dominated the headlines for the rest of the month. On Aug. 26 the General Accounting Office, Congress' fiscal watchdog, reported "apparent violations" of the federal Election Campaign Act by the Nixon re-election committee. Banner headlines trumpeted official documentation that a $350,000 cash fund had been kept in Stans' re-election office safe.

Still no outcry. Damning as these collective reports had been on a daily basis over more than two months, and ominous as were the implications, the American public did not believe. In crossing the country during the month of September interviewing voters in their homes, a team of eight Washington Post reporters would go for days without hearing a single person voluntarily bring up the Watergate case. The people did not want to face the implications, did not want to believe them, or did not want to acknowledge that they could be anything more than another example of dirty tricks employed by all politicians.

Believing the Denials

If they followed the case at all, they evidently believed the official denials which had begun immediately following the break-in news and which continued as each episode was unveiled. They believed because they wanted to believe. It was unthinkable that such a massive pattern of lying could be conducted from so high a level.

June 18, John Mitchell, commenting on the break-in and the knowledge that McCord worked for his committee: "The person involved is the proprietor of a private security agency who was employed by our committee months ago to assist with the installation of our security system. He has, as we understand it, a number of business clients and interests and we have no knowledge of these relationships . . . There is no place in our campaign, or in the electoral process, for this type of activity and we will not permit it nor condone it."

June 20, Ken W. Clawson, deputy director of commmunications at the White House, commenting on the fact that Hunt had been hired at Charles Colson's recommendation in the White House: "I've looked into the matter very thoroughly and I am convinced that neither Mr. Colson nor anyone else at the White House had any knowledge of, or participation in this deplorable incident at the DNC. Hunt, he stressed, had been working as a White House consultant on declassification of the Pentagon Papers and most recently on narcotics intelligence.

June 21, Ronald Ziegler: "We don't know where Mr. Hunt has been because he has not been involved in a consulting capacity with the White House since March." He added that President Nixon was not concerned "about any allegation of the committing of a crime" and that "the appropriate investigations of that are taking place."

July 8, Mitchell, after resigning "to devote more time to his wife and family" and being praised by the President for making "a most substantial sacrifice, personal and financial," answering whether his departure was in any way connected with Watergate: "On the contrary, if my own investigation had turned up a link between the White House and the raid, I would have wanted to stick around and clear it up." His own Watergate inquiries, he went on, "have not produced much more than the private agencies or the newspapers have," but he was satisfied that no one in authority in the Republican apparatus had anything to do with it.

An Explosive Report

The disclosures and denials came ever more quickly through September and October, and still it was the denials which were believed.

There were allegations about destruction of Nixon committee financial records after the June break-in, of Mitchell controlling a secret fund used to pay for gathering information on the Democrats, of eavesdropping logs being delivered to the committee after the "bugs" had been implanted in Democratic headquarters before the arrests, of an attempt to place more "bugs" in McGovern's Capitol Hill campaign headquarters. More names surfaced: Jeb Stuart Magruder, Robert C. Mardian, Frederick La Rue, Alfred C. Baldwin.

Then, on Tuesday, Oct. 10, 1972, Carl Bernstein and Bob Woodward of The Post disclosed the most explosive evidence to that time:

"FBI agents have established that the Watergate bugging incident stemmed from a massive campaign of political spying and sabotage conducted on behalf of President Nixon's re-election and directed by officials of the White House and the Committee for the Re-election of the President. The activities, according to information in FBI and Department of Justice files, were aimed at all the major Democratic presidential contenders and—since 1971—represented a basic strategy of the Nixon re-election effort."

They reported that hundreds of thousands of dollars in Nixon campaign contributions had been set aside to pay for an extensive undercover campaign aimed at discrediting individual Democratic presidential candidates and disrupting their campaigns. These activities, which they described as "unprecedented in scope and intensity," included following members of Democratic candidates' families and assembling dossiers on their personal lives; forging letters and distributing them under the candidates' letterheads; leaking false and manufactured information to the press; throwing campaign schedules into disarray; seizing confidential campaign files and looking into the lives of dozens of Democratic campaign workers; planting provocateurs among groups preparing to demonstrate at both the Republican and Democratic conventions; and investigating potential donors to the Nixon campaign before their contributions were solicited.

The Sharpest Response

Five days later, the Post reporters disclosed that Dwight Chapin, the President's appointments secretary, was one of the "spy" contacts for Donald Segretti, who was paid for his undercover work by the President's personal lawyer, Herbert W. Kalmbach. And five days after that, they reported that Haldeman, the President's strong right-hand man and most trusted counselor, was among the officials authorized to approve payments from a secret espionage and sabotage fund.

These stories drew the sharpest response of all. "The Post had maliciously sought to give the appearance of a direct connection between the White House and the Watergate—a charge The Post knows—and a half dozen investigations have found—to be false," said Clark MacGregor, chairman of the re-election committee.

And the people still wanted to believe the White House, still could not accept what had happened. Even today, after all the disclosures, many Americans do not want to believe it.

Of all the voices raised thousands of miles apart on the same day last week, two undoubtedly expressed the thoughts of many citizens. In California, Ronald Reagan said those responsible for Watergate should not be considered criminals. They are not, he said, "criminals at heart." In Washington, Melvin Laird said if the gravest suspicion—that the President himself in fact was involved—were proved true, that kind of disclosure "would be very bad for the country." There are some things, he added, that "I don't want to know."

In short, we should believe the best, not the worst.

Thus, at the heart of the Watergate affair lies more than a case study of power misused and trust misplaced. Watergate betrays an attitude. The President touched on it in his speech last week when he said: "I know that it can be very easy under the intensive pressures of a campaign for even well-intentioned people to fall into shady tactics, to rationalize this on the grounds that what is at stake is of such importance to the nation that the end justifies the means."

This is precisely the cast of mind—that the ends do justify the means, that the most powerful people know what is best, that the system is served most effectively by those who are convinced that *their* motives, *their* goals, *their* methods justify the actions taken—that has resulted in the shaking of America's belief in the presidency.

The Nixon Tone

In the commentaries on Watergate, much has been made of the grimly determined, disciplined, humorless, arrogant Nixon loyalists who have now become implicated, but, unpalatable though it may be, the President cannot easily disassociate himself from the attitudes of his subordinates. The tone in the Nixon White House has been set from the top down. It is a tone that has consistently articulated the idea that only *we* know what's best, *we* have the wisest sense of the country's course, *we* alone will make the necessary judgment and decisions, *we* will not brook criticism or dissent.

Thus, Richard Nixon: "The average American is just like the child in the family. You give him some responsibility and he is going to amount to something. He is going to do something. If, on the other hand, you make him completely dependent and pamper him and cater to him too much, you are going to make him soft, spoiled and eventually a very weak individual."

Thus, H. R. Haldeman: "He [the President] is naturally concerned by the kind of criticism that can get in the way of what he's trying to do, and that would be unfair criticism. Or the kind of criticism—you get a very good case in point right now where we're faced with the President having the other night on television very carefully explained . . . the background and the present status of his peace negotiations . . . and before that talk on television you could say that his critics, people who were opposing what he was doing, were unconsciously echoing the line that the enemy wanted echoed."

Thus, John Ehrlichman telling the FBI that he knew that G. Gordon Liddy and E. Howard Hunt had broken into the office of Daniel Ellsberg's psychiatrist in September of 1971 and that he had merely instructed them "not to do this again."

Thus, John Mitchell, after repeatedly denying that he knew anything about the Watergate break-in, conceding that while still chief legal officer of the United States, he twice participated in private meetings in which illegal activities were raised and discussed, but clearly took no steps to prosecute them.

Thus, Richard Kleindienst as attorney general telling a Senate hearing that the President has the power to forbid 2.5 million federal employees from testifying before Congress under any circumstances, including the commission of a crime, and saying: "If it feels he is exercising power like a monarch you could conduct an impeachment proceeding."

Thus, Charles W. Colson, in a memo to the White House staff 72 days before the 1972 presidential election: "Think to yourself at the beginning of each day, 'What am I going to do to help the President's re-election today?' and then at the end of each day think what you did in fact do to help the President's re-election . . . Just so you understand me, let me point out that the statement in last week's UPI story that I was once reported to have said that 'I would walk over my grandmother if necessary' is absolutely accurate."

Thus, Dwight Chapin, before the grand jury: "I had the authority to do a lot of things; I had the authority to plan a presidential trip to China; I sure as hell had the authority to go and do some other things." When a juror noted that Segretti had been paid "pretty high" ($16,000) for "such low-grade work," he asked about Segretti's work before he had been discharged from the Army. He hadn't been getting the salary in the Army, had he? Chapin was asked. "As a taxpayer I would like to complain if he was," Chapin said. After the prosecutor suggested the taxpayers might be justified in complaining about the kind of work Segretti was doing as an alleged political saboteur, Chapin haughtily retorted: "That's none of their concern. This is private enterprise."

Thus, DeVan L. Shumway, director of information for the Committee for the Re-election of the President, refusing to make available for questions the man who hired James W. McCord Jr., "because he is not a public figure."

Such was the anything-goes attitude, the imperiousness, the utter disdain that emanated from the Nixon White House. And, even more frightening, for a long time most Americans were not outraged. Perhaps they were weary after a decade of Vietnam abroad and civil strife at home. Perhaps they were willing to pay any price for a sense of stability and security. At any rate, most Americans just did not want to believe that such statements were an accurate reflection of the thinking of the men around the President.

They certainly did not want to believe that these attitudes were in any way associated with the President himself. Whatever Richard Nixon's problems in the past—over Helen Gahagan Douglas, the 1952 secret Nixon fund and Checkers, over his unsuccessful 1962 gubernatorial campaign and the later finding of a San Francisco court that he and Haldeman had authorized an effort to sabotage his opponent among registered Democrats —in 1972 American voters were saying they had confidence and respect in him. Now, a little more than three months after his second inauguration, the President finds a dramatic change in public attitudes toward him. On Friday, for example, half of all those interviewed in a special Gallup Poll said they believe that Mr. Nixon participated in a coverup of Watergate. The President not only has changed his own personal standing, but it seems certain that he has diminished the public love and respect for his office— and maybe he has reduced presidential power as well.

Now that the President and his men have been overtaken by Watergate and so many unthinkable thoughts have turned out to be true, there is a disposition to regard the Nixon team as an aberrant breed. They are, as Michael Davie suggested recently, "Orange County" men, men on the make, men of limited vision. They are the hacks and flacks of the advertising-PR world, swollen with power, contemptuous of critics whether in the Congress or the press.

There is some truth in this view. Certainly Watergate, as we now understand it, was an audacious attempt to use any means—including subverting the entire political process, the judiciary and the press—and a willingness to destroy anyone and anything that stood in the way of realizing the final desired end: retaining the presidency. In scope and scale, America has never experienced anything like it. But the Nixon people are not the prototypes of a political animal we have never seen before. Nor is Watergate, unfortunately, entirely alien to the American political experience.

Precursors of Watergate

Watergate flows out of a historical background of sleazy tactics and uneasy ethical standards in the employment of money, dirty tricks and assaults on character—all in the pursuit of political power. The mentality of Watergate also comes after a period in which men of highest power in the American government have often employed an end-justifies-the-means philosophy. For years, the end was safeguarding the country from alien threats, from the Communists, if you will, and the means has sometimes been to violate our treaty obligations by attempting to subvert or overthrow foreign governments (Guatemala, 1954; Cuba, 1961; South Vietnam, 1963; Chile, 1970). At home, the Justice Department, the FBI and the Pentagon have engaged in illegal acts, have spied on American citizens, have attempted to impair reputations (wiretapping, Army dossiers on "suspect" citizens, Martin Luther King). And ever since the U-2 spy plane incident, there has been a history of U.S. spokesmen publicly lying or trying to cover up embarrassing facts (the Cuban missile crisis, the Pentagon Papers, Watergate). All, always, in the apparent belief that the government knew best, that in employing dubious means it was nevertheless achieving desirable ends.

So it was, it appears, with the Nixon men who planned and executed Watergate and the broader campaign of espionage and sabotage. They were not motivated by desire for personal gain, for their own Swiss bank accounts or villas on the Riviera. They were acting because they sincerely believed that the end—re-electing the man they thought the best leader—justified the means of keeping him in office.

That may explain the rationale for Watergate, but it does not answer the specific questions of when it began and why it was thought necessary. We do not know, at this point, all those details. There are, however, strong clues.

The Rehearsal: 1970

It seems now that for an explanation of Watergate one can look back to the congressional campaign of 1970, in which President Nixon and his chief political operatives made a bold attempt to fashion the beginnings of their long-hoped-for "new majority." It was an ugly campaign, a campaign of smears and scare tactics, of appeals to fears of crime and violence, of the most lavish expenditure of funds in American history, of slogans and epithets directed against the Democrats, the press and the "radiclibs," the "impudent snobs," the "effete elite" and the "rotten apples." The Nixon administration, led by the President himself with Spiro Agnew as a principal spokesman, vigorously criss-crossed the country seeking to gain control of the Senate and improve the Republican position in the House and governorships. It was also a try-out for 1972.

On Wednesday morning, Nov. 4, 1970, after the ballots had been counted, the President's efforts had failed: The Democrats had solidly retained control of the Senate and House and totally erased the Republicans' two-to-one majority in the nation's governorships. Richard Nixon was in trouble. It was quite possible that he would turn out to be a one-term president. The polls, for instance, showed Sen. Edmund Muskie beating him in head-to-head encounters, and Sen. Edward Kennedy and Hubert Humphrey running even with him. On Feb. 1, 1971, The Harris Survey showed Muskie beating Nixon 43 to 40. In March, it was Muskie 44 to 39. In May, it was Muskie 48 to 39.

There is evidence that the Nixon political operatives were spurred on in their espionage and sabotage campaign by the 1970 political results and the polls showing the President losing to the leading Democrat.

Listen, for instance, to these remarks by a man who had been personally close to Mr. Nixon, and who knew intimately the White House operation and state of mind:

"The President was walking into a one-term presidency in the summer of '71—on almost every issue," he said. "Wallace had always been a threat. Muskie had come out of the '70 campaign with roses. Muskie was at his peak and Nixon was moving to his nadir. The fellows [in the White House] looking at the political landscape were saying one threat is Muskie; one threat is Wallace. Those were the big things around."

"Extraordinarily Able People"

Then, referring to Watergate, he said, "I can see how it happened. Early in '71 you say the guy who can hurt me the worst is Muskie. The guy who can hurt me the least is McGovern. So help me, we'll nominate McGovern. There is a whole bunch of extraordinarily able people they [the Nixon political apparatus] have to accomplish it."

Perhaps he was right. We do not know.

The President has now addressed himself in public to what he called "this whole sordid affair" and to "how far this false doctrine" of the end justifying the means can take us. And he has made this pledge:

"I will do everything in my power to insure that the guilty are brought to justice and that such abuses are purged from our political processes in the years to come long after I have left this office."

In that, Americans who have lost such faith in their leaders and institutions in recent years firmly do want to believe.

THE MINDS OF THE "MANAGERS"

Richard J. Whalen

During the transition period in the winter of 1968–69, a then-assistant to President Johnson recalls giving John Ehrlichman a tour of the White House. In a basement office he pointed to the ceiling and said impishly: "The trap-door in front of the President's desk is overhead. The bodies fall

Source: *The Washington Post* (May 6, 1973). © The Washington Post. Reprinted by permission.

down here and we carry them out the back way." Ehrlichman looked up, all seriousness. Finally the Johnson man signaled the visitor by laughing at his own joke.

Figuratively speaking, Ehrlichman, Bob Haldeman and several others have now slid through that trap-door and left the White House in disgrace, their fall from giddy heights of personal power uncushioned by President Nixon's heartfelt farewell.

Whether they have committed any crimes remains to be determined. Unquestionably, they have brought shame on the institution of the presidency and the man they served, perhaps to an irreparable degree. Of all the many questions still to be answered in the Watergate affair, perhaps the most troubling are: How did such men get where they were, and why did they stay so long? Some of the answers, it seems to me, ought to quiet the murmurs of self-congratulation passing through the ranks of the "free and vigorous press."

Haldeman, Ehrlichman & Company, who came to be known as "the Germans," rose on the side of politics furthest removed from the electorate: the behind-the-scenes realm of the managers, schedulers, advance-men, image manipulators, and assorted technicians who package and merchandise a presidential candidate. This was congenial work for Haldeman, the former manager of J. Walter Thompson's Los Angeles office, and he recruited cronies (such as Ehrlichman) and advertising agency underlings (such as Ron Ziegler and Dwight Chapin) into the Nixon *apparat*. He gave "the Boss" slavish loyalty and he demanded the same from those below.

The stage-managers, operating in a closed and secretive environment, had a natural antipathy to politicians, including those who were supposedly their collaborators. Through the closing months of the 1968 campaign and afterward in Washington, the Haldeman *apparat* waged jealous cold war against the politicians grouped around pipe-smoking John Mitchell, Mr. Nixon's former law partner and a relative newcomer to his inner circle.

But the hostile Haldeman and Mitchell factions joined forces to ruthlessly oppose the men inside and outside the Nixon organization, a miscellany of intellectuals and elected politicians, who supposed that "issues" mattered both in campaigning and governing. Shortly after Mr. Nixon's nomination in late August, 1968, when I resigned from his staff, a purge began that drove all "issue men" either out of his entourage completely or off to the lonely periphery. At the same time, party politicians, regardless of past loyalty and service to Mr. Nixon, were fenced off from him.

As a result, the men who did much to put Nixon in the White House had him almost completely to themselves after he arrived there, and they continued to give him the benefit of their experience and expertise. This was fine for them but very bad, on the evidence, for him and the presidency. For they regarded governing as little more than an extension of campaigning.

Campaign politics, regardless of party and candidate, is inherently conspiratorial. Because the only purpose and binding force of the enterprise is victory, almost any means toward that all-important end can be justified with a modest amount of rationalization. Everyone not a part of the conspiracy is, by definition, not to be trusted. Since that is where the public and the press stand, the attitude toward them follows automatically.

Long before the abortive burglary of the Democratic Party headquarters, the Watergate was a symbol. The chosen nesting-place of John and Martha and other well-heeled members of the Nixon hierarchy, it symbolized the transience and insularity of men who had taken power almost without bothering to unpack, men basically disinterested in the business of government whose hearts belonged in Westchester and points west, where big money and the good life waited.

To be sure, the right of a high official to eventually cash in on his experience and connections in Washington is established by long Democratic precedent. But Democrats who have come to office harboring the cynical ambition to exploit their public service have usually shown patience and a self-protecting prudence. They have known what to expect in Washington, and—far more important—what would be expected of them. They realized, as their unknowing Republican successors did not, that they would be *watched*.

Elected politicians, as a breed, are cautious men because their minds run naturally to the sometimes distant consequences of words and deeds. Intellectuals and "issues men" generally are advocates and want an audience. The former expect scrutiny and the latter crave it. But the *apparatchik,* lacking a constituency or an ideological commitment, does not understand scrutiny—*he* is the watcher and prier into secrets. And the conspiratorial campaign politician, who reduces all problems to power brokerage behind closed doors, is contemptuous of it. Sadly for Nixon, he had only these two kinds of men around him—the ignorant and the arrogant.

Haldeman and Ehrlichman and their buttoned-down, scurrying aides had the mission of protecting the President from disorder and enabling him to make the most effective use of his limited time and energy. Haldeman, as manager of Mr. Nixon's losing bid for the California governorship in 1962, had seen him come apart under pressure, and he was resolved to prevent it from happening in the White House.

What this actually meant, Haldeman once described in an interview with a friendly reporter:

"We started out trying to keep political coloration as much as possible out of policy and hiring matters. However, we realize that these things make for variety in decision-making, and so within reasonable limits we have tried to keep a spread of opinion on the staff, so that no one is to the left of the President at his most liberal or to the right of the President at his most conservative. . . . Ehrlichman, Kissinger and I do our best to make sure that all points of view are placed before the President. We do act as a screen, because there is a real danger of some advocate of an idea rushing in to the President . . . if that person is allowed to do so, and actually managing to convince [him] in a burst of emotion or argument . . ."

Can you imagine Marvin Watson saying something like that about Lyndon Johnson? Or Kenny O'Donnell presuming to enter John Kennedy's mind and judge the "reasonable limits" of what he wanted to hear? By Haldeman's own assertion, his dependency on the President, great as it was, was matched by President Nixon's dependence on him to protect him against his own inner weakness and irresolution.

Ehrlichman on Nixon

From entering the President's mind, it was but a short step for his protectors to go even further and *speak* the President's mind. Quite early in the Nixon administration, a shaken Cabinet-level official and old friend of the President's described to me a White House meeting at which Ehrlichman had proposed a new domestic program. The official challenged him, saying that the proposal contradicted what he knew of Nixon's values and philosophy. Ehrlichman coldly informed the official that the President didn't have any philosophy—he did what was feasible and tactically rewarding.

"Ehrlichman didn't realize what he was saying," the official told me. "*I* know Nixon has values and a philosophy, but why doesn't Ehrlichman? And why does Nixon rely on a man like that?"

The President's dependence for political counsel on Mitchell—called in his heyday "El Supremo"—led him into a succession of avoidable confrontations and disasters. Republican leaders in the Congress, who were ordered to close ranks behind the likes of Supreme Court nominee G. Harrold Carswell, had no voice in the councils leading to such gross misjudgments. Yet the conservative barons of the Senate—Barry Goldwater, John Tower, Strom Thurmond—who had played a decisive role in Mr. Nixon's nomination and election, kept their fury bottled up long after they saw both ideology and political common sense betrayed by Mitchell and his client in the White House.

Where, in all this, were the professional scrutinizers, the watchmen of the press? They were, for the most part, in a state of culture-shock brought about by the election of the first Republican administration they had encountered. And they were without a frame of reference to even begin describing the men who had taken over the White House. Because this was a Republican administration, the prevailing assumption was that it must be "conservative"—whatever that meant. On the eve of the first Hundred Days, a senior White House staff member boasted to a reporter about the administration's fundamental aimlessness: "There is no ideology, no central commitment, no fixed body of thought." He knew that he could dismiss idealism with impunity.

Influenced by the New Frontier to admire tough-minded, hard-boiled pragmatism, the White House press corps thought they saw it in Ehrlichman especially. They accepted the facade of neatness, discipline and managerial efficiency erected by "the Germans." Haldeman's crew cut and brisk manner were noted, but none of the watchers asked what kind of man this really was, and what, if anything, he believed in beyond serving "the Boss" and hermetically sealing him off from distractions. While the reporters panted after such colorful figures as Henry Kissinger and (while he lasted) Pat Moynihan, there was almost no critical scrutiny of the extraordinary White House organization structure and the unprecedented concentration of power in the hands of a few men unknown to the public.

A Press in the Dark

Early in the fall of 1969, one of the surviving "issues men" confided his despair to me. "The Germans are ready to bring the whole thing under their control. Moynihan is out, and so is Bryce Harlow. Ehrlichman will run a Domestic Affairs Council. Haldeman will be the only man between him and the President. You know what's so frustrating? The damned lazy press doesn't have a clue about what's happening. The only guy on the outside who understands the role of Haldeman and Ehrlichman is John Osborne of The New Republic."

So it was, but even the industrious Osborne had not found anyone inside to tell him the rest of what my former colleagues told me: "Haldeman and Ehrlichman shield the President by monopolizing him. One of them is present at every meeting—he sees no one alone. He's made himself their captive. Sometimes 'the Germans' don't carry out Nixon's orders, or they let papers sit on their desks for a while, because they're certain he won't find out. How *can* he find out? All the channels flow back to Haldeman."

From another member of the White House staff, in those same early months of the administration, came this assessment and unwitting prophecy: "The Boss likes things simple and uncomplicated, and that's the way Haldeman and Ehrlichman serve them up. It will take a catastrophic error to change it."

Even if they could not get insiders to speak so candidly to them, reporters covering the White House had daily evidence that they were pressing their noses against a plastic P.R. shell. Behind it was nothing resembling a coherent conservatism—or anything else, for that matter. There were only mediocrities conniving to derive what satisfactions they could from incumbency before their mistakes overtook them. But the press was inert. The same reporters who swore during the 1968 campaign that they would get rid of press secretary Ron Ziegler "within three months" were still showing up years later to accept his handouts and double-talk.

The White House press failed to analyze what it saw and to make moral judgments on that performance. In a remarkably prescient speech in 1962, the late Lawrence Fanning of the Field newspapers of Chicago worried about the elitism of the Kennedy administration and the lack of reaction by the docile press: "It boils down to government by an intellectual elite, and the policies can only be as good as the members of the elite. What happens if the elite is replaced by a venal, arrogant, or power-mad cabal? What happens if it is replaced by an elite of the stupid?"

What has happened is the Watergate. After all the bodies have vanished through the trap-door and been piled up behind the White House, it will remain for the Washington press to ask itself why a police-beat story was needed to break the truth about what had been going on in the White House for four years.

Can a President Govern Effectively Who Systematically Alienates Himself from the Rest of Official Washington?

Nelson W. Polsby

In reflecting from a distance upon the tragedy of Watergate one of the most striking phenomena is the satisfaction that nearly everyone in Washington seems to be expressing over the dismantling of the high command of the Nixon administration. Assistants to the President—even cabinet officers—have fallen from grace before, but never, it appears, to such sustained bipartisan applause from McLean to Chevy Chase, from Georgetown to Hollin Hills. One wonders if the reasons for this can be found in certain characteristics of the pre-Watergate Nixon presidency.

It has been a strong presidency, but one uncommonly devoted to enhancing its power by attempting to cripple, discredit or weaken competing power centers in national politics. In certain respects, this aggressive posture toward competing power centers has been dictated by considerations of policy; in other respects it has been the consequence of President Nixon's administrative style; and in other ways, it appears to be the product of a genuine spirit of alienation between Mr. Nixon's values and those of his

Source: *The Washington Post* (June 3, 1973). © The Washington Post. Reprinted by permission.

closest associates on the one hand, and the values and attitudes that dominate the thinking of leaders of most other Washington elite groups on
the other.

For the nation at large, the unfolding Watergate revelations present a
profound challenge to the people's sense of trust in their government. Even
before Watergate, however, many leaders in our national political life just
outside the presidential orbit may well have had to come to terms with
a fundamental unease about the course of the Nixon administration.

This unease did not have anything to do with suspicions of wrongdoing.
Rather, what has been at issue is the question of the commitment of the
Nixon administration to the underlying legitimacy of government agencies
and their rules, the media and their criticism, cabinet-level officials and their
linkages with interest-group constituencies, Congress and its constitutional
prerogatives, or the rest of the Republican Party and its political needs.

An Occupation Army

In successive waves over a five-year period, President Nixon has
attempted various schemes to govern the executive branch in the manner of
a small army of occupation garrisoned amid a vast and hostile population.

The first major Nixon reorganization pulled two trusted lieutenants—
Secretaries Shultz and Finch—out of day-to-day departmental responsibilities and brought them into the White House. The second move was to
change the name of the Budget Bureau and strengthen its powers over
government departments. Third, there has been a noticeable slowdown in
the staffing of the top levels of departments whose programs are given a
low priority by the administration. And, finally, there has been an effort
to move people without any notable background, experience, interests or
qualifications into top levels of various government agencies, apparently to
provide listening posts for the White House.

Programmatic commitments appear to lie at the heart of the Nixon
administration's seeming distrust of many parts of the national government.
It is a fairly reliable rule of thumb that government agencies retain forever
the political coloration that they have when they are founded, given their
central missions and initially staffed. Undeniably, also, the great expansions
of federal agencies have taken place under Democratic presidents. Thus a
Republican president is bound to feel at least a little like he is surrounded
by career-long Democratic bureaucrats, all hot in pursuit of the basically
Democratic objectives of their housing, education, welfare, transportation,
urban development and science programs.

A Matter of Degree

Once written into law and placed in the charge of a government agency, of course, it can be argued that programs are no longer Democratic or Republican but simply government programs, and whoever runs the government is obliged to see to them. This rather simple-minded, traditional view was sharply challenged by the Nixon administration decision to dismantle the Office of Economic Opportunity while the law embodying the agency was still in force. It is uncertain how this questionably legal maneuver struck the leaders of other government agencies, but to the OEO staff itself the attack must have seemed flagrant and somehow outside the rules of the game.

Leaders of Congress have expressed themselves in similar terms on the issues of impoundment and executive privilege. It is not that the Nixon administration, in asserting executive privilege and in impounding funds, has done unprecedented things. It is that it has done these things to an unprecedented degree, so much so that a matter of degree is transformed into a difference in kind and has an impact on the normal relations of comity and trust between Congress and the presidency.

As we all know, Congress and the President were meant to do battle. In the end, their capacity to do business at all rests upon a set of mutual restraints and accommodations, because in the last analysis, either branch can do the other in.

A Question of Politics

It is a matter of the utmost sadness that serious people in Washington and elsewhere are beginning to speak unflinchingly of ultimate sanction, and specifically of the impeachment or resignation of the President. Before Watergate, it is now clear, the mutual accommodations and understandings that must exist for orderly business to be done between Congress and the President were deeply eroded.

There was the ludicrous and intemperate claim of executive privilege for virtually everybody in the executive branch and on virtually all issues. There was the matter of impoundment—for example, of all public works projects added by Congress to the budget as presented by the President. Likewise, grant and loan programs for water lines and sewers, open spaces and public facilities were impounded, apparently to coerce the Congress into enacting the administration's special revenue-sharing bill. And there was the attempt to cancel the Rural Environmental Assistance Program.

What is at issue in all of these actions is not whether they represent good public policy or even whether they were legal. Rather, the question is whether they were good politics. The answer must be framed not only in terms of the goals of national constituencies and interest groups but also in terms of whether or not the President thinks he needs to get along with Congress.

Using Up Credit

The Nixon administration attacks on newspapers, on television commentators and the networks, and on the so-called "elitist" Eastern press—somehow these, too, got out of hand. Again, different observers might well draw somewhat different bills of particulars. Some would include as unwise the attempts to get injunctions enforcing prior restraint on publication of what turned out to be innocuous Pentagon Papers. Others remember the petty and futile exclusion of The Washington Post's Dorothy McCardle from coverage of routine White House social functions, and the clumsy investigation of Daniel Schorr of CBS, followed by the patently dishonest rationalizations of the White House press spokesman. Somewhere in between these were the famous speeches of Vice President Agnew, or opaque references to "ideological plugola" by a White House functionary, accompanied but not-so-opaque administration plans to exert political influence over public broadcasting.

Less noticeable to casual readers was the fact that, well before Watergate, President Nixon was also using up sizable amounts of credit with Republican Party leaders. There is always an election-year competition for campaign funds between presidential candidates and other party standard-bearers further down the ticket. In this contest, the presidential candidate —especially an incumbent—usually wins. It is then up to him to take the initiative and spread any extra cash around to help the party win some key Senate and House races, once he is fairly certain that his own campaign can be paid for.

This Mr. Nixon apparently neglected to do. Moreover, in his low-profile campaign he made few personal efforts to help fellow Republicans. Now that they are able to see the uses made of some of the money that could have paid for more conventional campaign expenses, it is no wonder that not a few Republican stalwarts are angry.

"Peace at the Center"

Some of the disagreeable relations between Mr. Nixon and the rest of official Washington are, as I have indicated, the result of programmatic differences. His dismantling of the President's scientific advice apparatus, for example, can be explained as simply a wish to rid himself of spokesmen for an interest group whose interests he did not wish to gratify. Likewise, his dismissal of the American Bar Association as a clearinghouse for future

Supreme Court justices came only after the relevant committee of the Association found fault with a couple of his prospective nominees.

Other problems are evidently the inescapable product of Mr. Nixon's work style. His intense desire for "peace at the center," for orderly, private, unharried decision-making, thrust a great burden on his most intimate staff. Not only have they had to protect the President, ruthlessly filter the stimuli to which he is subjected, meanwhile bringing him options and decisions to make, but they have also had to face outward, to deny access to congressmen, Cabinet officers and others whose responsibilities include shares in the ordering of various aspects of the public business. As time has gone on, it has become evident that there has been too much "peace at the center."

The Washington Subculture

A major by-product of the extreme insularity of this President has been a growing inability to come to terms with the ongoing subculture of official Washington, that noisy little world inhabited by the congressmen, agency heads, journalists, interest-group leaders, party dignitaries, lawyers, embassy folk and others, some of whom have been harshly dealt with by the Nixon administration. Of course, these few thousand people are not "the" people, those whom Presidents address on television and who vote by the millions in national elections. But does this mean that official Washington consists of nothing but "nattering nabobs"?

Some of these nabobs are themselves duly elected officials under the Constitution. Others are employed at activities contemplated under statutes of the U.S. government. Still others are doing work that manifestly aids in the proper discharge of governmental functions.

Can a President govern effectively or at all if he systematically alienates himself from most of the rest of official Washington? Can his feelings of alienation, or those of his closest advisers, lead to excessive suspicion, to a frame of mind that encourages the taking of extraordinary precautions, to worries about political opponents that verge on the obsessive? If Mr. Nixon's style of work tended to alienate him from official Washington before Watergate, can we reasonably expect that the trauma of Watergate will decrease his alienation from this indispensable community sufficiently to restore to him the capacity to govern?

The Swelling of the Presidency

Thomas E. Cronin

The advent of Richard Nixon's second term in the White House is marked by an uncommon amount of concern, in Congress and elsewhere, about the expansion of presidential power and manpower. Even the President himself is ostensibly among those who are troubled. Soon after his re-election, Mr. Nixon announced that he was planning to pare back the presidential staff. And in recent days, the President has said he is taking action to cut the presidential workforce in half and to "substantially" reduce the number of organizations that now come under the White House. Mr. Nixon's announcements have no doubt been prompted in part by a desire to add drama and an aura of change to the commencement of his second term. But he also seems genuinely worried that the presidency may have grown so large and top-heavy that it now weakens rather than strengthens his ability to manage the federal government. His fears are justified.

The presidency has, in fact, grown a full 20 per cent in the last four years alone in terms of the number of people who are employed directly under the President. It has swelled to the point where it is now only a little short of the State Department's sprawling domestic bureaucracy in size.

This burgeoning growth of the presidency has, in the process, made the traditional civics textbook picture of the executive branch of our government nearly obsolete. According to this view, the executive branch is more or less neatly divided into Cabinet departments and their secretaries, agencies and their heads, and the President. A more contemporary view takes note of a few prominent presidential aides and refers to them as the "White House staff." But neither view adequately recognizes the large and growing coterie that surrounds the President and is made up of dozens of assistants, hundreds of presidential advisers, and thousands of members of an institutional amalgam called the Executive Office of the President. While the men and women in these categories all fall directly under the President in the organizational charts, there is no generally used term for their common terrain. But it has swelled so much in size and scope in recent years, and has become such an important part of the federal government, that it deserves its own designation. Most apt perhaps is the Presidential Establishment.

The Presidential Establishment today embraces more than twenty support staffs (the White House Office, National Security Council, and Office of Management and Budget, etc.) and advisory offices (Council of Eco-

Source: *Saturday Review* (January 20, 1973), pp. 30–36. Copyright © 1973 by Saturday Review, Inc. First appeared in *Saturday Review of the Society,* January 20, 1973. Used with permission.

nomic Advisers, Office of Science and Technology, and Office of Telecommunications Policy, etc.). It has spawned a vast proliferation of ranks and titles to go with its proliferation of functions (Counsel to the President, Assistant to the President, Special Counselor, Special Assistant, Special Consultant, Director, Staff Director, etc.). "The White House now has enough people with fancy titles to populate a Gilbert and Sullivan comic opera," Congressman Morris Udall has reasonably enough observed.

There are no official figures on the size of the Presidential Establishment, and standard body counts vary widely depending on who is and who is not included in the count, but by one frequently used reckoning, between five and six thousand people work for the President of the United States. Payroll and maintenance costs for this staff run between $100 million and $150 million a year. (These figures include the Office of Economic Opportunity (OEO), which is an Executive Office agency and employs two thousand people, but not the roughly fifteen thousand-man Central Intelligence Agency, although that, too, is directly responsible to the Chief Executive.) These "White House" workers have long since outgrown the White House itself and now occupy not only two wings of the executive mansion but three nearby high-rise office buildings as well.

The expansion of the Presidential Establishment, it should be emphasized, is by no means only a phenomenon of the Nixon years. The number of employees under the President has been growing steadily since the early 1900s when only a few dozen people served in the White House entourage, at a cost of less than a few hundred thousand dollars annually. Congress's research arm, the Congressional Research Service, has compiled a count that underlines in particular the accelerated increase in the last two decades. This compilation shows that between 1954 and 1971 the number of presidential advisers has grown from 25 to 45, the White House staff from 266 to 600, and the Executive Office staff from 1,175 to 5,395.

But if the growth of the Presidential Establishment antedates the current administration, it is curious at least that one of the largest expansions ever, in both relative and absolute terms, has taken place during the first term of a conservative, management-minded President who has often voiced his objection to any expansion of the federal government and its bureaucracy.

Under President Nixon, in fact, there has been an almost systematic bureaucratization of the Presidential Establishment, in which more new councils and offices have been established, more specialization and division of labor and layers of staffing have been added, than at any time except during World War II. Among the major Nixonian additions are the Council on Environmental Quality, Council on International Economic Policy, Domestic Council, and Office of Consumer Affairs.

The numbers in the White House entourage may have decreased somewhat since November when the President announced his intention to make certain staff cuts. They may shrink still more if, as expected, the OEO is shifted from White House supervision to Cabinet control, mainly under the Department of Health, Education, and Welfare. Also, in the months ahead, the President will probably offer specific legislative proposals, as he has done before, to reprogram or repackage the upper reaches of the executive.

Even so, any diminution of the Presidential Establishment has so far been more apparent than real, or more incidental than substantial. Some aides, such as former presidential counselor Robert Finch, who have wanted to leave anyway, have done so. Others, serving as scapegoats on the altar of Watergate, are also departing.

In addition, the President has officially removed a number of trusted domestic-policy staff assistants from the White House rolls and dispersed them to key sub-Cabinet posts across the span of government. But this dispersal can be viewed as not so much reducing as creating yet another expansion—a virtual setting up of White House outposts (or little White Houses?) throughout the Cabinet departments. The aides that are being sent forth are notable for their intimacy with the President, and they will surely maintain direct links to the White House, even though these links do not appear on the official organizational charts.

Then, too, one of the most important of the President's recent shifts of executive branch members involves an unequivocal addition to the Presidential Establishment. This is the formal setting up of a second office—with space and a staff in the White House—for Treasury Secretary George Shultz as chairman of yet another new presidential body, the Council on Economic Policy. This move makes Shultz a member of a White House inner cabinet. He will now be over-secretary of economic affairs alongside Henry Kissinger, over-secretary for national security affairs, and John Ehrlichman, over-secretary for domestic affairs.

In other words, however the names and numbers have changed recently or may be shifted about in the near future, the Presidential Establishment does not seem to be declining in terms of function, power, or prerogative; in fact, it may be continuing to grow as rapidly as ever.

Does it matter? A number of political analysts have argued recently that it does, and I agree with them. Perhaps the most disturbing aspect of the expansion of the Presidential Establishment is that it has become a powerful inner sanctum of government, isolated from traditional, constitutional checks and balances. It is common practice today for anonymous, unelected, and unratified aides to negotiate sensitive international commitments by means of executive agreements that are free from congressional oversight. Other aides in the Presidential Establishment wield fiscal authority over billions of dollars in funds that Congress has appropriated, yet the President refuses to spend, or that Congress has assigned to one purpose and the administration routinely redirects to another—all with no semblance of public scrutiny. Such exercises of power pose an important, perhaps vital, question of governmental philosophy: Should a political system that has made a virtue of periodic electoral accountability accord an ever-increasing policy-making role to White House counselors who neither are confirmed by the U.S. Senate nor, because of the doctrine of "executive privilege," are subject to questioning by Congress?

Another disquieting aspect of the growth of the Presidential Establishment is that the increase of its powers has been largely at the expense of the traditional sources of executive power and policy-making—the Cabinet members and their departments. When I asked a former Kennedy-Johnson Cabinet member a while ago what he would like to do if he ever returned to government, he said he would rather be a presidential assistant than a Cabinet member. And this is an increasingly familiar assessment of the relative influence of the two levels of the executive branch. The Presidential Establishment has become, in effect, a whole layer of government between the President and the Cabinet, and it often stands above the Cabinet in terms of influence with the President. In spite of the exalted position that Cabinet members hold in textbooks and protocol, a number of Cabinet members in recent administrations have complained that they could not even get the President's ear except through an assistant. In his book *Who Owns America?*, former Secretary of the Interior Walter Hickel recounts his combat with a dozen different presidential functionaries and tells how he needed clearance from them before he could get to talk to the President, or how he frequently had to deal with the assistants themselves because the President was "too busy." During an earlier administration, President Eisenhower's chief assistant, Sherman Adams, was said to have told two Cabinet members who could not resolve a matter of mutual concern: "Either make up your mind or else tell me and I will do it. We must not bother the President with this. He is trying to keep the world from war." Several of President Kennedy's Cabinet members regularly battled with White House aides who blocked them from seeing the President. And McGeorge Bundy, as Kennedy's chief assistant for national security affairs, simply sidestepped the State Department in one major area of department communications. He had all important incoming State Department cables transmitted simultaneously to his office in the White House, part of an absorption of traditional State Department functions that visibly continues to this day with presidential assistant Henry Kissinger. Indeed, we recently witnessed the bizarre and telling spectacle of Secretary of State William Rogers insisting that he *did* have a role in making foreign policy.

In a speech in 1971, Sen. Ernest Hollings of South Carolina plaintively noted the lowering of Cabinet status. "It used to be," he said, "that if I had a problem with food stamps, I went to see the Secretary of Agriculture, whose department had jurisdiction over that problem. Not anymore. Now, if I want to learn the policy, I must go to the White House to consult John Price [a special assistant]. If I want the latest on textiles, I won't get it from the Secretary of Commerce, who has the authority and responsibility. No, I am forced to go to the White House and see Mr. Peter Flanigan. I shouldn't feel too badly. Secretary Stans [Maurice Stans, then Secretary of Commerce] has to do the same thing."

If Cabinet members individually have been downgraded in influence, the Cabinet itself as a council of government has become somewhat of a relic, replaced by more specialized comminglings that as often as not are presided over by White House staffers. The Cabinet's decline has taken place over several administrations. John Kennedy started out his term declaring his intentions of using the Cabinet as a major policy-making body, but his change of mind was swift, as his Postmaster General, J. Edward Day, has noted. "After the first two or three meetings," Day has written, "one had the distinct impression that the President felt that decisions on major matters were not made—or even influenced—at Cabinet sessions, and that discussion there was a waste of time. . . . When members spoke up to suggest or to discuss major administration policy, the President would listen with thinly disguised impatience and then postpone or otherwise bypass the question."

Lyndon Johnson was equally disenchanted with the Cabinet as a body and characteristically held Cabinet sessions only when articles appeared in the press talking about how the Cabinet was withering away. Under Nixon, the Cabinet is almost never convened at all.

Not only has the Presidential Establishment taken over many policy-making functions from the Cabinet and its members, it has also absorbed some of the operational functions. White House aides often feel they should handle any matters that they regard as ineptly administered, and they tend to intervene in internal departmental operations at lower and lower levels. They often feel underemployed, too, and so are inclined to reach out into the departments to find work and exercise authority for themselves.

The result is a continuous undercutting of Cabinet departments—and the cost is heavy. These intrusions can cripple the capacity of Cabinet officials to present policy alternatives, and they diminish self-confidence, morale, and initiative within the departments. George Ball, a former undersecretary of state, noted the effects on the State Department: "Able men, with proper pride in their professional skills, will not long tolerate such votes of no-confidence, so it should be no surprise that they are leaving the career service, and making way for mediocrity with the result that as time goes on it may be hopelessly difficult to restore the Department. . . ."

The irony of this accretion of numbers and functions to the Presidential Establishment is that the presidency is finding itself increasingly afflicted with the very ills of the traditional departments that the expansions were often intended to remedy. The presidency has become a large, complex bureaucracy itself, rapidly acquiring many dubious characteristics of large bureaucracies in the process: layering, overspecialization, communication gaps, interoffice rivalries, inadequate coordination, and an impulse to become consumed with short-term, urgent operational concerns at the expense of thinking systematically about the consequences of varying sets of policies and priorities and about important long-range problems. It takes so much of the President's time to deal with the members of his own bureaucracy that it is little wonder he has little time to hear counsel from Cabinet officials.

Another toll of the burgeoning Presidential Establishment is that White House aides, in assuming more and more responsibility for the management of government programs, inevitably lose the detachment and objectivity that is so essential for evaluating new ideas. Can a lieutenant vigorously engaged in implementing the presidential will admit the possibility that what the President wants is wrong or not working? Yet a President is increasingly dependent on the judgment of these same staff members, since he seldom sees his Cabinet members.

Why has the presidency grown bigger and bigger? There is no single villain or systematically organized conspiracy promoting this expansion. A variety of factors is at work. The most significant is the expansion of the role of the presidency itself—an expansion that for the most part has taken place during national emergencies. The reason for this is that the public and Congress in recent decades have both tended to look to the President for the decisive responses that were needed in those emergencies. The Great Depression and World War II in particular brought sizable increases in presidential staffs. And once in place, many stayed on, even after the emergencies that brought them had faded. Smaller national crises have occasioned expansion in the White House entourage, too. After the Russians successfully orbited *Sputnik* in 1957, President Eisenhower added several science advisers. After the Bay of Pigs, President Kennedy enlarged his national security staff.

Considerable growth in the Presidential Establishment, especially in the post-World War II years, stems directly from the belief that critical societal problems require that wise men be assigned to the White House to alert the President to appropriate solutions and to serve as the agents for implementing these solutions. Congress has frequently acted on the basis of this belief, legislating the creation of the National Security Council, the Council of Economic Advisers, and the Council on Environmental Quality, among others. Congress has also increased the chores of the presidency by making it a statutory responsibility for the President to prepare more and more reports associated with what are regarded as critical social areas —annual economic and manpower reports, a biennial report on national growth, etc.

Most recently, President Nixon responded to a number of troublesome problems that defy easy relegation to any one department—problems like international trade and drug abuse—by setting up special offices in the Executive Office with sweeping authority and sizable staffs. Once established, these units rarely get dislodged. And an era of permanent crisis ensures a continuing accumulation of such bodies.

Another reason for the growth of the Presidential Establishment is that occupants of the White House frequently distrust members of the permanent government. Nixon aides, for example, have viewed most civil servants not only as Democratic but as wholly unsympathetic to such objectives of the Nixon administration as decentralization, revenue sharing, and the curtailment of several Great Society programs. Departmental bureaucracies are viewed from the White House as independent, unresponsive, unfamiliar, and inaccessible. They are suspected again and again of placing their own, congressional, or special-interest priorities ahead of those communicated to them from the White House. Even the President's own Cabinet members soon become viewed in the same light; one of the strengths of Cabinet members, namely their capacity to make a compelling case for their programs, has proved to be their chief liability with Presidents.

Presidents may want this type of advocacy initially, but they soon grow weary and wary of it. Not long ago, one White House aide accused a former Labor Secretary of trying to "out-Meany Meany." Efforts by former Interior Secretary Hickel to advance certain environmental programs and by departing Housing and Urban Development Secretary George Romney to promote innovative housing construction methods not only were unwelcome but after a while were viewed with considerable displeasure and suspicion at the White House.

Hickel writes poignantly of coming to this recognition during his final meeting with President Nixon, in the course of which the President frequently referred to him as an "adversary." "Initially," writes Hickel, "I considered that a compliment because, to me, an adversary is a valuable asset. It was only after the President had used the term many times and with a disapproving inflection that I realized he considered an adversary an enemy. I could not understand why he would consider me an enemy."

Not only have recent Presidents been suspicious about the depth of the loyalty of those in their Cabinets, but they also invariably become concerned about the possibility that sensitive administration secrets may leak out through the departmental bureaucracies, and this is another reason why Presidents have come to rely more on their own personal groups, such as task forces and advisory commissions.

Still another reason that more and more portfolios have been given to the presidency is that new federal programs frequently concern more than one federal agency, and it seems reasonable that someone at a higher level is required to fashion a consistent policy and to reconcile conflicts. Attempts by Cabinet members themselves to solve sensitive jurisdictional questions frequently result in bitter squabbling. At times, too, Cabinet members themselves have recommended that these multi-departmental issues be settled at the White House. Sometimes new presidential appointees insist that new offices for program coordination be assigned directly under the President. Ironically, such was the plea of George McGovern, for example, when President Kennedy offered him the post of director of the Food-for-Peace program in 1961. McGovern attacked the buildup of the Presidential Establishment in his campaign against Nixon, but back in 1961 he wanted visibility (and no doubt celebrity status) and he successfully argued against his being located outside the White House— either in the State or Agriculture departments. President Kennedy and his then campaign manager Robert Kennedy felt indebted to McGovern because of his efforts in assisting the Kennedy presidential campaign in South Dakota. Accordingly, McGovern was granted not only a berth in the Executive Office of the President but also the much-coveted title of special assistant to the President.

The Presidential Establishment has also been enlarged by the representation of interest groups within its fold. Even a partial listing of staff specializations that have been grafted onto the White House in recent years reveals how interest-group brokerage has become added to the more traditional staff activities of counseling and administration. These specializations form a veritable index of American society:

Budget and management, national security, economics, congressional matters, science and technology, drug abuse prevention, telecommunications, consumers, national goals, intergovernmental relations, environment, domestic policy, international economics, military affairs, civil rights, disarmament, labor relations, District of Columbia, cultural affairs, education, foreign trade and tariffs, past Presidents, the aged, health and nutrition, physical fitness, volunteerism, intellectuals, blacks, youth, women, "the Jewish community," Wall Street, governors, mayors, "ethnics," regulatory agencies and related industry, state party chairmen, Mexican-Americans.

It is as if interest groups and professions no longer settle for lobbying Congress, or having one of their number appointed to departmental advisory boards or sub-Cabinet positions. It now appears essential to "have your own man right there in the White House." Once this foothold is established, of course, interest groups can play upon the potential political backlash that could arise should their representation be discontinued.

One of the more disturbing elements in the growth of the Presidential Establishment is the development, particularly under the current administration, of a huge public-relations apparatus. More than 100 presidential aides are now engaged in various forms of press-agentry or public relations, busily selling and reselling the President. This activity is devoted to the particular occupant of the White House, but inevitably it affects the presidency itself, by projecting or reinforcing images of the presidency that are almost imperial in their suggestions of omnipotence and omniscience. Thus the public-relations apparatus not only has directly enlarged the presidential workforce but has expanded public expectations about the presidency at the same time.

Last, but by no means least, Congress, which has grown increasingly critical of the burgeoning power of the presidency, must take some blame itself for the expansion of the White House. Divided within itself and ill-eqiupped, or simply disinclined to make some of the nation's toughest political decisions in recent decades, Congress has abdicated more and more authority to the presidency. The fact that the recent massive bombing of North Vietnam was ordered by the President without even a pretense of consultation with Congress buried what little was left of the semblance of that body's war-making power. Another recent instance of Congress's tendency to surrender authority to the presidency, an extraordinary instance, was the passage by the House (though not the Senate) of a grant to the President that would give him the right to determine which programs are to be cut whenever the budget goes beyond a $250 billion ceiling limit —a bill which, in effect, would hand over to the President some of Congress's long-cherished "power of the purse."

What can be done to bring the Presidential Establishment back down to size? What can be done to bring it to a size that both lightens the heavy accumulation of functions that it has absorbed and allows the Presidential Establishment to perform its most important functions more effectively and wisely?

First, Congress should curb its own impulse to establish new presidential agencies and to ask for yet additional reports and studies from the President. In the past Congress has been a too willing partner in the enlargement of the presidency. If Congress genuinely wants a leaner presidency, it should ask more of itself. For instance, it could well make better use of its own General Accounting Office and Congressional Research Service for chores that are now often assigned to the President.

Congress should also establish in each of its houses special committees on Executive Office operations. Most congressional committees are organized to deal with areas such as labor, agriculture, armed services, or education, paralleling the organization of the Cabinet. What we need now are committees designed explicitly to oversee the White House. No longer can the task of overseeing presidential operations be dispersed among dozens of committees and subcommittees, each of which can look at only small segments of the Presidential Establishment.

Some will complain that adding yet another committee to the already overburdened congressional system is just like adding another council to the overstuffed Presidential Establishment. But the central importance of what the presidency does (and does not do) must rank among the most critical tasks of the contemporary Congress. As things are organized now, the presidency escapes with grievously inadequate scrutiny. Equally important, Congress needs these committees to help protect itself from its own tendency to relinquish to the presidency its diminishing resources and prerogatives. Since Truman, President have had staffs to oversee Congress; it is time Congress reciprocated.

Similar efforts to let the salutary light of public attention shine more brightly on the presidency should be inaugurated by the serious journals and newspapers of the nation. For too long, publishers and editors have believed that covering the presidency means assigning a reporter to the White House press corps. Unfortunately, however, those who follow the President around on his travels are rarely in a position to do investigative reporting on what is going on inside the Presidential Establishment. Covering the Executive Office of the President requires more than a President watcher; it needs a specialist who understands the arcane language and highly complex practices that have grown up in the Presidential Establishment.

Finally, it is time to reverse the downgrading of the Cabinet. President Nixon ostensibly moved in this direction with his designation several days ago of three Cabinet heads—HEW's Caspar W. Weinberger, Agriculture's Earl L. Butz, and HUD's James T. Lynn—as, in effect, super-secretaries of "human resources," "natural resources," and "community development" respectively. The move was expressly made in the name of Cabinet consolidation, plans for which Mr. Nixon put forward in 1971 but which Congress has so far spurned.

The three men will hold onto their Cabinet posts, but they have been given White House offices as well—as presidential counselors—and so it may be that the most direct effect of the appointments is a further expansion of the Presidential Establishment, rather than a counter-bolstering of the Cabinet. But if the move does, in fact, lead to Cabinet consolidation under broader divisions, it will be a step in the right direction.

Reducing the present number of departments would strengthen the hand of Cabinet members vis-à-vis special interests, and might enable them to serve as advisers, as well as advocates, to the President. Cabinet consolidation would also have another very desirable effect: it would be a move toward reducing the accumulation of power within the Presidential Establishment. For much of the power of budget directors and other senior White House aides comes from their roles as penultimate referees of interdepartmental jurisdictional disputes. Under consolidated departments, a small number of strengthened Cabinet officers with closer ties to the President would resolve these conflicts instead. With fewer but broader Cabinet departments, there would be less need for many of the interest-group brokers and special councils that now constitute so much of the excessive baggage in the overburdened presidency.

Meantime, the presidency remains sorely overburdened—with both functions and functionaries—and needs very much to be cut back in both. Certainly, the number of presidential workers can and should be reduced. Harry Truman put it best, perhaps, when he said with characteristic succinctness: "I do not like this present trend toward a huge White House staff. . . . Mostly these aides get in each other's way." But while the number of functionaries is the most tangible and dramatic measure of the White House's expansion, its increasing absorption of governmental functions is more profoundly disturbing. The current White House occupant may regard cutting down (or transferring) a number of his staff members as a way of mollifying critics who charge that the American presidency has grown too big and bloated, but it is yet another thing to reduce the President's authority or his accumulated prerogatives. As the nation's number-one critic of the swelling of government, President Nixon will, it is hoped, move—or will continue to move if he has truly already started—to substantially deflate this swelling in one of the areas where it most needs to be deflated—at home, in the White House.

Chapter 6
SUGGESTED TOPICS FOR CLASS DISCUSSION

1. Are public opinion polls becoming such a threat to democratic elections that they should be legally prohibited?
2. Do Presidential preference primaries make the electoral process more democratic? Should we have these primaries in all states, thus replacing the convention nomination? What would be some advantages and disadvantages?
3. Republican party spokesmen dismissed attempts to sabotage the Democratic campaign as silly actions by overzealous workers. Was it no more serious than that? Suppose both parties went all-out every election to sabotage the other. What could be the results?
4. What happened to the old Democratic coalition in 1972? What was the reason: candidates? or had the coalition shown signs of falling apart before this?
5. The Republicans recovered from the debacle of 1964 to elect a President in just four years. Do you think the Democrats can make as dramatic a recovery?
6. What kind of campaign might a challenger use to off-set the enormous advantages of an incumbent President?

Chapter 7

Congressional Politics

The United States Congress is a huge, complex institution. Its work is done through a complicated process of committee hearings, proposals, voting, and amendments. It is a process marked by delay, compromise, and conciliation. In extreme cases, it can be paralyzed by delay tactics such as the filibuster.

Because of what many people believe to be the archaic structure and procedures of Congress, critics of Congress have developed a series of indictments of the Congressional system as it now operates and have proposed literally thousands of reforms over the past half century. In general, it is true that Congress has been slow to change. But has it, as many claim, lost its role as one of the great legislative bodies of modern government?

Despite many valid criticisms—such as those of the seniority system and of delay tactics—Congress is as important now as ever. Even though the President usually takes the initiative in proposing policy changes, Congress still determines the basic outlines of national policy.

Congress is the focal point of a vast number of political pressures. Because the journey through Congress of a policy proposal is so complex, there are many points at which opponents and proponents may be heard. This is where most lobbyists concentrate their efforts to influence national policy. But at the same time, the relatively open access to virtually all who wish to be heard makes Congress the most representative branch in the government. Though it is also true that the legislature cannot accede, sometimes even partially, to the wishes of all interests, it does offer them a hearing not obtainable elsewhere and as such can be an important factor in the management of conflict.

There are many other points to consider in better understanding Congress. How do members of the House and Senate conceive of their own roles? Should they be primarily representatives of their constituents or representatives of the nation as a whole? Is there such a clear-cut difference in these interests? What can Congress do to initiate corrective policy measures in such matters as executive war-making and executive impoundment of funds authorized by Congress? Just how does the legislative process work? Can it be improved?

The cases in this chapter take a look at some of the issues just raised.

On Becoming a United States Senator

James L. Buckley

On January 22, 1971, Jacob Javits, pursuant to custom, escorted me down the center aisle of the United States Senate Chamber. Vice President Agnew swore me in, and I was handed a pen with which I entered my name on the books of the Senate. I then walked a few steps to my desk on the Republican side of the aisle. I had become the Junior Senator from the State of New York. Or, as senatorial courtesy puts it, the distinguished and honorable Senator from the great State of New York.

Rarely has anyone, distinguished and honorable—or otherwise—entered the United States Senate so innocent of the mechanisms of a legislative body or of the impact of politics on the legislative process. Prior to my election I had never held public office or participated in any organized political effort other than the third-party mayoral and senatorial campaigns of the brothers Buckley.

Source: *National Review* (February 2, 1973), pp. 141–147. Reprinted by permission of *National Review*.

Shortly after my election Clif White, my campaign manager and guide into the political world, organized a private dinner with a few of the senior Republican senators so that I might acquire a better feel for the life I was about to enter. I had hoped to get specific advice on how to go about the job of being an effective senator. What I got instead were affable assurances to the effect that anyone capable of winning election to the Senate would find no difficulty in getting along once in it. This was all, in its own way, reassuring; but I did not emerge from that dinner with the mother lode of hard, practical information that would help me thread my way through the complexities of the senatorial life.

The first formal business for a senator-elect is the meeting with the Sergeant at Arms and the Secretary of the Senate, who give you the basic housekeeping instructions, take from you sample signatures for franking privileges, and explain insurance and retirement benefits, as well as such perquisites as the right to a District of Columbia license plate, numbered according to one's rank in the Senate pecking order—plus one, Number One being reserved for the Vice President. (My rank was 99 because I had no prior service as a congressman or governor, which adds into the calculation of seniority. I beat out Lawton Chiles of Florida because New York has the larger population.) At that meeting I was presented with three books: *The Rules and Manual of the United States Senate;* an exegesis thereof by the chief parliamentarian, Dr. Floyd Riddick; and the *Congressional Directory* for the second session of the prior Congress. I determined to spend the next few weeks mastering the parliamentary rules, but was soon bogged down in their intricacy. I would learn to my relief that the Senate operates in a reasonably free and tolerant manner, and that much of its business is conducted not so much by the rule book as by continuing recourse to unanimous-consent agreements. Those who do know the rule book, however, are equipped, at critical moments, to take the parliamentary advantage.

New senators learn that they are expected to carry the principal burden of presiding over the Senate. For someone like me, who had never presided over any function, nor even scanned *Robert's Rules of Order,* the prospect seemed ominous. It isn't all that difficult, however, because sitting immediately in front of the Chair is one of the three parliamentarians, who whispers up the appropriate instruction. The most difficult task is to learn the identity of eighty or ninety brand new faces, together with state of origin, so that one can recognize the Senator from So-and-so without any excessive or obvious fumbling.

During this orientation period, I introduced myself to the Senate Republican leadership—to Minority Leader Hugh Scott, Minority Whip Bob Griffin, Chairman Gordon Allott of the Republican Policy Committee, and Chairman Margaret Chase Smith of the Republican Conference.

One important call was at the office of Senator Wallace Bennett, Chairman of the Republican Committee on Committees, in order to learn how committee assignments were made, and to register my preferences. The process is in fact mechanical. Once the minority vacancies on the various committees become known, the Republican members of the incoming class line up in order of seniority, and take their pick. Each senator is appointed to two major committees, and often to one or more minor ones. My own initial assignments were to Public Works, Space, and the District of Columbia.

The Committee Shuffle

It was in committee work that I first came to appreciate the enormous volume of business that courses through the Congress, and its implications. It is not unusual to find meetings or hearings involving as many as three committees or subcommittees of which one is a member scheduled for the same time, each involving business of some importance. One either spreads himself thin by putting in token appearances at each, or devotes himself to one meeting, relying on an overworked staff member to keep abreast of what is going on in the other two. I have yet to be convinced that there isn't somewhere in the bowels of the Capitol a computer programmed to arrange as many conflicting appointments as possible.

The committee system constitutes a delegation of responsibility for legislative work in designated areas. It should not be assumed, however, that a given committee will be representative of the Senate as a whole. Senators naturally tend to gravitate to those committees that interest them most or whose work is most important to their particular constituencies, and a committee can become as "mission-oriented" as an executive agency. Given the broad range of viewpoints represented on each side of the aisle, the requirement that each committee have a majority and minority membership roughly comparable to that of the Senate as a whole is no guarantee that it will reflect the political spectrum in any other sense. Thus committee reports are too often "selling documents" that do not provide other senators with the kind of balanced information needed to help them reach a reasonably educated opinion regarding a particular bill's merits.

It isn't long—especially if controversial and complex legislation is being worked on—before a newcomer senses the enormous influence wielded by committee staffs. These are usually heavily loaded in favor of the majority party, in terms both of outlook and of availability to committee members. Time and again after new points are raised in committee, the staff will disappear to return the next day with what is often a significantly new or considerably refocused bit of legislation.

It can be extraordinarily difficult for committee members, even those particularly concerned with the legislation in question, to keep up with what is happening to it. There simply isn't time for a member to rethink and reconsider every interlocking provision of a complex bill each time a substantive change is made—hence the heavy reliance on staff. Furthermore, committees often work under enormous time pressures to report out particular pieces of legislation by certain deadlines which at times are set not so much by the natural rhythm of the legislative process as by political considerations.

Thus major legislation is often rushed through committee, reported out on the floor of the Senate, and put to a vote with few senators fully understanding it. It must be understood that it is virtually impossible for a senator to keep up with most—let alone all—of the significant legislation being considered by committees other than his own. I do not refer to legislation that grabs the headlines and occasions national debate: A senator has to examine such legislation in some detail if only to answer his mail and reply to reporters' questions. It is, after all, by his positions on conspicuous legislation that he establishes his political identity.

Most of the bills considered by the Senate are relatively inconspicuous —though by no means unimportant. They may involve new programs that will have an enormous impact on American society, on the states, or on the economy; programs that in time may grow into multibillion-dollar commitments. Yet many of these bills will be enacted with little real examination by most of the senators who will have to vote yea or nay on them, and with less than adequate comprehension of what the bill involves.

The average senator simply does not have sufficient legislative help to get a proper analysis of every bill that issues from the legislative mill. Too many bills are called to a vote before the ink has dried on the explanatory report. Thus, all too often a senator's vote is based simply on a summary description of the bill (which can be totally inadequate), plus whispered conversations with colleagues who may or may not have detailed information as to its content—all in the fifteen-minute period allowed for voting after the bells ring to summon him to the floor.

Technically speaking, any senator can insure that adequate time is allowed for debate of any bill. He can simply register his refusal to agree to a unanimous-consent agreement limiting the time allotted for debate. This presupposes, however, that he has had enough advance warning of the particular mischief at hand to record a timely objection to any agreement to which he is not a party. It also presupposes that he will be able to educate and energize a sufficient number of his all-too-preoccupied colleagues to assure himself of sufficient floor support to make the effort worthwhile.

I recall two cases in my own experience—although there are, unfortunately, many more—that dramatize the pressures under which the Senate operates.

In early 1971, Governor Daniel Evans of Washington suggested the need for legislation to cope with economic disasters similar to existing legislation designed to cope with natural disasters. The law he proposed would be narrow in its focus, providing relief on a short-term, emergency basis to help communities ride out sudden economic catastrophes.

Two bills incorporating this approach were introduced, and hearings on them were held by the Public Works Committee. Several months later the Committee met in executive session to consider the legislation as revised by staff after the hearings. To the astonishment of at least some, the draft bill differed in fundamental respects from both of the measures that had been introduced. The basic concept had shifted from bringing maximum effort to bear on specific emergency situations, to an amorphous bill that would also cover areas of chronic unemployment or chronically low economic activity for which there already existed thirty or forty other federal programs. The definition of areas which could be made subject to the legislation was such that even a neighborhood could qualify for the most exotic kinds of federal help.

Nevertheless, this basically new legislation was approved in a single day by the full committee, and reported out. The legislation was then rushed to the floor of the Senate, debated before a largely empty chamber, and put to a vote—all within a day or two of the time printed copies of the bill and of the accompanying committee report had become available to senators. This legislation opened up a whole new area of federal intervention; it carried no price tag; and it was approved by senators only a few of whom had any grasp of its scope.

The second example concerned a new program of a truly sweeping nature, enacted by an overwhelming majority of senators, many of whom I am convinced had little understanding of the real issues involved. Just before the August recess in 1971, the Committee on Labor and Public Welfare reported out a measure innocuously titled "A Bill To Extend the Equal Employment Opportunity Act 1968 and Other Purposes." The "other purposes" turned out to be the inauguration of a comprehensive federal program for "child development" services designed ultimately to embrace a very large proportion of pre-school-age children regardless of financial need. Whereas in its first year the new program would cost a mere $100 million (chickenfeed these days), the Committee report placed the figure for the second year at $2 billion—an amount significantly greater than the projected cost of all the rest of the OEO's activities. Furthermore, the report stated that the cost of the child-development program would double every two years thereafter for some time hence. Secretary Elliot Richardson, then of the Department of Health, Education, and Welfare, estimated that the annual cost of the new program would come to $20 billion before the end of the decade.

Thanks to an interested housewife who had followed the progress of the bill in committee, my office was alerted to its implications. Because of the recess, we had time to examine its horrors and I was in a position to argue on the basis of expert opinion against the child-development section. (The bill had been scheduled as the first order of business on the day Congress returned, and was voted on in the Senate the next day, "other purposes" and all.)

Senators who had happened to be on the floor to hear the debate would have learned that there was substantial controversy among professionals over the child-development section, a fact they would not have discovered from reading the report. They would have learned that a number of experts in the field questioned the need for such a vast undertaking, and, in fact, warned that permanent harm could be done to younger children placed in the impersonal "warehouse" environment of the kind of day-care facility that was apt to result from the legislation. They would have learned also that the expert opinion heard in committee was entirely one-sided, and that even among the experts who favored the program, one had remarked that its far-reaching provisions would revolutionize the concept of the family in American life.

Unfortunately, almost no one besides the sponsors of the bill and the two or three senators arguing for the elimination or modification of the child-development section were on hand to hear the debate. Thus when the time came to vote, most senators voted aye on the assumption that nothing significant was involved in the bill beyond a simple two-year extension of existing OEO programs. (This bill, incidentally, was later vetoed.)

This rush of business with little or no time allowed for legislative pause, thought, or deliberation brings to mind another aspect of the Senate's current way of conducting its affairs. I speak of the phenomenon of the amendment—printed or unprinted—offered from the floor with little or no notice, which can cover the range from purely technical corrections of statutory language to the most far-reaching changes in the legislation under consideration.

There is usually little check on the scope of amendments that can be offered from the floor, and no opportunity for the relevant committees and their staffs to study them so that some measure of expert analysis can be brought to bear in arguing their merits for the benefit of the Senate—always assuming other senators are on hand to hear the debate. Thus all too often, especially when the Senate is operating under unanimous agreements severely limiting the time for debate on amendments, they are apt to be adopted or rejected on the basis of their emotional or political appeal. So it was with the floor amendments that last October added $4 billion, or more than 27 per cent, to the cost of the Welfare-Social Security bill reported out by the Senate Finance Committee; with the amendments that added, in one day's time last June, almost $2 billion to the HEW-Labor appropriations bill.

Surely there is a better way in which to conduct the nation's vital legislative business short of the highly restrictive rules that obtain in the House.

Too Much Business

All of which brings me to certain observations about the Senate today.

At the root of most of the problems of the Senate is the enormous expansion of federal activites in recent years. A recent study by the Association of the Bar of the City of New York found that the workload of members of Congress had doubled every five years over the past several decades. The Congress, like the Federal Government itself, is simply trying to handle more business than it can digest. The results too often are waste, conflicts, inconsistencies, and superficiality.

Once upon a time Congress was in session only six or seven months a year. There is every reason to believe that during these months there was time and opportunity to think, to study, to argue, and to come to educated conclusions. As the volume of work increased, the Congress was able to cope by extending the length of its sessions. But now, as a result of the explosion of federal activity resulting from the War on Poverty and other programs of the 1960s, it is conceded that Congress is in session essentially on a year-round basis.

One consequence of these increasing demands on senators' time is that it can no longer be said of the Senate that it is a club, exclusive or otherwise. Members once were able to spend unhurried time together, to get to know one another and develop a sense of fraternity while working toward common goals in a highly civil environment. I do not mean to suggest that all of this has disappeared. Real friendships and a sense of belonging do develop, but the sense of community which must once have existed has certainly been dissipated by the preoccupations that tend to keep senators concentrating on their own separate concerns except as their work requires them to come together. It is difficult, in fact, to come to know members of the opposition party who do not happen to serve on one's committees.

Whether the situation can be changed, only time and a differently constituted Congress will tell. But even assuming that the volume of business can be held at present levels, there remains the fact that each senator has only so many hours per day to devote to his job. A senator must be able not only to bring effective judgment to bear on his legislative duties, but also to maintain contact with his own constituency so as to find out what are the real problems people are faced with, and what are the real effects of the legislation he has helped enact.

All of this, in turn, takes adequate staff and office space. Mundane as this may seem, one quickly finds that staffing and space can become important factors in determining just how good a job he is going to be able to do.

A new senator from a state like New York quickly learns that the Senate places great emphasis on the equal sovereign dignity of each individual state; which is a polite way of saying that when it comes to allocating rooms and funds, senators from the larger states invariably feel short-changed. It should be kept in mind that the volume of work that must be handled by a senator's office depends largely on the size of his constituency. I speak of handling mail and constituent problems (the so-called case work), which have been increasing at an enormous rate as the Federal Government has become more and more intrusive into its citizens' lives.

Case work involves such things as immigration problems, chasing down Social Security checks, helping municipalities process their applications for this or that program, helping businesses thread their way through red tape —you name it. Whereas the office workload of a senator from New York may not be sixty times as heavy as that of a senator from Alaska, it certainly involves significantly more than two or three times the volume of work. Yet when I entered the Senate in 1971, the smallest number of rooms assigned to any senator was five and the largest (California and New York), seven. As I started out with a staff of 35 and needed one room for myself, this created a degree of congestion. In like manner, my allowance for hiring staff was less than twice the allowance for the smallest state. It is of course true that each senator bears an equal legislative responsibility and needs equal facilities to keep track of legislative matters and to help him do his individual and committee work. But this doesn't explain the disparity (or lack thereof) in space and staff allowances. In my own case, for example, staff members directly involved in legislative matters are less than one-fifth of the total.

Easing the Workload

Committee problems, time problems, space problems . . . it would seem from my description that a senator's lot is not entirely a happy one. There are, of course, compensations, not the least of which is the pervasive air of civility and mutual respect with which the business of the Senate is conducted. But even the extraordinary civility and respect that are the hallmark of the institution cannot overcome organizational and structural complexities that make a difficult job even more difficult.

What, if anything, can be done about the ever-increasing workload that is at the heart of the Senate's problems? I am not so romantic as to believe that we can dismantle the Departments of HEW and HUD in the immediate future and return most of their functions to the states and localities. Therefore another approach to restructuring the work and the flow of business in the Senate must be considered if senators are to be able to use their scarce time more effectively, and if they are to bring a maximum degree of thought to bear on legislation.

One useful approach might be to place as much of the legislative business of the Congress as possible on a two-year cycle. One year might be devoted to debate and action on bills reported out of committees the prior year, and to the holding of public hearings to assemble information for committee consideration in the succeeding year. (Ideally, both of these activities, which are of a very public nature and which tend to attract headlines, would be scheduled in non-election years so that the participants would not needlessly be distracted from the business at hand. There are, however, technical difficulties with this.) The alternate years would then be available for detailed consideration in executive session of new legislative proposals without arbitrary deadlines requiring hurried, patchwork approaches to important bills, and for the important work of legislative oversight.

A system that would require committees to report out legislation one year, and to have that legislation considered on the floor the next, would allow ample time for special-interest groups, for the public at large, and for members of individual senatorial staffs to digest what it is that the senator will be asked to vote upon when the legislation reaches the floor. It would also provide a period within which amendments could be introduced sufficiently in advance of debate to enable the members of the relevant committees to study them and to give the Senate as a whole the benefit of their expert assessment.

Whether the appropriation process could also be placed on a biennial basis, I do not know; and of course, any fundamental reordering of business would have to make special provision for the handling of emergencies. But if the work of the Senate could be organized in some such manner—and I see no reason why it is necessary to enact routine legislation every year instead of every other year—then the conflicts between committee hearings and executive sessions could be eliminated or greatly reduced, the members of the Senate would have time to participate more fully in floor debate, and it ought to be possible—at least every other year—to adjourn the Congress early enough to provide senators with a greater opportunity to return to their states to listen and to observe.

In this connection, I believe the Congress should schedule more "free" time for its members—at least a week each month—for consecutive thought, for planning, for study, for travel, for meaningful contact with their constituents. All of this is necessary if a senator or representative is to bring the best that is in him to bear on his work as a legislator. This would also help with the problem of absenteeism, as senators would be able to schedule their out-of-town engagements during these periodic recesses.

No discussion of possible changes in the way the Senate goes about its business would be complete without further mention of the committees.

As I have already pointed out, although the Senate relies heavily on its committee system for the conduct of its business, there is no assurance that the membership of a committee will reflect the views of the Senate as a whole. Thus it will very often happen that legislation that is highly controversial in nature will be reported out unanimously, or with appended minority views that are more concerned with details of the legislation than with its basic merit. This means that in too many cases the report which accompanies a new bill is not nearly as informative as it ought to be, and fails to alert the Senate as a whole to its controversial features.

This is especially true of committees that have a tradition of trying to iron out all differences of opinion within the committee so that legislation may be reported out unanimously. This practice has a certain utility in that it results in a genuine effort within the committee to reach reasonable compromises among conflicting views. Yet I wonder if the interests of the Senate are necessarily best served by this drive to consensus; for it encourages a sense of commitment to the end product which inhibits any public expression of misgivings by individual committee members. Thus the Senate is apt to be deprived of the candid insights of those senators who are best informed about the weaknesses of the legislation in question.

It might be desirable to require that every committee report outline as objectively as possible the principal arguments for *and* against each new legislative proposal, even when the bill is in fact unanimously supported by the entire committee. I also feel that whenever a member of a committee has strong reservations about any feature of a proposed bill, he has an obligation to the Senate to spell them out in a minority view printed in the committee report.

One recommendation I will not make is that the seniority system be abolished. This does not mean that I find it in all respects to my liking, or that I will not support (as I did) such sensible proposals for restricting its application as the one recently offered by Senator Howard Baker (and adopted by the Senate Republican Conference) which affects the selection of a committee's ranking member. Rather it means that I find greater potential problems with the alternatives thus far advanced. An often overlooked fact is that the seniority system was introduced some years ago as a reform measure to minimize politicking and power plays within the Congress. The system as it operates within the Senate today is reasonably benign; and I, as a most junior senator, have not found myself unduly abused by it. There are far more important targets, it seems to me, for a reformer's zeal.

The Balance Wheel

I have often been asked whether I find work in the Senate frustrating, and whether I have found any surprises. I have not found the work frustrating because I had few illusions as to what a very junior member of the minority party could accomplish on his own. Nor have I experienced any really major surprises, although I was not at all prepared for the enormous demands that would be made on my time seven days a week, or for my loss of anonymity (the unsurprising result of six hundred or so thousand well-deployed dollars on television advertising during my campaign, reinforced by periodic meetings with the press since election.)

Early on, I was struck by the number of extracurricular demands on a senator's time, especially one who lives as close to millions of constituents as does a senator from New York: invitations to speak which for one good reason or another cannot be declined, ceremonial visits, people with problems whom one must see and cannot refer to staff, people in the Federal Government to get to know, and so on. The day begins to be splintered into all kinds of pieces, even before the business of legislative work begins.

One thing that in my innocence I had not anticipated was the intensely political atmosphere that prevails within the Senate, the great impact of purely political considerations on specific actions taken by individual senators. It may well be, of course, that mine was an unusual introduction to the institution, as at least a half-dozen of my colleagues were beginning to jockey for position in the presidential race within months after I had been sworn in. This had an inevitable influence on how they orchestrated their performance in the Senate. Also there was the fact that the Senate was controlled by one party and the White House by the other; and as the presidential elections approached, the political atmosphere palpably intensified.

But these unusual considerations notwithstanding, I early learned that many senators tend to cast their votes with a view toward minimizing future political controversy or embarrassment. When a senator's vote is clearly not critical to the fate of a bill, it is often deployed for future political convience on the grounds that it "wouldn't count anyway." Thus the Senate will often cast a lopsided vote on quesions on which public opinion and the real opinion within the Senate is much more evenly divided.

This protecting of political flanks seems harmless enough, but it vitiates what I have discovered to be the important educational function of the Senate. If citizens see that members of the Senate have voted overwhelmingly in favor of this or that piece of legislation, many not entirely certain of their own ground may decide that they have in fact been wrong or backward or insensitive. Yet if on such issues each member of the Senate had voted his true convictions, the breakdown might have been, say, 55 to 45 instead of 70 to 30. I can't help but wonder to what extent this form of political expediency may affect the public's perception of the issues.

There may be another reason why the opinion of the Senate—even when accurately recorded—is very often at odds with what I, at least, take to be the current mood of the American people. Without having researched the point, I suspect that the Senate incorporates a cultural lag of ten or fifteen years; that it is out of phase by a period approximately equivalent to the average tenure of its membership.

A·decade or so ago, the Senate was considered by some to be a backward, conservative body whose Republican-Southern Democrat coalition lay athwart progress and the will of the people. Others viewed it as a necessary brake on the rasher impulses of the House of Representatives. Today the situation is quite the reverse. The liberals in the Senate are clearly in the majority, and they do not reflect the growing public skepticism over federal initiatives; and today, for example, it is the House which tends to blow the whistle on the excessive spending approved by the Senate.

There is a reason for this cultural lag, if it indeed exists. A member of the House of Representatives is up for election every two years and studies the views of his constituency with particular care. Also, because each member of the House represents a relatively compact area, his constituency tends to be more homogeneous than a senator's and there is less of an impulse to cater to the fringe groups within it. A member of the Senate, on the other hand, represents an entire state incorporating a multitude of conflicting claims and interests. For better or worse (I suspect the latter) a senator tends to pay a disproportionate amount of attention to the loudest voices, to editorial writers and commentators, to the pressure groups. Furthermore, once in office, he tends to stay there. Thus a senator may be less sensitive than a representative to basic shifts in the underlying mood of the electorate as a whole.

I make this comment by way of observation and not of criticism. The Founding Fathers intended, after all, that the Senate be a balance wheel which would moderate the impulses of the moment. This function it in fact performs, even though at any point of time those who believe the current impulses are the correct ones may tend to impatience. The Senate, however, is not an institution to which the impatient should gravitate. It has its own pace; and, under the present rules, it takes a little maturing on the vine of seniority to be in a position to have a large impact on the body politic.

It would be inaccurate, however, and unfair to the institution to suggest that the newest members are without the power to do more than register their 1 per cent of the Senate's total vote. The ancient tradition that stated that freshman senators were to be seen and not heard has disappeared. Somewhat to my surprise, on my initial rounds I was encouraged by the most senior members to speak out when I felt I had learned the ropes and had something to say—which was not, I hasten to say, an invitation to be brash.

In point of fact, I soon learned that there are a number of ways in which even Number 99 can make his imprint on the law of the land. If he is willing to do the necessary homework on a bill before his committee, if he attends meetings, if he presents arguments for or against specific provisions, he does have a chance to mold its final form. I have found that my own views will be given as careful a hearing as those of any other member of the committees on which I have served; again the essential courtesy of the Senate comes to the fore. It is also possible, by submitting appropriate amendments, to shape legislation after it has reached the floor.

It will also occasionally be the lot of a senator to come across an idea of such universal appeal that it will whisk through the legislative process in record time—witness two bills I introduced involving certain benefits for prisoners of war and those missing in action in Indochina. Each immediately attracted more than sixty co-sponsors, and each has since been signed into law.

Finally, there are the educational opportunities—and hence, responsibilities—which the Senate opens up to the newest of senators. These had not occurred to me when I first decided to run for office, but it did not take long for me to appreciate the skill with which some of the more liberal members were utilizing their office to reach the public. They would schedule time on the Senate floor, often in tandem, to deliver themselves of learned or impassioned speeches to an empty chamber. Their wisdom might be wasted on the Senate air, but the exercise enabled them to alert the press that Senator So-and-so would deliver remarks on such-and-such a topic at the scheduled time. Copies of the speech would be distributed, and the gist of the senator's argument and the points he wished to make would become part of the nation's informational bloodstream. I also noted that conservative-minded senators were generally not so alert in this regard.

Whether utilized or not, the opportunity does exist for a senator to present his views on the important issues with some reasonable assurance that they will not be totally lost. Only by exploiting these opportunities for public education can he expect to help the electorate become more adequately informed on the basic issues. This in turn bears on the legislative process because, in the last analysis, public opinion dictates the outside limits of the options available to the Congress. By joining in the public debate and articulating the arguments in support of his own positions, a new senator —even one labeled "Conservative-Republican"—can contribute to the educational process which ultimately finds its reflection in national policy.

Snuff and Civility

These, then, are the random impressions of the United States Senate by one of its newest members: It is a deliberative body in which there is too little time to deliberate. It is a place where a senator is entitled to free haircuts (although he is expected to tip the barber a dollar) in a barbershop which keeps a shaving mug with his name on it. It is a place where on each desk there is a little inkwell, a wooden pen with steel nibs, and a glass bottle filled with sand with which to blot writing, and where on either side of the presiding officer's desk is a spittoon and a box of snuff.

Yet it is also a place where the rules of civility are still observed, and the rights and independence of each individual still respected. It is a place where many of the major decisions affecting the shape of our times are made; a place where even the least of its members may have a hand in making them.

It is, all in all, a good place to be.

ONE DAY IN THE LIFE OF GUY VANDER JAGT (R.-MICH.)

John Corry

The Congressman is ready to tie his shoelaces, having waited, as he does every morning, until he has stepped on the escalator that rises out of the bowels of the Longworth House Office Building, where he has parked his car, and is ascending to the basement, where he can take an elevator to his office on the second floor. The Congressman ties his shoelaces with a certain grace and style, the idea being that before he gets on the escalator going up, he will glance at the escalator coming down, and see if there is anyone on it he knows. The Congressman is an affable man, which is one reason he is a successful politician, and he knows a good many people in and about the House of Representatives, which is one reason he is a sound Congressman, and if he bends too quickly to tie his shoelaces while he is on the up escalator, he might pass without seeing someone on the down escalator to whom he might want to nod. There is a lot of civility in the House of Representatives; and while this can be one man's bullshit, it is another man's good manners, and without it the Congressmen might fly at one another's throats and never get around to doing any business at all. On this particular morning the Congressman, an intensely disorganized man who can get on the escalator with a pair of socks or Jockey shorts in one hand because he has forgotten to pack them in the overnight bag he is carrying in the other hand, is completely unencumbered, and so with both hands free, and after saying hello to a Congressman who was on the down escalator, he bends, ties his shoelaces, and straightens himself up at that precise

Source: *Harper's Magazine* (April 1971), pp. 70–79. Copyright © 1971, by Minneapolis Star and Tribune Co., Inc. Reprinted from the April, 1971 issue of *Harper's Magazine* by permission of the author.

moment he reaches the top. "There," he says, "I used six seconds that I might have wasted."

Now, this is whimsy, a ritual observed by the Congressman only because he enjoys observing it, and on this particular morning there is hardly any need to save time at all. It is a day in December, the election is past, and a new House, with fifty-six new members, will convene in less than a month. In fact, the Congress, having been sluggish in its duties in the past year, is meeting now mostly so that it can pass appropriations bills that will keep the great creaking machinery of government from going flat broke, and there is not much of a sense of urgency about even that. The Congressman, whose name is Guy Vander Jagt, and who is a thirty-nine-year-old Republican from the Ninth District in Michigan, will spend his day not being caught by the great questions of war and peace, but by things that few people outside his office have even heard of, which, as any Congressman will tell you, are the things that usually engage Congressmen anyway. A Congressman, you understand, is seldom allowed to be apocalyptic, which is a privilege ordinarily extended only to writers, ideologists, and a few show-business personalities; and although the messianic complex is rampant in the House of Representatives, it is considered bad form to show it, and a good Congressman does not. Consequently, on this quiet day in the House, when, among other things, seven bills and two resolutions will be introduced, when thirteen bills will be reported, a dozen committees will meet, and an uncounted number of Congressmen will either fall flat on their faces or run up some small and modest triumphs, Congressman Vander Jagt, recognizing it all as a slow day, will not hurry to his office, but will tarry, saying hello to as many people as he chooses, and move through the Longworth House Office Building with the sure tread of a man who is absolutely delighted to be precisely where he is.

Vander Jagt was made to hold office, being an old farm boy from Cadillac, Michigan who was graduated from Yale Divinity School, then left a pulpit to become a television news commentator, and then left that to go through law school and become a trial lawyer. In 1965 he ran for the State Senate, first telling the voters that if he won he would hold no other job than elected office, and be only a servant of the people. He did win, and subsequently the members of the press gallery chose him as the outstanding freshman in the State Senate. When Senator Patrick McNamara died in 1966, Congressman Robert P. Griffin was selected to fill the vacancy, leaving open his own seat in the Ninth District, and Vander Jagt chose to run for that. The district, made up of eleven counties on the western shore of Michigan, begins about a third of the way up the coast of the lower part of the state and stretches into the Straits of Mackinac, which is close to the wonderfully desolate Upper Peninsula of Michigan. The nice thing about

Michigan is that while politically it is thought of as being mostly Detroit and a few outlying communities, it includes virtually every class and condition of American, and Vander Jagt's own district, which is mostly rural and Republican, includes a county that is mostly urban and Democratic. Despite that county, which he carries anyway, the only truly difficult election contests that Vander Jagt has been in have been Republican primaries, the first when he ran for the State Senate, and the second when he ran for Griffin's seat. In that second primary, his opponent's people distributed a particularly scurrilous broadside which charged, among other things, that Vander Jagt had been in and out of mental institutions and that his wife had had some unknown number of husbands before she met him. In fact, Vander Jagt had never suffered an emotional ailment and his wife had never been married before, and other than introducing Vander Jagt to the particular ugliness that gets entwined in the political process, the broadside induced a good many Republicans to vote for him. The Michigan Ninth has a large number of what are sometimes called burghers, who do not much care for dirty pool, and the things that get to them the most are the things that can either be dismissed as home-and-motherhood stuff or be recognized as the serious concerns of serious people, which as often as not is what they are. Possibly, these concerns are most apparent in Ottawa County, the southernmost county in Vander Jagt's district, where a man must search long and hard to find a fifth of Scotch, and where most of the people, like Vander Jagt, are of Dutch descent.

Vander Jagt, in fact, won his first campaign in Ottawa County, getting elected president of the student body at Hope College in the town of Holland, when a particularly astute campaign manager used the slogan "Fly High With Guy," and insisted that the candidate appear before him each morning fully and suitably clothed, Vander Jagt even then having an unusual tendency to look as if he had stood in the middle of a room and his clothes had dropped on him at random. At Hope, Vander Jagt also won nearly every speech contest that was open to a college student, which was interpreted as a sign that he could later make it in any of the entertainment arts, all of which he more or less did, while finding only politics sustaining enough to stay with. Vander Jagt stayed at Yale Divinity School largely because Richard Niebuhr was there, and he regarded Richard as a more interesting man than his brother Reinhold. Later, he left the pulpit of his Congregational church in Cadillac because he could find nothing suitable to preach about death. He left television because that was just another branch of show business, and he went through the University of Michigan Law School mostly out of perversity. A dean had called him in on his arrival and said that Michigan was the finest and toughest law school about and that it was impossible to get through without the utmost devotion to law books and classes. The hell, Vander Jagt had said, and subsequently made it a point not to open too many books, and not to be particularly diligent about classes either. (Philip A. Hart, the senior Senator from Michigan, is supposed to have gone through Michigan Law School without opening *any* books. He was graduated No. 1 in his class; Vander Jagt, however, only made it into the top quarter.)

When Vander Jagt left law school, he went with Warner, Norcross & Judd, the biggest and most properous law firm in Western Michigan, and he was doing just fine, until one night, answering his own secret urgings, he summoned his wife Carol and announced that he wanted to go into politics. He did, running that first race for the State Senate, and being fortunate enough to have as his Democratic opponent a civilized doctor with money, who said to him, I have means, and you have none; I shall not try to outspend you, but we will debate together, and try the campaign on the issues. This they did, arriving separately with their wives at the schools, Legion halls, and churches of Western Michigan, there to talk about issues and call each other skunks and blackguards, and then to steal away separately and unite for a drink in some place where they would not be recognized. The doctor is still the most formidable opponent Vander Jagt has faced in a general election, and the Democratic party in the Michigan Ninth is a frail vessel indeed. Once Vander Jagt ran against a former minister, possessed of an enormous voice, an old Phi Beta Kappa key that he jangled a lot, and a firm conviction that the only thing worth talking about was the peril of extending aid to parochial schools. Another time he faced an apple farmer, who began each of his speeches by saying, "Hip, hip, hooray for America," and never got much beyond that; and in this last election he was up against a union official, who hardly said anything at all.

Nonetheless, Vander Jagt has remained an assiduous campaigner. In 1970, he returned to his district forty-nine times, speaking whenever he could get even two or three to gather in his name, and faithfully listening, nodding, and trying to accede to each request from a constituent, no matter how loony. In the spring of the year, Carol Vander Jagt organized a "Fry for Guy," which was a bratwurst roast in the sand dunes alongside Lake Michigan, charged admission at $100 a couple, and raised $14,000 for the campaign. There was to be no other money, although the Democratic organization in the Ninth, which is really labor and its Committee on Political Education (COPE), had more, and it was able to use unions, their members and halls, and their mimeograph machines too. This made the Ninth one of the few districts in the country where the Democrats spent more than the Republicans, although any Congressman from the Ninth would still cherish an endorsement from the conservative Americans for Constitutional Action infinitely more than he would one from the AFL-CIO. Vander Jagt, in fact, had even asked Americans for Constitutional Action for an endorsement, and throughout the campaign he carried a copy of their telegram

in his back pocket, ready to whip it out at first sight of an outraged conservative. Vander Jagt had voted for the rat-control bill, and he had voted
against the supersonic transport. He had voted for the House version of
the Cooper-Church resolution, which would have required the withdrawal
of American troops from Cambodia, and in his finest and most independent
hour he had been the only Republican to vote against a miiltary appropriations bill. Still, a defeat was inconceivable, and he knew it, and the Democrats knew it, and so did everyone else. COPE's campaign had not been
particularly good, and there were defections in its ranks. One night Vander
Jagt debated a union leader who stood up and said, "Well, I want you to
know that Vander Jagt is my friend and I like him. In fact, I can't think
of much bad to say about him. In fact, I can't think of anything bad to
say at all." Then he sat down. Still, politicians' hopes are the most fragile
of things, and politicians plunge easily into despair. On election night,
the first return was from a Democratic precinct in the Democratic city of
Muskegon; "214 for Rogers, 115 for Vander Jagt," a voice on the phone
said. "Don't tell Guy. It will only worry him," Mrs. Vander Jagt said,
looking stricken herself. Then she told him anyway, and he looked
stricken too. When it was all over, however, he had won with 67 per cent
of the vote, and he had even carried Muskegon easily. The next morning
Vander Jagt was outside the gates of a factory, awaiting the men as they
came to work, and then thanking them for their support.

So, on this slow day in the House, Vander Jagt enters the office on the second
floor into which he and his staff lately have moved from an office on the
first floor. The new office is next to the one occupied by John Buchanan of
Alabama, and Buchanan is supposed to have the best-looking secretaries on
the Hill, one of whom had reached an ephemeral kind of fame by being
dropped from the staff of Senator Joseph Tydings after she had worked as
a bunny in a Playboy club. Now, *machismo* is important to Congressmen,
being one of the things they use to unite themselves when politics divides
them, and a Congressman is only paying another Congressman a compliment when he suggests that he, too, is full of *machismo*. For days after he
had moved in next to Buchanan, Vander Jagt was visited by Congressmen
who would say, "Guy, you old rascal, how did you ever manage to get this
office?" All of this upset Vander Jagt's own girls, who are good-looking
themselves, and Vander Jagt, trying to do the right thing, told them that
they probably were more efficient than Buchanan's girls, which did no good
at all. A Congressman's staff is enormously important to him, handling his
requests from constituents and other supplicants, and more or less seeing to
it that the Congressman does not disappear under a welter of trivia. Among
his other allowances, a Congressman is permitted to hire up to thirteen
people, and to pay them a total of $135,000. Vander Jagt has four secre-

taries and an administrative assistant working for him in Washington, and one full-time man and three part-time people in his district. Every so often, he gets in other people for specific tasks (addressing Christmas cards, for example), and he is planning to hire a former professor of political science, who will be something of an idea man. The Congressional bureaucracy measures and operates itself under rules that no one man can ever know, or for that matter ever want to know. A Congressman, for example, is allowed to get a new steamer trunk at the start of each session of Congress and one plant a month from the Botanical Gardens. He is allowed to spend up to $3,500 a year for stationery, but if he takes the money and puts it in his pocket, it is to be considered income. The long distance calls from his office are measured by units, with one minute on the phone being four units, and the office may use up to 150,000 units every two years. However, if the calls are made after 5:00 P. M. or before 9:00 A. M. on something called the Federal Telecommunications System, they are free. Salaries for staff people are figured on a base pay, and although the base pay of, say, an administrative assistant may be only $7,500, his actual salary may be $27,000. A Congressman is allowed one free trip home every month, while members of his staff are allowed two a year. When Vander Jagt first reached the House, he had to supply his own curtains and wastebaskets. Subsequently, the bureaucracy shuddered into action, and now gnomes from somewhere bring them in for free.

"Guy, these are the calls so far," Peg Martin says to Vander Jagt. Mrs. Martin is the doyenne of the staff, a pretty woman with gray hair who reached the Hill in 1939, became enchanted by it, and never left. She is a discreet woman, married to a lobbyist for the oil industry, and one way or another she may know everyone in government. When her husband gave a party for her on her thirtieth anniversary in Congress, even Wilbur Mills, chairman of the Ways and Means Committee, came to celebrate, and Mills is a man with such small use for parties that he would grumble when President Kennedy would invite him to dinner at the White House. Now Mrs. Martin gives Vander Jagt his messages, arranging them so that the first he sees is one from Russell Train, the President's adviser on environmental problems. Vander Jagt calls Train, listens, and says, "Russell, that's just wonderful. I'm absolutely delighted, and thank you, thank you, for calling." Vander Jagt, you see, is the ranking Republican on the Conservation and Natural Resources Subcommittee, and about six months ago, the subcommittee went to the White House environmental people and discussed with them an old law that forbade industry from befouling interstate waters. The law, in fact, had been passed in 1899, but, like so many things in government, had lain moldering until good men would put their hands to it. Henry Reuss, a Democrat, who is the chairman of the subcommittee, brought the law up in hearings, wrote letters about it, and then went around and made speeches about it. Vander Jagt, being a Republican, and therefore closer to the White House, kept talking to the people there, and two weeks ago he got to Train at a cocktail party and insisted to him that the 1899 law should indeed be resurrected. Now Train had called to tell him that the Administration would soon issue an Executive Order, declaring that the old law was official policy and that enforcement machinery for it would be set up. There is nothing simple about government, and in the end the 1899 law will involve three or four agencies (all of which will have their own lobbyists), the Army Corps of Engineers, a couple of Congressional committees, and the delicate considerations of partisan politics. Jobs will be created, reputations will collapse, and some staff people will weep with frustration. Government is like that, and it is easier to be apocalyptic than to try to understand it.

So, feeling well pleased by Train's call, and after having disposed of some matters of no consequence, Vander Jagt leaves his office for the House gym. The gym, deep in the recesses of the Rayburn Building, is unmarked, and it is open only to Congressmen, who, in fact, do a good deal of business there. It is where they can be good fellows together and where even the least of the Congressmen can approach a committee chairman, naked and alone in the steam room, and ask for a favorable ruling on his bill. Some Congressmen spend more time in the gym than do others, and the Republican minority on the Public Works Committee, for example meets there in a more or less permanent caucus. Vander Jagt himself is the president of the gym, which he became when the other Congressmen voted him the Bullshot of the Year Award. This is an engraved cup that ostensibly is given to the Congressman who cheats the most at a game called paddle ball, and argues more over questionable line calls; actually, it is given as a mark of esteem, and Vander Jagt treasures it. The only duty of the president is to preside each year over the gym's annual dinner, which has been held in eighteen different places in twenty years, few establishments being willing to have the Congressmen as guests more than once. At some point in the dinners, Congressmen begin to soak their napkins in their water glasses, and then hurl them at other Congressmen. The hilarity increases after that, and otherwise dignified men get themselves sodden and bespotted, although the Great Republic itself always survives.

Nonetheless, there is a majesty about the House, even if it is not always apparent in its members. It must always be remembered that the curious ways of politics in the House, unlike the Senate, do not allow for much majesty, which is why Congressmen are infinitely more interesting and proportionately more productive than Senators, who must strike postures a lot. In the House, it is sweatier, so to speak, and more intimate, and there is more room for caprice. Vander Jagt's chief and abiding interest, for example, has been the environment, and his most notable project has been the establishment of the Sleeping Bear Dunes National Park, a tract of 61,000 acres on the shore of Lake Michigan. For years, Phil Hart had been introducing a Sleeping Bear bill in the Senate, and for years the Senate had been passing it. In the House, however, the bill never got beyond the Interior and Insular Affairs Committee, whose chairman, Wayne Aspinall of Colorado, always declined to report it unless the full Michigan delegation, Republicans and Democrats, would support it. This the delegation always declined to do, and Sleeping Bear would always die. Shortly after the '68 elections, however, Vander Jagt began to negotiate with the Secretary of the Interior and with the Park Service over a new Sleeping Bear bill, one that might please everyone, and after ten months of negotiation he produced it, staying all the time in touch with Hart, who was still laboring for Sleeping Bear in the Senate. This annoyed James O'Hara, a Democrat, who was Hart's closest colleague in the Michigan Congressional delegation, and he said that Hart should be dealing with him and not with Vander Jagt, who was, after all, a Republican. Consequently, O'Hara said, he would have nothing to do with Vander Jagt's bill, which meant, of course, that Aspinall would then reject it because the Michigan delegation would be divided. Subsequently, a lobbyist for the Wilderness Society got to O'Hara and suggested that he introduce his own bill, which the Michigan Democrats could sign, while the Michigan Republicans could go with Vander Jagt. O'Hara did, confusing nearly everyone, and inducing John Dingell, another Democrat, to say the hell with it and sign both bills. Meanwhile, the Interior Department, which had been working with Vander Jagt on his bill, suddenly and inexplicably said that it liked O'Hara's better. This enraged Vander Jagt, who, on demanding an explanation, was told that the man in the Interior Department who knew all about Sleeping Bear was on vacation and that someone had made a mistake. The department then reversed itself, and the O'Hara bill was so amended that it really became the Vander Jagt Bill, even though O'Hara's name was still on it. Chairman Aspinall, however, said that a bill amended that much was a mess, and he demanded that the Michigan delegation produce a clean bill. Of course, he said, it would still have to be supported by the full delegation. During all these peregrinations, Martha Griffiths of Detroit, a Democrat, had been lobbying for her own bill on women's rights, which was stuck off in another committee. Mrs. Griffiths wanted everyone to sign a discharge petition to force the committee to release the bill, but O'Hara, very sensibly saying that it was a bad bill, would not sign. This so angered Mrs. Griffiths that she said she would not support the Sleeping Bear bill. But, Martha, Vander Jagt said, that's *my* bill. I know, Mrs. Griffiths said, but that man's name is on it. But, Martha, Vander Jagt said. No, Mrs. Griffiths said. Nonetheless, Mrs. Griffiths said that she would visit Aspinall, and she did, telling him that she really did like the bill, but that she simply would not sign anything that said O'Hara on top.

Aspinall, who is seventy-four, rather liked the idea of Mrs. Griffiths coming to him that way, and so he said that his committee would report the bill out, even without her signature.

Faithfully, the committee did report the bill, sending it to the Rules Committee, which was to decide when it would be sent to the House floor, where its passage would be assured. There was, of course, no reason to think the Rules Committee would delay the bill, which had been the fruit of so much labor and passion, but in the mysterious ways of Congress it did, and once again Sleeping Bear was languishing. Baffled, Vander Jagt approached various members of the Rules Committee, asking them why, and was told that "Charlotte didn't like the bill," although no one knew quite why. Now, Charlotte is Congresswoman Charlotte Reid of Illinois, and she is not a member of the Rules Committee, but she is a sunny woman, much admired and liked, who was once the vocalist on Don McNeill's old *Break-fast Club* radio program. The members of the Rules Committee could not possibly know much about Sleeping Bear, but they did know Mrs. Reid, who has a summer cottage in the Sleeping Bear area, and they wanted to please her. Therefore, they were holding the bill back, and they kept holding it back until Mrs. Reid and Vander Jagt appeared formally to argue their cases. Then the committee locked its doors and voted in secret. When the doors were opened, it was announced that Sleeping Bear, finally, had triumphed.

It is noontime, and Vander Jagt is just sitting down in the House restaurant, and on the floor of the House the chaplain is praying over those few members who have gathered to open the day's session. Three staff people from the White House happen by, and one of them glumly tells Vander Jagt that "even cannons couldn't get the Buchanan bill out of the Rules Committee." Congressman Buchanan has sponsored a bill that would put a new consumer-protection agency more or less under the control of the White House, while a competing bill by a Democrat would make the agency more autonomous, which the staff people plainly don't want. A buzzer sounds in the restaurant, and Vander Jagt frowns. The buzzer means that a quorum call has been put forth on the floor and that a clerk is about to read the roll. The Constitution says that Congress cannot be in session unless a majority of its members are present, and so any Congressman, at any time and for the most frivolous of reasons, can ask the Speaker to check and make sure there is a majority. There are quorum calls because a Congressman simply is feeling irritable, or because he wants to delay the day's business, or because he has a friend who is making a speech and he wants to roust the other Congressmen out to hear it. There are quorum calls because a Congressman is lonely and wants to see his peers milling about him, and there are quorum calls because someone wants to empty the paddle-ball courts in the gym and then dash down and get the center court. (For his own reasons, H. R. Gross of Iowa asks for more quorum calls than anyone else, and the other Republicans, accepting H. R., sometimes call him the "conscience of the House." Mostly, however, H. R. is just being cranky.) Consequently, Congressmen spend a good part of their days walking rapidly along the underground corridors that lead from their office buildings to the Capitol, where they run out on the House floor, shout "Present," and then leave. It is usually a great exercise in futility, and the Congressmen resent it, but no one has been able to think of a way to stop it. Quorum calls are part of a man's record, and they are just not very well understood outside of Congress. A Congressman does not want his opponent in an election to be able to ask where he was when the roll was called that day, and so he goes on making the quorum calls. "In politics," Vander Jagt says, "if you even have to *answer* a charge, then you've already lost."

Vander Jagt waits until the buzzer rings a second time, which means that the clerk reading the roll is up to the letter Q. Vander Jagt has nicely calculated from all parts of the Hill exactly how much time it will take him to reach the floor after that second buzzer rings; from the restaurant, allowing for all vagaries, he knows that he can wait about two minutes, walk to an elevator, and get there just as the clerk is ready to intone "Vander Jagt." Today this gives him time to swallow his soup, unnecessarily tell the waiter he will be back, and start for the House floor in a dignified way. Allard K. Lowenstein, the liberal New Yorker who had just been defeated for re-election after one term, wants to make the quorum call too, and he is running. "Guy," he says, "can you think of anything more foolish than a lame-duck Congressman in a lame-duck session trying to answer a quorum call?" Everyone knows Lowenstein, and for days now, conservatives who might be expected to want to crucify a man of his proclivities have been coming up and saying how much they will miss him. Congress is a tough house to play to, but Lowenstein, who as much as any man had been responsible for Lyndon Johnson's decision not to run again, was something of a celebrity when he arrived, and Congressmen like to have celebrities about. Moreover, in terms of Congressional politics, Lowenstein was an authentic radical, and conservatives always are pleased when they meet someone they suppose to be a radical—and then find he is a decent, pleasant man. For one thing, it makes a conservative feel good, convincing him that he can get along with any man; for another, it makes him feel daring. Every two years, the Congressmen measure up all the new boys, and if a new boy is supposed to have a special dimension about him, he is measured up all the more quickly. Ideologists do not come out well, but Lowenstein showed he was a genuine reformer, and certainly not just another liberal politician, and the old boys respected him for it. On Lowenstein's first day in the

House, the late L. Mendel Rivers accosted him and almost immediately began waving three fingers in his face. Ho, ho, the reporters in the gallery said, Rivers is telling Lowenstein not to try any fancy New York-Jewish-liberal stuff here. Actually, Rivers was very courteously telling Lowenstein there were three synagogues in his district in South Carolina.

It is the 190th quorum call that Vander Jagt has answered this year, and he shouts "Present" and starts to move off the floor. Congressman Garry Brown stops him and says he needs his vote on an amendment he will offer in the afternoon. "I'll be there, Garry," Vander Jagt says. Congressman Don Clancy moves in hurriedly and says, "Guy, don't go away. I've been designated to seek your support for Sam Devine for chairman of the House Republican Conference." Now, this is a move by the more conservative Republicans to put one of their own in a job held by John Anderson, who is a moderate. It is largely a ceremonial job, but most Congressmen are moderates, and both the right and left wings of Congress place great stress on ceremonial victories. "I'm sorry, Don," Vander Jagt says, "but John Anderson is a friend of mine. I've been in his home, and he's been in mine." "Okay, Guy, I understand," Clancy says, and almost certainly he does, friendship and personal loyalty being recognized in the House as things beyond ideology, and sufficient to justify nearly any position. So Clancy does not try to persuade, and Vander Jagt returns to lunch. He has made the round trip in four minutes. There is nothing but routine in front of him, and he is a little bored, even though he is a man who loves the House. "Sometimes," he says, "I feel as if I should be paying for the *privilege* of being here." Congressman Pete McCloskey stops by, exchanges pleasantries, and mentions something about the Government Operations Committee. A few days before, in an interview with a reporter for the *Los Angeles Times,* McCloskey had said that it would be a good thing for everyone if Nixon were challenged in some Presidential primaries in 1972. Now, McCloskey has lean, tough good looks, and the residue of a national reputation left over from the time he beat Shirley Temple Black in a primary. Moreover, he is a liberal Republican, and he was endorsed by the *New York Times* in the last election, which he then won with 78 per cent of the vote. In the interview he had not said that *he* would enter a primary against Nixon, and in fact he had said that he wouldn't be right for it at all. Still, to be young, and to be a politician, is to have a sense of the possibility of all things, and it is also to think of all the other politicians who could get in your way. So, what is McCloskey *really* thinking? Another reporter wanders up to him and Vander Jagt. "Congressman McCloskey," he says, "have you had any trouble from the White House on that statement about Nixon?" "I said it because I *wanted* to make some trouble," McCloskey says, moving away, and looking leaner and tougher than ever. "It was a good answer to a bad question," the reporter says to Vander Jagt, "except that it didn't mean anything." Vander Jagt, who is young, and a politician, and gets mentioned himself when the Michigan Republicans count their candidates, looks speculative and says nothing at all.

It is early afternoon, and Vander Jagt is alone in his inner office with Bud Nagelvoort, his administrative assistant. Nagelvoort, who was a market research assistant for a baby food manufacturer in Michigan before he joined Vander Jagt in Washington, speaks very softly and very cautiously. He is superb at details and mustering all the small pieces of information that go into legislation, and like many politicians, Vander Jagt is not. Nagelvoort and Mrs. Martin are the only ones in the office who will call Vander Jagt by his first name, the secretaries always saying "Congressman," which is what Nagelvoort and Mrs. Martin do, too, when strangers are about. There is a deference shown to Congressmen, and one of the truly sad things in Washington is a Congressman who has just lost an election and must now forgo that deference forever. It is one reason so many of them never return to their districts, but linger on in Washington, wraiths around their old privileges.

The police stop traffic on Independence Avenue so a Congressman can cross and walk to the Capitol, even if it is only for one of H. R.'s quorum calls, and they will give him a number his secretary can call to fix his traffic tickets. The clerks at Washington National Airport will delay a flight for him, and the telephone company will put "The Honorable" after his name in the phone book. A Congressman can find someone to do something for him nearly any time, and while this may not corrupt him, it can easily confuse him. Politicians, like lawyers, want to be loved for themselves, but a politician can never be entirely sure that this is why he is loved, and so he has a harder time than most of us. Like all great institutions, official Washington sorts out men by their positions, and the positions determine the esteem one man shows for another. There is nothing wrong with this, and the Sacred College of Cardinals does it too. In Washington, however, there are more positions to go around than there are in the College, and while the cardinals only get together once in a while, the Washington people keep seeing one another all the time. Since only the strongest among them do not judge themselves mostly by the way the others treat them, they are all greatly dependent on one another. Unhappily for a politician, however, he cannot be sure whether he is treated the way he is because of himself or because of his position, and so he carries a burden that most of us do not. In his soul, it vexes him.

Bud Nagelvoort, meanwhile, is shuffling pieces of paper. "Guy," he says, "we have this." It is a confrontation they have each day, Nagelvoort carrying in to Vander Jagt the most recent memos, proposals, requests, and stray pieces of information he thinks he should know about, and Vander Jagt, after considering each one, saying either yes, no, let me see it, or put it aside. This day there is a memo on the United States and Soviet space programs. Vander Jagt wants to see it. There is more information on the Administration plan to help the railroads. He hesitates, and Nagelvoort suggests that perhaps he has read enough about it in the newspapers. It is put aside. Someone will propose a bill to increase the number of family doctors. Vander Jagt is interested. There is a statement by another Michigan Congressman. He is not interested. The Government Operations Committee will vote on something while he will be out of town. He will send a proxy. The committee is sponsoring a trip to Puerto Rico. He is interested. The offer expired last Sunday. Oh. There are clippings on the Hope College choir, new Republican officials in Michigan, and pollution in the Great Lakes, and there is a report on the Muskegon County sewage system. He is interested in all of them. There is a cable from a friend, a black artist, who is on a trip to Africa. He has just been invited for a showing in the Soviet Union. Should he go. Certainly. There are twenty-three pieces of paper, each one of considerable moment to someone or other, and if Vander Jagt stops to be thoughtful over each one he will do nothing else for the rest of the day. His talent, however, is to extrapolate, and then to decide quickly, which a good politician ought to be able to do. On larger matters, of course, it is more difficult. When Vander Jagt voted against the supersonic transport, the White House was for it; Gerry Ford, being the House minority leader, was for it too, although like any sensible leader he had said no more than, "Guy, we'd like your support on this one." Furthermore, a factory in Muskegon fabricated metal parts for the SST, and the Republican county chairman even worked there. What if the chairman were to lose a stock option, or even his job, if the SST were canceled? It was the kind of question that can get to a Congressman and gnaw at him. Vander Jagt brooded, wavered, and still voted against the SST. Shortly afterward, he learned that the men who ran the factory had never cared for him anyway, and indeed had supported his opponent. This made his vote more tolerable to him, although he wished he had known about it before.

Now, of all things that can sway a Republican Congressman, a Republican White House is probably the greatest. The White House, however, is not one man; it is a warren, a separate culture, of assistants, special assistants, counselors, and all their deputies. Their roles are unclear, and their authority never exactly defined, but they can be the ultimate source of favors and dispensations. A Congressman, for example, is supposed to be something of a public-relations man for his district, and Vander Jagt once worked his White House sources for five months to be allowed to present a pair of wooden shoes to President Nixon as a gift from the people of Holland, Michigan, who every year hold a Tulip Festival. (Vander Jagt also decided to give the President a recording made by an orchestra at

Interlochen, a summer music camp in his district. When he walked into Nixon's office, the wooden shoes in one hand, the recording in the other, he said, "Mr. President, I'd like to present you with this wooden record.") In 1969, on a trip home, Vander Jagt met with some ecologists, urban planners, and Muskegon County officials who were trying to establish a new kind of sewage system to take the sewage that was wasting Lake Michigan and divert it to fertilize barren land. It was a stunning plan, with implications for every city in the country, and it was being delayed by opposition in the state capital. When Vander Jagt returned to Washington, he met with the federal people involved, and then finally, and most importantly, with John Ehrlichman, Nixon's assistant on domestic affairs. Ehrlichman is one of the better people in the White House; his soul is not always torn by fear that his President might not be re-elected, and he can consider an issue on its merits. Moreover, the Ehrlichmans are friends and neighbors of the Vander Jagts, and Ehrlichman's daughter is their babysitter, and from more slender circumstances than these the fate of nations, much less that of a sewage system, has been decided. Vander Jagt and Nagelvoort talked to Ehrlichman for two hours about the Muskegon proposal, and shortly thereafter the whole federal bureaucracy became more interested in it. Nonetheless, the state government in Michigan still was not ready to accept it until Vander Jagt carried a letter from Nixon to Governor William Milliken at his summer home in Traverse City. The President told the Governor that he was personally interested in the sewage system, and although this was unlikely—the sewage system being a highly complicated project, and Presidents generally not having the time to study such things—it was *Realpolitik*. Subsequently, Milliken visited Muskegon, the state decided it supported the sewage system, and the federal government announced a $2 billion grant to get it started. Vander Jagt came out ahead too, when the League of Conservation Voters, which is interested in how *effective* a politician is, named him as one of only seven Congressmen it was endorsing for re-election.

A buzzer has sounded, signifying that a vote is forthcoming on the House floor, and Vander Jagt leaves his office, falling into step, as he does, with his neighbor, Congressman John Buchanan. "John," Vander Jagt says, "I talked to my man at the White House, and his reading is that they couldn't get your bill out of the Rules Committee with cannons." "That's just not true," Buchanan says, "and I got an even more optimistic report only an hour ago." Vander Jagt speculates. This Administration has not distinguished itself when it has counted votes beforehand, and maybe it is wrong again. "Well, I hope you're right, John," Vander Jagt says. "I certainly hope so." Vander Jagt crosses Independence Avenue (the policeman stops traffic for him, of course) and he sees coming toward him a Congressman he does not like, and who, for that matter, does not like him. They ignore each other as long as they can, and then at precisely the same moment, and almost imperceptibly, they both nod. Vander Jagt keeps walking until he is in the shadow of the Capitol. "I'll never be able to get along with that guy," he says moodily. Vander Jagt quickens his pace, afraid he will miss the vote, and when he gets to the floor he enters on the Democratic, and not the Republican, side. The clerk reading the roll is up to Udall, and across the floor Vander Jagt sees the Republican doorkeeper, William Bonsell, grinning, and then very gravely taking his index finger and poking himself in the eye with it. Vander Jagt stops and ponders. He is there to vote for a resolution that will limit the debate on a housing bill that afternoon to two hours. It is the 176th time this year he has appeared for a record vote, and he understands the resolution and knows how he will vote. Sometimes, however, dashing in from a committee meeting, or getting up from lunch, or running in from the paddle-ball court, he has not known what the hell he was supposed to be voting on, and even if he has known, he has not known how he wanted to vote. Bills tumble over one another in the House, and some of them are so complicated that only the staff, and perhaps a few Congressmen, ever know what is in them. There is no way that even the most conscientious Congressmen can sort them all out, but they are supposed to try, and so the Republicans, at least, will turn to Bonsell. "How are we going?" Vander Jagt will say as he runs past him. "Well," Bonsell will say, "Les and Gerry voted yes"—Les being Leslie Arends, the Republican whip—or "Everyone's voting no," Bonsell will say, sounding a little cavalier about it. So, there is Bonsell, still sticking his finger in one eye and looking at Vander Jagt with the other one, only now he is grinning. *His eye.* Vander Jagt understands. "Mr. Vander Jagt," the clerk calls. *"Aye,"* Vander Jagt says.

The afternoon is waning, and Vander Jagt is back in his office. A brigadier general from the Corps of Engineers, paying a courtesy call, was awaiting him when he returned from the House, and they exchanged pleasantries, the general saying that the Corps only took directions and did not set policy, and Vander Jagt agreeing, saying that of late the Corps had been doing a marvelous job against pollution. Then the two Democratic counsels to the Conservation and Natural Resources Subcommittee came by to talk about the 1899 law that Russell Train had called about in the morning. The two counsels are capable men who work well with Vander Jagt and Nagelvoort, but after they left, neither Vander Jagt nor Nagelvoort were exactly sure why they had come. The two counsels, after all, are Democrats, and they had been concerned about who would administer the 1899 law, and at bottom this is a political question. Vander Jagt and Nagelvoort did not quite see it as a political question, and they did not talk about it after the two Democrats had left, but that was because of the convention that allows party politics to be present in all things in Washington, while at the same time never acknowledged. It is a sensible convention, and it allows men to work together when they might otherwise be inclined to argue.

Now Vander Jagt is returning telephone calls. One is to a manufacturer in his district, who wants to object to an Administration plan for the Federal Aviation Agency. The second is to a Republican county chairman in Michigan, who wants his support on a candidate for the bench, and who finishes by saying, "Vander Jagt for Senator in '76." The third is from a friend, who wants a favor for *his* friend. The friend's friend is a Democratic county chairman in Vander Jagt's district, who has just discovered that he cannot get a loan from the Federal Housing Administration for a home on a private road. The Democrat thinks this is unfair, but he would feel foolish calling a Republican Congressman about it, and so has asked someone else to do it. Vander Jagt, who knows that perhaps a third of the homes in the county are on private roads, agrees with the caller and says that he will check into it. Now, it happens that Vander Jagt plays paddle ball regularly with the chairman of the FHA, and after a game sometime he will talk to him about it. The chairman may or may not think that the law should be changed, but either way the Democratic county chairman will have his day in court. Vander Jagt says it is a perfect example of the way things get done in Washington.

The members of Congress are scattered about the floor of the House. They are meeting in what is called the Committee of the Whole House, and they are about to consider the Housing and Urban Development Act of 1970. In appearance, Congressmen are disparate, although they like to have their suits well pressed, and there is an uncommon number of cufflinks among them. There are Congressmen who look like aging juvenile delinquents, and there are Congressmen who look like wheezing, belching rustics (and who, in fact, turn out to be experts in the arcanum of the tax structure, say, or the tariff). Here there is a Congressman with a spiky Kaiser Wilhelm moustache, who quotes Shakespeare, and over there is a Congressman who won two Olympic gold medals, and a little further on is a Congressman who steals money. There are Congressmen who can imagine themselves in no other place than the House, and there are Congressmen, a smaller number of them, who say the House makes their souls wither within them. Here is one, a younger man, exorcising his devils: "There are three kinds of Congressmen. First, there are the talented and gifted who will get out because they can't stand the system. Then there are the men with no talent, but they have a good job and so they stay. And then there are the men who are bright and they stay, but for the wrong reasons. The Rayburn dictum still works—if you want to get along, go along—but the more docile you are the more resentful you become, and it becomes corrosive."

There are Congressmen known by every man and woman in the House, and there are Congressmen so obscure they are known by hardly anyone. Their single devotions to the commonweal vary widely, and there are some easily indictable on the grounds of moral turpitude, but there is almost none who will break his word to another Congressman. That is considered the greatest of all sins, and the second greatest is to sell another Congressman on an absolutely lousy idea. Therefore, not everything produced by the House will have a great deal of merit, but very little will have no merit at all. It is a system that makes the House handle smaller issues better than it does larger ones; and a dedicated, conscientious man can work his will on small things, while he can wreck himself fighting for large things. Here is a Congressman, complaining of his impotence: "When I first got here I was shocked at the rudeness that committee members would show to Administration witnesses, and then gradually I became that way myself. Look, I checked, and there are only three computers in the House, and there are 3,700 in the Executive branch. You wait two hours so you can get a shot in at the Secretary of Defense, and then it lasts only five minutes. The only thing you know is that you're getting bullshit from him, and there's nothing you can do about it. My committee's staff is loyal to the chairman, and the chairman will go along with the Secretary. It gets down to where you ask yourself, Should you even bother going to a meeting when you know you won't get anything from it?"

So, on this day, assembled to consider the housing act, are people of many temperaments and persuasions, most of them seriously involved in their own separate projects and few of them with deep knowledge of a housing act, but none of them capable of much surprise at what their colleagues will bring forth. It is a big and complex bill they are dealing with, and it has been drawn up by the Housing Subcommittee of the Banking and Currency Committee. That is, the original bill was drawn up by the subcommittee, but at the moment Congressman Robert Stephens is rising to offer what is called an amendment in the nature of a substitute, which is 132 pages long and which would replace the subcommittee's bill, and he is doing it with the subcommittee's approval. Now Congressman Charles Jonas stands, and asks if he can offer three amendments to the Stephens amendment, and he is told he can, but that he must wait. Congressman Frank Brasco, however, is on his feet, offering an amendment to the Stephens amendment, and it is accepted. Now Congressman Garry Brown is up, having waited so far for tactical purposes, and he proposes a substitute amendment for the Stephens amendment, which, remember, was a substitute for the subcommittee's bill. Congressman Benjamin Blackburn, in turn, rises to offer an amendment to the Brown amendment, and then Stephens is up again to say that he thinks Congressman Blackburn is attaching his amendment to the wrong other amendment. Then Congressman Olin Teague

is recognized, so that he can propose his amendment to the Stephens amendment, and Congressman Blackburn is making a parliamentary inquiry:
whatever happened to his amendment? Congressman Robert Sikes then offers an amendment to the Brown amendment; if that amendment loses, he
says, he will propose it for the Stephens amendment. At this point there can
be no more than a few members who clearly know what is happening, and
things are not helped greatly when it is announced that "the question is on
the substitute amendment, as amended, offered by the gentleman from
Michigan for the amendment in the nature of a substitute offered by the
gentleman from Georgia." It is a time for visceral instincts, and Vander
Jagt knows only that, respecting Garry Brown as he does, he will vote for
whatever it is he is proposing. Brown, meanwhile, has demanded a teller
vote, and he and Congressman Willian Barrett, who opposes his amendment,
are appointed as tellers. They withdraw up an aisle, and the members who
support Brown, the aye votes, start to pass by in single file. Brown taps himself on the chest, saying "One," and then taps each Congressman on the
back as he passes by: "two, three, four." Barrett, as is the custom, is keeping his own count, and so they are standing there in the aisle, antagonists in
a kind of numbers game, with the other Congressmen running by as markers.
"Ninety-four," Brown says finally, and then Barrett starts counting his no
votes. He is up to ninety-six, and waiting, when five more Congressmen,
found and summoned from God knows where, come running up the aisle,
their arms outstretched, and point first to Barrett, and then to Brown, and
then back to Barrett again. "One hundred one," Barrett says. In fact, he is
confused, and so is Brown, and so are two of the five Congressmen, who had
wanted to be on Brown's side. It does not matter, of course, because Brown
would still have lost; but he is a professional, and so his pride is a little
touched.

However considerable his talents, Vander Jagt is among the most forgetful
of men, seldom wearing an overcoat, for example, because he knows he
will leave it somewhere behind him, and often leaving home in the morning
without his wallet, keys, or anything else that might persuade a policeman
he is not a simple vagrant. Moreover, no matter how readily he may grasp
a complicated piece of legislation, he is baffled by nearly any inanimate
object, and by timetables and maps as well. On Election Day he was minutes
getting into and out of the voting booth because he was defeated by a
lever, and when he was new in Washington he once had to call the police
to guide him back to his home because he had more or less forgotten the
way. Recognizing these things, his staff compensates for them, and now
Vander Jagt is sitting at his desk while a secretary reads from a list. "Keys?"
she says, and Vander Jagt pats his pocket. "Tickets?" she says, and he
picks up the envelope in front of him. Vander Jagt is leaving town later in

the evening so he can speak in Chicago the next day, and the secretary is leaving nothing to chance. A call is put through from his outer office, and Vander Jagt gets on the phone to talk to a friend at the White House. The Rules Committee has tied, 7 to 7, on Buchanan's bill for the new consumer-protection agency, and while this means the White House won't be able to get it now, it also means that it won't have to accept Democrat Rosenthal's bill, and for this it is grateful.

Vander Jagt is not scheduled to leave Washington until 8:00 P.M., and there are now more than two hours stretching in front of him, which means that he has time to go to a party. If Vander Jagt chose to, he could go to a party, or a reception, every night, a Congressman always being in demand for something, but he has long since learned that there is no profit in this, and so he exercises discretion. Tonight the National Space Club is holding a reception in the Caucus Room of the Cannon Office Building so that it can present trophies to Wernher von Braun and the widow of Dr. Robert H. Goddard, and as a member of the House Committee on Science and Astronautics, Vander Jagt has been asked to attend. The president of the Space Club is a man from Texas Instruments, and the first vice president is from Boeing, and the host for the evening is Congressman George P. Miller, chairman of the Committee on Science and Astronautics. It is a lobbying effort, and like most lobbying in Washington it is terribly *en famille*. (Washington, in fact, is terribly *en famille*.) When Vander Jagt enters, the first person he sees is Von Braun. "Wernher," he says, "the last time I saw you, you were leading a conga line in New Orleans." Von Braun smiles, acknowledges the memory, and then he is talking to someone about the stars, a fine flicker of fanaticism lighting his face, and Vander Jagt is plainly impressed. "Damn it," he says, "I know it's emotional, but I want to be exposed to the emotional part of it." A lobbyist wanders by, and tells Vander Jagt that the word is that George Bush of Texas will be the next head of NASA. (Two days later, Bush is appointed Ambassador to the United Nations.) Bill Anders, who flew an Apollo spacecraft around the moon, falls into conversation, and he says that when he speaks to college students he emphasizes the *spiritual* part of his journey. "Guy," he says, "when I looked back at the earth, then, boy, I knew I wasn't the center of things." In the corner of the room, Von Braun is introducing his young son to Neil Armstrong, and Mrs. Goddard is talking about her late husband, and a Texas Congressman is hustling a secretary from NASA. Vander Jagt is feeling warm and sustained, and as he leaves to go to the airport he begins to talk about his vision of a federal medical academy. He has at the moment a great sense of the possibility of all things.

Amphetamine Politics on Capitol Hill

James M. Graham

The American pharmaceutical industry annually manufactures enough amphetamines to provide a month's supply to every man, woman and child in the country. Eight, perhaps ten, billion pills are lawfully produced, packaged, retailed and consumed each year. Precise figures are unavailable. We must be content with estimates because until 1970, no law required an exact accounting of total amphetamine production.

Amphetamines are the drug of the white American with money to spend. Street use, contrary to the popular myths, accounts for a small percentage of the total consumption. Most of the pills are eaten by housewives, businessmen, students, physicians, truck drivers and athletes. Those who inject large doses of "speed" intravenously are but a tiny fragment of the total. Aside from the needle and the dose, the "speed freak" is distinguishable because his use has been branded as illegal. A doctor's signature supplies the ordinary user with lawful pills.

All regular amphetamine users expose themselves to varying degrees of potential harm. Speed doesn't kill, but high sustained dosages can and do result in serious mental and physical injury, depending on how the drug is taken. The weight-conscious housewife, misled by the opinion-makers into believing that amphetamines can control weight, eventually may rely on the drug to alter her mood in order to face her monotonous tasks. Too frequently an amphetamine prescription amounts to a synthetic substitute for attention to emotional and institutional problems.

Despite their differences, all amphetamine users, whether on the street or in the kitchen, share one important thing in common—the initial source of supply. For both, it is largely the American pharmaceutical industry. That industry has skillfully managed to convert a chemical, with meager medical justification and considerable potential for harm, into multi-hundred-million-dollar profits in less than 40 years. High profits, reaped from such vulnerable products, require extensive, sustained political efforts for their continued existence. The lawmakers who have declared that possession of marijuana is a serious crime have simultaneously defended and protected the profits of the amphetamine pill-makers. The Comprehensive Drug Abuse Prevention and Control Act of 1970 in its final form constitutes

Source: *Society* (January 1972), Vol. 9, No. 3, pp. 14–16, 18–22, 53. Published by permission of Transaction Inc. from *Transaction,* Vol. 9 (January 1972). Copyright © by Transaction Inc. James M. Graham received his J.D. from the University of Michigan Law School in 1971 and is a staff attorney with the Institute for Public Interest Representation at Georgetown University Law Center in Washington, D.C.

a victory for that alliance over compelling, contrary evidence on the issue of amphetamines. The victory could not have been secured without the firm support of the Nixon Administration. The end result is a national policy which declares an all-out war on drugs which are *not* a source of corporate income. Meanwhile, under the protection of the law, billions of amphetamines are overproduced without medical justification.

Hearings in the Senate

The Senate was the first house to hold hearings on the administration's bill to curb drug abuse, The Controlled Dangerous Substances Act (S-3246). Beginning on September 15, 1969 and consuming most of that month, the hearings before Senator Thomas Dodd's Subcommittee to Investigate Juvenile Delinquency of the Committee on the Judiciary would finally conclude on October 20, 1969.

The first witness was John Mitchell, attorney general of the United States, who recalled President Nixon's ten-point program to combat drug abuse announced on July 14, 1969. Although that program advocated tighter controls on imports and exports of dangerous drugs and promised new efforts to encourage foreign governments to crack down on production of illicit drugs, there was not a single reference to the control of domestic manufacture of dangerous drugs. The president's bill when it first reached the Senate placed the entire "amphetamine family" in Schedule III, where they were exempt from any quotas and had the benefit of lesser penalties and controls. Hoffman-LaRoche, Inc. had already been at work; their depressants, Librium and Valium, were completely exempt from any control whatsoever.

In his opening statement, Attorney General Mitchell set the tone of administrative policy related to amphetamines. Certainly, these drugs were "subject to increasing abuse"; however, they have "widespread medical uses" and therefore are appropriately classed under the administration guidelines in Schedule III. Tight-mouthed John Ingersoll, director of the Bureau of Narcotics and Dangerous Drugs (BNDD), reaffirmed the policy, even though a Bureau study over the last year (which showed that 92 percent of the amphetamines and barbiturates in the illicit market were legitimately manufactured) led him to conclude that drug companies have "lax security and recordkeeping."

Senator Dodd was no novice at dealing with the pharmaceutical interests. In 1965 he had steered a drug abuse bill through the Senate with the drug industry fighting every step of the way. Early in the hearings he recalled that the industry "vigorously opposed the passage of (the 1965) act. I know very well because I lived with it, and they gave me fits and they gave all of us fits in trying to get it through."

The medical position on amphetamine use was first presented by the National Institute of Mental Health's Dr. Sidney Cohen, a widely recognized authority on drug use and abuse. He advised the subcommittee that 50 percent of the lawfully manufactured pep pills were diverted at some point to illicit channels. Some of the pills, though, were the result of unlawful manufacture as evidenced by the fact that 33 clandestine laboratories had been seized in the last 18 months.

Dr. Cohen recognized three categories of amphetamine abuse, all of which deserved the attention of the government. First was their "infrequent ingestion" by students, businessmen, truck drivers and athletes. Second were those people who swallowed 50-75 milligrams daily without medical supervision. Finally, there were the speed freaks who injected the drug intravenously over long periods of time. Physical addiction truly occurs, said Dr. Cohen, when there is prolonged use in high doses. Such use, he continued, may result in malnutrition, prolonged psychotic states, heart irregularities, convulsions, hepatitis and with an even chance of sustained brain damage.

As the hearings progressed, the first two classes of abusers described by Dr. Cohen would receive less and less attention, while the third category —the speed freaks—would receive increasing emphasis. The amphetamine industry was not at all unhappy with this emphasis. In fact, they would encourage it.

Ingersoll had already said that BNDD statistics indicated that only 8 percent of illicit speed was illegally manufactured. Thomas Lynch, attorney general of California, testified that his agents had in 1967 successfully negotiated a deal for one-half million amphetamine tablets with a "Tijuana café man." Actual delivery was taken from a California warehouse. All of the tablets seized originated with a Chicago company which had not bothered to question the authenticity of the retailer or the pharmacy. Prior to the 1965 hearings, the Food and Drug Administration completed a ten-year study involving 1,658 criminal cases for the illegal sale of amphetamines and barbiturates. Seventy-eight percent of all convictions involved pharmacists, and of these convictions 60 percent were for illicit traffic in amphetamines.

The pharmacists were not the source of illicit diversion, according to the National Association of Retail Druggists (NARD) and the National Association of Chain Drug Stores. Indeed, NARD had conducted an extensive educational program combating drug abuse for years, and, as proof of it, introduced its booklet, "Never Abuse—Respect Drugs," into the record. Annual inventories were acceptable for Schedule I and II drugs, NARD continued, but were unwarranted for the remaining two schedules which coincidently included most of their wares—unwarranted because diversion resulted from forged prescriptions, theft and placebo (false) inventories.

The amphetamine wholesalers were not questioned in any detail about diversion. Brief statements by the National Wholesale Druggists Association and McKesson Robbins Drug Co. opposed separate inventories for dangerous drugs because they were currently comingled with other drugs. Finally, the massive volume of the drugs involved—primarily in Schedule III—was just too great for records to be filed with the attorney general.

Dodging the Diversion Issue

The representative of the prescription drug developers was also not pressed on the question of illicit diversion. Instead, the Pharmaceutical Manufacturers' Association requested clarifications on the definitional sections, argued for formal administrative hearings on control decisions and on any action revoking or suspending registration, and endorsed a complete exemption for over-the-counter non-narcotic drugs.

With some misgivings, Carter-Wallace Inc. endorsed the administration bill providing, of course, the Senate would accept the president's recommendation that meprobamate not be subjected to any control pending a decision of the Fourth Circuit as to whether the drug had a dangerously depressant effect on the central nervous system. On a similar special mission, Hoffman-LaRoche Inc. sent two of its vice-presidents to urge the committee to agree with the president's recommendation that their "minor tranquilizers" (Librium and Valium) remain uncontrolled. Senator Dodd was convinced that both required inclusion in one of the schedules. The Senator referred to a BNDD investigation which had shown that from January 1968 to February 1969, three drug stores were on the average over 30,000 dosage units short. In addition, five inspected New York City pharmacies had unexplained shortages ranging from 12 to 50 percent of their total stock in Librium and Valium. Not only were the drugs being diverted, but Bureau of Narcotics information revealed that Librium and Valium, alone or in combination with other drugs, were involved in 36 suicides and 750 attempted suicides.

The drug company representatives persisted in dodging or contradicting Dodd's inquiries. Angry and impatient, Senator Dodd squarely asked the vice-presidents, "Why do you worry about putting this drug under control?" The response was as evasive as the question was direct: There are hearings pending in HEW, and Congress should await the outcome when the two drugs might be placed in Schedule III. (The hearings had begun in 1966; no final administrative decision had been reached and Hoffman-LaRoche had yet to exercise its right to judicial review.)

In the middle of the hearings, BNDD Director Ingersoll returned to the subcommittee to discuss issues raised chiefly by drug industry spokesmen. He provided the industry with several comforting administrative interpretations. The fact that he did not even mention amphetamines is indicative of the low level of controversy that the hearings had aroused on the issue. Ingersoll did frankly admit that his staff had met informally with industry representatives in the interim. Of course, this had been true from the very beginning.

The president of the American Pharmaceutical Association, the professional society for pharmacists, confirmed this fact: His staff participated in "several" Justice Department conferences when the bill was being drafted. (Subsequent testimony in the House would reveal that industry participation was extensive and widespread.) All the same, the inventory, registration and inspection (primarily "no-knock") provisions were still "unreasonable, unnecessary and costly administrative burden(s)" which would result in an even greater "paper work explosion."

For the most part, however, the administration bill had industry support. It was acceptable for the simple reason that, to an unknown degree, the "administration bill" was a "drug company bill" and was doubtless the final product of considerable compromise. Illustrative of that give-and-take process is the comparative absence of industry opposition to the transfer of drug-classification decision and research for HEW to Justice. The industry had already swallowed this and other provisions in exchange for the many things the bill could have but did not cover. Moreover, the subsequent windy opposition of the pill-makers allowed the administration to boast of a bill the companies objected to.

When the bill was reported out of the Committee on the Judiciary, the amphetamine family, some 6,000 strong, remained in Schedule III. Senator Dodd apparently had done some strong convincing because Librium, Valium and meprobamate were now controlled in Schedule III. A commission on marijuana and a declining penalty structure (based on what schedule the drug is in and whether or not the offense concerned trafficking or possession) were added.

Debate in the Senate—Round I

The Senate began consideration of the bill on January 23, 1970. This time around, the amphetamine issue would inspire neither debate or amendment. The energies of the Senate liberals were consumed instead by unsuccessful attempts to alter the declared law enforcement nature of the administration bill.

Senator Dodd's opening remarks, however, were squarely directed at the prescription pill industry. Dodd declared that the present federal laws had failed to control the illicit diversion of lawfully manufactured dangerous drugs. The senator also recognized the ways in which all Americans had become increasingly involved in drug use and that the people's fascination with pills was by no means an "accidental development": "Multihundred million dollar advertising budgets, frequently the most costly ingredient in the price of a pill, have, pill by pill, led, coaxed and seduced post-World War II generations into the 'freaked-out' drug culture. . . . Detail men employed by drug companies propagandize harried and harassed doctors into pushing their special brand of palliative. Free samples in the doctor's office are as common nowadays as inflated fees." In the version adopted by the Senate, Valium, Librium and meprobamate joined the amphetamines in Schedule III.

Hearings in the House

On February 3, 1970, within a week of the Senate's passage of S-3246, the House began its hearings. The testimony would continue for a month. Although the Senate would prove in the end to be less vulnerable to the drug lobby, the issue of amphetamines—their danger and medical justification—would be aired primarily in the hearings of the Subcommittee on Public Health of the Committee on Interstate and Foreign Commerce. The administration bill (HR 13743), introduced by the chairman of the parent committee, made no mention of Librium or Valium and classified amphetamines in Schedule III.

As in the Senate, the attorney general was scheduled to be the first witness, but instead John Ingersoll of the BNDD was the administration's representative. On the question of amphetamine diversion, Ingersoll gave the administration's response: "Registration is . . . the most effective and least cumbersome way" to prevent the unlawful traffic. This coupled with biennial inventories of all stocks of controlled dangerous drugs and the attorney general's authority to suspend, revoke or deny registration would go a long way in solving the problem. In addition, the administration was proposing stronger controls on imports and exports. For Schedules I and II, but not III or IV, a permit from the attorney general would be required for exportation. Quotas for Schedules I and II, but not III or IV, would "maximize" government control. For Schedules III and IV, no approval is required, but a supplier must send an advance notice on triple invoice to the attorney general in order to export drugs such as amphetamines. A prescription could be filled only five times in a six-month period and thereafter a new prescription would be required, whereas previously such precriptions could be refilled as long as a pharmacist would honor them.

The deputy chief counsel for the BNDD, Michael R. Sonnenreich, was asked on what basis the attorney general would decide to control a particular drug. Sonnenreich replied that the bill provides one of two ways: Either the attorney general "finds *actual street abuse* or an interested party (such as HEW) feels that a drug should be controlled." (Speed-freaks out on the street are the trigger, according to Sonnenreich; lawful abuse is not an apparent criterion.)

The registration fee schedule would be reasonable ($10.00—physician or pharmacist; $25.00—wholesalers; $50.00—manufacturers). However, the administration did not want a formal administrative hearing on questions of registration and classification, and a less formal rule-making procedure was provided for in the bill.

Returning to the matter of diversion, Sonnenreich disclosed that from July 1, 1968 to June 30, 1969 the BNDD had conducted full-scale compliance investigations of 908 "establishments." Of this total, 329 (or about 36 percent) required further action, which included surrender of order forms (162), admonition letters (38), seizures (36) and hearings (31). In addition to these full-scale investigations, the Bureau made 930 "visits." (It later came to light that when the BNDD had information that a large supply of drugs was unlawfully being sold, the Bureau's policy was to warn those involved and "90 percent of them do take care of this matter.") Furthermore, 574 robberies involving dangerous drugs had been reported to the Bureau.

Eight billion amphetamine tablets are produced annually, according to Dr. Stanley Yolles, director of the National Institute of Mental Health, and although the worst abuse is by intravenous injection, an NIMH study found that 21 percent of all college students had taken amphetamines with the family medicine cabinet acting as the primary source—not surprising in light of the estimate that 1.1 billion prescriptions were issued in 1967 at a consumer cost of $3.9 billion. Of this total, 178 million prescriptions for amphetamines were filled at a retail cost of $692 million. No one knew the statistics better than the drug industry.

Representing the prescription-writers, the American Medical Association also recognized that amphetamines were among those drugs "used daily in practically every physician's armamentarium." This casual admission of massive lawful distribution was immediately followed by a flat denial that physicians were the source of "any significant diversion."

The next witness was Donald Fletcher, manager of distribution protection, Smith Kline & French Laboratories, one of the leading producers of amphetamines. Fletcher, who was formerly with the Texas state police, said his company favored "comprehensive controls" to fight diversion and stressed the company's "educational effort." Smith Kline & French favored federal registration and tighter controls over exports (by licensing the exporter, *not* the shipment). However, no change in present record-keeping requirements on distribution, production or inventory should be made, and full hearings on the decisions by the attorney general should be guaranteed.

The committee did not ask the leading producer of amphetamines a single question about illicit diversion. Upon conclusion of the testimony, Subcommittee Chairman John Jarman of Oklahoma commented, "Certainly, Smith Kline & French is to be commended for the constructive and vigorous and hard-hitting role that you have played in the fight against drug abuse."

Dr. William Apple, executive director of the American Pharmaceutical Association (APhA), was the subject of lengthy questioning and his responses were largely typical. Like the entire industry, the APhA was engaged in a massive public education program. Apple opposed the inventory provisions, warning that the cost would be ultimately passed to the consumer. He was worried about the attorney general's power to revoke registrations ("without advance notice") because it could result in cutting off necessary drugs to patients.

Apple admitted organizational involvement "in the draft stage of the bill" but all the same, the APhA had a "very good and constructive working relationship" with HEW. Apple argued that if the functions are transferred to Justice, "We have a whole new ball game in terms of people. While some of the experienced people were transferred from HEW to Justice, there are many new people, and they are law-enforcement oriented. We are health-care oriented." Surely the entire industry shared this sentiment, but few opposed the transfer as strongly as did the APhA.

Apple reasoned that since the pharmacists were not the source of diversion, why should they be "penalized by costly overburdensome administrative requirements." The source of the drugs, Apple said, were either clandestine laboratories or burglaries. The 1965 Act, which required only those "records maintained in the ordinary course of business" be kept, was sufficient. Anyway, diversion at the pharmacy level was the responsibility of the pharmacists—a responsibility which the APhA takes "seriously and (is) going to do a better job (with) in the future."

Congress should instead ban the 60 mail-order houses which are not presently included in the bill. (One sub-committee member said this was "loophole big enough to drive a truck through.") The corner druggist simply was not involved in "large-scale diversionary efforts."

The Pharmaceutical Manufacturers' Association (PMA) was questioned a bit more carefully in the House than in the Senate. PMA talked at length about its "long and honorable history" in fighting drug abuse. Its representative echoed the concern of the membership over the lack of formal hearings and requested that a representative of the manufacturing interests be appointed to the Scientific Advisory Committee. Significantly, the PMA declined to take a position on the issue of transfer from HEW to Justice. The PMA endorsed the administration bill. PMA Vice-President Brennan was asked whether the federal government should initiate a campaign, similar to the one against cigarettes, "to warn people that perhaps they should be careful not to use drugs excessively." Brennan's response to this cautious suggestion is worth quoting in full:

> I think this is probably not warranted because it would have the additional effect of giving concern to people over very useful commodities. . . . There is a very useful side to any medicant and to give people pause as to whether or not they should take that medication, particularly those we are talking about which are only given by precription, I think the negative effect would outweigh any sociological benefit on keeping people from using drugs.

"Limited Medical Use"

There was universal agreement that amphetamines are medically justified for the treatment of two very rare diseases, hyperkinesis and narcolepsy. Dr. John D. Griffith of the Vanderbilt University School of Medicine testified that amphetamine production should be limited to the needs created by those conditions: "A few thousand tablets (of amphetamines) would supply the whole medical needs of the country. In fact, it would be possible for the government to make and distribute the tablets at very little cost. This way there would be no outside commercial interests involved." Like a previous suggestion that Congress impose a one cent per tablet tax on drugs subject to abuse, no action was taken on the proposal.

The very next day, Dr. John Jennings, acting director of the Food and Drug Administration (FDA), testified that amphetamines had a "limited medical use" and their usefulness in control of obesity was of "doubtful value." Dr. Dorothy Dobbs, director of the Marketed Drug Division of the FDA further stated that there was now no warning on the prescriptions to patients, but that the FDA was proposing that amphetamines be labeled indicating among other things that a user subjects himself to "extreme psychological dependence" and the possibility of "extreme personality changes . . . (and) the most severe manifestation of amphetamine intoxication is a psychosis." Dr. Dobbs thought that psychological dependence even under a physician's prescription was "quite possible."

Congressman Claude Pepper of Florida, who from this point on would be the recognized leader of the anti-amphetamine forces, testified concerning a series of hearings which his Select Committee on Crime had held in the fall of 1969 on the question of stimulant use.

Pepper's committee had surveyed medical deans and health organizations on the medical use of amphetamines. Of 53 responses, only one suggested that the drug was useful "for *early* stages of a diet program." (Dr. Sidney Cohen of NIMH estimated that 99 percent of the total legal prescriptions for amphetamines were ostensibly for dietary control.) Pepper's investigation also confirmed a high degree of laxness by the drug companies. A special agent for the BNDD testified that by impersonating a physician, he was able to get large quantities of amphetamines from two mail-order houses in New York. One company, upon receiving an order for 25,000 units, asked for further verification of medical practice. Two days after the agent declined to reply, the units arrived. Before Pepper's committee, Dr. Cohen of NIMH testified that amphetamines were a factor in trucking accidents due to their hallucinatory effects.

Dr. John D. Griffith from Vanderbilt Medical School, in his carefully documented statement on the toxicity of amphetamines, concluded "amphetamine addiction is more widespread, more incapacitating, more dangerous and socially disrupting than narcotic addiction." Considering that 8 percent of all prescriptions are for amphetamines and that the drug companies make only one-tenth of one cent a tablet, Dr. Griffith was not surprised that there was so little scrutiny by manufacturers. Only a large output would produce a large profit.

Treatment for stimulant abuse was no easier than for heroin addiction and was limited to mild tranquilization, total abstinence and psychiatric therapy. But, heroin has not been the subject of years of positive public "education" programs nor has it been widely prescribed by physicians or lawfully produced. A health specialist from the University of Utah pointed out that the industry's propaganda had made amphetamines: "One of the major ironies of the whole field of drug abuse. We continue to insist that they are good drugs when used under medical supervision, but their greatest use turns out to be frivolous, illegal and highly destructive to the user. People who are working in the field of drug abuse are finding it most difficult to control the problem, partly because they have the reputation of being legal and good drugs."

The thrust of Pepper's presentation was not obvious from the questioning that followed, because the subcommittee discussions skirted the issue. Pepper's impact could be felt in the subsequent testimony of the executive director of the National Association of Boards of Pharmacy. The NABP objected to the use of the word "dangerous" in the bill's title because it "does little to enhance the legal acts of the physician and pharmacist in diagnosing and dispensing this type of medication." (The Controlled Dangerous Substances Act would later become the Comprehensive Drug Abuse Prevention and Control Act of 1970.)

As in the Senate hearings, Ingersoll of the BNDD returned for a second appearance and, this time, he was the last witness. Ingersoll stated that he wished "to place . . . in their proper perspective" some "of the apparent controversies" which arose in the course of testimony. A substantial controversy had arisen over amphetamines, but there was not a single word on that subject in Ingersoll's prepared statement. Later, he did admit that there was an "overproduction" of amphetamines and estimated that 75 percent to 90 percent of the amphetamines found in illicit traffic came from the American drug companies.

Several drug companies chose to append written statements rather than testifying.

Abbott Laboratories stated that it "basically" supported the administration bills and argued that because fat people had higher mortality rates than others, amphetamines were important to the public welfare, ignoring the charge that amphetamines were not useful in controlling weight. Abbott then argued that because their products were in a sustained-release tablet, they were "of little interest to abusers," suggesting that "meth" tablets per se cannot be abused and ignoring the fact that they can be easily diluted.

Eli Lilly & Co. also endorsed "many of the concepts" in the president's proposals. They as well had "participated in a number of conferences sponsored by the (BNDD) and . . . joined in both formal and informal discussions with the Bureau personnel regarding" the bill. Hoffman-LaRoche had surely watched, with alarm, the Senate's inclusion of Librium and Valium in Schedule III. They were now willing to accept all the controls applying to Schedule III drugs, including the requirements of record-keeping, inventory, prescription limits and registration as long as their "minor tranquilizers" were not grouped with amphetamines. Perhaps, the company suggested, a separate schedule between III and IV was the answer. The crucial point was that they did not want the negative association with speed and they quoted a physician to clarify this: "If in the minds of my patients a drug which I prescribe for them has been listed or branded by the government in the same category as 'goofballs' and 'pep pills' it would interfere with my ability to prescribe . . . and could create a mental obstacle to their . . . taking the drug at all."

When the bill was reported out of committee to the House, the amphetamine family was in Schedule III, and Hoffman-LaRoche's "minor tranquilizers" remained free from control.

Debate in the House—Round I

On September 23, 1970, the House moved into Committee of the Whole for opening speeches on the administration bill now known as HR 18583. The following day, the anti-amphetamine forces led by Congressman Pepper carried their arguments onto the floor of the House by way of an amendment transfering the amphetamine family from Schedule III into Schedule II. If successful, amphetamines would be subject to stricter import and export controls, higher penalties for illegal sale and possession and the possibility that the attorney general could impose quotas on production and distribution. (In Schedule III, amphetamines were exempt from quotas entirely.) Also, if placed in Schedule II, the prescriptions could be filled only once.

Pepper was convinced from previous experience that until quotas were established by law the drug industry would not voluntarily restrict production.

Now the lines were clearly drawn. The House hearings had provided considerable testimony to the effect that massive amphetamine production coupled with illegal diversion posed a major threat to the public health. No congressman would argue that this was not the case. The House would instead divide between those who faithfully served the administration and the drug industry and those who argued that Congress must act or no action could be expected. The industry representatives dodged the merits of the opposition's arguments, contending that a floor amendment was inappropriate for such "far reaching" decisions.

"Legislating on the floor . . . concerning very technical and scientific matters," said subcommittee member Tim Lee Carter of Kentucky, "can cause a great deal of trouble. It can open a Pandora's Box" and the amendment which affected 6,100 drugs "would be disastrous to many companies throughout the land."

Paul G. Rogers of Florida (another subcommittee member) stated that the bill's provisions were based on expert scientific and law enforcement advice, and that the "whole process of manufacture and distribution had been tightened up." Robert McClory of Illinois, though not a member of the subcommittee, revealed the source of his opposition to the amendment:

> Frankly . . . there are large pharmaceutical manufacturing interests centered in my congressional district. . . . I am proud to say that the well known firms of Abbott Laboratories and Baxter Laboratories have large plants in my (district). It is my expectation that C.D. Searl & Co. may soon establish a large part of its organization (there). Last Saturday, the American Hospital Supply Co. dedicated its new building complex in Lake County. . . where its principal research and related operations will be conducted.

Control of drug abuse, continued McClory, should not be accomplished at the cost of imposing "undue burdens or (by taking) punitive or economically unfair steps adversely affecting the highly successful and extremely valuable pharmaceutical industries which contribute so much to the health and welfare of mankind."

Not everyone was as honest as McClory. A parent committee member, William L. Springer of Illinois, thought the dispute was basically between Pepper's special committee on crime and the subcommittee on health and medicine chaired by John Jarman of Oklahoma. Thus phrased, the latter was simply more credible than the former. "There is no problem here of economics having to do with any drug industry."

But economics had everything to do with the issue according to Representative Jerome R. Waldie of California: "(T)he only opposition to this amendment that has come across my desk has come from the manufacturers of amphetamines." He reasoned that since the House was always ready to combat crime in the streets, a "crime that involved a corporation and its profits" logically merits equal attention. Waldie concluded that the administration's decision "to favor the profits (of the industry) over the children is a cruel decision, the consequences of which will be suffered by thousands of our young people." Pepper and his supporters had compiled and introduced considerable evidence on scientific and medical opinions on the use and abuse of amphetamines. It was now fully apparent that the evidence would be ignored because of purely economic and political considerations. In the closing minutes of debate, Congressman Robert Giaimo of Connecticut, who sat on neither committee, recognized the real issue: "Why should we allow the legitimate drug manufacturers to indirectly supply the (sic) organized crime and pushers by producing more drugs than are necessary? When profits are made while people suffer, what difference does it make where the profits go?"

Pepper's amendment was then defeated by a voice vote. The bill passed by a vote of 341 to 6. The amphetamine industry had won in the House. In two days of debate, Librium and Valium went unmentioned and remained uncontrolled.

Debate in the Senate—Round II

Two weeks after the House passed HR 18583, the Senate began consideration of the House bill. (The Senate bill, passed eight months before, continued to languish in a House committee.) On October 7, 1970, Senator Thomas Eagleton of Missouri moved to amend HR 18583 to place amphetamines in Schedule II. Although he reiterated the arguments used by Pepper in the House, Eagleton stated that his interest in the amendment was not solely motivated by the abuse by speed freaks. If the amendment carried, it would "also cut back on abuse by the weight-conscious housewife, the weary long-haul truck driver and the young student trying to study all night for his exams."

The industry strategy from the beginning was to center congressional outrage on the small minority of persons who injected large doses of diluted amphetamines into their veins. By encouraging this emphasis, the drug companies had to face questioning about illicit diversion to the "speed community," but they were able to successfully avoid any rigorous scrutiny of the much larger problem of lawful abuse. The effort had its success. Senator Thomas J. McIntyre of New Hampshire, while noting the general abuse of the drugs, stated that the real abuse resulted from large doses either being swallowed, snorted or injected.

Senator Roman Hruska of Nebraska was not surprisingly the administration and industry spokesman. He echoed the arguments that had been used successfully in the House: The amendment seeks to transfer between 4,000 and 6,000 products of the amphetamine family; "some of them are very dangerous" but the bill provides a mechanism for administrative reclassification; administration and "HEW experts" support the present classification and oppose the amendment; and, finally, the Senate should defer to the executive where a complete study is promised.

It would take three to five years to move a drug into Schedule II by administrative action, responded Eagleton. Meanwhile amphetamines would continue to be "sold with reckless abandon to the public detriment." Rather than placing the burden on the government, Eagleton argued that amphetamines should be classed in Schedule II and those who "are making money out of the misery of many individuals" should carry the burden to downgrade the classification.

Following Eagleton's statement, an unexpected endorsement came from the man who had steered two drug control bills through the Senate in five years. Senator Dodd stated that Eagleton had made "a good case for the amendment." Senator John Pastore was sufficiently astonished to ask Dodd pointedly whether he favored the amendment. Dodd unequivocally affirmed his support. Dodd's endorsement was clearly a turning point in the Senate debate. Hruska's plea that the Senate should defer to the "superior knowledge" of the attorney general, HEW and BNDD was met with Dodd's response that, if amphetamines were found not to be harmful, the attorney general could easily move them back into Schedule III. In Schedule II, Dodd continued, "only the big powerful manufacturers of these pills may find a reduction in their profits. The people will not be harmed." With that, the debate was over and the amendment carried by a vote of 40 in favor, 16 against and 44 not voting.

Dodd may have been roused by the House's failure, without debate, to subject Librium and Valium to controls which he had supported from the beginning. Prior to Eagleton's amendment, Dodd had moved to place these depressants in Schedule IV. In that dispute, Dodd knew that economics was the source of the opposition: "It is clearly evident . . . that (the industry) objections to the inclusion of Librium and Valium are not so much based on sound medical practice as they are on the slippery surface of unethical profits." Hoffman-LaRoche annually reaped 40 million dollars in profits—"a tidy sum which (they have) done a great deal to protect." Senator Dodd went on to say that Hoffman-LaRoche reportedly paid a Washington law firm three times the annual budget of the Senate subcommittee staff to assure that their drugs would remain uncontrolled. "No wonder," exclaimed Dodd, "that the Senate first, and then the House, was overrun by Hoffman-LaRoche lobbyists," despite convincing evidence that they were connected with suicides and attempted suicides and were diverted in large amounts into illicit channels.

By voice vote Hoffman-LaRoche's "minor tranquilizers" were brought within the control provisions of Schedule IV. Even Senator Hruska stated that he did not oppose this amendment, and that it was "very appropriate" that it be adopted so that a "discussion of it and decision upon it (be) made in the conference."

The fate of the minor tranquilizers and the amphetamine family would now be decided by the conferees of the two houses.

In Conference

The conferees from the Senate were fairly equally divided on the issue of amphetamine classification. Of the eleven Senate managers, at least six were in favor of the transfer to Schedule II. The remaining five supported the administration position. Although Eagleton was not appointed, Dodd and Harold Hughes would represent his position. Hruska and Strom Thurmond, both of whom had spoken against the amendment, would act as administration spokesmen.

On October 8, 1970, before the House appointed its conferees, Pepper rose to remind his colleagues that the Senate had reclassified amphetamines. Although he stated that he favored an instruction to the conferees to support the amendment, he inexplicably declined to so move. Instead, Pepper asked the conferees "to view this matter as sympathetically as they think the facts and the evidence they have before them will permit." Congressman Rogers, an outspoken opponent of the Pepper amendment, promised "sympathetic understanding" for the position of the minority.

Indeed, the minority would have to be content with that and little else. All seven House managers were members of the parent committee, and four were members of the originating subcommittee. Of the seven, only one would match support with "sympathetic understanding." The other six were not only against Schedule II classification, but they had led the opposition to it in floor debate: Jarman, Rogers, Carter, Staggers and Nelsen. Congressman Springer, who had declared in debate that economics had nothing to do with this issue, completed the House representation. Not a single member of Pepper's Select Committee on Crime was appointed as a conferee. On the questions of reclassification, the pharmaceutical industry would be well represented.

Hoffman-LaRoche, as well, was undoubtedly comforted by the presence of the four House subcommittee conferees: The subcommittee had never made any attempt to include Valium and Librium in the bill. On that question, it is fair to say that the Senate managers were divided. The administration continued to support no controls for these depressants.

At dispute were six substantive Senate amendments to the House bill: Three concerned amphetamines, Librium and Valium; one required an annual report to Congress on advisory councils; the fifth lessened the penalty for persons who gratuitously distributed a small amount of marijuana; and the sixth, introduced by Senator Hughes, altered the thrust of the bill and placed greater emphasis on drug education, research, rehabilitation and training. To support these new programs, the Senate had appropriated $26 million more than the House.

The House, officially, opposed all of the Senate amendments.

From the final compromises, it is apparent that the Senate liberals expended much of their energy on behalf of the Hughes amendment. Although the Senate's proposed educational effort was largely gutted in favor of the original House version, an additional 25 million dollars was appropriated. The bill would also now require the inclusion in state public health plans of "comprehensive programs" to combat drug abuse and the scope of grants for addicts and drug-dependent persons was increased. The House then accepted the amendments on annual reports and the possession charge for gratuitous marijuana distributors.

The administration and industry representative gave but an inch on the amphetamine amendment: Only the liquid injectible methamphetamines, speed, would be transferred to Schedule II. All the pills would remain in Schedule III. In the end, amphetamine abuse was restricted to the mainlining speed freak. The conference report reiterated the notion that further administrative action on amphetamines by the attorney general would be initiated. Finally, Librium and Valium would not be included in the bill. The report noted that "final administrative action" (begun in 1966) was expected "in a matter of weeks." Congress was contented to await the outcome of those proceedings.

Adoption of the Conference Report

Pepper and his supporters were on their feet when the agreement on amphetamines was reported to the House on October 14, 1970. Conferee Springer, faithful to the industry's tactical line, declared that the compromise is a good one because it "singles out the worst of these substances, which are the liquid, injectible methamphetamines and puts them in Schedule II." If amphetamine injection warranted such attention, why, asked Congressman Charles Wiggins, were the easily diluted amphetamine and methamphetamine pills left in Schedule III? Springer responded that there had been "much discussion," yes and "some argument" over that issue, but the conferees felt it was best to leave the rest of the amphetamine family to administrative action.

Few could have been fooled by the conference agreement. The managers claimed . . . to have taken the most dangerous and abused member of the family and subjected it to more rigorous controls. In fact, as the minority pointed out, the compromise affected the least abused amphetamine: Lawfully manufactured "liquid meth" was sold strictly to hospitals, not in the streets, and there was no evidence of any illicit diversion. More importantly, from the perspective of the drug manufacturers, only five of the 6,000 member amphetamine family fell into this category. Indeed, liquid meth was but an insignificant part of the total methamphetamine, not to mention amphetamine, production. Pepper characterized the new provision as "virtually meaningless." It was an easy pill for the industry to swallow. The Senate accepted the report on the same day as the House.

Only Eagleton, the sponsor of the successful Senate reclassification amendment, would address the amphetamine issue. To him, the new amendment "accomplish(ed) next to nothing." The reason for the timid, limpid compromise was also obvious to Eagleton: "When the chips were down, the power of the drug companies was simply more compelling" than any appeal to the public welfare.

A week before, when Dodd had successfully classified Librium and Valium in the bill, he had remarked (in reference to the House's inaction): "Hoffman-LaRoche, at least for the moment, have reason to celebrate a singular triumph, the triumph of money over conscience. It is a triumph . . . which I hope will be shortlived."

The Bill Becomes Law

Richard Nixon appropriately chose the Bureau of Narcotics and Dangerous Drugs offices for the signing of the bill on November 2, 1970. Flanked by Mitchell and Ingersoll, the president had before him substantially the same measure that had been introduced 15 months earlier. Nixon declared that America faced a major crisis of drug abuse, reaching even into the junior high schools, which constituted a "major cause of street crime." To combat this alarming rise, the president now had 300 new agents. Also, the federal government's jurisdiction was expanded: "The jurisdiction of the attorney general will go far beyond, for example, heroin. It will cover the new types of drugs, the barbiturates and amphetamines that have become so common *and are even more dangerous because of their use*" (author emphasis).

The president recognized amphetamines were "even more dangerous" than heroin, although he carefully attached the qualifier that this was a result "of their use." The implication is clear: The president viewed only the large dosage user of amphetamines as an abuser. The fact that his full statement refers only to abuse by "young people" (and not physicians, truck drivers, housewives or businessmen) affirms the implication. The president's remarks contained no mention of the pharmaceutical industry, nor did they refer to any future review of amphetamine classification. After a final reference to the destruction that drug abuse was causing, the president signed the bill into law.

The American Constitution and the Air War

Anthony D'Amato

The bombing in North and South Vietnam, Laos, and Cambodia . . . has taken place under the orders not of Congress but of the President of the United States. The President has stated that he acts as "Commander in Chief" of the armed forces in ordering the bombing. Currently, the main rationale for continuing the bombing is that it "protects the lives of American servicemen" whom the Chief Executive had previously sent to fight the undeclared war in Indochina.

Clearly, the constitutionality of the air war in Indochina is a part of the broader question whether the President had the power to involve this nation's armed forces in a war that had not been declared by Congress—though air warfare is presently in many ways a more dangerous and destabilizing aspect of power politics than the use of ground forces. Every bombardment could result in attacks on the perceived vital interests of other major powers. The threat of nuclear escalation in bombing missions is always present. Moreover, air warfare—by its very nature, as demonstrated in Indochina—tends to expand across boundaries more readily than ground warfare.

There is, indeed, a substantial question whether this air warfare, as conducted by the United States in Indochina, is in violation of international law. . . . In any event, it is clear that the Executive's use of air warfare, on a scale that has already exceeded the total tonnage of bombs dropped in the Second World War and the Korean War, raises an issue of profound importance under the United States Constitution.

To examine this question of constitutionality, we should look at the words of the Constitution, the meaning that the Framers intended that the

Source: *The Air War in Indochina,* Raphael Littauer and Norman Uphoff (eds.) (Boston: Beacon Press, 1972). From *The Air War in Indochina,* Raphael Littauer and Norman Uphoff, Editors. Copyright © 1972 by Cornell University Program on Peace Studies. Reprinted by permission of Beacon Press. All footnotes have been deleted.

words should have, and the development of constitutional interpretation since 1789. But before examining the document itself, let us first consider the argument that apart from whatever the Framers intended, the Constitution has necessarily been changed and modified to meet the exigencies of the modern age. This argument is an interesting one in light of recent Supreme Court cases in the areas of civil rights, where the Court has often justified the expression of constitutional protection in light of progressive societal demands and needs. One is tempted to say that in the modern world the President is the only efficient controller of foreign policy. Whatever his constitutional powers, he should be given the tools to deal with other nations flexibly and efficiently in the light of national interest as defined by him. An example that readily comes to mind is President Roosevelt's handling of preparations for the Second World War in the face of unenlightened Congressional demands for neutrality.

The problem with allowing one branch of the government to expand its constitutional powers at the expense of another branch is not the same as the Court's expansion of its judicial powers in the areas of civil rights and criminal justice. To say that we have a "living Constitution" may be perfectly satisfactory for the expansion of national powers at the expense of states in a federal system—which is what has occurred in the civil rights and criminal area. But it is not sound with respect to the separation of powers and the equilibrium of checks and balances among the branches of the national government. If, for example, the courts were to allow the President to encroach upon Congressional powers by appeals through the mass media, we pretty soon would have a one-man government. The courts have indicated the precise opposite. In the famous Steel Seizure Case, the Supreme Court held during the undeclared Korean War that the President could not resort to "Emergency Powers" or to "Commander-in-Chief Powers" to validate executive seizure of the steel mills when the Congress had not explicitly granted its own legislative powers of seizure to the President. In the course of that case, the Justice Department contended, on behalf of President Truman, that a number of prior instances of "executive seizures" and other decisive "executive actions" during national emergencies had not been struck down by the courts; these prior acts thus amounted to precedents for Truman's seizures. The Justice Department argued that the Constitution had been, and was being, expanded by these assertions of Presidential powers and that by 1950 such actions were clearly constitutional. The Supreme Court, however, did not agree with this argument. Instead, the Court indicated that no amount of "precedents" of this sort could amend the Constitution. In other words, a history of gradually increasing encroachments by one branch of the government upon another could not result in a permanent reallocation of constitutional powers. A case that challenged any of these encorachments, such as the Steel Seizure

Case, if upheld by the courts, would result in judicial restoration of the Constitution's balance among the branches of government.

Turning, then, to the question of the constitutionality of the undeclared war in Vietnam, let us ask first what argument can be made to support total Presidential authority to decide upon, and then to conduct, such a war.

The best case that can be made for the President is that he is Commander in Chief, and can also (with Senate concurrence) make treaties and appoint ambassadors. Do these powers mean that the President can decide upon war? Alexander Hamilton, that staunch proponent of executive power, wrote in *The Federalist* that the Commander-in-Chief role meant simply that the President was to be the top general of the army and the chief admiral of the navy. And Abraham Lincoln, surely one of the outstanding proponents of the expansion of Presidential powers, wrote that

> Kings had always been involving and impoverishing their people in wars, pretending generally, if not always, that the good of the people was the object. This our Constitution understood to be the most oppressive of all kingly oppressions; and they resolved to so frame the Constitution that no one man should hold the power of bringing this oppression upon us.

A study of the debates of the Constitutional Convention bears out these viewpoints. The Framers, it must be remembered, modified but did not overthrow the setup that had obtained under the Articles of Confederation. Unlike the Articles, the Constitution gave more powers to the central government, particularly in the areas of commerce and national defense. But the pervading principle was one of representative, legislative government, for the Framers had been through a revolution against nonrepresentation and "kingly" oppression; Congress was given vast powers over commerce and national defense. The new Constitution added a President as chief executive, but the powers of the President were carefully limited. The decision whether to go to war was given solely to the new Congress in the power "to declare war," a phrase taken from the Articles of Confederation which, too, had given to "the United States in Congress Assembled" the power to declare war.

That the intention of the Framers was to give only Congress the power to decide upon war—and not the President, who was only to be the top general and chief admiral—follows also from the various state constitutions at the time of the adoption of the national Constitution. A reading of the constitutions of the thirteen states reveals a consistent pattern of *legislative* determination of matters of military duty. Citizens of the pre-1789 sovereign states could volunteer for military duty, but if they were to be called in for such duty (as members of the state militia), an act of the legislature was the necessary prerequisite. Again, one gets the sense of a pervading philosophy that the most important questions of life and death were to be handled by a representative, legislatlve government. The Framers, and with them all of the people, were not about to entrust matters of war and peace to a single governor or President but instead insisted that the legislature alone could make such decisions.

The Constitution as finally adopted clearly reflects this opinion. We have already seen how few foreign-affairs powers wcrc actually given to the President. In contrast, Congress was given the power in Section 8 of Article 1 to tax to provide for the common defense, to define offenses against the law of nations, to declare war, to make rules concerning captures on land and water, to raise and support armies and provide a navy, and to call forth the militia when needed.

Clearly, if it were not for Korea and Vietnam, no reasonable man looking at the Constitution and at the intent of its Framers could conclude that the President, and not Congress, could lead this nation on his own initiative into a protracted foreign war, including bombing of the sort carried out in Indochina. At the very most, a President might order his troops to act in an emergency of brief duration, such as immediate self-defense, but only until Congress might have a chance to act. This "emergency" exception can easily be read into the Constitution without covering the cases of Korea and Vietnam, which were long wars with ample time for Congressional action. Indeed, the war in Indochina is the longest war in American history.

Some observers, however, insist upon focusing solely upon the Congressional power to "declare war." They argue as if this were the only power that Congress had in the war area—when, as we have just seen, there are many powers authorized—and they then proceed to give this one power an emasculated meaning. For example, some attorneys in the Department of Justice have claimed that the Congressional power to declare war means only that if a war is going on, Congress may or may not decide to declare that it really is a war. They argue further that this is not an entirely meaingless gesture. Various insurance contracts that people may have on their lives or property might have escape clauses depending on whether a war is going on. Moreover, certain international treaty obligations that the United States may have, or other commitments under customary international law, may depend upon whether the United States is an official "belligerent" in an actual war.

This argument gives to the term "declare war" such a trivial meaning as to rob it of the substance intended by the Framers in a way which no one would do to the terms "regulate commerce" and "coin money" (which are also found in the same section of the Constitution as the declaration-of-war clause). In its own terms, however, the argument is never actually supported. *Which* insurance policies depend upon a declaration of war by Congress? Insurance policies typically define "war" in terms other than whether or not Congress has declared it, and we even have some Federal cases arising after the Korean War that held it was a "war" for the purposes of insurance policies even though Congress had not declared it to be a war. Also, *what* treaties and *what* rules of international law depend upon a Congressional declaration of war? No treaties have been cited; and as for customary international law, such law has never depended upon what a nation unilaterally decides are facts, such as a Congressional decision that a given situation is a "war."

A different argument denigrating the effect of the declaration-of-war clause is that in this modern age, the President needs great flexibility to engage this nation in limited wars and other forms of limited military engagements. For Congress to come along and "declare war" would be to escalate the situation and perhaps make a total war out of a delicate limited war. According to this line of argument, the declaration-of-war clause is irrelevant to the needs of the modern age.

It is interesting to look at the implications of this argument. Apparently, if the United States is to engage in limited wars—of whatever duration and involving whatever number of casualties—Congress' power to declare war is anachronistic. On the other hand, if the United States were to engage in a total war of nuclear annihilation, then and only then would it be appropriate for Congress to declare war. No one explains in this argument how and under what conditions Congress could be called upon to deliberate and act in a total-war situation which, as we are told, could involve the destruction of the human race in a nuclear exchange that might last a couple of hours. The war itself could be irrevocably set off in fifteen minutes. Perhaps it is comforting to know that in the opinion of some learned jurists, Congress would truly have full power to declare total war, even if the circumstances make it unlikely that anyone at the time would be paying attention to what Congress might or might not be doing.

In this view, the Korean and Indochina wars are examples of limited, "Presidential" wars—the modern sort of wars that are irrelevant to Congress. The Congressional role is thus reserved for World Wars I, II, and lastly, III. Is it reasonable to believe, knowing what we know about the background and language of the Constitution, that its Framers had only these total wars in mind when they gave Congress the power to declare war? Merely to state the question suggests its absurdity. To the Framers of our Constitution, limited wars were natural, plentiful, easily contemplated, and totally forseeable. In those days we engaged in a limited war against France, and soon later in a limited war against England. Moreover, the European countries were constantly involved in limited wars against each other. Total fight-to-the-death wars were rare, and of course the twentieth century's versions had not yet happened. Thus, contrary to the view propounded above, the Framers of the Constitution were dealing precisely with limited wars (such as those in Korea and Vietnam) when they gave Congress the power to declare war.

Finally, even in those days Congress did not always "declare war" in such terms. A limited war was "authorized" against France, for example. The declaration-of-war clause does not require Congress to "declare" war as an all-out effort, but, sensibly, to "authorize" it in whatever language Congress deems appropriate. This is a point which the apologists for Presidential power conviently overlook in their insistence that Congress can only "declare" war.

Some lawyers for the government are still heard to claim that Congress in fact declared war when it passed the Tonkin Gulf Resolution in 1964. But as Congressional investigating committee later reported, that Resolution was obtained on the basis of executive misrepresentations to Congress. Additionally, the language of the Resolution is too broad and vague to be construed as a declaration of war. In any case, the Gulf of Tonkin Resolution was repealed by both houses of Congress in 1971.

What we have in Indochina is an undeclared war, a war initiated by the President (successive incumbents, actually) acting under his own authority under color of law. But, nevertheless, one might ask: has not Congress, by passing military appropriations and by renewing the Selective Service, in fact *consented* to the war? Declarations of war aside, this is in effect, according to such reasoning, as much a Congressional war as a Presidential war and hence it is indeed constitutional. If Congress does not like what is going on over Laos, it can cut off the funds and force the President to stop the bombing of that country. By its power of the purse, one might argue, Congress in fact controls the war-making power.

This line of reasoning has been upheld by the Federal court of appeals in New York in the case of *Orlando v. Laird* (1971). The Supreme Court declined to review the *Orlando* case in October 1971, and hence it stands as an affirmation of the "appropriations" argument, which would bypass the declaration-of-war clause. In another case which is moving slowly through the Federal courts, thirteen United States Congressmen have challenged the appropriations argument, filing affidavits that the expenditure of monies for the war in Indochina is not at all equivalent to the power to decide upon war. This case of *Mitchell v. Laird* is unique in that it is the first time in history that Congressmen have sued the executive branch of the government directly over an issue of constitutional separation of powers and the rights of the legislative branch.

Attorneys for the Congressmen argue first of all that the decision to initiate war is far more important than any subsequent decision to consent to the war or to ratify it. Once the President gets the country into a war, the momentum changes; supporting the war becomes, for many legislators, a matter of national responsibility. In the first year or two of any war there is vast public support, however unreasoning, based simply on a conviction that the President must know what he is doing. It is vastly more difficult by cutting off funds to stop a war that has been started than to decline to go to war in the first place. There is little on the public record to suggest that a President could have gotten Congress to authorize war in Indochina; that is why the executive branch backed into the war or sneaked into it, depending upon how one interprets the *Pentagon Papers.*

Congressmen will appropriate funds for a war for reasons other than a sense of national responsibility. For humanitarian reasons they do not want to cut off support for troops in the field. Moreover, they will renew the Selective Service Act so that troops can be rotated out of combat. Many Congressmen, in voting for defense appropriations, have stated on the floor of Congress that they were opposed to the war but felt that they could not cut off funds for a war that had already been started. Other Congressmen have stated that it is inappropriate, under Congressional procedures, to make substantive decisions in the debate to appropriate money. In other words, if the "power of the purse" were pushed to its limit, there would be no need for any committee in Congress other than the Finance and Appropriations Committees. Instead, long tradition has it that the appropriations process should be confined to questioning the dollar amount of appropriations and not the substantive policies for which the appropriations are allocated.

Another fault with the "appropriations" argument is that military defense expenditures—due to the power of conservative leadership of appropriations committees—come in a lump sum. It is difficult, and in some cases impossible, to separate out those appropriations that are related to Indochina from the nongeographical categories that are used in the defense bills. Of course, it is possible to put a rider on an appropriations bill cutting off the funds for Indochina—possible but not likely, since amendments are given very short shrift by the tight rules of the House of Representatives. But then the President could veto the entire bill and send it back, and one may be sure that Congress would not fail to appropriate the overall funds needed for national defense (missiles, submarines, troops all around the world, military pay, etc.). Thus the President effectively has a veto over any attempted fund cutoff, whereas he could have no veto over the *failure* of Congress to declare war in the first instance.

As for renewals of the Selective Service Act, one of the Congressmen who is a plaintiff in *Mitchell v. Laird* points out in his affidavit that the Selective Service Act has been renewed continuously since 1940, in time of peace as well as war.

But when all is said and done, the fact remains that Congress has certainly been implicated in the support of the war in Indochina. There may be many Congressmen now who are joining in the opposition to the war, as it has become unpopular with the public, but their public position four, six, and eight years ago was one of acquiescence or even endorsement of the war. Even now, while many Congressmen are advocating "bringing the boys home," they are not talking about bringing the pilots home or halting the planes and helicopters flown continuously over Indochina. Should we conclude, therefore, that Congress "really" consented to the war even if Congress did not initiate it, and that it is therefore absurd to say that the war is unconstitutional?

On the contrary, the consitutional argument is fundamentally one of procedure. The Constitution *requires* that *Congress* declare or authorize a war. This requirement was built in because the Framers wanted to make sure that such a grave question would be decided in the glare of national debate by legislators who would have to stand up and be counted on the issue, justifying their position on the question to their constituents. The Framers specifically tried to avoid the kind of subterfuge that has in fact happened with respect to Vietnam, where a President takes the initiative and Congressmen "reluctantly" go along. The Framers were well aware of the British experience where kings got their nations into unwanted wars and Parliament came along after the fact and paid the bills. A mere copying of the appropriations "power of the purse" from Parliament to Congress surely would not correct the unenviable British experience. Thus the Framers put in a separate clause—that Congress must declare war.

This *was* different from the unwritten British constitution, and for good reason. It is historically, and constitutionally, unsound to argue that we can read the declaration-of-war clause out of the Constitution because Congress has the power of the purse. Rather, the Constitution as written' *forced* Congress either to authorize war or to suffer the consequences of not going to war. In the words of a leading commentator on the Constitution, the Framers intended to make it difficult for this nation to get into war but easy to get out of war. In the past two decades, for whatever reasons, this nation's government has effectively reversed the clear intent of the Framers and the manifest meaning of the Constitution. The characteristics of air war have reinforced this trend, since they make it easier to get into such a war than into one limited to ground forces.

One may then ask, if all this is so, why have not the courts declared the war to be unconstitutional? The simple answer is that the courts have been as reticent as Congress. Indeed, despite President Nixon's pronounced preference for "strict construction" of the Constitution, he has sought out appointees to the Supreme Court who would not consider reversing his war. In fact, before Chief Justice Burger was nominated, he joined in an opinion in the Federal court of appeals, where he was sitting as a judge, to the effect it was a "waste of judicial time" to hear arguments on the unconstitutionality of the Vietnam war. In that opinion, the Court summarily dismissed a case of draft resisters challenging the war without even pausing to examine their arguments on the merits.

In fact, except for two lower-court cases, the courts have thrown out all cases involving the constitutionality of the war without going into the arguments—some observers believe, because the arguments are pretty much irrefutable. One exception has been mentioned—the court of appeals in New York, which held the war constitutional because of Congressional appropriations. The other exception was a case tried by District Judge Sweigert on the West Coast, who actually held that the plaintiffs—three law students in the reserves—had made out a *prima facie* case that the war in fact *was* unconstitutional. His decision, however, was immediately appealed by the Department of Justice, which then filed several motions in the court of appeals to delay the hearing of the case, with the result that only after a year had passed did the court of appeals hear oral arguments; apparently, it is taking considerable time in studying the matter prior to announcing a decision.

Many years from now, historians will surely look back upon this war and note the great failure of the courts to uphold the plain meaning of the Constitution. They will also note the failure of Congress to assert its own powers in the face of Presidential monopolization of authority in foreign affairs. But this is of little significance at the present. What is important is that the courts' failure to rule upon the question of the constitutionality of the war not be taken to mean that the issue is a trivial one or that the war is *ipso facto* constitutional.

The question of constitutionality is a fundamental one, and the more Americans conclude for themselves that the war violates our Constitution, the less support there will be for its continuation. Even if the courts will not declare the war unconstitutional, the American people can do this in effect through political channels, giving a vote of confidence to the Constitution as written and not as amended *de facto* by the executive branch with the tacit consent of a diffident legislature and an indifferent judiciary.

CHAPTER 7
SUGGESTED TOPICS FOR CLASS DISCUSSION

1. Does the account of Congressman Guy Vander Jagt's day in the House sustain former Speaker Sam Rayburn's dictum "if you want to get along, go along?"
2. Many critics of Congress maintain that Congressional hearings are no more than window dressing and that nothing ever results from them. What are the strengths and weaknesses of the hearing procedure reflected in the cases in this chapter?
3. Since 1900 the President has occupied a paramount position in foreign relations and this position has seldom been challenged. Such challenges have

usually come in a war situation. Should Congress be more active in determining foreign policy? Should the courts try to encourage this by enforcing the separation of powers, as suggested by Anthony D'Amato?

4. What does the case on amphetamine legislation show about the workings of the two houses of Congress? About the interests of members? Did the majority really believe that the bill was in the public interest? Could you detect any hypocritical attitudes?

Chapter 8

The President and the Executive Branch

The President of the United States occupies the most important and power-
ful elective office in the world. He operates at the center of a vast executive
establishment that generates a continuing flow of decisions and recom-
mendations affecting the people of the United States and directly or in-
directly the people of almost every other nation in the world.

He does not play one role but many: chief executive, commander-in-
chief of the armed forces, chief legislator (in that a great deal of draft legis-
lation is prepared in the Executive Branch), director of American foreign
policy, leader of his party, and moral and ideological leader of the nation.
If he is to perform these roles well, the President must organize the Execu-
tive Branch so that it functions effectively. Recent Presidents have sought
to broaden the scope of decision-making performed in the White House, and
this has led to, among other things, the emergence of Presidential assistants
who are semi-anonymous, who wield power far beyond that of many tra-
ditional cabinet secretaries, and who are part of the President's White

*House family and need not therefore be confirmed by Congress or appear
before Congress in answer to its summonses.*

*A President needs power and authority if he is to do his job well,
but is it possible that Presidents are proving too successful at drawing
power to themselves and to their subordinates in the White House? Is the
effectiveness and power of the Presidency being gained at the expense of
other elements in the political system, such as of Congress and of the independent press?*

NIXON II: POWER SEESAW

Elizabeth Drew

Last summer, during the Republican convention in Miami, a brief item
appeared in the *Wall Street Journal*'s "Washington Wire" column headed
"Who's Up?" which said a lot about both the Nixon Administration and
how the press reports on it. "The White House staff is up," the item revealed. The evidence: "Members attending the Republican convention ate
in the Doral Hotel's elegant main dining room, at party expense. Cabinet
officers were relegated to the downstairs coffee shop, had to pay their own
bills." What are commonly referred to as "Washington observers"—those
sifters of tea leaves and traders in gossip who interpret the government to
each other and to a presumably breathless public—know their signals and
symbols. The *Wall Street Journal* item signified how it was within the Nixon
Administration, and furthermore how it would be, and how, in fact, it
would have been no matter who had been in power.

The President's recent "reorganization" of the government continued
a trend toward gathering power within the White House that has accompanied the growth of government itself. When the President announced from
Camp David, his Maryland retreat, in November that "we are going to put
greater responsibility on individual Cabinet members for various functions
that previously had been that of the White House staff," experienced and
skeptical (which may be a redundancy) reporters were presented with a
difficult dilemma. It is one which confronts them frequently when an official
announces something which they believe in their bones to be untrue. If a
President announces that the world is flat, it is their job to report that "the

Source: Originally entitled, "The *Atlantic* Report: Washington," *The Atlantic Monthly*
(February 1973), pp. 6, 8, 12, 14, 16–17. Copyright © 1973, by The Atlantic Monthly
Company, Boston, Massachusetts. Reprinted with permission.

President announced today that the world is flat," and not, in print, to call him a liar. It is even indelicate to suggest, in the course of their stories, that there is another view of the matter. This is left largely to the columnists and to the "analysis" stories, which may or may not catch up with the official announcement, and may or may not be believed. Many Washington journalists have come to understand that their word is not held to be much more sacred than that of politicians.

Powerhouse

When Robert Finch, in a press conference just before his departure from the Administration in December, confirmed that all was not well between the White House and the Cabinet, the transcript was collected eagerly by White House reporters. "I think that is one of the biggest stories you will have to cover," Finch said, "how that tension between the White House staff and the Cabinet works." He tried to mitigate this bit of candor by saying that the tensions between the White House and the Congress and the story of the tensions between the White House and State Houses, and the story of revenue sharing, would be interesting, too. But Finch had spilled the beans, and this was something the reporters could report.

President Nixon is not the first President to accrue power in the White House and to take some pains to deny it. The purposes of the exercise, it seems, are to throw journalists and congressmen off the scent, to betray no unseemly penchant for power, and to convey the impression of frugality with public funds. While previous Presidents had their powerful and famous White House assistants, it remained for Lyndon Johnson, as was his wont, to multiply the effect. Yet the precise size of the White House staff was one of the mysteries of the Johnson Administration. Through a nice piece of legerdemain, several White House aids were "on loan" from other agencies, and their salaries were charged elsewhere.

When President Nixon took office four years ago, it may be recalled, he displayed his new Cabinet officers on television, and described them as men of "extra dimension." His assistants told reporters that "there will be no Califano here," referring to Joseph Califano, Mr. Johnson's powerful assistant for domestic affairs. This was, among other things, part of a concerted effort to establish that Mr. Nixon was going to be very different from Mr. Johnson. Much was made of the facts that the lights were on again at the White House, and that the three television sets had been removed from the President's Oval Office.

The inevitable accretion of power in the White House stems in part from the fact that there is really no other way to run the government. The more the government does, the more there must be a central body to coordinate its workings. The major issues of the day—such as the economy, race, cities, foreign policy, balance of payments—are not divisible into neat parcels to be distributed among the various Cabinet departments. An issue of trade relations can involve the Departments of Treasury, State, and Commerce, and the White House offices dealing with domestic and international economics and trade negotiations. A domestic issue of any consequence can involve the Departments of Justice, of Housing and Urban Development, of Transportation, of Health, Education and Welfare, and perhaps even Interior or Agriculture or what remains of the Office of Economic Opportunity (the poverty program). The White House and its executive arm, the Office of Management and Budget, must bring them together. Whatever rare efforts have been made by agencies to coordinate among themselves have been resisted by the OMB. The power to coordinate is power indeed.

Moreover, the budget itself is power. In the course of drawing up the budget, the President and his staff make crucial decisions about the arrangement of priorities, policy, and authority. The failure of the Congress to examine or shape the budget coherently also supplies a vacuum into which the executive and its budget makers have moved. Therefore, the Budget Bureau, which was a Wilsonian reform proposal finally adopted in 1921, has grown in importance in tandem with the White House which it serves. As the Johnson Administration piled up the programs and responsibilities, one weary Cabinet officer surveyed the scene and concluded that "Califano and Schultze [Charles Schultze, then director of the Budget Bureau] are holding the whole rickety business together."

The Nixon Administration, its protestations notwithstanding, had little alternative but to go along with the trend. Mr. Nixon moved his budget director from the Executive Office Building into the White House West Wing—a move which "Washington observers" knew to be significant. Subsequently it was said that the budget office would also "manage" the programs. It was understood in Washington that the terminological move from "coordinate" to "manage" was meaningful. Two axioms applied: the more powerful the Budget Bureau is, the weaker are the Cabinet agencies; the more proximity the budget officials have to the White House, the more politicized their decisions become.

There is also the factor of human nature. People who seek the presidency, and people who help them attain it, do not tend to be uninterested in power. White House assistants, moreover, have the unparalleled advantage of access to the king's ear. As George Ball once put it, "Nothing propinques like propinquity." As inevitable as the sunrise and traffic jams are the stories out of Washington of the complaints of congressmen and Cabinet officers about the inaccessibility of the President and the arrogance of his assistants who block their path to the Oval Office. Only the names of the offenders change: Sherman Adams, Kenneth O'Donnell, Marvin Watson, and Joseph Califano have been succeeded by Robert Haldeman and John

Ehrlichman. Presidents need such people. In the constant struggle for power in Washington, those who inhabit the White House hold the cards.

The Chasm

The way in which the executive branch is managed, and its internal distribution of power, are also determined by the personal characteristics of the people at the center. The traditional rationales for regular Cabinet meetings no longer exist. Another reason why the Cabinet hardly ever meets anymore is that the President does not like meetings. His distaste for confrontations tends to place Cabinet officers with persistent disagreements out of sight and favor, and any President prefers some personalities to others. In the Nixon Administration's first term, the only Cabinet officers who gained any real access and power were John Mitchell, John Connally, George Shultz, and Melvin Laird.

Cabinet officers in any administration may have difficulty straddling the great divide that can exist between the President at whose pleasure they serve and the bureaucracy over which they preside. Robert Finch, who began at HEW, fell into the chasm; from time to time his successor, Elliot Richardson, teetered on the brink. This problem is exacerbated in the Nixon Administration, especially on domestic issues. At first there was a theory prevalent in Washington that the Nixon Administration was not interested in governing. In retrospect, it is more accurate to say that the people in the new Administration were less familiar with government than were their predecessors and had, inevitably, a different set of assumptions about its purposes. The exercise of power by the Nixon White House grew in direct proportion to its familiarity with the terrain. But whereas the Johnson White House was likely to intervene in the bureaucratic processes to propel a program along, the Nixon White House was likely to intervene to slow it down. Any White House will interfere with the bureaucracy on behalf of its political allies, but the allies will differ from administration to administration.

Yet the Nixon White House does have a kind of them-versus-us view of the bureaucracy, based in part on misapprehension of the nature of the federal bureaucracy. The prevailing characteristic of that bureaucracy is not so much (as many in the Nixon White House believe) that it is populated largely by Democrats but rather that its members tend to believe in what they do. The dispenser of vocational education grants believes in vocational education; the civil rights enforcer believes in enforcing civil rights; the administrators of the highway program believe in building highways; the procurer of aircraft carriers is convinced of the importance of procuring more aircraft carriers. The experienced Washington bureaucrat cultivates his allies in Congress and the interest groups, and understands the techniques of survival. What to the White House appears to be subversion of its goals is, to the bureaucrat, protection of a worthy activity.

Every White House has had problems with the bureaucracy; the Nixon Administration, strapped for money, skeptical of federal programs, has many. The Nixon men therefore tend to suspect the bureaucracy, to shut it out of policy considerations, and to try to fill it with Republicans. (The latter effort is a matter of some controversy in Washington. There are many reports that people entering the bureaucracy at levels where, by law, their politics are supposed to be irrelevant are asked about their party affiliation. There were reports of this sort of questioning during the Johnson Administration, too. Republicans perhaps have to try harder because Republicans, by definition, are less attracted to government. Whatever the case, their suspicions about the large number of Democrats in the bureaucracy are not without basis, given the many years of Democratic control of it.)

Seesaw

The exigencies of coherent governing, plus the White House penchant for seclusion and suspicion, shaped the recent rearrangements. They also added to Washington terminology. The job description that signifies power was raised a notch. It no longer suffices to be a Cabinet officer, or even a White House assistant; one must be a "czar." This term does not show up in official announcements, of course, but everyone knows who the "czars" are: George Shultz, John Ehrlichman, Henry Kissinger, and Roy Ash, the new director of the Office of Management and Budget. ("Czars," by the way, do not have to be confirmed by Congress. Shultz needed confirmation to become Secretary of the Treasury, but by presidential fiat his economic policy domain now extends far beyond that.) These are the people with whom the President will deal on policy matters; they will bring him the information and transmit his decisions to the rest of the government. Cabinet officers will have to be content with operating within this framework.

There was a very large question as to how consequential were all of the changes of personnel and organization announced during the transition from Nixon I to Nixon II. Even though the "Washington observers" knew this, the changes inevitably became the stuff of headlines, speculation, and talk. In spite of the fact that the policies of Nixon II already were pretty clear— or perhaps *because* of the fact that the policies were known and there was therefore little else to talk about—the new appointments filled many column inches and hours of conversation.

For example, when Elliot Richardson was transferred from the Secretary's chair at HEW to that at Defense, Washington observers considered a number of possibilities. The appointment might be viewed in the context of the relationship between Richardson and Henry Kissinger, which, when

Richardson was Undersecretary of State at the beginning of the Nixon Administration, had been good. But that raised the question of whether that was good or bad for Richardson, in light of the rumor then making the rounds that Kissinger's standing with the President might not be as high as it once was. This was based on speculation, aired in a syndicated column by Tom Braden, that in his dealings with the North Vietnamese, Kissinger had exceeded his presidential charter. (Thus, according to this theory, he had announced that peace was "at hand" when it was not, since he had reached terms which were agreeable to neither Messrs. Thieu nor Nixon.) Richardson was chosen over Kenneth Rush, the Deputy Defense Secretary, one theory went, because Henry (all self-respecting Washington observers, whether or not they have ever met the man, refer to Kissinger as "Henry") had a low opinion of Rush. This, of course, assumed that Kissinger was in good standing. But then what did it mean when Rush was subsequently named Deputy Secretary of State? Was Rush being shunted aside (Kissinger is up) or being positioned to succeed William Rogers (Kissinger is down)? Was Richardson being sent to Defense to slash its budget or to provide a liberal camouflage for its continued growth?

The columnists play an important part in the process of deciding these things. Those "Washington observers" read the columnists with a sharp eye out for tales officials are telling and for who is doing what to whom. James Reston, for example, wrote a column in early December entitled "And What Now About Henry?" (Reston, of course, does know Kissinger, and anyone worth talking to in Washington knew that the column was based upon a conversation with him.) Reston said that despite the reappointment of Rogers (Kissinger is up), Kissinger's future was unsettled in his own mind. Reston had some hard news. Kissinger was troubled, the column said, by the wide extent of his influence, and by being shielded by executive privilege from questioning by the Congress. Until the column appeared, Kissinger's anguish over these matters had not been a subject of much speculation.

Perilous

Guidance on the Richardson question was provided in columns by the writing team of Rowland Evans and Robert Novak. From them it was learned that Richardson's deputy at Defense, William Clements, a Texas conservative, had been selected not by Richardson but by the White House. This was a crucial signal. For Washington observers know that leaders who cannot choose their deputies are without power. The message to the civilian and military bureaucracy was that the new Secretary could be circumvented, and the Pentagon bureaucracy cannot be outdone at circumvention. A week later, the "defense community" was reported by the columnists to be in "a frenzy." It seemed that Richardson might exercise the option of choosing his own assistant secretaries, and was considering two young men who had opposed the war and certain defense spending. Washington observers knew that someone in the "defense community," where the columnists are known to have good sources, was trying to sandbag the appointments and hog-tie Richardson.

It was, as the columnists said, "a classical Washington power struggle" —the sort of thing Washington observers love to read about over breakfast and talk about over lunch and dinner.

Although many in Washington had forgotten that the Department of Commerce existed, the removal of Peter Peterson as its Secretary became an important subject. It was known—such things become known—that Peterson had not asked to leave. The question, therefore, was why Peterson's career in the Nixon Administration had been derailed. Was it a move by the White House to curb the drive for the 1976 presidential nomination by Charles Percy, Peterson's former employer at Bell & Howell, and not exactly a White House favorite? While this was considered possible, other factors were given more weight. Peterson's style was too flamboyant; he spent too much time cultivating (successfully) the press; he turned up too often in Georgetown (for which read: homes of liberal journalists). It is perilous to negotiate the long passage from the White House to the Washington community of fashionable liberal journalists and politicians. One must tell the journalists and politicians just enough to interest and amuse them without arousing, back at the office, suspicions of disloyalty. Kissinger and presidential speechwriter William Safire, relying on their brains and disarming wit, succeeded. For others, the attempt proved fatal.

There may even have been policy considerations surrounding Peterson's demise. Had he, an advocate of liberal trade policies, run afoul of the protectionist-minded businessmen who are the Commerce Department's clientele? (While some Cabinet officers get in trouble for representing their Department's clientele too well, others can fall from grace for pleasing them insufficiently. Such was said to have been the fate of James Hodgson, who was removed as Secretary of Labor and replaced by Peter Brennan, a leader of a construction trade union and symbol of the Administration's hopes for a new Republican coalition. When Ronald Ziegler, the President's press secretary, announced that John Volpe would be named Ambassador to Italy, he pointed out that Volpe "started at the bottom of the construction trades as a hod carrier.")

The manner in which the announcements about personnel changes were made also told much about the capital during the period of transition from the first Nixon Administration to the second. The Cabinet appointments, once the subject of a television spectacular, were left to Ziegler. Neither the President nor the appointees were present. The communications between Ziegler and the press corps sank deeper and deeper into the trivia (the age, ninety-six, of a Pennsylvania state senator who was meeting with the President) and tired jokes (Kissinger's women) that have come to characterize these exchanges. Reporters who tired of waiting outside the formidable sets of fences at Camp David for Ziegler's news gathered in the White House press room, where the briefings were piped in over a loudspeaker. The scene was surreal. Reporters took notes and tape-recorded the disembodied voices. Perhaps in reaction to being at this still further remove from the realities of government, the reporters made wisecracks back to the loudspeaker. One day, the following exchange between the press secretary to the President of the United States and a member of the free press, guardians of democracy, came over the loudspeaker in the White House press room:

> Q. The last time the President was up here he was reported to be seen strolling around in a pair of flared purple trousers. I wonder if you are prepared to confirm that he has such a pair.
> A. Well, he wears sports clothes up here from time to time. I think "flared" is a little exaggerated. Some of his slacks don't have cuffs on them [*laughter*]. I mean he's a regular guy. He wears sports clothes [*laughter*].
> Q. Does he have a purple pair?
> A. I don't know if he has a purple pair. He has other colors. He has blue, maroon, and other colors. . . .

THE BALANCE OF MUTUAL WEAKNESS

Henry Brandon

The tapestry of American foreign policy in the seventies will be woven out of a clearer understanding of the limitations of American power, whether military, financial, or economic; a fatigue with foreign commitments and a disenchantment with the world; a rebellion against the American values of the last fifty years, noisy on the left, quiet in the center, resisted on the right; a despair about the intractability of domestic problems; an overall disposition to retrench and retreat.

President Nixon shifted the gears of U.S. foreign policy into reverse, but at the same time he put his foot on the brakes to slow the backing up, when his Democratic critics would have had him step hard on the accelera-

Source: *The Atlantic Monthly* (January 1973), pp. 35–42. "The Balance of Mutual Weakness" from *The Retreat of American Power*, copyright © 1972 by Henry Brandon. Reprinted by permission of Doubleday & Company, Inc.

tor. The actual pace of the American retreat will be faster than he is willing to admit and slower than they want it to be. But the President's sense of pace—typified by the stop-go retreat from Vietnam—was confirmed by his overwhelming election victory. With Henry Kissinger at his side, at least for now, he is in the ascendancy.

The first half of the seventies is a period of transition and experimentation, a search for new fixed points of orientation. It is a period of uncertainty as to the role the American public wishes the United States to play in the world, the amount of influence it wants to preserve. The intellectuals, when President Nixon came to power, withdrew to their ivory towers to contemplate the mistakes of the past and the lessons to be drawn from them for the future. And the indications are that the foreign-policy elite, having found overseas affairs their undoing, are now turning inward and are more interested in becoming a domestic-policy elite, under the impulse of the overriding problems that any American government will be facing at home in the seventies. Europeans and the Japanese tend to underestimate these problems; Americans perhaps tend to overestimate them.

The new generation of Americans is coming to power with a different experience and a different outlook. It is hardly aware of the Communist coup in Czechoslovakia in 1947; it has no memory of the Berlin blockade, the invasion of Korea, or the suppression of Hungrary. Uppermost in its mind is the catastrophe of Vietnam. The poison from that war will circulate in the American body and the American conscience for some time to come; the war's character and conduct are bound to remain part of the American experience and may leave an imprint as lasting as that of the Civil War. To this new generation it is damning evidence that the far-flung responsibilities of the United States have been executed in a reckless manner, that the limitations of American power have not been correctly assessed, and that American domestic needs have been badly neglected. The aim of this new generation will be to change the priorities of the past. Between those who do not understand the game of world power politics and those who exaggerate the need for overkill capacity, a great political struggle is developing in the seventies. There are many eloquent spokesmen among this new generation for the urgent American domestic needs, but for internationalism there are as yet none who can command the respect of this generation as well as of Congress. The kind of last-ditch defense the Nixon Administration mounted by sending the old guard of internationalists to do battle against Senate Majority Leader Mike Mansfield's attempt to cut drastically American troop commitments in Europe will be difficult to repeat.

This new generation became the engine behind the shifts and changes in the Democratic Party for the presidential campaign, and by 1976, with many more million young people enfranchised, its impact, of course, will become increasingly effective. Their influx into active politics has profoundly upset many political assumptions, and the consensus that for twenty-five years gave American foreign policy continuity, bipartisan support, and a remarkable stability has, as a consequence, been badly undermined. There are many who believe that an entirely fresh start has to be made, that every priority, every commitment, every assumption needs to be re-examined. The very idea of continuity, which has been the basis on which the world viewed American foreign policy with either confidence or awe, has become an albatross around the neck of the United States.

Some revered and idealistic concepts, such as the Atlantic Alliance, have been elbowed aside by the march of events. The United Nations, one of those great idealistic hopes, strongly promoted by the United States, that rose from the destruction of World War II, has been shunted onto the side-tracks of history. As a guardian of international security it has lost its significance. It will linger on as an international meeting ground and, who knows, could once again become a useful instrument when the challenge of the Third World to the industrial world becomes more acute.

The momentum for big ideas which accompanies the aftermath of great catastrophic wars has petered out. The young of today may be idealistic, but it is with an inner-directed idealism. They have no feeling for, no understanding of, no commitment to the world that created the United Nations.

Americans are now sharply divided on the U.S. role in the world, and any President in this decade will find it difficult to enter into new commitments, least of all any that could lead to sending American fighting forces abroad again, unless there should be a very drastic change in the international situation. Such change seems to me to be unlikely because, despite their overweening power, the United States and the Soviet Union are confined by a mutual vulnerability of which they have become well aware. It is this balance of mutual weakness that has raised hopes around the world that the seventies will be a period of relative peace and stability. Not only are there the weapons of infinite power, which compel the superpowers to coexist because neither can use them to impose its will on the other, but there is also the lesson the superpowers are beginning to grasp: that it is in their own interest to keep tension down and to avoid getting too deeply involved in peripheral conflicts. Diplomacy, as Henry Kissinger defines it, "is the art of restraining the exercise of power."

In that sense President Nixon's foreign policy has been extraordinarily successful. And success very much affects the way the public views foreign policy. Had the American intervention in Vietnam, for instance, ended in victory, it would not have aroused the opposition and revulsion it has, and American foreign policy would not have come under the kind of barrage of criticism it has. Whatever public controversy it engendered would have been soon forgotten in the wake of a successful conclusion. That is why some of the controversial, but successful, foreign-policy moves found easy acceptance.

Nixon met the public desire for a shift away from the cold-war outlook that had dominated American foreign policy throughout the post-World War II period by actively pursuing a détente with Moscow and Peking. In the process he and his impresario Henry Kissinger introduced a new diplomatic approach, balance-of-power diplomacy, at least as far as the United States, Russia, and China were concerned. It meant a far more radical change in the conduct of American diplomacy than is as yet fully recognized. The acknowledgment of the existence of a mutual weakness, the fading of the cold war, the weakening of the old rigid framework of coalition diplomacy, and the public pressures everywhere for exploring a détente policy, all contributed to this new approach. Kissinger described it in 1968 as follows: ". . . Political multipolarity, while difficult to get used to, is the precondition for a new period of creativity. . . . The shape of the future will depend ultimately on the conviction which far transcends the physical balance of power . . . part of the reason for our difficulties is our reluctance to think in terms of power and equilibrium."

By opening up relations with China, Nixon made the Soviet Union suspicious and jealous, and so eager to hold the Moscow summit that the Soviet leaders were prepared to swallow the affront of the mining of Haiphong harbor. It became important to them to make certain that the balance of power in the seventies would be three-cornered, and to demonstrate that the relationship between the United States and the Soviet Union was more important than that between the United States and China. When Kissinger squared the triangle by returning to Peking after the Moscow summit, he wondered, as he flew toward the China coast, whether he would get the same cordial reception as previously. But in spite of Moscow's smiles and Haiphong's mines, he was received even more warmly than before.

The world of the seventies is not so compact as the early-nineteenth-century political world which has been Kissinger's life study, and it is accordingly much more difficult, in his own phrase, "to respond to change with counter-adjustment." He readily admitted this when he told members of Congress in June, 1972: "This Administration's policy is occasionally characterized as being based on the principles of the classical balance of power. To the extent that that term implies a belief that security requires a measure of equilibrium, it has a certain validity. . . . But to the extent that balance of power means constant jockeying for marginal advantages over an opponent, it no longer applies. The reason is that the determination of national power has changed fundamentally in the nuclear age. Throughout history, the primary concern of most national leaders has been to accumulate geopolitical and military power. It would have seemed inconceivable, even a generation ago, that such power once gained could not be translated directly into advantage over one's opponent. But now both we and the Soviet Union have begun to find that each increment of power does not necessarily represent an increment of usable political strength."

This became painfully obvious during the Indo-Pakistan crisis, when all the counteradjustments were not enough to prevent war from breaking out. Still, as Nixon and Kissinger have shown, at least as regards the United States, the Soviet Union, and China, scales for balancing relations can be a valid instrument in the diplomatic toolbox, even in the complex world of today.

However, to pursue a balance-of-power concept a clear definition of basic interests is needed. Britain, at the height of its Empire days, was ruled by an elite which could forge its foreign policy on the basis of what it thought was in Britannia's interest—irrespective of public opinion. These interests were so clearly defined that even after the introduction of universal suffrage, the British public had an instinctive understanding of what was best for the Empire. No similar instinctive understanding is to be found in the United States today. The Nixon Doctrine is too vague a definition of American interests and priorities. It does not offer enough guidance about how new priorities should be adjusted between U.S. domestic and international responsibilities and commitments, how to marshal resources to maintain the balance-of-power equation with the Soviet Union, even if it is only a balance of mutual weakness. What complicates these calculations and adds to the pressures for a new approach is the recognition that has begun to sink in among economic planners—the fact that economic growth, which used to absorb the rising social costs of government, cannot do so anymore, and that new ways must be sought of finding the resources for the kind of new undertakings that are increasingly being talked about by leading politicians, from a new welfare program and a national health scheme to income redistribution, to mention the costliest. Americans have come to accept a much more extensive interventionist policy by the federal government in dealing with social problems, but they have not yet found ways to fund new programs adequately.

The most obvious target in the search for funds for domestic needs is the defense budget. Half of that budget goes to paying for the forces on active duty. The conventional force structure therefore is constantly eyed for possible savings. It means that the defense requirements of Western Europe are increasingly exposed to attacks, especially as the détente becomes a settled state of mind. American interests and defense commitments therefore are under review, the cost of the so-called "bargaining chip" policy is frowned upon, and the margins of safety are bound to be narrowed. But there is something of a vicious circle between the security that is desirable and the cost of military expenditures to ensure it. Opinions as to how large an insurance premium the United States should pay vary enormously if one compares, for instance, the Nixon and McGovern views. The Nixon Doctrine, being designed for all seasons, offers arguments to justify defense cuts, but that aspect of it has been obscured for the present by the requests for new weapons included in the defense budget. Even sympathetic critics at the Brookings Institution wonder whether these new weapons systems are not being determined before the nature of the threat is fully analyzed—in other words, whether they are not being pressed prematurely.

It has become obvious, therefore, that with American economic means limited, greater stringencies will have to be imposed, and they will have their effect not only on defense and foreign policy but also on American foreign economic policy.

A much more pervasive economic nationalism is making itself felt as a consequence of the costs of American defense commitments abroad, the heavy balance-of-payments deficits, and the influence foreigners can exert on the dollar. But just as the liberal Establishment has lost influence because of its misjudgments in Vietnam in the past ten years, so the international economic Establishment is now coming under increasing criticism for not deploying enough of its financial resources in the United States, for not being nationalistic enough.

John Connally, when he was Secretary of the Treasury, reflected the revival of economic nationalism, which had not been respectable for a generation or more. Even an internationalist such as Senator Hubert Humphrey thought it expedient to adopt an economic nationalist slogan during the California presidential primary of 1972; he admonished American investors to "make the dollar more patriotic." What he meant was that Americans should invest at home rather than abroad, so that Americans rather than foreigners would benefit.

Connally's outlook was not isolationist, but a mixture of nationalism and protectionism. It troubled not only foreign governments but also American business corporations, which are, with their multinational operations and vast holdings overseas, the last American globalists. His views were not typical, but they nevertheless reflected the views in the U.S. Treasury and of many in Congress. Mr. Nixon considers himself an expert in foreign policy, and so does Kissinger, but neither has a real understanding of overseas economic affairs. As a consequence there has been an unfortunate lack of American leadership in this field. Mr. Connally, while in power, was primarily interested in tactics, not long-term strategy. Still, he presented the President with a highly controversial, still unpublished proposal for a dollar bloc as a counter to the potential power of the European Economic Community. The EEC, he was convinced, would increasingly threaten American interests and exploit weaknesses in the overall American eco-

nomic situation. What he underrated was the extent to which these weaknesses were mutual and therefore created an interdependence. He saw the
harnessing of dollar power as the best way to stave off the threat. It was
difficult, however, to see the practicality of a dollar bloc, and easy to predict
that to play the balance-of-monetary-power game would lead to trade and
monetary wars and would inevitably jeopardize not only international economic relations but political relations as well. It was an idea that certainly
did not fit the Kissinger scheme of things.

There was anyway a danger that relations between the United States and the
Western European alliance would deteriorate. Nixon and Kissinger, preoccupied with their diplomatic forays to Peking and Moscow, had little time
—except during the dollar crisis after August 15, 1971—to think about
future economic, financial, military, and nuclear relations with their European allies. These relations were of a lower priority to Nixon and Kissinger,
engaged as they were in overarching balance-of-power maneuvers, because
Western Europe did not figure as a great power. What added to the Europeans' feeling of being on the outside was the realization that, in order to
gain a freer hand for this great-power diplomacy, the Nixon Administration
tended to behave like a mother bird toward its allies and friends to make
them more aware of the future need to fly on their own wings. They wondered whether the Gaullist view—that it was interests, not friends, that
mattered—had come to inspire American diplomacy. The American view
of the world, in the quest for flexibility, seemed to have become an extension
of the weaknesses that Nixon and Kissinger share—a difficulty in committing themselves intimately to other people, a desire to have no firm commitments and to have the freedom of several options. The European allies
made their own contribution to the alienation with Washington by being
too insensitive on their part to American problems. As a result, allied relationships have deteriorated and have been unnecessarily hurt. Kissinger
once quipped that "the worst fate that can befall one is being an ally of
the United States." Even if this was said facetiously, the detached U.S.
attitude toward her allies did come as a surprise after the impressions Mr.
Nixon left behind on his first European tour in February, 1969. There was
also an implicit assumption that countries like West Germany (and Japan)
had nowhere else to go, so they had to stay, in their own interests, close to
the United States, and an assumption, too, that self-interest was a more
enduring basis for relationships between governments than the sentimentality of a feeling of friendship. But mutual confidence, I, being a bit of a
romantic, believe, does play a role in international relations and to undermine it is a loss to both sides. The British in their Empire days ruled
supreme, convinced they did not need to consult with anybody. But when
the Empire was transformed into the Commonwealth and Britain became

primus inter pares, it consulted more and more, because it correctly concluded that a cooperative Commonwealth would help to make up for Britain's declining influence.

The continuing American interest in the Western alliance is to make certain that the most powerful industrial complex outside the United States does not come under Soviet control, but Americans also have a cultural conscience about the fate of Europe and, with so many other U.S. interests at stake, they want to keep their oars in European affairs.

One of the serious dangers, as the spirit of the Atlantic Alliance continues to fade in the seventies, is that the United States and Western Europe will come to see each other as competitors and not as allies. There are important men on both sides who are either anti-European or anti-American, and an unfortunate coincidence of chain reactions could play into the hands of those so prejudiced. A major American troop withdrawal, for instance, without proper consultation with NATO, a breakdown in the negotiations about EEC preferential tariffs followed by new protectionist legislation in Congress—just to dip into a basket of eels—could set in motion forces on both side of the Atlantic that would be difficult to restrain.

Western Europe cannot become a military equal of the United States or the Soviet Union and should not even try to. What will decide its power position in the seventies, whatever efforts are made to create a European Defense Community, is whether it can acquire a unified foreign, economic, and monetary policy. Whether it will have the political will to achieve that remains uncertain, but in seeking it the Europeans will have to be careful not to overplay their hand in dealing with American interests. There is an interdependence between economic and security relationships, and alienating one could lead to alienating the other.

The United States is not prepared anymore to pay a high economic price for the political benefits of European unity. A growing number of Americans have strong reservations about how desirable a new independent European power is, especially from the U.S. economic point of view. There is almost no area where the United States feels a more acute sense of vulnerability than in its economic relationship with Western Europe and Japan. The danger exists that the uncooperative behavior of the United States's main trading partners or of the United States in monetary affairs, with both blaming each other, will make for transatlantic and transpacific friction. Moreover, the United States, which for so many years shunned trading with Communist countries, will become a major competitor for Europeans, who used to have this market virtually to themselves. The United States also enjoys better communications with Russia today than do most European governments, and American interests in preserving this duopoly are also bound to conflict at times with the interests of the Western alliance.

The pressures at home for withdrawals of American troops from Europe will add to the strains between the United States and the rest of NATO. There is no evidence that these pressures reflect a desire for change in the relationship toward Western Europe. When the most vocal senators, such as Mansfield, Fulbright, or Church, raise the issue, they see it more as a housekeeping problem. Nor are there any public pressures for a change in the relationship. What troubles Congress is the disparity between the American defense effort and that of the Europeans, and the cost of maintaining that many troops under arms. One way to delay the congressional pressures for a troop withdrawal from Europe (which are mainly budgetary) would be to deactivate those forces stationed in the United States that are assigned for the defense of Europe; they represent about half of the expense, and it costs the United States as much to keep them in uniform at home as it would in Europe. Withdrawing the troops actually in Europe would not in itself save money. And since there is no logic in maintaining American troops in Europe as a "bargaining chip" for the negotiations with the Russians about mutual and balanced force reductions, this would be a practical way for the U.S. government to approach this problem. Furthermore, there is a new reason for maintaining sufficient conventional forces in Europe: the advent of nuclear parity between the two superpowers could become a temptation to the Russians to use their conventional forces, if not for military ends, then for political pressures.

The advocates of troop withdrawals reject the accusation, usually from across the Atlantic, that such withdrawals would throw doubts on the reliability of the American security guarantee. They are believers in the tripwire theory, which holds that even a handful of American soldiers in Europe would be enough to activate the guarantee. Still, this accusation raises a more fundamental question—how reliable, in fact, is this guarantee in the era of mutual weakness? Men like Kissinger believe that the Europeans, to be safer, should create their own nuclear deterrent. The British, in contrast to the French, used to oppose this in the belief that it would give the Americans a tempting escape clause, or that at any rate it would lessen the psychological deterrence of the American commitment. Kissinger is a Realpolitiker; the British tend to believe more in the mystique of power, though Edward Heath is the first British Prime Minister also to favor a European nuclear deterrent. It is impossible to decide who is right. Kissinger and Heath may be, in the light of the balance of mutual weakness and vulnerability between the great powers; but then it may be more important to preserve the psychology of the American guarantee in the Russian mind. The best hope, of course, is that the test as to which is the better choice will never occur.

Europe in many ways has become politically more stable. Written agreements usually are nothing more than the codification of an already existing situation, but the treaty on Berlin and the agreements of the Federal Republic of Germany with the Soviet Union and with Poland are the equivalent of a peace settlement of World War II. The territorial gains made by the Soviet Union and Poland are now legally confirmed and, since the Russians attach great importance to legality, they will help lessen tension in the center of Europe. Berlin, the symbol of these tensions for so many years, is likely to become more a symbol of relaxation, and, as the frontiers between the two Germanies harden, will become something of a bridge. The psychology of the division of Germany is changing. What used to be regarded as a forcibly imposed division, arousing frustrations and illusions about the unrequited promises of unification, will be viewed instead as a recognition of the existence of two German states with two different and deepening identities. This is not likely to be a permanent solution, but probably one that will last through the seventies, and one that will be equally welcome to the Russians and the West Europeans. It will help the Russians to maintain control over Eastern Europe and at the same time it will strengthen West Germany's sense of belonging to the European community.

Unquestionably, therefore, the United States will want to maintain an influence in Western Europe, though the relationship will come to rest more on psychological than institutional foundations. As the power of NATO declines and the U.S. security guarantee seems to become open to question, this psychological relationship will provide the necessary index. If it is good, then so will be the deterrent value of the guarantee; if it deteriorates, then the guarantee will be devalued with it. The growing fluidity in international relations will not make all this any easier.

In the Middle East the Israelis, though lacking a formal guarantee, will continue to rely on the United States to counterbalance Soviet power. When Egypt's President Sadat told Secretary of State William Rogers in 1971 that he would never allow the Russians to remain in his country indefinitely, Rogers was encouraged and impressed, but his elation was met with skepticism inside and outside the Administration. Yet a year later, to everybody's surprise, the Russians had been "expelled." The Middle East, with so many irreconcilable elements, so many people driven by emotion, so much smoldering hatred, is bound to remain a crisis area. But Mr. Nixon's luck in foreign affairs held even in this unpredictable area, and he and Mr. Rogers can take solace in the fact that they were able at least to begin the seventies by preserving a cease-fire along the Suez Canal. However simple it seems to many Israelis that the status quo is better than any settlement Israel could negotiate with its neighbors, the Arab-Israeli territorial conflict cannot go on indefinitely. Because of the enormous costs in men, material, and money to Israel, and the slow but growing strength of Egypt, however relative to the past the latter may be, something will have to give somewhere sooner or later. American policy will continue to aim at preserving a balance of power to prevent Israel from being destroyed. The Israelis would feel readier to give up territory that reinforces their security and their frontiers if they were more certain about the extent and consistency of this U.S. protection. What Israeli policy makers must take into consideration, and American planners increasingly talk about, is that by the end of this decade the United States will be facing a very serious energy crisis. And since so much of the needed oil comes from the Middle East, the Arabs will by then be in a powerful bargaining position with the United States.

In Asia, U.S. and Chinese interests are nowhere in serious conflict, except for Taiwan, and that problem has been defused. The Chinese do not mind the world behaving as it pleases, so long as it does not impinge on their interests. The two powers that could impinge on them are the Soviet Union and Japan, and with both of them the United States can exert an important influence—most importantly, to give the Chinese a certain reassurance that neither the Soviet Union nor Japan will attack them.

The Chinese, for instance, were very much concerned about the outcome of the Indo-Pakistan war, which involved Chinese interests, but Peking proved unable to give the support its Pakistani allies expected. The United States, whose interests were also involved, was not able to prevent war from truncating Pakistan, but it nevertheless played an important hand, much more than China. In Washington the United States was seen as defending American interests, but in Peking it also seemed to be defending Chinese interests in the situation. Thus Peking does not mind the United States maintaining a position in Asia, because it imposes certain limitations on Russia's freedom to extend her influence. Actually, the Russians have been careful enough not to get tied too closely to a weak country like India; what probably matters most to them is to ensure that India does not fall under Chinese influence. It was not surprising that the Indo-Pakistan war was compared to the old Balkan wars and the roles of the United States, Russia, and China to those that Austria, Prussia, and Russia played then. What actually happened to India and Pakistan seemed of lesser interest to the observers of big-power play. It was the maneuvers among the big powers that aroused the greatest attention, and not in the sense of who was gaining geographical advantages, but who was cleverer in preventing the other from gaining any. The Indo-Pakistan war experience points at the danger of small, limited wars among minor powers, as did the Arab-Israeli war, and at the risks and temptations they create for the great powers. It may be even more difficult to prevent them, now that big-power intervention is fraught with so much danger and therefore cannot dictate their settlement. The great powers are also learning that the developing world is hard to deal with. The Russians have learned that lesson in Indonesia, in the Sudan, and, above all, in Egypt; the United States learned it in Vietnam. It is bound to moderate their outlook and appetite.

If the Russians desist from moving against China—and they may already be too late—then China, probably with some technological support from the United States, will gradually move toward great-power status (Chou En-lai still refers to China as a developing country). If the United States continues to play its cards well and does not try to play off China against the Soviet Union, then it will place the Russians in a position where they will want to maintain not only the détente in Europe but also a modus vivendi in the gray areas where their interests overlap.

U.S.-Japanese relations have markedly deteriorated under the Nixon Administration, and although the United States would like Japan to assume the leading role in the Pacific region, no well-defined concept for this has yet developed in either country. Certainly in Washington the war in Vietnam and the initiative toward China took up too much of the time and effort of Kissinger and his staff to leave room for much else. Whatever frustrations were caused by the Vietnam War were compensated for by the exhilaration of the new relationship with China. For the rest of Asia, as for the Third World, no time was left on Kissinger's calendar, which, he once remarked, "was so crowded that it left no time for war."

The majority of Americans, despite the new relationship with Moscow and Peking, remain very conscious of the risks and dangers of cutting too deeply into the muscle of American power. Just as the forces for change in the United States are formidable, so are the forces of resistance. Robert W. Tucker, in his small book *A New Isolationism*—which he advocates with so much persuasiveness to American ears—admits that "the mood of the public is clearly ambivalent, the American people show little propensity to impose a massive veto on Presidential action on foreign policy, at least so long as this action avoids a repetition of the events associated with Vietnam." Whether interventionist or isolationist, Americans remain power-conscious and power-proud. A drastic reduction of the military budget soon is therefore unlikely; even if desired, it could not be accomplished except over a period of three to five years. The trade unions, the military-industrial complex, the military and congressional forces will slow it down. After all, the USSR is not sitting complacently on its achievement of nuclear parity. What the great debate in Washington will be about is not whether the United States should protect whatever qualitative lead it has in nuclear weapons, but the degree to which it should try to keep ahead. The next phase of the SALT talks ought to make this easier to decide.

But I have no doubt that the United States will, in the next few years, cut its overseas commitments more closely according to the cloth at its disposal. Nixon and Kissinger became very conscious of the fact that the United States no longer had the capacity to fulfill the range of commitments it had acquired after World War II, when the balance of power among the leading nations was quite different. There were commitments America was bound to live up to, but there were others it was prepared to jettison if necessary. The two therefore came to feel that they were acting from a hand that was, as they saw it, vulnerable. It is not impossible that in the recesses of his mind Kissinger occasionally compared his own situation to that of the Iron Chancellor Bismarck, who, at least after 1871, applied his mastery of the balance-of-power game to protect a vulnerable Prussia against any hostile coalition. The feat of developing good relations with China and the Soviet Union at the same time was alone one that would have been quite a challenge to Bismarck or Metternich; Kissinger succeeded because he knew how to restrain the contending forces by manipulating their antagonisms.

What presents a serious problem for the future is the intricate weave of the Nixon and Kissinger diplomacy and the difficulty of anybody else's assuming its management. Abram Chayes, the Harvard Law School professor who headed a task force to develop McGovern's foreign policy during the election campaign, called Kissinger a virtuoso for whom there was no obvious successor because there was simply no one, he thought, who had the same command of diplomacy and who could play the balance-of-power game with the same skill and success. Nothing worries Kissinger more than the fear that a President will come to power in this decade who will not understand his scheme of things, who will see the world quite differently and tear down the pillars of the power relationship he built. Essential to his thinking is the belief that you do not cut your strength and then fashion policy accordingly, but that you maintain or build up your resources and then negotiate about limiting or reducing them, if they can be limited or reduced. He has more faith in the power than in the prospects of limiting it; he is convinced of human fallibility. But it is a policy that increases rather than decreases budgets, and therefore it will become more difficult to follow.

What may alleviate this problem is that the two superpowers have in common the urgent need to deal with demands for domestic reform, as have China and Japan. This *Drang* for reform is most obvious, though, in the United States and the USSR, the two societies that have prided themselves for so long on being "classless." They have become more class-ridden than they are willing to admit, and the leaders in both countries have come to recognize that they must do more to alleviate these pressures for the sake of internal peace and order. It is a vital element in the balance of mutual weakness. The rebellions in the American ghettos and among the workers in Poland were signals no government could ignore. What happened in Poland, where police power is almost as strict as in the Soviet Union, could happen in the Soviet Union itself tomorrow.

In the Soviet Union the raising of the standard of living is still a relatively simple problem of more and better consumer goods; in the United States the problem is how to restrain the glut of inessential consumer goods that eat up an inordinate amount of raw materials, and how to reduce the ever widening gap between the rich and the poor. Americans could say with Churchill, "We are stripped bare by the curse of plenty." The focus may shift between the schools, the cities, the environment, the welfare program, but all are aspects of the redistribution of wealth, which will be the great social struggle in the United States in the seventies. What this requires is a Kissinger for domestic policy who can undertake the kind of long-term economic planning that this requires; Mr. Nixon lacked such an equivalent.

The retreat of American power will continue to prove a traumatic experience for Americans, their friends, and even their enemies. This does not mean, however, that the Western world will not continue to look to the United States for leadership, or will not watch with some anxiety whether the retrenchment will be managed wisely and how much the polarization of forces on the right and left will be kept under control. The stability of the Western world will continue to depend on the quality of American leadership. In a period of détente, which the seventies promise to be, and in an even more complex world than the one we are used to, it will be more difficult to keep a steady rudder than it was in a period of tension, when the answers often imposed themselves automatically. It will require a careful balancing between preserving the essentials of the older policy principles and making sufficient allowances for the new public mood. Whoever is in charge during the rest of this decade will have to remember that people do not forgive their leaders when they err, even if their errors reflect the popular preferences.

The seventies will go down in history as representing a watershed in the American relationship to the rest of the world. This relationship will prove to be more restrained, more impersonal, more detached, more self-centered. After a period when everyone knew where everyone else stood, when diplomacy was played to well-established rules, and a certain intimacy and interdependence were observed within the alliance, the world of the seventies will be less predictable. But the basic design of the retreat of American power is drawn. Only its pace and limits remain in doubt.

Nixon's Haldeman: Power Is Proximity

Christopher S. Wren

His title—Assistant to the President of the United States—is outrageously deadpan. It hints at so much, reveals so very little. That is appropriate enough for Harry Robins Haldeman, an adamantine Californian who serves President Richard M. Nixon as the White House chief of staff. After 15 years with Nixon, Haldeman is still viewed through a glass darkly, though his presence pervades the hallways of power. Whoever and whatever enters the President's Oval Office, whoever and whatever emerges must pass through Bob Haldeman. His colleague, John Ehrlichman, likens him to the Lord Chamberlain of yore, and another White House staffer privately calls him "by far the second most important man in government."

Haldeman does not accept the latter accolade: "All the power in the White House is in one man. I don't think there are seconds or thirds or fourths." He is not trying to mislead. Haldeman sees himself as just a faithful toiler in the Administration vineyards, though he concedes: "There's an adage about power relating to proximity, and the people most in touch with the President are going to have more influence. . . ."

Such men are a handful: John D. Ehrlichman, Assistant to the President for Domestic Affairs; Henry A. Kissinger, Assistant to the President for National Security Affairs; George P. Shultz, Director of the Office of Management and Budget; John N. Mitchell, Attorney General; and H. R. Haldeman, who keeps the wheels of the Presidency turning.

"People say Haldeman doesn't have a policy role," says an associate. "However, there's no major decision out of the President's office that he hasn't participated in." Nixon and Haldeman have been compared to twin prongs on a tuning fork. In fact, Haldeman is calibrated so precisely on the President's frequency that he can scout solutions to problems not yet pondered, like a sort of intellectual advance man. "I track well with him," explains Haldeman in the White House argot.

Not surprisingly, Haldeman calls himself "a Nixon Republican. I don't have much trouble with Nixon's positions. Of course, as you become integrally involved in forming them, you become pretty much convinced. . . ."

Bob Haldeman, at 44, is lean, unfaddishly crew-cut and tanned (a result of his thirst for sunshine). When he breaks into a hungry grin, he can charm, but more often he appears formidably preoccupied. He dresses in neat Ivy League suits with white button-down-collar shirts at a time when

Source: *Look* (August 24, 1971), Vol. 35, No. 17, pp. 15–19. *Look* Magazine, copyright © Cowles Communications, Inc., 1971. Reprinted by permission.

fashion color riots outside on Pennsylvania Avenue. His regimental striped ties are throttled with a gold Nixon-signature tie clasp. A small enamel American flag lives in his lapel. Haldeman resembles less the savvy pol than some diligent combat commander returned from the Asian wars to a civilian world that has drifted on in his absence.

Then, consider the mind. It is just plain remarkable. He can concentrate in assorted directions at once. When he reads, he gobbles words at up to 2,500 a minute. Some years ago, Haldeman heard about Mensa, a society that purports to restrict its ranks to the smartest two percent of the human race. He was curious enough to take the tests, passed of course, and then having learned he was brilliant, let his membership lapse.

That Henry Kissinger, the bespectacled Harvard professor, has been seized upon by the press as this Administration's "swinger" gives some measure of how straight the White House crowd is. Even among them, Haldeman stands like Caesar's wife, above suspicion. His wife Jo may be a stronger Christian Scientist than he, but Haldeman has no tolerance for dissipation. He tried to smoke a pipe, couldn't keep it lit. He doesn't really drink or party, and hoards his sparse free time with his family in the Republican suburban redoubt of Kenwood, Md. For kicks, he shoots home movies and plays a guitar; he digs the Beatles and Johnny Cash over the glib Washington social gossip. "He hates small talk," says Hugh Sutherland, a Los Angeles ad man who has been Haldeman's chum since boyhood. "I can envision Bob standing in the middle of a cocktail party and being completely bored."

Though his Dutch, German and Swiss ancestry has been kneaded into a cliché, Haldeman more accurately reflects the conservative side of Beverly Hills, Calif., where he grew up. He was an ROTC company commander in prep school, enrolled at the University of Redlands, switched to USC and wound up at UCLA.

Haldeman took a job in advertising, moving to San Francisco, New York and back to Los Angeles with the J. Walter Thompson agency. Other Thompson alumni have migrated from L.A. to the White House: press secretary Ronald Ziegler, appointments secretary Dwight Chapin, and Haldeman's own aides, Lawrence Higby and Bruce Kehrli. "It's easy to knock an ad man," says Dwight Chapin, "but a good advertising man is a good marketing man, and he knows what's going on."

That was true of Haldeman, who rose fast, to an account supervisor for insecticides, waxes and shaving creams, then to manager of the L.A. office, the youngest man ever in that spot. He ran a taut outfit, trusted by his subordinates and—more important—by the clients.

But politics kept wooing him away. "When I was at UCLA," says Haldeman, "I was fascinated by the Communist-front organizations, what they were trying to do." His grandfather had been militantly anti-Communist, and Haldeman rooted for the Mundt-Nixon bill pushing through Congress. Anti-Communism brought him to Richard M. Nixon. "I volunteered for the '52 campaign, but I was unable to work out any role at that time. I faded away and came back in 1956. I was enormously impressed by Nixon, the tremendous overall ability of the man, the way he deals with people, his intellectual ability, his articulation. To a degree, you can judge a man by his enemies as well as his friends."

On leave from J. Walter Thompson, Haldeman signed aboard as an advance man for three months each in the 1956 and 1958 campaigns. He devoted an entire year to Nixon's 1960 presidential campaign. Back in California after that defeat, Haldeman helped research Nixon's book, *Six Crises*. He urged Nixon not to run for governor of California in 1962; then, overruled by Republican leaders, he faithfully managed the campaign. "I think it was fortunate for the country and for him that he didn't win," Haldeman says now. "If he had, he would have been propelled into running [for President] in 1964, and the chances of winning that election weren't very good."

Others wrote Nixon off. Haldeman didn't. "As long as I've known Nixon, I've felt he should be President. I didn't have any supernatural premonitions. I felt that despite the events of the '60's, he was not through." After the 1968 Oregon primary, Haldeman joined Nixon once more, toting a yellow legal pad choked with notes, as chief of the campaign staff.

When Haldeman forsook advertising for the White House, he took a "substantial" salary cut to his current $42,500 and threw away perquisites like stock options. That Haldeman would want to be assistant to anyone, even the President, surprised some colleagues, but Hugh Sutherland, who succeeded Haldeman as office manager, recalls a bull session one day: "I asked him, 'If you had it to do over again, what would you do?' He said, 'I'd like to be the executive secretary of a major corporation.' He's got that in spades."

Organization is Haldeman's particular talent, though as an architect rather than a technician. He had designed the current infrastructure on the campaign trail before the election was secured.

"Why you have a White House staff," he says, "is to make it possible for the President to deal with the things he should be doing. His charge to us was to recognize that some things could be handled better by other people than by him.

". . . The President has been in public life for a long time. We have a pretty good codification of what his principles are. It's not difficult in most cases to know what his judgment would be. There are hundreds of thousands of decisions to be made by the White House. Most of them are routine. Only a small fraction would require his direct attention."

On paper, the staff is the biggest in White House history. Haldeman insists it is smaller than those of prior Administrations, who padded the ranks with employees borrowed from other departments. "We decided to bite the bullet and submit an honest budget," Haldeman typically puts it. "I felt it was something we had to do." He calls the current budget—about $8.5 million—a "ridiculous" bargain.

"A really good presidential staff is one that has no coloration of its own," suggests John Ehrlichman, "but simply reflects the needs of the President in office." Haldeman has no exact precedent for his own job. The closest may be that set by Sherman Adams during the Eisenhower years, but Haldeman is not the sort who adapts to a cozy prior style, if only because his authority transcends mere administration. As Haldeman sees it: "Everything comes to a point where it goes to the President and comes to a point where it comes out from the President, and that's basically where I fit."

Haldeman functions as a taxing but fair straw boss. "Bob's approach is to find good people and then give them a helluva lot of responsibility, but then hold them strictly accountable for the results," says Fred Malek, who recruits White House talent. "While you have this responsibility and all the trappings that go with it, you damn well better produce."

The staff considers President Nixon a thoroughly kind person to work for, in small measure because Haldeman wields the discipline. He does not tolerate prima donnas or suffer time-wasters: "I get impatient with trivia and I get impatient with people who don't figure out their own solutions and get them done." Despite Haldeman's penchant for bluntness, the younger staffers approach him by first name and seem to dote on him. "I don't want someone waltzing me around the ball park before he tells me what he wants me to do," says Fred Malek. "You can't expect a man in Bob's position to sit down and wonder how he can correct something without hurting feelings. He'll just lay it out, whether you're right or wrong."

Aware that the President wants time for uninterrupted concentration, Haldeman zealously protects the sanctity of the Oval Offce. A staffer recalls Haldeman's assertion: "Even John Mitchell comes through me." When Henry Kissinger joined the pre-Inaugural staff back at the Hotel Pierre in New York, he popped in to consult with Nixon through the day on each new concern. Haldeman took Kissinger aside and laid out the rules. Lesser unfortunates who try to end-run Haldeman on a dash to the ear of the President invariably find themselves slammed into the sidelines. "He's a nice guy, until you get in his way," one learned.

Consequently, Haldeman has become the lightning rod for recurrent charges of overprotectiveness. "He's *the* isolation of the President," insists a former staffer. "He's what they're complaining about." Haldeman doesn't see it that way. "I think my function is not one of isolating him but [of] making it possible for him to get the maximum exposure on the things that are productive. You've got to work out a way of using his time where it will do the most good. I don't see my job as keeping people out but getting them in."

Accessibility does not necessarily cure isolation, says Haldeman. "The test of isolation is not how much exposure he gets but the quality of exposure. I think I have a way of providing him with a range of useful exposure that makes him unisolated. If his door was always open and anyone who wanted could come in, then you'd call him unisolated. But then anyone—pressure groups or a pressure group—could completely dominate, and he would be much more isolated. . . .

"It's important that the President initiate, not simply react, and that requires some self-discipline and some planning."

The workdays of Bob Haldeman and Richard Nixon interlock. A black Chrysler from the White House motor pool picks up Larry Higby at 7:15 A.M. Haldeman slips into the left rear seat 15 minutes later. The limousine collects Dwight Chapin on the way downtown. They scan the daily news summary and begin paper work.

Nixon has already arrived in his Oval Office when Haldeman assembles the senior staff in the Roosevelt Room at 8:15. Haldeman otherwise avoids formal meetings. "One of Bob's primary responsibilities is being available to the President," says Larry Higby. "A man who's in meetings can't be available." That over, Haldeman, his familiar yellow pad tucked inside a brown-leather folder, walks in to see the President. "His inside pocket here," Haldeman gestures, "is full of papers that he's written notes on. He'll pull the news summary and there are things he frequently wants to discuss. It lasts a half hour to an hour." (Sometimes the session runs an hour and a half.) John Ehrlichman and Henry Kissinger follow to discuss domestic questions on the schedule for that day, that kind of thing. He'll have read those out and go through that. He'll have things for me to take care of— and foreign matters respectively. Haldeman may sit in. "He's sort of the conscience of us all in terms of the timeliness of the work," says Ehrlichman. "We try to take as many surprises as possible out of the President's day."

Unless there is a meeting with the National Security Council, the Cabinet or Republican leaders, the formal appointments begin at 10 A.M. These have been culled by Dwight Chapin under Haldeman's eye. "The decision who he's going to see isn't something I make in a vacuum," says Haldeman. "It's the result of the decision of staff people, his own instructions and external requests. . . . It's my job to balance things out so he has time to see who he has to see and, more important, has sufficient time to do his own work."

Where Johnson pushed for consensus, Nixon would rather listen to the opposing briefs argued before him, then make a decision. Haldeman may join in as devil's advocate. He has cogently presented viewpoints that he feels should be heard, though they are not his. "Someone here has to question everything," says Dwight Chapin. "Bob will sit in the President's office, and if he sees someone lobbying and can't answer them, he will call for someone who can. It's not unusual for him to come out and say, 'Will you get Robert Finch or George Shultz in here?' "

When the appointments end at 12:30, Haldeman meets with Nixon for up to another hour. The President eats his lunch, usually cottage cheese and pineapple, alone in an alcove of the Oval Office, or in the Executive Office Building next door. Haldeman adjourns with Larry Higby to his own working lunch, also cottage cheese and pineapple with a glass of milk, in his new office. An oil portrait of Nixon beside an American flag hangs on the green wall. The clock radio is tuned to an FM country-music station. The old office was next to the President's; Haldeman moved when traffic got too heavy.

While Nixon reads and signs paperwork, Haldeman wades through his own correspondence. The presidential buzzer on his green telephone often intrudes. Haldeman sees Nixon again before the longer appointments resume at 3:30. Later, Haldeman breaks for a cup of Constant Comment tea.

"At the end of the day," says Haldeman, "between six and seven, I go in. There are more notes on a yellow pad. He also makes notes all over everything that goes in." Haldeman turns these over for transcription by the secretaries.

In the limousine homeward, Haldeman checks tomorrow's schedule with Chapin and Higby. He was absent from his family so much on the campaigns that "by contrast, that I get home at all is pretty much an improvement." After dinner, he works into the evening. The President usually calls him on a direct line from the Lincoln Sitting Room back at the White House. If Haldeman goes out, Nixon finds him. After Larry Hibgy's daughter was born last January, the Haldemans stopped by the hospital. The White House phoned, and for several minutes, Higby listened to the President of the United States and his top assistant swap baby anecdotes.

"The one thing [Presidents] Johnson and Eisenhower both told me was that my greatest contribution would be to get him to take time off," says Haldeman of his boss. "But I'm not overly concerned. He doesn't need much time off. He doesn't enjoy it." A change of scene suffices. When Nixon flies to San Clemente, Calif., or Key Biscayne, Fla., Haldeman travels too. The meetings at San Clemente run for hours on such heavy subjects, like the budget. At Key Biscayne, Nixon has more time of his own to write his speeches or read historical biographies. His favorite Presidents: Lincoln, Wilson and Teddy Roosevelt. (Haldeman's favorite, after his boss, is FDR.)

"He doesn't watch television," says Haldeman of Nixon. "Oh, sometimes he will watch sports. He never watches the news shows and he doesn't have a wire ticker in his office. He feels it necessary to have some perspective. He thinks it's better to get a report on it afterward.

"They're so wrong most of the time. Today's analysis of today's news can be very wrong, especially when they're under the pressure of getting a show together night after night. He realizes its value as a means of communication. He knows what was on last night. He gets a better feel from the summary than you would if you watched [TV]." The news summary—a distillation of 50 newspapers, the wire services and TV news—that Nixon receives daily also includes a selection of editorials and political cartoons. Haldeman terms the latter "brutality for the sake of brutality. Herblock wouldn't exist if he didn't have nasty cartoons of Nixon, nor would Conrad."

Over the years, Haldeman's own patience with the press has stretched thin. He concedes that any President is going to be regarded critically by reporters, but he nonetheless sees a distinction: "I think, unfortunately, Nixon may have a greater number of the press interested in his un-success, and I think it's accentuated with this President. He's got a more hostile press corps among the working press. The great bulk of the working press are Democrats, so there's a party difference to begin with. Ideologically, they have a liberal-versus-conservative approach to things. . . . I think, on a personal basis, a commentator or reporter who finds out he's wrong doesn't like to be proved wrong. Nixon's been written off a number of times and has refused to go away. That leaves those who wrote him off in an awkward situation."

Haldeman wonders if the message is penetrating what he considers the hostile ether of the press: "There's two supreme ironies in the way this Administration is viewed. We're supposed to be a public relations oriented Administration, but we're doing more with less public relations than others have done. The Kennedy Administration had a lot of great goals but got very little through Congress. Johnson got a lot through Congress, but he didn't accomplish what he wanted to do. We've gotten legislation through Congress that will accomplish what we set out to do.

"The other irony is the interpretation that everything Nixon does is for a political purpose. You could argue that the things he's done in so many major areas, rather than being big PR or political coups, have had negative political effects—but they were done in spite of this because they were right." Haldeman details them, from postal reform to the war with its incursions into Cambodia and Laos.

"Only the narrow decisions get to the President," explains Haldeman. "Almost by definition, a presidential decision is a decision made between two narrow alternatives. It would be decided on a lower level if it weren't. It's also made with the outlook the President has. But the chances of his being right are greater than someone else being right. If he's a good President, he'll be right more often. He has a better perspective than most of how narrow the decision is."

During the demonstrations last spring, Haldeman invited a score of students from Williams College into the White House. For two and a half hours, they argued in the Roosevelt Room. No minds were changed, but Haldeman hopes the students found him sincere. "I had a feeling I was ruining their day. I tried several times to end, so that they could go out and demonstrate, but they kept wanting to talk. These were basically a really solid group of kids. Oh, a couple of them were way out and said so. One was quoting Che Guevara and giving all the Red rhetoric. It's hard to argue with an ideologue." (Ironically, Hugh Sutherland recalls Haldeman reached that same conclusion after confronting some John Birchers at a meeting in West Los Angeles a few years ago.) Still, Haldeman thought it important enough to share a dialogue with youth inside the White House. "My feeling is that if we have a problem, that's where it is. But," he is quick to add, "I don't believe youth has slipped away."

Haldeman never doubts that Nixon will run again in 1972. "We're still wrapping up the nightmares, but the dreams are going to take time too. There's very much the need for a second term to provide time for what he's trying to do.

". . . We've got the genius and drive to accomplish what we need to domestically if we have a time of peace to do it. His whole objective is [the] achieving of a generation of peace." Thus, Nixon's intended visit to China. "The China thing is an example where he's worked behind the scenes," says Haldeman, "laying the groundwork and quietly moving on it over a period of years—with the results just now beginning to show."

The time will come, if not in 1972, then in 1976, when Haldeman will be out of a job. Employment as a presidential assistant doesn't offer any tenure. Haldeman has no interest in parlaying the experience into a political career for himself, nor does he want to write a book. He will withdraw from Washington, though not back to advertising.

Ambition has possessed Bob Haldeman, but in a manner almost surgically selfless. He drives himself to meet the destiny that he senses awaits the man he follows:

"Just as I've always thought he was going to be President, I think he's become President at the right time. Times are changing. The great leaders are gone. The towering leaders are going. There aren't any great leaders now, except Richard Nixon."

The Convenience of Secrecy

Francis E. Rourke

Richard Nixon, his biographers commonly report, is an extraordinarily private man, whose bitterness over the exposure of the "Nixon fund" in the 1952 Presidential campaign was directed not least at the fact that it forced him to reveal intimate details about his economic circumstances. As Garry Wills puts it in *Nixon Agonistes:* "The public self-revelation for which Nixon would be blamed in later years was . . . forced on him, against all his own inclinations, personal and political. By temperament and conditioning, Nixon is reserved, with Quaker insistence on the right of privacy."

As President, Nixon's passion for privacy has been very much in evidence and has had a striking effect upon the structure and operation of the American political system. Institutions like the Executive departments, which cannot be trusted to keep Presidential secrets, have been downgraded. At the same time, the office of the Special Assistant for National Security Affairs has been given a commanding position in American government, largely because its activities can more easily be hidden from the public eye.

Moreover, his successful use of secrecy has greatly helped Nixon to frustrate the expectation widely held when he took office that the steady flow of power to the White House during the past four decades would finally be reversed. From 1932 to 1965 Presidential power rode the crest of successive waves of domestic and international crises. Few except unregenerate reactionaries questioned the assumption that what was good for the President was good for the country. But by 1968 a radically different attitude had begun to emerge. In Vietnam Presidential wisdom had proven quite fallible, and Executive power suddenly loomed as a source of danger as well as salvation. If the outbreak of World War II had seemed to confirm Executive wisdom and Congressional ignorance during the foreign policy debate of the 1930s, Vietnam in the 1960s appeared to furnish equally dramatic proof of the need to limit Presidential authority and to allow Congress and the public a greater voice in policy decisions.

Nixon's preservation of Presidential hegemony in the face of the discouraging prospects that prevailed when he took office in 1969 was a remarkable feat. A key element in that success has been the use of Executive secrecy to protect and ultimately to expand Presidential authority. Nixon's record thus far demonstrates that the ability of Presidents to operate in secret is one of their most durable sources of power in the American political system.

Source: *The Nation* (July 24, 1972), pp. 39–42. Reprinted by permission.

At the outset of his Administration Nixon moved quickly to exclude the regular Executive departments from major decisions on foreign affairs. This was an administrative coup of some magnitude. Previous Presidents had been able to limit Congressional and public involvement in foreign policy, but Nixon has gone them one better—he has managed to keep his decisions secret from the bureaucracy as well. Thus the Executive departments, which have traditionally been regarded as the major source of rules and regulations imposing secrecy in government, have now become one of its chief victims, a position of exclusion deeply resented by organizations like the State Department. Power which once rested in their hands has been shifted to the palace guard in the White House.

To be sure, all modern Presidents have been irritated by the many nooks and crannies in the large executive agencies through which information can leak to the outside world. In his memoirs President Johnson complains about the unauthorized disclosure by government officials at the time of the Tet offensive in 1968 of General Westmoreland's request for additional reinforcements for the half-million American troops then under siege by the North Vietnamese. From the Presidential perspective, Executive departments have always had far too much interchange with reporters and Congressmen to be trusted with confidential information.

What Nixon and other President's commonly fail to recognize is the extent to which such leaks serve the public interest—however much they may inconvenience the Chief Executive. Before the disclosure of Westmoreland's request for additional troops, American policy in Vietnam had moved steadily upward along a path of escalation in the apparent pursuit of military victory. After public exposure of the Westmoreland proposal the policy of escalation was halted, and the Johnson administration made proposals to the North Vietnamese which led eventually to the beginning of negotiations in Paris and a reduction of the American presence in Vietnam. Thus, what Presidents may regard as the pathological inability of large Executive departments to keep secrets may actually serve the healthy function of allowing the public to exert some influence over the development of foreign policy. This is especially useful in a democracy where the success of policy may ultimately depend upon public support.

In Nixon's eyes the bureaucratic leak has always been particularly obnoxious because it links together in hostile conspiracy two occupational groups in American society for which he has always cherished the most profound distrust—newsmen and career bureaucrats. Back in 1958 when he was serving as Vice President in the Eisenhower administration, Nixon charged the State Department with "undercutting" and "sabotage" of official policy when it released a breakdown of mail from constituents which showed heavy public opposition to an American commitment to defend the islands of Quemoy and Matsu off the Chinese mainland. This 1958 incident must have haunted Nixon in 1972 when the most celebrated leak on the internal deliberations of his Administration occurred—the disclosure of secret American efforts to assist Pakistan at a time when the Administration had publicly pledged itself to neutrality in the India-Pakistan war.

As noted, the institution which has chiefly benefited from Nixon's distrust of the established Executive departments is Kissinger's office of the Special Assistant for National Security Affairs. There are many attractive aspects of this office from Nixon's point of view, including the fact that it has no constituency other than the President himself. It can claim no allies in Congress and has no bureaucratic interests or identity of its own to advance or protect.

But it is the secretive way in which Kissinger's office can function that chiefly accounts for Nixon's decision to give it responsibility for the execution of his major foreign policy initiatives. Alone among key foreign policy officials Kissinger is protected by the doctrine of Executive privilege from having to appear or testify before Congress. It did not take long for Kissinger to be generally recognized as the President's chief deputy on all matters of salient importance in foreign affairs—by the public, by other participants in the foreign policy process, and even the heads of foreign governments.

The value of this highly secretive style of governmental operation is that it provides Nixon with a capacity for maneuver and surprise that he could never achieve acting through the ordinary Executive departments. It is obviously much easier to prevent leaks from his own staff than from the career civil service; it is hard to imagine how the great coup of this Administration—Kissinger's secret trip to China in 1971—could have been managed through the ordinary bureaucratic apparatus without a leak occurring at some point in the process. However, it is equally hard to see why it was necessary to carry out this venture in such secrecy, except for the opportunity it gave Nixon to reap political profit by springing a dramatic surprise on the American public.

Mr. Nixon's long-standing aversion to leaks does not, of course, apply to disclosures that he himself contrives. As it was in earlier administrations, the leak is eminently valuable to Nixon as a means of shaping public opinion at home or sending signals abroad. In the 1971 controversy over the publication by *The New York Times* of the Pentagon Papers, the newspaper was able to demonstrate without much difficulty that the government freely disclosed military "secrets" when doing so enhanced its ability to win an argument with its critics or mobilize public support for steps it wished to take in international politics.

Thus, for Nixon as for other Presidents, the real power of secrecy comes from the support it provides for effective publicity. To be sure, such secrecy does permit him to conceal information that, if released, might reveal flaws in his performance or arouse opposition to sub rosa policies he is following. But it is even more important as a means by which he can selectively release information on timely occasions so as to mold the public mind.

In May, for example, after the mining of Haiphong Harbor and the resumption of large-scale bombing of North Vietnam, the dispatches from Hanoi by *New York Times* correspondent Anthony Lewis appeared to suggest that morale remained high in the enemy capital in spite of these American military activities. Quickly the Administration arranged a background briefing for reporters by Gen. Alexander Haig, a Kissinger deputy on the National Security Council staff. Haig released intelligence data to the newsmen present that was designed to show that the North Vietnamese were actually in considerable disarray as a result of the military escalation.

The role of reporters in this case suggests the way in which the media of communication can be made to serve as instruments of Presidential power, providing channels through which the Chief Executive can mobilize and manipulate public attitudes. Indeed, from the point of view of some Presidential aides, the proper role of the media in foreign affairs is to provide the White House with just such an avenue through which it can transmit messages to the public. As Maxwell D. Taylor once put it, "Without strong, articulate information media, the government cannot communicate with the electorate, or win popular support for the needs of national security."

But, as the war in Vietnam strikingly reveals, the media also impose a tremendously effective check upon the ability of executive agencies to manipulate mass opinion. Throughout the war, the coverage by reporters on the scene has provided the public with information on the events taking place which on frequent occasion proved more accurate than the data released by the government. Correspondents also exposed information in the hands of executive officials that not even Congress had been successful in ferreting out. Witness, for example, the Pentagon Papers disclosure in 1971, when the press made available to the public a record of the early history of the war that most legislators had never been allowed to see.

When Nixon came to office, he inherited a wide credibility gap from the previous administration. The truthfulness of the government was under challenge from the press, Congress and a variety of private citizens and organizations. Nixon's response to this problem was certainly not to decrease official mendacity. The record of his Administration for lying may be no worse than that of some of its predecessors, but it is certainly no better.

What Nixon did instead was to attempt to create a credibility gap for the media of communications as well as the government. Vice President Agnew was the principal instrument of this strategy, with his repeated and strident attacks on the objectivity and reliability of leading news organizations and correspondents. The television networks were particularly singled out for charges of bias and distortion in their coverage of the news. This tactic of countering a charge with a countercharge of similar wrong-doing has been followed by the Administration in a number of other cases—most notably in the ITT affair, where it was suggested that the Democrats had questionable relationships with ITT.

Thus, rather than seeking to dispel the widespread suspicion that the government is telling lies, the Administration has sought to suggest instead that the public is also being lied to by the large news organizations. Since the media generate the principal pressure for open government in a democratic society, a successful effort to weaken their standing in the public eye will greatly increase the capacity of an administration to govern in secret.

Nixon clearly regards secrecy as enormously advantageous for the performance of his role as President. Living most of his adult life in the bath of publicity that normally surrounds party politics and election campaigns in the United States, Nixon nonetheless senses the value of secrecy for the actual task of governance once a politician has been elected to office. From de Gaulle, whom he and Kissinger so much admire, Nixon has learned that a certain remoteness on the part of the ruler and the process by which he rules exerts an irresistible fascination for the public—creating an air of mystery about a regime whose activities in the full light of day seem quite prosaic.

Moreover, secrecy creates distance, and distance helps a political leader conceal limitations and imperfections. Certainly it is more useful in this regard than constant exposure to interrogation by frequently hostile reporters. It is not surprising, therefore, that the President did not schedule a formal televised press conference from June of 1971 to June of 1972. Last year only nine ad hoc meetings with reporters were held, as compared to the twenty-four to thirty-five such conferences Presidents have conducted during each of the past twenty-five years.

Secrecy also permits Nixon to strengthen the impression of competence surrounding his Administration. The fact that he was acting on secret information in some of his major decisions in the past often seems to have provided the country with more reassurance than anything revealed in public. This is true in spite of the fact—noted by George Reedy in his *Twilight of the Presidency*—that the Chief Executive often makes his decisions on the basis of information no better than that available to the ordinary newspaper reader. Moreover, a secret trip abroad by a Presidential emissary always seems to promise more than a publicly announced visit. For the traditional American belief that secrecy in government conceals corruption and incompetence, we have now substituted the notion that it signifies a masterful control of processes too complex for public understanding.

For this reason secrecy has been extremely useful to Nixon as a means of immobilizing domestic critics of his performance in office. With respect to problems for which no public solution has yet been offered—Vietnam, for example—the Administration has always been able to claim that great things were being done in secret. If nothing else, the prospect that secret plans may actually be afoot prevents political opponents at home from pressing their attack. What can they do or say today without risking the possibility that the President will pull the rug out from under them to-morrow? Thus, while the rationale for secrecy has long been that it creates uncertainty and paralysis on the part of foreign adversaries, in point of fact it creates as much if not more confusion in domestic politics.

The most paradoxical aspect of Executive secrecy as it is practiced under Nixon is that more is now communicated to adversaries abroad about the foreign policy of the United States and the intentions of its President than is shared with the American public itself. Great care is taken to send Kissinger to Moscow and Peking, so that the rulers of these states will not misunderstand what it is that America is up to when it mines the harbors of North Vietnam and pulverizes it from the air. No such equivalent efforts are undertaken in this country. How much better informed we would all be if Brezhnev and Chou would share with us what they have learned from Kissinger about recent decisions in American foreign policy!

Where does all this leave us who are—happily or unhappily—Nixon's constituents? It leave us essentially where we have been since Franklin Roosevelt—residents in a political system which concentrates more power in the hands of a single ruler than the world has ever before seen. Writing a while ago, Ernest Barker characterized democracy as "government by discussion." We cannot escape a bleak question: is there a major political system anywhere today in which momentous decisions can be taken in secret by a single ruler with less prior discussion than in the United States?

SPIRO

Frank Trippett

The Vice President's notorious Des Moines assault on TV news—
   *The audience of seventy million Americans gathered to hear the Presi-
dent . . . was inherited by a small band of network commentators and
self-appointed analysts, the majority of whom expressed . . . their hostility*

Source: *Look* (September 7, 1971), Vol. 35, pp. 28–29. *Look* Magazine, copyright © Cowles Communications, Inc., 1971.

*to what he had to say. . . . The views of the majority of this fraternity do
not—and I repeat, not—represent the views of America. . . . Perhaps it is
time that the networks were made more responsive to the views of the nation. . . . Now I want to make myself perfectly clear. I'm not asking for
Government censorship. . . .*

—stirred up great alarm, and naturally so, for here was a coarse and
blatant attack upon the very idea of a free press or a free tube, whichever.
And what was perfectly clear, in addition to the picture that the networks
carried of the Vice President in Iowa, was the primitive and unmistakable
menace in Mr. Agnew's language. His effort to disclaim any intent to
censor was obvious bunk. "When the criticism is directed by the second
highest ranking elected official in the nation's Government," as commentator Joseph McCaffrey put it, "there is a fine, if not indiscernible line
between criticism and censorship." So alarm was justified, and I could
share in it and in the widespread dismay at the character of the Vice
President's language. Yet, it was not his language that finally left me
apprehensive.

What left me wondering then and later was not this man's much-studied
way of *saying* things but his peculiar way of *seeing* things. The peculiarities
of Mr. Agnew's vision have been much too little examined, and I come forward here to help fill this gap.

Mr. Agnew sees things in a very special way that I find intriguing and
instructive. What he sees on the television news is but a single example.
There he sees chronic hostility in the reporting and commentary wherein I
tend to see a seldom interrupted struggle of blandness against fatuousness.

Economic vistas, to take another example, unfold in a special way in
Mr. Agnew's vision. "The rise in prices," he saw in the fall of 1970, "has
been definitely curbed." To my eyes, prices still seemed to be rising. In
broader terms, Mr. Agnew has testified that he sees vast improvements in
the national economy under the Administration of Richard Nixon. Now, this
does not raise still another question about Mr. Agnew's controversial
rhetoric. This raises a question about his vision. It is his mode of perception
that deserves more analysis. Once Mr. Agnew's special mode of vision is
understood, his rhetoric becomes more comprehensible. What he says, after
all, must flow from what he sees.

Many Americans scanning their nation see a plethora of evils, and the
catalogue of these is familiar. There are poverty and racism and militarism
and unemployment and decrepit cities and runaway technology and hunger
and pollution, to reiterate a few. To some Americans, it seems self-evident
that we must focus steadily upon such evils if we are to remedy them. This
attitude is as elementary as that of a loving parent who realizes that he must
see and concentrate on the ills that a child suffers if they are to be remedied.

The Vice President, however, does not see it this way. In fact, he regards it as "masochistic" to see the evils that exist in this country. Mr. Agnew has made his witness on this point over and over.

Not long after his inaugural, the Vice President made a springtime visit to Oklahoma. There he told a gathering of fellow Republicans:

"It is time to end this masochistic binge—this senseless whining over what's wrong with America!"

A few months later in New Orleans came Mr. Agnew's celebrated speech attacking "impudent snobs." That phrase tended to stick in everybody's mind more vividly than the sentence in which it occurred. The sentence follows:

"A spirit of national masochism prevails, encouraged by an effete corps of impudent snobs who characterize themselves as intellectuals."

Soon after that, Mr. Agnew went to Mississippi and attacked "liberal intellectuals" who criticized the national leadership. He said:

"They have a masochistic compulsion to destroy their country's strength whether or not [it] is exercised constructively."

Just this year, of course, Mr. Agnew vented his displeasure over the doubts expressed in the news media that the invasion of Laos had been entirely successful. This, too—these doubts—he called "masochism" that would "destroy us as a nation."

On the face of it, the allegation (or diagnosis) of masochism is an uncommon charge for a leader to level again and again at Americans who simply see certain evils in the society and focus upon them with the hope of remedy in mind. How would Mr. Agnew address a loving parent observing and discussing potentially lethal ailments in a child? Granted consistency in his way of seeing this situation, he would be obliged to say:

"It is time to end this masochistic binge—this senseless whining over what's wrong with your child!"

What is, in any event, perfectly clear from his insistent reiteration is that this is how Mr. Agnew sees many critics of the American society. If we see poverty and pollution, in other words, the vision of these evils is supposed to cause us pain. As masochists, however, we experience this pain as pleasure. Because we are masochists, therefore, we tend to see poverty and pollution over and over because each time it brings us pain and hence pleasure.

Mr. Agnew, obviously, sees not a sick society but simply sick critics. It may be that by reiteration he hopes to make the critics feel sick or encourage uncritical Americans to regard them as sick. This technique is one that Mr. Agnew himself has discussed, suggesting, in fact, that the critics themselves were employing it. He said:

"If critics repeat often enough that a society is sick, then some easily frightened members of that healthy society are going to get a little green around the gills. Then others, observing these, will wonder whether they're sick too. Men in positions of power who keep bewailing our outcast state could cause the condition they profess to see."

I assume that Mr. Agnew acts on his own insights. This accounts for the way he has elected to appeal to those Americans who cannot bring themselves to look coolly and squarely at what is happening in the country. Agnew offers them a comforting concept: Those fellow countrymen who keep forcing unpleasant information upon them are sick. The favorable popular response to Mr. Agnew suggests the existence of many Americans who are susceptible to this kind of comfort.

I suspect that Americans almost always respond to the accumulation of hideous conditions in the society with pain, but I question that many of us masochistically translate it into pleasure. Most of us seek to alleviate the pain in two entirely human ways, some by actively seeking a solution to the problem, others simply by closing their eyes to the source of it.

This latter course, common in individuals or in groups, arises not from sloth or indifference but out of a more complex psychological defense instinct. Among many, the mere acknowledgement of certain hideous conditions tends to present a disturbing challenge to their vision of what America is like. These defend themselves simply with an eyes-closed denial of the disturbing information.

Lately, of course, a widely cherished concept of America has been radically challenged and disturbed by accumulating events and conditions, all smashing into the national consciousness for two straight decades. Information about such things is received instinctively as an attack by Americans who tend to take their personal identity from some cherished notion of the country. That old image has been taking a battering, of course.

Thinking of ourselves as a generous people, we are being forced to see that we perpetuate vast hunger and poverty amidst unprecedented affluence.

Thinking of ourselves as a tolerant people, we are being forced to acknowledge that we have structured racism into the fabric of our very institutions.

A self-proclaimed just people, we are forced to see ourselves crushing the dissenting young with clubs and guns. Many prefer to redefine justice rather than acknowledge the brutal injustices committed at Kent State and Jackson State.

We are fond of thinking of ourselves as individualistic, yet are being compelled to see the individual increasingly submerged in the vast and impersonal organizations of the technology.

Liberty- and privacy-loving, in our fond self-image, we are being forced to recognize ourselves as the acquiescent authors of wide-spread governmental spying on citizens, of massive illegal arrests, of the preventive-detention concept of imprisoning people not for something done but for what might be done, of direct governmental attacks on the free press. Dr. Frank Stanton has to promise to go to jail if need be to protect CBS from the intimidating excursion of a congressional committee, and the New York *Times* and Washington *Post* have to go to court to secure elementary First Amendment rights to print news without prior censorship.

We have supposed ourselves to be a people in love with the land, too, but now are discovering that in truth we have been ravagers of the land and poisoners of the waters and the very air we breathe.

We have been, or have thought of ourselves, as the great stewards of peace. Now for years we have witnessed ourselves as the architects of a veritably incomprehensible war in Southeast Asia.

Finally, America has ever nursed the dream of itself as invincible. But now, to encounter an almost impregnable resistance to a new image-crushing truth, comes the very simple and unmistakable fact of looming defeat in Vietnam.

It is easy to see across the land an enormous resistance to such harsh and fresh truths about ourselves. To many Americans, such truths smack of humiliation as well as defeat. And as the late Thurman Arnold perceptively wrote, those who come to power in times of humiliation and defeat tend to express and intensify the resulting popular persecution manias.

Mr. Agnew comes before us as a man whose peculiar way of seeing things appeals to those Americans who are impelled to avoid rather than confront this assortment of unpleasant truths.

Actually, as LOOK Editor William B. Arthur said in a recent speech to Sigma Delta Chi, Mr. Agnew and the Administration are not merely at war with the press and television. They are at war with the truth itself. And the ultimate danger is not the direct effect that they may have on American journalism, which is likely in the long run to be slight, but the effect that they have upon the willingness and capacity of the people to see their society as it is.

What it is useful to see, because of his role, is the way Mr. Agnew sees, the peculiar personal vision that he invites the American people to share. His way of seeing the press and TV is merely a small part of it. The Vice President tends to see all people with views divergent to his in either one of three ways. He sees them as sick, or he sees them as enemies—or he sees them as loathsome objects. What he says does, of course, flow from what he sees. And it is his vision of many fellow human beings as loathsome objects that spawns the rhetoric of loathing. Mr. Agnew's critics, however, have spent too much energy analyzing the rhetoric and too little grasping the vision that produces it.

Mr. Agnew sees Democrats complaining about inflation as "germs complaining about disease," and he sees some "totalitarian ptomaine dispensed by those who disparage our system," and a "perverted nationwide college competition for violence." He sees faculties and students in some "catatonic trance." He is forever Dr. Agnew in diagnostics with an eye out for loathsome infestations. He variously describes human beings of divergent views as "garbage" or "rotten apples" or, collectively, as a "cancer."

The striking and fearful thing is not the rhetoric, not the ugly name-calling, but the remedial ideas to which his visions impel him. Over and again, when Mr. Agnew sees human beings as loathsome objects, his instinct is to reach for and commend some terminal way of dealing with them.

Hence when some demonstrators from the opposition appeared at one of his political rallies in Illinois, Mr. Agnew declared that it was "time to sweep that kind of garbage out of our society."

The prior year, when Mr. Agnew scrutinized America's young dissenters, he said: "We can . . . afford to separate them from our society—with no more regret than we should feel over discarding rotten apples from a barrel."

In Houston in 1970, Mr. Agnew looked upon campus activists generally and said: "It is my honest opinion that this hard core of faculty and students should be identified and dismissed from the otherwise healthy body of the college community lest they, like a cancer, destroy it."

Repeatedly and consistently, when Dr. Agnew sees the loathsome political opposition he is impelled to think in terms of eradication or extermination. What he has in mind for American television—the termination not of its existence nor of his frequent appearance on it but merely of its right to criticize freely—is mild in comparison with what, by his own testimony, he sees as the way to deal with human beings holding views he detests. To sweep out the "garbage," to pluck out the "rotten apples," to cut out the "cancer"—this kind of vision occurs only in a man who is scarcely attuned to the American idea of tolerance.

Chapter 8
SUGGESTED TOPICS FOR CLASS DISCUSSION

1. The President wants to organize the Executive Branch so that it works efficiently. What is the standard by which efficiency is to be measured? Should it apply just to the functioning of the Executive Branch or apply to the functioning of the political system as a whole?
2. The drafters of the Constitution did not anticipate that great power would come to be wielded by men in the White House who are not elected, are little known to the public, and do not have to answer to Congress. What problems does this development create?
3. Certain roles of Presidents are well known, such as chief executive, chief

legislator, and ceremonial head of state. Can you identify other roles that Presidents may sometimes seem to play?

4. Both Presidents Lyndon Johnson and Richard Nixon created Administrations notable for being close-mouthed and secretive. From their point of view, what might be the advantage in this? From a broader perspective, what are some of the problems associated with it? What is a *credibility gap* and why has the term been used so much in recent years?

Chapter 9
Courts, Judges, and Justice

The Constitution provides that "the judicial power of the United States shall be vested in one Supreme Court, and in such inferior courts as the Congress may from time to time ordain and establish. . . ." Under the scheme of separation of powers, this allocation of power means that judges along with legislators, chief executives, and heads of major Administrative departments share the political power and responsibility to determine public policy. Hence, the Supreme Court is and always has been a political institution. Many of us find this hard to accept, yet an objective appraisal of the kinds of questions brought to the Supreme Court must lead one to conclude that it cannot escape being a policy-making body. Though it is true that a few of its cases involve narrow legal questions, such as those in the terms of a contract, by far the most numerous are concerned with such policy questions as apportionment, with its allocation of political power; the schools; public accommodations; voting rights; and procedural rights in arrests and trials.

The most spectacular exercise of the policy-making role of the judiciary has been through the use of judicial review. Since Marbury v. Madison, *the proper exercise of this review power has been the subject of controversy. Should the Supreme Court use its power only as a recorder of existing law, or should it use it to bring about social change by expanding the meaning of the Constitution?*

The popular view of the Supreme Court seems to be that it should be the guardian of the Constitutional process and the provider of fixed, certain, and timeless law. This implies a kind of mechanistic application of law and leaves little discretion to the Justices. Implicit in this view is the use of judicial self-restraint. The other view recognizes that the judiciary is, after all, one of the governing bodies and, as such, is basically a political institution and that its obligation to help bring about social change within the legal framework is no less than that of the Congress and the President.

But between these two positions, the Supreme Court sometimes finds itself in a political crossfire between the Congress and the President; if it appears that the Supreme Court cannot win, it may resort to the "political question" doctrine as an escape from the embarrassing predicament of either having its decision ignored and not enforced or being subjected to an onslaught of criticism or even threats. Nevertheless, it will sometimes accept a case that involves certain, strong reactions to its decision.

Though national attention is focused on the Supreme Court, the judicial system is composed of a great many lower courts, both federal and state, where all but a fraction of cases begin and end. It is at this level that the judicial process defines what we can and cannot do without punishment, regulates our economic activities, embodies our rights, provides ways they can be asserted, and establishes the means for their protection. It is at this level also that the individual judge, and especially the trial judge, becomes living justice. Usually presiding alone, he has great latitude in directing the outcome of the trial and in assessing punishment or providing an equitable settlement.

The cases in this chapter illustrate a number of issues relating to separation of powers, judicial review, the functioning of the courts, the role of judges, judicial activism and self-restraint, and questions of protection of the individual.

BIRTH OF JUDICIAL REVIEW

Marbury v. Madison

The most celebrated case in Constitutional history has never been quite able to outlive the charge of partisan politics and the usurpation of power by the Supreme Court to "supervise" both legislative and executive functions.

Fearing the excesses of the new Jeffersonian Republicans, the Federalists suddenly found great virtues in the nonelective branch of government and made a number of "midnight" judicial appointments to hold the fort until the Federalists could regain control of the government. Marbury, one of the midnight appointees, went directly to the Supreme Court to secure a commission that John Marshall, then Secretary of State and at the time of the suit, Chief Justice, had neglected to deliver.

The Court was faced with a serious dilemma: If it issued the order Jefferson was certain to ignore it. On the other hand, an admission by the Court that it could not interfere in executive matters would be a surrender to what Marshall called "speculative theorists and absolute terrorists" and might set a precedent for the supremacy of elective government. The stakes were high. What Marshall succeeded in doing was (1) to condemn his political opponent, (2) to declare the power of the court to set aside legislative acts (and by implication executive as well) all the while admitting that the Court had no jurisdiction!—A. M. S. and E. W.

Mr. Justice Marshall delivered the opinion of the Court.

At the last term, on the affidavits then read and filed with the clerk, a rule was granted in this case, requiring the Secretary of State to show cause why a mandamus should not issue, directing him to deliver to William Marbury his commission as a justice of the peace for the county of Washington, in the District of Columbia.

No cause has been shown, and the present motion is for a mandamus. The peculiar delicacy of this case, the novelty of some of its circumstances, and the real difficulty attending the points which occur in it, require a complete exposition of the principles on which the opinion to be given by the court is founded.

These principles have been, on the side of the applicant, very ably argued at the bar. In rendering the opinion of the court, there will be some departure in form, though not in substance, from the points stated in that argument.

Source: *Marbury* v. *Madison*, Secretary of State of the United States 1 Cranch 137; 2 L. Ed. 60 (1803).

In the order in which the court has viewed this subject, the following questions have been considered and decided.

1. Has the applicant a right to the commission he demands?

2. If he has a right, and that right has been violated, do the laws of his country afford him a remedy?

3. If they do afford him a remedy, is it a *mandamus* issuing from this court?

. . . It is . . . the opinion of the court,

1. That, by signing the commission of Mr. Marbury, the President of the United States appointed him a justice of peace, for the county of Washington in the District of Columbia; and that the seal of the United States, affixed thereto by the Secretary of State, is conclusive testimony of the verity of the signature, and of the completion of the appointment; and that the appointment conferred on him a legal right to the office for the space of five years.

2. That, having this legal title to the office, he has a consequent right to the commission; a refusal to deliver which, is a plain violation of that right, for which the laws of his country afford him a remedy.

It remains to be enquired whether,

3. He is entitled to the remedy for which he applies. This depends on,

1. The nature of the writ applied for, and,

2. The power of this court.

. . . This, then, is a plain case for a mandamus, either to deliver the commission, or a copy of it from the record; and it only remains to be enquired, whether it can issue from this court.

The act to establish the judicial courts of the United States authorizes the Supreme Court "to issue writs of mandamus in cases warranted by the principles and usages of law, to any courts appointed, or persons holding office, under the authority of the United States."

The Secretary of State, being a person holding an office under the authority of the United States, is precisely within the letter of the description, and if this court is not authorized to issue a writ of mandamus to such an officer, it must be because the law is unconstitutional, and therefore absolutely incapable of conferring the authority, and assigning the duties which its words purport to confer and assign.

The Constitution vests the whole judicial power of the United States in one supreme court, and such inferior courts as Congress shall, from time to time, ordain and establish. This power is expressly extended to all cases arising under the laws of the United States; and, consequently, in some form, may be exercised over the present case; because the right claimed is given by a law of the United States.

In the distribution of this power it is declared that "the Supreme Court shall have original jurisdiction in all cases affecting ambassadors, other public ministers and consuls, and those in which a state shall be a party. In all other cases, the Supreme Court shall have appellate jurisdiction."

It has been insisted, at the bar, that, as the original grant of jurisdiction to the supreme and inferior courts, is general, and the clause assigning original jurisdiction to the Supreme Court contains no negative or restrictive words, the power remains to the legislature to assign original jurisdiction to that court in other cases than those specified in the article which has been recited; provided those cases belong to the judicial power of the United States.

If it had been intended to leave it in the discretion of the legislature to apportion the judicial power between the supreme and inferior courts according to the will of that body, it would certainly have been useless to have proceeded further than to have defined the judicial power, and the tribunals in which it should be vested. The subsequent part of the section is mere surplusage, is entirely without meaning, if such is to be the construction. If Congress remains at liberty to give this court appellate jurisdiction, where the Constitution has declared their jurisdiction shall be original; and original jurisdiction where the Constitution has declared it shall be appellate, the distribution of jurisdiction made in the Constitution is form without substance.

Affirmative words are often, in their operation, negative of other objects than those affirmed; and in this case, a negative or exclusive sense must be given to them, or they have no operation at all.

It cannot be presumed that any clause in the Constitution is intended to be without effect; and, therefore, such a construction is inadmissible unless the words require it.

. . . To enable this court, then, to issue a mandamus, it must be shown to be an exercise of appellate jurisdiction, or to be necessary to enable them to exercise appellate jurisdiction.

It has been stated at the bar that the appellate jurisdiction may be exercised in a variety of forms, and that, if it be the will of the legislature that a mandamus should be used for that purpose, that will must be obeyed. This is true, yet the jurisdiction must be appellate, not original.

It is the essential criterion of appellate jurisdiction that it revises and corrects the proceedings in a cause already instituted, and does not create that cause. Although, therefore, a mandamus may be directed to courts, yet to issue such a writ to an officer for the delivery of a paper is in effect the same as to sustain original action for that paper, and, therefore, seems not to belong to appellate, but to original jurisidiction. Neither is it necessary, in such a case as this, to enable the court to exercise its appellate jurisdiction.

The authority, therefore, given to the Supreme Court by the act establishing the judicial courts of the United States, to issue writs of mandamus of public officers, appears not to be warranted by the Constitution; and it becomes necessary to inquire whether a jurisdiction so conferred can be exercised.

The question, whether an act repugnant to the Constitution can become the law of the land, is a question deeply interesting to the United States; but, happily, not of an intricacy proportioned to its interest. It seems only necessary to recognize certain principles, supposed to have been long and well established, to decide it.

That the people have an original right to establish, for their future government, such principles as, in their opinion, shall most conduce to their own happiness is the basis on which the whole American fabric had been erected. The exercise of this original right is a very great exertion; nor can it, nor ought it, to be frequently repeated. The principles, therefore, so established, are deemed fundamental. And as the authority from which they proceed is supreme, and can seldom act, they are designed to be permanent.

This original and supreme will organizes the government, and assigns to different departments their respective powers. It may either stop here, or establish certain limits not to be transcended by those departments.

The government of the United States is of the latter description. The powers of the legislature are defined and limited; and that those limits may not be mistaken, or forgotten, the Constitution is written. To what purpose are powers limited, and to what purpose is that limitation committed to writing, if these limits may, at any time, be passed by those intended to be restrained? The distinction between a government with limited and un-limited powers is abolished if those limits do not confine the persons on whom they are imposed, and if acts prohibited and acts allowed are of equal obligation. It is a proposition too plain to be contested, that the Constitution controls any legislative act repugnant to it; or, that the legislature may alter the Constitution by an ordinary act.

Between these alternatives there is no middle ground. The Constitution is either a superior paramount law, unchangeable by ordinary means, or it is on a level with ordinary legislative acts, and, like other acts, is alterable when the legislature shall please to alter it.

If the former part of the alternative be true, then a legislative act con-trary to the Constitution is not law: if the later part be true, then written constitutions are absurd attempts on the part of the people to limit a power in its own nature illimitable.

Certainly all those who have framed written constitutions contemplate them as forming the fundamental and paramount law of the nation, and consequently, the theory of every such government must be, that an act of the legislature, repugnant to the Constitution, is void.

This theory is essentially attached to a written constitution, and is, con-sequently, to be considered by this court as one of the fundamental principles of our society. It is not therefore to be lost sight of in the further consideration of this subject.

If an act of the legislature, repugnant to the Constitution, is void, does it, notwithstanding its invalidity, bind the courts, and oblige them to give it effect? Or, in other words, though it be not law, does it constitute a rule as operative as if it was a law? This would be to overthrow in fact what was established in theory; and would seem, at first view, an absurdity too gross to be insisted on. It shall, however, receive a more attentive consideration.

It is emphatically the province and duty of the judicial department to say what the law is. Those who apply the rule to particular cases must, of necessity, expound and interpret that rule. If two laws conflict with each other, the courts must decide on the operation of each.

So if a law be in opposition to the Constitution; if both the law and the Constitution apply to a particular case, so that the court must either decide that case conformably to the law, disregarding the Constitution; or conformably to the Constitution, disregarding the law; the court must determine which of these conflicting rules governs the case. This is of the very essence of judicial duty.

If, then, the courts are to regard the Constitution, and the Constitution is superior to any ordinary act of the legislature, the Constitution, and not such ordinary act, must govern the case to which they both apply.

Those, then, who controvert the principle that the Constitution is to be considered, in court, as a paramount law, are reduced to the necessity of maintaining that courts must close their eyes on the Constitution, and see only the law.

This doctrine would subvert the very foundation of all written constitutions. It would declare that an act which, according to the principles and theory of our government, is entirely void, is yet, in practice, completely obligatory. It would declare that if the legislature shall do what is expressly forbidden, such act, notwithstanding the express prohibition, is in reality effectual. It would be giving to the legislature a practical and real omnipotence, with the same breath which professes to restrict their powers within narrow limits. It is prescribing limits and declaring that those limits may be passed at pleasure.

That it thus reduces to nothing what we have deemed the greatest improvement on political institutions—a written Constitution—would of itself be sufficient, in America, where written Constitutions have been viewed with so much reverence, for rejecting the construction. But the peculiar expressions of the Constitution of the United States furnish additional arguments in favour of its rejection.

The judicial power of the United States is extended to all cases arising under the Constitution.

Could it be the intention of those who gave this power to say that, in using it, the Constitution should not be looked into? That a case arising under the Constitution should be decided without examining the instrument under which it rises?

This is too extravagant to be maintained.

In some cases, then, the Constitution must be looked into by the judges.

THE ROLE OF THE COURTS: CONSCIENCE OF A SOVEREIGN PEOPLE

Judge J. Skelly Wright

There is abroad in this country a major debate concerning the role of the courts in expanding individual freedom and in increasing respect for human rights.

One school of thought, known as the advocates of judicial restraint, has advised the judges to move cautiously. Judges cannot give the people more freedom than the people themselves want or deserve, they tell us. And whatever freedom the people want or deserve cannot be kept from them by the judges. So from this point of view, it is useless for the judges to concern themselves with expanding the sphere of human freedom. It may be worse than useless, for judicial protection of individual rights may well encroach on the powers and prerogatives of other branches of our government, thereby upsetting our Constitutional system of checks and balances. Thus, it is said, it is to state legislatures and to Congress, rather than to the courts, that the people must look for the protecion of their rights. Moreover, if the judges take the burden of defending and expanding freedom upon their own shoulders, then the people may grow lazy and less vigilant, and neglect their own duties in protecting freedom. It is the efforts of the people themselves, expressed through the election of their chosen representatives, which underlie whatever freedom exists in our nation. Or so the advocates of judicial restraint would have it.

But the rival school of thought, derisively called the judicial activists, has taken quite a different view. For them, it is the duty of the courts to do all in their power to protect those freedoms which our Constitution grants. The courts will not be able to do all that is necessary by themselves. The courts have no army like the President, nor can the judiciary declare

Source: *The Reporter* (September 26, 1963). Reprinted by permission.

war as Congress can. But the courts can act as the collective conscience of a sovereign people—just as once nations had chancellors to act as conscience to the king. With courts performing their duty of proclaiming the eternal rights and liberties of the people, the people will not be slow to defend the banners raised by the courts. And the President and Congress will fall in line. This judges must do, according to the judicial activist, in deciding the cases and controversies involving the rights of human beings.

Moreover, freedom under our Constitution is not subject to any elections, state or Federal. The fundamental freedoms announced in the Bill of Rights are inalienable, and the protection of those rights, by the Constitution itself, is consigned to the courts. With the late Justice Robert H. Jackson the activists say:

"The very purpose of a Bill of Rights was to withdraw certain subjects from the vicissitudes of political controversy, to place them beyond the reach of majorities and officials and to establish them as legal principles to be applied by the courts. One's right to life, liberty, and property, to free speech, a free press, freedom of worship and assembly, and other fundamental rights may not be submitted to vote; they depend on the outcome of no elections."

Witnesses and the Flag

Perhaps the most dramatic demonstration of the difference between these two schools of thought occurred during the Second World War, when the Jehovah's Witnesses experienced a wave of persecution in our country because of their unusual religious beliefs and practices. Matters reached a climax when a number of local school boards required that schoolchildren —including Jehovah's Witnesses—give a daily pledge of allegiance to the flag. The Jehovah's Witnesses refused to do this, for they felt that such an act was contrary to the Bible's command "Thou shalt have no other gods before me." As a consequence of this refusal, Jehovah's Witnesses across the country faced the prospect of having their children expelled from school, arrested as truants, taken from their parents, and sent to reform schools.

Eventually this problem arrived at our highest tribunal, the Supreme Court, as it seems almost every major social problem does today. In a straightforward statement of the views of the advocates of judicial restraint, the Supreme Court announced that it would not interfere with the requirement of the pledge of allegiance. It recognized a major conflict between the freedom of belief of the individual child and his parents versus the power of the state to command allegiance. But, said the court, the reconciliation of that conflict must be left to the people and their elected representatives —this could not be done for them by judges. If the responsibility for protecting the freedom of the individual were left to the people, said the court, the people would rise to that responsibility.

But without guidance from the Supreme Court, the people misread their responsibilities. From the standpoint of religious freedom and respect for human rights, the effect of that Supreme Court decision in the first flag-salute case was disastrous. School board after school board adopted new requirements commanding the flag salute, on pain of expulsion or other penalties. And often the school boards would quote the very words of the Supreme Court opinion in justification of their action. In many cases the salute to the flag was used simply as a device to expel the unpopular Jehovah's Witnesses. The words of the Supreme Court, that the protection of freedom could best be left the responsibility of local authorities, were perverted and used as an excuse for what was in effect religious persecution by the local school boards.

At the same time, and worse than the official action against the Jehovah's Witnesses, was the nation-wide wave of mob violence, attempts at lynching, and physical brutality against the Witnesses—all in the name of patriotism and support for the Supreme Court's opinion. Conditions were such that within three years after the first flag-salute case was decided, a second one reached the Supreme Court. In a dramatic reversal, the court ruled that no authority, state or Federal, could dictate the religious beliefs of any citizen. Schoolchildren could not be coerced into reciting pledges of allegiance when to do so would violate their freedom of religion. Specifically, the children of Jehovah's Witnesses could not be expelled from school because their religious beliefs prevented them from giving the flag salute.

The Supreme Court decision was honored by the local boards. Much of the official persecution of the Jehovah's Witnesses diminished. The new Civil Rights Section of the Department of Justice—founded by the former Attorney General, later Mr. Justice Frank Murphy—helped communicate the Supreme Court ruling to local authorities, and to the people, explaining that the freedom of belief of the Witnesses was protected by law. The rest is history. The Jehovah's Witnesses have been let alone. At least they have been allowed to practice their religion.

Thus, in the very midst of the Second World War, a court defended—indeed expanded upon—Constitutional freedoms. It did so despite the opposition of political authorities. It did so in behalf of a very small and very unpopular minority. And it did so in behalf of one of the most unpopular of freedoms—especially in wartime—the freedom *not* to salute the flag.

The Supreme Court's defense of freedom of religion did not cease with the war. The school-prayer cases of the very recent past demonstrate once again that the Court is alert to even minor abridgments of fundamental freedoms. Once again the apostles of judicial restraint have been critical. But religious freedom in this country is safer today because the Supreme

Court has shown the people why even a minor inroad on religious freedom cannot be tolerated.

Protection for the Poor

The courts have also been expanding the sphere of human freedom in the field of criminal law. It has often been said that "History will judge the quality of a civilization by the manner in which it enforces its criminal laws." The Supreme Court has taken the lead in ensuring that our enforcement of criminal law receives the approbation of history. In decision after decision it has sought to upgrade and civilize the manner in which our criminal laws, state and Federal, have been enforced.

The court has demonstrated a determination to diminish the part that poverty plays in the administration of criminal justice—the type of trial a man gets must not depend on whether he is rich or poor. Following this thesis, the court has recognized the right to counsel in both Federal and state criminal trials and has required the state and the national governments to supply a lawyer for the indigent person. More than this, the Supreme Court has required the state and Federal governments to provide a proper appeal for indigents by paying the costs thereof, including a transcript of the testimony taken at the trial. Thus the court has sought to remove the handicap of poverty so that the indigent, too, may receive a fair trial under our law.

Coerced confessions have also received the condemnation of the current court. Under the Anglo-Saxon system of criminal justice, as distinguished from the Continental system, a defendant has a right to remain silent, not only at the time of trial but, most importantly, after his arrest before trial. The Supreme Court has been at pains to condemn, as uncivilized and as a reproach to our system of criminal justice, not only physical pressure, but psychological pressure as well, designed to force an accused to confess.

Perhaps the keynote case on the subject of coerced confessions and third degree is *Chambers* v. *Florida*. There a young Negro was accused of committing a heinous crime that had excited a large number of the white citizens of Florida. Without access to a lawyer or even to members of his family, young Chambers was questioned by the police for days on end while a mob bent on his destruction roamed outside the jail. Under these circumstances, it was said that he confessed to the crime. After his conviction in the state courts of Florida, the Supreme Court heard the case. In reversing that conviction and in denouncing the conditions under which a confession was extracted from Chambers, Mr. Justice Hugo L. Black sounded what has come to be the new creed for the court:

"Under our constitutional system, courts stand against any winds that blow as havens of refuge for those who might otherwise suffer because they are helpless, weak, outnumbered, or because they are nonconforming victims of prejudice and public excitement. . . . No higher duty, no more solemn responsibility, rests upon this Court, than that of translating into living law and maintaining this constitutional shield deliberately planned and inscribed for the benefit of every human being subject to our Constitution—of whatever race, creed or persuasion."

The Supreme Court has not satisfied itself with merely outlawing confessions that are demonstrably involuntary. Taking cognizance of the fact that most confessions are obtained while the accused is alone in police custody immediately after arrest and before being transferred to judicial custody by a committing magistrate, the court has held that where there is unnecessary delay in bringing the accused before the committing magistate, any confession made during this period of unnecessary delay shall not be received in evidence. Thus the court has sought to outlaw not only coerced confessions but also confessions obtained under circumstances presumptively coercive.

In the protection of rights under the Fourth Amendment against unreasonable searches and seizures, the Supreme Court has also been active. The midnight knock on the door, the hallmark of the totalitarian police, does not pass muster in this country. The court not only has outlawed evidence obtained from unreasonable searches and illegal arrests. By an application of the so-called fruit-of-the-poisoned-tree doctrine, it has ordered excluded from the trial of a criminal case all evidence derived from the evidence illegally obtained. "Knowledge gained by the government's own wrong cannot be used by it," says the court.

Through its decisions in criminal law, the court has given rich meaning to our ideal of equal justice under law. Persons accused of crime, as a class, have little claim to sympathy with the public or to influence with political authorities. It would be easy, even popular, to constrict the rights of those who stand at the bar of justice. But the courts have reminded us that the rights of all citizens are safe only to the extent that the rights of each accused person are protected. The phrase "It's his Constitutional right" has entered the common language as a link between the ideals of our civilization and the recognition of the rights of the lowliest offender.

Of course, these civilizing advances in the manner of enforcing criminal justice have also been the subject of criticism. The court itself has been condemned for recognizing the rights of "criminals." What the detractors fail to recognize, of course, is that the Bill of Rights outlined in the first eight Amendments to the United States Constitution are the rights of all citizens of the United States, and until an accused is proved guilty beyond a reasonable doubt after a fair trial, he also, as a citizen, is entitled to those rights.

Equal Votes

The reapportionment cases mark another important area in which the Supreme Court has affected our freedom. When we say "This is a free country," one of the things we mean is that we are a free people who govern ourselves. In order for us to govern ourselves, we require fair apportionment. If, for practical purposes, it were primarily the farmers and small-town residents who voted, and the votes of city people hardly counted at all, then to that extent we would be less a free country.

Reapportionment cases highlight the debate on the role of judges in preserving freedom. And these cases point out the importance of general acceptance, of popular support, of aid from Executive and legislature, and of reaffirmation by the national conscience. For many years, judges would not decide reapportionment cases—no matter how unfair the apportionment, no matter what laws or Constitutional provisions were violated, no matter how many people were denied an effective right to vote. Judges would not decide such cases because, as some of them saw it, a court decision about legislative apportionment could have no effect unless the legislature and the people accepted the decision. And no one could count on, or predict, whether there would be legislative or popular support. And so, though as a matter of law the courts had the power to decide apportionment cases, as a matter of judicial wisdom they generally abstained from these issues. Reapportionment was held to be a political issue that addressed itself to the people.

But the Supreme Court has now declared that such cases are proper for judicial decision. The court has now found that in many areas the political system restrained the people from acting, that there was developing in this country a condition in some respects similar to the rotten-borough system that disgraced England two centuries ago. So the court, in effect, authorized the courts in each state to hear apportionment cases as they came up and to apply to voting the principle of equal protection our Constitution ordains. Some people predicted that the court's decree would be ignored or mocked, that the legislatures and the people would resist to the end the court's efforts in this field, and that the nation's refusal to accept the challenge and rise to the responsibility given them by the courts would become a national disgrace. But the results have been quite different, and the response to the judicial spark has been broader and stronger than anyone could have predicted. In state after state, citizens' groups have stepped forward, swiftly and effectively, to demand enforcement of the Constitutional principles of equality of which the Supreme Court had reminded them. Soon local courts took up the matter of reapportionment. And in some states, even before the question came before the local courts, legislators and governors have supported reapportionment proposals of their own.

Now, by and large, citizens generally—from the man in the street to newspapers and preachers—have said "at long last" to the principle that a state's apportionment must conform to the standards of equality required by our Constitution.

Making a Truism True

Of the areas in which courts, particularly the Supreme Court, have been active in promoting the freedom of us all, the one of first concern to us today is racial justice. The Supreme Court decisions in the field of racial equality have attempted to secure an actual freedom for the Negro from the bonds of discrimination and bigotry—and a freedom for the white from having to live in a society where such injustices occur. That these freedoms belong to the white and to the Negro is solid Constitutional law—nothing could be more clear than that the Thirteenth, Fourteenth, and Fifteenth Amendments to the Constitution were adopted exactly for the purpose of raising the former slave to the level of first-class citizen. The court decisions of our day are but long-delayed steps forward in giving actual effect to that Constitutional law.

The question remains, Will these decisions receive the support of the people, or will they remain only words in the mouths of the judges? Will the other branches of the Federal government, the Executive and Congress —and the state and local governments—respond to the challenge of these Supreme Court decisions and make a reality today the promise of a hundred years ago?

In pleading for passage of the Civil Rights Act of 1963, the Attorney General of the United States began his remarks to the Congress with this statement:

"For generations, Americans have prided themselves on being a people with democratic ideals—a people who pay no attention to a man's race, creed, or color. This very phrase has become a truism. But it is a truism with a fundamental defect: it has not been true." Is there an honest person in this country today who will deny this statement? Are there enough people in this country today so depraved that the Supreme Court's efforts in behalf of racial justice shall be in vain?

In answering these questions, we should first take notice that the landmark 1954 school-desegregation case has received both more support and more opposition than any other case in our century. The support it has received is tremendous. Organizations sprang up to implement its philosophy, people who had been apathetic to all things public suddenly took a new interest in the commonwealth, a wave of idealism swept the country— especially among college youth—to see the old Constitutional principle of equal justice given effect in the problems of the day. Even foreign nations looked at us with new respect as we began to practice what for so long we had merely preached.

But the civil-rights cases also provoked opposition. Men whose positions had been entrenched upon the foundation of old injustices resisted the righting of wrongs. Unthinking men, men used to old customs and old thoughts, refused to alter their ways. And many others were fearful; being unused to change, they were not ready to accept what was for them a revolution in their lives.

And so these court decisions that have inspired such enthusiasm from many of our citizens stand in need of even further support. The voices of the judges have struck a note of conscience in the breast of America, and America has been stirred to new efforts in behalf of an old idealism. But so entrenched an evil is not so easily overcome. The rock of selfishness, the hard core of racial injustice, is not so easily dissolved. Idealism alone is not enough. There must be a recognition by all our people that we have been wrong, morally wrong, in our treatment of the Negro. There must be a day of repentance. There must be a determination to redress the injustice of the past and a firm resolve by all branches of the government, and by the people, that the long suffering of the Negro shall not have been in vain.

Thus we see that in the areas of religious freedom, criminal law, reapportionment, and racial justice the courts have indeed played a leading role in expanding human freedom in our time. And for this they, particularly the Supreme Court, have been subjected to a barrage of calumny and vilification in some parts of our country. Even some thinking men, men of good will whose roots in the fight for human freedom go very deep, deplore the leadership the current Supreme Court has given in the fight for social and political justice. They say they fear the rule of judges. I say their fears are foolish fancies. In expanding human freedom, the judges have nothing to enforce their rule but the conscience of America. And as long as we are ruled by the informed and challenged conscience of America, we have nothing to fear.

The Case of the Pentagon Papers:
Knee Deep in the "Political Thicket"

New York Times v. United States

In June, 1971, The New York Times *began publication of a large part of a 47-volume Pentagon study on the origins and conduct of the war in Vietnam. These documents, still classified "Top Secret—Sensitive" by the Defense Department, had been released to the* Times *by Professor Daniel Ellsberg and had been in the possession of the newspaper for several months, during which time its staff had edited, analyzed, and prepared the papers for publication. On June 18, The* Washington Post *also began to publish the documents. The government urged the newspapers to stop publication in the interest of national security. Both refused. The government then sought injunctions in the federal district courts in New York and the District of Columbia. Both district courts denied the injunctions. The court of appeals in Washington D.C., upheld the district courts' action, but the court of appeals in the second New York circuit issued a restraining order against the* Times *in order for the government to appeal to the Supreme Court; the court of appeals in Washington D.C., then followed suit and restrained the* Post *from publication pending review by the Supreme Court. Both cases were brought to the Supreme Court on writs of* certiorari. *On June 26, the Supreme Court held hearings even though the written briefs from the lower courts arrived less than two hours beforehand. Four days later the Supreme Court handed down its* per curiam *decision, followed by individual opinions by each Justice.*

The controversy surrounding the publication of the Pentagon Papers involved a number of important political and legal issues: separation of powers, the power of the President in foreign policy-making, judicial policy-making involving judicial activism as opposed to restraint, and freedom of the press. The case is also an excellent example of the Supreme Court's entering the political thicket, *a term long used to describe an issue that, in the opinion of the Supreme Court, would be better left to the "political" branches of government or to the people themselves. In such cases the Supreme Court usually justifies its intervention on the grounds that there is the "threat of imminent harm" to the claimant or that there is "no other available remedy."—A. M. S. and E. W.*

PER CURIAM.
We granted certiorari in these cases in which the United States seeks to

Source: *New York Times* v. *United States* 403 U.S. 713 (1971).

enjoin the *New York Times* and the *Washington Post* from publishing the contents of a classified study entitled "History of U.S. Decision-Making Process on Viet Nam Policy."

"Any system of prior restraints of expression comes to this Court bearing a heavy presumption against its constitutional validity." *Bantam Books, Inc.* v. *Sullivan.* . . ; see also *Near* v. *Minnesota.* . . . The Government "thus carries a heavy burden of showing justification for the enforcement of such a restraint." *Organization for a Better Austin* v. *Keefe.* . . . The District Court for the Southern District of New York in the *New York Times* case and the District Court for the District of Columbia and the Court of Appeals for the District of Columbia Circuit in the *Washington Post* case held that the Government had not met that burden. We agree.

The judgment of the Court of Appeals for the District of Columbia Circuit is therefore affirmed. The order of the Court of Appeals for the Second Circuit is reversed and the case is remanded with directions to enter a judgment affirming the judgment of the District Court for the Southern District of New York. The stays entered June 25, 1971, by the Court are vacated. The mandates shall issue forthwith.

So ordered.

Mr. Justice Black, with whom Mr. Justice Douglas joins, concurring.

I adhere to the view that the Government's case against the *Washington Post* should have been dismissed and that the injunction against the *New York Times* should have been vacated without oral argument when the cases were first presented to this Court. I believe that every moment's continuance of the injunctions against these newspapers amounts to a flagrant, indefensible, and continuing violation of the First Amendment. . . . In my view it is unfortunate that some of my Brethren are apparently willing to hold that the publication of news may sometimes be enjoined. Such a holding would make a shambles of the First Amendment. . . .

In the First Amendment the Founding Fathers gave the free press the protection it must have to fulfill its essential role in our democracy. The press was to serve the governed, not the governors. . . . Only a free and unrestrained press can effectively expose deception in government. And paramount among the responsibilities of a free press is the duty to prevent any part of the government from deceiving the people and sending them off to distant lands to die of foreign fevers and foreign shot and shell. In my view, far from deserving condemnation for their courageous reporting, the *New York Times,* the *Washington Post,* and other newspapers should be commended for serving the purpose that the Founding Fathers saw so clearly. . . .

Mr. Justice Douglas with whom Mr. Justice Black joins, concurring. . . .

The dominant purpose of the First Amendment was to prohibit the widespread practice of governmental suppression of embarrassing information. It is common knowledge that the First Amendment was adopted against the widespread use of the common law of seditious libel to punish the dissemination of material that is embarrassing to the powers-that-be. . . . The present cases will, I think, go down in history as the most dramatic illustration of that principle. A debate of large proportions goes on in the Nation over our posture in Vietnam. That debate antedated the disclosure of the contents of the present documents. The latter are highly relevant to the debate in progress.

Secrecy in government is fundamentally anti-democratic, perpetuating bureaucratic errors. Open debate and discussion of public issues are vital to our national health. On public questions there should be "open and robust debate." . . .

Mr. Justice Brennan, concurring.

I write separately in these cases only to emphasize what should be apparent: that our judgment in the present cases may not be taken to indicate the propriety, in the future, of issuing temporary stays and restraining orders to block the publication of material sought to be suppressed by the Government. . . .

The error which has pervaded these cases from the outset was the granting of any injunctive relief whatsoever, interim or otherwise. The entire thrust of the Government's claim throughout these cases has been that publication of the material sought to be enjoined "could," or "might," or "may" prejudice the national interest in various ways. But the First Amendment tolerates absolutely no prior judicial restraints of the press predicated upon surmise or conjecture that untoward consequences may result. . . . Thus, only governmental allegation and proof that publication must inevitably, directly and immediately cause the occurrence of an event kindred to imperiling the safety of a transport already at sea can support even the issurance of an interim restraining order. In no event may mere conclusions be sufficient: for if the Executive Branch seeks judicial aid in preventing publication, it must inevitably submit the basis upon which that aid is sought to scrutiny by the judiciary. And therefore, every restraint issued in this case, whatever its form, has violated the First Amendment—and none the less so because that restraint was justified as necessary to afford the court an opportunity to examine the claim more thoroughly. Unless and until the Government has clearly made out its case, the First Amendment commands that no injunction may issue.

Mr. Justice Stewart, with whom Mr. Justice White joins, concurring. . . .

In the absence of the governmental checks and balances present in other areas of our national life, the only effective restraint upon executive policy and power in the areas of national defense and international affairs may lie in an enlightened citizenry—in an informed and critical public opinion which alone can here protect the values of democratic government. . . .

Yet it is elementary that the successful conduct of international diplomacy and the maintenance of an effective national defense require both confidentiality and secrecy. . . .

I think there can be but one answer to this dilemma, if dilemma it be. The responsibility must be where the power is. If the Constitution gives the Executive a large degree of unshared power in the conduct of foreign affairs and the maintenance of our national defense, then under the Constitution the Executive must have the largely unshared duty to determine and preserve the degree of internal security necessary to exercise that power successfully. . . . [I]t is clear to me that it is the constitutional duty of the Executive—as a matter of sovereign prerogative and not as a matter of law as the courts know law—. . . to protect the confidentiality necessary to carry out its responsibilities in the fields of international relations and national defense. . . .

. . . [I]n the cases before us we are asked neither to construe specific regulations nor to apply specific laws. We are asked, instead, to perform a function that the Constitution gave to the Executive, not the Judiciary. . . . I join the judgments of the Court.

Mr. Justice White, with whom Mr. Justice Stewart joins, concurring.

I concur in today's judgments, but only because of the concededly extraordinary protection against prior restraints enjoyed by the press under our constitutional system. I do not say that in no circumstances would the First Amendment permit an injunction against publishing information about government plans or operations. Nor, after examining the materials the Government characterizes as the most sensitive and destructive, can I deny that revelation of these documents will do substantial damage to public interests. Indeed, I am confident that their disclosure will have that result. But I nevertheless agree that the United States has not satisfied the very heavy burden which it must meet to warrant an injunction against publication in these cases, at least in the absence of express and appropriately limited congressional authorization for prior restraints in circumstances such as these. . . .

Mr. Justice Marshall, concurring. . . .

The problem here is whether in this particular case the Executive Branch has authority to invoke the equity jurisdiction of the courts to protect what it believes to be the national interest. . . .

It would . . . be utterly inconsistent with the concept of separation of power for this Court to use its power of contempt to prevent behavior that Congress has specifically declined to prohibit. . . .

Either the Government has the power under statutory grant to use traditional criminal law to protect the country or, if there is no basis for arguing that Congress has made the activity a crime, it is plain that Congress has specifically refused to grant the authority the Government seeks from this Court. In either case this Court does not have authority to grant the requested relief. It is not for this Court to fling itself into every breach perceived by some Government official nor is it for this Court to take on itself the burden of enacting law, especially law that Congress has refused to pass. . . .

Mr. Chief Justice Burger, dissenting. . . .

Only those who view the First Amendment as an absolute in all circumstances—a view I respect, but reject—can find such a case as this to be simple or easy.

This case is not simple for another and more immediate reason. We do not know the facts of the case. No District Judge knew all the facts. No Court of Appeals judge knew all the facts. No member of this Court knows all the facts. . . .

I suggest we are in this posture because these cases have been conducted in unseemly haste. Mr. Justice Harlan covers the chronology of events demonstrating the hectic pressures under which these cases have been processed and I need not restate them. . . .

The consequence of all this melancholy series of events is that we literally do not know what we are acting on. As I see it we have been forced to deal with litigation concerning rights of great magnitude without an adequate record, and surely without time for adequate treatment either in the prior proceedings or in this Court. . . . I agree with Mr. Justice Harlan and Mr. Justice Blackmun but I am not prepared to reach the merits.

I would affirm the Court of Appeals for the Second Circuit and allow the District Court to complete the trial aborted by our grant of certiorari meanwhile preserving the *status quo* in the *Post* case. I would direct that the District Court on remand give priority to the *Times* case to the exclusion of all other business of that court but I would not set arbitrary deadlines. . . .

Mr. Justice Harlan, with whom the Chief Justice and Mr. Justice Blackmun join, dissenting. . . .

With all respect, I consider that the Court has been almost irresponsibly feverish in dealing with these cases. . . .

Forced as I am to reach the merits of these cases, I dissent from the opinion and judgments of the Court. . . .

It is plain to me that the scope of the judicial function in passing upon the activities of the executive Branch of the Government in the field of foreign affairs is very narrowly restricted. This view is, I think, dictated by the concept of separation of powers upon which our constitutional system rests. . . .

I agree that, in performance of its duty to protect the values of the First Amendment against political pressures, the judiciary must review the initial Executive determination to the point of satisfying itself that the subject matter of the dispute does lie within the proper compass of the President's foreign relations power. . . . Moreover, the judiciary may properly insist that the determination that disclosure of the subject matter would irreparably impair the national security be made by the head of the Executive Department concerned—here the Secretary of State or the Secretary of Defense—after actual personal consideration by that officer. . . .

THE TRIAL JUDGE

Harry W. Jones

"In the long run," wrote Judge Cardozo, "there is no guarantee of justice except the personality of the judge." Basic reforms in court organization and sound and imaginative new procedures for handling the mounting flow of civil claims and criminal prosecutions are indispensable conditions for meeting today's crisis in the courts. But law can never be much better than the men who administer and apply it. Legal rules and procedures do not operate automatically, nor cases decide themselves.—H. W. J.

A certain Bishop of Paris, known throughout Europe for his great learning and humility, came to the conclusion that he was unworthy of his high

Source: "The Trial Judge—Role Analysis and Profile," *The Courts, the Public, and the Law Explosion,* Harry W. Jones (ed.) (New York: The American Assembly, Columbia University, and Englewood Cliffs, N.J., Prentice-Hall, Inc., 1965), pp. 124–145. Reprinted by permission of The American Assembly.

place in the Church and successfully petitioned the Pope for reassignment to service as a simple parish priest. The legend is regrettably vague as to whether this happened in the twelfth century or the thirteenth, or indeed as to whether our almost unbecomingly humble prelate was bishop in Paris or some place else, but it is perfectly clear as to what came of the reassignment. After less than a year of parish work, the former bishop was back in Rome with another petition, this one praying for his restoration to episcopal status, and for good and sufficient reason. "If I am unworthy to be Bishop of Paris," he said,

> how much more unworthy am I to be priest of a parish. As bishop, I was remote from men and women of lowly station, my shortcomings and weaknesses concealed from them by distance and ecclesiastical dignity. But as parish priest, I move intimately each day among the members of my flock, endeavoring by comfort, counsel and admonition to make their hard lot on earth seem better than it is. I *am* the Church to them; when my faith flags or my wisdom fails or my patience wears thin, it is the Church that has failed them. *Demote* me, Your Holiness, and make me a bishop again, for I have learned how much easier it is to be a saintly bishop than to be a godly priest.

The trial judge is the parish priest of our legal order. The impression that prevails in society concerning the justice or injustice of our legal institutions depends almost entirely on the propriety, efficiency, and humaneness of observed trial court functioning. "Important as it is that people should get justice," said the Victorian chancellor, Lord Herschell, "it is even more important that they be made to feel and see that they are getting it." This profound truth about law in society is deeply rooted in the common-law tradition, and it fully justified the focus of this book on trial courts and what they do. The typical citizen will never see an appellate court in action, but there is every likelihood that he will sooner or later be drawn into the operation of one or another of our trial courts, whether as litigant, witness, or juryman.

The Trial Judge as a Representative of Justice

Aristotle was surely right when he said that members of the public look upon the judge as "living justice," that is, as the personification of the legal order. For better or worse, it is the trial judge upon whom this representative responsibility falls in our society. He *is* the law for most people and most legal purposes. Whenever a trial judge fails in probity, energy, objectivity, or patience, his failure is observable and cannot but impair public fidelity to law. This is true even and particularly of the minor magistrate in a police court or a small-claims tribunal. He may be at the bottom of the judicial totem pole, but it is there that the exposure is often greatest and the strains of the judge's role manifest for all to see.

Indeed, a case can be made that a judge's importance as a justice representative varies inversely with his rank in the judicial hierarchy. There is a public welfare perspective in which the personality of the appellate-court justice seems less significant than that of the trial judge of general jurisdiction, and the personality of the police-court magistrate more significant than either of them. Thoughtful citizens are concerned and apprehensive about the decreasing respect for law and social order evidenced by mounting crime statistics, particularly by the sharp rise in arrests for petty offenses, narcotics addiction, drunkenness, and juvenile delinquency. These are offenses of social alienation. The juvenile delinquent and the narcotics addict are not professional criminals, at least not yet. It is a great task of the legal order to win back for society as many of the alienated as are not irretrievably lost to it.

Scholars of society advise us that great symbolic importance, for good or for harm, can attach to the juvenile offender's or the alcoholic's early encounters with the institutions of the legal order, and particularly with the judge in his case. . . . When the young or petty offender's first encounter with the legal order takes the form of a mass shape-up, with each subject for adjudication taking his place in a long queue for split-second disposition of his case by a tired, bored, or irascible magistrate, the social effects can be disastrous. If organized society treats a petty offender or a neglected child as if he were a blank for machine processing, there may be no getting him back from social alientation into useful citizenship.

To be sure, unbearable time pressures are imposed on our so-called "inferior courts" by the quantitative explosion in criminal law administration. It is reckless parsimony for an affluent society to withhold the modest expenditures that would be necessary to create the reality and appearance of compassionate deliberation in the operations of our lower criminal courts. Available judicial manpower there must be increased at least three-fold, and speedily before further irremediable damage is done. But the problem calls for more than an increase in undifferentiated units of judicial manpower. It is equally important that the new judges brought to the lower criminal courts not be professional misfits or clubhouse hacks, but men and women of understanding, firmness, and imagination, genuinely concerned about the social consequences of their adjudicative work and earnestly determined to do something constructive about it.

There are all sorts and conditions of trial judges, ranging in professional status from prestigious United States district judges and state judges of general jurisdiction to lowly magistrates whose social importance is hardly grasped at all by the legal profession or the public at large. There are many areas of judicial specialization, each requiring that its judges be persons of unusual and particular competence and experience: divorce courts, probate or surrogate's courts, children's courts, and many others. What these sorts and conditions of trial judges have in common is that they are all engaged in bringing law's general principles and commands down to the people law governs and serves. A legal order without trial judges of high professional and moral qualifications is like an army without dependable field-grade combat officers or a school system without able and devoted classroom teachers. Planning and policy coordination must come from headquarters (in law from the appellate courts) but it is out in the field that the day-to-day work is done.

It will be a thesis of this essay that genuinely effective service as a trial judge calls for qualities of mind, heart, and character that may differ from but are in no way inferior to the qualities required for effective service on a high appellate court, even a state court of last resort or the Supreme Court of the United States. When and how can it be brought home to the legal profession and to the public generally that a man unworthy by character and temperament to be an appellate judge is, in a real sense, even more unworthy to be entrusted with the highly visible powers and responsibilities of a trial judge? There is a growing recognition of this in the selection of judges for high-prestige trial courts of general jurisdiction and for courts charged with responsibility in delicate matters of juvenile behavior and family law. But the recognition has been slow in coming and has still not been extended to awareness of the importance of far higher standards than now prevail in the recruitment of personnel for the inferior courts at the bottom rung of the judicial hierarchy.

The Central Importance of Trial Courts in Adjudication

Suppose that we were to get the appraisal of a thoughtful and experienced trial judge on what has been said so far about the role of the trial judge as a kind of justice representative. In all probability, he would concede that he inevitably carries a certain responsibility as one of the law's principal representatives and witnesses to society, although it might make him a bit uneasy in his daily courtroom work if he thought too much about it. But he would insist that his role as representative of public justice is only incidental to his main job and that his main job is the business of adjudication. This is a sensible and thoroughly professional way of looking at the matter, and no one could quarrel too much with it. Certainly judges are appraised by their peers not in terms of their sensitivity to human relations but in terms of their effectiveness as adjudicative officials. We turn, then, to an analysis of the trial judge's basic role as a decision-making and decision-influencing officer of the legal order.

Common Misconceptions of the Judge's Role

How important, really, is the work of the trial judge qua adjudicative official? The question is not as fanciful or simple-minded as it might seem to be on first impression, and it is often pressed by non-lawyers, even by behavioral scientists of considerable legal sophistication, at conferences on judicial selection and law administration. Such doubts as to whether a particular trial judge's qualifications, or lack of them, make any genuine difference as to the ultimate outcome of a case seem to proceed from two more or less related preconceptions: *First,* that ours is a "government of laws and not of men," from which the inference is readily drawn that one judge will read the law's mandate about the same way as another will, if it be assumed that both of them are men of probity and learned enough in formal legal sources to have passed a bar examination; and *Second,* that a trial judge, in any event, has several tiers of appellate courts above him, and his appellate betters will surely catch and correct any misreading of the law of which he may be guilty at the trial stage of a controversy. On this showing, say the doubters, how can a civil suit or criminal prosecution be affected, as to its final result, by the circumstance that the particular trial judge before whom it comes is, or is not, a man of resourcefulness, wisdom, and uncommon professional skill?

The question just put is, of course, a crucial one for the current proposals . . . that are designed to improve prevailing standards of judicial selection in the United States. If the intellect and personality of the trial judge make relatively little difference on how cases are finally decided, why should the public generally be too much concerned about judicial selection, at least about the qualifications, questions of elementary honesty aside, of aspirants for the trial bench? In fact, the prevailing public attitude, even among leaders of community opinion, may be about as suggested. If this is not the prevailing attitude, it is curious that reasonably alert citizens and civic groups should be as acquiescent as they are about the not infrequent appointment of second- or third-rate lawyers to first-rate trial courts and that intelligent people should go to the polls and vote for a party-leader-nominated slate of trial-court judges, without having the foggiest notion of the intellectual and moral qualifications of the candidates.

The conceptions that contribute to this widespread under-appraisal of the work of the trial courts have no support whatever in the realities of the adjudicative process. A trial judge's intellect, energy, and character, or his deficiencies in any of these qualities, will make a great difference, can make all the difference in the world, on how the cases tried before him are finally decided. The trial judge is the key man in our system of adjudication. In the great bulk of litigated cases, he is by far the most important and influential participant, and this whether or not the case at hand is a jury case, whether or not it is appealed from trial-court judgment to one or more higher appellate courts, and whether or not the legalities of the controversy involve the interpretation of a federal or state statute or a question of common law.

Legal Rules and Concrete Cases: The Inescapability of Choice

We need not pause too long to dispose of the hoary fiction that judges have no discretion, no choices between alternative decisions, in "a government of laws and not of men." The notion that a juge merely pronounces results already preordained and fixed by the rules of the legal system is the long-discarded "slot machine" theory of the judicial process and almost as misdescriptive of the trial judge's work as it is of the work of appellate courts. This is not to say that the established substantive law is always or usually uncertain in its application to the particular controversies that reach the courts for decision. In most cases it is doubtless true that there is little room for argument as to the legal rule that controls the dispute between the parties, once the facts of the case are "found" by the judge, or by the jury under the judge's guidance and supervision. Legislative foresight is finite, however, and there is no limit to the variety of situations that can arise in a complex and dynamic society. No legal code, no aggregate of statutory directions and judge-made precedents, can ever furnish explicit and unambiguous commands for every conceivable case.

If the law were truly and everywhere as certain as the "government of laws and not of men" formula would have it, why would businessmen of good sense hire lawyers of distinction to advise and represent them, at fees running into six figures, when the services of a low-status professional might be secured for a few hundred dollars? Why, for that matter, would the Supreme Court of the United States divide as often as it does, by five to four or six to three? No, on any account of the judicial process, there is a substantial incidence of cases in which the law is unclear, that is, in which the judge has no clear mandate to decide one way or the other and must choose between the alternative decisions open to him on the basis of his own best judgment as to which decision is fair between the parties and sound as a matter of generally applicable public policy. Whatever the incidence of these hard or "unprovided for" cases may be—even if it be calculated very conservatively at no more than one-fifth or even one-tenth of the cases that reach the courts—it is indisputable that the work of a judge involves the high art of prudential judgment. To quote Cardozo:

> It is when the colors do not match, when the references in the index fail, when there is no decisive precedent, that the serious business of the judge begins.

A trial judge lacking in social insight, prudence, and intellectual resourcefulness is incapable of measuring up to the challenge of this aspect of his serious business. It must be kept in mind that in any hard case in which his decision on the troublesome question of law is not appealed to a higher court, the trial judge's error of law and wisdom can effect an irremediable miscarriage of justice.

The Upper-Court Myth

What of the other preconception that underlies public discounting of the importance of the trial judge's role as an adjudicative official? What merit is there in the suggestion that the center of gravity of American adjudication is really in the appellate courts and that the determinations of trial judges are provisional only and subject to ready correction on appeal? The realities of the American judicial system have been obscured, in scholarly writing as in public discussion, by the stubborn persistence of what the late Judge Jerome Frank called the "upper-court myth," the notion that everything will be all right in the house of justice so long as appeals from trial-court decisions are freely available and the upper courts manned by judges of wisdom, experience, and professional competence. In this view, which has been contributed to by the almost exclusive preoccupation of American legal education with the reported opinions of appellate courts, the trial-court stage of a civil suit or criminal prosecution seems a mere preliminary bout; the main event will not begin until the case reaches the appellate court of last resort. Political scientists have absorbed the upper-court myth as uncritically as their scholarly brothers in the law schools. For every book or article analyzing the functioning of the trial courts as agencies of government and large-scale public administration, there are a dozen or more given to charting the batting averages of individual justices of the Supreme Court of the United States on this or that issue of constitutional law or to developing the logical or policy subtleties of striking pieces of rhetoric in Supreme Court opinions.

The extent to which the upper-court myth distorts the relative significance of trial-court functioning and appellate-court functioning is manifest even if we put aside, for the moment, the assembly-line operations of police courts, traffic courts, small claims courts, and the like and consider only the traditional and substantial civil and criminal cases that are heard, as of first instance, in trial courts of general jurisdiction. It is a safe guess that at least 90 per cent of even these blue ribbon controversies are determined and controlled, as to practical outcome, by rules of law applied and facts "found" at the trial-court stage, as against 10 per cent at most that are controlled in result by what happens to them in the appellate courts. It is in the appellate courts that precedents are forged for the future and statutes given their authoritative interpretation and effect, but, as concerns the ultimate adjudicative fate of litigated controversies, the trial courts outweigh the appellate courts by at least nine to one.

RELATIVELY FEW CASES ARE APPEALED. The quantitative appraisal just recorded may be surprising to a non-lawyer reader. Since a right to appeal is generously, perhaps too generously, afforded in our judicial system, how can it be maintained that the practical outcome of a substantial lawsuit is set and determined, ninety times out of a hundred, by what happens to the controversy in the trial court? The first and obvious point in the explanation is that relatively few cases, perhaps 10 per cent at most, are ever appealed at all. Although our procedural system does not discourage appeals, as the English system does by assessing heavy fees and costs against an unsuccessful appellant, appeals are expensive and time-consuming, and the statistical evidence warns sufficiently that incomparably more trial-court decisions are affirmed on appeal than reversed. Even in jurisdictions where the ratio of appeals to trials is far higher (as in the federal courts) than one in ten, a substantial number of appeals are taken with no great expectation of success, either as a delaying tactic to impose pressure for settlement of the case at less than the amount of trial-court judgment or as a means of assuring a disappointed and indignant client that every possible step is being taken in his behalf.

FINDINGS OF FACT CAN BE DECISIVE. The rising incidence of appeals . . . suggests this question: Would the work of the trial courts become less significant if a full third or more of trial-court decisions were taken on appeal to a higher court? Even this would require no drastic modification of the proposition that the ultimate fate of most cases, whether appealed or not, is determined by what happens to them at the trial stage. It is in the trial court that the facts of a case are "found," and for most cases the findings of fact are decisive. Of the mine-run of controversies that reach the courts, relatively few—one in five, perhaps, as we have seen—turn on questions as to what the "law" of the case is. The usual dispute is as to what the true facts are. Consider, for example, the automobile accident-personal injury cases that have inundated trial courts of general jurisdiction throughout the United States. The central issue in dispute between the plaintiff and the defendant (or the defendant's liability insurance company) is rarely an issue of substantive law, that is, rarely a question whether, on some agreed or conceded set of facts, the law of the state concerned would or would not authorize a judgment for damages in the plaintiff's favor. The crucial issues are far likelier to be factual in character: Was the defendant driving sixty-five miles an hour in a thirty-five-miles-an-hour speed zone, as the plaintiff asserts, or was the defendant proceeding at a cautious thirty-miles an hour, as he contends he was? Had the red light changed to green before the plaintiff started to cross the intersection, as he and his witnesses swear that it had, or was the green light still in defendant driver's favor, as he and the passengers in his car swear that it was? Is the injured plaintiff permanently disabled for his former employment, as he and his physician testify, or is his injury temporary and capable of simple surgical correction, as the defendant's medical witnesses declare?

Similarly, in commercial litigation and in criminal prosecutions, the central issue in dispute is far more often what lawyers call an "issue of fact" than an "issue of law." What precisely did the property owner say when the contractor came to his office and told him that the construction would not be ready by the date fixed in the contract, or could not be completed for the originally agreed contract price? Did the seller call the buyer's attention specifically to the presence of an arbitration clause embedded in the fine print on the back of the seller's standard contract form? The seller says yes, the buyer says no, and which of them is to be believed? Or, in a criminal case, was the accused really in Peoria on the day of the bank robbery, as his alibi witnesses swear that he was, or are the prosecution's eyewitnesses testifying truthfully and accurately when they say that they saw him that day running out of the held-up bank? Questions like these are the grist of the adjudicative mill, even in cases of first magnitude to the parties involved. Once the factual dispute has been resolved, the facts "found" in favor of one party or the other, the result of the case, more often than not, is foreordained.

When injustice occurs in our legal system, it is less often because of some archaicism or unfairness in the general law than because of some error in the ascertainment of facts, that is, from some failure in the reconstruction at the trial of what had actually happened outside the courtroom. Here is Judge Frank's appraisal:

> Trained lawyers know the "jurisprudence" relevant to murder trials or automobile accident trials and can prophesy with a high degree of reliability what rules will be applied in such litigation. But what of it? The layman wants to know whether these rules will be applied to the actual facts. . . . If a man, defeated in a suit because of a mistake about the facts, goes to jail or the electric chair or loses his business, will it solace him to learn that there was no possible doubt concerning the applicable legal principles?

The trial court, as the agency of the state for the hearing and determination of disputed issues of fact, holds the central position in the practical administration of justice.

FINDINGS OF FACT NOT REVIEWABLE ON APPEAL. . . . appellate courts rarely undertake to review trial-court findings of fact. The appealing party may be able to secure reversal of a trial-court judgment against him if he can persuade the appellate court that the trial judge was wrong on his "law," as where the jury was given an instruction embodying an erroneous view of the substantive law, or inadmissible and prejudicial evidence was admitted at the trial over the appellant's objection. But there are relatively few situations in which an appellate court will listen to an argument that the version of the facts accepted as true by the jury, or by the trial judge sitting as trier of the facts without a jury, was a false version or one against the weight of the evidence at the trial. Reasons both of tradition and of good sense explain this general limitation of the appellate process to legal (as distinguished from factual) issues. There would be no end to litigation if factual disputes could be recontested at each successive tier of the judicial hierarchy, and appellate judges, having only a printed record before them, are properly reluctant to second-guess a trial judge or a panel of jurymen who observed the demeanor of the witnesses at the trial and heard their examination and cross-examination. Thus the factual element in a case, the element which, as we have seen, is the decisive one in most litigated controversies, is decided with substantial finality in the trial court. This should be enough to dispose of the upper-court myth.

Relation of the Trial Judge to Jury Fact-Finding

Nothing a trial judge does in his role as an adjudicative official is more important than his work in relation to the determination of disputed issues of fact. This is clear enough when the trial judge is himself the sole trier of the facts, as he often is when the case is of a category which, historically, does not call for the summoning of a jury (e.g., a suit for an injunction or other "equitable remedy") or when the parties to a civil suit or the accused in a criminal case "wave" the right to jury trial and consent to have the case's issues of fact as well as its issues of law determined by the court without a jury. But how important is the judge's role when the issues of fact are for the "twelve good men and true" in the jury box? In a jury case, is the trial judge much more than a keeper of order and master of ceremonies?

The institution of the jury trial retains greater vitality in the land of its transplantation than in the land of its historical origin. In England, jury trials have been abolished for almost all civil litigation; in the United States, federal and state constitutional provisions preserve the jury institution not only for serious criminal prosecutions but also for the generality of civil cases. Even in this country, however, the trial judge is far from a passive bystander in a jury case. Through his rulings on questions of the admissibility of evidence, he controls or largely influences the testimonial data from which the jury will draw its inferences as to the truth of the plaintiff's and the defendant's competing versions of the facts of the case. The trial judge, within certain more or less defined limits, may set aside the jury verdict in a civil suit and order a new trial of the case when he believes that the verdict at which the jury arrived was capricious or wholly unsupported by the evidence before it. He may do this, too, in a criminal case if the jury comes in with a verdict of guilty, although our legal system, for reasons of fairness symbolized by the phrase "double jeopardy," gives conclusiveness and finality to a jury verdict of not guilty. Most important of all the forms of the trial judge's participation in jury fact-finding is his "charge" or instruction to the jury, in which he expounds the law to be applied by the jury in reaching its verdict, telling the jurymen, in effect, the facts they must find to be true (beyond a reasonable doubt in criminal cases or, in civil cases, supported by the preponderance of the evidence) before they can bring in a verdict for one side or the other in the controversy.

If the personality of the trial judge is such that he can establish a working rapport with the juries empaneled in his courtroom, the judge becomes the jury's effective guide and counselor, virtually a full partner in the jury's discharge of its decisional responsibility. Top flight trial judges have always been able to establish close working relations with their juries, but this achievement requires that the judge be possessed of unusual talents of communication, talents not widely shared by members of the legal profession. The high art of charging a jury furnishes a good illustration of the point at hand. A run-of-the-mill trial judge will phrase his instruction to the jury in impenetrably technical terms; a charge so worded is a pure ritual, hardly more influential on the jury's deliberations than it would have been if delivered in classical Greek. A genuinely qualified trial judge has the capacity to translate legal jargon into English intelligible to lay jurymen and can, without endangering the legal soundness of his instruction, give the jury a useful analysis of the task it has ahead of it. Sensitivity to jury relations and skills at communication are among the qualities that are most imperative for effective service as a trial judge. It is regrettable that these attributes are taken account of as infrequently as they are in professional and public discussions of the qualifications for judicial office.

Strains and Demands in the Role of the Trial Judge

A lawyer raised to the bench by appointment or election comes at once under the influence of a great and continuing tradition of craftsmanship and social accountability, perhaps the most powerful craft tradition that survives in contemporary society. If the lawyer was a good man before his elevation, he will almost certainly be a better man after it, at least as goodness is measured in the legal universe. If he was mediocre before, appointment or election to the bench is likely to make him less mediocre. Even if he was the kind of lawyer who should never have been made a judge, and many such unpromising candidates reach the bench every year, his temperament and character will probably show at least some improvement after he dons the robe.

This demonstrable fact about the tendency of judicial office to elevate the moral and intellectual standards of the men and women who attain it is sometimes drawn on to support a kind of argument that there is no reason for great concern about the professional and moral qualifications of judicial hopefuls, that the tradition will somehow ennoble even the least qualified man. This wildly overoptimistic suggestion claims too much even for the great adjudicative tradition of our common law. To be sure, the tradition can transform an indifferent lawyer into a somewhat less indifferent judge, but in law, as elsewhere in life, one cannot make a silk purse out of a sow's ear. Nowhere in the whole range of public office are weaknesses of character, intellect, or psychic constitution revealed more mercilessly than in the discharge of the responsibilities of a trial judge. The strains and demands of the role could be illustrated in a dozen different contexts; we will consider two of them, the tensions involved in the trial judge's relations with the lawyers appearing before him, and the burdens he must sustain in the sentencing of persons convicted on criminal charges.

Judge-Lawyer Relations in an Adversary System of Litigation

American court procedures, like the English system from which it springs, is adversary in character both in its approach to the determination of contested issues of law and in its approach to the even more important matter, for most cases, of determining the truth of disputed issues of fact. The opposed parties appear in the trial court through advocates, professional champions, each of whom is pledged to present the legal theory, or the version of the disputed facts, favorable to his client's side of the case. It is only in a limited sense that the trial lawyer is an "officer of the court"; actually the advocacy model embodied in the common law canons of professional ethics is that of the honorable partisan who fights honestly and fairly but wholly in his client's cause. This trial by forensic combat strikes most laymen as a curious, even eccentric, way of going about the hearing and determination of controversies. Most lawyers feel, as I most assuredly do, that the adversary system, with all its conceded shortcomings, is a better procedure than any other yet devised for arriving at the sound development of legal principles and the substantial justice of particular litigated cases. There are certain postulates, however, on which even we lawyers base our confidence in the adversary system. The premise of our system of adjudication is that the adversary performance will go on with a cast of characters composed of an equally powerful advocate for each side and a trial judge who is at least the equal of either of them in legal acumen, energy, and force of character.

DEFECTS OF RESOLUTION. In American procedural theory, the conventional description characterizes the trial judge as the "umpire" of the contest. Few American judges intervene as actively as their English common law predecessors did in the examination of witnesses and other aspects of trial management. This is true today as concerns jury trials in criminal cases in the two countries; it is suggestive of the difference that the English idiom speaks of a criminal case as tried *by* the judge, while we speak of it as tried *before* the judge. But the role of umpire in an adversary court proceeding is not one that can be played effectively by a judge who is mediocre in intellect or professional skill, lacking in decisiveness, or in any way emotionally insecure. Courtroom decorum has to be maintained with a firm hand if cases are to be tried fairly and expeditiously, and as a case proceeds the trial judge is called upon to make many rulings that are of great strategic and tactical importance for the outcome of the litigation. These rulings, characteristically, have to be made by the trial judge "from the hip," that is, under the pressures of the trial and without opportunity for extended consultation of the formal authorities in the law books. Many trial judges who have later moved up to high appellate courts have spoken gratefully of the more relaxed pace and opportunity for reflection they found in appellate work after years of the hurly-burly of trial court proceedings. It is as if a teacher had suddenly been translated from a classroom assignment in a problem high school to the relative tranquility of a post as assistant superintendent of schools.

Former President Truman's classic injunction, "If you can't stand the heat, get out of the kitchen," applies superbly to trial judges and particularly to judges of the trial courts of general jurisdiction. The trial judge who is shaky in professional understanding, imperfect in moral resolution, or unduly conciliatory in personality will inevitably be overpowered and overborne by forceful and aggressive trial counsel. The evil that weak judges do, less often from partiality, as commonly supposed, than from simple psychic inability to stand up to abrasive or stronger willed leaders of the trial bar is a bitter but largely untold story in the administration of justice. If the adversary system is to work justly, the trial judge must command the respect, not necessarily the affection, of every advocate who may appear before him, however powerful or distinguished the advocate may be. This status he can never attain unless he has every resource of self-respect: confidence in his judgment, willingness to act on the balance of probabilities, and inner assurance of his authenticity in the role he has undertaken. The umpire who thinks himself inferior to any player on the field will never be able to call 'em as he sees 'em.

THE SIN OF ARROGANCE. In inadequate men of other psychic constitutions, the tensions of the trial judge's role can be manifested in a quite different way but one equally violative of the postulates of the adversary system. Every multi-judge trial court of general jurisdiction has at least one tyrant in residence. Sometimes he is a short-tempered man of professional ability and irascible disposition. If his technical qualifications are outstanding, they may compensate in large degree for the unpleasantness of his personality, although the execessively crusty judge will leave a bad taste with litigants, witnesses, and jurymen, however impressive his technical endowments may be to the lawyers in the casc.

Far more often, as would be expected, the judicial tyrant is a man of inferior intellect and professional skill whose impatient and overbearing manner reflects deeply rooted feelings of his own inferiority. In any metropolitan community, arrogant judges of this second category are readily identified by experienced trial lawyers. There are regular ways by which the sophisticated advocate manages to avoid having his cases assigned to them for trial, with the ironical consequence that the worst judges are likely to get more than their ratable share of the cases in which trial counsel are inferior or inexperienced, and so least able to cope with impatience, oppression, or undue interference from the bench.

The very real values inherent in the adversary system of litigation are undermined when the trial judge in a case is a man of arrogant and abusive temperament. The lawyers in the controversy find it impossible to develop their cases in an effective and orderly way. Witnesses become confused or defiantly resentful. They expect harsh treatment on cross-examination by opposing counsel, but not from the judge, to whom they look for comfort and support in their unusual ordeal. The clarity and accuracy of their testimony suffers accordingly. Jurymen are estranged and disinclined to follow the instructions of their heavy-handed preceptor. The entire trial process is distorted, and the parties, certainly the losing party and often the winner, leave the courtroom with a distinct impression that their dignity has been assailed and their claims and grievances inadequately heard. In the administration of justice, Roscoe Pound once wrote, "men count more than machinery." His text applies perfectly to the trial of a civil action or criminal prosecution.

THE STRAINS OF THE ROLE ON THE BEST OF JUDGES. It has been seriously suggested now and then that aspirants to the bench should be required to go through some kind of psychoanalytic screening, as is now required of psychoanalysts themselves and gradually being extended to students preparing for the ministry, candidates for certain sensitive government positions, and a few other socially critical employments. This is not a derogatory suggestion or in any way unflattering to the men and women who now preside over American trial courts. It is rather a recognition of the critical social importance of the work of the courts and of the strains imposed by judicial office not only on problem personalities like our unduly conciliatory judge and his tyrannical opposite number but also on men and women of average or better than average patience and psychic endurance.

As claimants, defendants, and accused persons pass before him, a trial judge meets and has to put up with many more scoundrels, cheats, and liars than most other men encounter in their vocations. His work is not calculated to make him excessively optimistic concerning the natural inclinations of human nature. The lawyers who appear as counsel before him are often incompetent or barely competent, and the trial judge of first-rate intellectual and professional attainments has the good craftsman's proper impatience with shoddy work and wishes that the sorry advocates before him would get on with their business. It is hard for an able man to suffer fools gladly when they are certified members of his own profession. Sometimes the trial judge has the even more painful awareness that one of his fellow professionals of the practicing bar is trying to mislead him into acceptance of a fraudulent claim or defense or trying to badger him into some error that will cause the reversal of the trial court judgment on appeal. And, all the while, the conscientious trial judge is striving to maintain unbroken concentration on a flow of complex and conflicting evidence that may extend over many days.

The strains and psychic demands of the trial judge's role were illustrated dramatically some fifteen years ago when the leaders of the American communist party came up for trial before Judge Harold Medina, now a judge of the United States Court of Appeals, for violation of the Smith Act. The trial lasted for months, and the several counsel for the defendants did everything they could, day after wearying day, to break Judge Medina down or to taunt or exhaust him into some reversible error of trial procedure. We have wondered since whether any other lawyer of our time would have had the resilience and psychic durability to complete that trial as Judge Medina did, or even to survive it. The case was out of the ordinary, but it serves admirably to make the point that our adversary system of litigation can on occasion impose burdens that challenge the patience, spirit, and endurance of the strongest of trial judges.

The Burden of Sentencing in Criminal Cases

Severe demands are made on a trial judge's moral resources, in this case on his sensitivity and compassion, by his duty to determine and impose the sentences of persons found guilty of a crime. The judge's discretion and responsibility are large, since the general statutory precept, more likely than not, will authorize a wide range of permissible treatment of the offender: "Punishable by fine not to exceed $10,000 or by imprisonment from one to five years, or by both such fine and such imprisonment" is not an untypical sentencing provision of our day. In short, the legal rule merely fixes the outside bounds for the inescapable act of judicial discretion. Shall the offender before the court be sent to prison for five years, or one, or for some period in between, or is it perhaps appropriate that he be put on probation during good behavior and not sent to prison at all? The trial judge must decide. Nowhere else in our society is one man invested with so awful a power over the life and freedom of another man.

Two things must be understood at the outset if the trial judge's role as sentencing official is to be seen in full perspective. The first of these is that the overwhelming majority of the persons up for criminal sentence plead guilty. . . . When the accused enters a plea of guilty to the charge against him, the determination of the sentence to be imposed is the only significant decision made by a court in his case. Thus, by any quantitative standard, the trial judge's exercise of his sentencing authority far outweighs everything else he does as a participant in the administration of criminal justice.

The second essential insight is that the severity of the punishment that will be imposed on a convicted criminal offender depends in very large measure on the personality and social attitudes of the particular judge before whom the offender comes for sentence. A crime that strikes one judge as deserving of a long prison term may seem appropriate for far milder punishment to another judge on the same bench. Contemporary sentencing statistics demonstrate that there are dramatic differences from judge to judge in the imposition of penalties in similar criminal cases. This is no news to persons familiar with the realities of criminal law administration. A study made fifty years ago of the records of the then forty-one criminal magistrates of the City of New York revealed that the percentage of cases in which the accused person was discharged without any penalty at all varied from 74 per cent for the most permissive of the magistrates to less than 7 per cent for the most punitive and austere of the forty-one. In disorderly conduct prosecutions, one magistrate heard more than five hundred cases and discharged only one of the accused without penalty. Another magistrate, in an adjoining court, discharged more than half of the disorderly conduct charges brought before him. The criminal court as a whole convicted and imposed penalties on 92 per cent of the 17,000 persons brought up on charges of drunkenness, but one sympathetic magistrate convicted only 20 per cent of the drunks summoned to trial before him. It would be useless to belabor the point with additional statistics. The social view of the particular judge can be the most important single factor in the sentencing equation.

In the literature of law and criminology, penal sanctions are analyzed and appraised from many different perspectives, sometimes as instruments of deterrence, sometimes as means of treatment and social rehabilitation of the offender, occasionally as measures of retribution visited on the offender for the moral and social wrong of his unlawful act. However one may interpret the purpose or purposes of the criminal law, it is evident that sentencing determinations are socially critical decisions. What qualities of mind and character would we want our sentencing judge to have, and how should he go about the demanding and often painful task? There is no simple answer to either of these questions.

The sentencing burden will be easiest on the judge if he can find some way to routinize it, to make punishments fit categories of crime without too much attention to the particular offender and his personal and family circumstances. This seems, superficially at least, a technique for administering equal justice, and there are trial judges whose sentencing practice is more or less along these lines—so many years for embezzlements, so many days in city jail for drunken and disorderly conduct, and the like. But this way of easing the strain of sentencing is barred to the thoughtful judge by his awareness that discriminating individualization in the handling of specific cases is an essential element in our tradition of justice. Shall the sentencing judge, then, avoid or minimize the burdens of his responsibility by making it his practice to impose whatever penalty may be recommended in the probation report on the offender? Conceivably, some time in the future, the judicial function in criminal cases may be cut down so that only issues of guilt or innocence are left for determination by judge or jury and decisions as to punishment referred to boards of experts in criminology, psychiatry, and other relevant fields of knowledge, as parole matters are handled under modern procedures. Over the years a good many judges and scholars have urged that our system of criminal justice would operate more fairly and effectively if the guilt-determining function were separated from the sentencing function and all issues concerning a convicted offender's penalty resolved less hurriedly and by specialists better qualified for the task than most judges are. But this is not the existing situation. The judge still carries ultimate sentencing responsibility, within the bounds fixed for the offense by the legislature, and he must exercise that responsibility as best he can.

The demands and strains of the sentencing role bear hardest on the sensitive and compassionate trial judge, who cannot help seeing the patterns of human tragedy in the cases that come before him. Would it be better if all the judges of our criminal trial courts were as detached and hard boiled as many of them are, or make out to be, in sentencing matters? There is respectable authority, tracing back at least to Thomas Hobbes, that charity and compassion are no part of legal justice and that the sentencing judge must learn to steel himself against humanitarian impulses. But would we be content with a trial bench of judges who, by personality and character, find no burden or psychic strain in the sentencing task? Is a man worthy of judicial office, whatever his other qualifications, if he is entirely insensitive to the searching implications of the chastening injunction, "Judge not, that ye be not judged"?

And Who Is "Qualified"?

Bar associations and other civic groups undertake from time to time to determine whether particular candidates for appointment to the bench are or are not "qualified"—variously, "well qualified" or "exceptionally well qualified"—for judicial office. No person or organization has yet been rash enough to offer an authoritative definition of the crucial word "qualified" or even an all-inclusive checklist of the attributes to be kept in mind in appraising the qualifications of a lawyer who aspires to join the company of the judiciary. This essay was certainly not designed as a systematic analysis of judicial qualifications, but our examination of the role of the trial judge in the administration of justice should suggest at least a few of the attributes of mind, heart, and character that are essential to the task.

Probity

To be authentic in his role, the trial judge must be an unusually honest man, a man of exceptional integrity financially, politically, and socially. This is usually put first in discussions of qualifications for judicial office, and rightly so. But honesty is hardly a sufficient qualification or even one unique to the judicial branch of public service. It has been taken for granted throughout our analysis of the trial judge's role that a judge who is susceptible to bribery in any form, or who favors his relatives, cronies, or political sponsors either in the conduct of litigation or in the award of lucrative commissions like guardianships and receiverships, is unworthy of his post, and, for that matter, unworthy of membership in the legal profession. The ugliest words in the administration of justice are "the fix is in" or any remote equivalent.

The stress on personal honesty in most discussions of judicial qualifications seems quite unflattering to the legal profession, and one searches for an explanation of the prominence of the theme. Certainly a list of qualifications for appointment as a superintendent of schools or director of a scientific laboratory would not put comparable emphasis on elementary probity as a *sine qua non*. There are several possible explanations. Insistence on personal integrity as an indispensable qualification, almost as *the* indispensable qualification, for judicial office reflects an apprehensive awareness in the legal profession of the immensity of the damage that can be done to the legal order by judicial corruption. If a physician or a professor or a businessman is discovered to be a thief or an influence peddler, the disclosure will not put medicine, higher education, or business into general disrepute. But judges are different and more representative; revelations of judicial corruption create suspicion and loss of confidence in legal processes generally and endanger public respect for law.

The further explanation of the heavy emphasis usually put on personal honesty as a judicial qualification is, I think, that it reflects a great and continuing uneasiness, in the legal profession and in the public generally, about the dominance of political considerations in judicial selection. These considerations weigh heavily, and are known by the public to have this weight, even when judicial offices are filled by executive appointment, as in some states by the governor, and in the federal court system by the President on recommendation of the Attorney General. In states where judges are elected, it is common knowledge that party politicians are the effective nominators of judicial candidates, and there is ground for concern, or at least for suspicion, that judges so chosen may be vulnerable to political pressures in the performance of their high social duties. Perhaps we worry as much as we do about the personal honesty of candidates for the bench because of a certain feeling in our society that a man who has been active enough in party politics to have earned the reward of a coveted judgeship may not be as righteous as he ought to be. The greatest single objection to our prevailingly political system of judicial selection is that it makes our judges subject to the suspicions that members of the public entertain about politicians and political processes generally. If there were a flat rule that no one would be eligible for judicial office if he had ever been active in party politics, many of our ablest trial judges would have been lost to the administration of justice. But it is unlikely that as much would be heard as is heard today about personal honesty as the indispensable requirement for judicial office.

Professional Skill and Acumen

Only a good lawyer, a genuinely good one, is qualified for service on a substantial trial court. This was plain at every step in our analysis of the importance, difficulty, and strain of the trial judge's role, and it would be unprofitable to repeat the points already made in that analysis or readily inferable from it. Civic groups and bar associations have been far too generous, by and large, in their ratings of judicial candidates. "Qualified" has come to be used much as teachers use the *C* grade, as signifying a passable minimum of proficiency; the grade *B* candidates are characterized as "well qualified" and the *A* men as "exceptionally well qualified." If such in-group appraisals of judicial candidates are to have political value and influence, "qualified" must have the signification of professional excellence, a degree of intellect and technical proficiency equal to that possessed by the best members of the practicing bar. A man who is pretty good but not good enough is not "qualified" for appointment or election to the trial bench.

Professional excellence on a trial court of general jurisdiction means at least: 1) wide ranging analytical power comparable to that of the qualified internist in medical practice; 2) mastery, or the intellectual capacity to achieve mastery, of the intricacies of legal procedure and evidence; 3) unusual discernment in dealing with facts and weighing conflicting testimony; and 4) unusual skill at communication with jurymen and witnesses. The judge presiding over a juvenile court, family relations court, or other court of specialized jurisdiction does not have to be a "generalist" to this extent, since his cases will involve fewer different areas of substantive law and formal trials will be less important in his work, but he has the corresponding intellectual burden of the specialist, familiarity in depth with a relevant and ever increasing body of medical and behavioral-science knowledge. Professional excellence of the specialist sort is called for, too, in the lower criminal courts. Only a man of first rate capacity can make sound split-second decisions on questions of criminal law and procedure, exercise sentencing responsibilities thoughtfully and wisely under exhausting pressures of time, and improvise procedures to make assembly-line law enforcement seem less cut and dried.

In this connection, the creation, less than two years ago, of the National College of State Trial Court Judges in Boulder, Colorado is one of the happiest developments in the recent history of legal institutions. The new College extends to recently selected trial judges opportunities for intensive study of their role comparable to the educational opportunities that have been provided to appellate judges for some years by the School of Law of New York University. There are other significant signs of serious interest in the study of trial-court processes by the men and women who actually conduct them. The ambitious and well planned judges' training program of the National Council of Juvenile Court Judges is an important recent enterprise in point.

Judicial education can help greatly in improving trial-court processes but, as in education generally, as much depends on the innate ability of the students as on the quality of the instruction. A great university can keep its student quality high by selective admission procedures. This form of quality control is manifestly unavailable to a college for judicial education; the prospective student is already in office, and the less qualified he is the greater his need for the training. . . .

Character, Energy, and Personality

In any sizeable community there will be many lawyers of complete financial probity and genuinely first rate professional skill and acumen. Some of these able men would be very bad trial judges. It has been a central thesis of this essay that the role of the trial judge calls for uncommon qualities of personality and character. The demands and strains of his courtroom task require unusual emotional stability, exceptional firmness and serenity of temperament, and not infrequently great intellectual and psychic endurance. In his relations with jurymen, witnesses, and litigants, the trial judge has to be empathetic and endlessly patient. As a sentencing official, his action must be compassionate without being mushy-headed, and his demeanor must be at once sensitive and austere. These are not attributes that can be measured on a quantitative scale or in any precisely objective way. But they are essential to performance of the role in accordance with the best traditions of common law adjudication.

By these criteria, has any lawyer ever been "qualified" for selection as a trial-court judge? *Fully* qualified? Of course not, any more than men are every fully qualified in mind, heart, and character for the ministry, or for high military command, or for management of a great governmental or business enterprise. But every lawyer knows at least a few trial judges who have come wonderfully close to the ideal, partly through their own natural qualities as human beings and partly through the influence and support of the common law judicial tradition. And the statement of an ideal provides a standard to measure the extent to which particular aspirants to judicial office approach or fall short of the ideal.

Only a brave and good man, or a stupid one, will put himself forward as worthy of designation as a representative and witness of public justice. There is much talk in contemporary literature about improving the "image" of justice. Justice is not a commodity to be marketed by such means. The way to improve the image of justice is to improve the reality of justice in the trial courts of the United States. That depends, above all, on the intellectual, moral, and personal quality of the men and women who are called to serve as our trial judges.

THE BAIL SYSTEM: MONEY JUSTICE

Lynn Walker

One out of every four Americans is arrested at some time in his life, and in Black communities, the chances of arrest and involvement with the criminal process are even greater. The purpose of arrest is to secure the defendant's presence for trial and for punishment in the event of conviction. Arrest is usually accompanied by detention, and therefore, one of the most

Source: *Essence* (January 1973), Vol. 3, No. 9, pp. 24, 56. Reprinted by permission of Lynn Walker.

vital and immediate concerns of any arrested person and of his family and friends is always how to arrange for the defendant's release from custody. Bail and other pretrial release methods are vital areas about which Black people must be informed, not only so that we will know what to do if confronted with an arrest situation personally, but also because, as will be seen, the bail system falls with discriminatory and often devastating effect upon our own.

Most states and the federal jurisdictions have statutes requiring that a defendant be brought before a magistrate, judge, or some other authority within a very brief period of time after arrest, for purposes of entering a plea to the charges, (guilty or non-guilty) and for purposes of considering what measures are necessary to assure the defendant's presence for trial. This procedure is called the preliminary hearing.

The United States Supreme Court has never ruled that there is "a right to bail." The Eighth Amendment to the United States Constitution, prohibits "excessive bail" but it does not expressly recognize the underlying right to have bail set. Many courts, including the Supreme Court, have assumed that a defendant has such a right, and virtually all the states have provided for it in their state constitutions or by statute in all but capital cases.

The purpose of bail, as of arrest, is to secure the defendant's presence at trial. The United States Supreme Court in *Stack* v. *Boyle* has held that bail should be fixed in each individual case in view of the defendant's circumstances in an amount no greater than is necessary to accomplish that purpose. Many of the state statutes allowing a right to bail give discretion wholly to the magistrates or judges to fix the amount of bail and provide no guidelines, but some contain schedules for the fixing of amounts of bail based on the offenses involved. The statutes may also describe the allowable form of bonds, the charges therefore and define the conditions for forfeiture of bail. A number of states have statutes permitting the police in some minor cases, to release arrested persons on "station-house" bail, and in those cases, the police determine the amount of bail.

The factors most often mentioned in the statutes to be considered in determining the amount of bail are: 1. the nature of the offense, including the gravity of the possible penalties, facts surrounding the offense in aggravation or mitigation thereof; 2. the defendant's character, reputation and past record; 3. the defendant's employment history, *i.e.,* whether he is stable and trustworthy; 4. the defendant's family status and roots in the community, including the length of time that he has lived there and the whereabouts of his family and friends; and 5. the defendant's financial assets.

If the defendant is poor, frequently the attorney assigned to handle his bail application will be with the Legal Aid Society or a Public Defender's Office. Often these attorneys will have very little, if any, time to confer with the defendant prior to trial. Indeed, they will probably meet the defendant for the first time at the hearing. Even a private attorney may have very little time to prepare a bail application.

It is important that the attorneys be given the type of information about the defendant mentioned in the statutes. If for any reason, you or a member of your family is arrested, you should try to speak with the attorney who will make the bail application and tell him about as many of these factors as possible. Sometimes, it is useful just to write down this information where it is favorable and give it to the attorney to study before trying to arrange for bail.

If it is a court-appointed attorney, you may have to be aggressive and persistent with him so that he will "find" the time to familiarize himself with the case, but it is worth it. Keep one thing in mind. *If you are silent, your case or that of your loved one may get swallowed up in the crush of the court's work or that of the attorney and not get fair consideration at all.* This is one stage of the criminal process where persistence and family interest may pay off. In this connection, it is important to remember that courts, magistrates, and attorneys, like everyone else, may be impressed by a strong expression of support by the defendant's family and friends. You should always arrange for as many interested persons as possible to be present at the bail hearing, and you should ask the attorney to tell the magistrate or judge who you are and that you are there to provide support to the defendant to aid in his supervision if released, and to verify the fact of the defendant's roots in the community.

In large metropolitan areas, there are sometimes organizations called "Bail Projects" that may investigate a defendant's background immediately after arrest to determine whether, under their standards, the defendant should be released. Usually their services are limited to minor offenses by those who are not transients. Often the courts or magistrates give great weight to the recommendations of such projects. These projects may be located in or near the criminal courts and are certainly worth checking into. Your local bar association can probably tell you whether there are such projects in your vicinity and where to find them.

After hearing from the parties, the magistrate or judge usually has several alternative courses of action open to him. He can either set bail, release the defendant on his own bond, his own recognizance, or into the custody of another person. This latter alternative is most frequently used in cases involving minors.

When a defendant is ordered released on his own bond, it means that he makes a promise to pay a certain amount of money, to be named by the court or magistrate, if he should fail to appear when required. Release on his own recognizance, or R.O.R. means merely that the defendant has made a simple promise to appear when required. For the poor person, bail obviously is the least favorable pretrial release device. To be released on bail, the defendant or his family must post a bail bond, and cash, securities, pledges of personal or real property must be put up to guarantee the bond. Sometimes the court will just accept a certain amount of cash. Some states additionally require that another person go on the bond with the defendant and post additional property or funds. Usually a surety company or bail bondsman will do this for a premium of about 10% of the face amount of the bond.

These bondsmen are regulated by law, but they have latitude in determining whether to post a defendant's bond and sometimes refuse to do so in civil rights or political cases. The premium is a fee to the bondsman and is not recoverable. Bondsmen may also require some additional collateral before consenting to post the bond.

Too often, the magistrate or court will set bail in an amount which cannot be raised by a poor defendant. Indeed, in many cases, they plainly ignore the constitutional conception of bail set forth by the Supreme Court, and instead of considering the limited function of bail as a means of assuring the defendant's presence at trial, set bail only with regard to the seriousness of the offense and the defendant's prior criminal record. They do this in order to insure that the defendant will not be released, sometimes because they consider him "dangerous," sometimes to give him "a taste of jail." To the extent that these authorities deliberately set bail beyond a poor man's capacity to make, they are perverting the bail system into a system of preventive detention. But more than that, they are blatantly discriminating against the poor defendant. A poor man who has been charged with assault, for example, may not be able to raise $500.00 bail. A rich man who has committed an assault and who may be equally as dangerous as the former can raise the $500.00 bail and be released. Black people, who constitute the bulk of poor defendants are therefore constantly being treated unequally in this regard. Cases which have made the argument that the money bail system discriminates against poor people have, however, been uniformly rejected by the courts in the past. There are some legal challenges to the bail system still pending, but their likelihood of success is questionable.

The nation's pretrial detention facilities are thus overcrowded and swollen with poor Black people who cannot raise money to secure their release on bail. They swelter in ancient facilities like the Tombs in New York City without adequate recreation, visiting facilities, sanitation, medical services, and decent food. The 1970 prisoner riot at the Tombs was sparked by the brutal conditions in that facility, and there have been other similar uprisings across the country. The court systems in urban areas, clogged hopelessly by backlogs of hundreds of cases, cannot bring these pretrial detainees to trial, and so the pressure builds on the incarcerated man, innocent or guilty, to plead guilty to the criminal charges against him in order to escape, among other things, the deplorable conditions of pretrial detention.

But increased plea bargaining is not the only by-product of the inability of poor defendants to make bail. Time spent in jail also means lost wages, frequently lost jobs and disturbance of family life. Goldfarb, in his book, *Ransom,* documents the case of a defendant accused of taking $14.05 from a subway change booth who was jailed for six months because he could not afford the bondsman's fee of $105.00 for his $2,500 bond. The defendant was subsequently acquitted of the charge, but in the interim had lost his apartment, his job, and had spent half a year in jail with a drug addict, a homosexual, and a lifelong felon. In another case documented by Goldfarb, the accused was jailed for 54 days because he could not raise $1,300 bail for driving without a license. The maximum sentence for the offense was 5 days. These cases can be duplicated again and again.

It has been said that "there can be no equal justice where the kind of trial a man gets depends upon the kind of money he has." There is now a great deal of valid research which indicates that persons who are not released on bail are more likely to be convicted than their released counterparts and/or to receive longer sentences. This is, then, the most outrageous and tragic by-product of the discriminatory bail system. Not only is the indigent defendant punished pretrial, in flagrant violation of the presumption of innocence, by incarceration in inhuman detention facilities with all the detriment that it causes, but additionally, the outcome of his case is skewed against his interest.

Of course, most states do permit renewed motions for reduction of bail, and where bail has been set in an amount beyond the defendant's means, repeated applications for reduction should be made. Again, for those represented by court-appointed or recalcitrant private counsel, they should be urged to renew bail applications. If a defendant is released on bail and does not appear when required, his bail is revoked and forfeited. Sometimes, however, the courts or magistrate will reinstate bail when there is an appropriate explanation for the defendant's absence. If a defendant does not jump bail, the bonds, or property put up for his bail are returned to him or the person who pledged them at the conclusion of the case.

In the final analysis, nothing short of the total restructuring of the pretrial release system will remedy its many abuses. The Bail Reform Act of 1966, applicable in federal cases, makes money bail a last alternative, not to be demanded unless other forms of conditional release are insufficient to secure the accused's presence at trial. It is a step in the right direction, but only a small one. Black people, as the bail system's greatest victims, must become much more aggressive in their manipulation of the bail system as presently constituted, all the while working for its fundamental alteration. This means speaking out against the bail system, urging the powers-that-be to change it, and supporting some of the proposals now being advanced to reform or abolish the system. Remember, as Frederick Douglass has said, "the limits of tyrants are prescribed by the endurance of those whom they oppress."

DOES THE LAW OPPRESS WOMEN?

Diane B. Schulder

Introduction

Law is a reflection and a source of prejudice. It both enforces and suggests forms of bias. In earlier times, the United States Constitution blatantly described the black man as three-fifths of a man and the Supreme Court decided that black people did not qualify as "citizens." That black people have been thought of and treated as chattel is clear from a reading of the laws. An understanding of the attitudes toward women and the objective facts of women's oppression can similarly be found in an examination of the laws.

Sometimes, prejudices linger on long after corrective legislation is passed or decisions rendered—such as the 1954 Supreme Court (*Brown*) decision requiring desegregation of schools. Sometimes, oppressive laws remain on the books although public opinion has moved ahead of them— such as the abortion laws.

In the 1960's, most respected legal minds would, at least theoretically, profess the view that black people should be treated as citizens, as people, as equals, and not denied equal opportunity or equal protection under the laws. Not so for women! Goals, nature, and function are still very much in dispute. Technological advances, the economic structure, and the political situation have reached a point now, however, that permit women to examine the thinking in this area more carefully, and to analyze the supporting rationalizations and mythology.

In the following pages I touch on some of the legislation, court decisions, administrative practices, and underlying rationale that support this discrimination.[1]

Source: *Sisterhood Is Powerful: An Anthology of Writings from the Women's Liberation Movement,* Robin Morgan (ed.) (New York: Vintage Books, A Division of Random House, Inc., September 1970), pp. 139–157. Reprinted by permission of Diane B. Schulder.

[1] Space permits the presentation of selected examples only.

Civil Rights

Dr. Benjamin Spock was tried in June 1968 for conspiring to aid draft resistance. Would the case have been decided differently if he, a man of peace and the world's foremost baby doctor, had not been tried by an all-male jury? Leonard Boudin, his attorney, discovered that it had been the practice of the jury clerk in the federal court in Boston to take a list of the population, which is evenly divided between men and women, and to send jury eligibility questionnaires to approximately three times as many men as women.[2] Along the way, additional administrative hanky-panky led, eventually, to a very lopsided jury panel and, in this case, to a jury devoid of women. This practice (although in existence for years) had never before been challenged.

The law has never been partial to women serving on juries. The rule at Common Law was that juries were composed of "twelve good men." One exception was made, however: when a pregnant woman faced execution, a jury of twelve women was convened to decide whether she should be executed *before* or *after* giving birth to her child. (Some commentators add that a jury of twelve men was convened simultaneously, anyway, to stand by and make sure the women reached the right decision.)

To the present day, the United States Supreme Court has not ruled it unconstitutional for women to be excluded from a jury.[3]

In 1879, when the Supreme Court ruled it was unconstitutional to exclude Negroes from state juries, it hastened to add:

> A state may prescribe . . . the qualifications of its jurors . . . *It may confine the selection to males,* to freeholders . . .[4]

In one of its more recent pronouncements on the subject, in 1961, the Supreme Court dealt with a Florida statute that allows women on a jury only if they go to the Courthouse and request to be put on a special list. The procedure for men is automatic. The number of women on the Florida juries had been, of course, negligible. The Court said:

> At the core of appellant's argument is the claim that the nature of the crime of which she was convicted peculiarly demanded the inclusion of persons of her own sex on the jury. She was charged with killing her husband by assaulting him with a baseball bat . . . The affair occurred in the context of a marital upheaval involving, among other

---

[2] *U.S.* v. *Spock* (1968) Record at 456–474. See also, Brief of Defendant-Appellant, Spock, in United States Court of Appeals for the First Circuit, at 49ff.

[3] But, *cf. White* v. *Crook,* 251 F. Supp. 401 (N.D. Ala. 1966).

[4] *Stauder* v. *U.S.,* 100 U.S. 303 (1879), at 310.

things, the suspected infidelity of appellant's husband, and culminating in the final rejection of his wife's efforts at reconciliation. It is claimed, in substance, that women jurors would have been more understanding or compassionate than men in assessing the quality of appellant's act and her defense ... [5]

The Court dismissed her pleas and upheld her conviction by an all-male jury. In this instance, the Court found it convenient to minimize differences between men and women (as jurors).[6]

Not mentioned in the opinion was a recent study by Professor Hans Zeisel of the University of Chicago showing that jurors do vote differently, based on whether they are old or young, black or white, men or women. The Court justified its ruling in the Florida case by saying that "woman is still regarded as the center of home and family life." [7]

There are many other areas of civil rights that could be studied. Women are not covered in the public accommodations section of the Civil Rights Act nor does the law currently protect them from being discriminated against by schools or universities. A group of women law students at New York University Law School, as recently as 1969, had to petition their school to open the Root-Tilden scholarships, $3,500 yearly stipends which had formerly been restricted to "young men who showed promise of being outstanding members of the Bar." [8] Dorms, of course, are still segregated, and colleges pretend to be able to exercise much more authority over their women than their men students.[9] Needless to say, women did not secure the right to vote until the Nineteenth Amendment in 1920—sixty-five years after it had been granted to people of any race.[10]

Myths built up to perpetuate the inferior status of women and black people are similar:

As in the Negro problem, most men have accepted as self-evident, until recently, the doctrine that women had inferior endowments in

---

[5] *Hoyt* v. *Florida,* 368 U.S. 57 (1961), at 58.

[6] *Cf. Ballard* v. *U.S.* 329 U.S. 187 (1946). Therein, Justice Douglas, in a case finding exclusion of women in *federal* juries to be illegal although not unconstitutional, stated: "But if the shoe were on the other foot, who would claim that a jury was truly representative of the community if all men were intentionally and systematically excluded from the panel. The truth is that the two sexes are not fungible; a community made up exclusively of one is different from a community composed of both ... " (at 193, 194).

[7] *Hoyt* v. *Florida, supra,* at 62.

[8] See The Women's Rights Committee, "Fair and Equal Treatment for Women at New York University Law School" (1969).

[9] The *Linda LeClair* case, for example, would never have happened to a male student at Columbia University.

[10] In many countries the fundamental right to vote is still withheld from women. See Kanowitz, "Sex-based Discrimination in American Law," 11 St. Louis L.J. 293 (1967) at 294.

most of those respects which carry prestige, power, and advantages in society, but that they were, at the same time, superior in some other respects. The arguments, when arguments were used, have been about the same: smaller brains, scarcity of geniuses and so on. The study of women's intelligence and personality has had broadly the same history as the one we record for Negroes. As in the case of the Negro, women themselves have often been brought to believe in their inferiority of endowment. As the Negro was awarded his "place" in society, so there was a "woman's place." In both cases the rationalization was strongly believed that men, in confining them to this place, did not act against the true interest of the subordinate groups. The myth of the "contented women," who did not want to have suffrage or other civil rights and equal opportunities, had the same social function as the myth of the "contented Negro." [11]

Employment

Presented below are some key quotes from a few of the older United States Supreme Court cases. I would like the reader to see the source material, and to experience the process whereby the Court's prejudices become ossified into law and practice. Judges in those days were most honest, direct, and expansive about expressing their prejudices. *Moreover, the Supreme Court has not since overruled itself as to rights due women under the United States Constitution.* Some lower courts have ruled otherwise.[12] Legislation has improved. But practice remains.

As with many of the pernicious laws relating to women, judges explain their reasoning as being "protective" of women. In 1908, in upholding an hour-limitation statute for working women, the Supreme Court stated:

> That woman's physical structure and the performance of maternal functions place her at a disadvantage in the struggle for subsistence is obvious. This is especially true when the burdens of motherhood are upon her. Even when they are not, by abundant testimony of the medical fraternity, continuance for a long time on her feet at work, repeating this from day to day, tends to injurious effects upon the body, and, as healthy mothers are essential to vigorous offspring, the physical well-being of woman becomes an object of public interest and care in order to preserve the strength and vigor of the race.
>
> Still again, history discloses the fact that woman has always been dependent upon man. He established his control at the outset by superior physical strength, and this control in various forms, with diminishing intensity, has continued to the present. As minors, though not to the

---

[11] Gunner Myrdal, *An American Dilemma,* cited in Eastwood and Murray, "Jane Crow and the Law, Sex Discrimination and Title VII," 34 Geo. Wash. L. Rev. 232 (1966), at 234.

[12] See, e.g., *Rosenfeld* v. *Southern Pacific Co., 37* LW 1089 (Cent. D. Cal., 1968).

same extent, she has been looked upon in the courts as needing especial care that her rights may be preserved. Education was long denied her, and while now the doors of the schoolroom are opened and her opportunities for acquiring knowledge are great, yet even with that and the consequent increase of capacity for business affairs it is still true that in the struggle for subsistence she is not an equal competitor with her brother. Though limitations upon personal and contractual rights may be removed by legislation, there is that in her disposition and habits of life which will operate against a full assertion of those rights . . . looking at it from the viewpoint of the effort to maintain an independent position in life, she is not upon an equality . . . she is properly placed in a class by herself . . . It is impossible to close one's eyes to the fact that she still looks to her brother and depends upon him. Even though all restrictions on political, personal, and contractual rights were taken away, and she stood, so far as statutes are concerned, upon an absolutely equal plane with him, it would still be true that she is so constituted that she will rest upon and look to him for protection: that her physical structure and a proper discharge of her maternal functions—having in view not merely her own health, but the well-being of the race—justify legislation to protect her from the greed as well as the passion of man. The limitations which this statute places upon her contractual powers, upon her right to agree with her employer as to the time she shall labor, are not imposed solely for her benefit, but also largely for the benefit of all . . .

We have not referred in this discussion to the denial of the elective franchise of the state of Oregon, for while that may disclose a lack of political equality in all things with her brother, that is not of itself decisive. The reason runs deeper and rests in the inherent difference between the two sexes, and in the different functions in life which they perform.[13]

In 1948, the Supreme Court reaffirmed its protective approach, in not allowing a woman to be a bartender unless she was "the wife or daughter of the male owner." The Court explained:

The fact that women may now have achieved the virtues that men have long claimed as their prerogatives and now indulge in vices that men have long practiced, does not preclude the states from drawing a sharp line between the sexes, certainly in such matters as the regulation of liquor traffic. *The Constitution does not require legislatures to reflect sociological insight, or shifting social standards, any more than it requires them to keep abreast of the latest scientific standards.*[14]

In 1963, many Congressmen tried to block the Equal Pay Act, the purpose of which was to give people, regardless of sex, equal pay for equal

[13] *Muller* v. *Oregon,* 208 U.S. 412 (1908), at 421–423.
[14] *Goesart* v. *Cleary,* 335 U.S. 464 (1948), at 466 (italics mine).

work. In 1964, when Congress was debating Title VII of the Civil Rights Act, forbidding discrimination in hiring, certain Southern Congressmen decided on a tactic to defeat the entire bill—add a clause prohibiting discrimination because of "sex" as well as a clause prohibiting discrimination because of "race"! Real supporters of women's rights opposed the amendment, in an effort to save the bill. Congressmen, generally, considered it some sort of obscene joke.[15]

In a polite understatement as to the present over-all condition of women and employment, the Committee on Private Employment of the President's Commission on the Status of Women noted:

> Although women in the work force have a somewhat higher-than-average schooling than men, they, more generally than men, work in jobs far below their native abilities or trained capabilities. Barriers to women's employment and to their occupational progress generate feelings of injustice and frustration.[16]

The recently established Equal Employment Opportunity Commission should not have been surprised (as it was) to find that at times 50 percent of the complaints it received were from women.[17]

Recently, a study was conducted of all women law school graduates of the years 1956–1965.[18] Approximately half of the women stated that they had been the object of discrimination by employers. Average income differed sharply, based on sex [19] [see the chart on the next page].

How has the Supreme Court treated women lawyers? In an opinion that might sound to some like a parody of sexism written by the Women's Liberation Movement, the Court upheld state legislation barring women from the practice of law.

A married woman from Illinois attacked the state law that forbade her from practicing law, and the Supreme Court answered her thusly:

> The claim of the plaintiff, who is a married woman, to be admitted
> to practice as an attorney and counselor-at-law, is based upon the sup-

[15] See Caroline Bird, *Born Female or The High Cost of Keeping Women Down* (New York: David McKay, 1968), chapter 1.

[16] President's Commission on the Status of Women, *Report of the Committee on Private Employment* (1963).

[17] Caroline Bird, *Born Female,* pp. 205–206, 268. Her information comes from various newspaper articles and the *First Annual Report* of the Equal Employment Opportunity Commission, House Document No. 86, for the year ending June 30, 1966.

[18] White, "Women in the Law," 65 Mich. L. Rev. 105 (1967) at 1068.

[19] White, *ibid.,* 1055. Contrary to expectation, full-time employed married women earned significantly more money than did the unmarried women. White, *ibid.,* 1067. Reprinted by permission of Professor James J. White.

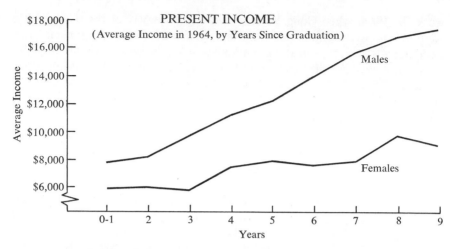

PRESENT INCOME
(Average Income in 1964, by Years Since Graduation)

posed right of every person, man or woman, to engage in any lawful employment for a livelihood. The Supreme Court of Illinois denied the application on the ground that, by the common law, which is the basis of the laws of Illinois, only men were admitted to the bar . . .

The claim that (under the Fourteenth Amendment of the Constitution, which declares that no state shall or enforce any law which shall abridge the privileges and immunities of citizens of the United States) the statute law of Illinois, or the common law prevailing in that state, can no longer be set up as a barrier against the right of females to pursue any lawful employment for a livelihood (the practice of law included). assumes that it is one of the privileges and immunities of women as citizens to engage in any and every profession, occupation, or employment in civil life.

It certainly cannot be affirmed, as an historical fact, that this has ever been established as one of the fundamental privileges and immunities of the sex. On the contrary, the civil law, as well as nature herself, has always recognized a wide difference in the respective spheres and destinies of man and woman. Man is, or should be, woman's protector and defender. The natural and proper timidity and delicacy which belongs to the female sex evidently unfits it for many of the occupations of civil life. The constitution of the family organization, which is founded in the divine ordinance, as well as in the nature of things, indicates the domestic sphere as that which properly belongs to the domain and functions of womanhood. The harmony, not to say identity, of interests and views which belong, or should belong, to the family institution is repugnant to the idea of a woman adopting a distinct and independent career from that of her husband. So firmly fixed was this sentiment in the founders of the common law that it became a maxim of that system of jurisprudence that a woman had no legal existence separate from her husband, who was regarded as her head and representative in the social state; and notwithstanding some recent modifications of this civil status, many of the special rules of law flowing from and dependent upon this cardinal principle still exist in full force in most states. One of these is, that a married woman is incapable, without her husband's consent, of making contracts which shall be binding on her or him. This very incapacity was one circumstance which the Supreme Court of Illinois deemed important in rendering a married woman incompetent fully to perform the duties and trusts that belong to the office of an attorney and counselor.

It is true that many women are unmarried and not affected by any of the duties, complications, and incapacities arising out of the married state, but these are exceptions to the general rule. *The paramount destiny and mission of woman are to fulfill the noble and benign offices of wife and mother.* This is the law of the Creator. And the rules of civil society must be adapted to the general constitution of things, and cannot be based upon exceptional cases.

The humane movements of modern society, which have for their object the multiplication of avenues for woman's advancement, and of occupations adapted to her condition and sex, have my heartiest concurrence. But I am not prepared to say that it is one of her fundamental rights and privileges to be admitted into every office and position, including those which require highly special qualifications and demanding special responsibilities . . . in my opinion, in view of the peculiar characteristics, destiny, and mission of woman, it is within the province of the legislature to ordain what offices, positions, and callings shall be filled and discharged by men, and shall receive the benefit of those energies and responsibilities, and that decision and firmness which are presumed to predominate in the sterner sex.

For these reasons I think that the laws of Illinois now complained of are not obnoxious to the charge of abridging any of the privileges and immunities of citizens of the United States.[20]

Twenty-two years later, a Miss Belva Lockwood was denied entry to the bar in Virginia. In its opinion this time, the Supreme Court decided that it is reasonable for a state court to find that a "woman" is not a "person":

> It was for the Supreme Court of Appeals to construe the statute of Virginia in question, and to determine whether the word *"person"* as therein used is *confined to males,* and whether women are admitted to practice law in that Commonwealth. Leave denied.[21]

Marital Relationship

In 1966, a bank in Texas got a raw deal. The Supreme Court found fit to uphold the Texas law providing that a married woman did not have the

[20] *Bradwell* v. *Illinois,* 83 U.S. (16 Wall) 130 (1872), at 140–142.

[21] *In re Lockwood,* 154 U.S. 116 (1894), at 117 (italics mine).

capacity to enter into a binding contract (and, therefore, the bank could not collect the $4,000 she had promised to pay it).

In a dissenting opinion, Justice Black stated:

> The Texas law of "coverture" . . . rests on the old common-law fiction that the husband and wife are one. This rule has worked out in reality to mean that though the husband and wife are one, the one is the husband. This fiction rested on what I had supposed is today a completely discredited notion that a married woman, being a female, is without capacity to make her own contracts and do her own business . . . It seems at least unique to me that this Court in 1966 should exalt this archaic remnant of a primitive caste system to an honored place among the laws of the United States.[22]

Can a woman keep her own name upon remarrying? It seems that in some places she can if she has her husband's permission, but an Illinois court, in 1945, refused to let a woman vote in her maiden name, holding:

> The facts that a married woman practiced law for some years, became widely known as an attorney in her neighborhood, took active part in political activities thereof, was admitted to practice in various courts, and had certificates issued to her in her maiden name, were irrelevant on question of her statutory duty to cancel her registration under such name and reregister in her husband's surname in order to preserve her right to vote.[23]

Additionally, the Common Law tradition of loss of her legal personality when a woman marries, has raised, among others, the issues of right to a separate domicile; capacity to sue and be sued; change in citizenship upon marriage to an alien, cause of action for "loss of consortium" to one spouse only. Today, controversies center around men claiming to be discriminated against in the laws of alimony and child custody. "My wife sued to divorce me, and I had to pay for her lawyer!" complained a man recently. (There seems to be a trend among young women today not to request alimony if they can possibly afford not to.) Rights and obligations in marriage are currently under serious reconsideration.[24] Whether it is fair, or even wise—for children, husband, and wife—that the woman have complete responsibility as caretaker of the children is also being reconsidered.[25]

[22] *U.S.* v. *Yazell,* 382 U.S. 341 (1966), at 361.

[23] *Peo* v. *Lipsky,* 327 Ill. App. 63, 63 N.E. 2d 642 (1945).

[24] Sayre, "A Reconsideration of Husband's Duty to Support and Wife's Duty to Render Services," 29 Va. L. Rev. 857 (1943); Paulson, "Support Rights and Duties Between Husband and Wife," 9 Va. L. Rev. 709 (1956).

[25] See Philip Roth, *Portnoy's Complaint* (New York: Random House, 1969).

A supposed breakthrough was made in French law in February 1966, after heated debate. As a result of this new French law, "a wife, without asking the permission of her husband, can take a job or open a checking account. The husband can no longer simply choose housing without consulting his wife, nor make all the decisions about the children's education." [26]

Changes in the law cannot take place without changes in societal structure.[27]

Welfare Law

> " . . . we have two systems of family law . . . different in origin, different in history, different in administration, different in orientation and outlook."—one for the rich and one for the poor.[28]

One of the most flagrant abuses in recent years has been the searching of homes to find out if a welfare mother was having a sexual relationship and, if she was, then cutting her off welfare. The rule came to be known by various names, such as "substitute father" or "man in the house" rule. There was never, of course, any "woman in the house" rule. Raids to check out the situation were conducted as follows:

> Much more generally used than mass arrests are night calls, popularly known as "night raids," "bed checks," and "operations week-end." They may be made at the home of only one recipient but often they are a mass operation. The purpose is usually to determine whether there is an unreported man in the home of the recipient—whether he be husband, father, stepfather, or man assuming the role of spouse—whose presence may, on the one hand, determine eligibility or the amount of the grant, and on the other hand constitute an element in the crime of welfare fraud or theft. Such calls are frequently made between 10:00 P.M. and 4:00 A.M. The normal procedure is this: Investigators working in two-man teams approach the front and back of the house simultaneously and ring the doorbell; the investigator identifies himself, asks to be admitted, not specifically to look for a man or to make a routine check of the conditions of the home and the children; once inside, the investigator admits his partner and the two then conduct a minute search of the house looking into the children's and mother's bedrooms, in and under the beds, the attic, cellar, shower, closets, drawers, and medicine chest, searching

---

[26] *New York Times,* 2 February 1966. For n65–570 due 13 Juillet 1965, [1965] J. O. 6044 (1); Recueil Dalloy Sirey, 31 Août 1965, p. 233; effective on February 1, 1966.

[27] For a brilliant discussion of how women's roles change in the course of revolutionary struggle, see Frantz Fanon's *Studies in a Dying Colonialism* (New York: Grove Press, 1967).

[28] Ten Broek, "California's Dual System of Family Law," 16 Stan L. Rev. 257 (1964).

for a man or evidence of his presence. Adults and children in the home are interviewed, notes taken, and sometimes signed statements are secured without explanation of their intended use.[29]

In the case which finally destroyed the "substitute father" theory rule,[30] a lawyer representing a welfare mother questioned a case-work supervisor:

Q: Now, the regulation provides: " . . . though not living in the home regularly, he visits frequently for the purposes of cohabiting." What is your understanding of what the term "regularly" means in that provision?

A: Well, I think it means on a continuing basis.

Q: In other words, though not living in the home, on a continuing basis?

A: Yes.

Q: If a man is not living in a home on a continuing basis, but visits the house once a month for the purpose of cohabiting, is that, so far as your understanding of the regulation, sufficient to be presumptive evidence of a substitute father?

A: Well, I think it would depend upon the intent of the persons involved, whether they intended to have a continuing relationship or not.

. . . .

Q: How would you go about finding this out? . . .

A: Well, I think that the worker would talk with the mother and also with the father if it were indicated.

Q: What kind of questions would be asked?

A: Well, how she felt about the man, what her intentions were, whether she intended to keep on with her relationship, or whether it was just a casual thing, or whether it had meaning.

. . .

Q: Assuming, now, that the mother and the substitute parent said that, although they cohabited only once every two months, they intended to do this on a permanent basis: would that be a basis for a *prima facie* presumption that the substitute parent rule should apply?

A: . . . we never have had an actual case that I can recall where they said it was once a month; but I assume that if it were considered permanent, as you say, that it would be considered a substitute parent.

Q: And that would be irrespective of whether the sexual relationship was in the home or outside of the home—is that right?

A: Yes.

Q: And so, if parties engaged in sexual relations once every two

[29] Ten Broek, "California's Dual System of Family Law," 17 Stan L. Rev. 257 (1965), at 667, 668.

[30] This rule (which operated to deprive indigent women of a sex life), deems the men with whom she is fucking to be her children's "father" (although he is not). Ergo, he has to support them. Ergo, they are cut off welfare.

months outside of the home, but told you that they intended to continue to do this, it would be sufficient to warrant that they be denied aid under the regulation?

A: Now, do you mean with the same man, or do you mean different men?

Q: With the same man.

A: I would think that they would consider that—

Q: —*prima facie*—

A: —a marital relationship, if they continued to do this.

Q: Would your answer be the same if it were once every four months, and if the woman and the substitute parent told you that they intended to have these sexual relationships once every four months?—would that be sufficient *prima facie* proof to deny aid?

A: I believe I would have to call the State Department on that and see what they say about that.[31]

Criminal Law

Legislation and case law still exist in some parts of the United States permitting the "passion shooting" by a husband of a wife;[32] the reverse, of course, is known as homicide. Italy, on December 20, 1968, abolished a law under which a woman could be jailed for adultery for one year, while her husband could be unfaithful with impunity.[33] On December 12, 1968, the United States Supreme Court considered the case of a girl who was imprisoned for "lascivious carriage." It considered the constitutionality of a 1905 Connecticut law authorizing imprisonment of young women if they are "in manifest danger of falling into habits of vice or leading a vicious life."[34] Thus, we see sex discrimination in the very definition of crimes.[35]

---

[31] See *King v. Smith,* 329 U.S. 309 (1968). The above questioning was in a deposition taken on March 9, 1967. Martin Garbers, Esq., is questioning Jean M. Johnson, casework supervisor of Aid to Dependent Children in Dallas County.

[32] See, N.M. Stat. Ann. sec. 40A–2–4(7) (Repl. 1964); Texas Penal Code art 1220 (Vernon's 1961): Utah Code Ann. sec. 76–30–10 (5) (1953); *State* v. *Williams,* 47 Utah 320, pll04 (1917). See also the film *Adam's Rib.*

[33] *New York Times,* 20 December 1968.

[34] See *New York Times,* 12 December 1968.

[35] The criminal prosecution of witches is not very common today, but it was at one time, and there are many volumes of legal writing on the subject. Why were most of the convicted witches women? Is it because religious and political heresy, or even independence of opinion, is less to be tolerated in women than men? Some groups are now researching the proposition that witches were actually early women revolutionaries. A book written in England in 1680 by Sir Robert Filmer would seem to support this conclusion. The book is entitled *The Freeholders Grand Inquest.* Its summary includes a review of the following subjects: Observations upon forms of Government; Directions for obedience to governors in dangerous and doubtful times; Observations on Anarchy; An advertisement to the jury-men of England, touching witches; Observations upon: Aristotle's *Politiques,* Hobbes's *Leviathan,* Milton against Salmasius, Grotius, *De Jure Belli & pacis;* The Anarchy of a limited or mixed Monarchy; A difference between an English and Hebrew witch.

Laws also exist providing for different lengths of jail sentences for the same crime, depending on whether the perpetrator is male or female.[36]

More studies are needed in the area of criminal law and criminology to determine why some crimes are committed more often by men (e.g., violent crimes, shootings) and other crimes by women (e.g., shoplifting). Studies should also be conducted concerning comparative treatment inside jails. A counselor working with imprisoned women drug addicts told me recently that it is much more difficult working with female prisoners, partly because it is less possible to train them for work after release that would pay reasonably well. A woman confined for three years at one of these "re-habilitation centers" wrote to me on June 21, 1968:

> On May 27, 1968, I *volunteered* to Manhattan Rehabilitation Center [a center for drug addicts] . . . I volunteered to this program under the assumption that I would receive professional psychiatric and medical care at all times. I have found, much to my disappointment, that I receive very little medical care and no psychiatric treatment whatsoever.
>
> I have also found myself locked up in a building that was condemned by the Fire Department as a fire hazard.
>
> As a mere drug user, I understand I am legally considered "sick," yet here I am treated as a hardened criminal.
>
> For many reasons I feel this Center would be detrimental, not sup-plemental, to my health.[37]

In the area of sex and reproduction, the law has an effect on women more directly than on men. In many states, dispensing birth-control in-formation is a crime. Thus, Bill Baird, for example, faced five years in jail in Massachusetts, for handing someone a can of "contraceptive" foam. Under recent New York abortion laws, a person who performed an abortion on another was guilty of a felony, and a woman who submitted herself to an abortion was guilty of a misdemeanor.[38] The abortion Statutes are in a section of the New York Penal Law entitled "Homicide, abortion, and related offenses."

One of the areas where the criminal law operates most discriminatorily relates to prostitution. In New York City, policemen actively entrap women and then charge them with prostitution. A defendant (who was acquitted) testified to a typical example:

---

[36] See *Commonwealth* v. *Daniels,* 37 L. W. 2064 Pa. Sup. Ct. 7/1/68 (reversing L. W. 2004).

[37] Letter to Liane B. Schulder, Esq. (italics mine) See also Father Daniel Egan S. A., *The Junkie Priest* (New York: Pocket Books, 1965), for a description of the life of drug addiction and prostitution.

[38] N. Y. Penal Law Section 125.40. The only exception was when it was necessary to save the mother's life.

He came up behind me first and asked me was I going out, and I really didn't have too much to say to him at first, and then he started walking alongside me and we both started a small conversation, and I told him that he looked like a police officer, and he told me that he wasn't, he was a shoe salesman or something from Minnesota, and he showed me some identification . . . It was like a name tag with a plastic covering over it or something. He took it out of his jacket pocket. He was wearing a suit and carrying a valise . . . Then there was a lot of other small talk and then he told me that he was spending twenty dollars . . . [39]

The officer testified:

I hailed a cab and we got into the cab, and she said, "Driver, go along Seventh Avenue," and as we drove away I said to the driver, "Forget about that, driver, take me to the 18th Precinct." [40]

A directive was issued, not too long ago, to policemen in New York City not to entrap male homosexuals; no such relating to female prostitutes. Nor, of course, do policewomen in disguise try to entrap businessmen seeking to exploit the indigent women who walk the streets.

In a recent pronouncement, a Criminal Court judge characterized the women prostitutes as "hardened criminals" and said "one could not equate their activity with that of their customers." [41] This, despite the fact that New York law states that prostitutes and their customers are guilty of equal violations.[42] The New York District Attorney's office has also chosen not to prosecute the men customers.[43] Both deterrence and fairness, however, would be served if this were done. In another country, a strikingly successful campaign in the suppression of prostitution was carried out as follows:

Whenever officers raided a place of vice—whether it was a house, a tavern, or simply a dark street—they were to take down the names, addresses, and place of employment of all men found there. The cus-

---

[39] Trial Transcript, *Peo* v. *Dixon,* trial in N.Y. Criminal Court, Part 1C, on July 18, 1968, at p. 14ff.

[40] *Peo* v. *Dixon, supra,* at 3. Policemen often testify in court that women approach them and ask, "Do you want to get laid?" This is often a lie, used to secure a conviction, and frequently judges will close their eyes to this tactic. There have been speculative rumors, as well, that some vice squads participate in vice with their arrestees.

[41] *New York Times,* 27 January 1968.

[42] N.Y. Penal Law, Sections 230ff. The New York law making it an equal offense for the man who participates was added in 1967. The stated purposes of this new addition are "deterrence" and "fairness."

[43] An attorney friend of mine noted recently that if the police were too successful in deterrence, big business conventions would cancel out of New York City and go elsewhere.

tomers were not to be arrested. But on the following day, and for a specified period, those men would have their names and identifying information posted in a public place, under the heading "Buyers of the Bodies of Women." These lists were to be prominently displayed outside public buildings or on factory bulletin boards.[44]

Other countries, such as England, have legalized prostitution.[45] As has been suggested before (but not practiced), "The stigma and consequence of crime must . . . be either removed from the woman or affixed to the man." [46]

Conclusion

Thus, prejudice (the mythology of class oppression) is enshrined in laws. Laws lead to enforcement of practices. Practices reinforce and lead to prejudice. The cycle continues . . . Women who feel oppressed, women involved in the fight for women's liberation, are not paranoid. Their feelings of oppression are not imaginary. Indeed their oppression, in more areas than generally realized, is built into the law.

[44] Carter, *Sin and Science* (1945) at 56–57, describing action in the Soviet Union.

[45] Another judge in the New York Criminal Court believes this is the proper solution. See *New York Times,* 27 January 1969.

[46] Abraham Flexner, *Prostitution in Europe* (New York: Century Co., 1914), p. 103. As Flexner says (p. 107): ". . . as a matter of history, no proposition aiming at punishment of prostitution has ever involved both participants. The harlot has been branded as an outcast and flung to the wolves: she alone,—never the man, her equal partner in responsibility."

Chapter 9
SUGGESTED TOPICS FOR CLASS DISCUSSION

1. Critics of the Supreme Court, among them members of Congress, frequently accuse the Supreme Court of "political" activism and of usurping the powers of Congress by legislating. What forces tend to draw the Supreme Court into "legislative" activity? Is there any alternative in a system under which every law is subject to being declared constitutional or unconstitutional?
2. It has for many years been an accepted idea that the Supreme Court is an essentially undemocratic institution functioning in a democracy. Is this necessarily true? Does the fact that Justices are not elected make the Supreme Court undemocratic? Is it possible that its record as the defender of minority rights makes it the most democratic institution?
3. When the Supreme Court is aware that basic freedoms are being denied persons by the state governments, should it still rely on the legislatures to correct the evil? If they do not, should the Supreme Court close its eyes?

4. With the trial judge playing such a crucial role in the administration of justice, how should he be chosen, by appointment or election? What are the advantages and disadvantages of each?

5. Sex discrimination supported by state statutes is more prevalent now than against any other identifiable group. What can the courts do to help eliminate such discrimination? Can the Thirteenth, as well as the Fourteenth, Amendment be used?

Chapter 10
Civil Rights: Liberty and Authority

This chapter is concerned with the central problem of government: Liberty v. Authority. *In any democratic society lines must be drawn to reconcile individual freedoms with the rights of the community. But these lines are not easily drawn, because how, where, and when they will be applied can never be resolved to the satisfaction of the entire community. Both must be preserved, but too much authority leads to a loss of liberty; too much liberty leads to an instability in which few can be secure.*

A democratic society such as ours, based on a government of limited powers under a written constitution, depends upon majority rule with protection of minority rights. But such principles do not, of course, exist in a vacuum; it is inevitable that individual freedoms will at times conflict with the rights of the community at large. The conflicts have become more numerous in recent years, arising from the cry for more law and order, from civil rights activities, from war protests, and from a seeming willingness of both national and state authorities to by-pass some of the long-held substantive and procedural rights of individuals. Such by-passing is especially true when there seems to be considerable popular support for such actions. But the support, even if it is nearly unanimous, does not give government, in the name of the majority, the right to deprive individuals of Constitutionally protected rights. As Judge Jerome Frank observed, "The test of the moral quality of a civilization is its treatment of the weak and the powerless." *Justice Robert H. Jackson probably put it best:

> If there is any fixed star in our constitutional constellation, it is that no official, high or petty, can prescribe what shall be orthodox in politics, nationalism, religion, or other matters of opinion or force citizens to confess by word or act their faith therein. . . . The very purpose of a Bill of Rights was to withdraw certain subjects from the vicissitudes of political controversy, to place them beyond the reach of majorities and officials and to establish them as legal principles to be applied by the courts. One's right to life, liberty, and property, to free speech, a free press, freedom of worship and assembly, and other fundamental rights may not be submitted to vote; they depend on the outcome of no elections.†

The problems of protecting civil liberties are further aggravated by the federal system. It is obvious that most of the laws regulating individual actions are applied by states; hence, most deprivations of liberties and of procedural protections have occurred at that level. Even so, it was not until 1927 that the Supreme Court began to apply the protections of the Bill of Rights against state actions.

Another factor further aggravating the whole problem of individual rights and liberties is the more subtle forms of deprivations. What does liberty mean? Only protection of the more obvious activities: those of religion, speech, right to counsel, trial by jury? Or should liberty include freedom of choice, of opportunity in such areas as housing, employment, and education beyond the public schools?

The law explosion of the past two decades is itself the best indicator that the problems of protecting civil liberties continue. New rights are being claimed; new social interests are pressing for recognition before the bar; groups long without knowledge or resources to seek relief now have legal spokesmen who are asserting grievances long suppressed. The Supreme Court has since 1937 been heavily involved in these questions, so much so that now more than 45 percent of all cases decided by the Supreme Court deal with basic human liberties.

* United States v. Murphy 22 F. 2d 698 (1955).
† West Virginia State Board of Education v. Barnette 319 U.S. 624 (1943).

HELLO DOLLY: A CASE FOR SELECTIVE INCORPORATION

Mapp v. Ohio

It comes as a shock to most Americans to learn for the first time that the Bill of Rights is a restraint on the federal government only. Relying upon the history of the ratification of the amendments that make up the Bill of Rights, Chief Justice John Marshall, speaking for the Supreme Court in Barron v. Baltimore (1833) said, in part, "These amendments demanded security against apprehended encroachments by the general government— not against those of the local governments. . . ." Whenever a Constitutional provision was meant to affect the states "words are employed which directly express that intent. . . . These (first eight) amendments contain no expression indicating an intention to apply them to state governments. This Court cannot so apply them." This interpretation has been fully incorporated into American Constitutional development.

But one of the strongest motives in drafting the post Civil War protective amendments, and especially the Fourteenth, with its prohibitions on the states against denial of due process and equal protection of the laws, was to liquidate the effects of the Barron decision.

Despite a number of narrow interpretations of the scope of protections afforded by the Fourteenth Amendment, since the middle 1920's the Court has proceeded toward "nationalization" of the Bill of Rights by incorporating many of its protections as prohibitions against states' denials of due process and equal protection as commanded by the Fourteenth Amendment.

As a result of the Supreme Court's decision in the case that follows, the protection against illegal search and seizure afforded by the Fourth Amendment is now imposed upon the states. In reaching its decision, the Supreme Court followed the principle of incorporation provided in Palko v. Connecticut by concluding that this liberty is one of those that are "implicit in the concepts of ordered liberty which lie at the base of all of our civil and political institutions."

Miss Dollree Mapp was convicted in Ohio of having obscene materials in her possession in violation of state statute. After the Ohio Supreme Court upheld the conviction, Miss Mapp brought an appeal to the Supreme Court.
—A. M. S. and E. W.

Mr. Justice Clark Delivered the Opinion of the Court.

. . . On May 23, 1957, three Cleveland police officers arrived at appellant's residence in that city pursuant to information that "a person [*was*]

Source: *Mapp* v. *Ohio* 367 U.S. 643; 81 Sup. Ct. 1684; 6 L. Ed. 2d (1961).

hiding out in the home who was wanted for questioning in connection with a recent bombing, and that there was a large amount of policy paraphernalia being hidden in the home." Miss Mapp and her daughter by a former marriage lived on the top floor of the two-family dwelling. Upon their arrival at that house, the officers knocked on the door and demanded entrance but appellant, after telephoning her attorney, refused to admit them without a search warrant. They advised their headquarters of the situation and undertook a surveillance of the house.

The officers again sought entrance some three hours later when four or more additional officers arrived on the scene. When Miss Mapp did not come to the door immediately, at least one of the several doors to the house was forcibly opened and the policemen gained admittance. Meanwhile Miss Mapp's attorney arrived, but the officers, having secured their own entry, and continuing in their defiance of the law, would permit him neither to see Miss Mapp nor to enter the house. It appears that Miss Mapp was halfway down the stairs from the upper floor to the front door when the officers, in this highhanded manner, broke into the hall. She demanded to see the search warrant. A paper, claimed to be a warrant, was held up by one of the officers. She grabbed the "warrant" and placed it in her bosom. A struggle ensued in which the officers recovered the piece of paper and as a result of which they handcuffed appellant because she had been "belligerent" in resisting their official rescue of the "warrant" from her person. Running roughshod over appellant, a policeman "grabbed" her, "twisted [*her*] hand," and she "yelled [*and*] pleaded with him" because "it was hurting." Appellant, in handcuffs, was then forcibly taken upstairs to her bedroom where the officers searched a dresser, a chest of drawers, a closet and some suitcases. They also looked into a photo album and through personal papers belonging to the appellant. The search spread to the rest of the second floor including the child's bedroom, the living room, the kitchen and a dinette. The basement of the building and a trunk found therein were also searched. The obscene materials for possession of which she was ultimately convicted were discovered in the course of that widespread search.

At the trial no search warrant was produced by the prosecution, nor was the failure to produce one explained or accounted for. At best, "there is, in the record, considerable doubt as to whether there ever was any warrant for the search of defendant's home." . . .

The State says that even if the search were made without authority, or otherwise unreasonably, it is not prevented from using the unconstitutionally seized evidence at trial, citing *Wolf* v. *Colorado,* 338 U.S. 25 (1949), in which this Court did indeed hold "that in a prosecution in a State court for a State crime the Fourteenth Amendment does not forbid the admission of evidence obtained by an unreasonable search and seizure." . . .

I

Seventy-five years ago, in *Boyd* v. *United States,* 116 U.S. 616, 630 (1886), considering the Fourth and Fifth Amendments as running "almost into each other" on the facts before it, this Court held the doctrines of those Amendments

> apply to all invasions on the part of the government and its employees of the sanctity of a man's home and the privacies of life. It is not the breaking of his doors, and the rummaging of his drawers, that constitutes the essence of the offense; but it is the invasion of his indefeasible right of personal security, personal liberty and private property. . . . Breaking into a house and opening boxes and drawers are circumstances of aggravation; but any forcible and compulsory extortion of a man's own testimony or of his private papers to be used as evidence to convict him of crime or to forfeit his goods,, is within the condemnation . . . [of those Amendments]. . . .

Less than 30 years after Boyd, this Court, in *Weeks* v. *United States,* 232 U.S. 383 (1914), stated that

> the Fourth Amendment . . . put the courts of the United States and Federal officials, in the exercise of their power and authority, under limitations and restraints [*and*] . . . forever secure[*d*] the people, their persons, houses, papers and effects against all unreasonable searches and seizures under the guise of law . . . and the duty of giving to it force and effect is obligatory upon all entrusted under our Federal system with the enforcement of the laws. . . .

Specifically dealing with the use of the evidence unconstitutionally seized, the Court concluded:

> If letters and private documents can thus be seized and held and used in evidence against a citizen accused of an offense, the protection of the Fourth Amendment declaring his right to be secure against such searches and seizures is of no value, and, so far as those thus placed are concerned, might as well be stricken from the Constitution. The efforts of the courts and their officials to bring the guilty to punishment, praiseworthy as they are, are not to be aided by the sacrifice of those great principles established by years of endeavor and suffering which have resulted in their embodiment in the fundamental law of the land. . . .

Finally, the Court in that case clearly stated that use of the seized evidence involved "a denial of the constitutional rights of the accused." . . . Thus, in the year 1914, in the Weeks case, this Court "for the first time" held that "in a federal prosecution the Fourth Amendment barred the use of evidence secured through an illegal search and seizure." . . . This Court has ever since required of federal law officers a strict adherence to that command which this Court has held to be a clear, specific, and constitutionally required—even if judicially implied—deterrent safeguard without insistence upon which the Fourth Amendment would have been reduced to "a form of words." . . . It meant, quite simply, that "conviction by means of unlawful seizures and enforced confessions . . . should find no sanction in the judgments of the courts. . . ."

There are in the cases of this Court some passing references to the Weeks rule as being one of evidence. But the plain and unequivocal language of Weeks—and its later paraphrase in Wolf—to the effect that the Weeks rule is of constitutional origin, remains entirely undisturbed. . . .

II

In 1949, 35 years after Weeks was announced, this Court, in *Wolf* v. *Colorado,* supra, again for the first time, discussed the effect of the Fourth Amendment upon the States through the operation of the Due Process Clause of the Fourteenth Amendment. It said:

> [W]e have no hesitation in saying that were a State affirmatively to sanction such police incursion into privacy it would run counter to the guaranty of the Fourteenth Amendment. . . .

Nevertheless, after declaring that the "security of one's privacy against arbitrary intrusion by the police" is "implicit in the 'concept of ordered liberty'—and as such enforceable aagint the States through the Due Process Clause," *cf. Palko* v. *Connecticut,* 302 U.S. 319 (1937), and announcing that it "stoutly adhere[d]" to the Weeks decision, the Court decided that the Weeks exclusionary rule would not then be imposed upon the States as "an essential ingredient of the right." . . .

III

Some five years after Wolf, in answer to a plea made here Term after Term that we overturn its doctrine on applicability of the Weeks exclusionary rule, this Court indicated that such should not be done until the States had "adequate opportunity to adopt or reject the [*Weeks*] rule." . . .

Today we once again examine Wolf's constitutional documentation of the right to privacy free from unreasonable state intrusion, and, after its dozen years on our books, are led by it to close the only courtroom door remaining open to evidence secured by official lawlessness in flagrant abuse of that basic right, reserved to all persons as a specific guarantee against that very same unlawful conduct. We hold that all evidence obtained by searches and seizures in violation of the Constitution is, by that same authority, inadmissible in a state court.

IV

Since the Fourth Amendment's right of privacy has been declared enforceable against the States through the Due Process Clause of the Fourteenth, it is enforceable against them by the same sanction of exclusion as is used against the Federal Government. Were it otherwise, then just as without the Weeks rule the assurance against unreasonable federal searches and seizures would be "a form of words," valueless and undeserving of mention in a perpetual charter of inestimable human liberties, so too, without that rule the freedom from state invasions of privacy would be so ephemeral and so neatly severed from its conceptual nexus with the freedom from all brutish means of coercing evidence as not to merit this Court's high regard as a freedom "implicit in the concept of ordered liberty." At the time that the Court held in Wolf that the Amendment was applicable to the States through the Due Process Clause, the cases of this Court, as we have seen, had steadfastly held that as to federal officers the Fourth Amendment included the exclusion of the evidence seized in violation of its provisions. . . . [T]he admission of the new constitutional right by Wolf could not consistently tolerate denial of its most important constitutional privilege, namely, the exclusion of the evidence which an accused had been forced to give by reason of the unlawful seizure. To hold otherwise is to grant the right but in reality to withhold its privilege and enjoyment. Only last year the Court itself recognized that the purpose of the exclusionary rule "is to deter—to compel respect for the constitutional guaranty in the only effectively available way—by removing the incentive to disregard it." . . .

Indeed, we are aware of no restraint, similar to that rejected today, conditioning the enforcement of any other basic constitutional right. The right to privacy, no less imporant than any other right carefully and particularly reserved to the people, would stand in marked contrast to all other rights declared as "basic to a free society." . . . The Court has not hesitated to enforce as strictly against the States as it does against the Federal Government the rights of free speech and of a free press, the rights to notice and to a fair, public trial, including, as it does, the right not to be convicted by use of a coerced confession, however logically relevant it be, and without regard to its reliability. . . . We find that, as to the Federal Government, the Fourth and Fifth Amendment and, as to the States, the freedom from unconscionable invasions of privacy and the freedom from convictions based upon coerced confessions do enjoy an "intimate relation" in their perpetuation of "principles of humanity and civil liberty [secured] . . . only after years of struggle." . . .

V

Moreover, our holding that the exclusionary rule is an essential part of both the Fourth and Fourteenth Amendments is not only the logical dictate of prior cases, but it also makes very good sense. There is no war between the Constitution and common sense. Presently, a federal prosecutor may make no use of evidence illegally seized, but a State's attorney across the street may, although he supposedly is operating under the enforceable prohibitions of the same Amendment. Thus the State, by admitting evidence unlawfully seized, serves to encourage disobedience to the Federal Constitution which it is bound to uphold. . . . In nonexclusionary States, federal officers, being human, were by it invited to and did, as our cases indicate, step across the street to the State's attorney with their unconstitutionally seized evidence. Prosecution on the basis of that evidence was then had in a state court in utter disregard of the enforceable Fourth Amendment. If the fruits of an unconstitutional search had been inadmissible in both state and federal courts, this inducement to evasion would have been sooner eliminated. . . .

Federal-state cooperation in the solution of crime under constitutional standards will be promoted, if only by recognition of their now mutual obligation to respect the same fundamental criteria in their approaches. "However much in a particular case insistence upon such rules may appear as a technicality that inures to the benefit of a guilty person, the history of the criminal law proves that tolerance of shortcut methods in law enforcement impairs its enduring effectiveness." . . . Denying shortcuts to only one of two cooperating law enforcement agencies tends naturally to breed legitimate suspicion of "working arrangements" whose results are equally tainted. . . .

The ignoble shortcut to conviction left open to the State tends to destroy the entire system of constitutional restraints on which the liberties of the people rest. Having once recognized that the right to privacy embodied in the Fourth Amendment is enforceable against the States, and that the right to be secure against rude invasions of privacy by state officers is, therefore, constitutional in origin, we can no longer permit that right to remain an empty promise. Because it is enforceable in the same manner and to like effect as other basic rights secured by the Due Process Clause, we can no longer permit it to be revocable at the whim of any police officer who, in the name of law enforcement itself, chooses to suspend its enjoyment. Our decision, founded on reason and truth, gives to the individual no more than that which the Constitution guarantees him, to the police officer no less than that to which honest law enforcement is entitled, and to the courts, that judicial integrity so necessary in the true administration of justice.

The judgment of the Supreme Court of Ohio is reversed and the cause remanded for further proceedings not inconsistent with this opinion.

Reversed and remanded.

Mr. Justice Black, Concurring.

I am still not persuaded that the Fourteenth Amendment, standing alone, would be enough to bar the introduction into evidence against an accused of papers and effects seized from him in violation of its commands. For the Fourth Amendment does not itself contain any provision expressly precluding the use of such evidence, and I am extremely doubtful that such a provision could properly be inferred from nothing more than the basic command against unreasonable searches and seizures. Reflection on the problem, however, in the light of cases coming before the Court since *Wolf,* has led me to conclude that when the Fourth Amendment's ban against unreasonable searches and seizures is considered together with the Fifth Amendment's ban against compelled self-incrimination, a constitutional basis emerges which not only justifies but actually requires the exclusionary rule.

The close interrelationship between the Fourth and Fifth Amendments, as they apply to this problem, has long been recognized and, indeed, was expressly made the ground for this Court's holding in *Boyd* v. *United States.* There the Court fully discussed this relationship and declared itself "unable to perceive that the seizure of a man's private books and papers to be used in evidence against him is substantially different from compelling him to be a witness against himself." It was upon this ground that Mr. Justice Rutledge largely relied in his dissenting opinion in the *Wolf* case. And, although I rejected the argument at that time, its force has, for me at least, become compelling with the more thorough understanding of the problem brought on by recent cases. In the final analysis, it seems to be that the Boyd doctrine, though perhaps not required by the express language of the Constitution strictly construed, is amply justified from an historical standpoint, soundly based in reason, and entirely consistent with what I regard to be the proper approach to interpretation of our Bill of Rights. . . .

The Court's opinion, in my judgment, dissipates the doubt and uncertainty in this field of constitutional law and I am persuaded, for this and other reasons stated, to depart from my prior views, to accept the Boyd doctrine as controlling in this state case and to join the Court's judgment and opinion which are in accordance with that constitutional doctrine.

Mr. Justice Douglas, Concurring.

. . . *Wolf* v. *Colorado* . . . was decided in 1949. The immediate result was a storm of constitutional controversy which only today finds its end.

I believe that this is an appropriate case in which to put an end to the asymmetry which *Wolf* imported into the law. . . . It is an appropriate case because the facts it presents show—as would few other cases—the casual arrogance of those who have the untrammelled power to invade one's home and to seize one's person. . . .

Memorandum of Mr. Justice Stewart.

Agreeing fully with Part I of Mr. Justice Harlan's dissenting opinion, I express no view as to the merits of the constitutional issue which the Court today decides. I would, however, reverse the judgment in this case, because I am persuaded that the provision of Section 2905.34 of the Ohio Revised Code, upon which the petitioner's conviction was based, is, in the words of Mr. Justice Harlan, not "consistent with the rights of free thought and expression assured against state action by the Fourteenth Amendment."

Mr. Justice Harlan, whom Mr. Justice Frankfurter and Mr. Justice Whittaker Join, Dissenting.

In overruling the *Wolf* case the Court, in my opinion, has forgotten the sense of judicial restraint which, with due regard for stare decisis, is one element that should enter into deciding whether a past decision of this Court should be overruled. Apart from that I also believe that the *Wolf* rule represents sounder Constitutional doctrine than the new rule which now replaces it.

I

From the Court's statement of the case one would gather that the central, if not controlling, issue on this appeal is whether illegally state-seized evidence is Constitutionally admissible in a state prosecution, an issue which would of course face us with the need for re-examining *Wolf*. However, such is not the situation. For, although that question was indeed raised here and below among appellant's subordinate points, the new and pivotal issue brought to the Court by this appeal is whether Section 2905.34 of the Ohio Revised Code making criminal the mere knowing possession or control of obscene material, and under which appellant has been convicted, is consistent with the rights of free thought and expression assured against state action by the Fourteenth Amendment. That was the principal issue which was decided by the Ohio Supreme Court, which was tendered by appellant's Jurisdictional Statement, and which was briefed and argued in this Court.

In this posture of things, I think it fair to say that five members of this Court have simply "reached out" to overrule *Wolf*. With all respect for the views of the majority, and recognizing that stare decisis carries different weight in Constitutional adjudication than it does in nonconstitutional decision, I can perceive no justification for regarding this case as an appropriate occasion for re-examining *Wolf*.

The action of the Court finds no support in the rule that decision of Constitutional issues should be avoided wherever possible. For in overruling *Wolf* the Court, instead of passing upon the validity of Ohio's Section 2905.34, has simply chosen between two Constitutional questions. . . .

The occasion which the Court has taken here is in the context of a case where the question was briefed not at all and argued only extremely tangentially. The unwisdom of overruling *Wolf* without full-dress argument is aggravated by the circumstances that that decision is a comparatively recent one (1949) to which three members of the present majority have at one time or other expressly subscribed; one to be sure with explicit misgivings. I would think that our obligation to the States, on whom we impose this new rule, as well as the obligation of orderly adherence to our own processes would demand that we seek that aid which adequate briefing and argument lends to the determination of an important issue. It certainly has never been a postulate of judicial power that mere altered disposition, or subsequent membership on the Court, is sufficient warrant for overturning a deliberately decided rule of Constitutional law.

Thus, if the Court was bent on reconsidering *Wolf*, I think that there would soon have presented itself an appropriate opportunity in which we could have had the benefit of full briefing and argument. In any event, at the very least, the present case should have been set down for reargument, in view of the inadequate briefing and argument we have received on the *Wolf* point. To all intents and purposes the Court's present action amounts to a summary reversal of *Wolf*, without argument.

I am bound to say that what has been done is not likely to promote respect either for the Court's adjudicatory process or for the stability of its decisions. Having been unable, however, to persuade any of the majority to a different procedural course, I now turn to the merits of the present decision.

II

I would not impose upon the States this federal exclusionary remedy. The reasons given by the majority for now suddenly turning its back on *Wolf* seem to me notably unconvincing. . . .

Our concern here, as it was in *Wolf*, is not with the desirability of that rule but only with the question whether the States are constitutionally free to follow it or not as they may themselves determine, and the relevance of the disparity of views among the States on this point lies simply in the fact that the judgment involved is a debatable one. . . .

The preservation of a proper balance between state and federal responsibility in the administration of criminal justice demands patience on the part of those who might like to see things move faster among the States in this respect. Problems of criminal law enforcement vary widely from State to State. One State, in considering the totality of its legal picture, may conclude that the need for embracing the Weeks rule is pressing because other remedies are unavailable or inadequate to secure compliance with the substantive Constitutional principle involved. Another though equally solicitous of Constitutional rights, may choose to pursue one purpose at a time, allowing all evidence relevant to guilt to be brought into a criminal trial, and dealing with Constitutional infractions by other means. Still another may consider the exclusionary rule too rough and ready a remedy, in that it reaches only unconstitutional intrusions which eventuate in criminal prosecution of the victims. Further, a State after experimenting with the Weeks rule for a time may, because of unsatisfactory experience with it, decide to revert to a nonexclusionary rule. And so on. . . . For us the question remains, as it has always been, one of state power, not one of passing judgment on the wisdom of one state course or another. In my view this Court should continue to forebear from fettering the States with adamant rule which may embarrass them in coping with their own peculiar problems in criminal law enforcement. . . .

Our role in promulgating the Weeks rule and its extensions . . . was quite a different one than it is here. There, in implementing the Fourth Amendment, we occupied the position of a tribunal having the ultimate responsibility for developing the standards and procedures of judicial administration within the judicial system over which it presides. Here we review State procedures whose measure is to be taken not against the specific substantive commands of the Fourth Amendment but under the flexible contours of the Due Process Clause. I do not believe that the Fourteenth Amendment empowers this Court to mold state remedies effectuating the right to freedom from "arbitrary intrusion by the police" to suit its own notions of how things should be done. . . .

A state conviction comes to us as the complete product of a sovereign judicial system. Typically a case will have been tried in a trial court, tested in some final appellate court, and will go no further. In the comparatively rare instance when a conviction is reviewed by us on due process grounds we deal then with a finished product in the creation of which we are allowed no hand, and our task, far from being one of overall supervision, is, speaking generally, restricted to a determination of whether the prosecution was constitutionally fair. The specifics of trial procedure, which in every mature legal system will vary greatly in detail, are within the sole competence of the States. I do not see how it can be said that a trial becomes unfair simply because a State determines that evidence may be considered by the trier of fact, regardless of how it was obtained, if it is relevant to the one issue with which the trial is concerned, the guilt or innocence of the accused. Of course, a court may use its procedures as an incidental means of pursuing other ends than the correct resolution of the controversies before it. Such indeed is the Weeks rule, but if a State does not choose to use its courts in this way, I do not believe that this Court is empowered to impose this much-debated procedure on local courts, however efficacious we may consider the Weeks rule to be as a means of securing Constitutional rights. . . .

I regret that I find so unwise in principle and so inexpedient in policy a decision motivated by the high purpose of increasing respect for Constitutional rights. But in the last analysis I think this Court can increase respect for the Constitution only if it rigidly respects the limitations which the Constitution places upon it, and respects as well the principles inherent in its own processes. In the present case I think we exceed both, and that our voice becomes only a voice of power, not of reason.

YOUR PHONE IS A PARTY LINE

Ira Glasser and Herman Schwartz

> They that can give up essential liberty to obtain a little temporary safety deserve neither liberty nor safety.
>
> —BENJAMIN FRANKLIN

Your son has just turned eighteen, and the Vietnam war is raging. You call up your local draft-counseling center, run by the Quakers, and make an appointment. It's important to know what your son's options are under the law, according to a friend of yours who is a lawyer. "The Selective Service law is very complicated," he tells you, "just like the tax law. At tax time, you go to a specialist, so when it's draft time for your son, you should do the same." The advice sounds reasonable and you are worried.

The local police are worried too, but not about your son. They are concerned about subversives and hippies, so they are watching everyone who comes and goes at the draft-counseling center. They are keeping political dossiers on the people who run the center and are even considering planting an undercover police agent inside who himself will provide advice while he checks out everyone else. Just to be on the safe side, they've got

Source: *Harper's Magazine* (October 1972), pp. 106–108, 111–112, 114. Copyright © 1972, by Minneapolis Star and Tribune Co., Inc. Reprinted from the October 1972 issue of *Harper's Magazine* by permission of the authors.

a tap on the center's phones. When you call about your son, your conversation is recorded.

You are a United States Congressman, and you have just discovered that the environment is becoming a big political issue. Environment groups are organizing a massive demonstration in Washington called Earth Day. You figure it would be a good idea to attend. Overhead, Army helicopters are taking aerial photos of the participants. Later, as a result of Congressional hearings, you discover that your activities have been closely followed and recorded in the files of Army intelligence.

You are married and the mother of a fourteen-month-old little girl, Cathy. You have a small house in the suburbs, and your husband works hard, but runaway prices aren't making it any easier to make ends meet. The last thing in the world you and your husband want is another baby, so one night while he is out bowling, you decide to attend a lecture about birth control. Baby-sitters are very expensive, and the meeting is early, so you take Cathy along. The lecture is fascinating, and despite some apprehension you had, she behaves well.

In the audience, however, are undercover police agents, watching everything, listening, and taking pictures with hidden cameras. After the meeting, you are arrested, charged with endangering the morals of a minor because you exposed your fourteen-month-old daughter to demonstrations of birth-control devices.

You are a member of and occasional contributor to a minority political party, one of the many splinter groups that have always existed on the fringe of American politics. Along with many other groups, your party is organizing a few buses to go to Washington to participate in a demonstration against the war. The FBI is nervous and decides to check up on the demonstrators. FBI agents persuade officials at the party's bank to let them see the names of officers of the party, these authorized to sign checks, and those who posted bond for the buses. Your name is among them. Soon your phone is tapped in the interests of national security.

You are a construction worker, and life isn't easy. After a hard day's work in the hot sun, you like to stop off at the local tavern for a cold beer. When you can you take the beer at a ball park, or at the track. Sometimes you don't mind placing a small bet on your favorite team, or on a horse. There's this bookie you know, and once in a while, if the odds are right and the hunch irresistible, you give him a call and put down a few dollars. It makes the evening a little more interesting, and when you win, the beer tastes a little bit colder.

But the police (who will tell you, if you ask them, that gambling should be legalized so they can spend their time catching real criminals) have every bookie they know tapped. Your bookie is one of the unlucky ones. When you call (and when his wife, his mother, his daughter, or his girl-friend calls), the conversation is recorded. If you call often enough, maybe your phone will be tapped too. Just to be on the safe side.

You are an Army doctor, serving out your two years on an Army base in the South, taking care of the mostly minor ailments of Army men and their wives. Like most Army doctors, you are privileged to have the rank of captain, and you are permitted to live off-base. You decide to spend your time off (out of uniform, of course) working with a local civil-rights group in a voter-registration campaign. While engaged in this work, you attract the attention of a civilian Army counterintelligence agent, who happens to live in the same town. Before long, there's a thick dossier on you, the magazines you subscribe to are noted, and a tap is placed on your phone.

All these examples of government surveillance are true. Aside from some anecdotal details, all actually happened. Although surveillance of phone conversations (wiretapping) took place in some cases and not in others, all of them—any many others like them—document the government's pro-miscuous desire to snoop.

Contrary to news reports and editorial hosannas, the government's pas-sion for snooping is unlikely to be cooled by the Supreme Court's recent decision requiring federal agents to obtain judge-signed warrants before they can tap the phones of alleged suspects in cases of "domestic national security." To be sure, the Court's decision was a strong reaffirmation of the Fourth Amendment—and a stern rebuttal of former Attorney General John Mitchell's arrogant argument that he was empowered to wiretap political dissenters with no judicial supervision whatever. As we shall see, though, the decision is sufficiently narrow that government snooping is almost certain to continue virtually unabated, at least under the Nixon Administra-tion. The future looks bright for everyone in the official surveillance busi-ness—local police, Army intelligence, and various civilian federal agencies, from the FBI to the IRS.

A growing sense that government is watching is not the paranoid de-lusion of a few discontented left-wingers. According to Justice William O. Douglas: "Those who register dissent or who petition their government for redress are subjected to scrutiny by grand juries, by the FBI, or even by the military. Their associates are interrogated. Their homes are bugged and their telephones are wiretapped. They are befriended by secret government informers." Douglas' concerns are warmly shared by old-fashioned con-servatives like Senator Sam J. Ervin, Jr., the North Carolina Democrat who is generally recognized as the Senate's foremost authority on constitutional law. Interestingly enough, Ervin, who is chairman of the Senate Sub-committee on Constitutional Rights, originally supported the 1968 bill that authorized wiretapping and electronic eavesdropping. After watching the surveillance system in action for four years, however, Senator Ervin had this to say: "Knowledge that the government is engaged in surveillance of its citizens creates an atmosphere of fear, which is inimical to freedom . . . Democracy cannot survive if the people are sullen, scared and rebellious."

Writs of Assistance

Wiretapping is nothing else but an electronic search. If the government wished to have one of its agents provided with a key to your house, to come and go as he pleased, listening to whatever interested him, we would all be quite properly frightened. But if the development of technology allows the government to achieve the same result by using a powerful microphone or by electronically intercepting the signal on a telephone wire, it doesn't seem to bother us as much. (A few polls have indicated widespread hostility to wiretapping, but the hostility has remained silent, and as a result many legislators throughout the country have voted and spoken for wiretapping.)

The lack of public fright or outrage over government wiretapping is especially puzzling in light of the fierce defense of privacy that formed much of the early American colonial struggle against Britain. British colonial reve-nue officers, for example, were granted wide discretionary powers by Par-liament to search in suspected places for smuggled goods by means of "writs of assistance." The fight by American colonists against these hated writs was described by John Adams as "the first act of opposition to the arbitrary claims of Great Britain." Colonial revulsion against British searches led the Founding Fathers to write the Fouth Amendment to our Constitution, which bans general searches and narrowly limits the granting of search warrants except under very special and particular conditions.

Unfortunately, however, wiretapping was for years not considered by the Supreme Court to be a "search" within the meaning of the Fourth Amendment. The Court, in a 5-4 decision handed down in 1928, ruled that there was no search when the building was not actually penetrated physi-cally. In these days of parabolic microphones, miniature electronic devices, and hidden cameras, such a view seems quaint and wildly unrealistic. In any case, due to that decision, the chief protection from government wire-tapping had to come from Congress. In 1934, Congress passed a law pro-hibiting wiretapping. Ever since then, the battle has been on.

For more than thirty years, law-enforcement officials lobbied hard for bills that would relax the total ban on wiretapping. Such bills always failed (although many law-enforcement officials continued to tap wires illegally, spurred on perhaps by the ambiguous attitude of Supreme Court decisions).

But then, in 1968, Congress enacted the Omnibus Crime Control and Safe Streets Act, which permitted all state and federal police to obtain warrants in order to tap phones and bug rooms for an almost unlimited number of crimes ranging from marijuana possession and cockfighting to murder.

Time, Money, and Liberty

Is wiretapping necessary? Is it so crucial to effective law enforcement that it is worth risking our right to privacy? Does wiretapping snoop only on criminals, or do innocent citizens have cause to fear? How much does wiretapping cost? How many criminals does it catch? How much wiretapping actually goes on, and for what purposes?

Until recently, it was not possible to answer these questions with any certainty. If legislators were forced to balance the claims of privacy against the claims of law enforcement, they usually had nothing to go on but the strong opinions of law-enforcement officials. Is wiretapping necessary? Certainly, according to New York District Attorney Frank Hogan, who repeatedly claimed that electronic surveillance was the "single most valuable weapon" in fighting organized crime. Does wiretapping help catch a lot of criminals? Certainly, according to former FBI Director J. Edgar Hoover, who just before his death claimed that "much of the credit for [increased convictions in 1971] should go to court-approved electronic surveillance devices." Is wiretapping especially useful for really serious crimes like homicide and kidnapping? Certainly, according to Mr. Justice Lewis Powell, who wrote an article in August 1971, before he was appointed to the Supreme Court, arguing that federal surveillance was used largely for crimes like homicide and kidnapping.

For the first time, however, facts are available that show that Hogan, Hoover, and Powell were exaggerating grossly. And the facts prove that wiretapping is not a very useful, much less a necessary, tool of law enforcement; that it is extraordinarily expensive; that relatively few convictions are linked to wiretapping; and that of those few convictions, an almost negligible number have been for serious crimes like murder or kidnapping.

These data are available from the federal government. The Omnibus Crime Control and Safe Streets Act of 1968 that authorized expanded bugging and tapping also required full government reports to Congress detailing the annual costs, results, and number of wiretaps conducted. The reports have now been issued for the years 1968 to 1971, and they prove conclusively that wiretapping is at best of very little value.

Here are the facts:[1]

---

[1] For some reason, the government reports contain very few overall totals. Our figures were obtained by multiplying the average number of conversations and people overheard per wiretap by the total number of taps.

- In 1968, when there was no federal eavesdropping, state officials listened in on 66,716 conversations.
- In 1969, when both federal and state officials eavesdropped, 173,711 conversations were overheard.
- In 1970, the amount of eavesdropping doubled to 381,865 conversations.
- In 1971, at least 498,325 conversations were overheard, a jump of 30 per cent over 1970.

What were the results?

- In 1968, out of 66,716 overheard conversations, *no* convictions were reported.
- In 1969, out of 173,711 conversations, 294 convictions resulted.
- In 1970, out of 381,865 conversations, 538 convictions resulted.
- In 1971, out of at least 498,325 conversations, 322 convictions have resulted so far.

In the four years since the bill was passed, 93,080 people have been spied upon, and thus far, only 1,154 have been reportedly convicted—*barely more than 1 per cent.*[2]

In 1971, the reported cost of such surveillance was over $5 million. The average federal tap in 1971 cost $7,500; in 1970, it was $12,106. Neither of these figures includes the many, many hours spent by lawyers, judges, and investigators in preparing applications and keeping records. It also omits the cost of so-called "national security" surveillance, which if included would increase the total enormously.

It is true, of course, that the rate of convictions is not yet complete, because there is a lag between the time the tap occurs and the time the case is disposed of in court. But certainly one can assume that most arrests that took place in 1968 and 1969 have by now been disposed of and their results reported; and even if there turned out to be twice as many convictions as have so far been reported, the rate would still be under 2.5 per cent of the persons overheard.

Law-enforcement officials are not happy about these meager results, which do not exactly support their constant clamor for wiretapping power. They would rather use statistics on arrests, which are somewhat more favorable to their point of view. Arrests, however, prove nothing about guilt or in-

[2] It is not at all clear that even these few convictions were achieved by wiretapping. It is quite possible that many or all of them could have been obtained without it. We don't know, and the government reports don't say. We do know of several examples, however, where convictions were obtained and wiretapping was used, although wiretapping had nothing to do with the convictions.

nocence and are often made incorrectly at the discretion of the police officer. During the May Day demonstrations in Washington last year, for example, thousands of arrests were made and later dismissed as "mistakes."

Furthermore, wiretap warrants may not be constitutionally issued unless there is already enough evidence to arrest at least someone. So the fact that wiretaps lead to a large number of arrests is hardly surprising. Even so, if arrest rates are used instead of conviction rates as a measure of wiretapping's usefulness, the results are remarkably thin. Out of more than 1.1 million tapped conversations involving 93,080 people from 1968 to 1971, only 6,131 arrests were made, less than 7 per cent of the people overheard. Of those few arrests, less than 20 per cent have resulted in convictions, but even if *all* the arrests had resulted in convictions the returns would still not be very impressive.

The kinds of crimes in which wiretapping is used are equally unimpressive. Mr. Justice Powell's assertion that federal surveillance was used largely for serious crimes like homicide and kidnapping is baseless. In 1970 and 1971, there was not a single federal tap for either crime; in 1969, only one tap even arguably involved kidnapping, and as of December 31, 1971, not even an arrest had resulted in that case. On the state level, the results are similar. From 1968 to 1971, only three taps used by state officials involved kidnapping, and while murder was involved in a few state wiretaps, only one conviction has yet been reported for any of them.

The overwhelming bulk of court-ordered tapping is not for crimes of violence but for gambling and drugs. In 1971, gambling alone accounted for 90 per cent of federal tapping; drugs accounted for another 6 per cent, and all other offenses only 4 per cent. It cannot even be argued that the bosses of organized crime are the target; most taps in gambling cases snoop on bookies and their customers. It is hard to believe that many top figures in organized crime operate out of bookmaking parlors.

Is it worth the cost, in both dollars and liberty, to listen in on many thousands of conversations and people merely to obtain 1 per cent convictions, and most of those in petty gambling cases? Certainly, we should not be spending millions of dollars, invading the privacy of tens of thousands of people, and risking basic liberties for the sake of so little return in law enforcement.

Why, then, have John Mitchell, William Rehnquist, and Richard Kleindienst pressed so hard for wiretapping powers? Some people believe that the government has used the fear of violent crime to gain widespread social acceptance of electronic surveillance in order to use it to spy on and ultimately control political behavior, and especially dissent. An analysis of the government's recent vigorous attempt to spy on political dissidents without a warrant lends some support for that view.

National Security and Political Freedom

So far, all of the analysis of wiretapping has been based upon official government reports of court-ordered taps. However, these reports *do not include wiretaps and electronic surveillance undertaken in the name of "national security."* In fact, until this past June when the Supreme Court struck it down, the Attorney General claimed the power to wiretap *without court order* on any group or person he considered "dangerous" (whatever that means). Moreover, the government admitted in court that in national-security wiretapping, it is not even looking for criminals but rather is seeking "intelligence." So no question of crime generally arises. FBI agents freely conceded that such taps check up not on criminals but on the activities and associations of political suspects. Indeed, G. Robert Blakey, chief counsel to Senator John McClellan, has said that such surveillance "is sometimes used to determine the influence of extremist groups in other legitimate organizations." The best example of this was the tapping of Martin Luther King's phone, which went on until a few days before his death and which did not remotely have anything to do with crime. Unfortunately, the King example was not an isolated one.

If the reported results of court-ordered wiretapping (where warrants must be issued and reports made) show so much promiscuous government wiretapping with so little result for law enforcement, imagine what has gone on with national-security wiretapping, where no warrants have been required and no reports need be made.

Until December 1971 there was no way to tell. The Administration kept assuring us in public statements that very few national-security taps took place. President Nixon repeatedly said that there were no more than fifty such taps per year in operation at any one time during 1970 and 1971. For example, in April 1971 Nixon told the annual convention of the American Society of Newspaper Editors: "Now in the two years that we have been in office—now get this number—the total number of taps for national-security purposes by the FBI . . . has been less than fifty a year." And in its brief filed before the Supreme Court, the government told the court that only thirty-six warrantless wiretaps were operated in 1970.

These claims, however, have been completely contradicted by correspondence between the Justice Department and Senator Edward M. Kennedy, in which the government admitted to far more extensive spying. A study of that correspondence and related public materials, released last December by Senator Kennedy, shows that:

- During 1969–70, there were almost as many national-security wiretaps as there were court-ordered wiretaps.
- The average duration of such warrantless taps was from *three to nine times longer* than the average duration of court-approved taps.

- The total number of people overheard by federal electronic eaves-dropping without court permission thus probably *far exceeds* the number overheard by eavesdropping with court permission.

In the Supreme Court, the government admitted to some incredibly lengthy surveillance. In one case, it eavesdropped on a single target for fourteen months, intercepting nearly 1,000 phone calls and overhearing who knows how many people. If this example and others like it are typical—and Senator Kennedy's study lends some support to such an assumption—then the number of people overheard on these national-security taps is in the tens of thousands. These people are not criminals but political suspects, people whose political activities the Attorney General thinks bear watching.

The frightening thing about the government's rationale in support of its power to wiretap without a warrant was that it could equally be used to extend to other forms of obtaining "intelligence," such as entering and searching someone's home or office or desk—dangerously close to the hated "writs of assistance" we fought against during the American Revolution. The true dimension of the government's position as argued in the Supreme Court revealed an open demand for vast, lengthy, unsupervised, and unchecked powers to invade the privacy of many, many people having no link, or only the remotest link, to any criminal activity.

This demand proved to be too much even for the Nixon Court, despite its domination by a "law and order" majority. Without a dissent (although Justice Rehnquist abstained), the Court ruled that the government could not eavesdrop on domestic groups with "no significant connection with a foreign power, its agents or agencies" unless a court-ordered warrant was obtained first. As the Court said in an opinion by Mr. Justice Powell:

> Official surveillance, whether its purpose be criminal investigation or on-going intelligence gathering, risks infringement of constitutionally pro-tected privacy of speech. Security surveillances are especially sensitive because of the inherent vagueness of the domsetic security concept, the necessarily broad and continuing nature of intelligence gathering, and the temptation to utilize such surveillance to oversee political dissent.

The Powell opinion, however, left the government a good many loop-holes. First, it prohibited warrantless taps only on purely *domestic groups,* leaving open the question of whether a warrant is required in investigations concerning foreign intelligence. This opening is dangerous because the defi-nition of "foreign intelligence" is pretty vague and because foreign intelligence investigations can involve domestic groups. J. Edgar Hoover justified spying on Martin Luther King by referring to "Communist in-fluence." The Justice Department justified taps on the Jewish Defense League either because of the League's "links" to Israel or because of its actions in behalf of Soviet Jewry against Russian diplomats in the United States.

After the Court's decision last June, Attorney General Richard Kleindienst declared that he would not tap domestic groups based on tenuous links with foreign powers. But when the temptation arises, can the government be trusted not to rely on possible relationships between the Black Panthers and Algeria, the Jewish Defense League and Israel, and various peace groups and North Vietnam or Cuba when it wishes to justify uncontrolled surveillance? Given the record of this Administration, it does not seem very safe to trust the promises of Richard Kleindienst. It would have been better if the Court had instead closed all the doors to warrantless tapping.

Even where warrants are required, Justice Powell's opinion was somewhat ominous. Normally, a wiretapping warrant cannot be issued unless there is probable cause to believe that a crime has been committed. That is the same standard used to justify an arrest. But in national-security wiretapping, the government has admitted that it frequently has no evidence of crime but is only looking for "intelligence." Under the usual standards, such taps would not qualify for a warrant. In his opinion, however, Justice Powell virtually invited Congress to relax the standard and make it easier to issue a warrant in cases involving domestic-intelligence surveillance. If the standards are lowered, the requirement of prior court approval might turn out not to mean much.

As a matter of fact, our experience with wiretapping warrants, and with conventional search warrants as well, shows that the courts are remarkably cooperative. From 1968 to 1971, out of 1,891 federal and state applications for wiretap warrants, only *two* were turned down. As Philadelphia District Attorney Arlen Specter has delicately put it:

> Judges tend to rely upon the prosecutor . . . Experience in our criminal courts has shown the prior judicial approval for search and seizure warrants is more a matter of form than of substance in guaranteeing the existence of probable cause to substantiate the need for a search . . . Some judges have specifically said they do not want to know the reasons for the tap so that they could not be accused later of relaying the information to men suspected of organized crime activities.

Under the even more relaxed standards suggested by Justice Powell, the government will probably be able to tap whenever and as long as it wants, if it is willing to go through the motions of getting prior judicial approval. And that should be easy.

Once, long ago, we were afraid of British officials invading our homes on warrantless searches, and so we erected the Fourth Amendment to protect us. Today, in a time of social disorganization, we have other fears—

racial, generational, economic—but mostly we fear crime. Not all crime. We don't fear white-collar crime, and we don't even fear the violent gang-land shootouts in New York. Random mugging and burglary—the crimes of social disorganization—are what we fear, and there are those who would manipulate that fear and panic us into dismantling the Fourth Amendment. If they succeed, we will be less, not more, safe.

No Right to Liberty

In Re Gault

Mr. Justice Fortas delivered the opinion of the Court.

This is an appeal under 28 U.S.C. Sec. 1257(2) from a judgment of the Supreme Court of Arizona affirming the dismissal of a petition for a writ of habeas corpus. . . . The petition sought the release of Gerald Francis Gault, petitioners' 15-year-old son, who had been committed as a juvenile delinquent to the State Industrial School by the Juvenile Court of Gila County, Arizona. The Supreme Court of Arizona affirmed dismissal of the writ. . . . The court agreed that the constitutional guarantee of due process of law is applicable in such proceedings. It held that Arizona's Juvenile Code is to be read as "impliedly" implementing the "due process concept." . . . It concluded that the proceedings ending in commitment of Gerald Gault did not offend those requirements. We do not agree, and we reverse. We begin with a statement of the facts.

On Monday, June 8, 1964, at about 10 A.M., Gerald Francis Gault and a friend, Ronald Lewis, were taken into custody by the Sheriff of Gila County. Gerald was then still subject to a six months' probation order. . . . The police action on June 8 was taken as the result of a verbal complaint by a neighbor of the boys, Mrs. Cook, about a telephone call made to her in which the caller or callers made lewd or indecent remarks. It will suffice for the purposes of this opinion to say that the remarks or questions put to her were of the irritatingly offensive, adolescent, sex variety.

At the time Gerald was picked up, his mother and father were both at work. No notice that Gerald was being taken into custody was left at the home. No other steps were taken to advise them that their son had, in effect, been arrested. Gerald was taken to the Children's Detention Home. . . . The deputy probation officer, Flagg, who was also superintendent of the Detention Home, told Mrs. Gault "why Jerry was there" and said that a

Source: *In Re Gault* 387 U.S. 1; 18 L. Ed. 2d 527; 87 Sup. Ct. 1428 (1967).

hearing would be held in Juvenile Court at 3 o'clock the following day, June 9.

Officer Flagg filed a petition with the Court on the hearing day, June 9, 1964. It was not served on the Gaults. Indeed, none of them saw this petition until the habeas corpus hearing on August 17, 1964. The petition was certainly formal. It made no reference to any factual basis for the judicial action which it initiated. It recited only that "said minor is under the age of 18 years and in need of the protection of this Honorable Court [and that] said minor is a delinquent minor." It prayed for a hearing and an order regarding "the care and custody of said minor." . . .

On June 9, Gerald, his mother, his older brother, and Probation Officers Flagg and Henderson appeared before the Juvenile Judge in chambers. Gerald's father was not there. He was at work out of the city. Mrs. Cook, the complainant, was not there. No one was sworn at this hearing. No transcript or recording was made. No memorandum or record of the substance of the proceedings was prepared. Our information about the proceedings and the subsequent hearing on June 15, derives entirely from the testimony of the Juvenile Court Judge, Mr. and Mrs. Gault, and Officer Flagg at the habeas corpus proceedings conducted two months later. From this, it appears that at the June 9 hearing Gerald was questioned by the judge about the telephone call. There was conflict as to what he said. His mother recalled that Gerald said he only dialed Mrs. Cook's number and then handed the telephone to his friend, Ronald. Officer Flagg recalled that Gerald had admitted making the lewd remarks. Judge McGhee testified that Gerald "admitted making one of these [lewd] statements." At the conclusion of the hearing, the judge said he would "think about it." Gerald was taken back to the Detention Home. . . . On June 11 or 12, after having been detained since June 8, Gerald was released and driven home.[1] There is no explanation in the record as to why he was kept in the Detention Home or why he was released. At 5 P.M. on the day of Gerald's release, Mrs. Gault received a note signed by Officer Flagg. It was on plain paper, not letterhead. Its entire text is as follows:

> Mr. Gault:
> Judge McGhee has set Monday June 15, 1964 at 11:00 A.M. as the date and time for further Hearings on Gerald's delinquency
> /s/ Flagg

At the appointed time on Monday, June 15, Gerald, his father and mother, Ronald Lewis and his father, and Officers Flagg and Henderson

---

[1] There is a conflict between the recollection of Mrs. Gault and that of Officer Flagg. Mrs. Gault testified that Gerald was released on Friday, June 12, Officer Flagg that it had been on Thursday, June 11. This was from memory; he had no record, and the note was undated.

were present before Judge McGhee. Witnesses at the habeas corpus proceedings differed in their recollections of Gerald's testimony at the June 15 hearing. Mr. and Mrs. Gault recalled that Gerald again testified that he had only dialed the number and that the other boy had made the remarks. Officer Flagg agreed that at this hearing Gerald did not admit making the lewd remarks. But Judge McGhee recalled that "there was some admission again of some of the lewd statements. He—he didn't admit any of the more serious lewd statements." Again, the complainant, Mrs. Cook, was not present. Mrs. Gault asked that Mrs. Cook be present "so she could see which boy had done the talking, the dirty talking over the phone." The Juvenile Judge said "she didn't have to be present at that hearing." The judge did not speak to Mrs. Cook or communicate with her at any time. Probation Officer Flagg had talked to her once—over the telephone on June 9.

At this June 15 hearing a "referral report" made by the probation officers was filed with the court, although not disclosed to Gerald or his parents. This listed the charge as "Lewd Phone Calls." At the conclusion of the hearing, the judge committed Gerald as a juvenile delinquent to the State Industrial School "for the period of his minority (that is, until 21), unless sooner discharged by the process of law." . . .

No appeal is permitted by Arizona law in juvenile cases. On August 3, 1964, a petition for a writ of habeas corpus was filed with the Supreme Court of Arizona and referred by it to the Superior Court for hearing.

At the habeas corpus hearing on August 17, Judge McGhee was vigorously cross-examined as to the basis for his actions. He testified that he had taken into account the fact that Gerald was on probation. He was asked "under what section of . . . the code you found the boy delinquent?" . . .

. . . In substance, he concluded that Gerald came within [the state statute] which specifies that a "delinquent child" includes one "who has violated a law of the state or an ordinance or regulation of a political subdivision thereof." . . . The judge also testified that he acted under [the statutory provision] which includes in the definition of a "delinquent child" one who, as the judge phrased it, is "habitually involved in immoral matters." . . .

The Superior Court dismissed the writ, and appellants sought review in the Arizona Supreme Court. . . .

The Supreme Court handed down an elaborate and wide-ranging opinion affirming dismissal of the writ. . . . [Appellants] urge that we hold the Juvenile Code of Arizona invalid on its face or as applied in this case because, contrary to the Due Process Clause of the Fourteenth Amendment, the juvenile is taken from the custody of his parents and committed to a state institution pursuant to proceedings in which the Juvenile Court has virtually unlimited discretion, and in which the following basic rights are denied:

1. Notice of the charges;
2. Right to counsel;
3. Right to confrontation and cross-examination;
4. Privilege against self-incrimination;
5. Right to a transcript of the proceedings; and
6. Right to appellate review.

. . .

This Court has not heretofore decided the precise question. In *Kent* v. *United States,* 383 U.S. 541, 86 S.Ct. 1045, 16 L.Ed. 2d 84 (1966), we considered the requirements for a valid waiver of the "exclusive" jurisdiction of the Juvenile Court of the District of Columbia so that a juvenile could be tried in the adult criminal court of the District. . . . [We] emphasized the necessity that "the basic requirements of due process and fairness" be satisfied in such proceedings. *Hale* v. *State of Ohio,* 332 U.S. 596, 68 S.Ct. 302, 92 L.Ed. 224 (1948), involved the admissibility, in a state criminal court of general jurisdiction, of a confession of a 15-year-old boy. The Court held that the Fourteenth Amendment applied to prohibit the use of the coerced confession. Mr. Justice Douglas said, "Neither man nor child can be allowed to stand condemned by methods which flout constitutional requirements of due process of law." . . . Accordingly, while these cases relate only to restricted aspects of the subject, they unmistakably indicate that, whatever may be their precise impact, neither the Fourteenth Amendment nor the Bill of Rights is for adults alone.

. . .

From the inception of the juvenile court system, wide differences have been tolerated—indeed insisted upon—between the procedural rights accorded to adults and those of juveniles. In practically all jurisdictions, there are rights granted to adults which are withheld from juveniles. In addition to the specific problems involved in the present case, for example, it has been held that the juvenile is not entitled to bail, to indictment by grand jury, to a public trial or to trial by jury. It is frequent practice that rules governing the arrest and interrogation of adults by the police are not observed in the case of juveniles.

. . .

The right of the State, as *parens patriae,* to deny to the child procedural rights available to his elders was elaborated by the assertion that a child, unlike an adult, has a right "not to liberty but to custody." He can be made to attorn to his parents, to go to school, etc. If his parents default in effectively performing their custodial functions—that is, if the child is "delinquent"—the state may intervene. In doing so, it does not deprive the child of any rights, because he has none. It merely provides the "custody" to which the child is entitled. On this basis, proceedings involving juveniles were described as "civil" not "criminal" and therefore not subject to the requirements which restrict the state when it seeks to deprive a person of his liberty.

. . . Juvenile court history has . . . demonstrated that unbridled discretion, however benevolently motivated, is frequently a poor substitute for principle and procedure. . . . The absence of substantive standards has not necessarily meant that children receive careful, compassionate, individualized treatment. The absence of procedural rules based upon constitutional principle has not always produced fair, efficient, and effective procedures. Departures from established principles of due process have frequently resulted not in enlightened procedure, but in arbitrariness.

. . .

. . . [I]t is urged that the juvenile benefits from informal proceedings in the court. The early conception of the juvenile court proceeding was one in which a fatherly judge touched the heart and conscience of the erring youth by talking over his problems, by paternal advice and admonition, and in which, in extreme situations, benevolent and wise institutions of the State provided guidance and help "to save him from a downward career." Then, as now, goodwill and compassion were admirably prevalent. But recent studies have, with surprising unanimity, entered sharp dissent as to the validity of this gentle conception. They suggest that the appearance as well as the actuality of fairness, the partiality and orderliness—in short, the essentials of due process may be a more impressive and more therapeutic attitude so far as the juvenile is concerned. . . . While due process requirements will, in some instances, introduce a degree of order and regularity to juvenile court proceedings to determine delinquency, and in contested cases will introduce some elements of the adversary system, nothing will require that the conception of the kindly juvenile judge be replaced by its opposite, nor do we here rule upon the question whether ordinary due process requirements must be observed with respect to hearings to determine the disposition of the delinquent child.

Ultimately, however, we confront the reality of that portion of the juvenile court process with which we deal in this case. A boy is charged with misconduct. The boy is committed to an institution where he may be restrained of liberty for years. It is of no constitutional consequence—and of limited practical meaning—that the institution to which he is committed is called an Industrial School. The fact of the matter is that, however euphemistic the title, a "receiving home" or an "industrial school" for juveniles is an institution of confinement in which the child is incarcerated for a greater or lesser time. His world becomes "a building with white-washed walls, regimented routine and institutional laws. . . ." Instead of mother and father and sisters and brothers and friends and classmates, his world is peopled by guards, custodians, state employees, and "delinquents" confined with him for anything from waywardness to rape and homicide.

In view of this, it would be extraordinary if our Constitution did not require the procedural regularity and the exercise of care implied in the phrase "due process." Under our Constitution, the condition of a boy does not justify a kangaroo court. The traditional ideas of juvenile court procedure, indeed, contemplated that time would be available and care would be used to establish precisely what the juvenile did and why he did it—was it a prank of adolescence or a brutal act threatening serious consequences to himself or society unless corrected? Under traditional notions, one would assume that in a case like that of Gerald Gault, where the juvenile appears to have a home, a working mother and father, and an older brother, the Juvenile Judge would have made a careful inquiry and judgment as to the possibility that the boy could be disciplined and dealt with at home, despite his previous transgressions. Indeed, so far as appears in the record before us, except for some conversation with Gerald about his school work and his "wanting to go to . . . Grand Canyon with his father," the points to which the judge directed his attention were little different from those that would be involved in determining any charge of violation of a penal statute. The essential difference between Gerald's case and a normal criminal case is that safeguards available to adults were discarded in Gerald's case. The summary procedure as well as the long commitment were possible because Gerald was 15 years of age instead of over 18.

If Gerald had been over 18, he would not have been subject to Juvenile Court proceedings. For the particular offense immediately involved, the maximum punishment would have been a fine of $5 to $50, or imprisonment in jail for not more than two months. Instead, he was committed to custody for a maximum of six years. If he had been over 18 and had committed an offense to which such a sentence might apply, he would have been entitled to substantial rights under the Constitution of the United States as well as under Arizona's laws and constitution. The United States Constitution would guarantee him rights and protections with respect to arrest, search, [sic] and seizure, and pretrial interrogation. It would assure him of specific notice of the charges and adequate time to decide his course of action and to prepare his defense. He would be entitled to clear advice that he could be represented by counsel, and, at least if a felony were involved, the State would be required to provide counsel if his parents were unable to afford it. If the court acted on the basis of his confession, careful procedures would be required to assure its voluntariness. If the case went to trial, confrontation and opportunity for cross-examination would be guaranteed. So wide a gulf between the State's treatment of the adult and of the

child requires a bridge sturdier than mere verbiage, and reasons more persuasive than cliché can provide. . . .

We now turn to the specific issues which are presented to us in the
present case.

NOTICE OF CHARGES

. . .

We cannot agree with the court's conclusion that adequate notice was
given in this case. Notice, to comply with due process requirements, must
be given sufficiently in advance of scheduled court proceedings so that
reasonable opportunity to prepare will be afforded, and it must "set forth
the alleged misconduct with particularity." . . . The "initial hearing" in
the present case was a hearing on the merits. Notice at that time is not
timely; and even if there were a conceivable purpose served by the deferral
proposed by the court below, it would have to yield to the requirements
that the child and his parents or guardian be notified, in writing, of the
specific charge or factual allegations to be considered at the hearing, and
that such written notice be given at the earliest practicable time, and in
any event sufficiently in advance of the hearing to permit preparation. Due
process of law requires notice of the sort we have described—that is, notice
which would be deemed constitutionally adequate in a civil or criminal
proceedings. . . .

RIGHT TO COUNSEL

Appellants charge that the Juvenile Court proceedings were fatally defective because the court did not advise Gerald or his parents of their right
to counsel, and proceeded with the hearing, the adjudication of delinquency
and the order of commitment in the absence of counsel. . . . The Supreme
Court of Arizona pointed out that "[t]here is disagreement [among the
various jurisdictions] as to whether the court must advise the infant that
he has a right to counsel." . . . It referred to a provision of the Juvenile
Code which it characterized as requiring "that the probation officer shall
look after the interests of neglected, delinquent and dependent children,"
including representing their interests in court. The court argued that "The
parent and the probation officer may be relied upon to protect the infant's
interests." . . . It said that juvenile courts have the discretion, but not the
duty, to allow such representation. . . . We do not agree. Probation officers, in the Arizona scheme, are also arresting officers. They initiate proceedings and file petitions which they verify . . . alleging the delinquency
of the child; and they testify . . . against the child. And here the probation
officer was also superintendent of the Detention Home. The probation officer
cannot act as counsel for the child. His role in the adjudicatory hearing, by

statute and in fact, is as arresting officer and witness against the child. Nor can the judge represent the child. . . . A proceeding where the issue is whether the child will be found to be "delinquent" and subjected to the loss of his liberty for years is comparable in seriousness to a felony prosecution. The juvenile needs the assistance of counsel to cope with problems of law, to make skilled inquiry into the facts, to insist upon regularity of the proceedings, and to ascertain whether he has a defense and to prepare and submit it. The child "requires the guiding hand of counsel at every step in the proceedings against him."

. . .

CONFRONTATION, SELF-INCRIMINATION, CROSS-EXAMINATION

Appellants urge that the writ of habeas corpus should have been granted because of the denial of the rights of confrontation and cross-examination in the Juvenile Court hearings, and because the privilege against self-incrimination was not observed. . . .

Our first question, then, is whether Gerald's admission was improperly obtained and relied on as the basis of decision, in conflict with the Federal Constitution. For this purpose, it is necessary briefly to recall the relevant facts.

Mrs. Cook, the complainant, and the recipient of the alleged telephone call, was not called as a witness. Gerald's mother asked the Juvenile Court Judge why Mrs. Cook was not present and the judge replied that "she didn't have to be present." So far as appears, Mrs. Cook was spoken to only once, by Officer Flagg, and this was by telephone. . . . Gerald had been questioned by the probation officer after having been taken into custody. The exact circumstances of this questioning do not appear in the record. Gerald was also questioned by the Juvenile Court Judge at each of the two hearings. The judge testified in the habeas corpus proceeding that Gerald admitted making "some of the lewd statements . . . [but not] any of the more serious lewd statements." . . .

We shall assume that Gerald made admissions of the sort described by the Juvenile Court Judge. . . . Neither Gerald nor his parents was advised that he did not have to testify or make a statement, or that an incriminating statement might result in his commitment as a "delinquent." . . .

. . . Specifically, the question is whether, in such a proceeding, an admission by the juvenile may be used against him in the absence of clear and unequivocal evidence that the admission was made with knowledge that he was not obligated to speak and would not be penalized for remaining silent. In light of *Miranda* v. *Arizona,* . . . we must also consider whether, if the privilege against self-incrimination is available, it can effectively be waived unless counsel is present or the right to counsel has been waived.

. . .

It would indeed be surprising if the privilege against self-incrimination were available to hardened criminals but not to children. The language of the Fifth Amendment . . . is unequivocal and without exception. And the scope of the privilege is comprehensive.

. . .

Against the application to juveniles of the right to silence, it is argued that juvenile proceedings are "civil" and not "criminal," and therefore the privilege should not apply. It is true that the statement of the privilege in the Fifth Amendment . . . is that no person "shall be compelled in any *criminal* case to be a witness against himself." However, it is also clear that the availability of the privilege does not turn upon the type of proceeding in which its protection is invoked, but upon the nature of the statement or admission and the exposure which it invites. . . .

It would be entirely unrealistic to carve out of the Fifth Amendment all statements by juveniles on the ground that these cannot lead to "criminal" involvement. . . . [J]uvenile proceedings to determine "delinquency," which may lead to commitment to a state institution, must be regarded as "criminal" for purposes of the privilege against self-incrimination. To hold otherwise would be to disregard substance because of the feeble enticement of the "civil" label-of-convenience which has been attached to juvenile proceedings. Instead, in over half of the States, there is not even assurance that the juvenile will be kept in separate institutions, apart from adult "criminals." . . . For this purpose, at least, commitment is a deprivation of liberty. It is incarceration against one's will, whether it is called "criminal" or "civil."

. . .

We conclude that the constitutional privilege against self-incrimination is applicable in the case of juveniles as it is with respect to adults. We appreciate that special problems may arise with respect to waiver of the privilege by or on behalf of children, and that there may well be some differences in techniques—but not in principle—depending upon the age of the child and the presence and competence of parents. The participation of counsel will, of course, assist the police, juvenile courts and appellate courts in administering the privilege. If counsel is not present for some permissible reason when an admission is obtained, the greatest care must be taken to assure that the admission was voluntary, in the sense not only that it has not been coerced or suggested, but also that it is not the product of ignorance of rights or of adolescent fantasy, fright or despair.

. . .

. . . We now hold that, absent a valid confession, a determination of delinquency and an order of commitment to a state institution cannot be sustained in the absence of sworn testimony subjected to the opportunity for cross-examination in accordance with our law and constitutional requirements.

. . .

*Judgment reversed and cause
remanded with directions.*

Mr. Justice Stewart, dissenting.

The Court today uses an obscure Arizona case as a vehicle to impose upon thousands of juvenile courts throughout the Nation restrictions that the Constitution made applicable to adversary criminal trials. I believe the Court's decision is wholly unsound as a matter of constitutional law, and sadly unwise as a matter of judicial policy. Whether treating with a delinquent child, a neglected child, a defective child, or a dependent child, a juvenile proceeding's whole purpose and mission is the very opposite of the mission and purpose of a prosecution in a criminal court. The object of the one is the correction of a condition. The object of the other is conviction and punishment for a criminal act.

. . .

The inflexible restrictions that the Constitution so wisely made applicable to adversary criminal trials have no inevitable place in the proceedings of those public social agencies known as juvenile or family courts. And to impose the Court's long catalog of requirements upon the country is to invite a long step backwards into the Nineteenth Century. In that era there were no juvenile proceedings, and a child was tried in a conventional criminal court with all the trappings of a conventional trial. So it was that a 12-year-old boy named James Guild was tried in New Jersey for killing Catherine Beakes. A jury found him guilty of murder, and he was sentenced to death by hanging. The sentence was executed. It was all very constitutional.

A state in all its dealings must, of course, accord every person due process of law. And due process may require that some of the restrictions which the Constitution has placed upon criminal trials must be imposed upon juvenile proceedings. For example, I suppose that all would agree that a brutally coerced confession could not constitutionally be considered in a juvenile court hearing. But it surely does not follow that the testimonial privilege against self-incrimination is applicable in all juvenile proceedings. Similarly, due process clearly requires timely notice of the purpose and scope of any proceedings affecting the relationship of parent and child. . . . But it certainly does not follow that notice of a juvenile hearing must be framed with all the technical niceties of a criminal indictment. . . .

In any event, there is no reason to deal with issues such as these in the present case. The Supreme Court of Arizona found that the parents of Gerald Gault "knew of their right to counsel, to subpoena and cross examine witnesses against Gerald and the possible consequences of a finding of delinquency." . . . It further found that "Mrs. Gault knew the exact nature of the charge against Gerald from the day he was taken to the detention home." . . . And . . . no issue of compulsory self-incrimination is presented by this case.

I would dismiss the appeal.

THE CASE OF DEMETRIO RODRIGUEZ

William Allen

SAN ANTONIO, Tex.—Demetrio P. Rodriguez, the principal plaintiff for what could become one of the more far-reaching Supreme Court cases in history, didn't want the interview to take place at his home. When I called from Dallas to ask if I could drive down to talk to him and his family, he said, in a Spanish accent, "Yes, sir, that will be fine. But maybe I better meet you someplace. You see, I don't think you could find the house. A lot of the street signs around here have been torn down." I told him I thought I could find it if he would give me the directions, and he said, "Well, sir, the thing is this. My wife, she don't speak no English at all. She'll be all in a dither. She'll say, 'How can we welcome this man when I don't even speak English?' "

It was an awkward moment. So far, to me, Rodriguez was just a name on the upcoming case—*Demetrio P. Rodriguez* v. *San Antonio Independent School District*—and the whole point of my trip was to find out something about the man whose pending suit will test whether levying local property taxes to finance public education is legal. I persisted, and Demetrio finally said quietly, "Yes, sir. I tell her to get things ready."

The Edgewood School District, in which Demetrio lives, is crisscrossed by dusty and sometimes nameless streets lined with tiny, run-down frame houses. It is one of the poorest districts in the country, next to Watts, with unusually low property values and low taxes. As I drove up and down the streets the next day, I felt sure that a better example of an impoverished

Source: *Saturday Review* (September 9, 1972), Vol. 55, pp. 6, 8, 10, 13. Copyright © 1972 by Saturday Review, Inc. First appeared in *Saturday Review of the Arts,* September, 1972. Used with permission.

school district couldn't be found. The neighborhood seemed almost deserted, except for an occasional person sitting on a porch or working under a car, and I thought everyone must be inside because of the parching, 100-degree heat. Later I learned that 45 per cent of the community were migrant workers up in Minnesota or in the Dakotas, harvesting crops.

Finally, I found Demetrio's small, neat, white-and-blue frame house, located about one block from the Edgewood Elementary and Junior High School, which two of Demetrio's children attend. There was a sign on the gate saying BAD DOG, but Demetrio stuck his head out the screen door and called, "Don't pay no attention to that. That just keeps the robbers away." He was a short, stocky Mexican-American, with a quick, energetic walk and an easy smile. A few streaks of silver in his thick hair were the only hint that he was forty-six. We shook hands, and he ushered me inside to where his wife and three young boys were lined up for introductions. Genaro Cano, a Mexican-American friend of Demetrio's, was also there. After everybody had been introduced, the boys—all with fresh haircuts and wearing their best slacks and short-sleeved shirts—sat silent and attentive in a row on the floor. Demetrio's wife left the room, then returned with a baby girl, and sat in a small adjoining dining area.

The water-cooled fan in the window was putting out more noise than air, and we spoke loudly about my drive down, the terrible heat, and how I liked San Antonio. I made polite comments about the bric-a-brac around the little room. Demetrio showed me a lacquered leather plate his sister had sent him from Mexico City. Then he cleared his throat and said, "You know, you really should be talking to my lawyer instead of me. He could tell you more facts about the case than I ever could."

Since I had already talked on the phone to Demetrio's lawyer, a San Antonio attorney named Arthur Gochman, as well as to several authorities on constitutional law, the facts and the possible consequences of the case were clear to me: School financing in most states relies in large part on local property taxes. The result is that poor districts, such as Edgewood, have considerably less money to spend on their school systems than, for instance, Beverly Hills in California. The state tax and local property tax allocated for each pupil in Edgewood is $264, one of the lowest amounts in Texas— and in the whole country, for that matter. (In one Texas community, which has more oil wells than students, per-pupil allocations go as high as $5,334; in the more affluent districts of San Antonio, though, the average is about twice that of Edgewood.) The result is inferior education for children in the impoverished areas, and the contention of the complaints is that this is a denial of the children's constitutional rights.

Nearly fifty suits similar to the Rodriguez suit are pending in more than thirty states, but the Texas case, which the state lost early in 1971, will be the first to be tested by the Supreme Court. It is scheduled to be heard in the term beginning this October. If the ruling of the lower courts, in favor of Rodriguez, is upheld, every state in the Union that presently relies on local property taxes for educational financing will have to come up with ways that will provide an equal education for all its children.

Demetrio said to me, "You're going to have to help me along here about what to say. I mean, I ain't no journalist or nothing. All I know is the average property-tax bill around here is about thirty dollars a year, and some pay a lot less. Just a few dollars. You can't run schools on money like that."

He ran his finger around the leather plate he was still holding. "See, I do know a lot about this issue, but sometimes it's hard for me to get it out in the right words. I grew up on a farm near a Texas border town that wasn't no more than a post office. I only went to the eighth grade. But one thing I want you to be sure and know is that I'm not the only person involved in this. It's just my name on the case. A whole lot of people have worked real hard on this."

Demetrio's friend, Genaro, an officer on a program called Civil Rights for Migrant Workers, leaned forward in his chair and said, "I'd like to say something about that." He was eight years younger than Demetrio and much taller and had more of a slow Texas drawl than a Spanish accent. He spoke with compelling earnestness about his friend. "I've known Demetrio here for a long time, and he's just being modest. He really spearheaded the movement. He might not use good grammar or things like that, but you ought to hear him give a speech. He knows how to get our people together and get them to work for their rights. Almost every night he's out at one meeting or another."

Genaro began to count on his fingers. "He belongs to SANYO—that means San Antonio Neighborhood Youth Organization. He's a board member of the Bexar County Migrant Farm Workers Association. He's a member of the Bexar County Civic Action Committee. He's president of the Nathan Hale Community Action Council. He's very active in combating glue sniffing here. He's trying to get the manufacturers to put something in the glue so that the kids can't stand the smell of it."

He paused for breath, and Demetrio used the lull to turn the attention away from himself. "Well, Jimmy," he said to one of his sons on the floor, "how did you like your summer school?"

"Fine."

"What did you learn there?"

"The sound of the letters."

"He's been in kindergarten this summer," Demetrio explained. "He's going to start this year in the first grade. Carlos, what grade are you in?"

"Fourth grade."

"All my kids are going to grow up to speak good English. Not like me.

You know, I took the high school certificate test twice and flunked it both times. It's the grammar and punctuation that get me. I got a chance to go to night school cheap, but I'm so wrapped up in these different groups now I don't have time."

I asked Demetrio just how the lawsuit came about and how he got involved with it. "It all started in 1968," he said. "We were having a lot of trouble with the Edgewood school superintendent. You wouldn't believe how terrible the schools were run. The kids were let to run wild. Nobody cared if they learned anything or not. The books were old and all tore up. They didn't have no toilet paper. Well, we organized the Edgewood Concerned Parents Association, and we walked all the kids out—and it worked. The superintendent had to resign.

"But things didn't get much better, and that's when we went to see Mr. Gochman. He set us straight right away on what was wrong. He said you could get rid of as many people as you wanted and it wouldn't do no good. The real trouble was that we weren't getting our fair share of the money. After we got through talking, he asked us if we wanted him to help us file suit. I said, 'Wait a minute. Before we sign anything, what's it going to cost us?' See, we didn't have no money at all. He told us it wouldn't cost us a penny; he would do it for nothing. So far he's already spent over ten thousand dollars on the case out of his own pocket."

Genaro waved his hand, wanting to clarify a point. "But after the suit was filed, the Edgewood Concerned Parent Association did get a little money from the Mexican American Unity Council—for a phone and an office. See, the Unity Council has funds from the Ford Foundation to give to some of our organizations."

"Then," Demetrio went on, "we started selling food at these festivals we have in San Antonio. We rent booths and sell tamales, tacos, things like that. So far we've raised enough to give out three five-hundred-dollar scholarships to kids who want to go to college."

Genaro suggested that it might be a good idea to take a drive around the neighborhood and look at the schools. I agreed, and, to Mrs. Rodriguez's obvious relief, Demetrio, Genaro, and I said goodbye and headed for my car. As we were getting in, Demetrio said, "You know, my wife, she's not even an American citizen."

First we pulled into a Stop-and-Go drive-in grocery for a six-pack of beer to sip while cruising around. "Look who's going there," Demetrio said to Genaro a few minutes later. "Ain't that a priest in that new car?"

"That's a priest, all right. It's air-conditioned, too. See? The windows are up."

Demetrio laughed. "The priests do okay around here, but that's about all. You know what the average income in Edgewood is? Three to four thousand a year for big families."

We drove by the Edgewood Elementary and Junior High School, a con-
glomeration of shabby buildings with broken windows and peeling paint. The
grounds were overgrown with weeds, the fences torn away. "You ought
to go inside," Genaro said, "It's even worse. And *hot?* I don't blame the
teachers for not staying."

"This shows you why we had to have the walkout," Demetrio said. "People told us it was very indecent what we were doing—marching and demonstrating and everything. You know, a lot of our people are ashamed of
the way we have to live. They want to hide it. But we know now that's
not the answer. You got to bring it out in the open if you want to get
anything done. But everything we do here is nonviolent. We don't burn
or nothing like that. We just focus the problem. We have police escorts.
We have permits."

"We're opening up to you now," Genaro said. "The Chicano has really
been taken advantage of by some of the gringos down here. We've always
been kept down. Till we got organized, a Mexican couldn't even hold a manager's position in a supermarket, even if just Chicanos traded there."

"Tell him about those two supermarkets," Demetrio said, grinning.

Genaro rolled his eyes. "Man oh man. It's almost too much to believe.
There's these two identical supermarkets, see. One of the rich north side of
town and one on this side. They're part of a chain. The one on this side
didn't have no package boys, no nothing, but Demetrio and me compared
the prices in both stores, and the prices on the rich north side was actually
lower. Can you believe that? We called the managers and said we wanted
to talk, but they wouldn't have nothing to do with us. So then we got a
camera and took pictures of a package boy carrying out this tiny little bag
for an elderly Anglo lady on the north side. Then we got pictures at the other
store of an ancient old Mexican woman with *only one arm* staggering out
with a huge sack of groceries. We sent copies to the managers, and you
should have seen them jump. They came running over to Demetrio's house,
giving out candy to the kids in the neighborhood, everything. They was
really scared."

"They got our prices lowered, and now we've got package boys, too,"
Demetrio said.

We drove around a while longer, talking and looking at the various
schools. With the exception of one fairly new high school, they all had the
rundown look of abandoned or condemned buildings. Demetrio pointed out
a signal light, a drainage ditch, one shopping center—all improvements the
neighborhood organizations had worked for. As we drove up and down
the dismal back streets of the neighborhood, the two men described how
some of the migrants boarded up their houses while they were gone and
others rented theirs out. I heard about how bad the gang fights and killings
had been in the area until the War on Poverty program came along and
helped to solve the problem by setting up youth organizations.

Finally, we had seen all there was to see, the beer was gone, and we returned to Demetrio's house and said goodbye. He and Genaro got out. Then Demetrio came around to my window. "Listen," he said, "I know I told you before, but I want to say it again. It ain't just me doing this. It's all the people of Edgewood. And don't forget Mr. Gochman, our lawyer. He don't have to do this. He's doing it because he cares."

I told him I wouldn't forget, and we shook hands. He was about to go through the gate with BAD DOG on it when it occurred to me I hadn't asked what he did for a living. I asked him, and he said, "I'm a sheet-metal worker. At Kelly Air Force Base. But I wish you wouldn't make too much of that. You see, I'm one of the few that have done okay, I learned a trade in the service. Most of my people aren't so fortunate. I'm one of the lucky ones."

FREEDOM OF SPEECH FOR BIGOTS?

Brandenburg v. Ohio

> *It is a fair summary of history to say that safeguards of liberty have been forged in controversies involving not very nice people.**
> —A. M. S. and E. W.

A leader of a Ku Klux Klan group spoke at a Klan rally at which a large wooden cross was burned and some of the other persons present were carrying firearms. His remarks included such statements as: "Bury the niggers," "the niggers should be returned to Africa," and "send the Jews back to Israel." He was convicted under the Ohio Criminal Syndicalism statute of "advocating . . . the duty, necessity, or propriety of crime, sabotage, violence, or unlawful methods of terrorism as a means of accomplishing industrial or political reform" and of "voluntarily assembling with any society, group or assemblage of persons formed to teach or advocate the doctrines of criminal syndicalism." On appeal, he challenged the constitutionality of the statute under the First and Fourteenth Amendments, but the appellate court of Ohio affirmed, without opinion, and the Supreme Court of Ohio dismissed his appeal.

PER CURIAM. . . .

In 1927, this Court sustained the constitutionality of California's Criminal Syndicalism Act, . . . the text of which is quite similar to that of the laws of Ohio. *Whitney* v. *California*. . . The Court upheld the statute on

Source: *Brandenburg* v. *Ohio* 395 U.S. 444 (1969).
* *United States* v. *Rabinowitz* 339 U.S. 56 (1950).

the ground that, without more, "advocating" violent means to effect political and economic change involves such danger to the security of the
State that the State may outlaw it. . . . But *Whitney* has been thoroughly
discredited by later decisions. See *Dennis* v. *United States.* . . . These later
decisions have fashioned the principle that the constitutional guarantees of
free speech and free press do not permit a State to forbid or proscribe advocacy of the use of force or of law violation except where such advocacy
is directed to inciting or producing imminent lawless action and is likely to
incite or produce such action. As we said in *Noto* v. *United States,* . . .
"the mere abstract teaching . . . of the moral propriety or even moral
necessity for a resort to force and violence, is not the same as preparing a
group for violent action and steeling it to such action." . . . A statute
which fails to draw this distinction impermissibly intrudes upon the freedoms
guaranteed by the First and Fourteenth Amendments. . . .

. . . [W]e are here confronted with a statute which, by its own words
and as applied, purports to punish mere advocacy and to forbid, on pain
of criminal punishment, assembly with others merely to advocate the described type of action. Such a statute falls within the condemnation of the
First and Fourteenth Amendments. The contrary teaching of *Whitney* v.
California, supra, cannot be supported, and that decision is therefore overruled.

Reversed

Should Government Prescribe Morality?

Stanley v. Georgia

Mr. Justice Marshall delivered the opinion of the Court.

An investigation of appellant's alleged bookmaking activities led to the
issuance of a search warrant for appellant's home. Under authority of this
warrant, federal and state agents secured entrance . . . [W]hile looking
through a desk drawer in an upstairs bedroom, one of the federal agents,
accompanied by a state officer, found three reels of eight-millimeter film.
Using a projector and screen found in an upstairs living room, they viewed
the films. The state officer concluded that they were obscene and seized
them. Since a further examination of the bedroom indicated that appellant
occupied it, he was charged with possession of obscene matter and placed
under arrest. He was later indicted for "knowingly hav[ing] possession

Source: *Stanley* v. *Georgia* 394 U.S. 557 (1969).

of obscene matter" in violation of Georgia law. Appellant was tried before a jury and convicted. The Supreme Court of Georgia affirmed. . . .

It is now well established that the Constitution protects the right to receive information and ideas. . . . This right to receive information and ideas, regardless of their social worth . . . is fundamental to our free society. Moreover, in the context of this case—a prosecution for mere possession of printed or filmed matter in the privacy of a person's own home—that right takes on an added dimension. For also fundamental is the right to be free, except in very limited circumstances, from unwanted governmental intrusions into one's privacy. . . .

These are the rights that appellant is asserting in the case before us. He is asserting the right to read or observe what he pleases—the right to satisfy his intellectual and emotional needs in the privacy of his own home. He is asserting the right to be free from state inquiry into the contents of his library. Georgia contends that appellant does not have these rights, that there are certain types of materials that the individual may not read or even possess. Georgia justifies this assertion by arguing that the films in the present case are obscene. But we think that mere categorization of these films as "obscene" is insufficient justification for such a drastic invasion of personal liberties guaranteed by the First and Fourteenth Amendments. Whatever may be the justifications for other statutes regulating obscenity, we do not think they reach into the privacy of one's own home. If the First Amendment means anything, it means that a State has no business telling a man, sitting alone in his own house, what books he may read or what films he may watch. Our whole constitutional heritage rebels at the thought of giving government the power to control men's minds.

And yet, in the face of these traditional notions of individual liberty, Georgia asserts the right to protect the individual's mind from the effects of obscenity. We are not certain that this argument amounts to anything more than the assertion that the State has the right to control the moral content of a person's thoughts. To some, this may be a noble purpose, but it is wholly inconsistent with the philosophy of the First Amendment. . . . Whatever the power of the state to control public dissemination of ideas inimical to the public morality, it cannot constitutionally premise legislation on the desirability of controlling a person's private thoughts. . . .

[Reversed and remanded.]

Mr. Justice Black, concurring. . . .

Mr. Justice Stewart, with whom Mr. Justice Brennan and Mr. Justice White join, concurring in the result. . . .

Even in the much criticized case of *United States* v. *Rabinowitz* . . . the Court emphasized that "exploratory searches . . . cannot be undertaken by officers, with or without a warrant." . . . This record presents a bald violation of that basic constitutional rule. To condone what happened here is to invite a government official to use a seemingly precise and legal warrant only as a ticket to get into a man's home, and, once inside, to launch forth upon unconfined searches and indiscriminate seizures as if armed with all the unbridled and illegal power of a general warrant. . . .

Is There a "Private" Right to Discriminate?

Jones v. Alfred Mayer Co.

Mr. Justice Stewart delivered the opinion of the Court.

"All citizens of the United States shall have the same right, in every State and Territory, as is enjoyed by white citizens thereof to inherit, purchase, lease, sell, hold, and convey real and personal property."

[Petitioners filed a complaint in federal court alleging that the respondents had refused to sell them a home in the Paddock Woods community of St. Louis County for the sole reason that petitioner Jones is a Negro. Petitioners sought injunctive and other relief. The District Court dismissed and the Court of Appeals affirmed, concluding that Sec. 1982 applies only to state action and does not reach private refusals to sell.]

At the outset, it is important to make clear precisely what this case does *not* involve. Whatever else it may be, 42 U.S.C. Sec. 1982 is not a comprehensive open housing law. In sharp contrast to the Fair Housing Title (Title VIII) of the Civil Rights Act of 1968, . . . 82 Stat. 73, the statute in this case deals only with racial discrimination and does not address itself to discrimination on grounds of religion or national origin. It does not deal specifically with discrimination in the provision of services or facilities in connection with the sale or rental of a dwelling. . . . It does not empower a federal administrative agency to assist aggrieved parties. It makes no provision for intervention by the Attorney General. And, although it can be enforced by injunction, it contains no provision expressly authorizing a federal court to order the payment of damages. . . .

On its face . . . Sec. 1982 appears to prohibit *all* discrimination against Negroes in the sale or rental of property—discrimination by private owners as well as discrimination by public authorities. Indeed, even the respondents seem to concede that, if Sec. 1982 "means what it says"—to use the words of the respondents' brief—then it must encompass every racially motivated

Source: *Jones* v. *Alfred Mayer Co.* 392 U.S. 409 (1968).

refusal to sell or rent and cannot be confined to officially sanctioned segregation in housing. Stressing what they consider to be the revolutionary implications of so literal a reading of Sec. 1982, the respondents argue that Congress cannot possibly have intended any such result. Our examination of the relevant history, however, persuades us that Congress meant exactly what it said. [The opinion here treats the history of the 1866 Act and concludes that private discrimination was within the reach of Congress' purpose in enacting the law.]

The remaining question is whether Congress has power under the Constitution to do what Sec. 1982 purports to do: to prohibit all racial discrimination, private and public in the sale and rental of property. Our starting point is the Thirteenth Amendment, for it was pursuant to that constitutional provision that Congress originally enacted what is now Sec. 1982. . . .

As its text reveals, the Thirteenth Amendment "is not a mere prohibition of State laws establishing or upholding slavery, but an absolute declaration that slavery or involuntary servitude shall not exist in any part of the United States." . . . It has never been doubted, therefore, "that the power vested in Congress to enforce the article by appropriate legislation," *ibid.,* includes the power to enact laws "direct and primary, operating upon the acts of individuals, whether sanctioned by State legislation or not." . . .

Thus, the fact that Sec. 1982 operates upon the unofficial acts of private individuals, whether or not sanctioned by state law, presents no constitutional problem. If Congress has power under the Thirteenth Amendment to eradicate conditions that prevent Negroes from buying and renting property because of their race or color, then no federal statute calculated to achieve that objective can be thought to exceed the constitutional power of Congress simply because it reaches beyond state action to regulate the conduct of private individuals. The constitutional question in this case, therefore, comes to this: Does the authority of Congress to enforce the Thirteenth Amendment "by appropriate legislation" include the power to eliminate all racial barriers to the acquisition of real and personal property? We think the answer to that question is plainly yes. . . .

Reversed.

Chapter 10
SUGGESTED TOPICS FOR CLASS DISCUSSION

1. Some of the Justices of the Supreme Court have been urging that it, at the next opportunity, move all the protections of the Bill of Rights under the Fourteenth Amendment and thereby secure these liberties against encroachment by all governments. Do you agree with this position? Should state gov-

ernments be free to do what the national government cannot do? What would be some objections to this change?

2. Should tax payments be used to accomplish equal protection of the laws in such matters as equality of schools?

3. For many years we have been told that the problem of racial discrimination is one of attitude and not a legal or political one at all, that it is a problem whose solution can only be hurt rather than helped by legislation. Do you agree?

4. Do the laws of the states regulating juvenile "trials" need to be drastically changed?

5. What role should the national government, including the courts, assume in the protection of the rights of individuals, especially in such areas as private housing?

6. What role should the government play in enforcing morality? Whose morality? Should it be permitted to censor books, magazines, movies, television?

Chapter 11

The Politics of Discrimination and Liberation

The United States has a long tradition of being a melting pot—understandably so, because its population is overwhelmingly composed of descendants of immigrants. As waves of immigrants fell upon the shores of the United States, the normal pattern was for each new incoming minority—Irish, Italians, Poles, Scandinavians, Slovaks—to struggle for a time and finally establish itself. Before long, as a rule, leadership emerged in each minority and the group went on to achieve a degree of assimilation and to participate in the social, political, and economic life of the country. Sometimes, however, the melting pot does not melt, or melts only imperfectly, and groups continue as objects of legal, illegal, and nonlegal discrimination. One of the cases in this chapter illustrates the way in which a minority group of Italians continues to have difficulties.

The assimilation of national groups has gone far more smoothly, on the whole, than has the assimilation of a racial group, the blacks. Some cases in this chapter deal with problems that blacks face, the growing political awareness among them, the emergence of new patterns of black political leadership, and some of the strategic questions blacks encounter as they become more involved in politics.

Women are a majority of the total population of the United States, yet they have been exploited and discriminated against as if they were a small and helpless minority. This discrimination has involved political, social, economic, family, and sexual realms. It has been supported by male prejudice, a variety of social, political, and economic practices (such as those involving the division of labor within marriage, the peripheral role of women in party politics, and discriminatory employment of women) and by formal legal actons such as laws and court decisions. In recent years this situation has been receiving increased attention, as cases in this chapter indicate, and changes are now beginning on a broad front.

The Women's Liberation Movement: Its Origins, Structures, and Ideas

Jo Freeman

Sometime in the 1920s, feminism died in the United States. It was a premature death. Feminists had only recently obtained their long-sought-for tool, the vote, with which they had hoped to make an equal place for women in this society. But it seemed like a final one. By the time the granddaughters of the women who had sacrificed so much for suffrage had grown to maturity, not only had social mythology firmly ensconced women in the home, but the very term "feminist" had become an epithet.

Social fact, however, did not always coincide with social mythology. During the era of the "feminine mystique" when the percentage of degrees given to women was dropping, their absolute numbers were rising astronomically. Their participation in the labor force was also increasing—even while their position within it was declining. Opportunities to work, the trend toward smaller families, plus changes in status symbols from a leisured wife at home to a second car and TV, all contributed to a basic alteration of the female labor force from one of primarily single women under twenty-five to one of married women and mothers over forty. Added to these de-

Source: *Recent Sociology No. 4: Family, Marriage, and the Struggle of the Sexes,* Hans Peter Drietzel (ed.) (New York: Macmillan Publishing Co., Inc., 1972), pp. 201–216. © Copyright 1971 by Jo Freeman. Reprinted by permission of the author.

velopments were an increased segregation of the job market, a flooding of traditional female jobs (e.g., teaching and social work) by men, a decrease of women's percentage of the professional and technical jobs by a third, and a commensurate decline in their relative income. The result was the creation of a class of highly educated, underemployed women.

In the early sixties feminism was still an unmentionable, but its ghost was slowly awakening from the dead. The first sign of new life came with the establishment of the Commission on the Status of Women by President Kennedy in 1961. Created at the urging of Esther Petersen of the Women's Bureau, in its short life the commission came out with several often radical reports thoroughly documenting women's second-class status. It was followed by the formation of a citizen's advisory council and fifty state commissions.

Many of the people involved in these commissions became the nucleus of women who, dissatisfied with the lack of progress made on commission recommendations, joined with Betty Friedan in 1966 to found the National Organization for Women.

NOW was the first new feminist organization in almost fifty years, but it was not the sole beginning of the organized expression of the movement. The movement actually has two origins, from two different strata of society, with two different styles, orientations, values, and forms of organization. In many ways there were two separate movements, which only in 1970–71 began to merge sufficiently for the rubric "women's liberation" to be truly an umbrella term for the multiplicity of organizations and groups.

The first of these I call the older branch of the movement, partially because it began first, and partially because the median age of its activists is higher. In addition to NOW it contains such organizations as the PWC (Professional Women's Caucus), FEW (Federally Employed Women), and the self-defined "right wing" of the movement, WEAL (Women's Equity Action League).

The participants of both branches tend to be predominantly white, middle-class, and college-educated, but the composition of the older is much more heterogeneous than that of the younger. In issues, however, this trend is reversed, with those of the younger being more diverse. While the written programs and aims of the older branch span a wide spectrum, their activities tend to be concentrated on the legal and economic difficulties women face. These groups are primarily made up of women who work and are substantially concerned with the problems of working women. Their style of organization has tended to be formal, with numerous elected officers, boards of directors, bylaws, and the other trappings of democratic procedure. All started as top-down organizations lacking in a mass base. Some have subsequently developed a mass base, some have not yet done so, and others don't want to.

In 1967 and 1968, unaware of and unknown to NOW or the state commissions, the other branch of the movement was taking shape. Contrary to popular myth it did not begin on the campus; nor was it started by SDS. However, its activators were, to be trite, on the other side of the generation gap. While few were students, all were "under thirty" and had received their political education as participants or concerned observers of the social-action projects of the last decade. Many came direct from New Left and civil rights organizations where they had been shunted into traditional roles and faced with the self-evident contradiction of working in a "freedom movement" but not being very free. Others had attended various courses on women in the multitude of free universities springing up around the country during those years .

At least five groups in five different cities (Chicago, Toronto, Detroit, Seattle, and Gainesville, Florida) formed spontaneously, independently of each other. They came at a very auspicious moment. In 1967 the blacks kicked the whites out of the civil rights movement, student power had been discredited by SDS, and the New Left was on the wane. Only draft-resistance activities were on the increase, and this movement more than any other exemplified the social inequities of the sexes. Men could resist the draft. Women could only counsel resistance.

There had been individual temporary caucuses and conferences of women as early as 1964, when Stokely Carmichael made his infamous remark that "the only position for women in SNCC is prone." But it was not until 1967 that the groups developed a determined, if cautious, continuity and began consciously to expand themselves. In 1968 they held their first, and so far only, national conference, attended by over two hundred women from around the United States and Canada on less than a month's notice. They have been expanding exponentially ever since.

This expansion has been more amoebic than organized because the younger branch of the movement prides itself on its lack of organization. Eschewing structure and damning the idea of leadership, it has carried the concept of "everyone doing her own thing" almost to its logical extreme. The thousands of sister chapters around the country are virtually independent of each other, linked only by the numerous journals, newsletters, and cross-country travelers. Some cities have a coordinating committee which attempts to maintain communication between the local groups and channel newcomers into appropriate ones, but none has any power over group activities, let alone group ideas. One result of this style is a very broad-based, creative movement, which individuals can relate to pretty much as they desire with no concern for orthodoxy or doctrine. Another result is a kind of political impotency. It is virtually impossible to coordinate a national action, assuming there could be any agreement on issues around which to coordinate one. Fortunately the older branch of the movement does have the structure necessary to coordinate such actions, and is usually the one to initiate them, as NOW did for the August 26, 1970, national strike.

It is a common mistake to try to place the various feminist organizations on the traditional left/right spectrum. The terms "reformist" and "radical" are convenient and fit into our preconceived notions about the nature of political organization, but they tell us nothing of relevance. As with almost everything else, feminism cuts through the normal categories and demands new perspectives in order to be understood. Some groups often called "reformist" have a platform which would so completely change our society it would be unrecognizable. Other groups called "radical" concentrate on the traditional female concerns of love, sex, children, and interpersonal relationships (although with untraditional views). The activities of the organizations are similarly incongruous. The most typical division of labor, ironically, is that those groups labeled "radical" engage primarily in educational work while the so-called reformist ones are the activists. It is structure and style rather than ideology which more accurately differentiate the various groups, and even here there has been much borrowing on both sides. The older branch has used the traditional forms of political action, often with great skill, while the younger branch has been experimental.

The most prevalent innovation developed by the younger branch has been the "rap group." Essentially an educational technique, it has spread far beyond its origins and become a major organizational unit of the whole movement, most frequently used by suburban housewives. From a sociological perspective the rap group is probably the most valuable contribution so far by the women's liberation movement to the tools for social change.

The rap groups serves two main purposes. One is traditional; the other is unique. The traditional role is the simple process of bringing women together in a situation of structured interaction. It has long been known that people can be kept down as long as they are kept divided from each other, relating more to those in a superior social position than to those in a position similar to their own. It is when social development creates natural structures in which people can interact with each other and compare their common concerns that social movements take place. This is the function that the factory served for the workers, the church for the southern civil rights movement, the campus for students, and the ghetto for urban blacks.

Women have been largely deprived of a means of structured interaction and been kept isolated in their individual homes, relating more to men than to each other. Natural structures are still largely lacking, though they have begun to develop, but the rap group has created an artificial structure which does much the same thing. This phenomenon is similar to the nineteenth-century development of a multitude of women's clubs and organizations around every conceivable social and political purpose. These organizations taught women political skills and eventually served as the primary communications network for the spread of the suffrage movement. Yet after the great crusade ended, most of them vanished or became moribund. The rap groups are taking their place and will serve much the same function for the future development of this movement.

They do more than just bring women together, as radical an activity as that may be. The rap groups have become mechanisms for social change in and of themselves. They are structures created specifically for the purpose of altering the participants' perceptions and conceptions of themselves and society at large. The means by which this is done is called "consciousness raising." The process is very simple. Women come together in groups of five to fifteen and talk to each other about their personal problems, personal experiences, personal feelings, and personal concerns. From this public sharing of experiences comes the realization that what was thought to be individual is in fact common; that what was thought to be a personal problem has a social cause and probably a political solution. Women learn to see how social structures and attitudes have molded them from birth and limited their opportunities. They ascertain the extent to which women have been denigrated in this society and how they have developed prejudices against themselves and other women.

It is this process of deeply personal attitude change that makes the rap group such a powerful tool. The need of a movement to develop "correct consciousness" has long been known. But usually this consciousness is not developed by means intrinsic to the structure of the movement and does not require such a profound resocialization of one's concept of self. This experience is both irreversible and contagious. Once one has gone through such a "resocialization," one's view of oneself and the world is never the same again, whether or not there is further active participation in the movement. Even those who do "drop out" rarely do so without first spreading feminist ideas among their own friends and colleagues. All who undergo "consciousness raising" virtually compel themselves to seek out other women with whom to share the experience, and thus begin new rap groups.

There are several personal results from this process. The initial one is a decrease of self and group depreciation. Women come to see themselves as essentially pretty groovy people. Along with this comes the explosion of the myth of individual solution. If women are the way they are because society has made them that way, they can only change their lives significantly by changing society. These feelings in turn create the consciousness of oneself as a member of a group and the feeling of solidarity so necessary to any social movement. From this comes the concept of sisterhood.

This need for group solidarity partially explains why men have been largely excluded from the rap groups. It was not the initial reason, but it has been one of the more beneficial by-products. Originally, the idea was borrowed from the black power movement, much in the public consciousness when the women's liberation movement began. It was reinforced by the unremitting hostility of most of the New Left men at the prospect of an independent women's movement not tied to radical organizations. Even when this hostility was not present, women in virtually every group in the United States, Canada, and Europe soon discovered that the traditional sex roles reasserted themselves in the groups regardless of the good intentions of the participants. Men inevitably dominated the discussions, and usually would talk only about how women's liberation related to men, or how men were oppressed by the sex roles. In segregated groups women found the discussions to be more open, honest, and extensive. They could learn how to relate to other women and not just to men.

Unlike the male exclusion policy, the rap groups did not develop spontaneously or without a struggle. The political background of many of the early feminists of the younger branch predisposed them against the rap group as "unpolitical," and they would condemn discussion meetings which "degenerated" into "bitch sessions." This trend was particularly strong in Chicago and Washington, D.C., which had been centers of New Left activity. Meanwhile, other feminists, usually with a civil rights or apolitical background, saw that the "bitch session" obviously met a basic need. They seized upon it and created the consciousness-raising rap group. Developed initially in New York and Gainesville, Florida, the idea soon spread throughout the country, becoming the paradigm for most movement organization.

To date, the major, though hardly exclusive, activity of the younger branch has been organizing rap groups, putting on conferences, and putting out educational literature, while that of the older branch has been using the "channels" and other forms of political pressure to change specific situations in inequity. In general, the younger branch has been organized to attack attitudes and the older branch to attack structures.

While the rap groups have been excellent techniques for changing individual attitudes, they have not been very successful in dealing with social institutions. Their loose, informal structure encourages participation in discussion, and their supportive atmosphere elicits personal insight; but neither is very efficient in handling specific tasks. Thus, while rap groups have been of fundamental value to the development of the movement, the more structured groups are the more visibly effective.

Individual rap groups tend to flounder when their members have exhausted the virtues of consciousness raising and decide they want to do something more concrete. The problem is that most groups are unwilling to change their structure when they change their tasks. They have accepted the ideology of "structurelessness" without realizing the limitations of its uses. This eventually caused an organizational crisis within the movement because the formation of rap groups as a major movement function is becoming obsolete. Due to the intense press publicity that began in the fall of 1969, as well as the numerous "overground" books and articles now being circulated, women's liberation has become a household word. Its issues are discussed and informal rap groups are formed by people who have no explicit connection with any movement group. Ironically, this subtle, silent, and subversive spread of feminist consciousness is causing a situation of political unemployment. With educational work no longer such an overwhelming need, women's liberation groups have to develop new forms of organizations to deal with new tasks in a new stage of development. This is necessitating a good deal of retrenchment and rethinking. Cities undergoing this process often give the impression of inactivity, and only time will tell what will be the result.

Initially there was little ideology in the movement beyond a gut feeling that something was wrong. NOW was formed under the slogan "Full equality for women in a truly equal partnership with men" and specified eight demands in a "Bill of Rights." It and the other organizations of the older branch have continued to focus around concrete issues, feeling that attempts at a comprehensive ideology have little to offer beyond internal conflict.

In the younger branch a basic difference of opinion developed quite early. It was disguised as a philosophical difference, was articulated and acted on as a strategical one, but actually was more of a political disagreement than anything else. The two sides involved included essentially the same people who differed over the rap groups, but the split endured long after the groups became ubiquitous. The original issue was whether the fledgling women's liberation movement would remain a branch of the radical left movement or be an independent women's movement. Proponents became known as "politicos" or "feminists," respectively, and traded arguments about whether "capitalism was the enemy," or the male-dominated social institutions and values. They also traded a few epithets, with politicos calling feminists politically unsophisticated and elitist, while in turn being accused of subservience to the interests of left wing men.

With the influx of large numbers of previously apolitical women an independent, autonomous women's liberation movement became a reality instead of an argument. The spectrum shifted to the feminist direction, but the basic difference in orientation still remained. Politicos now also call themselves feminists, and many have left the left, but most see women's issues within a broader political context while the original feminists continue to focus almost exclusively on women's concerns. Although much of the bitterness of the original dispute has subsided, politicos generated such distrust about their motives that they prejudiced many women against all concerns of left ideology. This has led some feminists to the very narrow outlook that politicos most feared they would adopt.

Meanwhile, faced with a female exodus, the radical left movement has forsaken the rhetoric of its original opposition without relinquishing most of its sexist practices. Embracing the position that women are a constituency to be organized, most New Left (and some Old Left) organizations have created women's caucuses to recruit women to "more important activities." These are very different from the women's caucuses of the professional associations that have also mushroomed into existence. The latter are concerned with raising feminist issues within their organizations. The New Left women's groups serve much the same function as traditional ladies' auxiliaries.

The widely differing backgrounds and perspectives of the women in the movement have resulted in as many different interpretations of women's status. Some are more developed than others, and some are more publicized, yet as of 1972 there is no comprehensive set of beliefs which can accurately be labeled women's liberationist, feminist, neofeminist, or radical feminist ideology. At best one can say there is general agreement on two theoretical concerns. The first is the feminist critique of society, and the second is the idea of oppression.

The feminist critique starts from entirely different premises than the traditional view, and therefore neither can really refute the other. The latter assumes that men and women are essentially different and should serve different social functions. Their diverse roles and statuses simply reflect these essential differences. The feminist perspective starts from the premise that women and men are constitutionally equal and share the same human capabilities. Observed differences therefore demand a critical analysis of the social institutions which cause them.

The concept of oppression brings into use a term which has long been avoided out of a feeling that it was too rhetorical. But there was no convenient euphemism and discrimination was inadequate to describe what happens to women and what they have in common with other groups. As long as the word remained illegitimate, so did the idea and it was too valuable not to use. It is still largely an undeveloped concept in which the details have not been sketched, but there appear to be two aspects to oppression which relate much the same as two sides of a coin—distinct, yet inseparable. The social-structural manifestations are easily visible, as they are reflected in the legal, economic, social, and political institutions. The social-psychological ones are often intangible, hard to grasp and hard to alter. Group self-hate and distortion of perceptions to justify a preconceived interpretation of reality are just some of the factors being teased out.

For women, sexism describes the specificity of female oppression. Starting from the traditional belief of the difference between the sexes, sexism embodies two core concepts.

The first is that men are more important than women. Not necessarily superior—we are far too sophisticated these days to use those tainted terms —but more important, more significant, more valuable, more worthwhile. This value justifies the idea that it is more important for a man, the "breadwinner," to have a job or a promotion than for a woman, more important for a man to be paid well, more important for a man to have an education and in general to have preference over a woman. It is the basis of the feeling by men that if women enter a particular occupation they will degrade it and that men must leave or be themselves degraded; and the feeling by women that they can raise the prestige of their professions by recruiting men, which they can only do by giving them the better jobs. From this value comes the attitude that a husband must earn more than his wife or suffer a loss of personal status, and a wife must subsume her interests to his or be socially castigated. From this value comes the practice of rewarding men for serving in the armed forces and punishing women for having children. The first core concept of sexist thought is that men do the important work in the world and the work done by men is what is important.

The second core concept is that women are here for the pleasure and assistance of men. This is what is meant when women are told that their role is complementary to that of men; that they should fulfill their natural "feminine" functions; that they are "different" from men and should not compete with them. From this concept comes the attitude that women are and should be dependent on men for everything, but especially for their identities, the social definition of who they are. It defines the few roles for which women are socially rewarded—wife, mother, and mistress—all of which are pleasing or beneficial to men, and leads directly to the "pedestal" theory, which extols women who stay in their place as good helpmates to men.

It is this attitude which stigmatizes those women who do not marry or who do not devote their primary energies to the care of men and their children. Association with a man is the basic criterion for participation by women in this society, and one who does not seek her identity through a man is a threat to the social values. It is similarly this attitude which causes women's liberation activists to be labeled as manhaters for exposing the nature of sexism. People feel that a woman not devoted to looking after men must act this way because of hatred or inability to "catch" one. This second core concept of sexist thought is that women's identities are defined by their relationship to men and their social value by that of the men they are related to.

The sexism of our society is so pervasive that we are not even aware of all its inequities. Unless one has developed a sensitivity to its workings, by adopting a self-consciously contrary view, its activities are accepted as "normal" and justified with little question. People are said to "choose" what in fact they never thought about. A good example is what happened during and after the Second World War. The sudden onslaught of the war radically changed the whole structure of social relationships as well as the economy. Men were drafted into the army and women into the labor force. Now desperately needed, women's wants were provided for as were those of the boys on the front. Federal financing of day-care centers in the form of the Landham Act passed Congress in a record two weeks. Special crash training programs were provided for the new women workers to give them skills they were not previously thought capable of exercising. Women instantly assumed positions of authority and responsibility unavailable only the year before.

But what happened when the war ended? Both men and women had heeded their country's call to duty to bring the war to a successful conclusion. Yet men were rewarded for their efforts and women punished for theirs. The returning soldiers were given the GI Bill and other veterans' benefits, as well as their jobs back and a disproportionate share of the new ones created by the war economy. Women, on the other hand, saw their child-care centers dismantled and their training programs cease. They were fired or demoted in droves and often found it difficult to enter colleges flooded with ex-GIs matriculating on government money. Is it any wonder that they heard the message that their place was in the home? Where else could they go?

The eradication of sexism and the practices it supports, like those above, is obviously one of the major goals of the women's liberation movement. But it is not enough to destroy a set of values and leave a normative vacuum. They have to be replaced with something. A movement only begins by declaring its opposition to the status quo. Eventually, if it is to succeed, it has to propose an alternative.

I cannot pretend to be even partially definitive about the possible alternatives contemplated by the numerous participants in the women's liberation movement. Yet from the plethora of ideas and visions feminists have thought, discussed, and written about, I think there are two basic ideas emerging which express the bulk of their concerns. I call these the Egalitarian Ethic and the Liberation Ethic, but they are not independent of each other, and together they mesh into what can only be described as a feminist humanism.

The Egalitarian Ethic means exactly what it says. The sexes are equal; therefore, sex roles must go. Our history has proved that institutionalized difference inevitably means inequity, and sex-role stereotypes have long since become anachronistic. Strongly differentiated sex roles were rooted in the ancient division of labor; their basis has been torn apart by modern technology. Their justification was rooted in the subjection of women to the reproductive cycle. That has already been destroyed by modern pharmacology. The cramped little boxes of personality and social function to which we assign people from birth must be broken open so that all people can develop independently, as individuals. This means that there will be an integration of social functions and life-styles of men and women as groups until, ideally, one cannot tell anything of relevance about a person's social role by knowing the sex of the person. But this increased similarity of the two groups also means increased options for individuals and increased diversity in the human race. No longer will there be men's work and women's work. No longer will humanity suffer a schizophrenic personality desperately trying to reconcile its "masculine" and "feminine" parts. No longer will marriage be the institution where two half-people come together in hopes of making a whole.

The Liberation Ethic says this is not enough. Not only must the limits of the roles be changed, but their content as well. The Liberation Ethic looks at the kinds of lives currently being led by men as well as women and concludes that both are deplorable and neither are necessary. The social institutions which oppress women as women also oppress people as people and can be altered to make a more humane existence for all. So much of our society is hung upon the framework of sex-role stereotypes and their reciprocal functions that the dismantling of this structure will provide the opportunity for making a more viable life for everyone.

It is important to stress that these two ethics must work together in tandem. If the first is emphasized over the second, then we have a women's rights movement, not one of women's liberation. To seek for only equality, given the current male bias of the social values, is to assume that women want to be like men or that men are worth emulating. It is to demand that women be allowed to participate in society as we know it, to get their piece of the pie, without questioning the extent to which that society is worth participating in. This view is held by some, but most feminists today find it inadequate. Those women who are more personally compatible in what is considered the male role must realize that that role is made possible only by the existence of the female sex role; in other words, only the subjection of women. Therefore, women cannot become equal to men without the destruction of those two interdependent, mutually parasitic roles. The failure to realize that the integration of the sex roles and the equality of the sexes will inevitably lead to basic structural change is to fail to seize the opportunity to decide the direction of those changes.

It is just as dangerous to fall into the trap of seeking liberation without due concern for equality. This is the mistake made by many of the left radicals. They find the general human condition to be so wretched that they feel everyone should devote energies to the Millennial Revolution in the belief that the liberation of women will follow naturally the liberation of people.

However, women have yet to be defined as people, even among the radicals, and it is erroneous to assume their interests are identical to those of men. For women to subsume their concerns once again is to ensure that the promise of liberation will be a spurious one. There has yet to be created or conceived by any political or social theorist a revolutionary society in which women are equal to men and their needs duly considered. The sex-role structure has never been comprehensively challenged by any male philosopher, and the systems they have proposed have all presumed the existence of a sex-role structure to some degree.

Such undue emphasis on the Liberation Ethic has also often led to a sort of Radical Paradox. This is a situation the politicos frequently found themselves in during the early days of the movement. They found repugnant the possibility of pursuing "reformist" issues which might be achieved without altering the basic nature of the system, and thus, they felt, only strengthen the system. However, their search for a sufficiently radical action and/or issue came to naught, and they found themselves unable to do anything, out of fear that it might be counterrevolutionary. Inactive revolutionaries are a good deal more innocuous than active "reformists."

But even among those who are not rendered impotent, the unilateral pursuit of liberation can take its toll. Some radical women have been so appalled at the condition of most men, and the possibility of becoming even partially what they are, that they have clung to the security of the role they know, to wait complacently for the revolution to liberate everyone. Some men, fearing that role reversal was a goal of the women's liberation movement, have taken a similar position. Both have failed to realize that the abolition of sex roles must be continually incorporated into any radical restructuring of society and thus have failed to explore the possible consequences of such role integration. The goal they advocate may be one of liberation, but it does not involve women's liberation.

Separated from each other, the Egalitarian Ethic and the Liberation Ethic can be crippling, but together they can be a very powerful force. Separately they speak to limited interests; together they speak to all humanity. Separately they are but superficial solutions; together they recognize that while sexism oppresses women, it also limits the potentiality of men. Separately neither will be achieved because its scope does not range far enough; together they provide a vision worthy of our devotion. Separately these two ethics do not lead to the liberation of women; together they also lead to the liberation of men.

NOW (National Organization for Women)
Bill of Rights

Adopted at NOW's first national conference, Washington, D.C., 1967

I. Equal Rights Constitutional Amendment
II. Enforce Law Banning Sex Discrimination in Employment
III. Maternity Leave Rights in Employment and in Social Security Benefits
IV. Tax Deduction for Home and Child Care Expenses for Working Parents
V. Child Day Care Centers
VI. Equal and Unsegregated Education
VII. Equal Job Training Opportunities and Allowances for Women in Poverty.
VIII. The Right of Women to Control Their Reproductive Lives

WE DEMAND:

I. That the U.S. Congress immediately pass the Equal Rights Amendment to the Constitution to provide that "Equality of rights under the law shall not be denied or abridged by the United States or by any State on account of sex," and that such then be immediately ratified by the several States.

II. That equal employment opportunity be guaranteed to all women, as well as men, by insisting that the Equal Employment Opportunity Commission enforces the prohibitions against racial discrimination.

III. That women be protected by law to ensure their rights to return to their jobs within a reasonable time after childbirth without loss of seniority or other accrued benefits, and be paid maternity leave as a form of social security and/or employee benefit.

IV. Immediate revision of tax laws to permit the deduction of home and child-care expenses for working parents.

V. That child-care facilities be established by law on the same basis as parks, libraries, and public schools, adequate to the needs of children from the pre-school years through adolescence, as a community resource to be used by all citizens from all income levels.

VI. That the right of women to be educated to their full potential equally with men be secured by Federal and State legislation, eliminating all discrimination and segregation by sex, written and unwritten, at all levels

Source: "NOW Bill of Rights," in Robin Morgan, ed., *Sisterhood Is Powerful: An Anthology of Writings from the Women's Liberation Movement* (New York: Vintage Books, A Division of Random House, Inc., September 1970), pp. 512–514. Reprinted by permission of National Organization for Women.

of education, including colleges, graduate and professional schools, loans and fellowships, and Federal and State training programs such as the Job Corps.

VII. The right of women in poverty to secure job training, housing, and family allowances on equal terms with men, but without prejudice to a parent's right to remain at home to care for his or her children; revision of welfare legislation and poverty programs which deny women dignity, privacy, and self-respect.

VIII. The right of women to control their own reproductive lives by removing from the penal code laws limiting access to contraceptive information and devices, and by repealing penal laws governing abortion.

REDSTOCKINGS MANIFESTO

I. After centuries of individual and preliminary political struggle, women are uniting to achieve their final liberation from male supremacy. Redstockings is dedicated to building this unity and winning our freedom.

II. Women are an oppressed class. Our oppression is total, affecting every facet of our lives. We are exploited as sex objects, breeders, domestic servants, and cheap labor. We are considered inferior beings, whose only purpose is to enhance men's lives. Our humanity is denied. Our prescribed behavior is enforced by the threat of physical violence.

Because we have lived so intimately with our oppressors, in isolation from each other, we have been kept from seeing our personal suffering as a political condition. This creates the illusion that a woman's relationship with her man is a matter of interplay between two unique personalities, and can be worked out individually. In reality, every such relationship is a *class* relationship, and the conflicts between individual men and women are *political* conflicts that can only be solved collectively.

III. We identify the agents of our oppression as men. Male supremacy is the oldest, most basic form of domination. All other forms of exploitation and oppression (racism, capitalism, imperialism, etc.) are extensions of male supremacy: men dominate women, a few men dominate the rest. All power structures throughout history have been male-dominated and male-oriented. Men have controlled all political, economic and cultural institu-

Source: "Redstockings Manifesto," in Robin Morgan, ed., *Sisterhood Is Powerful: An Anthology of Writings from the Women's Liberation Movement* (New York: Vintage Books, A Division of Random House, Inc., September 1970), pp. 533–536. Copyright © 1970 by Robin Morgan. Reprinted by permission of Robin Morgan.

tions and backed up this control with physical force. They have used their power to keep women in an inferior position. *All men* receive economic, sexual, and psychological benefits from male supremacy. *All men* have oppressed women.

IV. Attempts have been made to shift the burden of responsibility from men to institutions or to women themselves. We condemn these arguments as evasions. Institutions alone do not oppress; they are merely tools of the oppressor. To blame institutions implies that men and women are equally victimized, obscures the fact that men benefit from the subordination of women, and gives men the excuse that they are forced to be oppressors. On the contrary, any man is free to renounce his superior position provided that he is willing to be treated like a woman by other men.

We also reject the idea that women consent to or are to blame for their own oppression. Women's submission is not the result of brainwashing, stupidity, or mental illness but of continual, daily pressure from men. We do not need to change ourselves, but to change men.

The most slanderous evasion of all is that women can oppress men. The basis for this illusion is the isolation of individual relationships from their political context and the tendency of men to see any legitimate challenge to their privileges as persecution.

V. We regard our personal experience, and our feelings about that experience, as the basis for an analysis of our common situation. We cannot rely on existing ideologies as they are all products of male supremacist culture. We question every generalization and accept none that are not confirmed by our experience.

Our chief task at present is to develop female class consciousness through sharing experience and publicly exposing the sexist foundation of all our institutions. Consciousness-raising is not "therapy," which implies the existence of individual solutions and falsely assumes that the male-female relationship is purely personal, but the only method by which we can ensure that our program for liberation is based on the concrete realities of our lives.

The first requirement for raising class consciousness is honesty, in private and in public, with ourselves and other women.

VI. We identify with all women. We define our best interest as that of the poorest, most brutally exploited woman.

We repudiate all economic, racial, educational or status privileges that divide us from other women. We are determined to recognize and eliminate any prejudices we may hold against other women.

We are committed to achieving internal democracy. We will do whatever is necessary to ensure that every woman in our movement has an equal chance to participate, assume responsibility, and develop her political potential.

VII. We call on all our sisters to unite with us in struggle.

We call on all men to give up their male privileges and support women's liberation in the interest of our humanity and their own.

In fighting for our liberation we will always take the side of women against their oppressors. We will not ask what is "revolutionary" or "reformist," only what is good for women.

The time for individual skirmishes has passed. This time we are going all the way.

THE WHITE NIGGERS OF NEWARK

David K. Shipler

On the other side of the city, far from the rotting row houses of the black ghetto with its dropouts and junkies, safe in the sanctuary of the neat, white, working-class neighborhood, there is a grimy poolroom that is lit too brightly. The white kids with long, matted hair squint as they drift in from the night, forming knots around the two ratty little pool tables, their shrill laughter spilling out from under the scalding fluorescent lights onto darkened Bloomfield Avenue. Dropouts. A few junkies. Most are in dungarees, some in Levi jackets, as if it were a uniform. Only two girls are in the crowd, both expertly shooting pool, chewing gum seriously, tough girls in tight sweaters. On the sidewalk, kids flick glowing cigarette butts into the gutter as they lean against the poolroom's two huge storefront windows where the faded red letters from another time can still be seen spelling, "J & J Confectionery."

Most come here after spending their days looking fruitlessly for work and groping aimlessly for a way out of their own kind of ghetto. The twenty-two-year-old with the trimmed beard and the pleading, liquid eyes, who calls himself "J.B." and says he shoots heroin a couple of times a week, but gets turned away by methadone programs that are looking for harder addicts, especially blacks. The self-confident eighteen-year-old, Gerard Furrule, who works his way easily around a pool table, quit school in ninth grade, worked in a print shop for a dollar an hour, and now gets $1.90 in the mail room of a big company. In this candy store turned poolroom, he is considered a success. He is going to classes in the evening, trying

Source: *Harper's Magazine* (August 1972), pp. 77 83. Copyright © 1972, by Minneapolis Star and Tribune Co., Inc. Reprinted from the August 1972 issue of *Harper's Magazine* by permission of the author.

to get his high-school diploma. College? "Only niggers go to college," one of his buddies says morosely. Gerard smiles.

These kids are part of a dwindling white minority in Newark, New Jersey, where blacks are 54 per cent and Puerto Ricans 13 per cent of the 382,000 people and where, after long decades of powerlessness, blacks have taken political control. The result has been a new set of angry lines between whites and blacks, drawn as never before in an American city. Black power has been converted into reality with such headiness, and the outside white establishment has applauded the turnabout so vigorously, that many whites in Newark have been left with a corrosive sense of invisibility. Colleges that send recruiters to Newark do so in search of blacks, not working-class whites. Federal programs designed to help youngsters get jobs, keep them off drugs, provide them with recreation, and improve their schooling are aimed at blacks, staffed by blacks, and located in black neighborhoods. They do not reach the white kids who hang out at the J & J Confectionery.

But simple neglect fails to explain completely the difficulties of Newark's poor and working-class whites, just as it never fully summed up the black experience in America. The whites, especially the Italians, are deeply distrusted by many blacks who have attained power, including the city's first black mayor, Kenneth A. Gibson, who sees himself still struggling against the organized crime, corruption, and white racism that gripped the city government under his predecessor, Hugh J. Addonizio. Just before the 1970 election, Addonizio was indicted on sixty-four counts of extortion and conspiracy, along with several city councilmen, former public works directors, and reputed Mafia figures. The indictment, which led to a ten-year federal prison sentence for Addonizio and contributed to his defeat by Gibson, also contaminated all the city's Italians, even those who were disgusted by the corruption, for it reinforced—both to the blacks and to outsiders—a sinister stereotype.

Now, after all the shifts of power, going to Newark is like stepping into a hall of mirrors where familiar images are inverted and twisted into remarkable, confusing shapes that destroy any sense of equilibrium. The familiar American patterns of racism and exploitation dissolve into a mad array of reversals and contradictions.

Gibson is widely regarded by whites as a moderate, undramatic, conscientious man who hasn't the strength to resist the pressure of some militant blacks for the transformation of Newark into what they call "New Ark," a romantic vision of black nationalism and black pride. The mayor architect of this vision—and of Gibson's election—is the poet and playwright LeRoi Jones, who has adopted the African name of Imamu Baraka. His brilliant pursuit of political power and cultural strength for blacks has frightened many whites, who see in the dashikis of the black councilmen, the clenched-fist salutes of the Board of Education members, and the black-liberation flags in the schools the symbols of a new racism.

The institution most sensitive to this surge of black pride is the Board of Education, always in the past a crucial instrument of white power. Gibson's black appointees have proved more militant than the mayor, and since they constitute the majority of the board, some of them at public meetings sneer and laugh at the white members. Many white citizens say they no longer dare enter the board's hearing room with its dark-stained wood and curved, polished wooden dais. The few whites who do go to monthly hearings are often hooted and ridiculed by the black audiences, and their testimony is ignored by the predominantly black board.

In the spring of 1971, at the height of an emotional teachers' strike, a black physician, Dr. E. Wyman Garrett, rose at a public hearing, pointed to a white board member, John Cervase, and said: "Cervase, we know where you live. We're going to get you. We're really going to get you." Then he allegedly ordered several black men to beat up a white reporter who had written down his threat.

Amateur Racism

"We're the niggers now, that's what's happened," said Stephen N. Adubato. "It just is who's on top. The group that's second's gonna catch shit —they're gonna be niggers. This is what this country's really all about." Adubato hunched intently over his desk. "The blacks aren't so sophisticated with their racism. They're just learning what power is about, what America's about. They're more overt, and so are we—we're not sophisticated about our racism as Italians. We're amateurs too." Once a schoolteacher, Adubato is emerging as a political leader in Newark's North Ward, the stronghold of the city's remaining working-class Italian-Americans, who make up most of the city's white population. He spent his younger years fighting for the rights of blacks, and he campaigned for Gibson. But as the power of the blacks grew in the city, and as he discovered that nobody was trying to help the Italians, he turned his attention to his own people. He left teaching and won election as Democratic leader in the North Ward.

"Let me give you this analogy," he said. "I see the Italian community in Newark and the black community in Newark face to face, really in a crowd, lined up in a crowd. And the pressure, the momentum, is with the blacks, and they're pushing us backward, and we're not acting like other whites, 'cause we're fighting back, you know, clawing and punching and kicking in the balls and all the rest. But if you reach up and look beyond that line, that black line, you'll see all of the white liberals and do-gooders and the people who really won't meet the problem, pushing, encouraging, you know, and putting on more pressure. It's a nice picture, you can almost see it. D'ya see it?" He laughed.

"And of course we look bad because we're cursin' and swearin', and we say 'nigger' all the time, and the people in the back always said 'Negro' when that was right and now 'black.' They talk the right way, and they're actually assisting. Someone's got to be hurt, that's what I hear, someone's got to be hurt."

Adubato is full of statistics that show the extent of the hurt: a study by the Board of Education, for example, revealing that the percentage of white Newark high-school graduates going to college dropped from 50 per cent in 1969 to 45 per cent in 1970, while the proportion of blacks rose from 49 to 52 per cent.

"There's a great need in the black area for the things that are being done, and they're only scratching the surface," Adubato said. "But take two cases of terminal cancer. The black cancer is more acute, in six months it's terminal; the white cancer is less acute, it would take eighteen months before it's terminal. Now some asshole liberal by looking at that analogy, you know what he says? Well, the whites are three times better off. So what does he do? He goes on the black street exclusively. Nobody attends to the white cancer."

At Barringer High School, white teenagers—who make up about one-fourth of the student body—find themselves engulfed by a whirlwind of blackness: black history, black literature, black culture, black pride, all the components of self-assertion and identity that have been hailed as healthy for a people enslaved and beaten down and brutalized over the centuries. It is not so healthy for the whites. Every morning, "Swahili music" is played over the school's public address system, and some white students find it as offensive and threatening as blacks would find "Dixie." The day after the Board of Education voted to hang the black, red, and green flag of black liberation in every classroom with a majority of black students (a move ultimately barred by the courts), someone got on the PA system and said, "Brothers be cool, sisters be sweet, and others—well, just others."

Whites stay out of the cafeteria, which is black turf; they don't go to basketball games, since the team is black. And just as blacks used to avoid dances at school in Adubato's day, now whites avoid them, taking the cue from the dance posters in the hallways with pictures of black couples cut out of black magazines. "I never saw a sign in the school of a social event that applied to me," said Stephen Mustacchio, an eighteen-year-old senior. "The same thing with the school chorus: 'Brothers and sisters, if you want to find yourself, join the chorus.' I mean, you know, the white people can't join the chorus if they want to?" One boy ventured into a college recruiter's meeting where it had been announced, as usual, that "a representative will be here today to recruit black and Puerto Rican students," and found talk only of black clubs and black studies, "like I didn't belong there," he said. He didn't apply.

In English class, "you have to read black literature," Steve said. "They never give you any white literature to read. You have to read *Black Voices,* there's a book out called *Black Voices,* then we had to read Malcolm X, then there's another one about a black child. We don't have to read anything about a white person."

Most of the teachers at Barringer are white, but they are fearful of the black students declaring them "insensitive," which Adubato noted means insensitive not to Italians or to whites—just to blacks.

The sense of worthlessness and inferiority that has so long afflicted blacks now seems to threaten these white youngsters, many of whom are struggling to get to college, something their parents could not do. They and their parents see themselves in double jeopardy, a minority in their own city, yet too urban and too Italian to be part of the American mainstream, which they characterize as suburban and WASP.

"When you really feel this is like when you get into college," said Lucille Poet, a bright-eyed college sophomore whose father is a foreman in a factory. "You can't get a scholarship because you're not quite poor enough—well, really, you're not black. And you get into college and they look at you, you come from Newark, and you're caught in the middle: you're not rich enough to be really a white person, but you're not poor enough to be a colored person."

When she finished, a roomful of North Ward kids let the silence hang for a long moment.

But the kids fail to see the parallels between their experience and the complaints of blacks about predominantly white schools where no black literature is read and no blacks appear as characters in American history. When the similarity was suggested, Lucille's brother Maurice snapped, "Why should that affect us?" And Steve Mustacchio explained, "When I reached high school my whole attitude changed toward them, 'cause I wasn't really in too much contact with them. I went to a private white grammar school, I hardly spoke about them or anything, but when I got to high school, I had to go to school with them, I grew to hate them. When I got to school, and I saw who they were, I came to hate them."

In their candor, the Barringer kids contrast sharply with another group of white Newark teenagers, who go to Vailsburg High School, the last high school in the city in which whites still constitute the majority, and only 30 per cent of the students are black. Sitting in a circle one evening on the floor of a room belonging to a young divinity student who is trying to help organize the white community, about a dozen white Vailsburg students were asked if they had black friends. "Of course!" they shouted in an annoyed chorus. Pressed for specifics, the kids got tense. Only one girl could name a friend who was black, and her friend went to another school.

The Vailsburg kids have the luxury of fighting very hard to be, or at least to appear, open-minded. The same is often true of North Ward youngsters who have gone to mostly white private high schools. Everyone in that room could list clear differences between his own and his parents' attitudes toward blacks. Always the parents were bigots or racists.

By contrast, the Barringer teenagers generally agree with their parents' anti-black views, and Steve Mustacchio even disputes his mother's liberal attitude that "I work with them and I get along with them." "She works in a candy factory with the older type of people," Steve said. "She don't have to put up with everything."

Some kids try to resist black pressure, but others succumb. The Rev. John R. Sharp, a Presbyterian minister in the mostly white Vailsburg section, describes an effort his church made to organize a summer basketball team so white neighborhood youngsters would have a chance to take part in the downtown recreation programs, which are run mostly for blacks.

"Our kids would go down and get on the court and they would freeze, they couldn't play," Sharp said. "They'd lose their cool, they would get so uptight playing in an all-black neighborhood, and the blacks would continue to take advantage of that and just keep up a running commentary: 'You better go on back to white town' and laugh at 'em and call 'em honkies. And our kids would be on best behavior—they wouldn't respond. And they wouldn't go back next time."

Sharp counts himself among the few liberals in Newark. He resembles the young, moderate black leaders of a previous generation, striving to show the majority that his constituents are human beings who defy easy stereotypes, who present no threat. He is even hanging on in the face of open hostility, living in a mostly black neighborhood and suffering the telephone calls of some black parents who tell him, "Keep your honky kids away from our kids." Sharp explained that the blacks are worried about the white youngsters eroding the black identity of their children.

In response to the dominance of the city's black power structure, especially in the public schools, Sharp and other white leaders have tried to do what black leaders in many communities managed years ago—unite the diverse elements in their neighborhood to speak with one voice on selected issues. The result is an umbrella organization known as the Unified Vailsburg Committee, which contains not only liberals but John Birchers and Wallace supporters as well. "One of the conservatives said, 'We could probably be more moderate, Reverend, but if we did, they'd walk over us, and so what we do is go all the way to the right. We take a position, and we won't move, and we let you guys do all the negotiation.'"

This role as white organizer leads Sharp into some remarkable statements, the kind of statements that were not at all remarkable when black leaders used to make them about their own people. "If they felt they had a voice," Sharp said wistfully of his white constituency. "The great victory is to get the Board of Education to deal with the people and not deal with the stereotype—it's awful hard. Now it's a problem of trying to convince the black majority to be humane and just toward the white minority."

The symmetry of black and white response to power and powerlessness has translated a good many romantic notions into real political questions. "It's the same way as white pride has gotten bad," said Frank DonDiego, who grew up in Newark and now goes to college at Rutgers. "The blacks have gotten their pride, and it started in the beginning really beautiful, but now they've gone into the same white hangups; pride has become a superiority trip."

Adubato's response to the dominance of the blacks is considerably different from Sharp's, but no less pragmatic. He reaches back for his own roots as an Italian, arguing that as a minority ethnic group, Italians should be given the same kind of representation on public bodies, in City Hall, and in federal programs that blacks have won for themselves in cities where they are the minority. He scorns Gibson's two major Italian appointees—one a deputy mayor, one a school board member—as "Uncle Marios" who "think black."

Even though most teachers, policemen, and firemen are still white, the alleged preference of the city's institutions for blacks is an emotional, hate-filled topic of conversation at the Italian social clubs in the North Ward, where men gather in the evenings to watch ball games on television or shoot pool or drink or play cards or eat huge meals they cook themselves in ancient kitchens laden with enormous pots and greasy stoves. The rhetoric swirls back and forth between fact and myth.

"What about Newark Airport? The construction of the new airport? They held up construction for a year already, they stopped all construction on it, being that it's being built in Newark they want 50 per cent of the working force minorities, if they're qualified or not, because they're black or Puerto Rican. That means if I'm a qualified man, a bricklayer, I'm gonna lose a fuckin' job because I'm gonna be replaced by a shine that has no qualifications. But being it's being built in Newark, it's supposedly a majority of fuckin' shines, they want the shines to do the bricklayin', even if they're not qualified." Pete Cannestro, a young truck driver for Sears, shakes his head in disbelief. Then he repeats the complaint that many Italians voice in Newark, that the federal government and private lending institutions give blacks preference when it comes to mortgages or business loans. "They would turn me down and back the shine," Cannestro says. "I know about five people that had experiences like that."

Whether or not such tales are true, they exist with fiery credibility around the card tables in the Italian clubs. These are working men who generally make under $10,000, own $8,000 brick or wooden row houses on dingy streets, cannot get fire insurance because of the 1967 riots in the city's ghettos, pay one of the nation's highest property tax rates (nearly $10 per $100), and submit to what some of them bitterly term a "double tax," the tuition for the parochial schools they feel they owe their children. They are racists, sure, and they like George Wallace and Anthony Imperiale, the beefy white militant and vigilante leader who is now a state assemblyman from the North Ward. But simply to dismiss them as racists and thereby discard their anger and their hurt is to make a sad mistake, one for which they hate the news media and the Establishment in Washington and the suburban executives who crowd downtown Newark during daylight to run the businesses that exclude Italians at least as efficiently as they exclude blacks.

"The liberals are so good at understanding every other group, why don't they want to understand us?" Adubato asks. "Our mothers work in factories —we're the white pigs."

The Urge to Flee

Many whites who have decided to stay in Newark have begun to see themselves as victims not only of the new black power but also of the larger greed and indifference of outside white America. Many understand that they and the blacks are equal victims of the rampant blockbusting being attempted in white neighborhoods of their city, where they are barraged by letters and phone calls from real estate agents who spread fear and urge sales at low prices so that the houses can be resold at inflated levels to black families. Signs painted with the word "SOLD" in electric red or orange have been nailed up by real estate agents so that they stick out horizontally from houses, flagging the points of panic on an otherwise peaceful residential block. Some residents of Vailsburg, which has a lovely, more suburban look than the North Ward, have even begun countering with signs declaring, "This House Is NOT For Sale."

The whites who stay expose themselves to the pain of seeing their old neighborhoods, where they and their fathers and grandfathers once lived, ravaged by poverty and decay. They see it every time they drive into downtown Newark, past the old streets, the old corners, past the Boys' Clubs and the YMCAs where they spent hours as children, but where their children cannot go.

Sticking it out in Newark, stopping the trend that saw 10,000 whites leave in the 1960s, is a political strategy in Adubato's terms, essential to his goal of consolidating Italian power in the city. It is also a matter of pride to some, and it stirs sharp debate within families. In one of the shabby brick row houses on a narrow street in the North Ward, a forty-six-year-old man who works the nightshift in a Pabst Blue Ribbon brewery, his wife, and their twenty-two-year-old son talked through the question of leaving. They have lived all their lives in Newark, their parents having arrived there from Italy, but their block has become mostly Puerto Rican, and crime has increased in recent years. The father, a serious, well-read man although he had only two years of high school, was adamant about staying. The mother and the son, a college student who lives at home, wanted to leave. They asked that their names not be used.

"There's no magic in black skin, and some of us are beginning to realize you cannot run," the father said, "because if you run from Wakeman Avenue today, you're going to run from Mt. Prospect Avenue tomorrow, and if it's from Mt. Prospect Avenue tomorrow, you're gonna run from Llewellyn Park, which is an exclusive suburban residential area, the following day. When do you stop running?" He asked his daughter to get him the Scotch, and he poured some into a shot glass. The bottle in one hand, the glass in the other, he drank and gestured as he talked. His wife, fighting a cold, rubbed her raw nose with a handkerchief.

"I happen to be here all day," she said. "My husband is away at work, so I'm stuck with all the trials that go on, whether they be black or Spanish, so I have the inclination to run. I can cope with the winters, but the summer —it seems as if the warm weather sets everybody off. I don't enjoy the summers here at all. The winters, we close the door, it gets dark early and I'm glad."

"Pride," the son said to his father. "What is the sense of staying in a city, any city, right? Now Newark is just about the worst city in the country. I'm only living in Newark right now because I have to. I'm not running from Newark, I'm running from a bunch of garbage, which is alien to my nature and I don't want to be part of it."

"For you, son, this is okay," his father answered with a tone of finality. "I'm staying in Newark because I simply do not want someone pushing me out. I do not want the idea that I am running away."

Not all young Italians in Newark want to flee. Jim Cundari, for one, a handsome, twenty-seven-year-old lawyer whose family moved from the city a few years ago, found the suburbs barren and came back. "If you go to a shopping center community, you lose that little corner grocery store where you go and get your Italian cheeses and your sausage and bologna, and you lose the warmth and comfort of having the close row houses and the stoops and the kind of social activity. You just lose the closeness with your whole sense of your history and your traditions."

When Newark was authorized by the federal government to expand its Model Cities program to include not just the central ghetto but the entire city, Cundari, with Adubato's help, tried to get a job in the Newark Model

Cities agency to represent the Italians. He was refused; the agency remains virtually all black, and Model Cities funds are still not getting into white neighborhoods. Cundari found a post in the office of the city's Business Administrator, but the morning he showed up for work, he was met on the steps of City Hall by an aide to Mayor Gibson and informed that there was no job for him. During the months that followed, he was told repeatedly that the budget couldn't support him. "I was pretty well convinced that the reason I wasn't getting in was because I was Italian and they didn't want an Italian with a head on his shoulders being in a position of responsibility." Finally, through Gibson's personal intervention, Cundari was hired and put in charge of the city's lobbying efforts in Trenton, the state capital.

Gibson has tried hard to integrate his staff and limit patronage to the less crucial anti-poverty-type programs, but an acute apprehension seems to run through his efforts. He complains that white civil servants who cannot be fired subvert his policies by a kind of passive resistance, refusing to do anything they are not directly ordered to do. He has named whites to important posts, such as police director, fire director, and business administrator. But they are not Italians.

Gibson's nervousness is not exactly surprising. The City Council, still mostly Italians, opposes him at every turn. It insisted on retaining as city auditor an accountant who in twenty-four years had never found a problem with Newark's books and who, for the same length of time, had done the auditing for the family of Anthony (Tony Boy) Boiardo, named by law enforcement officials as the Mafia head in Newark. In addition, the most venomous hatred of blacks and of Gibson himself during his campaign came from Italians—the former police director, Dominick Spina, for example, and Anthony Imperiale, who warned of rapists and insurrectionists taking over the city if Gibson became mayor.

When Gibson came into office in July of 1970, he found city government a shambles, mangled to make corruption easy. There was almost no middle management to dilute the power of the top city officials, with the result that there was not much management at all. The city had not a single licensed engineer to check for error or fraud in work done by private firms on millions of dollars' worth of sewer and road projects. Virtually every city contract had been let with a 10 per cent kickback to city officials. Some sewers were built to nowhere, simply ending underground. Corruption heightened the special viciousness about Newark, the rawness in the racism of both whites and blacks. And it damaged the chances for reconciliation.

"There is no real concept of brotherhood in this city," Cundari said. "We all have our own agendas, for the simple reason that we all have such real problems. The consciousness of who you are and what you are is so rampant in the city, as soon as something becomes identified as yours, that's it.

There's no one going into an Italian barbershop and trying to challenge whether they'll cut a black man's hair. There's no one trying to implement busing to bring whites and blacks into closer community. It just doesn't work that way. No one wants it. In a city like this, people would be content with separate but equal facilities, and no one would challenge it."

Newark may be the real truth about America, the nation's subconscious finally stripped of its rationalizations and platitudes. The city wallows in the swath of stinking factories that belch filth from the Jersey flats into the shadow of the Statue of Liberty. It has also tarnished the other symbols of America by making hatred look like honesty, by making old dreams laughable.

BLACK POLITICS AT THE CROSSROADS

Alex Poinsett

Perhaps Sammy Davis Jr. had not been hipped to the confidential memo when he hugged President Richard M. Nixon so spontaneously. Perhaps the millions who watched that ecstatic television spectacular—many in utter disgust and outrage—also had not heard about it. Perhaps only Nixon Administration insiders were aware of the document which circulated around Washington, D. C., singling out blacks as the nation's most unpopular and disorganized minority, dismissing them as an impotent political force to be either patronized or passed over.

The confidential memo could have been a sort of script for this summer's Democratic and Republican conventions in Disneylandish Miami Beach, Fla. For blacks, generally, were either caught up in the illusion of political power or benignly neglected, as if both parties coveted their votes but not necessarily their participation as equals. Since their delegate strength had more than doubled from 209 in 1968 to 454, since they had made more than token appearances at the podium, since they had been prominent in behind-the-scenes maneuverings, black Democrats could boast of greater participation in an "open" convention. On the other hand, black Republicans sometimes apologized for their inconspicuousness, their near extinct role in the party's delicately programmed extravaganza. Still, in the euphoria of cocktail parties—first in the lavish hotels and then on the appropriately named "Cloud Nine" houseboat—black Republicans could rhapsodize over

Source: *Ebony* (October 1972), pp. 37–40, 42–43, 46–48. Reprinted by permission of *Ebony* Magazine, copyright 1972 by Johnson Publishing Company, Inc.

the ballooning of their delegates from 26 in 1968 to 56 and could speak of approaching some sort of symmetrical balance to genuine black participation in the two-party system. To be sure, individual black Democrats or black Republicans scored a Brownie point or two at Miami Beach. Like the political parties they represented, however, none produced a program relevant to the suffering, the impoverishment and the powerlessness of most blacks. For as one hardened political observer noted: "They came without an agenda. They came unprepared to ask for a damn thing. Therefore, they weren't organized to do a damn thing."

It had been precisely to avoid this sort of trap that a series of "closed-door" meetings had been held last winter and early spring of this year in response to thoughtful pleas from black thinkers for a political "map" rather than a "rap." Black leaders—that is, those who were sure enough serious—sought to construct a viable black political strategy for 1972 and beyond. Early on, Democratic presidential candidate Shirley Chisholm believed she had peeped a poorly-concealed hole card here and there. Perhaps angered at convention time by the scarcity of black support for her candidacy, she spoke mysteriously of $50,000 payoffs, charging that even as black leaders called their strategy meetings many were unable to put together a plan. "They were already in the man's pocket," she declared, derisively.

Well now, if you were one of those black leaders who had "sold out," like a certain fat cat seen nibbling cheese and crackers and sipping Scotch, you pretended as if the historic National Black Political Convention in Gary, Ind., never really occurred last March. You acted as if the Black Agenda produced there was never written. You revealed to a newsman that you had been asked to defend in Miami Beach, the Black Agenda's meticulous cataloging of black aspirations and demands that were to be the basis of black negotiations with the Democratic and Republican parties. You explained that, on the contrary, your political assignment in Miami Beach was to handle yachts. And when you completed your assignments, you grinned triumphantly. You were going to be cool. You weren't going to be no fool. You were going to get you some more cheese and crackers.

. . .

But the tide of history rolls over cool cheese eaters and the hot sands of Miami Beach. The Black Agenda had been formally ratified in Greensboro, N. C., last May. Imamu Amiri Baraka, who had co-convened the Gary convention along with Gary's Mayor Richard Hatcher and Congressman Charles Diggs, had pleaded with blacks that "from this point we can either pull together, build and rise, or else we can draw apart, splinter, polarize, and sink back to our abstract isolated 'correctness,' amidst the not so dignified 'right offs!' of our jolly enemies."

Baraka's warnings, however, had largely gone unheeded by those black leaders who repudiated sections of the Black Agenda, claiming the Gary Convention did not represent the black community because it included "too many militants." Then, as if to codify these objections, the Congressional Black Caucus had produced its own document—The Black Bill of Rights—a watered down and somewhat expanded version of the Gary Agenda. A caucus member had carefully explained that the Black Bill of Rights was more attuned to "the political circumstances of 1972" than the strident, manifesto-like Black Agenda. His had been a polite way of saying the Caucus disapproved of the Agenda's controversial anti-busing and anti-Israel resolutions.

Out of this background, then, black politicians had stepped into the conventions at Miami Beach. Many of the Democrats had left Gary generally agreeing to maximize their bargaining power by withholding support from front-running candidates until the last possible minute. For most, however, such political idealism remained checked with the unclaimed baggage at the Miami International Airport. Even before the Democratic convention got underway, black Democrats were supporting either Rep. Chisholm, Sen. Hubert Humphrey or hopping merrily on the steam roller created by Sen. George McGovern's spectacular victories in the primaries. And so Institute of the Black World political analyst William Strickland noted: "Some of our elected representatives were sincerely mistaken, others were hopelessly corrupt, but all, the best and the worst, including Shirley, delivered up our real and potential black political power. They delivered it up willingly, graciously, cleverly, in the belief, one supposes, that by advancing white politics they were somehow advancing our own."

. . .

In any case, Sen. McGovern was especially appealing to the convention's young blacks, because he had been the only presidential candidate bold enough to endorse—with some reservations—the spirit and substance of both the Congressional Caucus' Bill of Rights and the Black Agenda. That endorsement counter-balanced his lackluster civil rights record in Congress and the fact that so far as black psyches were concerned the senator hailed from a state located at some point outside the known universe. Throughout the spring primaries McGovern had done very little campaigning in the black community. True, he had made sporadic forays among blacks in California and Wisconsin. But by and large he had neglected the more numerous blacks in, for example, New York, Michigan and Ohio. On the other hand, in the convention itself he had tightened up his game plan and relied heavily on blacks to win the crucial fight over the seating of the entire California delegation.

Yet the blacks who had helped McGovern exercised practically no say-so in the selection of later-deposed Sen. Thomas Eagleton as the Democratic vice-presidential candidate. And McGovern's black aide, tall, tough, ex-Army paratrooper Yancy Martin had become so enraged at being systematically excluded from campaign policy making, he threatened to resign. At convention's end, McGovern and his staffers had planned a junket to the Black Hills of South Dakota. Some black politicians believed, innocently, that the trip would be for vacation purposes only.

"Man, don't kid yourself," warned a more experienced politician. "They're going there to plan the campaign and we won't be in on it." Hurriedly, McGovern's black supporters decided that Congressmen Walter Fauntroy and William Clay should join, even if it meant crashing the party.

"All the seats on the plane are taken," explained Frank Mankiewicz, one of McGovern's top strategists, speaking to Congressman Clay.

"That's all right," the congressman replied. "There's one seat for me."

"What do you mean?" Mankiewicz wanted to know. "The plane's full."

"I'll just take your seat."

"Okay! You win! I lose! You go!"

On a later plane trip, this time during the opening leg of his presidential campaign in New Hampshire, Connecticut, Rhode Island and New York. McGovern insisted he had to win the black vote overwhelmingly in order to gain the White House. Yet, he had just addressed a church rally in Hartford, sharing the stage only with white dignitaries while four prominent black politicians languished in the audience.

"That was a mistake," the Senator later confessed aboard his chartered jet. "That shouldn't have happened. That's mainly the fault of the local office in Hartford rather than our national office in Washington. We just gotta see that it doesn't happen again."

Sincerity accented his words. Nevertheless, it was clear that McGovern knew not much more about blacks than most liberal whites. The dialogue veered now into his qualified support of the Black Agenda. He agreed, for example, with its contention that blacks are politically under-represented. Instead of accepting the Agenda's novel formula to increase black representation, McGovern proposed to earmark 40 to 50 per cent of his voter registration funds for massive campaigns to sign up the nation's six million eligible, unregistered blacks. The funds were to be administered by local blacks rather than by state political parties. Also blacks were to be included for the first time in the South's patronage system, controlling at least 10 per cent of the patronage jobs.

A three-phase program of full employment, tax reform and a guaranteed income for persons unable to work was McGovern's answer to the Agenda's call for black economic empowerment. He dismissed as impractical proposals of a $6,500 income for a family of four. "I think Congress would just laugh you out of court," he explained, slouched down in his airliner seat. "You might aim at a figure of $6,500, but you're never going to get that through the Congress in the next administration. If we could get people up to the poverty level by the end of 1976, that would be as ambitious a goal as you could achieve."

As for the Black Agenda's advocacy of a National Black Development Agency, McGovern vigorously agreed that long years of neglect of the black community justified a compensatory program of low-interest credit and technical assistance for blacks. He also favored community control of schools.

"Have you had a chance to be advised by blacks regarding the concept?" came a question.

"Yes, I have." The senator paused momentarily, waiting out verbal competition from the plane's intercom. "As a matter of fact, Yancey Martin, who is on my staff, is very competent in this field. I talked about it at considerable length with people like Ken Gibson, the mayor of Newark, state Sen. Willie Brown of California, Congressman Walter Fauntroy in Washington and Congressman Bill Clay in St. Louis."

"But those are all political types. Have you talked with any black educators?"

Again Sen. McGovern paused thoughtfully, tuned out to the busy comings and goings of staff members sharing the first-class cabin with him. Finally he admitted: "I have not. Maybe that's a failing on my part that I haven't."

"But you intend to!"

"Yes! I do! I do! You know, I've talked to black educators, but not about that specific issue."

The athletically-built South Dakotan supported the Black Agenda's proposal for National Health Insurance, explaining that he had cosponsored with Sen. Ted Kennedy a bill that would provide complete hospital coverage. Half of its funding would come from the federal treasury, while the remainder would be contributions from citizens—matched by their employers, much like the social security program.

. . .

None of these proposals flowed from the Republican Convention in Miami Beach. Indeed, the Nixon Administration had flatly refused repeated requests to match Sen. McGovern and respond in writing to the Black Agenda, perhaps fearing reprisals from the Southern voters it had so successfully wooed. If the Democratic Convention had been spirited and somewhat freewheeling a month earlier, the Republican gathering was as staid and patterned as a Fischer/Spassky chess match timed by metronome. The difference was that the Republicans seemed to want to play their game only with white pieces. And they proved themselves grand masters at checkmating dissent. Thus, for example, black delegates who sought to hold black caucus meetings were effectively blocked by certain black Republican leaders. On one particular occasion, a caucus meeting was cleverly co-opted by the surprise appearance of Julie Nixon Eisenhower. But the applause she received shortly gave way to groans when she declared: "I am one of a small band, but growing band, who believes that this year the Republican Party will do much better among black voters. And I think the reason is the Nixon Administration—in a quiet and effective way—has really done the best that it can do for the black man in America. . . ."

Well now, just what has the Nixon Administration done on behalf of black people?

It takes credit for stimulating black capitalism by establishing the Office of Minority Business Enterprise (OMBE) early in 1969. But OMBE had no authority to grant loans, or fund, or even supervise economic development programs. The office's original director, Thomas F. Roesser, resigned in October, 1969, charging that the agency was being run by Administration "press agentry."

It is true, as the Nixon Administration proudly claims, that Federal aid to black colleges has increased 5 per cent since 1969 to $171 million. However, that sum represents only 4.4 per cent of all Federal aid to colleges. The Administration glories in the number of blacks appointed to what it calls "top policy making positions," as if the tired, old political ploy of empowering a few blacks is equivalent to empowering all of Black America. Besides, "top policy making" in this country is reserved almost exclusively for the President, his advisers, his cabinet and the Supreme Court justices.

President Johnson's cabinet included one black, HUD Secretary Robert C. Weaver. President Nixon's cabinet includes none. President Johnson appointed two Supreme Court judges, one of whom was "Mr. Civil Rights" himself, Justice Thurgood Marshall. President Nixon has appointed four men to the High Court and almost appointed the arch racists Clement F. Haynsworth and George H. Carswell. Voting as a block, Nixon's appointees seem bent on reversing liberal trends in interpreting the U. S. Constitution.

The President's highly touted appointments also include 12 black generals and admirals, but general rank officers, especially in the lower grades, are in the thousands. The number of blacks (and black casualties) in Vietnam suggests there should be not a handful but hundreds of black generals and top officers to reflect more accurately black presence in the military.

President Johnson pushed passage of such civil rights legislation as the Equal Employment Opportunity Act of 1964, the Voting Rights Act of 1965, and the housing rights bill in 1968. Any progress in these areas claimed by Nixon supporters is directly traceable to the legislative machinery which President Johnson—not President Nixon—set up. By contrast, the President's most memorable legislative accomplishment may be to ban busing for the purpose of integrating schools. It is true that President Nixon's civil rights budget ($235 million last year) is the highest in history, but compared to the magnitude of the problem and compared to the billions in the war defense budget and the billions spent supporting the Vietnam war, it is ridiculously small.

The Nixon Administration designed a pilot plan for the city of Philadelphia that set hiring quotas for contractors in an attempt to assure minority workers of jobs in federally-contracted or subsidized construction. But "the Philadelphia Plan" ran into problems. A 1971 report released by the Citizens Organization of Philadelphia made clear the plan had fallen short of its own hiring goals because contractors either abused or disregarded it. The Nixon Administration, in short, had not enforced its own guidelines.

In 1969, when extension of the Voting Rights Act was due in Congress, the Nixon Administration sought to undermine it by eliminating the crucial requirement that states covered by the act submit their election law changes to the Attorney General for approval. The White House also proposed moving exclusive jurisdiction over voting rights cases from federal courts in the District of Columbia to federal courts in the various states. These startling proposals would have allowed states to reinstate discriminatory voter registration practices on a massive scale.

Congress, however, extended the 1965 Voting Rights Act without the White House's crippling recommendations. Some of the most outspoken opposition to President Nixon's proposals came from Congressional Republicans unwilling to junk one of the most successful civil rights statutes in American history.

The checkered civil rights record of the Nixon Administration parallels the nation's rapidly accelerating slide to the political right. As Howard University political scientist Ronald Walters has noted: "We have seen it in the reaction to the revolt of the late 1960s which has resulted in increased police repression of all kinds, but most importantly in the trend toward the election of more conservative people to positions of policy making responsibility."

Dr. Walters observes further that some blacks hate President Nixon while others hate only the conservatism he represents. Still others dislike the Republican Party intensely, while others only dislike the policies they have had to endure for the past four years. But neither "likes" nor "dislikes" meet the immediate survival problem enmeshing blacks. Instead, the continuing gravity of that problem in this political crossroads year still merits the clearest, most unemotional calculation and political organizing possible in the black community, at least for the next four years. However dispiriting the Miami Beach disasters may have been, they were not signals for blacks to abandon traditional politics or duplicate 1968 by remaining away from the polls in droves on election day. Rather blacks must become more expert at traditional politics, pressing even harder for genuine participation from the grassroots level up. Thus, to cite a simple example, both black Republicans and black Democrats must see to it that every precinct and ward office is filled in the black community. For without this rudimentary base building there can be no black political participation with power either on the precinct and ward levels or on the county, state and national levels. And without participation with power on all levels, blacks can have no real say so about such important things as party slates, platforms, and the manning of Democratic and Republican party administrative machinery.

Ideally, 25 percent of black voters should be Democrats, another 25 per cent Republicans and the remaining 50 per cent should vote as independents—for men rather than for parties. Only then, perhaps, will both parties take blacks seriously. But this does not exhaust the broad outlines of black political strategy for the next four years. The Gary Convention created —on paper—a National Black Assembly to broker political power not just for individuals but for the entire black community. Because of post-Gary complications, that Assembly has yet to become an actuality.

Meanwhile, of the two presidential candidates, Sen. McGovern espouses the more liberal principles of government. Since his campaign has been sputtering and spattering and threatening to burn out, however, his election to the White House does not appear likely this year. "Perhaps his future is already behind him," observes Strickland, "his greatest achievement lying not in his near rise to the White House but in his rise to the top, if only temporarily, of the Democratic Party."

No Hope in Woodlawn

Seth S. King

CHICAGO, Ill.—"Now I'm going to show you a building that just makes me want to cry every time I look at it," Leon Finney said. We were riding in his black Volvo, weaving around the potholes as we drove through Woodlawn, the crumbling black neighborhood that abuts the southern edge of the University of Chicago.

Source: *Saturday Review* (August 19, 1972), Vol. 55, pp. 6, 12–13. Copyright © 1972 by Saturday Review, Inc. First appeared in *Saturday Review of Education*, August 19, 1972. Used with permission.

A lean, fast-moving, blunt, young black man who learned his neighborhood organizing from the late Saul Alinsky, Finney is the executive director of The Woodlawn Organization (TWO). He was showing me what was left of one of Chicago's once comfortable (and white) working-class neighborhoods. I could readily understand his desire to weep. Block after block of Woodlawn looked like old war ruins. Whole rows of solidly built three-story apartment buildings stood eviscerated, their windows shattered, their roofs sagging or already caved in, their yards piled with litter. The smell of human excrement penetrated the closed windows of the Volvo.

What we were seeing was a late phrase in the slow death of an urban community—one whose case history is all too familiar to urbanologists. As black families began to move into Woodlawn in the 1940s, the whites started to move out. The poorer blacks could not pay rents high enough to maintain the buildings. The buildings began to deteriorate. Those blacks who could afford to leave left; those who couldn't moved in with neighboring relatives. The vacant buildings were gutted by vandals, set afire by vagrants. Now only the hulks remain, either vacant or filled with squatter families living in appalling surroundings. In the two square miles of Woodlawn there are more than 200 abandoned apartment units, in which more than 1,200 people could live.

"There's the one I mean," said Finney, pointing to a gracefully proportioned structure of heavy, gray stone built around what had once been a cool, inviting courtyard. "Look at those wonderful, solid walls. We could make a beautiful building out of that wreckage, if we could just get the money."

He shook his head dejectedly. "Hell," he said, "we've spent more than thirty thousand dollars just boarding up some of these shells. But we've had to wait so long for money that most of it's down the drain. The boarded-up buildings have been broken into again and damaged further, and it'll cost us that much more to start again."

At the moment TWO is attempting to satisfy the technical requirements for a Department of Housing and Urban Development (HUD) loan to rehabilitate 118 abandoned apartment buildings in Woodlawn. These funds are about the only federal money left that could be used to clear the wretched slums that are spreading, like ugly oil slicks, through hundreds of blocks in the all-black ghettos of Chicago's South and Near West sides.

The Chicago Housing Authority, the city's own agency for building low-income public housing, could do the rehabilitation work. There are federal funds available right now that would permit the CHA to build 1,500 new units. The CHA could also have part of the $50 million available through HUD's Project Rehab, if the authority would apply for it and agree to relocate in white neighborhoods any tenants who might be displaced by the rehabilitation.

But for the past three years the CHA has not started a single unit of low-income family housing here because Mayor Richard J. Daley and his white-dominated city council, together with the white constituents the council represents, have vehemently refused to permit any such units in all-white neighborhoods. At the same time, however, a federal judge has ruled that not a dime of federal funds allocated for low-income housing shall be used by the CHA until at least 700 units are built outside the ghettos. After that, the CHA must put three units in a white neighborhood for every one it builds in an all-black or a "changing" neighborhood, the Chicago euphemism for mixed black and white.

Since it began building low-rent public housing in 1938, the CHA has produced a commendable record of constructions. It has completed 30,305 apartment units for low-income families and 10,500 units for couples or for the elderly. This is enough low-rent housing for 155,000 persons, making the CHA "city" within Chicago larger than Rockford, Peoria, or Springfield. But 92 per cent of all CHA low-rent apartments for families are presently located in predominantly, if not entirely, black neighborhoods. Chicago is the most tightly segregated large city in the nation, as the latest census makes clear. More than one million of its 3.3-million residents are black, and more than 800,000 of them live in neighborhoods that are 90 per cent black. The government of Chicago is determined that they'll stay there—or at least that any federally funded low-rent housing a poor black could afford will be erected within those ghettos.

Two of the largest low-rent housing projects are the up-to-nineteen-story rectangles of Cabrini-Green, on Chicago's Near West Side, and the twenty-eight slabs of the sixteen-story Robert Taylor Houses, which tower above the South Side's Dan Ryan Expressway. From a distance neither of these projects looks bad. Close up, though, one sees boarded-up windows, burned sills, rust-stained balconies, littered play yards, and smashed playground equipment. The orgy of high-rise public housing that produced Cabrini-Green and the Robert Taylor Homes, among others, was not, it must be said, the CHA's idea. The authority was only following the federal guidelines of the late 1950s. But the result has been a disaster. Completed in 1962, the gleaming rectangles developed, all too soon, into jungles in which tenants are afraid to ride the elevators alone, in which parents are afraid to let their children play on the high balconies, in which robberies, rapes, and murders are so common that they often go unreported.

Thus, about all that the millions of dollars in federal housing funds for CHA high rises have produced is vertical slums. Even at cheap rents these apartments are so undesirable that today there are 616 vacancies in Cabrini-Green and Robert Taylor alone. Even the wretchedly housed survivors in Woodlawn refuse to be moved into them.

The whole experience has been reduced to a formula that has become an essential tenet of the Chicago political catechism: Public housing means low-income housing; low-income housing means black housing; and black housing means inferior housing that will quickly destroy a white neighborhood.

As far back as 1949, when alert do-gooders realized the pattern CHA housing was taking, several Chicago civic groups and newspapers protested. The only result was a clever side step by the city council: They persuaded the state legislature to pass a special bill giving the council explicit veto power over all new public housing sites.

There is little doubt that the CHA, with the council's enthusiastic approval, would have gone right on concentrating its efforts in the ghettos if the American Civil Liberties Union and six Chicago blacks had not taken action. In 1966 they brought suit against the CHA in federal court, charging that for more than fifteen years the authority had selected public housing sites almost exclusively in black ghetto areas. This, they said, violated the civil rights of poor tenants, both black and white, by denying them a free choice of where they might live.

Chicago is a city not easily surprised by anything that happens in its courts or legislative halls. The findings cited in the ACLU suit, however, shook its political establishment so hard that cracks appeared in unlikely places. U.S. District Court Judge Richard B. Austin, for example, was, to all appearances, a reliable product of Chicago's Cook County Democratic Organization (Richard J. Daley, chairman). A former prosecuting attorney in Chicago, an unsuccessful Democratic gubernatorial candidate, then a Chicago criminal court judge, and, throughout, a friend of Mayor Daley. Judge Austin was presumed to be a safe venue for quelling the ACLU disturbance.

But then, in 1969, Judge Austin ruled that the CHA's actions were unconstitutional. Further, he found "incredible" the authority's assertion that its years-long confining of public housing for the poor to all-black areas was not a deliberate policy. He rejected the CHA's plea that it was not racist but was simply rolling with the political punches to get the housing built. As for the city's aldermen, he brushed aside their argument that they were entitled to reflect the views of their constituents on CHA sites, especially if those views excluded blacks from public housing in white neighborhoods.

Judge Austin's decision caused as much turmoil as the Chicago Fire. In the three years since Austin first spoke, the city council and the CHA, with Mayor Daley's concurrence, have slipped and slid and stalled on approving housing sites. The judge became so exasperated with these delays that he ordered a freeze on Chicago's $26 million in federal Model Cities funds until the CHA complied with his site edict. He even spoke harshly of Mr. Daley, saying that some chief executives in other parts of the country had stood in schoolhouse doors, "their faces livid and their wattles flapping." But, he went on, "It is an anomaly that the law-and-order chief executive of Chicago should challenge and defy the federal law."

His thrust had no visible effect on Mr. Daley. Last year the mayor and the CHA signed an elaborate "letter of intent" with HUD, promising to provide 4,300 units of low-income housing *throughout the city,* partly through new construction or rehabilitation, partly by leasing space for low-income tenants in moderate-income housing then being built on some of the 1,000 vacant areas (mostly in white neighborhoods) that the city had created for Urban Renewal projects. By last January, however, the city and the CHA had done so little to fulfill these promises that even HUD was moved to action. It took away $22 million of Chicago's urban renewal allotment and distributed it among other, presumably more deserving, cities in HUD's Midwest region.

The fallout from both Judge Austin's ruling and the 1968 Public Housing Act guidelines, which give blacks at least a fighting chance of getting into public housing in white areas, has now spread to other areas. Within the past year Federal District Judge Frank Battisti ruled that the white mayor of Cleveland had exceeded his authority when he canceled building permits for low-income housing scheduled for white sections of that city. Judge Battisti directed that the Cuyahoga Metropolitan Housing Authority could build no more low-income units until it put them in white areas. Another federal judge has ordered Atlanta's housing authority to publish a list of proposed housing sites as evidence of its intention to build new low-income units in white, as well as black, neighborhoods. Federal site guidelines have caused another uproar—the one still raging over the Lindsay administration's proposal to build scatter-site, low-income housing in the all-white section of New York City's Forest Hills.

In Chicago the federal guidelines and the Austin decision have produced the predictable circle of Pontius Pilates. The CHA says it can do nothing in the Chicago ghettos because Judge Austin won't let it. HUD says it is empowered to act only through local housing authorities and cannot give the CHA any funds until it meets the site-selection criteria. The city says it can't use its Urban Renewal funds because HUD took them away—and so on.

"We get the shaft from both ends." Mr. Finney said bitterly. "Each side blames the other, a perfect excuse for doing nothing."

In July the CHA took a timid first step by listing 518 sites in white neighborhoods where, it said, scatter-site, low-income housing *might* be feasible. And it authorized preparation of plans for 156 dwellings on twenty-four scatter sites in white areas.

In the meantime Chicago's whites have mobilized for continued inaction. An organization called the Nucleus of Chicago Homeowners Association (No-CHA), which says it speaks for 1,000 white homeowners, has filed a suit under the National Environmental Policy Act. It claims that the CHA would pollute middle-class white neighborhoods if it brought poor black families into their midst. "As a statistical whole, low-income families of the kind that reside in housing provided by the CHA possess certain social class characteristics which will be, and have been, inimical and harmful to the legitimate interests of the plaintiffs," the suit states in one of the more forthright explanations of why the blacks should be barred.

If there is any doubt about the effects of public housing stagnation in Chicago, the projections of a joint HUD-city study at the end of 1970 should dispel it. That study disclosed that so many low-income structures were being demolished in Chicago, either because they were uninhabitable or because the land had been appropriated for various purposes, and that so few replacements for poor families were available, that two years ago at least 4,300 low-income units would have had to be built as quickly as possible just to keep up with the demolitions and removals. This meant that even if the CHA had capitulated and built the 1,500 units for which funds are available, Chicago would still have been more than 2,800 units short—and the rot in the city has grown apace since this calculation was made in 1970.

I asked Mr. Finney how the blacks themselves felt about the great CHA debate and whether they would rather have something to live in, even if it were locked in a ghetto.

"I know you'll hear 'em say that the blacks really don't want to move into those hostile white neighborhoods," he said, after thinking carefully about my question. "Well, that's crap. If you give me a community that's safe, with good housing, good transportation to jobs, and good schools, then sure, black people are happy to be living there with other black people. But you can't tell me that a black family living in a goddamned slum that costs five times what it should wouldn't rather move to a decent house in a white neighborhood. We blacks, just like you whites, will get out of any poor neighborhood if we can."

Mr. Finney turned north from the smell of old feces and the staring skeletons of buildings to show me Woodlawn Gardens, a federally subsidized middle-income project TWO completed before the Austin ruling took effect. All of its 500 units were three-story walk-ups, imaginatively grouped around landscaped courts and playgrounds. A major share of the tenants, Mr. Finney told me, were now low-income families living there with federal rent subsidies.

"Man, it looks good, doesn't it?" he asked. "Well, we've had our troubles with it. Some of those people have to be persuaded, shall we say, to keep their places up. Some have trouble paying the rent. But nobody's desperate to get out. We don't have vacancies for very long there."

But the rest of Woodlawn and the other black neighborhoods won't see anything like it until the CHA, or somebody, begins building in the white areas. As the shock waves spread after Judge Austin's decisions, there were those pragmatic urbanologists, as well as Chicago politicians such as Rep. Roman Pucinski, now the Democratic party's candidate for the Senate, who were freely predicting that the ruling would mean the end of public housing, at least in Chicago. They may be right. The CHA is still appealing Judge Austin's directive to go on selecting sites in white neighborhoods whether or not the city council approves of them. Suppose that appeal should somehow be upheld. The CHA couldn't act because the city council hadn't approved, and so on, far into the night.

Chapter 11
SUGGESTED TOPICS FOR CLASS DISCUSSION

1. What was the effect of nonviolent resistance in drawing attention to the oppression of blacks? What role did violence play in dramatizing the situation?
2. What are the more prominent forms of black political involvement at present? What are some of the factors that help explain the changes in the pattern of political action that have taken place?
3. What are some of the ways in which women continue to be discriminated against in schools? in the professions? in marriage? in politics? Are the values and expectations of society determined largely by men and does this indeed tend to force women to play a series of roles that are not defined by them but are defined by men with little regard for women?
4. What is the explanation for the persistence of male discrimination against women?
5. What are some of the similarities in the position of women, blacks, and other minorities in American life? What are some of the more significant differences? What are the implications of these similarities and differences for the way in which each group should proceed politically?

Chapter 12
Foreign and Military Policy

The machinery that produces American foreign policy can never rest. It must generate a continuing flow of decisions, great and small, for there are over 125 nations that the United States must be concerned with, scores of international and regional organizations that it participates in, and count-less issues on which it must be prepared to take a stand. How can this nation organize for the making of foreign policy decisions in such a way that important issues are recognized and wise decisions concerning them are made? In an era of ICBM's, MIRV's, and multimegaton warheads, the margin for error is small.

The practical consequences of American decisions for other nations and peoples are often enormous, and the exercise of our national power should therefore be constrained by a strong sense of responsibility. Would foreign policy decision-making be better and more responsible if Congress had a greater share in the process? The United States has waged the longest and most expensive war in its history—and yet Congress never declared the war. A substantial proportion of Congressional opinion was opposed to this war for years, and yet Congress was not able to stop the war completely or even to interpose significant restraints on its conduct. Are there levers of Congressional power that could be used more effectively than at present or is the foreign policy contest with the President one in which Congress must always be hopelessly handicapped?

This chapter inspects legal precedents for Presidential war-making, the battle between the President and Congress over the control of foreign policy, the style and influence of Henry Kissinger, the problems of White House control over departmental bureaucracies, and the consequences of the decision to employ a policy of ecocide, that is, a policy of destroying the natural environment in which people live.

THE CONVENIENCE OF "PRECEDENT"

Francis D. Wormuth

The Presidential wars in Indochina have been the least publicized events in American history. The war, or rather the unopposed career of carnage, in Laos has never been acknowledged; there has been negligible official, and scanty unofficial, reporting of the military adventures in Vietnam and Cambodia. So obscure has been the history of our involvement that Robert McNamara, then Secretary of Defense, commissioned a study to discover what had happened. To maintain public ignorance, the Nixon Administration unsuccessfully sought to enjoin publication of the study.

There has been even greater official reticence on the constitutional questions involved. In 1966, a year after President Johnson's massive escalation of the war in Vietnam, the State Department supplied the Senate Committee on Foreign Relations with a memorandum, so slight as to be frivolous, in justification of Executive war making. The present Administration has been even less communicative. In various forums, Secretary of State Rogers, Solicitor General Griswold, and former Assistant Attorney General Rehnquist have defended Mr. Nixon's prosecution of the war; these brief statements exhaust the Administration's apologies for its conduct. They do not say much, but they say more than can be defended.

The framers of the Constitution attempted to put the question beyond doubt. At the Constitutional Convention, the committee of detail reported a proposal that the legislature be given the power "to make war." The Con-

Source: *The Nation* (October 9, 1972), pp. 301–304. Reprinted by permission.

vention changed the word "make" to "declare," so that the Executive might be free "to repel sudden attacks." This meant that war could be initiated in two ways: by joint resolution of Congress, and by the attack of an enemy. On issues arising from the war with France, 1798–1801, the Supreme Court held that it was for Congress to initiate all hostilities, whether general war or limited war, and that it was illegal for the President to exceed the authorization of Congress. In 1863, in the Prize Cases, the Court held that the President's power to resist sudden attack included response to insurrection; but it said that he had no power to initiate war.

According to Secretary Rogers, it follows from the power to repel attack that "in emergency situations, the President has the power and responsibility to use the armed forces to protect the nation's security." The emergency in Vietnam which purportedly called for independent Executive action has never been identified; in any case the Constitution authorizes Congress, and not the President, to determine when the nation's security is imperiled and when it is appropriate to use the armed forces to protect it.

But the Nixon Administration places its chief reliance on the Commander-in-Chief clause. This title was introduced in English military usage in 1639 and is still used by the British to describe the highest ranking officer in a military or naval hierarchy; this officer has always been subject to political superiors. When the Continental Congress made George Washington Commander in Chief in 1776, it instructed him "punctually to observe and follow such orders and directions, from time to time, as you shall receive from this, or a future Congress of these United Colonies, or committee of Congress." The Constitutional Convention adopted the term in the light of this usage. In 1850 the Supreme Court said of the position of the President, *after* Congress had declared war: "His duty and power are purely military. As commander-in-chief, he is authorized to direct the movements of the naval and military forces placed by law at his command, and to employ them in the manner he may deem most effectual to harass and conquer the enemy."

The Commander-in-Chief clause does not supplant the war clause, which gives the power to initiate war to Congress. And it must be read together with the clauses of the Constitution which authorize Congress to raise and support armies, to provide and maintain a Navy, and to make rules for the government and regulation of the land and naval forces. The Supreme Court has held that only Congress may raise armies, that the President may not require an officer to perform any duty not imposed on him by statute, that he may not alter a salary fixed by statute, that he may not discharge an officer contrary to statute, that court-martial jurisdiction over soldiers is limited to that authorized by Congress, that a soldier when drafted may be assigned duties only in the capacity which subjected him to the draft. Congress has obliged the President to assign command of troops to the highest ranking officer in the force; it has authorized the use of troops for some purposes and forbidden it for others; on several occasions it has forbidden that troops be sent to specified areas; when Theodore Roosevelt took the Marines off naval vessels, Congress obliged him to restore them. As David Dudley Field put it: "To command an army is to give it its orders. . . . To do what? That, and that only, which the laws allow; and the laws are made, not by him but by Congress. His function is executive."

No judicial precedents support the claim that the Commander-in-Chief clause authorizes the President to undertake acts of war. But the apologists for the war in Vietnam rely on purported Executive precedents. This argument developed in a curious way. In 1912 the Solicitor of the State Department, J. Reuben Clark, published a list of forty-one armed actions or displays of force abroad which had not been individually authorized by Congress. Two were illegal, but the other thirty-nine were naval actions to protect citizens. After "cursory consideration" Clark offered a legal theory to justify these actions, but he warned that "a more detailed and careful study" might not support it. This theory was the proposition that citizens were entitled to protection at international law, that international law was incorporated in the law of the United States, and that in protecting citizens the President was merely executing the laws of the United States. In 1934 the State Department republished Clark's study, updating the list of foreign interventions.

In 1941 there occurred a revolution in legal theory. Defending President Roosevelt's action in sending troops to Iceland, Senator Connally argued that the President as Commander in Chief might send troops wherever he wished, and cited the eighty-five cases from the 1934 revision of Clark's list as evidence. The Commander-in-Chief clause thus replaced the President's Executive power; the limitation to the protection of citizens disappeared, and with it Clark's misgivings about even this narrowly defined action. In 1950 the State Department used Connally's list of eighty-five cases as precedents for President Truman's unauthorized entry into the Korean War. In 1966 the State Department asserted that there were 125 precedents for President Johnson's unauthorized entry into the war in Vietnam. In 1967 the State Department offered a list of 137 "armed actions taken by the United States without a declaration of war." In 1971 Solicitor General Griswold said that the United States has formally declared war six times and had engaged in hostilities on 155 other occasions as well. On December 18, 1971, Senator Goldwater asserted that he had compiled a list of "192 military actions undertaken without a declaration of war, eighty-one of which involved actual combat or ultimatums tantamount to the use of force."

It is time to set the record straight. Congress has passed not six but thirteen formal declarations of general war against a named adversary. On eight occasions Congress has authorized hostilities short of general war against a named adversary. On thirteen occasions Congress has rejected or ignored Presidential requests for authority to engage in limited hostilities. On at least seven occasions the Executive has refused to undertake hostile action on the ground that Congress had not authorized it.

In all the lists of purported Executive precedents, about half the cases have been brief naval landings to protect citizens or their property in a foreign country in a time of riot or insurrection. All the lists are in error: there have in fact been 116 such landings, thirteen before 1865 and 103 thereafter. The thirteen were legally unauthorized, but in 1862 Congress empowered the Secretary of the Navy to make rules for the government of the Navy, and the rules issued in 1865 contained carefully limited instructions to protect citizens in foreign ports in case of need. The 103 landings after 1865 did not rest on the President's Executive power or the Commander-in-Chief clause. They rested on Congressional authorization.

Only fifty-six of these 103 landings appear in the 1967 State Department list. Nine of the other cases listed also had statutory authorization. Of the seventy-two remaining cases, most were trivial. Some were merely miniatory demonstrations at sea; some involved merely technical trespass. An unknown number were undertaken by Army or Navy officers without authorization from their superiors; if they prove anything about the war power, they prove that it belongs to every commissioned officer. On the other hand, some cases have been Presidential usurpations of great magnitude: six protracted occupations of Caribbean states, the Korean War, the Vietnamese War. These can be said to establish that the President possesses the war power only if the mere repetition of a crime legalizes a sequence of crimes.

However, the Nixon apologists do not rest solely on the Commander-in-Chief clause; they also argue that the President's "Executive power" authorizes him to engage in war. Justice Holmes said: "The duty of the President to see that the laws be executed is a duty that does not go beyond the laws or require him to achieve more than Congress sees fit to leave within his power." In the 1952 Steel Seizure Case, three Justices, led by Harry Truman's crony, Chief Justice Vinson, argued that the President's Executive power authorized him to seize the steel mills in order to maintain military production; but six Justices denied that he could act without a statute. In 1971 the President sought to enjoin the publication of the Pentagon Papers, but six Justices held that he could not do so without satutory authorization. The other three Justices took no position; they thought it premature to resolve the issues.

Apologists for Executive war making invariably refer to what Secretary Rogers has called "the President's constitutional authority to conduct the foreign relations of the United States." Of course, no such grant is to be found in the Constitution. The President shares the treaty-making power and the power to appoint ambassadors with the Senate. He shares the power over foreign commerce and all the war powers with the full Congress. Only two powers in foreign relations are assigned to him alone. He is Commander in Chief; but he acts in this capacity by and under the authority of Congress. And he has the power to receive foreign ambassadors. Alexander Hamilton said that this function was purely ceremonial; but it has come to entail recognition, which has legal consequences. But the power of recognition does not entail the war power. Presidents Madison, Monroe, Jackson, Grant, Cleveland and McKinley refused to recognize revolutionary governments in colonial countries because this might be regarded as an act of war by the mother country, and only Congress could authorize acts of war.

The 1966 State Department apology asserted that the SEATO treaty authorized, indeed obliged, the President to go to war in Vietnam. No one had noticed this feature of the treaty for twelve years after its negotiation in 1954. No treaty made by the President and the Senate can authorize war. In the Constitutional Convention, Charles Pinckney proposed that the war power be given to the Senate, but he found no second; it was given to the full Congress. Nor, if the Senate had the war power, could it delegate it *in futuro* to the President. Finally, no word of the SEATO treaty requires or permits the President to do anything whatever except to consult with the other signatories. In time of common danger, each signatory is to act "in accordance with its constitutional processes." Today no reliance is placed on the SEATO treaty. As far as this writer has been able to discover, only Presidential Assistant Harry Dent has offered the SEATO treaty as justification for President Nixon's prosecution of the war.

Obviously it is impossible to overcome the constitutional assignment of the war power to Congress. So the argument shifts. During the Johnson administration and the first two years of the Nixon Administration reliance was placed on the Tonkin Gulf Resolution of 1964, in which Congress said that the President might do whatever he liked, "including the use of armed force," to assist Cambodia, Laos, "the free territory of Vietnam," Australia, New Zealand, Pakistan, the Philippines, Thailand, Great Britain and France in the maintenance of their freedom. Under-Secretary of State Katzenbach called this resolution a "functional equivalent of a declaration of war." But a declaration of war always names an adversary; it makes hostilities mandatory; it specifies whether the war is general or limited. Tonkin Gulf attempted to delegate the war power wholesale to the President, at least as far as Southeast Asia was concerned.

Early in our history Chief Justice Marshall laid down the law of Congressional delegation. Certain functions are "strictly and exclusively legislative," and "these important subjects must be entirely regulated by the legislature itself." But Congress may authorize judical or Executive rule making on matters "of lesser interest, in which a general provision may be made, and power given to those who are to act under such provisions to fill up the details."

Clearly the initiation of war is legislative. In 1835 the Senate unanimously adopted a resolution drafted by Henry Clay which rejected a request of President Jackson for contingent authority to make reprisals on French shipping because the war power could not be delegated. Congress rejected for the same reason eight requests of President Buchanan for contingent authority to intervene militarily in Central America and Mexico.

Suppose, however, we agree with the spokesmen for the Johnson and Nixon Administrations that choosing an antagonist and launching a war is one of those topics of "lesser interest" on which Congress may delegate the power of decision to the Executive. As Chief Justice Hughes said in *Schechter Poultry Corp.* v. *United States,* in making such a delegation Congress must "perform its function in laying down policies and establishing standards, while leaving to selected instrumentalities the making of subordinate rules within prescribed limits and the determination of facts to which the policy as declared by the Legislature is to apply." In the Tonkin Gulf Resolution Congress laid down no policy and established no standard; the resolution was, as Senator Fulbright, who sponsored it in the Senate, said at a later date, "a blank check."

But in a strange opinion of 1936 by Justice Sutherland in *United States* v. *Curtiss-Wright Export Corp.* the Court had said that the limitations of the Constitution did not apply in foreign affairs, and that Congress might delegate to the President the power to make rules over foreign commerce without "laying down policies and establishing standards." Both the Johnson and Nixon Administrations have argued that the Tonkin Gulf Resolution was a valid delegation of the war power because in foreign affairs the rule against delegation does not apply.

Sutherland's statement was not law but dictum, and has been rejected in every subsequent decision. In *Reid* v. *Covert* in 1956 the proposition that the Constitution does not apply in foreign affairs was expressly repudiated. In two cases involving foreign commerce (the issue in *Curtiss-Wright*) and five cases involving matters "of lesser interest" under the war power (a curfew, price controls, rent controls and contract renegotiation) all decided since *Curtiss-Wright,* the Court has announced and applied the orthodox tests of the validity of delegation: Congress must lay down policy and establish standards. In *Zemel* v. *Rusk* (1956), Chief Justice Warren said that the *Curtiss-Wright* case "does not mean that simply because a statute deals with foreign relations, it can grant the Executive totally unrestricted freedom of choice." The dictum in *Curtiss-Wright* has neither paternity nor progeny.

In any case the Tonkin Gulf Resolution was repealed on January 12, 1971. Solicitor General Griswold, deprived of this purported statutory authorization, has aruged that Congressional appropriations for the support of troops in Vietnam have amounted to an implied ratification of the war. If these acts are ratifications, they too are uncontrolled delegations. But the argument ignores the law of ratification by appropriation laid down by Justice Douglas for the Court in *Ex Parte Endo*: "the ratification must plainly show a purpose to bestow the precise authority which is claimed." And it ignores the doctrine of the equity of the statute. This doctrine, which goes back at least to the 15th century, is the proposition that the policy of a statute must be given effect beyond its literal terms. As Justice Holmes said: "The Legislature has the power to decide what the policy of the law shall be, and if it has intimated its will, however indirectly, that will should be recognized and obeyed." A repealer statute repeals all statutes, though not named, which share the policy of the statute repealed. If earlier appropriation acts carried any implied endorsement of the war, the repeal of the Tonkin Gulf Resolution, to which the appropriation acts were tributary, revoked that endorsement.

Nor has Congress left this in doubt. In the National Procurement Authorization Act of November 17, 1971, Congress declared it the policy of the United States "to terminate at the earliest practicable date all military operations of the United States in Indochina, and to provide for the prompt and orderly withdrawal of all United States military forces at a date certain, subject to the release of all American prisoners of war. . . ." President Nixon in signing the bill announced his intention of defying it. Since then he has repeatedly said that he will end military operations in Vietnam only after an agreement to political terms stipulated by him. The war is being continued, not without Congress but in defiance of Congress. None of the policy arguments for Executive usurpation—"emergency" or "national security"—applies to this war. No constitutional provision and no Executive precedent justifies the President in continuing a war against the expressed will of Congress. The case is unprecedented.

Since there is no legal case for the Nixon Administration, its spokesmen have taken final refuge, not in the law but in the assertion that they are not accountable to law. The courts will not undertake to decide "political questions." Secretary Rogers has said that "There are relatively few judicial decisions concerning the relationship between the Congress and the President in the exercise of their respective war powers under the Constitution. The courts have usually regarded the subject as a political question and refused jurisdiction." Mr. Rogers must know that there are literally dozens of cases in which the courts have decided "concerning the relationship between the Congress and the President in the exercise of their respective war powers under the Constitution." It was never suggested until the Vietnamese War that the war power raised political questions. Rogers himself names only three cases, all concerned with this war. The Court of Appeals for the District of Columbia wrote a brief, confused opinion in *Luftig* v. *McNamara* in which it said, among other things, that the legality of the Vietnamese War was a political question which it might not decide. In *Mora* v. *McNamara* the same court followed this earlier decision without opinion. Rogers' third case is *Massachusetts* v. *Laird,* in which the Supreme Court refused to permit Massachusetts to file a bill of complaint to challenge the war. It wrote no opinion and we are left to guess what motive or motives may have prompted the majority. Justices Douglas, Harlan and Stewart dissented.

The first and central test of a political question which the courts may not adjudicate is, to use the language of Justice Brennan in *Baker* v. *Carr,* the existence of a "textually demonstrable constitutional commitment of the issue to a coordinate political department." The Constitution nowhere commits the decision of the constitutional issue of the power of the President to initiate war, or for that matter of the power of Congress to delegate its war power, to the President or to Congress. These are justiciable matters for the courts, which have repeatedly asserted that the President may not initiate war, and that Congress may not delegate legislative power to the President.

But there is a political question of another order, one which demands judicial solution: it is nothing less than the continuance of our republican form of government. As Justice Davis said, in holding Lincoln's declaration of martial law unconstitutional, "wicked men, ambitious of power, with hatred of liberty and contempt of law, may fill the place once occupied by Washington and Lincoln." Chief Justice Marshall in deciding, in *Cohens* v. *Virginia,* a question more dangerous politically to the Court than the war in Vietnam is to the present Court, said: "We have no more right to decline the exercise of jurisdiction which is given, than to usurp that which is not given. The one or the other would be treason to the Constitution." But our present Supreme Court continues to evade, by denial of certiorari, the most important constitutional question of the 20th century.

Congress and Foreign Policy

Arthur S. Miller

A foreign policy debate of potentially historic proportions is now taking place in the U.S. Senate. Not since the beginnings of the Republic, not even twenty years ago at the time of Senator Bricker's abortive amendment, have the lines been drawn so sharply. Essentially a struggle over who will control foreign policy—Congress or the President—its outcome could very well determine the direction and nature of American policy for the next generation. With the Javits war powers bill behind it and having dallied with efforts by Senators Mansfield, Cooper and Church to stay the course of the Vietnamese conflict, Senatorial attention is now focused on the President's agreement-making power—his power, as Chief Executive and Commander in Chief of the armed services, to commit the nation on his own authority. Major attempts to curb Presidential power have already been made; more may be expected.

Because of its silences, the Constitution invites battle over the privilege of directing foreign affairs. The Delphic language raises the question of who shall control, but does not answer it. One proposition, however, is entirely indisputable: there is divided authority—shared power—between Congress and the President, in this as in other policy areas. That, at least, was the way the document was written; later developments, particularly in the past thirty-five years, have greatly altered the original concept.

Every schoolchild knows that American Government is a "system" of checks and balances in which each branch purportedly offsets the others. "Ours is a government of divided authority," Justice Hugo Black once said, "on the assumption that in division there is not only strength but freedom from tyranny." That quaint bit of judicial mythology clouds the reality of Presidential hegemony over vast segments of governmental policy. It is truistic to assert that, whatever the intentions of those who wrote the Constitution, the Executive today is far and away the dominant branch—and becoming more so each year. The development finds the judiciary, speaking generally, impotent; and Congress has gracelessly abdicated much of its power. In 1885, Woodrow Wilson could call the chairmen of the standing committees of Congress the most powerful governmental officials. Less than a century later, one looks to the other end of Pennsylvania Avenue. Power radiates from the White House in concentric circles of influence that at times encompass members of Congress, but only as individuals and less so with each succeeding administration. As with all other modern

Source: *The Nation* (September 25, 1972), pp. 234–237. Reprinted by permission.

governments, the United States is essentially Executive-dominated, even Executive-controlled.

Domestically, the development is a thrice-told tale, requiring no present restatement other than to list some blatant examples of extra-Constitutional Presidential power. Included are the following illustrative instances: (*a*) casually bargaining away the spirit of the antitrust laws by entering into consent decrees that favor the acquisitve instincts of corporate and financial executives; (*b*) exercising "Executive privilege," a device to keep Congress and the public from knowing data pertinent to present and future policies; (*c*) "impounding" (as of spring 1971) more than $12 billion in funds appropriated by Congress, without a shadow of statutory authority to do so; (*d*) investing the Subversive Activities Control Board with new duties, even though its chairman says it is a "quasi-judicial" body, under legal theory an organ over which the President has no authority; (*e*) exercising a "pocket veto" over legislation (the Family Practice of Medicine Act of 1970) in circumstances of dubious constitutionality; (*f*) granting tax depreciation credits to business by Treasury Department fiat; (*g*) "reprogramming" hundreds of millions of dollars of appropriated funds, mainly in the Pentagon's budget; (*h*) slapping on a 10 per cent import surcharge in August 1971, contrary to the General Agreement of Tariffs and Trade; (*i*) asserting an "inherent" power to wiretap without legislative or judicial authority; and (*j*) attempting (with temporary success) to impose a prior restraint on newspaper publication (the case of the Pentagon Papers). The list need not be extended; the foregoing is enough to show an unmistakable Executive grab for power.

A similar pattern emerges in foreign affairs. For example, Presidents, both Democratic and Republican, have asserted a power to commit the armed forces without Congressional authorization. Sen. Jacob Javits' war powers bill is a last-ditch attempt to stay that course. Its success may be small and is certainly to be doubted, but at least it is an effort to curb a reckless Executive and bureaucracy.

Less evident but of fundamental importance is the President's power to conclude international agreements. The highly publicized accords with Russia, entered into by President Nixon in May, take the form of both formal treaties and "Executive agreements." One may welcome the move toward détente with the USSR and at the same time question an increasingly frequent use of the latter; often they are negotiated solely on the President's authority as Chief Executive, and are thus of questionable constitutionality; but they do obligate the United States under international law. Presumably, when mainland China is recognized, that act will be accompanied, as was President Franklin Roosevelt's recognition of the USSR, by a set of Executive agreements dealing with financial and trade matters.

Possibly, too, as Sen. Henry Jackson, among others, has intimated, the Nixon-Brezhnev accords include secret deals that will surface in due time.

Those highly visible "Summit" accommodations hide the fact that the "Executive" or "Presidential" agreement has become the usual way in which the United States formalizes its diplomatic relations. Under the Constitution the President has express authority to make treaties only "by and with the advice and consent of the Senate," but the tendency for several decades has been to use that instrument sparingly. In the period of 1946 to April 1, 1972, by the State Department's own statistics, 5,958 international agreements were concluded, only 368 of which were treaties. That means that about 94 per cent of American international compacts were, in the Department's ambiguous categorization, "international agreements other than treaties."

Although the range and type of agreements between and among nations are far more numerous, constitutional law recognizes only three basic categories of international accords. First in order of importance is the *treaty*, requiring approval by two-thirds of the Senate before ratification (which, despite usage to the contrary, is an Executive act, the Senate's task being that of consenting to ratification). Next comes the *Congressional-Executive agreement*, an accord made by the Executive pursuant to a prior statute or treaty. The usual illustrations here are the reciprocal trade agreements negotiated under a 1934 statute and the many subsidiary agreements concluded under the terms of the NATO treaty. Finally, there is the "pure" or "true" *Executive* (or Presidential) *agreement*, made solely on the basis of the President's power as Chief Executive. Recognition of foreign governments is often said to be of this nature, although there is no clear-cut law on the matter; and some assert that the settlement of claims incident to recognition is also of Presidential provenance. The so-called Litvinov assignment, concluded by Secretary of State Cordell Hull in 1933 with the then foreign minister of Russia, is an example. It led to two famous decisions that greatly exercised Senator Bricker, in which the Supreme Court held that the agreement was sufficiently like a treaty to override inconsistent state laws (on the ownership of assets of the Czar).

As a consequence of the Supreme Court's lawmaking on international agreements, the category of subjects that can be so dealt with internationally is open-ended (the landmark decision here is *Missouri* v. *Holland* in 1920, holding that a migratory bird treaty with Canada was valid and prevailed over state law, a decision that also made Bricker unhappy), and *all* international agreements are made "the supreme law of the land" under Article VI of the Constitution. What the United States cannot do by treaty or agreement, however, is bargain away the personal rights of its citizens. That was decided in 1957 when the Court held that dependents accompanying the armed forces abroad (to England) could not be tried by court-martial, even though England by agreement had ceded jurisdiction to the United States. That is the state of the law. It isn't very much. Certainly it does not begin to answer the ticklish separation-of-powers questions that are now coming to the fore.

The Constitution is not only an invitation to struggle between Congress and the President over the right to control foreign policies; it also fails to settle the way in which that battle will proceed or end. The Executive, by usage running back almost to the beginnings of the nation, has pre-empted ever larger segments of those policies. This has led to the second argument used to justify Executive action: other Presidents have concluded Executive agreements; accordingly, President Nixon can do so. Coupled with that (which in legal terms may be called making constitutional law by custom and usage) is the argument that the President has certain powers which, when added to an expanding notion of "inherent" Executive authority, enables him to direct and even control both the negotiation of international agreement and their content. Boiled down to its essentials, it is a naked grab for Executive power dressed up in legalese.

Government lawyers, not least of whom was Justice William H. Rehnquist when he was assistant attorney general, readily find a foundation in law and constitutional theory for that ploy. And indeed the law is sufficiently uncertain, with so many gaps in it, that no one can say absolutely that the Executive is wrong. What can be said, and what is being said with increasing insistence and persistence, is that Congress, too, has a foreign policy role under the Constitution and that it is past time for that body to begin to exercise it.

How to do so is the rub. In final analysis, Congress has few weapons at its command. Theoretically, it has the power of impeachment, a blundering, clumsy device that plays no role in the controversy. Other than that, only the ability to withhold funds is available, and that, too, is of dubious usefulness. By slow accretion, budgetary matters have become controlled or controllable by the Executive; it is difficult, perhaps impossible, to muster the votes necessary to cut off money for projects the President desires, and which he has promised to other nations. Considerations of national prestige, of the balance of power in a badly splintered world, accompanied by a tacit recognition of a Congressional lack of information and expertise, all contribute to deprive the appropriations power of its threat; it is, to paraphrase President Cleveland, merely a theory, not a condition. It exists but is not used, much as the power to enter into war is legislative in constitutional theory but Executive in fact.

If that be true historically, it is much more so today. Constitutional historian Alfred H. Kelly noted the development in these terms: "The destruction of the balance of power in Europe and the technological disintegration of the ocean barrier . . . plunged the United States after 1940 very heavily" into world politics. "The result was a vast increase in the foreign policy operations of the Executive branch of the government, operations which to considerable extent by their very nature tended to exclude the two houses of Congress from direct participation. The advent since 1945 of a bi-polarized world, in which the United States became the leader of a complex series of grand alliances intended to check and balance the power of the Soviet Union, substantially strengthened this tendency. Immersed as it now was in something like traditional balance-of-power diplomacy, the United States reacted in essentially the traditional fashion—by conducting extensive, intimate and generally secret Executive-to-Executive negotiations in the accepted style of Talleyrand, Metternich, or Castlereagh." For those three worthies read Henry Kissinger.

By its very nature, this process is anti-constitutional and anti-democratic. Lacking widespread publicity and public or legislative participation in the decisions, it is directly contrary to the doctrine of the separaton of powers in the American Constitution. Not that anyone is engaged in a sinister conspiracy to subvert the constitutional system, as those who adhere to what Richard Hofstadter called the "paranoid style in American politics" contend. The Executive decisions made during, say, the past thirty years were undoubtedly viewed in that branch as being in the national interest. But the cost, as Professor Kelly says, was borne by the internal constitutional processes. America has plunged into balance-of-power international politics at the price of greatly damaging the internal balance of power provided for by the constitutional system.

However, the phenomenon is much older than this development of the country's world role. Theodore Roosevelt, in effect, defied the Senate in 1905–07 when he arranged for an American financial protectorate over Santo Domingo by Executive agreement, even though the Senate had rejected a treaty drawn up for that very purpose. Interventions in the "banana republics" by American Marines for the purpose of protecting American investments were routine in the 1920s, as Gen. Smedley Butler has testified. Franklin Roosevelt in 1940 traded allegedly over-age destroyers to Great Britain for military bases, a deal of at best dubious legality (even though Atty. Gen. Robert Jackson dutifully produced an opinion justifying it), and at Yalta entered into secret agreements with Churchill and Stalin that carved up the world much as Napoleon and Czar Alexander divided it between them at Tilsit. Presidential agreements are always made in the national interest, as the Chief Executive sees it, but their substance can at times be challenged for overreaching or, in recent years, for an overweening desire for a *Pax Americana*. It is precisely because of such grotesque errors that some Senators are objecting violently.

Congress has reacted in a variety of ways. Led, often in a very lonely fashion, by Senator Fulbright (who has publicly regretted his part in the Tonkin Gulf Resolution that was rammed through Congress), the Senate has become the main Presidential antagonist. Perhaps that is because Senators feel comparatively secure from the ballot box; after all, a Representative is always running for office and is particularly susceptible to pressure from the White House. But though the Senate has pushed the counterattack, the effect, thus far at least, has been slight. Senator Fulbright's fulminations have perhaps helped to create, or at least to accelerate, a public disillusionment with the war in Vietnam, but little more than that has been accomplished by the Foreign Relations Committee.

Sen. Clifford Case has gotten deeply into the act. His bill, S. 596, requiring that Congress be notified of all Executive agreements "as soon as practicable," was passed unanimously by the Senate in February and got by the House in August. Now Public Law 92–403, it is a somewhat pathetic document; it does not require the President to consult with Congress, but merely to tell the legislature what he has done. As a further, more specific measure, Case has introduced S. R. 214, which, if passed, would require Executive agreements with Portugal and Bahrain to be submitted to the Senate as treaties. There is little chance that it will pass either body of the Congress. Even if it does, there is no way to enforce it, save by withholding appropriations.

The latest move is by a solid member of the Senate "club," Sam J. Ervin, Jr., of North Carolina. Ervin, who chairs the Subcommittee on Separation of Powers, has during the past few years held a number of significant hearings on excesses of Executive power. In April he introduced S. 3475, a bill to require submission of all international agreements other than treaties to Congress, where they would lie for at least sixty legislative days before going into effect. They would then go into force automatically unless both houses, by concurrent resolution, vetoed them. Hearings were held in May, at which time such notables as former Justice and U.N. Ambassador Arthur Goldberg and former Secretary of Defense Clark Clifford, as well as Senators Fulbright, Case and Symington, all testified in favor of the bill. Some, notably Fulbright, thought it too weak; others raised some minor points of objection. Predictably, the lawyers from the Executive branch lined up shoulder to shoulder in opposition. Should the bill clear the subcommittee, and also the full Judiciary Committee, it will then be referred to the Foreign Relations Committee, at which time Fulbright and Case will have a go at it.

Senator Ervin's bill has the merit of permitting agreements to become effective without express Congressional action. That should dispose of the bulk of them (always assuming favorable legislative action on the bill). But those few that raise serious questions, such as the agreements with Portugal and Bahrain and the secret agreement with Thailand, would subject to full public debate the nature of American commitments abroad. Perhaps the sixty-day period is too short; ninety or 120 days might be better. And the requirement of negative votes by both houses may well be too stringent. Senator Fulbright so believes; he would allow one house to "veto" agreements.

Whatever the ultimate result, there can be little doubt about the constitutionality of the bill in its general outlines. Some witnesses before the Ervin subcommittee suggested that certain agreements lie entirely within the province of the President, mentioning recognition of other governments and armistices at the end of hostilities as examples. But even there the law is uncertain at best, there being no Supreme Court decisions on the question. The State Department, adapting as do all bureaucracies, subtly shifted its position from opposing even the puny provisions of Senator Case's bill requiring mere notification to agreeing to such submissions. The unstated hope is that by agreeing to that inadequate procedure, it can stave off more drastic legislation.

Also unsettled constitutionally is the question of whether Congress by concurrent resolution, not subject to Presidential veto, can stop promulgation of Executive agreements. The argument here is that all bills, of whatever type, must be submitted to the White House. Possibly, if S. 3475 is enacted, it will take a subsequent Supreme Court decision to settle the matter. Historically, it is appropriate to mention that FDR thought that repeal of legislation (by analogy, that could include Executive agreements) by concurrent resolution was unconstitutional. Roosevelt so stated in a memorandum concerning Lend-Lease during World War II, published several years after the war was over.

On the other hand, "laying" proposed Executive or administrative actions before Congress for its scrutiny is not new. For example, Title VI of the Civil Rights Act of 1964 requires that before funds can be cut off to states that are alleged to be discriminating racially, the proposed decisions be submitted to appropriate Congressional committees. Presidential plans to reorganize Executive agencies are treated similarly, as are proposed changes in procedural rules governing the federal courts.

Fundamentally, however, the critical question is the extent to which the President has some type of "inherent" powers not touchable by legislation. Here, too, the constitutional picture is cloudy. The leading decision, concerning President Truman's seizure of the steel mills in 1952, settled little other than the invalidity of the specific action. Left unstated were the parameters of Executive power—*terra incognita* in constitutional law.

Ultimately, the problem is less "legal" than "practical." One can spin out legal arguments of almost equal persuasiveness for either side of the Congressional-Executive coin. That is so even though the original constitutional conception was for the foreign relations power to be shared—and for Congress to have a major role in foreign affairs. What Congress does not have, and what it must have if it is to become an effective instrument, is a means by which data can be obtained *and* assimilated in quantities sufficient to make the members privy to what they must know to make intelligent decisions. If, then, S. 3475 is enacted and if Congress moves further into the foreign affairs arena, its ability to gather, retain, and use relevant intelligence on many complex issues must be enhanced. At present, it must rely on the Executive to furnish it with that data, which is usually but not always done. The bureaucracy's penchant for secrecy includes even Congress.

How the institutional capability of Congress can be improved is far from self-evident. Despite the demonstrated need, acknowledged by scholars and Congressmen alike, no serious effort has thus far been made to modernize its procedures or to beef up its powers. The Congressional dragon still languishes deep in the 19th century, now and again switching its tail as it goes through its death throes. At times those lashes abort Executive action, as in the Haynsworth-Carswell nominations to the Supreme Court and the SST appropriation, but at a high price. Congress cannot go many times to that well. The debate over who is to control foreign policy is likely to find the President the victor. Whether Republican or Democrat, the Chief Executive is in charge of government. Institutions that do not adapt with fast-moving times—this includes Congress—are finding themselves swept aside as the winds of change steadily alter the social structure. This will not sit well with constitutional antiquarians. Nor should anyone applaud the development, for it means the desuetude (at least in part) of American constitutionalism. The ongoing foreign policy debate is apt to be more verbal pyrotechnics than substantive changes in programs. Only if Congress drags itself into the last part of the 20th century, sloughing off adherence to ancient practices, will it return, in foreign affairs as well as other areas, to being "equal in title and equal in dignity" to the Executive.

Nor will greater Congressional participation in foreign affairs necessarily help to preserve basic constitutional values. The shameful behavior of Congress over Vietnam is too well known to permit the luxury of believing that there is an easy or quick solution to a perennial problem of government. What would be preserved is the fragmentation of power over foreign policy. Only by an article of faith can one assume that such fragmentation, if it occurs, will produce results that are both viable and decent.

IN SEARCH OF KISSINGER

Joseph Kraft

"I'm not like Bill Moyers," he used to say of the former Presidential aide who virtually advertised himself as the liberal angel behind the scenes of the Johnson White House. "I don't believe I should take credit for all the good things the Administration does and blame the bad ones on the President." And the deep confidence game implicit in that remarkable disavowal expresses the finely filigreed complexity, the many-layered ambiguity, that envelops the role played by President Nixon's Assistant for National Security Affairs, Henry Kissinger.

For indirectly—by the company he keeps and the swinging figure he affects as well as by many confidence games—Kissinger tries to come on as the secret good guy of the Nixon foreign-policy Establishment. Actually, when set against the dovish temper of the country, the Congress, and the Cabinet, he works to reinforce and legitimize the President's hard-line instincts on most major international business. His closest friends and associates, in consequence, have come to see him as a suspect figure, personifying the treason of the intellectuals.

One thing no one doubts is the importance of Kissinger's role in the Nixon Administration. He sees the President alone almost every morning. He speaks to him on the phone two or three times during a routine day, and often takes a drink with him late in the afternoon. On special occasions such as trips abroad, or before speeches or press conferences, he is almost constantly with the President. He travels by Air Force plane only, and with a bodyguard. He inhabits a sumptuous ground-floor office a couple of doors down from the President's working rooms—a far cry from the severely utilitarian basement occupied by Walt Rostow and McGeorge Bundy, his predecessors under Presidents Johnson and Kennedy. He negotiates with heads of state, foreign ministers, and ambassadors galore. He does almost all the briefings attributed to high White House officials on major statements and big developments in foreign policy. He fights the President's battles with the Cabinet, the bureaucracy, the Eastern Establishment, and the intellectuals. It is perhaps not too much to say that he is the second most powerful man in the world.

Discovering exactly where he casts his influence is not so easy. For personal reasons, supplemented perhaps by experience of the Eisenhower staff system, President Nixon has a positive horror of making decisions

Source: *Harper's Magazine* (January 1971), pp. 54–61. Copyright © 1970, by Minneapolis Star and Tribune Co., Inc. Reprinted from the January 1971 issue of *Harper's Magazine* by permission of the author.

amidst the explicit pulling and hauling of rival bureaucratic groups. Kissinger does not stimulate such bureaucratic conflict, as McGeorge Bundy did for Kennedy; nor does he mine the bureaucracy for new ideas and slogans as Walt Rostow did for Lyndon Johnson. On the contrary, Kissinger's function is to screen the President from the raw bureaucratic pressures. It is for that purpose that there was devised the so-called "options system."

The basic idea is that long-range strategic objectives are defined in general policy statements such as the State of the World message delivered by the President to the Congress in February 1970, or the Presidential statement on the Far East which became known as the Guam Doctrine. With these goals identified, Kissinger and his staff consult with the various Departments and then serve up to the President various ways of reaching the objectives—the famous options. In making his choice, Mr. Nixon only selects among intellectually distinct alternatives, thereby avoiding the dirty business of having to favor one Department and its chief over another. And in a few areas—for example, the decisions to return Okinawa to the Japanese in 1972, and to renounce chemical and biological warfare—the options system plainly helped Mr. Nixon make decisions that would have been much harder if the opposition of the Joint Chiefs and their tribunes in the Congress and the press had been asserted, naked and unashamed.

But on major issues that keep cropping up over and over again, the President wants to gauge personally what Cabinet officers and military advisers really think. The options system cannot work—as indicated by the establishment of WSAG, or the Washington Special Action Group with top representatives of the chief agencies, for the daily management of such affairs as the Cambodian crisis of last spring or the Jordanian civil war of last fall. On all the big problems—on arms control, the Near East, and Vietnam—well-known bureaucratic positions have emerged. And in each case, Kissinger has tended to come down with the President and against most of the rest of the bureaucracy on the central issue of applying pressure to the Communists.

In the matter of arms control, the starting point was a policy put together by the Johnson Administration. The Johnson package provided for a freeze by both sides on strategic weapons with no allowance for new additions or qualitative improvements including further development of either the ABM or the MIRV (for Multiple Independently-Targeted Reentry Vehicles). Disarmers in the Congress, the State Department, and the Arms Control Agency wanted to go with that package as soon as the Nixon Administration came to office.

But Mr. Nixon had scant political interest in a Johnson package—the more so as he had backed the ABM and attacked the Democrats for allowing development of a "strategic gap." For different reasons Kissinger shared the President's skepticism. As a believer in the "linkage theory," he wanted no accord with the Russians on strategic weapons unless it was linked with Soviet cooperation in such political matters as the Near East and Vietnam.

As its first big decision in the arms-control field, the Nixon Administration dropped the Johnson package by moving for deployment of an ABM (redesigned, through the work of Kissinger and his staff, to protect this country's land-based missiles). Given that inch, the Pentagon came roaring back to claim the usual yard. Secretary of Defense Melvin Laird began putting out horror stories about a possible first strike by the Soviets with a new missile—the SS-9. Development of MIRV was pushed along, as were arguments for a full ABM system designed to protect the big cities against enemy missiles. President Nixon was plainly loath to overrule his military men directly, and at a press conference in January 1970, he even seemed to favor the full-scale ABM.

With pressure on the Russians thus mounted, Kissinger moved to channel it toward negotiations. He set up a Verification Panel that brought together heads of interested agencies, working under his leadership with materials prepared by his staff. He and his staff demolished Pentagon claims about tricks the Russians could play through secret deployment of new or improved weapons. They won general agreement for a set of new proposals. After soundings in Helsinki, the Administration put to the Russians last September in Vienna what is essentially a Nixon package. The Nixon package calls for a freeze at present levels, with limited deployment of ABM permitted and no provision for cutting off MIRV development. It is still being negotiated with the Soviet Union.

In the Near East, the starting point was a general concern that, as the President put it in his first press conference, local rivalries might draw the United States and the Soviet Union into a "nuclear confrontation." The State Department was given the task of arranging an easing of tension between Israel and the Arabs. The Department moved in two critical stages.

First, on December 9, 1969, Secretary of State William Rogers proposed that Israel withdraw from territories seized in the Six Day War in return for Arab recognition of her right to live in peace. Second, a peace initiative, put together by Assistant Secretary Joseph Sisco, was advanced on June 19 and accepted by Egypt, Jordan, and Israel on August 7. It provided for a ninety-day cease-fire and talks through the U.N. mediator.

President Nixon undoubtedly approved the general approach of the Department. But he apparently had misgivings that the Russians would use American actions to embarrass this country with the Arabs, while increasing Soviet influence. And whenever events seemed to vindicate those suspicions, Kissinger surfaced to warn the Russians they were moving into troubled waters.

In February, the State of the World message prepared by Kissinger warned that "the United States would view any effort by the Soviet Union to seek predominance in the Middle East as a matter of grave concern." In July, after the Russians started to assume the air defense of Egypt through new missiles and planes manned by Soviet pilots, Kissinger asserted at a background session at the Western White House that the American purpose was to "expel" the Soviet military presence from Egypt. After August 7, when the Russians violated the cease-fire by moving up missiles, and then allowed their Syrian friends to menace Jordan, Kissinger was in the thick of a flurry of moves to apply pressure on Moscow through the President's visit to the Sixth Fleet, the reinforcement of Israel, the very strong line taken about a possible Soviet submarine base in Cuba. Even after the death of Colonel Nasser, positions within the United States government remained as they were. While the State Department has been pushing for Israeli agreement to withdraw as a step toward peace, Kissinger has been working to keep up the pressure against any further Soviet penetration.

As to Vietnam, Kissinger set out his views in an article published in the January 1969 issue of *Foreign Affairs*. He believed there was no chance to crush the other side by military means: "The guerrilla wins if he does not lose." At the same time he felt that American prestige was deeply and adversely engaged in Vietnam. "The commitment of 500,000 Americans has settled the importance of Vietnam," he wrote.

Kissinger's answer to the problem thus posed was the answer of two-track negotiations. On one track, the Saigon regime would negotiate with the guerrillas, or National Liberation Front, a political status for South Vietnam that would encompass such concessions as had to be made. On the other, the United States and North Vietnam would negotiate a mutual withdrawal of forces that would register a peace without victory or defeat. In that way the war would end with the blow to American prestige minimized and camouflaged.

Technically Kissinger has never departed from that prescription. Inside the Nixon Administration, he has been the constant protagonist of negotiations. In the very first months he managed a secret effort through the Russians that collapsed ignominiously in June. He pushed an effort through the French after the death of Ho Chi Minh. When Prince Sihanouk fell, he worked through the Russians for an all-Indochina conference. After the Cambodian operations put the President under pressure to show a willingness to deal, it was Kissinger who came up with the idea of sending David Bruce to Paris as the new peace negotiator. And he was a principal architect last fall of the ceasefire offered on October 8.

But the Communist price for negotiations has been some sign of change in the Saigon government. While Secretary of State Rogers has repeatedly seemed to flirt with the idea of change in Saigon, President Nixon had been adamantly opposed to political concessions in South Vietnam. Negotiations have been acceptable to the President only on condition that the other side change its objectives. To that end, Kissinger, unlike Rogers, has repeatedly managed to square his interest in negotiations with the President's instinct for mounting pressure on Hanoi.

The first adjustment involved the gradual passage of the military burden from American troops to the forces of the Saigon government—Vietnamization. Kissinger combined negotiation with Vietnamization by developing the theory that as the other side saw the Saigon regime becoming stronger, it would be more and more pushed to deal with Washington. And suppose the other side used the occasion of the drawing down of American troops to launch a large-scale attack? Then, the President announced in what was certainly a threat devised by Kissinger, he would take "prompt and effective measures."

Next came the enormous swelling of public dissent in this country at the time of the Moratorium of October 15, 1969. The President met that head-on, asking the country in his speech of November 3 to choose between a sellout and a peace with honor. Mr. Nixon wrote much of the speech himself—including the appeal to the "great silent majority." But Kissinger was with him every step of the way. His office prepared drafts of the speech. He repeatedly asserted that the other side would only negotiate if it was convinced the President could hold the country's support. And when the tactic had worked, when the President's appeal had prevailed, no one was more pleased than Kissinger. "He didn't say a thing," a former staff man recalls. "He just smiled like the Cheshire cat."

Then there was the little matter of expanding the war into Cambodia. Secretary of Defense Melvin Laird and Secretary of State Rogers have both let it be known that they opposed the decision at some times and on some grounds. But how about Kissinger? Unlike Laird and Rogers, he participated in every phase of the decision making. At one point he convoked a meeting of five of his brightest young associates to get their views. All were against. One argued that expanded commitments to the Cambodian regime would weigh against any short-term military gains likely to accrue. Another described the internal upheavals likely to occur. Kissinger has indicated to at least one friend that he passed these views on to the President. But all the evidence suggests that he himself raised only feeble objections to the operation. He has expressed the belief that there wouldn't have been any serious trouble except for the shootings at Kent State. He has peddled to complaisant journalists the story that the whole purpose of the operation was to provide a cover for a more rapid pullout. And why? Once again the rationale seems to have been that Cambodia, by decreasing the other side's military capacity, would put pressure on Hanoi to enter negotiations. "I am," he once said in an allusion to his predecessor's unremitting faith in the possibility of victory in Vietnam, "the Walt Rostow of peace by negotiations."

That Kissinger should turn out to be a hard boy in the Nixon Administration is not really so surprising. Becoming tough is what his life story is all about. He was born in 1923 into a cozy and comfortable little world. His father, Louis Kissinger, was a teacher at the gymnasium, or prep school, in Fürth, a small town outside Nuremberg in Franconia. His mother was a formidable housekeeper. The family was unmistakably middle-class.

Middle-class Jews, however, in a Franconia that was a hotbed of nascent Nazism. Three years before Hitler took over in Berlin, the Nazis were in the saddle in Fürth. From 1930 through 1938, from the age of seven until he was fifteen, Kissinger lived as a despised pariah. He was denied entrance to the gymnasium and forced to go to an all-Jewish school. He or his school fellows were beaten up almost every day. His father was stripped of his post and humiliated. Twelve relatives eventually died at the hands of the Nazis. When the Kissingers got away in 1938, it was through the agency of his mother. For some time thereafter she supported the family, working as a cook for neighbors on the upper West Side of New York. His father had been broken in spirit. "He was a man of great goodness," Kissinger says now, "in a world where goodness had no meaning."

The reaction of the son was to go deep in his shell. From 1939 to 1943, when he was going to George Washington High School in New York, Kissinger seems to have made no friends—hence, probably, the survival of the German accent which most refugees who came over in their teens lost. He recalls that if he was walking down the street in New York and saw a group of boys approaching the other way, he would cross to the opposite sidewalk. Though he was plainly well-equipped intellectually, particularly in mathematics, he set his sights very low. "I worked in a shaving-brush factory during the days," he says, "so that I could go to school at nights to prepare for what was then the height of my ambition—becoming an accountant."

Not much changed when Kissinger was drafted into the Army in 1943 as a private in the infantry. The writer Theodore Draper, who served with Kissinger, recalls him as a "nice, quiet boy . . . a young fellow who didn't know what to do with his life." "He was totally withdrawn," says Fritz Kraemer, another member of the same unit who was to have a deep influence on Kissinger's later life. And Kissinger himself observes of that time: "Living as a Jew under the Nazis, then as a refugee in America, and then as a private in the Army isn't exactly an experience that builds confidence."

The depths of Kissinger's inward-turning, the glacial quality of his withdrawal are revealed by nothing so much as those who took him out of it. For they were not the ordinary sources of inspiration to bright young men— dedicated scholars like Christian Gauss or potent intellectuals in the mold of Felix Frankfurter. On the contrary, to shock Henry Kissinger out of the depths, to charge him with purpose and ambition required men who were themselves outsiders—a couple of flamboyant personalities, nostalgic for vanished features of an aristocratic life they presumed to embody, and full of snobbish contempt for present times.

One of these was Fritz Kraemer. "I am the last individual in a mass society," Kraemer said when I called him at the Pentagon where he works as an assistant to the Army Chief of Staff. "Journalists who come to see me about Henry go away disappointed." If the last phrase was a come-on, the first was only a slight exaggeration. Kraemer, the son of a Ruhr businessman, with the bearing and style of a Prussian, had left Germany in the late Twenties for schooling and adventure in a dozen different countries. After Pearl Harbor he enlisted as a private in the American Army and won a battlefield commission. He then set up a kind of military-government school for the officers and men of the 84th Division. Kissinger, a private in that division, attended one of the lectures and wrote Kraemer a fan letter. Kraemer asked him to come around.

"Within twenty minutes," Kraemer recalls, "I recognized that here was a rare political intelligence." He had Kissinger made an instructor in the school and a translator for the commanding general of the 84th Division. He took in hand the education of his protégé. Looking back he says, "A lot of junk has been written about how I put Henry into Harvard. What happened is this: I used to tell him, 'Henry, you understand everything but know nothing. You need an education.' One day he came to me and said he was going home—home to college. I said to him: 'Henry, gentlemen do not go to the College of the City of New York.' The rest he did himself. He won a New York State scholarship. Then he was admitted to Harvard."

The other crucial patron was William Yandell Elliott—a sometime Army officer, Presidential adviser, and professor of government, who, in Kissinger's own phrase, "lived as a grand seigneur in a world where eminence has become a technical achievement." Elliott became Kissinger's tutor at Harvard and much more. "We met every week for years," Kissinger recalled in a tribute written when Elliott retired from Harvard in 1963. "Bill Elliott made me discover Dostoevski and Hegel, Kant, Spinoza, and Homer. On many Sundays we took long walks in Concord. He spoke of the power of love, and said that the only truly unforgivable sin is to use people as if they were objects. He discussed greatness and excellence. And while I did not always follow his words, I knew that I was in the presence of a remarkable man."

One thing Kraemer and Elliott gave to Kissinger was the realization that he could do truly distinguished work in politics and philosophy—a sense of métier. Under their impulse he shot up the academic ladder at Harvard: A.B., 1950; M.A., 1952; Ph.D., 1954; Lecturer, 1957; Associate Professor, 1959; Professor, 1962. In 1949 he had married a refugee girl, Ann Fleischer. He could have settled down to the normal don's life of Cambridge.

But Kraemer and Elliott had also imparted to Kissinger something far more important—something that, as Helmut Sonnenfeld, a friend from Army days who now serves with Kissinger in the White House, perceives, "could not have been given by wild-eyed radicals." They delivered to him an antidote against the quietude of his early life, a reason for not being the victim he had been. They taught the principle, and embodied the practice, of struggle against anarchy. "A man," Kraemer said to me when ruminating about Kissinger, "does not know the world until he has been out alone on the docks of Marseilles, hungry and with only one suit, being stalked by another man who wants that suit. Then being reasonable or good doesn't matter. Then a man has to stand up for himself or die."

It was that do or die credo which struck fire with Kissinger. He had experienced in his own life shattering calamity. He had known the time when there was "no place for goodness." He understood the danger of unhappy endings. So he made it his life's work to show that force could be used to avert tragedy and catastrophe. He became not a mere diplomatic historian, but a defense intellectual or military schoolman, primarily concerned with power. In that role he made a name for himself at the Council on Foreign Relations, and then as a consultant to Nelson Rockefeller. His best-known books—*Nuclear Weapons and Foreign Policy* in 1957; *The Necessity for Choice* in 1961; *The Troubled Partnership* in 1965*—all argued the need for reshaping armies to provide a more stable world. The underlying logic he had set out even earlier in a Ph.D. thesis on Europe after Napoleon which was published later under the title, *A World Restored: The Politics of Conservatism in a Revolutionary Age.* In that work Kissinger identified as the leitmotif of modern history a running battle between forces of revolution and forces of conservatism. On the side of revolution were conquerors and prophets— "the great symbols of attacks on the legitimate order." In dialectic tension with these wreckers were the statesmen of conservatism who sought to restore "order and balance" through "a pattern of obligations sufficiently spontaneous to reduce to a minimum the necessity for the application of force."

Needless to say, Kissinger did not align himself with troublemakers—the Rousseaus and Napoleons who surfaced in latter days as Marxes and Lenins and Hitlers and Stalins. He cast his lot with the statesmen—with Castlereagh especially, and Metternich in the Napoleonic era; later, and less, with Bismarck; and most recently, with General de Gaulle. The practical payoff of all this was in large degree only an elegant generalization of Kraemer's specter of the man hunted on the docks of Marseilles. As Kissinger put it in *A World Restored:*

> Whenever peace—conceived as the avoidance of war—has been the primary objective of a group of powers, the international system has been at the mercy of the most ruthless member of the international com-

munity. Whenever the international order has acknowledged that certain principles should not be compromised, even for the sake of peace, stability based on an equilibrium of forces was at least conceivable.

Given those views, a man who came to Washington as Assistant to the President in 1969 had scant choice. Vietnam had prepared the *Zeitgeist*. All around were men prepared to compromise for the sake of peace. The Secretary of State favored almost any deal to get out of Vietnam, and wind down tension in the Near East. The Secretary of Defense was prepared to pull troops from Vietnam and Europe and everywhere else. Doves dominated the Congress and most of the Foreign Service. Inevitably, Kissinger was drawn to the hard-liner who showed least disposition to yield. Between the President and Kissinger there was established a professional and psychic bond far deeper than previous Presidents developed with their chief foreign-policy assistants. Kissinger became a Nixonite par excellence. But for many months and many people Kissinger obscured this commitment through a convoluted personality that, in the interests of not making enemies, projected a kind of double image.

At bottom there was that lack of grace known in modern times as insecurity. Superficially, at least, Kissinger is the prototype of Dr. Strangelove. He has the refugee background and marked accent. He speaks in slow, ponderous cadences—"like a man who has never had a childhood," Professor Richard Gardner of the Columbia Law School who has known him since Harvard remarks. He has a form (5 feet 9 inches tall, 160 pounds) and face (severe eyes behind heavy glasses and long nose under high brow rising to wavy, light-brown hair) that do not make much of an impression. Not surprisingly, he is rarely at ease with people. "Henry," his deputy, Brigadier General Alexander Haig, remarks with the caution appropriate to a deputy, "is not always sure he'll be accepted." "He doesn't really believe anybody likes him," Adam Yarmolinsky, a Harvard friend, once exclaimed. Kissinger himself repeatedly refers to his own "paranoia."

Jokingly, of course. Only the joke isn't all that funny. The Kissinger wit, which can be formidable, runs to a type. "I suppose," he used to tell lecture groups, "you all came here to find out just exactly how depraved a Harvard professor can be." "This will be good for my megalomania," he said when his students applauded a farewell statement he made before taking his present job. "Everything's going to plan—over the cliff," is one of his regular gags now that he's in office. A couple of days after it was reported that Attorney General John Mitchell had called him an "egotistical maniac," he told a group of reporters: "It took me eighteen years to achieve total animosity at Harvard. In Washington I did it in eighteen months." In all cases, Kissinger himself is the butt of the jokes, and they turn on some trait other people regard with misgivings, even alarm. Functionally, the gags work to probe an uncertain landscape, distinguishing friendlies from hostiles.

With the friendlies, Kissinger can be warm and patient to a rare degree. He takes remarkable pains to talk at their level to his young children—Elizabeth, eleven, and David, nine. I have listened to him spend a quarter of an hour explaining to them the role of a newspaper columnist. He has charm to burn for women he likes. "He's *süss,* a regular courtier," Mrs. John Sherman Cooper, wife of the Senator from Kentucky, says, using the German word for sweet with its sugary overtone. Former secretaries have been known to wait for hours just to have a chance to say hello. His big difficulty lies in breaking relations. He let an unhappy marriage drag on for years, and divorced in 1964 only after his wife took the initiative. "Henry," a colleague who knew him then explains, "doesn't like the idea of losing touch with people. He fears that cut loose they might turn hostile."

This fear finds expression in almost all of Kissinger's most prominent traits. His suspiciousness is proverbial. He once accused a Harvard colleague who suggested they dine together in a hotel room so they could talk without interruption of not wanting to be seen with him. Even in government few men are so secretive. "I never knew what Henry said to the President and I never will," Roger Morris, a former staff member whom Kissinger likened to a son, acknowledges.

Like many persons constantly on the watch for enemies, Kissinger is extremely reluctant to extend trust. Bayless Manning, now dean of the Stanford Law School, but once a rapporteur working under Kissinger on a Rockefeller Brothers Fund project, recalls that he and other rapporteurs nearly rebelled because Kissinger was redoing their work. Professors who taught courses with him were not allowed to invite guest lecturers without his approval.

Even at the White House Kissinger tries to do everything himself. He works at a phenomenal pace—often from seven in the morning to the wee hours. Recently, the draft of a guest column written for the *New York Times* by the Deputy Director of the Budget, Caspar Weinberger, elicited from Kissinger a fifteen-page critique. One evening after ten he told his appointments man, David Young, to "take the rest of the day off." Since he is always available to the President, but also tries to see practically everybody else who comes to town, his schedule is inevitably chaotic. "I spend each day canceling the appointments made the day before," Lawrence Eagleburger, who used to keep his schedule, once lamented. Even when the disorder of the office procedure had reached scandalous heights—with people waiting for hours and Cabinet officers complaining of calls not returned—Kissinger would not delegate authority. Though both his predecessors had deputies, it was only after eighteen months of disruption that Kissinger appointed General Haig to that post.

In one respect Kissinger's one-man-showmanship had undoubted consequences. He is the only one on his staff who has regular access to the

President. Nixon wants it that way, but so does Kissinger. He has never taken on his staff, as Bundy and Rostow did before him, individuals with the kind of personalities sure to command Presidential attention. The absence of staff access to the President has inevitably meant that only the problems of interest to Kissinger get the highest attention. Scant heed is paid at the Presidential level to Africa or Latin America or trade. When African, Latin American, or economic affairs come up, the White House, in effect, is out-to-lunch. Not a few of the numerous Kissinger staff resignations have come from men who came to feel that working for Kissinger was a kind of servitude. I once mentioned to a former Kissinger staff man that a couple of young technicians working in his communications office had used their passes to crash the White House party given for Prince Charles. The former staff man burst out, "Good for them. I'm glad somebody had the guts to stand up—even on that issue."

A curiously connected phenomenon is Kissinger's taste for high abstractions. Almost alone in the American academic community, Kissinger is literally a doctrinaire. His intellectual heroes are supreme theoreticians— Hegel and Kant. His constant charge against past policy makers was that they acted pragmatically to the point where, he wrote in *The Troubled Partnership,* "each event is a compartment analyzed and dealt with under pressure . . . without an adequate consideration of its relations to other occurrences." Back in 1957 he was arguing in *Nuclear Weapons and Foreign Policy* that "doctrine is important." In a paper on European policy published by the Brookings Institution just before he entered government he was again asserting: "In the years to come the most profound challenge to American policy will be philosophic."

Most Kissinger watchers put down this bent for generalization to a trait passed on from his father's academic background—the trait that made the Germans *das Volk der Denker.* But my strong impression is that Kissinger also uses high abstraction as a protective device—a system of rules that fence out the need for spontaneous adjustment in face-to-face contacts. Long ago, and it is a mark of high intellectual penetration, Kissinger concluded that the case he wanted to make—the conservative case for legitimacy—could not be well argued in the pragmatic spirit of self-interest. On the contrary, he wrote in *A World Restored* that "the case has to be made by fighting as anonymously as possible . . . so that the contest occurs at least on a plane beyond the individual." It is typical that on Vietnam he has ordered from his own staff and most of the rest of the government immensely complicated and highly structured studies on the progress of Vietnamization and pacification. And while everybody in government is running down those hares, Kissinger and his principal, President Nixon, are free to concentrate on the only interesting question—the question about the intention of the governments of Saigon and Hanoi.

Finally, in keeping with his wariness, secretiveness, and taste for camouflage, Kissinger has at all times sought to anticipate and propitiate potential foes. His capacity to profit from criticism is truly impressive. At Harvard, his closest colleague was Thomas Schelling, an economist who made his reputation by showing the danger of relying on the tactical nuclear weapons Kissinger had recommended in *Nuclear Weapons and Foreign Policy*. Though known as an associate of Nelson Rockefeller, Kissinger maintained ties with the White House intellectuals under Kennedy, notably Arthur Schlesinger and McGeorge Bundy. In the Johnson Administration, Robert McNamara used him to play a role in a major sounding of Hanoi, and he was regularly briefed on the progress of the Paris peace talks by the chief negotiator, Averell Harriman, and Under Secretary of State Nicholas Katzenbach. In the Nixon Administration he began playing almost instinctively, and even before accepting appointment, the role of ambassador to the intellectual community and the Eastern Establishment. He had known the appointment would probably come through long before election day 1968.

But when Nixon actually extended the offer, Kissinger asked for a week to think it over. He then went the rounds of his friends. He spoke to the Harvard and Kennedy intellectuals—Bundy, Galbraith, Schlesinger, Schelling, Yarmolinsky, Richard Neustadt, and a leading disarmament specialist, Paul Doty. He canvassed the Eastern Establishment at the Council on Foreign Relations and in the Rockefeller entourage. His explanation for this inquiry suggested that the near victim of Hitler had delicate scruples about a figure associated in the past with the Republican right-wing. "For people of my generation," Kissinger told me when I asked at the time about his hesitation, "Nixon had a certain reputation. I needed to assure myself that reputation was not deserved." But, of course, virtually everybody told Kissinger to take the job. The predictable result of the canvass was that he had for a little while anyhow lined up the support of the main centers of intellectual and Establishment opinion.

The same technique revealed itself in the appointment of the Kissinger staff. For day-to-day operational business he took men long inured to working in the system. General Haig, from the Pentagon, was in charge of liaison with the military. Helmut Sonnenfeld, an old friend, and Pete Vakey, John Holdridge, and Richard Smyser were pulled from the State Department to deal with Europe, Latin America, Asia, and Vietnam respectively. But amidst these, in free-floating positions, were a bunch of young men known in previous Administrations as critics of official policy—particularly in Vietnam. They included Daniel Davidson from Harriman's staff at the Paris peace talks; Anthony Lake and Lawrence Eagleburger from the staff of Under Secretary Katzenbach; Richard Moose from the National Security staff assembled by

Rostow; Roger Morris from the National Security staff assembled by Bundy; and Morton Halperin, Lawrence Lynn, and Winston Lord from the McNamara Pentagon. As the special feature of the staff, moreover, Kissinger set up under Halperin and Lynn a Systems Analysis unit—a transplant from the organization established by McNamara in the Pentagon to block out basic strategy through critical analysis of the various programs thrown up by the services.

Socially, Kissinger also cultivated the constituency on the other side. From the very first—from a small White House dinner he attended as "date" for Alice Roosevelt Longworth—he kept up his White House fences, particularly with Mrs. Nixon, it is said. But his best buddies seemed to be Washingtonians associated with earlier regimes. At his last birthday party, the guests were former Secretary of Defense and Mrs. McNamara; Richard Helms, who became head of the CIA under Lyndon Johnson, and Mrs. Helms; John Freeman, the former editor of the New Statesman who was made Ambassador to Washington by Labor Prime Minister Harold Wilson, and his wife; and Katherine Graham, publisher of the liberal Washington Post. On one occasion, Kissinger even asked Mary McGrory, columnist for the Washington Star, to arrange for him a private dinner with some leaders of the peace movement, including Sam Brown and David Mixner.

On top of all that, Kissinger cut out for himself a role foreign to every leading Nixonite but distinctly reminiscent of the "dancing professors" of the Kennedy regime. He began going out with well-known glamour girls—Barbara Howar in Washington, Gloria Steinem in New York, and Jill St. John in Hollywood. His luncheon dates at the Sans Souci became a regular subject of press gossip—the basic rule being that the more hairy the crisis, the more often Kissinger had a long-stemmed lovely to lunch. "I am," he himself announced at a party given for Miss Steinem by Mrs. Howar and full of journalists, "a secret swinger."

The secret swinger image with its underlying theme of secret good guy has had a certain impact with the media. CBS-TV did a special on him which featured his social life. But nobody close-in has been fooled. On the contrary, many have felt had; and there has been a steady flow of friends and associates away from Kissinger. At least a dozen of the best staff members left either because of inability to reach through Kissinger to the President or because of dissatisfaction with hawkish policies. Five—including two young foreign-policy experts whom he regarded with particular affection, Anthony Lake and Roger Morris—quit after Cambodia. A delegation of thirteen close Harvard colleagues—including Schelling, Kistiakowsky, Neustadt, Yarmolinsky—made a public visit to his office at that time to demonstrate their lack of support for his policies. Arthur Schlesinger and Carl Kaysen of the Institute for Advanced Study wrote him frankly that he should quit. When Kissinger revealed the dinner arranged by Miss McGrory, Sam Brown promised the peace movement would drive Kissinger from Cambridge if he ever tried to return. Even the glamour girls began to feel they were being used to win sympathy for Henry in sophisticated circles. When Barbara Howar was asked on the CBS special how somebody with her peacenik views could keep going out with Kissinger, she said, in a reply cut from the show, "Politics make strange bedfellows."

Some of the attacks shook Kissinger badly. "He had a couple of rocky days," General Haig says of the period after Cambodia. He allowed to go uncorrected—indeed he may well have stimulated—an inaccurate report by *Time* magazine that the visiting professors had threatened that he would not be allowed to return to his post at Harvard. He railed repeatedly against the intellectual community and the Eastern Establishment. "What the hell's an Establishment for," he once asked with great heat, "if not to support the President when he's in trouble?" Occasionally he even fell back on a pathetic version of the tyrant's plea. Cambodia he justified because otherwise President Nixon would be unseated by the superpatriots of the right. "The country," Kissinger said, "has destroyed its last two Presidents. It cannot stand destruction of a third President." Since the Cambodian affair the tension has eased. A first-rate man who also once served in the McNamara Pentagon, Wayne Smith, has taken the Systems Analysis post vacated by Lawrence Lynn. Kissinger has seen or lunched with most of his former academic colleagues. There is no doubt that he can go back to Harvard if he wants. But my sense is that the bitterness remains and a certain contempt for those who tried to exonerate themselves by jumping on him. When the time comes to step down, Kissinger will almost certainly want to one up the Harvards. A good guess is that he will probably accept a fellowship at All Souls, Oxford.

Meanwhile, no one can doubt that there remains a case to be made against Kissinger, a strong case. He has carefully camouflaged his true colors. He has betrayed the trust of innocent people, and induced a suspension of disbelief among normally vigilant persons. He has caused some of the very best men in government to leave government. Worst of all, perhaps, he has, particularly in the Cambodia business, become wrapped up in his own work to the point of seeing foreign affairs as a set of technical problems, not the stuff that engages the lives and passions of millions of people. Still, that is not the treason of the intellectuals.

While hardly exempt from moral criticism, intellectuals do not enter government to be nice guys. They are called upon to help Presidents get hold of problems that have got beyond their traditional managers. Much as economists helped Roosevelt and subsequent Presidents get hold of the business cycle that the bankers could not manage, foreign-policy intellectuals were called in by Kennedy, Johnson, and Nixon to get hold of security problems that the generals and diplomats could not solve. Far from presenting a case of intellectual treason, Kissinger has been true to his mission in remarkable degree. Others may be hotter to disengage, but Kissinger, and Kissinger alone, has provided a forum for careful analysis of how to manage a safe winding down of the American presence abroad. He has fenced off his President from bureaucratic pressures. He has helped Mr. Nixon achieve more mastery of foreign policy than was ever enjoyed by Johnson or Kennedy or Eisenhower or Truman. And for my own part, I find it scarcely credible that the Nixon Administration will be a better instrument of government when Kissinger finally takes his leave.

DIPLOMATIC NOTES

Leslie H. Gelb and Morton H. Halperin

The average reader of the *New York Times* in the 1950s must have asked: why don't we take some of our troops out of Europe? Ike himself said we didn't need them all there. Later, in 1961, after the tragi-comic Bay of Pigs invasion, the reader asked: how did President Kennedy ever decide to do such a damn fool thing? Or later about Vietnam: why does President Johnson keep on bombing North Vietnam when the bombing prevents negotiations and doesn't get Hanoi to stop the fighting?

Sometimes the answer to these questions is simple. It can be attributed squarely to the President. He thinks it's right. Or he believes he has no choice. As often as not, though, the answer lies elsewhere—in the special interests and procedures of the bureaucracy and the convictions of the bureaucrats.

If you look at foreign policy as a largely rational process of gathering information, setting the alternatives, defining the national interest, and making decisions, then much of what the President does will not make sense. But if you look at foreign policy as bureaucrats pursuing organizational, personal, and domestic political interests, as well as their own beliefs about what is right, you can explain much of the inexplicable.

In pursuing these interests and beliefs, bureaucrats (and that means everyone from Cabinet officials to political appointees to career civil servants) usually follow their own version of the Ten Commandments:

Source: *Harper's Magazine* (June 1972), pp. 28, 30–32, 36–37. Copyright © 1971, by Minneapolis Star and Tribune Co., Inc. Reprinted from the June 1972 issue of *Harper's Magazine* by permission of the authors.

1. Don't discuss domestic politics on issues involving war and peace.

On May 11, 1948, President Harry Truman held a meeting in the White House to discuss recognition of the new state of Israel. Secretary of State George Marshall and State Undersecretary Robert Lovett spoke first. They were against it. It would unnecessarily alienate forty million Arabs. Truman next asked Clark Clifford, then Special Counsel to the President, to speak. Arguing for the moral element of U.S. policy and the need to contain Communism in the Middle East, Clifford favored recognition. As related by Dan Kurzman in *Genesis 1948,* Marshall exploded: "Mr. President, this is not a matter to be determined on the basis of politics. Unless politics were involved, Mr. Clifford would not even be at this conference. This is a serious matter of foreign policy determination . . ." Clifford remained at the meeting, and after some hesitation, the U.S. recognized Israel.

The moral merits of U.S. support of Israel notwithstanding, no one doubts Jewish influence on Washington's policy toward the Middle East. And yet, years later, in their memoirs, both Truman and Dean Acheson denied at great length that the decision to recognize the state of Israel was in any way affected by U.S. domestic politics.

A powerful myth is at work here. It holds that national security is too important, too sacred, to be tainted by crass domestic political considerations. It is a matter of lives and the safety of the nation. Votes and influence at home should count for nothing. Right? Wrong. National security and domestic reactions are inseparable. What could be clearer than the fact that President Nixon's Vietnam troop reductions are geared more to American public opinion than to the readiness of the Saigon forces to defend themselves? Yet the myth makes it bad form for government officials to talk about domestic politics (except to friends and to reporters off the record) or even to write about politics later in their memoirs.

And what is bad form on the inside would be politically disastrous if it were leaked to the outside. Imagine the press getting hold of a secret government document that said: "President Nixon has decided to visit China to capture the peace issue for the '72 elections. He does not intend or expect anything of substance to be achieved by his trip—except to scare the Russians a little." Few things are more serious than the charge of playing politics with security.

Nevertheless, the President pays a price for the silence imposed by the myth. One cost is that the President's assumptions about what public opinion will and will not support are never questioned. No official, for example, ever dared to write a scenario for President Johnson showing him how to forestall the right-wing McCarthyite reaction he feared if the U.S. pulled out of Vietnam. Another cost is that bureaucrats, in their ignorance of Presidential views, will use their own notions of domestic politics to screen information from the President or to eliminate options from his consideration.

2. Say what will convince, not what you believe.

In the early months of the Kennedy Administration, CIA officials responsible for covert operations faced a difficult challenge. President Eisenhower had permitted them to begin training a group of Cuban refugees for an American-supported invasion of Castro's Cuba. In order to carry out the plan, they then had to win approval from a skeptical new President whose entourage included some "liberals" likely to oppose it. The CIA director, Allen Dulles, and his assistant, Richard Bissell, both veteran bureaucrats, moved effectively to isolate the opposition. By highlighting the extreme sensitivity of the operation, they persuaded Kennedy to exclude from deliberations most of the experts in State and the CIA itself, and many of the Kennedy men in the White House. They reduced the effectiveness of others by refusing to leave any papers behind to be analyzed; they swept in, presented their case, and swept out, taking everything with them. But there remained the problem of the skeptical President. Kennedy feared that if the operation was a complete failure he would look very bad. Dulles and Bissell assured him that complete failure was impossible. If the invasion force could not establish a beachhead, the refugees, well-trained in guerrilla warfare, would head for the nearby mountains. The assurances were persuasive, the only difficulty being that they were false. Less than a third of the force had had any guerrilla training; the nearby mountains were separated from the landing beach by an almost impenetrable swamp; and none of the invasion leaders was instructed to head for the hills if the invasion failed (the CIA had promised them American intervention).

Kennedy was told what would persuade him, not the truth or even what the CIA believed to be true. Bureaucrats like Dulles and Bissell are confident that they know what the national security requires. The problem is to convince an uninformed and busy President. To do that you do not carefully explain the reasoning that leads to your position, nor do you reveal any doubts you may have. Rather you seek to figure out what the President's problem is as he sees it and to convince him that what you want to do will solve it.

3. Support the consensus—Option B.

Vietnam policy under President Johnson exemplified the concept of Option B. The papers to the President went something like this: Option A— Use maximum force (bomb Hanoi and Haiphong and invade North Vietnam, Laos, and Cambodia). Recommend rejection on the ground that the Soviets and the Chinese might respond. Option C—Immediate unilateral American withdrawal. Recommend rejection because it will lead to a Communist victory in Vietnam. Option B—Bomb a little more each time and seek negotiations (even though the bombing was preventing negotiations). Turn more of the fighting over to the Saigon forces and send more U.S. troops (even though the American buildup obviated the need for the South Vietnamese to shoulder more of the burden). Press Saigon for reforms and give them all they want for the war effort (even though aid without conditions gave Saigon no incentive to reform). Option B triumphed.

Option B solves a lot of problems for the bureaucrat. Bureaucrats do not like to fight with each other. Option B makes everybody a winner (by letting everyone do the essence of what he wants), preserves the policy consensus, and provides ultimate comfort to the bureaucrat—deference to his expertise and direct responsibility. Very few will be so dissatisfied as to take their case to the public.

Unfortunately, while this process allows the President to keep his house happy, it also robs him of choice. The alternatives he is given are often phony, two ridiculous extremes and a jumbled, inconsistent "middle course." Unless a President knows enough and has the time to peel off the real alternatives from within Option B, he ends up being trapped by the unanimity of advice.

4. Veto other options.

Former Secretary of State Dean Acheson, summoned by President Kennedy to join the Executive Committee of the National Security Council debate on Soviet missiles in Cuba, favored a "surgical strike," a limited air attack designed simply to destroy the missiles before they could become operational. Each time the military was asked to come in with a plan for a surgical strike, they asserted that a limited air strike could not destroy all the missiles—despite their having the capability to do so. Instead, they produced a plan for their favored option—an all-out air assault on Cuba climaxed by a ground invasion. Their plan had something in it for each service—the Air Force and Navy would pound the island by sea and air, the Marines would storm ashore as the Army paratroopers descended—and the military would be left free to act as they chose. The military insisted that a surgical strike was "infeasible" in part because they assumed that Soviet missiles were "mobile" (i.e., capable of being moved in a few hours) rather than "movable" (i.e., their actual capability of being moved in a few days). Kennedy was intrigued by the surgical-strike option and met with the commander of the Tactical Air Command. When the commander solemnly assured the President face-to-face that the option was "infeasible," Kennedy with great reluctance abandoned it.

"Infeasibility" is one technique to disqualify an option; demanding full authority is another. Early in his administration, Kennedy confronted a deteriorating situation in Laos. He was reluctant to commit any American forces, but neither was he prepared to have Laos overrun. At a critical White House meeting he asked the military what could be done with various levels of force. The Joint Chiefs' answer was clear. They would not recommend any landing of American forces and could guarantee nothing unless the President was prepared to authorize the use of nuclear weapons whenever, in their judgment, that use was required. Kennedy reluctantly decided not to send any forces to Laos.

5. *Predict dire consequences.*

With the Chinese Communist guns firing at the tiny island of Quemoy three miles from the mainland and an invasion expected momentarily, President Eisenhower's principal advisers met to frame a recommendation. The problem, as they saw it, was to formulate an argument that would persuade the President that the U.S. must defend Quemoy. The advisers resorted to the prediction of dire consequences, recognizing that only if the alternative could be shown to be very adverse to American interests would Eisenhower agree to the use of force. They warned the President that in their unanimous judgment, if he permitted Quemoy to be captured, "the consequences in the Far East would be more far-reaching and catastrophic than those which followed when the United States allowed the Chinese mainland to be taken over by the Chinese Communists."

Did Eisenhower reject this prediction as absurd? On the contrary, he accepted it and defended Quemoy.

The uncertainties of international politics are so great that it is difficult to disprove any prediction. This puts the President in a bind. If he fails to act and things go badly, the overruled advisers are likely to leak their warnings. In fact, much of the dialogue within the government is in terms of worst cases. An advocate who does not warn of extreme consequences is often viewed as not seriously supporting his prediction.

6. *Argue timing, not substance.*

Although the advocates of the Bay of Pigs landing had convinced President Kennedy that the invasion of Cuba was worth a try, they recognized that they were not yet in the clear: they still had to persuade the President to act immediately. Presidents are, in the eyes of bureaucrats, notorious for putting off decisions or changing their minds. They have enough decisions to make without looking for additional ones. In many cases, all the options look bad and they prefer to wait. The Bay of Pigs plan called for an effective "now or never" argument, and the CIA rose to the occasion. The agency told Kennedy that the invasion force was at the peak of its effectiveness; any delay, and it would decline in morale and capability. More important, it warned the President that a vast shipment of Soviet arms was on the way to Cuba; the Castro forces would soon have such superior weapons that substantial American combat involvement would be necessary to bail out the anti-Castro Cuban invaders. Faced with these arguments, Kennedy gave the order to proceed.

Conversely, when a President wants to act, bureaucrats can stymie him by arguing that "now is not the time." President Eisenhower reported in his memoirs that he came into office believing, after having served as commander of the allied forces in Europe, that the United States should withdraw most of its forces there; he left office eight years later still believing that the U.S. had far too many troops assigned to NATO. Secretary of State John Foster Dulles knew better than to argue with the military substance of General Eisenhower's position. Instead he argued timing. Each time Eisenhower raised the issue, Dulles pointed to some current NATO difficulty. This was, he would argue, a critical moment in the life of the alliance in which one or another NATO country was experiencing a domestic crisis. For the U.S. to withdraw troops would be to risk political disintegration. The moment for troop withdrawals never arrived. To this day, pressures for some American withdrawals from Europe have been headed off by the same ploy.

7. Leak what you don't like.

We had a glimpse of this phenomenon last January with the publication of the Anderson Papers, in which we read about Henry Kissinger warning his State, Defense, and CIA colleagues: "The President does not believe we are carrying out his wishes. He wants to tilt in favor of Pakistan. He feels everything we do comes out otherwise." And, "The President is under the 'illusion' that he is giving instructions; not that he is merely being kept apprised of affairs as they progress." The President's subordinates disagreed with the President's policy toward the India-Pakistan crisis. They were undermining him by resisting his orders and then by leaking his policy. He knew it and did not like it; but apparently could not do much about it.

Although leaking the texts of many documents, à la Pentagon and Anderson papers, is relatively rare, much classified information regularly makes its way into the press. Presidents are surprised not when something leaks but rather when any hot item remains out of the press for even a few days. Providing information to the press—whether in press conferences, backgrounders, or leaks—is the main route by which officials within the executive branch bring their supporters in the Congress and the interested public into action. Only bureaucrats with potential outside support are tempted to leak. In some cases, it is sufficient to leak the fact that an issue is up for decision: in others, what is leaked is information on the positions of key participants. In many instances sufficient factual material must be leaked to convince Congressmen and others to join the fray.

Presidents don't like leaks by others and complain about them whenever they occur, often asking the FBI to run down the culprit. Such efforts almost always fail.

8. *Ignore orders you don't like.*

On March 20, 1948, President Harry Truman rose from bed early, as was his custom, and began scanning the morning newspapers. He was astonished to read that his ambassador to the United Nations, Warren Austin, had told the Security Council the previous day that "there seems to be general agreement that the plan [for the partition of Palestine] cannot now be implemented by peaceful means." Truman had agreed to no such thing. He was firmly committed to partition and on the previous day had reiterated his support in a private meeting with Chaim Weizmann, the leader of worldwide Zionism. Austin and the Arabists in the State Department did not know about the meeting with Weizmann, but they knew that the President wanted partition and believed that it could be carried out peacefully. Austin and his associates had no doubts about what the President wanted; they simply felt no obligation to do what he wanted them to do.

At the end of his term in office, Truman was acutely conscious of the limited ability of Presidents to have their orders obeyed, and he worried about his successor. "Poor Ike," he was heard to muse, "he'll sit here and say do this and do that and nothing will happen." And so it continues.

During the first week of the Cuban missile crisis, in October 1962, an adviser warned Kennedy that the Russians were likely to demand that the United States withdraw its missiles from Turkey in return for the Soviet withdrawal of its missiles from Cuba. Kennedy was astonished. Months before, he had ordered the missiles removed from Turkey and could not believe they were still there.

Most students of the Cuban missile crisis have emphasized the degree to which Kennedy controlled every detail of what the American Government did. However, a closer look by Graham Allison, in his book on the crisis, *Essence of Decision,* has shown that the bureaucracy was behaving otherwise, choosing to obey the orders it liked and ignore or stretch others. Thus, after a tense argument with the Navy, Kennedy ordered the blockade line moved closer to Cuba so that the Russians might have more time to draw back. Having lost the argument with the President, the Navy simply ignored his order. Unbeknownst to Kennedy, the Navy was also at work forcing Soviet submarines to surface long before Kennedy authorized any contact with Soviet ships. And despite the President's order to halt all provocative intelligence, an American U-2 plane entered Soviet airspace at the height of the crisis. When Kennedy began to realize that he was not in full control, he asked his Secretary of Defense to see if he could find out just what the Navy was doing. McNamara then made his first visit to the Navy command post in the Pentagon. In a heated exchange, the Chief of Naval Operations suggested that McNamara return to his office and let the Navy run the blockade.

Bureaucrats know that the President and his principal associates do not have the time or the information to monitor compliance with all Presidential orders. Often, the bureaucrats can simply delay or do nothing, and no one will notice. If the President is actively involved, they may find it necessary to obey the letter, but not the spirit, of his orders. As Henry Kissinger observed to a journalist recently, the problem is not to know what to do, but rather to figure out how to get the bureaucracy to do it.

9. Don't tell likely opponents about a good thing.

The commandments discussed thus far have all dealt with relations between the Departments and the White House. When issues get that far, one of the fundamental rules has already been violated: keep issues away from the President. Bureaucrats prefer to be left alone to do their own thing. They will not voluntarily bring issues to the attention of the President (or senior officials) unless they conclude that he is likely to rule in their favor in a conflict with another agency. Consider the case of surplus and long supply arms transfers to other countries.

One of Secretary McNamara's goals in the Pentagon was to reduce the level of military assistance, particularly to countries that did not need the weapons and could afford to pay for what they needed. A prime objective was Taiwan. McNamara and his office of International Security Affairs engaged in a yearly battle with the State Department and the military over the level of aid to Taiwan. The White House was drawn in because a number of influential Congressmen were strong supporters of aid to Taiwan. One year in the late 1960s a battle raged over whether Taiwan would get $30 million or $40 million in military assistance. During the same year, the military quietly shipped to Taiwan more than $40 million worth of military equipment, which the Pentagon had labeled "excess or long supply." No senior civilian official was aware of the fact that these transfers were taking place, and no junior official aware of what was going on felt obliged to report up. Thus while seniors officials argued over irrelevant ceilings on expenditures, Taiwan got more aid than anyone realized.

Observers sometimes assume that the bureaucracy bucks the hard choices to the President. Nothing could be further from the truth. Left alone, the bureaucracy will settle as many issues as it can by leaving each organization free to act as it chooses. When and if the President learns of an issue, bureaucrats will try to incorporate current behavior into "Option B."

10. Don't fight the consensus and don't resign over policy.

If an official strongly disagrees with a consensus or dislikes a key man behind the consensus, he might chance a leak to the press. But frontal assaults on a consensus happen only rarely. In the summer of 1965, Undersecretary of State George Ball was among the first to confirm this fact with respect to the policy of bombing North Vietnam. Ball thought U.S. bombing of the North was folly—and worse than that, would only stiffen Hanoi's will. But he did not propose a unilateral cessation. In a TV interview last year, Ball explained himself as follows: "What I was proposing was something which I thought had a fair chance of being persuasive . . . . if I had said let's pull out overnight or do something of this kind, I obviously wouldn't have been persuasive at all. They'd have said 'the man's mad.' "

Ball's remarks express at once the futility of resisting agreed policy and the bureaucrat's concern for his personal effectiveness. Ball knew he could not convince anyone if he revealed his true beliefs. He knew he would have been dismissed as "mad" and would not have been in a position to argue another day. So, he tempered his arguments and went along. Like all other bureaucrats, he hoped to preserve his effectiveness.

As it turned out, Ball's more moderate arguments were not persuasive either, but he did not resign over Vietnam and did not take his case to the public. No one resigned over Vietnam policy. Indeed, there seems to be no evidence that any civilian official has resigned over any foreign-policy matter since World War II.

The only officials with a record for resigning are the professional military. Generals Ridgeway, Taylor, and Powers are notable examples. What is more, they tour the hustings, write books, and complain out loud. Military officers feel strongly about the interests of their military organization and often believe that if the people of the country only knew "the truth," they would support the military's position. With this record on resigning and going to the public, it is no wonder the military has been so influential in Presidential decisions.

But again, it is the President and the nation who ultimately suffer. If the President remains confident that none of his civilian advisers will resign and take their case to the public, he has little incentive ever to question his own assumptions.

The Ten Commandments pose a serious problem for a President, who is after all the one who got elected and has the responsibility. Truman understood the problem but feared that Eisenhower would not. But evidence abounds that President Eisenhower, precisely because of his background in Army politics and international military negotiations, was far from a novice. President Kennedy was quite expert and attuned to the ways of the bureaucracy—especially after the Bay of Pigs fiasco. His famous calls to State Department desk officials made the point well. President Johnson was a master of such maneuvering. Even as he stepped up the bombing of North Vietnam he would say, "I won't let those Air Force generals bomb the smallest outhouse north of the 17th parallel without checking with me. The generals know only two words—spend and bomb."

The Nixon-Kissinger team is second to none in its sensitivity to bureaucratic behavior. The elaborate National Security Council decision-making apparatus they established is predicated on tight White House control of the bureaucracy. Their system is designed to neutralize narrow organizational interests (meaning the viewpoints of State and Defense), force the bureaucracy to suggest real alternatives and provide more accurate information (meaning, as has been done, to centralize the intelligence functions around Kissinger).

While this new system has been an improvement in some respects over the past, it has decisive costs and limitations. It has totally demoralized the State Department. The Department's expertise has been for naught, and its exclusion had led to a rash of pointless leaks from disgruntled Foreign Service Officers. With all its reins on the bureaucrat, the new system did not prevent part of the bureaucracy from tilting the "wrong way" (meaning against the President, as revealed in the Anderson papers) in the recent India-Pakistan crisis.

The problem, then, boils down to this: given the fact that the President cannot either chain the system or entirely work around it without serious costs, and given the judgment that a President strong enough to collar the bureaucracy would be too strong for the good of the nation, is there a better way to make foreign policy?

The answer is yes—probably. The President, we think, should make a determined effort to use the system. The personal and organizational interests of the bureaucrat are a reality. So are the different viewpoints on what is good policy. The President's main theme of operation should be to force bureaucratic differences out into the open. Pick strong and able men to lead State and Defense. Let them use their judgment and be advocates for their organizations. Encourage debate and contention rather than asking for agreed upon recommendations. Such tactics may be the only way for the President to ferret out hidden or conflicting information and to leave himself with real choices.

Perhaps, in the end, neither this suggested system nor any system will produce better decisions. Perhaps better decisions really depend on beliefs and events and guesses. But a fuller, more honest and open treatment of the bureaucracy might make for more honest and open treatment of the American people. Presidents might be less inclined to spend a good deal of their time denying differences and hiding policy. This would mean less deception and less manipulation. What better reason for trying it?

SILENT VIETNAM

Orville Schell, Jr.

The gradual dismemberment of Indochinese society has become a fact of life. Learned at first with disbelief and horror, and then integrated into the routines of our everyday existence, the destruction has become a cliché. Even to speak of the "Vietnam problem" or the "Indochina problem" is deceiving because it implies that there remains a real entity that can easily be restored to health with certain reasonable changes. But, like the bodies of men and women mangled by napalm, fragmentation bombs and phosphorous, the land and the peoples of Indochina will not readily recover from the wounds that America has inflicted, even if a peace is achieved.

The war reports speak of particular battles, an accidentally bombed village, a B-52 strike, a defoliated county, the body count and the increasing numbers of refugees. We have understood this conflict more in terms of isolated events rather than as a complex pattern. We have come to assume that the changed structure of a village, the altered chemistry of a jungle or river, the destroyed tissue of a napalmed child or the shattered economy of a nation do not affect each other. We still see the war in Indochina in terms of meaningless categories, of boundaries, programs, operations and invasions, without understanding that Indochina is an organic fabric in which all living things are tied together in innumerable ways.

If we look at all these disparate disasters as part of a whole, however, it begins to become apparent that our actions in Indochina have already gone far in committing what may well be a new kind of crime in the history of warfare—ecocide. Just as genocide is the crime of eliminating one of the earth's peoples, ecocide is the crime of destroying the natural environment in which people live. In the past, armies have often engaged in a "scorched earth" policy. But whereas a scorched-earth strategy killed and burned everything in its path, an ecocidal strategy, which has become possible only

Source: *Look* (April 6, 1971), pp. 55, 57–58. Reprinted by permission of the author.

through the recent technological transformation of warfare, destroys an environment for an extended period of time.

It is difficult now to recall Indochina before the ecocide began. Over the last few centuries, the countryside had changed little. South Vietnam was an area largely made up of small decentralized villages spread out over the coastal plain and the fertile Mekong River Delta in the South. The village was the essential unit of Vietnamese life. Most people seldom left their village. Fewer left their county or province. Most villages, although simple, gave one a sense of peace and beauty. Many were accessible only by path or canal. Small houses of split bamboo and thatch, many even on stone foundations, were clumped together in an agreeable way so as to allow for both privacy and communality. In spite of poverty and the absence of land reform, the inhabitants had worked out an accommodation with the natural world around them. They planted palm trees and bamboo groves around their houses for shade and shelter. Rice fields surrounded each village. And, of course, not far away, were the ancestral tombs. At his village, a peasant farmer was born, got married, raised his family, grew his rice crops and died. He lived in a simple universe, yet one that gave him dignity.

Now, ten years after the American military began to move into Vietnam, many crucial elements between man and nature have been destroyed. The two principal agents of this destruction have been a saturation bombing unprecedented in warfare, and the massive spraying of herbicides.

From the point of view of the Indochinese peasant, Vietnamization and President Nixon's claims of withdrawal have not meant an end to the destruction, but a clear escalation of the assault on the countryside by American air power, bombing and defoliation. Aerial bombardment has increased, and systematically replaced ground forces as they have withdrawn. Whatever selectivity the military once exercised in picking targets has disappeared with the massive, continuous bombing in Vietnam, Cambodia and Laos.

Indochinese society has become our target, and, in turn, our enemy. We are waging a war against an abstraction that has turned out to be a war against the people and the land itself. Gen. William C. Westmoreland's billion-dollar electronic battlefield for automated warfare has arrived. A year and a half ago, he told the Association of the U.S. Army, "I see battlefields on which we can destroy anything we can locate through instant communications and almost instantaneous application of highly lethal firepower. With first-round kill probabilities approaching certainty, and with surveillance devices that can continually track the enemy, the need for large forces to fix the opposition physically will be less important."

Technology and firepower have now allowed America to wage a wider war while reducing its own casualties, and thus hardly notice what it is doing.

With the replacement of General Westmoreland by Gen. Creighton W. Abrams, the much publicized "search and destroy" operations that were the heart and soul of the Westmoreland tenure began quietly to be phased out in favor of "cordon and search" and "reconnaissance in force" operations, which simply meant that large ground operations were phased out and technology substituted. The high U.S. casualties—over 1,500 during an average week—had become too great a political liability at home. There was a pullback on the ground away from the bloody Loc Ninh, Hamburger Hill, Khe Sanh battles, and the Junction City or Cedar Rapids type of military operation. Drug problems and insubordination among U.S. troops rendered such operations worthless. The war moved to the air. Planes that had been flying daily strikes over North Vietnam were diverted, after the bombing halt in October, 1968, to Laos and South Vietnam. B-52's began to be used as tactical weapons on daily runs. Bomb tonnage soared, and U.S. casualty figures dropped. Mr. Nixon began to speak effusively about withdrawal and of Vietnamization. But the tonnage still has reached amounts that are difficult to comprehend. *Le Monde* reported last July 29 that 1,387,000 tons of bombs were dropped on Indochina in 1969. During the first five months of last year, 594,171 tons of bombs were dropped. The total tonnage dropped during the war is now just under six million tons. (The U.S. dropped just over two million tons of bombs during the whole of World War II on Europe and Japan.) This does not even include artillery shells fired (for example, some 5,172,588 tons fired between January 1, 1968, and May 31, 1970). Since then, B-52's have been flying a thousand sorties and dropping up to 2,000 tons of bombs a day. Such figures stagger the imagination; we have dropped almost 20 tons of explosives for every square mile in Vietnam.

The war has shown that United States firepower is almost limitless. Our inability to win has not stemmed from an absence of ordnance but from an absence of targets. In this technological warfare, our lethal firepower has been turned on society itself, like a broad-spectrum antibiotic that makes no distinction between wanted and unwanted organisms. Target bombing and air support for ground operations have given way to saturation bombing. Artillery strikes, once called in on specific targets, have evolved into harassment and interdiction (H&I) fire that is shot around the clock into "free-fire zones" (now conveniently called "specified strike zones") from coastal and inland fire bases. Navy guns are now computerized to fire continuously at whole counties for several days running rather than just at isolated targets. Whole villages are incinerated by napalm strikes because of single snipers. Armed helicopters of days gone by have become "gun ships" capable of launching rockets, grenades and machine-gun fire. C-47's, now nicknamed "Puff-the-Magic-Dragons," have been armed with multiple "miniguns" that are capable of laying a withering blaze of fire, 18,000 rounds a minute.

One of the most disastrous, and least noticed, effects of our bombing has been the destruction of the irrigation system in rural Vietnam. The water works are one of the most important elements in inter-village life of South Vietnam, the one undertaking that makes cooperation within the village, and even between adjacent villages, absolutely essential. As in all Asian countries, the irrigation system for the rice fields is extremely complicated. Water runs down through scores of paddies on which hundreds of different people and families depend. Disruption at any point of the long chain threatens the survival of everyone further down the line.

More than anything else since the advent of Chinese hydraulic technology hundreds of years ago, the irrigation system made a social fabric out of the patchwork of villages in the Vietnamese countryside. Without the dams, dikes and canals to temper the heavy monsoon rains and assure a supply of water during the long dry months, tillable land, crops, and hence society, could not exist.

Almost without noticing it, the U.S. military have destroyed this system in Vietnam and much of Indochina. As one flies over the countryside, he sees brownish-yellow rivers and streams flowing aimlessly across paddies and eroded fields. Some areas are scorched dry and pitted with craters. One looks down on mile after mile of uncultivated rice fields pockmarked with millions of large craters filled with water in which malarial mosquitoes have been breeding in epidemic numbers. Reportedly, 2.5 billion cubic yards of earth have been removed. This is 25 times greater than the Suez Canal excavation. In the coastal areas of I Corps, one searches for signs of life in the vast "sanitized" free-fire zones. On the borders of fields, at the treeline, one can often see evidence of pathetic gardens where people attempt to grow basic foods like sweet potatoes, taro or squash. They do not dare work the rice fields for fear of being shot by Americans who are out "squirrel hunting" in bubble choppers. In free-fire zones, people are subject to bombardment 24 hours a day and live like moles in bomb-shelter holes beneath the ground.

While the bombing was being stepped up, the use of herbicides continued unabated. Beginning in 1961, the U.S. began the "experimental" use of herbicides in South Vietnam as a weapon to destroy crops. The initial objective was to deny food to the National Liberation Front. In 1962, herbicides became "a central weapon" in the overall chemical and biological warfare (CBW) strategy of America throughout Southeast Asia. Known as "Operation Ranch Hand," the project's motto became "Only we can prevent forests."

The defoliation program soon expanded into a critical aspect of the whole shift of strategy from ground to air power in South Vietnam. Besides destroying crops, defoliants began to be used to destroy the forest canopy that hid NLF forces from detection by air. The process is described in an Army Training Circular *#TC3-16 Employment of Riot Control Agents, Flame, Smoke, Antiplant Agents and Personnel Detectors in Counter Guerrilla Operations:* "Guerrilla operations rely heavily on locally produced crops for their food supply. Crop destruction can reduce the food supply and seriously affect the guerrilla's survival. Naturally dense vegetation in jungle areas is ideal for illusive hit and run tactics of guerrillas. Removal or reduction of this concealment limits the guerrilla's capability to operate in the defoliated area." A report released last December by the American Association for the Advancement of Science claims that in Vietnam, some 600,000 people have been deprived of their normal food supply by defoliation. The report claims that chemical agents sprayed by the U.S. have been responsible for killing over $500 million worth of prime hardwood, covering an area the size of Massachusetts. It states that some 400,000 acres of coastal mangrove forest have been killed, leaving lifeless swamps. These vast areas were once major sources of smaller species of fish and shrimp, on which larger kinds of seafood depend for life. The effect of this disruption in the food chain, and, consequently, of the livelihood of fishermen in the area, is not known.

Over 12 percent of South Vietnam's territory, including croplands and grazing lands, has been damaged or destroyed. Sen. Gaylord A. Nelson of Wisconsin reports that "The U.S. has sprayed [in South Vietnam] enough chemicals to amount to six pounds for every man, woman and child in that country."

Last spring, American military sources announced that after nine years, use of the deadliest herbicide, Agent Orange (some 60,000 tons had already been used), was suspended. The use of other herbicides continued. But in November, it was revealed that the 90th Chemical Attachment in Quang Ngai province had, in fact, continued to use Agent Orange and had defoliated thousands of acres in spite of the ban. As one soldier remarked, "Hell, we've been using it all through the summer." Sen. Stephen M. Young of Ohio quoted another young soldier, who had been asked where all the barrels of Agent Orange had disappeared: "If we ain't been using it, where do you think those missing barrels went? We sure ain't makin' milkshakes out of it."

On February 2, 1971, General Abrams and U.S. Ambassador Ellsworth Bunker issued a statement saying that herbicide spraying of crops by fixed-wing aircraft would cease, but that the program would continue, from the ground and from helicopters, around U.S. bases and in other "unpopulated areas." Most people, however, remain justifiably confused as to the real status of the herbicide program. Even, if the program were ended *in toto*, the indications are that many important aspects of the whole organic fabric of Vietnam have already been affected. Scientists are concerned that herbicides have damaged the soil by destroying the process through which foliage regularly falls to the ground, decays, and returns minerals and nutrients to the earth. As a result, plant life is unable to replenish itself, and erosion washes the essential soil nutrients away. Other scientists fear that a process called laterization may set in in many areas, turning the soil into a hard, rocklike substance in which nothing will grow.

Reports indicate that patterns of wild-animal life have been altered through the interruption of food chains and the near extinction of several rare species. The regeneration of vast jungle areas that are pollinated by animals and insects rather than air currents are affected in turn. Elephants, often used by both sides for transportaton, are shot on sight, while the tiger population has soared as a consequence of an abundant supply of fresh human meat.

There are even reports of women giving birth to monsters, though most occurrences are not reported because of nonexistent procedures for compiling statistics. The Saigon Ministry of Health classified the files of malformed babies as "secret" in 1969.

Quietly, the whole nature of Indochinese agriculture is being changed by the aerial destruction. In 1964, South Vietnam exported 48,563 metric tons of rice. The following year, largely because of bombing and spraying, South Vietnam *imported* 240,000 metric tons of rice. In 1968, the figure rose to 677,000 tons. The destruction of rice has meant the destruction of a culture. The people of Asia have been growing and eating rice for 5,000 years. Rice is central not only to their diet but to the entire spiritual relationship between the Vietnamese people and the natural world. If a Vietnamese has not eaten rice, though he may have eaten other foods that day, he considers himself not to have eaten at all. During the day, Vietnamese often greet each other with the words, "*Ăn Cơm Chửa?*" literally, "Eat cooked rice yet?"

The destruction of the rice crop has meant that the fundamental connection between peasant and earth is broken. Without the rice to plant, grow and harvest, the village is without function or meaning, even if it is not bombed or burned. A man forced off his land is left without reason to exist or connection with the world around him. He becomes a purposeless human being.

For the people of Vietnam, the immediate consequence of the bombing and the destruction of their crops has been the growth of the "refugee" camps. Such camps are usually located in "secure areas," away from trees or hills. They are placed in the baking sun on bulldozed lots surrounded by barbed wire. Small houses with tin roofs that cause them to heat up like ovens under the tropical sun are lined up like cars on a parking lot. U.S. surplus-commodities, dietary food and food banned in the U.S. because of cyclamates are brought in to replace the native rice. Here a refugee, or "detainee," frequently separated even from friends and family in the evacuation shuffle, is "resettled."

As with every other aspect of the war, statistics on refugees have almost no real meaning. Authorities in Vietnam have compiled "statistics" to give the illusion that the problem is not totally out of hand. Their figures give only an incomplete, shadowy picture of the devastating reality.

On December 28, 1967, the New York *Times* reported that although the military have "classified" two million Vietnamese as refugees, a "competent source" put the figure at four million. Meanwhile, officials claimed that 309,000 "classified" refugees were in camps and 475,000 were "elsewhere." Where is "elsewhere"? Journalists in Saigon are usually told that the refugees are "staying with relatives." One can understand what this means by seeing the squalid overcrowding of South Vietnamese cities.

In February, 1970, Rand Corporation anthropologist Gerald Hickey said "Just 15 years ago, all but 15 percent of the South Vietnamese people lived in rural areas. Now, 60 percent live in urban areas. Saigon has grown from a city of 300,000, which it was designed to be, to more than three million." The pattern is the same in most Vietnamese cities. Da Nang, for example, has grown from a city of 25,000 to 300,000 in five years. Similarly, Phnom Penh, the capital of Cambodia, has grown from half a million to two million in eight months. This kind of "urbanization" is a tactic that Samuel P. Huntington, chairman of the Department of Government at Harvard University, and a long-time supporter of the war, advocated in *Foreign Affairs,* July, 1968. He claimed that Vietcong support could be cut off if there were " 'direct application of mechanical and conventional power' . . . on such a massive scale as to produce a massive migration from countryside to city."

The city of Saigon perhaps best illustrates this tactic of forced urbanization. In December, 1964, an article in the *Christian Science Monitor* described Saigon as the "Paris of the East." In a scant two years, the same paper began to run articles describing Saigon as a city in which "labor shortages due to the war have made services worse than usual. The streets are very dirty. Huge piles of uncollected trash and rotting garbage lie about, and sanitation is sadly lacking." Saigon has become one of the ugliest and most congested cities in the world, with an average population of 140 persons per acre (Tokyo has 63).

The overriding problem of civilian dislocation, euphemistically called "pacification," is one that the American military have never taken seriously. The index of General Westmoreland's final report on the war includes five references to "Refugees"—all with the misleading subtitle, "Care of. . . ." There is no serious discussion or even statistical reference in that report to the disruption that has been taking place in the countryside because of U.S. firepower.

In June, 1969, John Hannah, head of the Agency for International Development, told Sen. Edward Kennedy's Subcommittee on Refugees that 3.2 million Vietnamese had "become homeless" since 1965. A chart accompanying the testimony lists 1,328,517 of them as "current temporary refugees" for 1968. Then, there is an asterisk referring to a footnote in minute print: "Refugees are defined as persons who leave their home for war related reasons, and have not yet reestablished a permanent home. Statistics do not include victims of the Tet and May offensives numbering in excess of 1,000,000."

Hannah's report further states that 612,101 of these "current temporary refugees" are "in camp." Another 600,105 are listed as "out of camp" or "elsewhere." It all sounds like a reasonably manageable proposition. But as any honest refugee adviser in the provinces of Vietnam is quick to point out (since he has to work with actual people, not fantasy-land figures), official statistics only deal with "classified" refugees. Conservative estimates place the figure of dislocated people at twice the number of those "classified." This means that, as of 1969, roughly seven million Vietnamese (or nearly half the population of South Vietnam) had become homeless.

According to Royal Laotian Government figures in 1970, 1.5 million people there have been displaced since the U.S. began intensive bombing of Pathet Lao-held territory in 1968. Laos has a population of only three million. According to Jacques Decornoy of *Le Monde,* who was in the province of Sam Noua, a Pathet Lao area, all but two villages there had been destroyed as early as 1968. Since then, the U.S. has been flying up to 20,000 sorties a month over Sam Neua. One can only guess the effect the February invasion of Laos has had on the already severe refugee crisis in that country.

In 1970, a report of the Senate Subcommittee on Refugees said that in Cambodia, with a population of seven million, one million refugees have already been "generated." We also know that the Lon Nol regime "generated" some 100,000 refugees from the ethnic Vietnamese population living in Cambodia just before the invasion of the NLF sanctuaries last spring. We also know that since then, the U.S. has provided unlimited air power to Lon Nol's tragicomic army. Whole cities like Snoul, where thousands of people lived, have been destroyed. And yet, in spite of this obvious escalation of the air war and the inevitable rural dislocation that must follow, U.S. authorities continue to claim, even with self-satisfaction, that the refugee problem is under control.

One wonders where all the refugees went. They began to disappear from our consciousness just as the B-52 raids increased. One is justified in conjecturing whether people are simply being killed in their villages without being brought into a pacificaton camp where they can be tabulated.

Fact has been piled on fact—few of them are new and fewer capable of shocking. The immensity of the destruction in the Indochinese war has led to a kind of national numbness that is only momentarily interrupted by another escalation or invasion. Government "experts" speak of "urbanization," "protective reaction," "crop control," and "Vietnamization." But the old words are incapable of conveying just what it is that the U.S. is doing to Vietnam and the rest of Indochina. The crime is a new one, ecocide, our addition to the annals of man's inhumanity to man.

Chapter 12
SUGGESTED TOPICS FOR CLASS DISCUSSION

1. In what ways can the public have a practical impact upon the making of foreign and military policy?
2. Several years ago there was a good deal of discussion about the role of the "military-industrial complex" in the making of foreign and military policy. What was the general idea behind this concept? Why has discussion of the military-industrial complex declined?
3. Recent Presidents have sought to concentrate major foreign policy decision-making in the White House. This has resulted in White House assistants wielding greater power than the Secretary of State. Congressional committees can call the Secretary of State before them, but the doctrine of executive privilege has been interpreted so as to prevent their summoning members of the White House staff. What problems does this create?
4. A President will want the American people to think well of his conduct of foreign affairs. Because the media have a great impact on the way the President's performance will be perceived, it is understandable that members of the White House staff should seek to influence the presentation of news and interpretation by the media. How far is it appropriate for the White House to go in this direction?
5. The conduct of foreign affairs will sometimes require secrecy, yet the proper functioning of a democracy assumes that the populace be reasonably well informed. How can the claims of confidentiality and security be satisfied at the same time as the claims of democracy?